STUDENT'S SOLUTIONS MANUAL

NANCY S. BOUDREAU
Bowling Green State University

STATISTICS FOR BUSINESS AND ECONOMICS
TWELFTH EDITION

James T. McClave
Info Tech, Inc.
University of Florida

P. George Benson
College of Charleston

Terry Sincich
University of South Florida

PEARSON

Boston Columbus Indianapolis New York San Francisco Upper Saddle River
Amsterdam Cape Town Dubai London Madrid Milan Munich Paris Montreal Toronto
Delhi Mexico City São Paulo Sydney Hong Kong Seoul Singapore Taipei Tokyo

Copyright © 2014, 2011, 2008 Pearson Education, Inc.
Publishing as Pearson, 75 Arlington Street, Boston, MA 02116.

ISBN-13: 978-0-321-82629-9
ISBN-10: 0-321-82629-9

1 2 3 4 5 6 EBM 16 15 14 13 12

www.pearsonhighered.com

Contents

Chapter 1
Statistics, Data, and Statistical Thinking

1.1   Statistics is a science that deals with the collection, classification, analysis, and interpretation of information or data. It is a meaningful, useful science with a broad, almost limitless scope of applications to business, government, and the physical and social sciences.

1.3   The four elements of a descriptive statistics problem are:

1.   The population or sample of interest. This is the collection of all the units upon which the variable is measured.
2.   One or more variables that are to be investigated. These are the types of data that are to be collected.
3.   Tables, graphs, or numerical summary tools. These are tools used to display the characteristic of the sample or population.
4.   Identification of patterns in the data. These are conclusions drawn from what the summary tools revealed about the population or sample.

1.5   The first major method of collecting data is from a published source. These data have already been collected by someone else and are available in a published source. The second method of collecting data is from a designed experiment. These data are collected by a researcher who exerts strict control over the experimental units in a study. These data are measured directly from the experimental units. The final method of collecting data is observational. These data are collected directly from experimental units by simply observing the experimental units in their natural environment and recording the values of the desired characteristics. The most common type of observational study is a survey.

1.7   A population is a set of existing units such as people, objects, transactions, or events. A variable is a characteristic or property of an individual population unit such as height of a person, time of a reflex, amount of a transaction, etc.

1.9   A representative sample is a sample that exhibits characteristics similar to those possessed by the target population. A representative sample is essential if inferential statistics is to be applied. If a sample does not possess the same characteristics as the target population, then any inferences made using the sample will be unreliable.

1.11   A population is a set of existing units such as people, objects, transactions, or events. A process is a series of actions or operations that transform inputs to outputs. A process produces or generates output over time. Examples of processes are assembly lines, oil refineries, and stock prices.

1.13   The data consisting of the classifications A, B, C, and D are qualitative. These data are nominal and thus are qualitative. After the data are input as 1, 2, 3, and 4, they are still nominal and thus qualitative. The only differences between the two data sets are the names of the categories. The numbers associated with the four groups are meaningless.

1.15   a.   The experimental unit for this study is a single-family residential property in Arlington, Texas.

        b.   The variables measured are the sale price and the Zillow estimated value. Both of these variables are quantitative.

c. If these 2,045 properties were all the properties sold in Arlington, Texas in the past 6 months, then this would be considered the population.

d. If these 2,045 properties represent a sample, then the population would be all the single-family residential properties sold in the last 6 months in Arlington, Texas.

e. No. The real estate market across the United States varies greatly. The prices of single-family residential properties in this small area are probably not representative of all properties across the United States.

1.17 a. The population of interest is all citizens of the United States.

b. The variable of interest is the view of each citizen as to whether the president is doing a good or bad job. It is qualitative.

c. The sample is the 2000 individuals selected for the poll.

d. The inference of interest is to estimate the proportion of all U.S. citizens who believe the president is doing a good job.

e. The method of data collection is a survey.

f. It is not very likely that the sample will be representative of the population of all citizens of the United States. By selecting phone numbers at random, the sample will be limited to only those people who have telephones. Also, many people share the same phone number, so each person would not have an equal chance of being contacted. Another possible problem is the time of day the calls are made. If the calls are made in the evening, those people who work in the evening would not be represented.

1.19 I. Qualitative; the possible responses are "yes" or "no," which are non-numerical.

II. Quantitative; age is measured on a numerical scale, such as 15, 32, etc.

III. Qualitative; the possible responses are "yes" or "no," which are non-numerical.

IV. Qualitative; the possible responses are "laser printer" or "another type of printer," which are non-numerical.

V. Qualitative; the speeds can be classified as "slower," "unchanged," or "faster," which are non-numerical.

VI. Quantitative; the number of people in a household who have used Windows 95 at least once is measured on a numerical scale, such as 0, 1, 2, etc.

1.21 a. Whether the data collected on the chief executive officers at the 500 largest U. S. companies is a population or a sample depends on what one is interested in. If one is only interested in the information from the CEO's of the 500 largest U.S. companies, then these data form a population. If one is interested in the information on CEO's from all U.S. firms, then these data would form a sample.

b. 1. The industry type of the CEO's company is a qualitative variable. The industry type is a name.

2. The CEO's total compensation is a meaningful number. Thus, it is a quantitative variable.

3. The CEO's total compensation over the previous five years is a meaningful number. Thus, it is a quantitative variable.

4. The number of company stock shares (millions) held is a meaningful number. Thus, it is a quantitative variable.

5. The CEO's age is a meaningful number. Thus, it is a quantitative variable.

6. The CEO's efficiency rating is a meaningful number. Thus, it is a quantitative variable.

1.23   Since the data collected consist of the entire population, this would represent a descriptive study. Flaherty used the data to help describe the condition of the U.S. Treasury in 1861.

1.25   a.   The population of interest is all individuals who earned MBA degrees since January 1990.

   b.   The method of data collection was a survey.

   c.   This is probably not a representative sample. The sample was self-selected. Not all of those who were selected for the study responded to all four surveys. Those who did respond to all 4 surveys probably have very strong opinions, either positive or negative, which may not be representative of all of those in the population.

1.27   a.   Length of maximum span can take on values such as 15 feet, 50 feet, 75 feet, etc. Therefore, it is quantitative.

   b.   The number of vehicle lanes can take on values such as 2, 4, etc. Therefore, it is quantitative.

   c.   The answer to this item is "yes" or "no," which is not numeric. Therefore, it is qualitative.

   d.   Average daily traffic could take on values such as 150 vehicles, 3,579 vehicles, 53,295 vehicles, etc. Therefore, it is quantitative.

   e.   Condition can take on values "good," "fair," or "poor," which are not numeric. Therefore, it is qualitative.

   f.   The length of the bypass or detour could take on values such as 1 mile, 4 miles, etc. Therefore, it is quantitative.

   g.   Route type can take on values "interstate," U.S.," "state," "county," or "city," which are not numeric. Therefore, it is qualitative.

1.29   a.   The process being studied is the distribution of pipes, valves, and fittings to the refining, chemical, and petrochemical industries by the Wallace Company of Houston.

   b.   The variables of interest are the speed of the deliveries, the accuracy of the invoices, and the quality of the packaging of the products.

   c.   The sampling plan was to monitor a subset of current customers by sending out a questionnaire twice a year and asking the customers to rate the speed of the deliveries, the accuracy of the invoices, and the quality of the packaging minutes. The sample is the total numbers of questionnaires received.

d.   The Wallace Company's immediate interest is learning about the delivery process of its distribution of pipes, valves, and fittings. To do this, it is measuring the speed of deliveries, the accuracy of the invoices, and the quality of its packaging from the sample of its customers to make an inference about the delivery process to all customers. In particular, it might use the mean speed of its deliveries to the sampled customers to estimate the mean speed of its deliveries to all its customers. It might use the mean accuracy of its invoices from the sampled customers to estimate the mean accuracy of its invoices of all its customers. It might use the mean rating of the quality of its packaging from the sampled customers to estimate the mean rating of the quality of its packaging of all its customers.

e.   Several factors might affect the reliability of the inferences. One factor is the set of customers selected to receive the survey. If this set is not representative of all the customers, the wrong inferences could be made. Also, the set of customers returning the surveys may not be representative of all its customers. Again, this could influence the reliability of the inferences made.

1.31   a.   The population of interest would be all accounting alumni of a large southwestern university.

b.   Age would produce quantitative data – the responses would be numbers.

Gender would produce qualitative data – the responses would be 'male' or 'female'.

Level of education would produce qualitative data – the responses could be categories such college degree, master's degree, or PhD degree.

Income would produce quantitative data – the responses would be numbers.

Job satisfaction score would produce quantitative data. We would assume that a satisfaction score would be a number, where the higher the number, the higher the job satisfaction.

Machiavellian rating score would produce quantitative data. We would assume that a rating score would be a number, where the higher the score, the higher the Machiavellian traits.

c.   The sample is the 198 people who returned the useable questionnaires.

d.   The data collection method used was a survey.

e.   The inference made by the researcher is that Machiavellian behavior is not required to achieve success in the accounting profession.

f.   Generally, those who respond to surveys are those with strong feelings (in either direction) toward the subject matter. Those who do not have strong feelings for the subject matter tend not to answer surveys. Those who did not respond might be those who are not real happy with their jobs or those who are not real unhappy with their jobs. Thus, we might have no idea what type of scores these people would have on the Machiavellian rating score.

1.33   a.   The experimental units for this study are engaged couples who used a particular website.

b.   There are two variables of interest – the price of the engagement ring and the level of appreciation. Price of the engagement ring is a quantitative variable because it is measured on a numerical scale. Level of appreciation is a qualitative variable. There are 7 different categories for this variable that are then assigned numbers.

c.   The population of interest would be all engaged couples.

    d.   No, the sample is probably not representative. Only engaged couples who used a particular web site were eligible to be in the sample. Then, only those with "average" American names were invited to be in the sample.

    e.   Answers will vary. First, we will number the individuals from 1 to 50. Using MINITAB, 25 random numbers were generated on the interval from 1 to 50. The random numbers are:

1, 4, 5, 8, 12, 13, 17, 18, 19, 20, 22, 26, 27, 30, 31, 33, 34, 35, 38, 39, 40, 42, 43, 46, 49

The individuals who were assigned the numbers corresponding to the above numbers would be assigned to one role and the remaining individuals would be assigned to the other role.

1.35   a.   Some possible questions are:

    1.   In your opinion, why has the banking industry consolidated in the past few years? Check all that apply.

        a.   Too many small banks with not enough capital.
        b.   A result of the Savings and Loan scandals.
        c.   To eliminate duplicated resources in the upper management positions.
        d.   To provide more efficient service to the customers.
        e.   To provide a more complete list of financial opportunities for the customers.
        f.   Other. Please list.

    2.   Using a scale from 1 to 5, where 1 means strongly disagree and 5 means strongly agree, indicate your agreement to the following statement: "The trend of consolidation in the banking industry will continue in the next five years."

        1 strongly disagree   2 disagree   3 no opinion   4 agree   5 strongly agree

    b.   The population of interest is the set of all bank presidents in the United States.

    c.   It would be extremely difficult and costly to obtain information from all bank presidents. Thus, it would be more efficient to sample just 200 bank presidents. However, by sending the questionnaires to only 200 bank presidents, one risks getting the results from a sample which is not representative of the population. The sample must be chosen in such a way that the results will be representative of the entire population of bank presidents in order to be of any use.

1.37   a.   The population of interest is the set of all people in the United States over 14 years of age.

    b.   The variable being measured is the employment status of each person. This variable is qualitative. Each person is either employed or not.

    c.   The problem of interest to the Census Bureau is inferential. Based on the information contained in the sample, the Census Bureau wants to estimate the percentage of all people in the labor force who are unemployed.

1.39   Answers will vary.

    a.   The results as stated indicate that by eating oat bran, one can improve his/her health. However, the only way to get the stated benefit is to eat only oat bran with limited results. People may change their eating habits expecting an outcome that is almost impossible.

b.   To investigate the impact of domestic violence on birth defects, one would need to collect data on all kinds of birth defects and whether the mother suffered any domestic violence or not during her pregnancy. One could use an observational study survey to collect the data.

c.   Very few people are *always* happy with the way they are. However, many people are happy with themselves most of the time. One might want to ask a series of questions to measure self-esteem rather than just one. One question might ask what percent of the time the high school girl is happy with the way she is.

d.   The results of the study are probably misleading because of the fact that if someone relied on a limited number of foods to feed her children it does not imply that the children are hungry. In addition, one might cut the size of a meal because the children were overweight, not because there was not enough food. One might get better information about the proportion of hungry American children by actually recording what a large, representative sample of children eat in a week.

e.   A leading question gives information that seems to be true, but may not be complete. Based on the incomplete information, the respondent may come to a different decision than if the information was not provided.

Chapter 2
Methods for Describing Sets of Data

2.1   First, we find the frequency of the grade A. The sum of the frequencies for all five grades must be 200. Therefore, subtract the sum of the frequencies of the other four grades from 200. The frequency for grade A is:

$$200 - (36 + 90 + 30 + 28) = 200 - 184 = 16$$

To find the relative frequency for each grade, divide the frequency by the total sample size, 200. The relative frequency for the grade B is 36/200 = .18. The rest of the relative frequencies are found in a similar manner and appear in the table:

Grade on Statistics Exam	Frequency	Relative Frequency
A: 90 –100	16	.08
B: 80 – 89	36	.18
C: 65 – 79	90	.45
D: 50 – 64	30	.15
F: Below 50	28	.14
Total	200	1.00

2.3   a.   The type of graph is a bar graph.

b.   The variable measured for each of the robots is type of robotic limbs.

c.   From the graph, the design used the most is the "legs only" design.

d.   The relative frequencies are computed by dividing the frequencies by the total sample size. The total sample size is $n = 106$. The relative frequencies for each of the categories are:

Type of Limbs	Frequency	Relative Frequency
None	15	15/106 = .142
Both	8	8 / 106 = .075
Legs ONLY	63	63/106 = .594
Wheels ONLY	20	20/106 = .189
Total	106	1.000

e.   Using MINITAB, the Pareto diagram is:

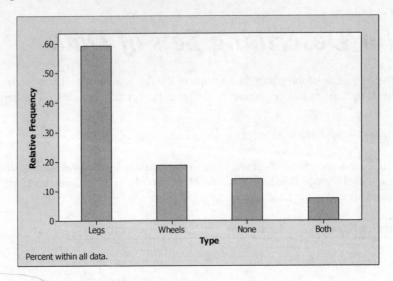

2.5   Using MINITAB, the Pareto diagram for the data is:

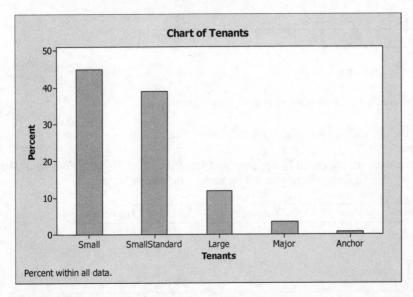

Most of the tenants in UK shopping malls are small or small standard. They account for approximately 84% of all tenants ([711 + 819]/1,821 = .84). Very few (less than 1%) of the tenants are anchors.

2.7   a.   Since the variable measured is manufacturer, the data type is qualitative.

b.   Using MINITAB, a frequency bar chart for the data is:

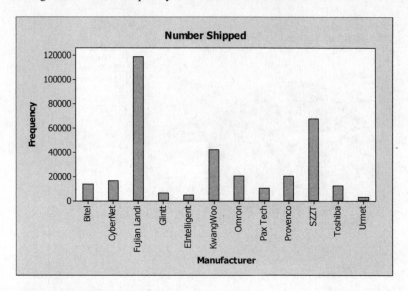

c.   Using MINITAB, the Pareto diagram is:

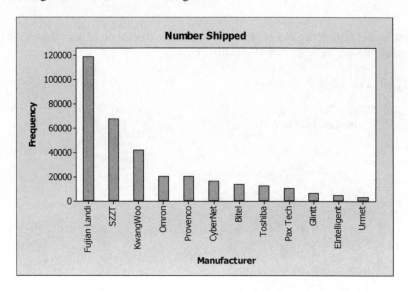

Most PIN pads shipped in 2007 were manufactured by either Fujian Landi or SZZT Electronics. These two categories make up (119,000 + 67,300)/334,039= 186,300/334,039 = .558 of all PIN pads shipped in 2007. Urmet shipped the fewest number of PIN pads among these 12 manufacturers.

2.9   Using MINITAB, the pie chart is:

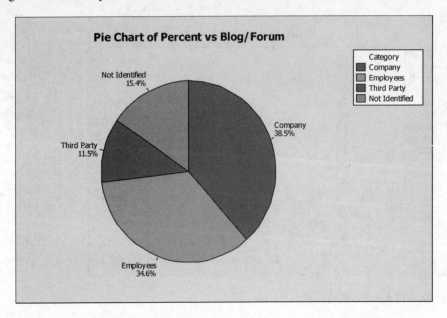

Companies and Employees represent (38.5 + 34.6 = 73.1) slightly more than 73% of the entities creating blogs/forums. Third parties are the least common entity.

2.11   a.   Using MINITAB, a pie chart of the data is:

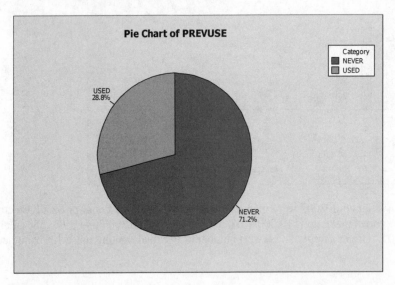

From the chart, 71.2% or .712 of the sampled physicians have never used ethics consultation.

b.   Using MINITAB, a pie chart of the data is:

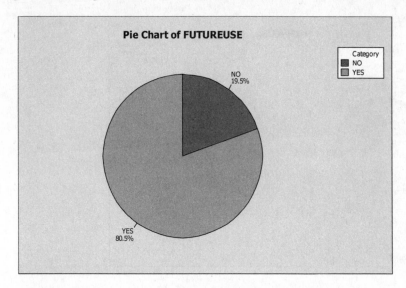

From the chart, 19.5% or .195 of the sampled physicians state that they will not use the services in the future.

c.   Using MINITAB, the side-by-side pie charts are:

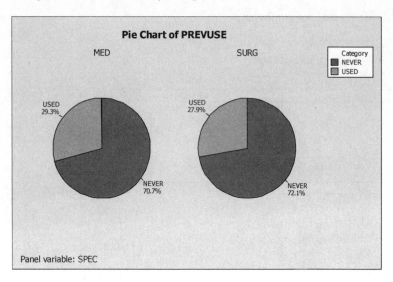

The proportion of medical practitioners who have never used ethics consultation is .707. The proportion of surgical practitioners who have never used ethics consultation is .721. These two proportions are almost the same.

d.   Using MINITAB, the side-by-side pie charts are:

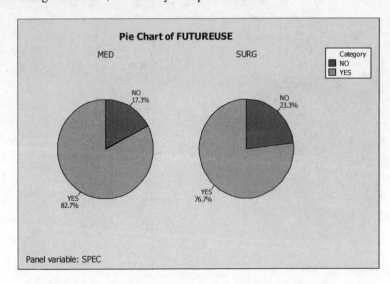

The proportion of medical practitioners who will not use ethics consultation in the future is .173. The proportion of surgical practitioners who will not use ethics consultation in the future is .233. The proportion of surgical practitioners who will not use ethics consultation in the future is greater than that of the medical practitioners.

2.13   Using MINITAB, the side-by-side bar graphs are:

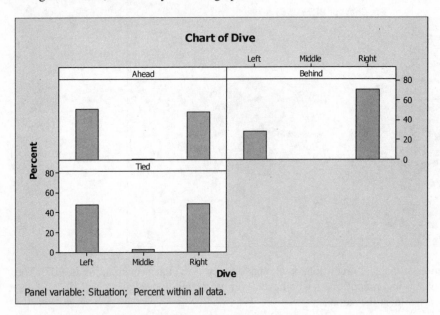

From the graphs, it appears that if the team is either tied or ahead, the goal-keepers tend to dive either right or left with equal probability, with very few diving in the middle. However, if the team is behind, then the majority of goal-keepers tend to dive right (71%).

2.15   a.   The variable measured by Performark is the length of time it took for each advertiser to respond back.

b.   The pie chart is:

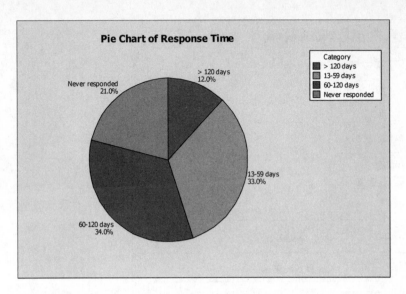

c. Twenty-one percent or $.21 \times 17,000 = 3,570$ of the advertisers never respond to the sales lead.

d. The information from the pie chart does not indicate how effective the "bingo cards" are. It just indicates how long it takes advertisers to respond, if at all.

2.17 a. Using MINITAB, bar charts for the 3 variables are:

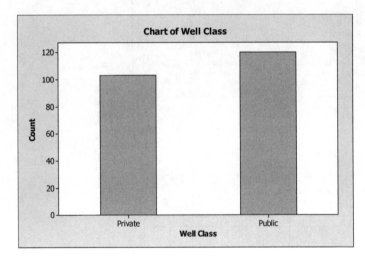

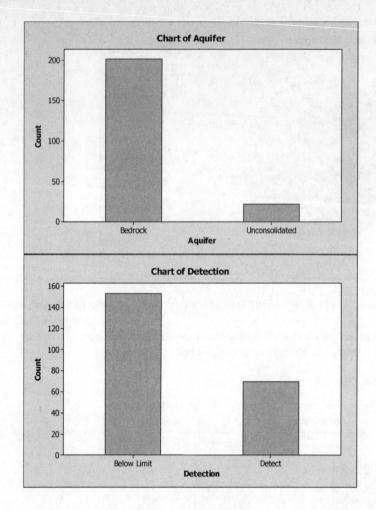

b.   Using MINITAB, the side-by-side bar chart is:

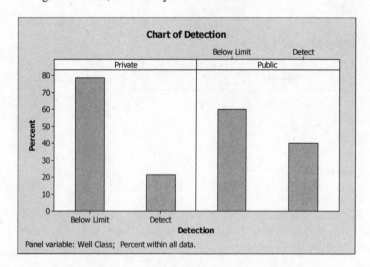

c. Using MINITAB, the side-by-side bar chart is:

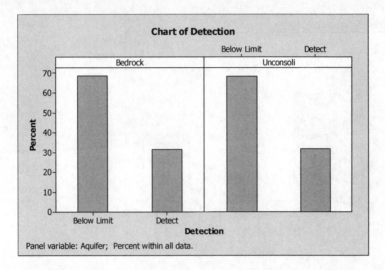

d. From the bar charts in parts a-c, one can infer that most aquifers are bedrock and most levels of MTBE were below the limit $(\approx 2/3)$. Also the percentages of public wells verses private wells are relatively close. Approximately 80% of private wells are not contaminated, while only about 60% of public wells are not contaminated. The percentage of contaminated wells is about the same for both types of aquifers $(\approx 30\%)$.

2.19 To find the number of measurements for each measurement class, multiply the relative frequency by the total number of observations, $n = 500$. The frequency table is:

Measurement Class	Relative Frequency	Frequency
.5 – 2.5	.10	500(.10) = 50
2.5 – 4.5	.15	500(.15) = 75
4.5 – 6.5	.25	500(.25) = 125
6.5 – 8.5	.20	500(.20) = 100
8.5 – 10.5	.05	500(.05) = 25
10.5 – 12.5	.10	500(.10) = 50
12.5 – 14.5	.10	500(.10) = 50
14.5 – 16.5	.05	500(.05) = 25
		500

Using MINITAB, the frequency histogram is:

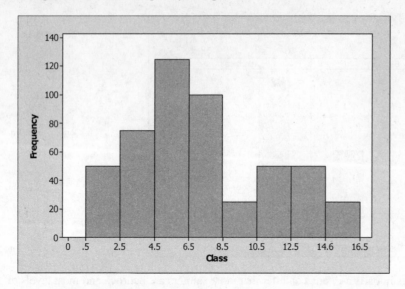

2.21   a.   This is a frequency histogram because the number of observations is graphed for each interval rather than the relative frequency.

b.   There are 14 measurement classes.

c.   There are 49 measurements in the data set.

2.23   a.   Since the label on the vertical axis is Percent, this is a relative frequency histogram. We can divide the percents by 100% to get the relative frequencies.

b.   Summing the percents represented by all of the bars above 100, we get approximately 12%.

2.25   a.   Using MINITAB, a dot plot of the data is:

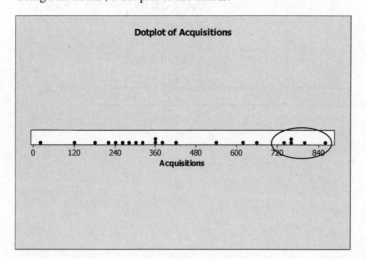

b.   By looking at the dot plot, one can conclude that the years 1996-2000 had the highest number of firms with at least one acquisition. The lowest number of acquisitions in that time frame (748) is almost 100 higher than the highest value from the remaining years.

2.27   a.   Using MINITAB, the frequency histograms for 2011 and 2010 SAT mathematics scores are:

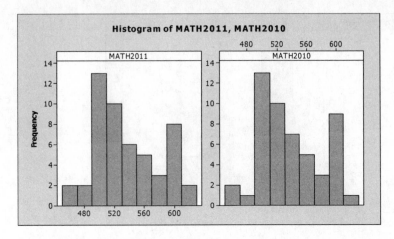

It appears that the scores have not changed very much at all. The graphs are very similar.

b.   Using MINITAB, the frequency histograms for 2011 and 2001 SAT mathematics scores are:

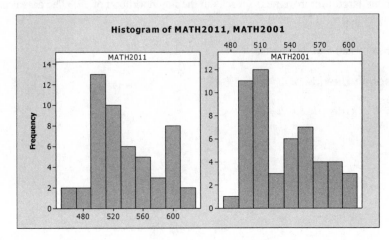

It appears that the scores have shifted to the right. The scores in 2011 appear to be somewhat better than the scores in 2011.

c.   Using MINITAB, the frequency histogram of the differences is:

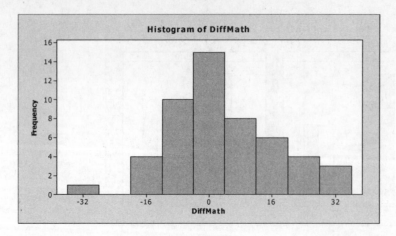

From this graph of the differences, we can see that there are more observations to the right of 0 than to the left of 0. This indicates that, in general, the scores have improved since 2001.

d.   From the graph, the largest improvement score is in the neighborhood of 32. The actual largest score is 32 and it is associated with Michigan.

2.29   Using MINITAB, the stem-and-leaf display is:

Stem-and-Leaf Display: Dioxide

```
Stem-and-leaf of Dioxide   N  = 16
Leaf Unit = 0.10


   5    0   12234
   7    0   55
  (2)   1   34
   7    1
   7    2   44
   5    2
   5    3   3
   4    3
   4    4   0000
```

The highlighted values are values that correspond to water specimens that contain oil. There is a tendency for crude oil to be present in water with lower levels of dioxide as 6 of the lowest 8 specimens with the lowest levels of dioxide contain oil.

2.31   Using MINITAB, the relative frequency histograms of the years in practice for the two groups of doctors are:

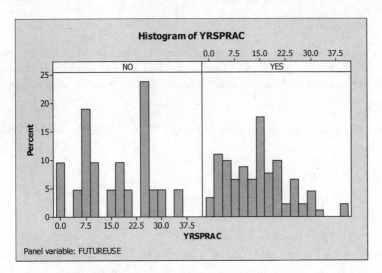

The researchers hypothesized that older, more experienced physicians will be less likely to use ethics consultation in the future. From the histograms, approximately 38% of the doctors that said "no" have more than 20 years of experience. Only about 19% of the doctors that said "yes" had more than 20 years of experience. This supports the researchers' assertion.

2.33   Using MINITAB, the histogram of the data is:

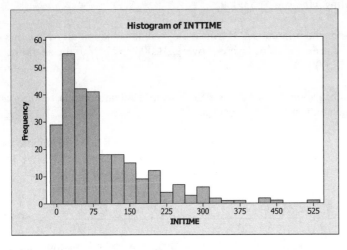

This histogram looks very similar to the one shown in the problem. Thus, there appears that there was minimal or no collaboration or collusion from within the company. We could conclude that the phishing attack against the organization was not an inside job.

2.35   Assume the data are a sample. The sample mean is:

$$\bar{x} = \frac{\sum x}{n} = \frac{3.2 + 2.5 + 2.1 + 3.7 + 2.8 + 2.0}{6} = \frac{16.3}{6} = 2.717$$

The median is the average of the middle two numbers when the data are arranged in order (since $n = 6$ is even). The data arranged in order are: 2.0, 2.1, 2.5, 2.8, 3.2, 3.7. The middle two numbers are 2.5 and 2.8.

The median is:

$$\frac{2.5+2.8}{2} = \frac{5.3}{2} = 2.65$$

2.37   The mean and median of a symmetric data set are equal to each other. The mean is larger than the median when the data set is skewed to the right. The mean is less than the median when the data set is skewed to the left. Thus, by comparing the mean and median, one can determine whether the data set is symmetric, skewed right, or skewed left.

2.39   Assume the data are a sample. The mode is the observation that occurs most frequently. For this sample, the mode is 15, which occurs three times.

The sample mean is:

$$\bar{x} = \frac{\sum x}{n} = \frac{18+10+15+13+17+15+12+15+18+16+11}{11} = \frac{160}{11} = 14.545$$

The median is the middle number when the data are arranged in order. The data arranged in order are: 10, 11, 12, 13, 15, 15, 15, 16, 17, 18, 18. The middle number is the 6th number, which is 15.

2.41   a.   For a distribution that is skewed to the left, the mean is less than the median.

   b.   For a distribution that is skewed to the right, the mean is greater than the median.

   c.   For a symmetric distribution, the mean and median are equal.

2.43   a.   The mean amount exported on the printout is 653. This means that the average amount of money per market from exporting sparkling wine was $653,000.

   b.   The median amount exported on the printout is 231. Since the median is the middle value, this means that half of the 30 sparkling wine export values were above $231,000 and half of the sparkling wine export values were below $231,000.

   c.   The mean 3-year percentage change on the printout is 481. This means that in the last three years, the average change is 481%, which indicates a large increase.

   d.   The median 3-year percentage change on the printout is 156. Since the median is the middle value, this means that half, or 15 of the 30 countries' 3-year percentage change values were above 156% and half, or 15 of the 30 countries' 3-year percentage change values were below 156%.

2.45   a.   The mean is $\bar{x} = \frac{\sum x}{n} = \frac{1,680,927+885,182+881,777+\cdots+563,967}{20} = \frac{15,192,021}{20} = 759,601.05$.

The average research expenditures for the top 20 ranked universities is 759,601.05 thousand dollars.

   b.   Since the number of observations is even, the median is the average of the middle 2 numbers once the data have been arranged in order. Since the data are already arranged in order, the median is $\frac{702,592+688,225}{2} = 695,408.5$.

Half of the institutions have a research expenditure less than 695,408.5 thousand dollars and half have research expenditures greater than 695,408.5 thousand dollars.

   c.   No, the mean from part a would not be a good measure for the center of the distribution for all

American universities. The data in part a come from only the top 20 universities. These universities would not be representative of all American universities.

2.47   a.   The median is the middle number (18th) once the data have been arranged in order because $n = 35$ is odd. The honey dosage data arranged in order are:

4,5,6,8,8,8,9,9,9,9,10,10,10,10,10,10,<u>11</u>,11,11,11,12,12,12,12,12,12,13,13,14,15,15,15,15,16

The 18th number is the median = 11.

b.   The median is the middle number (17th) once the data have been arranged in order because $n = 33$ is odd. The DM dosage data arranged in order are:

3,4,4,4,4,4,4,6,6,6,7,7,7,7,7,8,<u>9</u>,9,9,9,9,10,10,10,11,12,12,12,12,12,13,13,15

The 17th number is the median = 9.

c.   The median is the middle number (19th) once the data have been arranged in order because $n = 37$ is odd. The No dosage data arranged in order are:

0,1,1,1,3,3,4,4,5,5,5,6,6,6,6,7,7,7,<u>7</u>,7,7,7,7,8,8,8,8,8,9,9,9,9,10,11,12,12

The 19th number is the median = 7.

d.   Since the median for the Honey dosage is larger than the other two, it appears that the honey dosage leads to more improvement than the other two treatments.

2.49   a.   Skewed to the right. There will be a few people with very high salaries such as the president and football coach.

b.   Skewed to the left. On an easy test, most students will have high scores with only a few low scores.

c.   Skewed to the right. On a difficult test, most students will have low scores with only a few high scores.

d.   Skewed to the right. Most students will have a moderate amount of time studying while a few students might study a long time.

e.   Skewed to the left. Most cars will be relatively new with a few much older.

f.   Skewed to the left. Most students will take the entire time to take the exam while a few might leave early.

2.51   The mean is 141.31 hours. This means that the average number of semester hours per candidate for the CPA exam is 141.31 hours. The median is 140 hours. This means that 50% of the candidates had more than 140 semester hours of credit and 50% had less than 140 semester hours of credit. Since the mean and median are so close in value, the data are probably not skewed, but close to symmetric.

2.53   For the "Joint exchange offer with prepack" firms, the mean time is 2.6545 months, and the median is 1.5 months. Thus, the average time spent in bankruptcy for "Joint" firms is 2.6545 months, while half of the firms spend 1.5 months or less in bankruptcy.

For the "No prefiling vote held" firms, the mean time is 4.2364 months, and the median is 3.2 months. Thus, the average time spent in bankruptcy for "No prefiling vote held" firms is 4.2364 months, while half of the firms spend 3.2 months or less in bankruptcy.

For the "Prepack solicitation only" firms, the mean time is 1.8185 months, and the median is 1.4 months.

Thus, the average time spent in bankruptcy for "Prepack solicitation only" firms is 1.8185 months, while half of the firms spend 1.4 months or less in bankruptcy.

Since the means and medians for the three groups of firms differ quite a bit, it would be unreasonable to use a single number to locate the center of the time in bankruptcy. Three different "centers" should be used.

2.55   a.   Due to the "elite" superstars, the salary distribution is skewed to the right. Since this implies that the median is less than the mean, the players' association would want to use the median.

   b.   The owners, by the logic of part **a**, would want to use the mean.

2.57   a.   Range $= 4 - 0 = 4$

$$s^2 = \frac{\sum x^2 - \frac{\left(\sum x\right)^2}{n}}{n-1} = \frac{22 - \frac{8^2}{5}}{5-1} = 2.3 \qquad s = \sqrt{2.3} = 1.52$$

   b.   Range $= 6 - 0 = 6$

$$s^2 = \frac{\sum x^2 - \frac{\left(\sum x\right)^2}{n}}{n-1} = \frac{63 - \frac{17^2}{7}}{7-1} = 3.619 \qquad s = \sqrt{3.619} = 1.9$$

   c.   Range $= 8 - (-2) = 10$

$$s^2 = \frac{\sum x^2 - \frac{\left(\sum x\right)^2}{n}}{n-1} = \frac{154 - \frac{30^2}{10}}{10-1} = 7.111 \qquad s = \sqrt{7.111} = 2.67$$

   d.   Range $= 1 - (-3) = 4$

$$s^2 = \frac{\sum x^2 - \frac{\left(\sum x\right)^2}{n}}{n-1} = \frac{25.04 - \frac{(-6.8)^2}{17}}{17-1} = 1.395 \qquad s = \sqrt{1.395} = 1.18$$

2.59   a. $\sum x = 3 + 1 + 10 + 10 + 4 = 28 \qquad \sum x^2 = 3^2 + 1^2 + 10^2 + 10^2 + 4^2 = 226$

$$\bar{x} = \frac{\sum x}{n} = \frac{28}{5} = 5.6$$

$$s^2 = \frac{\sum x^2 - \frac{\left(\sum x\right)^2}{n}}{n-1} = \frac{226 - \frac{28^2}{5}}{5-1} = \frac{69.2}{4} = 17.3 \qquad s = \sqrt{17.3} = 4.1593$$

   b. $\sum x = 8 + 10 + 32 + 5 = 55 \qquad \sum x^2 = 8^2 + 10^2 + 32^2 + 5^2 = 1213$

$$\bar{x} = \frac{\sum x}{n} = \frac{55}{4} = 13.75 \text{ feet}$$

$$s^2 = \frac{\sum x^2 - \frac{\left(\sum x\right)^2}{n}}{n-1} = \frac{1213 - \frac{55^2}{4}}{4-1} = \frac{456.75}{3} = 152.25 \text{ square feet}$$

$$s = \sqrt{152.25} = 12.339 \text{ feet}$$

c. $\sum x = -1 + (-4) + (-3) + 1 + (-4) + (-4) = -15$ $\sum x^2 = (-1)^2 + (-4)^2 + (-3)^2 + 1^2 + (-4)^2 + (-4)^2 = 59$

$$\bar{x} = \frac{\sum x}{n} = \frac{-15}{6} = -2.5$$

$$s^2 = \frac{\sum x^2 - \frac{\left(\sum x\right)^2}{n}}{n-1} = \frac{59 - \frac{(-15)^2}{6}}{6-1} = \frac{21.5}{5} = 4.3 \qquad\qquad s = \sqrt{4.3} = 2.0736$$

d. $\sum x = \frac{1}{5} + \frac{1}{5} + \frac{1}{5} + \frac{2}{5} + \frac{1}{5} + \frac{4}{5} = \frac{10}{5} = 2$ $\sum x^2 = \left(\frac{1}{5}\right)^2 + \left(\frac{1}{5}\right)^2 + \left(\frac{1}{5}\right)^2 + \left(\frac{2}{5}\right)^2 + \left(\frac{1}{5}\right)^2 + \left(\frac{4}{5}\right)^2 = \frac{24}{25} = .96$

$$\bar{x} = \frac{\sum x}{n} = \frac{2}{6} = \frac{1}{3} = .33 \text{ ounce}$$

$$s^2 = \frac{\sum x^2 - \frac{\left(\sum x\right)^2}{n}}{n-1} = \frac{\frac{24}{25} - \frac{2^2}{6}}{6-1} = \frac{.2933}{5} = .0587 \text{ square ounce} \quad s = \sqrt{.0587} = .2422 \text{ ounce}$$

2.61   This is one possibility for the two data sets.

Data Set 1: 0, 1, 2, 3, 4, 5, 6, 7, 8, 9
Data Set 2: 0, 0, 1, 1, 2, 2, 3, 3, 9, 9

The two sets of data above have the same range = largest measurement − smallest measurement = 9 − 0 = 9.

The means for the two data sets are:

$$\bar{x}_1 = \frac{\sum x}{n} = \frac{0+1+2+3+4+5+6+7+8+9}{10} = \frac{45}{10} = 4.5$$

$$\bar{x}_2 = \frac{\sum x}{n} = \frac{0+0+1+1+2+2+3+3+9+9}{10} = \frac{30}{10} = 3$$

The dot diagrams for the two data sets are shown below.

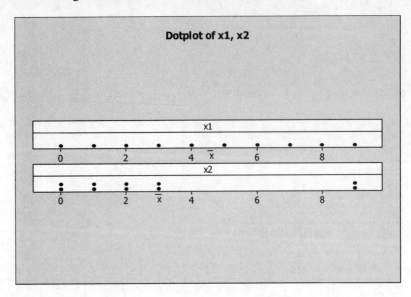

2.63   a.   Range = 3 − 0 = 3

$$s^2 = \frac{\sum x^2 - \dfrac{\left(\sum x\right)^2}{n}}{n-1} = \frac{15 - \dfrac{7^2}{5}}{5-1} = 1.3 \qquad\qquad s = \sqrt{1.3} = 1.14$$

b.   After adding 3 to each of the data points,

Range = 6 − 3 = 3

$$s^2 = \frac{\sum x^2 - \dfrac{\left(\sum x\right)^2}{n}}{n-1} = \frac{102 - \dfrac{22^2}{5}}{5-1} = 1.3 \qquad\qquad s = \sqrt{1.3} = 1.14$$

c.   After subtracting 4 from each of the data points,

Range = −1 − (−4) = 3

$$s^2 = \frac{\sum x^2 - \dfrac{\left(\sum x\right)^2}{n}}{n-1} = \frac{39 - \dfrac{(-13)^2}{5}}{5-1} = 1.3 \qquad s = \sqrt{1.3} = 1.14$$

d.   The range, variance, and standard deviation remain the same when any number is added to or subtracted from each measurement in the data set.

2.65   a.   The range is the difference between the largest observation and the smallest observation. From the printout, the largest observation is $4,852 thousand and the smallest observation is $70 thousand. The range is:

$R = \$4,852 - \$70 = \$4,882$ thousand

b.   From the printout, the standard deviation is $s = \$1,113$ thousand.

c.   The variance is the standard deviation squared. The variance is:

$s^2 = 1,113^2 = 1,238,769$ million dollars squared

2.67   a.   The range is 155. The statement is accurate.

b.   The variance is 722.036. The statement is not accurate. A more accurate statement would be: "The variance of the levels of supports for corporate sustainability for the 992 senior managers is 722.036."

c.   The standard deviation is 26.871. If the units of measure for the two distributions are the same, then the distribution of support levels for the 992 senior managers has less variation than a distribution with a standard deviation of 50. If the units of measure for the second distribution is not known, then we cannot compare the variation in the two distributions by looking at the standard deviations alone.

d.   The standard deviation best describes the variation in the distribution. The range can be greatly affected by extreme measures. The variance is measured in square units, which is hard to interpret. Thus, the standard deviation is the best measure to describe the variation.

2.69   a.   The range is the largest observation minus the smallest observation or $11 - 1 = 10$.

The variance is: $s^2 = \dfrac{\sum_i x_i^2 - \dfrac{\left(\sum_i x_i\right)^2}{n}}{n-1} = \dfrac{450 - \dfrac{78^2}{20}}{20-1} = 7.6737$

The standard deviation is: $s = \sqrt{s^2} = \sqrt{7.6737} = 2.77$

b.   The largest observation is 11. It is deleted from the data set. The new range is: $9 - 1 = 8$.

The variance is: $s^2 = \dfrac{\sum_i x_i^2 - \dfrac{\left(\sum_i x_i\right)^2}{n}}{n-1} = \dfrac{329 - \dfrac{67^2}{19}}{19-1} = 5.1520$

The standard deviation is: $s = \sqrt{s^2} = \sqrt{5.1520} = 2.27$

When the largest observation is deleted, the range, variance and standard deviation decrease.

c.   The largest observation is 11 and the smallest is 1. When these two observations are deleted from the data set, the new range is: $9 - 1 = 8$.

The variance is: $s^2 = \dfrac{\sum_i x_i^2 - \dfrac{\left(\sum_i x_i\right)^2}{n}}{n-1} = \dfrac{328 - \dfrac{66^2}{18}}{18-1} = 5.0588$

The standard deviation is: $s = \sqrt{s^2} = \sqrt{5.0588} = 2.25$

When the largest and smallest observations are deleted, the range, variance and standard deviation decrease.

2.71   a.   The unit of measurement of the variable of interest is dollars (the same as the mean and standard deviation). Based on this, the data are quantitative.

b.   Since no information is given about the shape of the data set, we can only use Chebyshev's Rule.

$900 is 2 standard deviations below the mean, and $2100 is 2 standard deviations above the mean. Using Chebyshev's Rule, at least 3/4 of the measurements (or $3/4 \times 200 = 150$ measurements) will fall between $900 and $2100.

$600 is 3 standard deviations below the mean and $2400 is 3 standard deviations above the mean. Using Chebyshev's Rule, at least 8/9 of the measurements (or $8/9 \times 200 \approx 178$ measurements) will fall between $600 and $2400.

$1200 is 1 standard deviation below the mean and $1800 is 1 standard deviation above the mean. Using Chebyshev's Rule, nothing can be said about the number of measurements that will fall between $1200 and $1800.

$1500 is equal to the mean and $2100 is 2 standard deviations above the mean. Using Chebyshev's Rule, at least 3/4 of the measurements (or $3/4 \times 200 = 150$ measurements) will fall between $900 and $2100. It is possible that all of the 150 measurements will be between $900 and $1500. Thus, nothing can be said about the number of measurements between $1500 and $2100.

2.73   According to the Empirical Rule:

a.   Approximately 68% of the measurements will be contained in the interval $\bar{x} - s$ to $\bar{x} + s$.

b.   Approximately 95% of the measurements will be contained in the interval $\bar{x} - 2s$ to $\bar{x} + 2s$.

c.   Essentially all the measurements will be contained in the interval $\bar{x} - 3s$ to $\bar{x} + 3s$.

2.75   Using Chebyshev's Rule, at least 8/9 of the measurements will fall within 3 standard deviations of the mean. Thus, the range of the data would be around 6 standard deviations. Using the Empirical Rule, approximately 95% of the observations are within 2 standard deviations of the mean. Thus, the range of the data would be around 4 standard deviations. We would expect the standard deviation to be somewhere between Range/6 and Range/4.

For our data, the range $= 760 - 135 = 625$.

The $\dfrac{\text{Range}}{6} = \dfrac{625}{6} = 104.17$ and $\dfrac{\text{Range}}{4} = \dfrac{625}{4} = 156.25$.

Therefore, I would estimate that the standard deviation of the data set is between 104.17 and 156.25.

It would not be feasible to have a standard deviation of 25. If the standard deviation were 25, the data would span $625/25 = 25$ standard deviations. This would be extremely unlikely.

2.77   a.   The interval $\bar{x} \pm 2s$ will contain at least 75% of the observations. This interval is $\bar{x} \pm 2s \Rightarrow 3.11 \pm 2(.66) \Rightarrow 3.11 \pm 1.32 \Rightarrow (1.79, 4.43)$.

b.   No. The value 1.25 does not fall in the interval $\bar{x} \pm 2s$. We know that at least 75% of all observations will fall within 2 standard deviations of the mean. Since 1.25 falls more than 2 standard deviations from the mean, it would not be a likely value to observe.

2.79   a.   The 2 standard deviation interval around the mean is:

$$\bar{x} \pm 2s \Rightarrow 141.31 \pm 2(17.77) \Rightarrow 141.31 \pm 35.54 \Rightarrow (105.77, \quad 176.85)$$

  b.   Using Chebyshev's Theorem, at least ¾ of the observations will fall within 2 standard deviations of the mean. Thus, at least ¾ of first-time candidates for the CPA exam have total credit hours between 105.77 and 176.85.

  c.   In order for the above statement to be true, nothing needs to be known about the shape of the distribution of total semester hours.

2.81   a.   The sample mean is: $\bar{x} = \dfrac{\sum\limits_{i=1}^{n} x_i}{n} = \dfrac{17,800}{186} = 95.699$

The sample variance is: $s^2 = \dfrac{\sum\limits_{i=1}^{n} x^2 - \dfrac{\left(\sum\limits_{i=1}^{n} x_i\right)^2}{n}}{n-1} = \dfrac{1,707,998 - \dfrac{17,800^2}{186}}{186-1} = 24.6332$

The standard deviation is: $s = \sqrt{s^2} = \sqrt{24.6332} = 4.9632$

  b. $\bar{x} \pm s \Rightarrow 95.699 \pm 4.963 \Rightarrow (90.736, \quad 100.662)$

$\bar{x} \pm 2s \Rightarrow 95.699 \pm 2(4.963) \Rightarrow 95.699 \pm 9.926 \Rightarrow (85.773, \quad 105.625)$

$\bar{x} \pm 3s \Rightarrow 95.699 \pm 3(4.963) \Rightarrow 95.699 \pm 14.889 \Rightarrow (80.810, \quad 110.558)$

  c.   There are 166 out of 186 observations in the first interval. This is $(166/186) \times 100\% = 89.2\%$. There are 179 out of 186 observations in the second interval. This is $(179/186) \times 100\% = 96.2\%$. There are 182 out of 186 observations in the second interval. This is $(182/186) \times 100\% = 97.8\%$.

The percentages for the first 2 intervals are much larger than we would expect using the Empirical Rule. The Empirical Rule indicates that approximately 68% of the observations will fall within 1 standard deviation of the mean. It also indicates that approximately 95% of the observations will fall within 2 standard deviations of the mean. Chebyshev's Theorem says that at least ¾ or 75% of the observations will fall within 2 standard deviations of the mean and at least 8/9 or 88.9% of the observations will fall within 3 standard deviations of the mean. It appears that our observed percentages agree with Chebyshev's Theorem better than the Empirical Rule.

2.83   The sample mean is:

$$\bar{x} = \frac{\sum\limits_{i=1}^{n} x_i}{n} = \frac{240.9 + 248.8 + 215.7 + \cdots + 238.0}{10} = \frac{2347.4}{10} = 234.74$$

The sample variance deviation is:

$$s^2 = \frac{\sum\limits_{i=1}^{n} x_i^2 - \dfrac{\left(\sum\limits_{i=1}^{n} x_i\right)^2}{n}}{n-1} = \frac{551,912.1 - \dfrac{2347.4^2}{10}}{9} = \frac{883.424}{9} = 98.1582$$

The sample standard deviation is: $\sqrt{s^2} = \sqrt{98.1582} = 9.91$

The data are fairly symmetric, so we can use the Empirical Rule. We know from the Empirical Rule that almost all of the observations will fall within 3 standard deviations of the mean. This interval would be:

$$\bar{x} \pm 3s \Rightarrow 234.74 \pm 3(9.91) \Rightarrow 234.74 \pm 29.73 \Rightarrow (205.01, \quad 264.47)$$

2.85   a.   The interval $\bar{x} \pm 2s$ for the flexed arm group is $\bar{x} \pm 2s \Rightarrow 59 \pm 3(4) \Rightarrow 59 \pm 12 \Rightarrow (47, 71)$. The interval for the extended are group is $\bar{x} \pm 2s \Rightarrow 43 \pm 3(2) \Rightarrow 43 \pm 6 \Rightarrow (37, 49)$. We know that at least 8/9 or 88.9% of the observations will fall within 3 standard deviations of the mean using Chebyshev's Rule. Since these 2 intervals barely overlap, the information supports the researchers' theory. The shoppers from the flexed arm group are more likely to select vice options than the extended arm group.

   b.   The interval $\bar{x} \pm 2s$ for the flexed arm group is $\bar{x} \pm 2s \Rightarrow 59 \pm 2(10) \Rightarrow 59 \pm 20 \Rightarrow (39, 79)$. The interval for the extended are group is $\bar{x} \pm 2s \Rightarrow 43 \pm 2(15) \Rightarrow 43 \pm 30 \Rightarrow (13, 73)$. Since these two intervals overlap almost completely, the information does not support the researcher's theory. There

2.87   Since we do not know if the distribution of the heights of the trees is mound-shaped, we need to apply Chebyshev's Rule. We know $\mu = 30$ and $\sigma = 3$. Therefore,

$$\mu \pm 3\sigma \Rightarrow 30 \pm 3(3) \Rightarrow 30 \pm 9 \Rightarrow (21, 39)$$

According to Chebyshev's Rule, at least $8/9 = .89$ of the tree heights on this piece of land fall within this interval and at most $1/9 = .11$ of the tree heights will fall above the interval. However, the buyer will only purchase the land if at least $\dfrac{1000}{5000} = .20$ of the tree heights are at least 40 feet tall. Therefore, the buyer should not buy the piece of land.

2.89   We know $\mu = 25$ and $\sigma = 1$. Therefore, $\mu \pm 2\sigma \Rightarrow 25 \pm 2(.1) \Rightarrow 25 \pm .2 \Rightarrow (24.8, 25.2)$

The machine is shut down for adjustment if the contents of two consecutive bags fall more than 2 standard deviations from the mean (i.e., outside the interval (24.8, 25.2)). Therefore, the machine was shut down yesterday at 11:30 (25.23 and 25.25 are outside the interval) and again at 4:00 (24.71 and 25.31 are outside the interval).

2.91   Using the definition of a percentile:

	Percentile	Percentage Above	Percentage Below
a.	75th	25%	75%
b.	50th	50%	50%
c.	20th	80%	20%
d.	84th	16%	84%

2.93   We first compute z-scores for each x value.

a. $z = \dfrac{x-\mu}{\sigma} = \dfrac{100-50}{25} = 2$

b. $z = \dfrac{x-\mu}{\sigma} = \dfrac{1-4}{1} = -3$

c. $z = \dfrac{x-\mu}{\sigma} = \dfrac{0-200}{100} = -2$

d. $z = \dfrac{x-\mu}{\sigma} = \dfrac{10-5}{3} = 1.67$

The above z-scores indicate that the x value in part **a** lies the greatest distance above the mean and the x value of part **b** lies the greatest distance below the mean.

2.95   The mean score of U.S. eighth-graders on a mathematics assessment test is 283. This is the average score. The 25th percentile is 259. This means that 25% of the U.S. eighth-graders score below 259 on the test and 75% score higher. The 75th percentile is 308. This means that 75% of the U.S. eighth-graders score below 308 on the test and 25% score higher. The 90th percentile is 329. This means that 90% of the U.S. eighth-graders score below 329 on the test and 10% score higher.

2.97   A median starting salary of $41,100 indicates that half of the University of South Florida graduates had starting salaries less than $41,100 and half had starting salaries greater than $41,100. At mid-career, half of the University of South Florida graduates had a salary less than $71,100 and half had salaries greater than $71,100. At mid-career, 90% of the University of South Florida graduates had salaries under $131,000 and 10% had salaries greater than $131,000.

2.99   Since the 90th percentile of the study sample in the subdivision was .00372 mg/L, which is less than the USEPA level of .015 mg/L, the water customers in the subdivision are not at risk of drinking water with unhealthy lead levels.

2.101   a.   The 10th percentile is the score that has at least 10% of the observations less than it. If we arrange the data in order from the smallest to the largest, the 10th percentile score will be the .10(75) = 7.5 or 8th observation. When the data are arranged in order, the 8th observation is 0. Thus, the 10th percentile is 0.

b.   The 95th percentile is the score that has at least 95% of the observations less than it. If we arrange the data in order from the smallest to the largest, the 95th percentile score will be the .95(75) = 71.25 or 72nd observation. When the data are arranged in order, the 72nd observation is 21. Thus, the 95th percentile is 21.

c.   The sample mean is: $\bar{x} = \dfrac{\sum_{i=1}^{n} x_i}{n} = \dfrac{393}{75} = 5.24$

The sample variance is: $s^2 = \dfrac{\sum_i x_i^2 - \dfrac{\left(\sum_i x_i\right)^2}{n}}{n-1} = \dfrac{5943 - \dfrac{393^2}{75}}{75-1} = 52.482$

The standard deviation is: $s = \sqrt{s^2} = \sqrt{52.482} = 7.244$

The z-score for a county with 48 Superfund sites is: $z = \dfrac{x - \bar{x}}{s} = \dfrac{48 - 5.24}{7.244} = 5.90$

d.   Yes. A score of 48 is almost 6 standard deviations from the mean. We know that for any data set almost all (at least 8/9 using Chebyshev's Theorem) of the observations are within 3 standard deviations of the mean. To be almost 6 standard deviations from the mean is very unusual.

2.103   a.   The z-score for Harvard is $z = 5.08$. This means that Harvard's productivity score was 5.08 standard deviations above the mean. This is extremely high and extremely unusual.

b.   The z-score for Howard University is $z = -.85$. This means that Howard University's productivity score was .85 standard deviations below the mean. This is not an unusual z-score.

c.   Yes. Other indicators that the distribution is skewed to the right are the values of the highest and lowest z-scores. The lowest z-score is less than 1 standard deviation below the mean while the highest z-score is 5.08 standard deviations above the mean.

Using MINITAB, the histogram of the z-scores is:

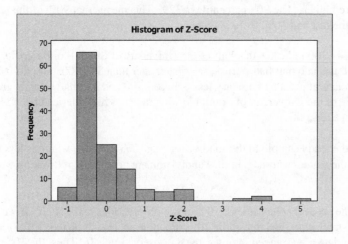

This histogram does imply that the data are skewed to the right.

2.105   Not necessarily. Because the distribution is highly skewed to the right, the standard deviation is very large. Remember that the z-score represents the number of standard deviations a score is from the mean. If the standard deviation is very large, then the z-scores for observations somewhat near the mean will appear to be fairly small. If we deleted the schools with the very high productivity scores and recomputed the mean and standard deviation, the standard deviation would be much smaller. Thus, most of the z-scores would be larger because we would be dividing by a much smaller standard deviation. This would imply a bigger spread among the rest of the schools than the original distribution with the few outliers.

2.107   The interquartile range is $IQR = Q_U - Q_L = 85 - 60 = 25$.

The lower inner fence $= Q_L - 1.5(IQR) = 60 - 1.5(25) = 22.5$.

The upper inner fence $= Q_U + 1.5(IQR) = 85 + 1.5(25) = 122.5$.

The lower outer fence $= Q_L - 3(IQR) = 60 - 3(25) = -15$.

The upper outer fence $= Q_U + 3(IQR) = 85 + 3(25) = 160$.

With only this information, the box plot would look something like the following:

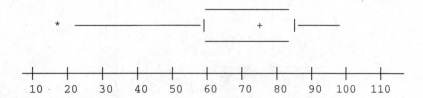

The whiskers extend to the inner fences unless no data points are that small or that large. The upper inner fence is 122.5. However, the largest data point is 100, so the whisker stops at 100. The lower inner fence is 22.5. The smallest data point is 18, so the whisker extends to 22.5. Since 18 is between the inner and outer fences, it is designated with a *. We do not know if there is any more than one data point below 22.5, so we cannot be sure that the box plot is entirely correct.

2.109   a.   Using MINITAB, the box plot for sample A is given below.

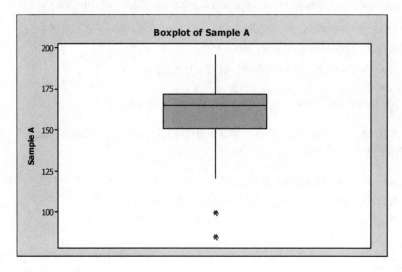

Using MINITAB, the box plot for sample B is given below.

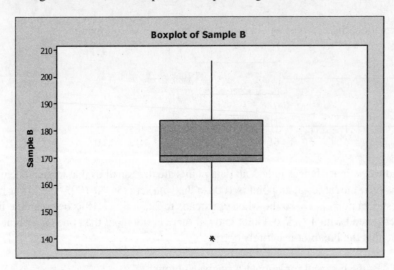

b.   In sample A, the measurement 84 is an outlier. This measurement falls outside the lower outer fence.

Lower outer fence = Lower hinge $-3(IQR) \approx 150 - 3(172 - 150) = 150 - 3(22) = 84$

Lower inner fence = Lower hinge $-1.5(IQR) \approx 150 - 1.5(22) = 117$

Upper inner fence = Upper hinge $+1.5(IQR) \approx 172 + 1.5(22) = 205$

In addition, 100 may be an outlier. It lies outside the inner fence.

In sample B, 140 and 206 may be outliers. The point 140 lies outside the inner fence while the point 206 lies right at the inner fence.

Lower outer fence = Lower hinge $-3(IQR) \approx 168 - 3(184 - 169) = 168 - 3(15) = 123$

Lower inner fence = Lower hinge $-1.5(IQR) \approx 168 - 1.5(15) = 145.5$

Upper inner fence = Upper hinge $+1.5(IQR) \approx 184 + 1.5(15) = 206.5$

2.111   a.   The average expenditure per full-time employee is $6,563. The median expenditure per employee is $6,232. Half of all expenditures per employee were less than $6,232 and half were greater than $6,232. The lower quartile is $5,309. Twenty-five percent of all expenditures per employee were below $5,309. The upper quartile is $7,216. Seventy-five percent of all expenditures per employee were below $7,216.

b. $IQR = Q_U - Q_L = \$7,216 - \$5,309 = \$1,907$.

c.   The interquartile range goes from the 25th percentile to the 75th percentile. Thus, $.5 = .75 - .25$ of the 1,751 army hospitals have expenses between $5,309 and $7,216.

2.113   a.   The z-score is: $z = \dfrac{x - \bar{x}}{s} = \dfrac{160 - 141.31}{17.77} = 1.05$

Since the z-score is not large, it is not considered an outlier.

b.   Z-scores with values greater than 3 in absolute value are considered outliers. An observation with a z-score of 3 would have the value:

$$z = \frac{x - \bar{x}}{s} \Rightarrow 3 = \frac{x - 141.31}{17.77} \Rightarrow 3(17.77) = x - 141.31 \Rightarrow 53.31 = x - 141.31 \Rightarrow x = 194.62$$

An observation with a z-score of -3 would have the value:

$$z = \frac{x - \bar{x}}{s} \Rightarrow -3 = \frac{x - 141.31}{17.77} \Rightarrow -3(17.77) = x - 141.31 \Rightarrow -53.31 = x - 141.31 \Rightarrow x = 88.00$$

Thus any observation of semester hours that is greater than or equal to 194.62 or less than or equal to 88 would be considered an outlier.

2.115   a.   Using MINITAB, the boxplots for each type of firm are:

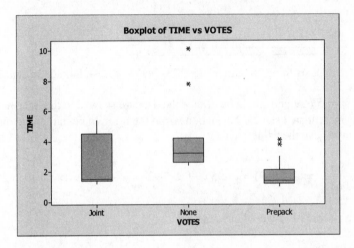

b.   The median bankruptcy time for Joint firms is about 1.5. The median bankruptcy time for None firms is about 3.2. The median bankruptcy time for Prepack firms is about 1.4.

c.   The range of the "Prepack" firms is less than the other two, while the range of the "None" firms is the largest. The interquartile range of the "Prepack" firms is less than the other two, while the interquartile range of the "Joint" firms is larger than the other two.

d.   No. The interquartile range for the "Prepack" firms is the smallest which corresponds to the smallest standard deviation. However, the second smallest interquartile range corresponds to the "None" firms. The second smallest standard deviation corresponds to the "Joint" firms.

e.   Yes. There is evidence of two outliers in the "Prepack" firms. These are indicated by the two *'s. There is also evidence of two outliers in the "None" firms. These are indicated by the two *'s.

2.117   a.   Using MINITAB, the boxplot is:

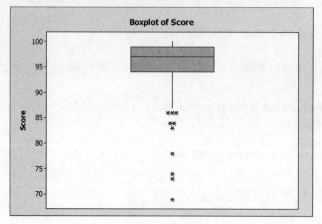

From the boxplot, there appears to be 10 outliers: 69, 73, 74, 78, 83, 84, 84, 86, 86, and 86.

b.   From Exercise 2.81, $\bar{x} = 95.699$ and $s = 4.963$. Since the data are skewed to the left, we will consider observations more than 2 standard deviations from the mean to be outliers. An observation with a z-score of 2 would have the value:

$$z = \frac{x - \bar{x}}{s} \Rightarrow 2 = \frac{x - 95.699}{4.963} \Rightarrow 2(4.963) = x - 95.699 \Rightarrow 9.926 = x - 95.699 \Rightarrow x = 105.625$$

An observation with a z-score of -2 would have the value:

$$z = \frac{x - \bar{x}}{s} \Rightarrow -2 = \frac{x - 95.699}{4.963} \Rightarrow -2(4.963) = x - 95.699 \Rightarrow -9.926 = x - 95.699 \Rightarrow x = 85.773$$

Observations greater than 105.625 or less than 85.773 would be considered outliers. Using this criterion, the following observations would be outliers: 69, 73, 74, 78, 83, 84, and 84.

c.   No, these methods do not agree exactly. Using the boxplot, 10 observations were identified as outliers. Using the z-score method, only 7 observations were identified as outliers. However, the 3 additional points that were not identified as outliers using the z-score method were very close to the cutoff value.

2.119   From the stem-and-leaf display in Exercise 2.34, the data are fairly mound-shaped, but skewed somewhat to the right.

The sample mean is $\bar{x} = \dfrac{\sum x}{n} = \dfrac{1493}{25} = 59.72$.

The sample variance is $s^2 = \dfrac{\sum x^2 - \dfrac{\left(\sum x\right)^2}{n}}{n-1} = \dfrac{96,885 - \dfrac{1493^2}{25}}{25-1} = 321.7933$.

The sample standard deviation is $s = \sqrt{321.7933} = 17.9386$.

The z-score associated with the largest value is $z = \dfrac{x - \bar{x}}{s} = \dfrac{102 - 59.72}{17.9386} = 2.36$.

Since the data are not extremely skewed to the right, this observation is probably not an outlier.

The observations associated with the one-time customers are 5 of the largest 7 observations. Thus, repeat customers tend to have shorter delivery times than one-time customers.

2.121   Using MINITAB, the scatterplot is:

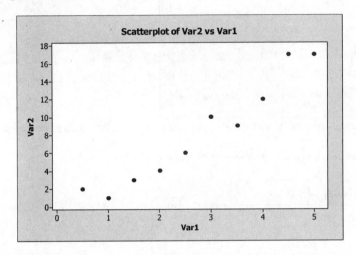

2.123.   From the scatterplot of the data, it appears that as the number of punishments increases, the average payoff decreases. Thus, there appears to be a negative linear relationship between punishment use and average payoff. This supports the researchers conclusion that "winners" don't punish".

2.125   Using MINITAB, a scattergram of the data is:

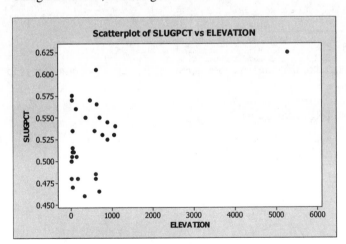

If we include the observation from Denver, then we would say there might be a linear relationship between slugging percentage and elevation. If we eliminated the observation from Denver, it appears that there might not be a relationship between slugging percentage and elevation.

2.127   a.   Using MINITAB, a scatterplot of JIF and cost is:

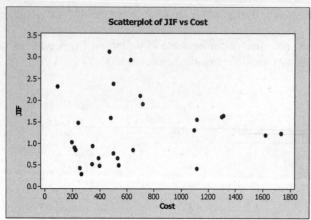

There is a slight negative linear trend to the data. As cost increases, JIF tends to decrease.

b.   Using MINITAB, a scatterplot of the number of cities and cost is:

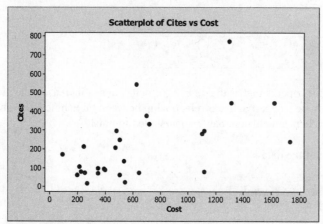

There is a moderate positive trend to the data. As cost increases, the number of cities tends to increase.

c.   Using MINITAB, a scatterplot of RPI and cost is:

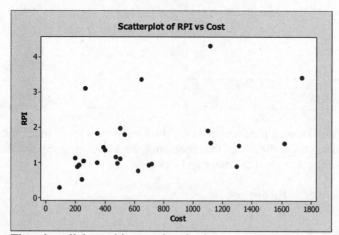

There is a slight positive trend to the data. As cost increases, RPI tends to increase.

2.129   a.   Using MINITAB, a scatterplot of the data is:

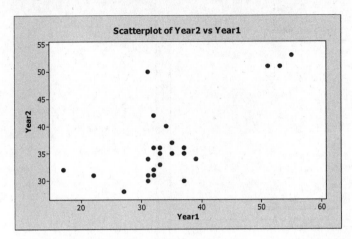

There is a moderate positive trend to the data. As the scores for Year1 increase, the scores for Year2 also tend to increase.

b.   From the graph, two agencies that had greater than expected PARS evaluation scores for Year2 were USAID and State.

2.131   a.   Using MINITAB, the scatterplot of the data is:

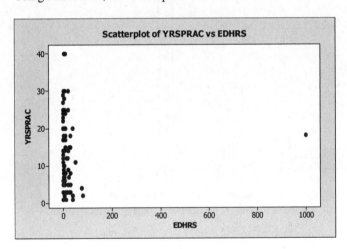

There does not appear to be much of a relationship between the years of experience and the amount of exposure to ethics in medical school.

b.   Using MINITAB, a boxplot of the amount of exposure to ethics in medical school is:

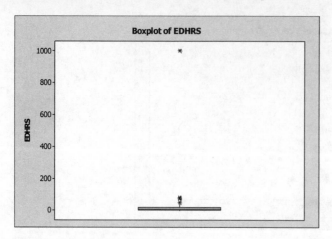

The one data point that is an extreme outlier is the value of 1000.

c.   After removing this data point, the scatterplot of the data is:

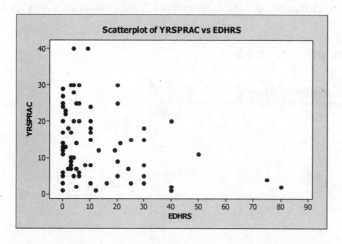

With the data point removed, there now appears to be a negative trend to the data. As the amount of exposure to ethics in medical school increases, the years of experience decreases.

2.133   One way the bar graph can mislead the viewer is that the vertical axis has been cut off. Instead of starting at 0, the vertical axis starts at 12. Another way the bar graph can mislead the viewer is that as the bars get taller, the widths of the bars also increase.

2.135   a.   The graph might be misleading because the scales on the vertical axes are different. The left vertical axis ranges from 0 to $120 million. The right vertical axis ranges from 0 to $20 billion.

b.   Using MINITAB, the redrawn graph is:

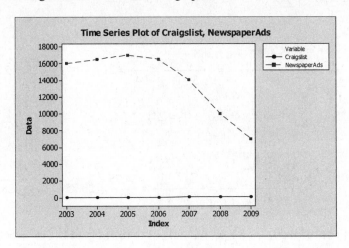

Although the amount of revenue produced by Craigslist has increased dramatically from 2003 to 2009, it is still much smaller than the revenue produced by newspaper ad sales.

2.137   The relative frequency histogram is:

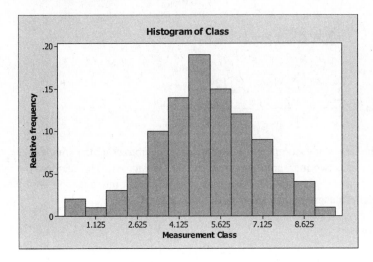

2.139   a. $z = \dfrac{x - \mu}{\sigma} = \dfrac{50 - 60}{10} = -1$ $z = \dfrac{70 - 60}{10} = 1$ $z = \dfrac{80 - 60}{10} = 2$

b. $z = \dfrac{x - \mu}{\sigma} = \dfrac{50 - 50}{5} = 0$ $z = \dfrac{70 - 50}{5} = 4$ $z = \dfrac{80 - 50}{5} = 6$

c $z = \dfrac{x - \mu}{\sigma} = \dfrac{50 - 40}{10} = 1$ $z = \dfrac{70 - 40}{10} = 3$ $z = \dfrac{80 - 40}{10} = 4$

d. $z = \dfrac{x - \mu}{\sigma} = \dfrac{50 - 40}{100} = .1$ $z = \dfrac{70 - 40}{100} = .3$ $z = \dfrac{80 - 40}{100} = .4$

2.141   a. $\sum x = 13 + 1 + 10 + 3 + 3 = 30$ $\sum x^2 = 13^2 + 1^2 + 10^2 + 3^2 + 3^2 = 288$

$$\bar{x} = \frac{\sum x}{n} = \frac{30}{5} = 6 \qquad s^2 = \frac{\sum x^2 - \frac{\left(\sum x\right)^2}{n}}{n-1} = \frac{288 - \frac{30^2}{5}}{5-1} = \frac{108}{4} = 27 \qquad s = \sqrt{27} = 5.20$$

b. $\sum x = 13 + 6 + 6 + 0 = 25$ $\sum x^2 = 13^2 + 6^2 + 6^2 + 0^2 = 241$

$$\bar{x} = \frac{\sum x}{n} = \frac{25}{4} = 6.25 \qquad s^2 = \frac{\sum x^2 - \frac{\left(\sum x\right)^2}{n}}{n-1} = \frac{241 - \frac{25^2}{4}}{4-1} = \frac{84.75}{3} = 28.25 \qquad s = \sqrt{28.25} = 5.32$$

c. $\sum x = 1 + 0 + 1 + 10 + 11 + 11 + 15 = 49$ $\sum x^2 = 1^2 + 0^2 + 1^2 + 10^2 + 11^2 + 11^2 + 15^2 = 569$.

$$\bar{x} = \frac{\sum x}{n} = \frac{49}{7} = 7 \qquad s^2 = \frac{\sum x^2 - \frac{\left(\sum x\right)^2}{n}}{n-1} = \frac{569 - \frac{49^2}{7}}{7-1} = \frac{226}{6} = 37.67 \qquad s = \sqrt{37.67} = 6.14$$

d. $\sum x = 3 + 3 + 3 + 3 = 12$ $\sum x^2 = 3^2 + 3^2 + 3^2 + 3^2 = 36$

$$\bar{x} = \frac{\sum x}{n} = \frac{12}{4} = 3 \qquad s^2 = \frac{\sum x^2 - \frac{\left(\sum x\right)^2}{n}}{n-1} = \frac{36 - \frac{12^2}{4}}{4-1} = \frac{0}{3} = 0 \qquad s = \sqrt{0} = 0$$

2.143   The range is found by taking the largest measurement in the data set and subtracting the smallest measurement. Therefore, it only uses two measurements from the whole data set. The standard deviation uses every measurement in the data set. Therefore, it takes every measurement into account—not just two. The range is affected by extreme values more than the standard deviation.

2.145   Using MINITAB, the scatterplot is:

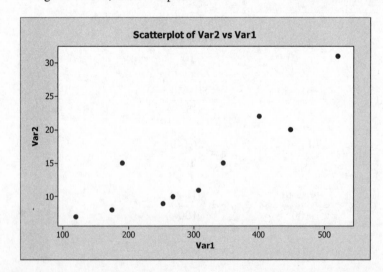

2.147 a. The relative frequency for each response category is found by dividing the frequency by the total sample size. The relative frequency for the category "Global Marketing" is 235/2863 = .082. The rest of the relative frequencies are found in a similar manner and are reported in the table.

Area	*Number*	*Relative Frequencies*
Global Marketing	235	235/2863 = .082
Sales Management	494	494/2863 = .173
Buyer Behavior	478	478/2863 = .167
Relationships	498	498/2863 = .174
Innovation	398	398/2863 = .139
Marketing Strategy	280	280/2863 = .098
Channels/Distribution	213	213/2863 = .074
Marketing Research	131	131/2863 = .046
Services	136	136/2863 = .048
TOTAL	2,863	1.00

Relationships and sales management had the most articles published with 17.4% and 17.3%, respectively. Not far behind was Buyer Behavior with 16.7%. Of the rest of the areas, only innovation had more than 10%.

b. Using MINITAB, the pie chart of the data is:

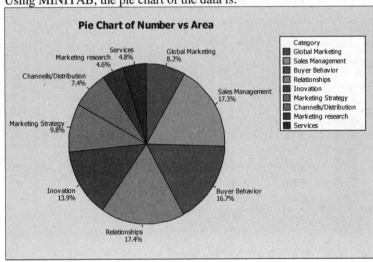

The slice for Marketing Research is smaller than the slice for Sales Management because there were fewer articles on Marketing Research than for Sales Management.

2.149   Using MINITAB, the pie chart is:

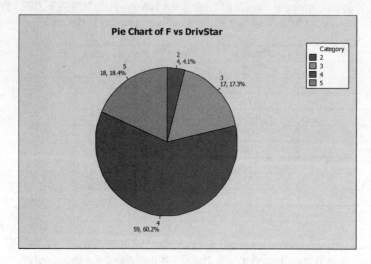

60% of cars have 4-star rating and only 4% have 2-star ratings.

2.151   a.   Using MINITAB, a Pareto diagram for the data is:

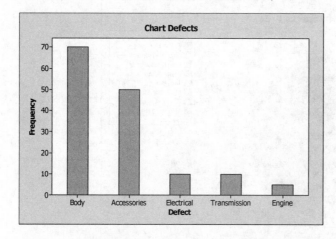

The most frequently observed defect is a body defect.

b.   Using MINITAB, a Pareto diagram for the Body Defect data is:

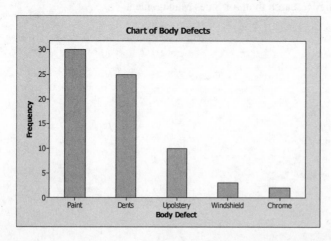

Most body defects are either paint or dents. These two categories account for $(30 + 25)/70 = 55/70 = .786$ of all body defects. Since these two categories account for so much of the body defects, it would seem appropriate to target these two types of body defects for special attention.

2.153   a.   From the information given, we have $\bar{x} = 375$ and $s = 25$. From Chebyshev's Rule, we know that at least three-fourths of the measurements are within the interval: $\bar{x} \pm 2s$, or (325, 425)

Thus, at most one-fourth of the measurements exceed 425. In other words, more than 425 vehicles used the intersection on at most 25% of the days.

b.   According to the Empirical Rule, approximately 95% of the measurements are within the interval:

$\bar{x} \pm 2s$, or (325, 425)

This leaves approximately 5% of the measurements to lie outside the interval. Because of the symmetry of a mound-shaped distribution, approximately 2.5% of these will lie below 325, and the remaining 2.5% will lie above 425. Thus, on approximately 2.5% of the days, more than 425 vehicles used the intersection.

2.155   a.   Using MINITAB, the stem-and-leaf display is:

```
Stem-and-Leaf of PENALTY            N = 38
Leaf Unit = 10

 (28)      0  0011111122222222333333344444899
  10       1  00239
   5       2
   5       3  0
   4       4  0
   3       5
   3       6
   3       7
   3       8  5
   2       9  3
   1      10  0
```

b.   See the highlighted leaves in part **a**.

c.   Most of the penalties imposed for Clean Air Act violations are relatively small compared to the penalties imposed for other violations. All but two of the penalties for Clean Air Act violations are below the median penalty imposed.

2.157   a.   Using MINITAB, the relative frequency histogram is:

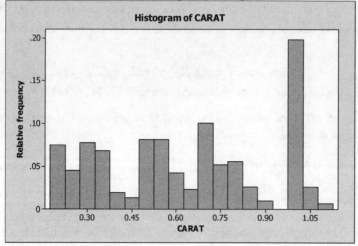

b.   Using MINITAB, the relative frequency histogram for the GIA group is:

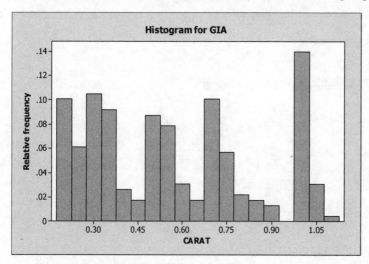

c.   Using MINITAB, the relative frequency histograms for the HRD and IGI groups are:

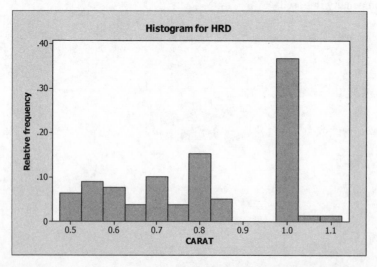

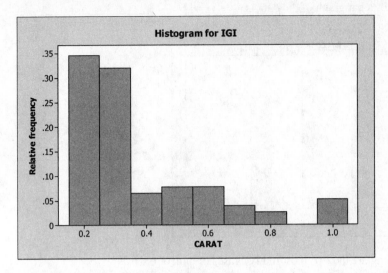

d. The HRD group does not assess any diamonds less than .5 carats and almost 40% of the diamonds they assess are 1.0 carat or higher. The IGI group does not assess very many diamonds over .5 carats and more than half are .3 carats or less. More than half of the diamonds assessed by the GIA group are more than .5 carats, but the sizes are less than those of the HRD group.

e. The sample mean is: $\bar{x} = \dfrac{\displaystyle\sum_{i=1}^{n} x_i}{n} = \dfrac{194.32}{308} = .631$

The average number of carats for the 308 diamonds is .631.

f. The median is the average of the middle two observations once they have been ordered. The 154th and 155th observations are .62 and .62. The average of these two observations is .62.

Half of the diamonds weigh less than .62 carats and half weigh more.

g The mode is 1.0. This observation occurred 32 times.

h. Since the mean and median are close in value, either could be a good descriptor of central tendency.

i. From Chebyshev's Theorem, we know that at least ¾ or 75% of all observations will fall within 2 standard deviations of the mean. From part e, $\bar{x} = .63$.

The variance is: $s^2 = \dfrac{\displaystyle\sum_{i} x_i^2 - \dfrac{\left(\displaystyle\sum_{i} x_i\right)^2}{n}}{n-1} = \dfrac{146.19 - \dfrac{194.32^2}{308}}{308-1} = .0768$ square carats

The standard deviation is: $s = \sqrt{s^2} = \sqrt{.0768} = .277$ carats

This interval is: $\bar{x} \pm 2s \Rightarrow .631 \pm 2(.277) \Rightarrow .631 \pm .554 \Rightarrow (.077,\ 1.185)$

2.159   a.   Using MINITAB, a bar graph of the data is:

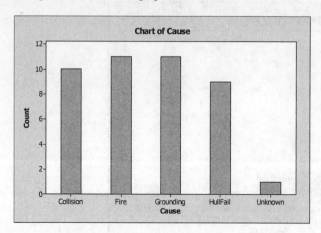

Fire and grounding are the two most likely causes of puncture.

b.   Using MINITAB, the descriptive statistics are:

Descriptive Statistics: Spillage

```
Variable    N    Mean   StDev   Minimum     Q1  Median      Q3  Maximum
Spillage   42   66.19   56.05     25.00   32.00   43.00   77.50   257.00
```

The mean spillage amount is 66.19 thousand metric tons, while the median is 43.00. Since the median is so much smaller than the mean, it indicates that the data are skewed to the right. The standard deviation is 56.05. Again, since this value is so close to the value of the mean, it indicates that the data are skewed to the right.

Since the data are skewed to the right, we cannot use the Empirical Rule to describe the data. Chebyshev's Rule can be used. Using Chebyshev's Rule, we know that at least 8/9 of the observations will fall within 3 standard deviations of the mean.
$\bar{x} \pm 3s \Rightarrow 66.19 \pm 3(56.05) \Rightarrow 66.19 \pm 168.15 \Rightarrow (-101.96, \ 234.34)$ or $(0, 234.34)$ since we cannot have negative spillage.

Thus, at least 8/9 of all oil spills will be between 0 and 234.34 thousand metric tons.

2.161   a.   Since no information is given about the distribution of the velocities of the Winchester bullets, we can only use Chebyshev's Rule to describe the data. We know that at least 3/4 of the velocities will fall within the interval:

$\bar{x} \pm 2s \Rightarrow 936 \pm 2(10) \Rightarrow 936 \pm 20 \Rightarrow (916, 956)$

Also, at least 8/9 of the velocities will fall within the interval:

$\bar{x} \pm 3s \Rightarrow 936 \pm 3(10) \Rightarrow 936 \pm 30 \Rightarrow (906, 966)$

b.   Since a velocity of 1,000 is much larger than the largest value in the second interval in part **a**, it is very unlikely that the bullet was manufactured by Winchester.

2.163   a.   One reason the plot may be interpreted differently is that no scale is given on the vertical axis. Also, since the plot almost reaches the horizontal axis at 3 years, it is obvious that the bottom of the plot has been cut off. Another important factor omitted is who responded to the survey.

b.   A scale should be added to the vertical axis. Also, that scale should start at 0.

2.165   a.   Since the mean is greater than the median, the distribution of the radiation levels is skewed to the right.

b. $\bar{x} \pm s \Rightarrow 10 \pm 3 \Rightarrow (7, 13)$; $\bar{x} \pm 2s \Rightarrow 10 \pm 2(3) \Rightarrow (4, 16)$; $\bar{x} \pm 3s \Rightarrow 10 \pm 3(3) \Rightarrow (1, 19)$

Interval	Chebyshev's	Empirical
(7, 13)	At least 0	≈68%
(4, 16)	At least 75%	≈95%
(1, 19)	At least 88.9%	≈100%

Since the data are skewed to the right, Chebyshev's Rule is probably more appropriate in this case.

c.   The background level is 4. Using Chebyshev's Rule, at least 75% or .75(50) ≈ 38 homes are above the background level. Using the Empirical Rule, ≈ 97.5% or .975(50) ≈ 49 homes are above the background level.

d. $z = \dfrac{x - \bar{x}}{s} = \dfrac{20 - 10}{3} = 3.333$

It is unlikely that this new measurement came from the same distribution as the other 50. Using either Chebyshev's Rule or the Empirical Rule, it is very unlikely to see any observations more than 3 standard deviations from the mean.

2.167   a.   Both the height and width of the bars (peanuts) change. Thus, some readers may tend to equate the area of the peanuts with the frequency for each year.

b.   Using MINITAB, the frequency bar chart is:

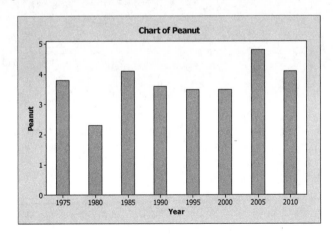

2.169   First we make some preliminary calculations.

Of the 20 engineers at the time of the layoffs, 14 are 40 or older. Thus, the probability that a randomly selected engineer will be 40 or older is 14/20 = .70. A very high proportion of the engineers is 40 or over.

In order to determine if the company is vulnerable to a disparate impact claim, we will first find the median age of all the engineers. Ordering all the ages, we get:

<u>29</u>, <u>32</u>, <u>34</u>, 35, <u>38</u>, 39, 40, 40, 40, <u>40</u>, <u>40</u>, 41, <u>42</u>, <u>42</u>, 44, <u>46</u>, 47, 52, <u>55</u>, 64

The median of all 20 engineers is $\dfrac{40+40}{2} = \dfrac{80}{2} = 40$

Now, we will compute the median age of those engineers who were not laid off. The ages underlined above correspond to the engineers who were not laid off. The median of these is $\dfrac{40+40}{2} = \dfrac{80}{2} = 40$.

The median age of all engineers is the same as the median age of those who were not laid off. The median age of those laid off is $\dfrac{40+41}{2} = \dfrac{81}{2} = 40.5$, which is not that much different from the median age of those not laid off. In addition, 70% of all the engineers are 40 or older. Thus, it appears that the company would not be vulnerable to a disparate impact claim.

2.171   There is evidence to support this claim. The graph peaks at the interval above 1.002. The heights of the bars decrease in order as the intervals get further and further from the peak interval. This is true for all bars except the one above 1.000. This bar is greater than the bar to its right. This would indicate that there are more observations in this interval than one would expect, suggesting that some inspectors might be passing rods with diameters that were barely below the lower specification limit.

Chapter 3
Probability

3.1   a.   Since the probabilities must sum to 1,

$$P(E_3) = 1 - P(E_1) - P(E_2) - P(E_4) - P(E_5) = 1 - .1 - .2 - .1 - .1 = .5$$

        b.

$$P(E_3) = 1 - P(E_1) - P(E_2) - P(E_4) - P(E_5) = 1 - P(E_3) - P(E_2) - P(E_4) - P(E_5)$$
$$\Rightarrow 2P(E_3) = 1 - .1 - .2 - .1 \Rightarrow 2P(E_3) = .6 \Rightarrow P(E_3) = .3$$

        c. $P(E_3) = 1 - P(E_1) - P(E_2) - P(E_4) - P(E_5) = 1 - .1 - .1 - .1 - .1 = .6$

3.3 $P(A) = P(1) + P(2) + P(3) = .05 + .20 + .30 = .55$

    $P(B) = P(1) + P(3) + P(5) = .05 + .30 + .15 = .50$

    $P(C) = P(1) + P(2) + P(3) + P(5) = .05 + .20 + .30 + .15 = .70$

3.5   a. $\binom{N}{n} = \binom{5}{2} = \dfrac{5!}{2!(5-2)!} = \dfrac{5 \cdot 4 \cdot 3 \cdot 2 \cdot 1}{2 \cdot 1 \cdot 3 \cdot 2 \cdot 1} = \dfrac{120}{12} = 10$

        b. $\binom{N}{n} = \binom{6}{3} = \dfrac{6!}{3!(6-3)!} = \dfrac{6 \cdot 5 \cdot 4 \cdot 3 \cdot 2 \cdot 1}{3 \cdot 2 \cdot 1 \cdot 3 \cdot 2 \cdot 1} = \dfrac{720}{36} = 20$

        c. $\binom{N}{n} = \binom{20}{5} = \dfrac{20!}{5!(20-5)!} = \dfrac{20 \cdot 19 \cdot 18 \cdots 3 \cdot 2 \cdot 1}{5 \cdot 4 \cdot 3 \cdot 2 \cdot 1 \cdot 15 \cdot 14 \cdot 13 \cdots 3 \cdot 2 \cdot 1} = \dfrac{2.432902008 \times 10^{18}}{1.569209242 \times 10^{14}} = 15{,}504$

3.7   a.   If we denote the marbles as B$_1$, B$_2$, R$_1$, R$_2$, and R$_3$, then the ten sample points are:

        (B$_1$, B$_2$) (B$_1$, R$_1$) (B$_1$, R$_2$) (B$_1$, R$_3$) (B$_2$, R$_1$) (B$_2$, R$_2$) (B$_2$, R$_3$) (R$_1$, R$_2$) (R$_1$, R$_3$) (R$_2$, R$_3$)

        b.   Each of the sample points would be equally likely. Thus, each would have a probability of 1/10 of occurring.

        c.   There is one sample point in A: (B$_1$, B$_2$). Thus, $P(A) = \dfrac{1}{10}$.

            There are 6 sample points in B: (B$_1$, R$_1$) (B$_1$, R$_2$) (B$_1$, R$_3$) (B$_2$, R$_1$) (B$_2$, R$_2$) (B$_2$, R$_3$).

            Thus, $P(B) = 6\left(\dfrac{1}{10}\right) = \dfrac{6}{10} = \dfrac{3}{5}$.

            There are 3 sample points in C: (R$_1$, R$_2$) (R$_1$, R$_3$) (R$_2$, R$_3$). Thus, $P(C) = 3\left(\dfrac{1}{10}\right) = \dfrac{3}{10}$.

3.9   a.   The sample points of this experiment correspond to each of the 6 possible colors of the M&M's. Let Br = brown, Y = yellow, R = red, Bl = blue, O = orange, G = green. The six sample points are: Br, Y, R, Bl, O, and G

49

b.   From the problem, the probabilities of selecting each color are:

$$P(Br) = 0.13, \quad P(Y) = 0.14, \quad P(R) = 0.13, \quad P(Bl) = 0.24, \quad P(O) = 0.2, \quad P(G) = 0.16$$

c.   The probability that the selected M&M is brown is $P(Br) = 0.13$

d.   The probability that the selected M&M is red, green or yellow is:

$$P(R \text{ or } G \text{ or } Y) = P(R) + P(G) + P(Y) = 0.13 + 0.16 + 0.14 = 0.43$$

e. $P(\text{not } Bl) = P(R) + P(G) + P(Y) + P(Br) + P(O) = 0.13 + 0.16 + 0.14 + 0.13 + 0.20 = 0.76$

3.11   Define the following events:

M: {Nanny who was placed in a job last year is a male}

$$P(M) = \frac{24}{4,176} = .0057$$

3.13   a.   The 5 sample points are the possible responses of a randomly selected person who participated in Harris Poll:

None, 1-2, 3-5, 6-9, 10 or more

b.   The probabilities are:

$$P(\text{none}) = 0.19, \ P(1-2) = 0.31, \ P(3-5) = 0.26, \ P(6-9) = 0.05, \ P(10 \text{ or more}) = 0.19$$

c.   Define the following event:

A: {Respondent looks for healthcare information online more than two times per month}

$$P(A) = P(3-5) + P(6-9) + P(10 \text{ or more}) = 0.25 + 0.05 + 0.19 = 0.50$$

3.15   a.   The international consumer is most likely to use the Certification mark on a label to identify a green product.

b.   Define the following events:

A: {Certification mark on label}
B: {Packaging}
C: {Reading information about the product}
D: {Advertisement}
E: {Brand website}
F: {Other}

$$P(A \text{ or } B) = P(A) + P(B) = .45 + .15 = .60$$

c. $P(C \text{ or } E) = P(C) + P(E) = .12 + .04 = .16$

d. $P(\text{not } D) = P(A) + P(B) + P(C) + P(E) + P(F) = .45 + .15 + .12 + .04 + .18 = .94$

3.17   a.   Define the following event:

   C: {Slaughtered chicken passes inspection with fecal contamination}

   $$P(C) = \frac{1}{100} = .01$$

   b.   Based on the data, $P(C) = \dfrac{306}{32,075} = .0095 \approx .01$

   Yes. The probability of a slaughtered chicken passing inspection with fecal contamination rounded off to 2 decimal places is .01.

3.19   a.   The probability that any network is selected on a particular day is 1/8. Therefore,

   $P($ ESPN selected on July 11 $) = 1/8$.

   b.   The number of ways to select four networks for the weekend days is a combination of 8 networks taken 4 at a time. The number of ways to do this is $\begin{pmatrix} 8 \\ 4 \end{pmatrix} = \dfrac{8!}{4!(8-4)!} = \dfrac{8 \cdot 7 \cdot 6 \cdot 5 \cdot 4 \cdot 3 \cdot 2 \cdot 1}{4 \cdot 3 \cdot 2 \cdot 1 \cdot 4 \cdot 3 \cdot 2 \cdot 1} = 70$.

   c.   First, we need to find the number of ways one can choose the 4 networks where ESPN is one of the 4. If ESPN has to be chosen, then the number of ways of doing this is a combination of one thing taken one at a time or $\begin{pmatrix} 1 \\ 1 \end{pmatrix} = \dfrac{1!}{1!(1-1)!} = \dfrac{1}{1 \cdot 1} = 1$. The number of ways to select the remaining 3 networks is a combination of 7 things taken 3 at a time or $\begin{pmatrix} 7 \\ 3 \end{pmatrix} = \dfrac{7!}{3!(7-3)!} = \dfrac{7 \cdot 6 \cdot 5 \cdot 4 \cdot 3 \cdot 2 \cdot 1}{3 \cdot 2 \cdot 1 \cdot 4 \cdot 3 \cdot 2 \cdot 1} = 35$. Thus, the total number of ways of selecting 4 networks of which one has to be ESPN is 1(35) = 35.

   Finally, the probability of selecting ESPN as one of the 4 networks for the weekend analysis is $35 / 70 = .5$.

3.21   Since one would be selecting 3 stocks from 15 without replacement, the total number of ways to select the 3 stocks would be a combination of 15 things taken 3 at a time. The number of ways would be

$$\begin{pmatrix} 15 \\ 3 \end{pmatrix} = \frac{15!}{3!(15-3)!} = \frac{15 \cdot 14 \cdot 13 \cdots 3 \cdot 2 \cdot 1}{3 \cdot 2 \cdot 1 \cdot 12 \cdot 11 \cdot 10 \cdots 3 \cdot 2 \cdot 1} = \frac{1.307674368 \times 10^{12}}{2874009600} = 455$$

3.23   a.   Since we want to maximize the purchase of grill #2, grill #2 must be one of the 3 grills in the display. Thus, we have to pick 2 more grills from the 4 remaining grills. Since order does not matter, the number of different ways to select 2 grill displays from 4 would be a combination of 4 things taken 2 at a time. The number of ways is:

$$\begin{pmatrix} 4 \\ 2 \end{pmatrix} = \frac{4!}{2!(4-2)!} = \frac{4 \cdot 3 \cdot 2 \cdot 1}{2 \cdot 1 \cdot 2 \cdot 1} = \frac{24}{4} = 6$$

   Let Gi represent Grill i. The possibilities are:

   $G_1 G_2 G_3, \ G_1 G_2 G_4, \ G_1 G_2 G_5, \ G_2 G_3 G_4, \ G_2 G_3\,G_5, \ G_2 G_4 G_5$

b.   To find reasonable probabilities for the 6 possibilities, we divide the frequencies by the total sample size of 124. The probabilities would be:

$$P(G_1G_2G_3) = 35/124 = .282 \qquad P(G_1G_2G_4) = 8/124 = .065 \qquad P(G_1G_2G_5) = 42/124 = .339$$

$$P(G_2G_3G_4) = 4/124 = .032 \qquad P(G_2G_3G_5) = 1/124 = .008 \qquad P(G_2G_4G_5) = 34/124 = .274$$

c. $P(\text{ display contained Grill \#1}) = P(G_1G_2G_3) + P(G_1G_2G_4) + P(G_1G_2G_5) = .282 + .065 + .339 = .686$

3.25   a.   The odds in favor of an Oxford Shoes win are $\frac{1}{3}$ to $1 - \frac{1}{3} = \frac{2}{3}$ or 1 to 2.

b.   If the odds in favor of Oxford Shoes are 1 to 1, then the probability that Oxford Shoes wins is

$$\frac{1}{1+1} = \frac{1}{2}.$$

c.   If the odds against Oxford Shoes are 3 to 2, then the odds in favor of Oxford Shoes are

2 to 3. Therefore, the probability that Oxford Shoes wins is $\frac{2}{2+3} = \frac{2}{5}$.

3.27   a.   The number of ways the 5 commissioners can vote is $2(2)(2)(2)(2) = 2^5 = 32$ (Each of the 5 commissioners has 2 choices for his/her vote – For or Against.)

b.   Let F denote a vote 'For' and A denote a vote 'Against'. The 32 sample points would be:

FFFFF   FFFFA   FFFAF   FFAFF   FAFFF   AFFFF   FFFAA   FFAFA   FAFFA   AFFFA
FFAAF   FAFAF   AFFAF   FAAFF   AFAFF   AAFFF   FFAAA   FAFAA   FAAFA   FAAAF
AFFAA   AFAFA   AFAAF   AAFFA   AAFAF   AAAFF   FAAAA   AFAAA   AAFAA   AAAFA
AAAAF   AAAAA

Each of the sample points should be equally likely. Thus, each would have a probability of 1/32.

c.   The sample points that result in a 2-2 split for the other 4 commissioners are:

FFAAF   FAFAF   AFFAF   FAAFF   AFAFF   AAFFF   FFAAA   FAFAA   FAAFA
AFFAA   AFAFA   AAFFA

There are 12 sample points.

d.   Let V = event that your vote counts. $P(V) = 12/32 = 0.375$.

e.   If there are now only 3 commissioners in the bloc, then the total number of ways the bloc can vote is $2(2)(2) = 2^3 = 8$. The sample points would be:

FFF   FFA   FAF   AFF   FAA   AFA   AAF   AAA

The number of sample points where your vote would count is 4: *FAF, AFF, FAA, AFA*

Let W = event that your vote counts in the bloc. $P(W) = 4/8 = 0.5$.

3.29   a.   A: {*HHH, HHT, HTH, THH, TTH, THT, HTT*}

B: {*HHH, TTH, THT, HTT*}

$A \cup B$: {*HHH, HHT, HTH, THH, TTH, THT, HTT*}

A^c: {*TTT*}

$A \cap B$: {*HHH, TTH, THT, HTT*}

b. $P(A) = \dfrac{7}{8}$ $P(B) = \dfrac{4}{8} = \dfrac{1}{2}$ $P(A \cup B) = \dfrac{7}{8}$ $P(A^c) = \dfrac{1}{8}$ $P(A \cap B) = \dfrac{4}{8} = \dfrac{1}{2}$

c. $P(A \cup B) = P(A) + P(B) - P(A \cap B) = \dfrac{7}{8} + \dfrac{1}{2} - \dfrac{1}{2} = \dfrac{7}{8}$

d.   No. $P(A \cap B) = \dfrac{1}{2}$ which is not 0.

3.31   a. $P(A) = P(E_1) + P(E_2) + P(E_3) + P(E_5) + P(E_6) = \dfrac{1}{5} + \dfrac{1}{5} + \dfrac{1}{5} + \dfrac{1}{20} + \dfrac{1}{10} = \dfrac{15}{20} = \dfrac{3}{4}$

b. $P(B) = P(E_2) + P(E_3) + P(E_4) + P(E_7) = \dfrac{1}{5} + \dfrac{1}{5} + \dfrac{1}{20} + \dfrac{1}{5} = \dfrac{13}{20}$

c. $P(A \cup B) = P(E_1) + P(E_2) + P(E_3) + P(E_4) + P(E_5) + P(E_6) + P(E_7)$

$$= \dfrac{1}{5} + \dfrac{1}{5} + \dfrac{1}{5} + \dfrac{1}{20} + \dfrac{1}{20} + \dfrac{1}{10} + \dfrac{1}{5} = 1$$

d. $P(A \cap B) = P(E_2) + P(E_3) = \dfrac{1}{5} + \dfrac{1}{5} = \dfrac{2}{5}$

e. $P(A^c) = 1 - P(A) = 1 - \dfrac{3}{4} = \dfrac{1}{4}$

f. $P(B^c) = 1 - P(B) = 1 - \dfrac{13}{20} = \dfrac{7}{20}$

g. $P(A \cup A^c) = P(E_1) + P(E_2) + P(E_3) + P(E_4) + P(E_5) + P(E_6) + P(E_7)$

$$= \dfrac{1}{5} + \dfrac{1}{5} + \dfrac{1}{5} + \dfrac{1}{20} + \dfrac{1}{20} + \dfrac{1}{10} + \dfrac{1}{5} = 1$$

h. $P(A^c \cap B) = P(E_4) + P(E_7) = \dfrac{1}{20} + \dfrac{1}{5} = \dfrac{5}{20} = \dfrac{1}{4}$

3.33   a. $P(A) = .50 + .10 + .05 = .65$

b. $P(B) = .10 + .07 + .50 + .05 = .72$

c. $P(C) = .25$

d. $P(D) = .05 + .03 = .08$

e. $P(A^c) = .25 + .07 + .03 = .35$ (Note: $P(A^c) = 1 - P(A) = 1 - .65 = .35$)

f. $P(A \cup B) = P(B) = .10 + .07 + .50 + .05 = .72$

g. $P(A \cap C) = 0$

h.   Two events are mutually exclusive if they have no sample points in common or if the probability of their intersection is 0.

$P(A \cap B) = P(A) = .50 + .10 + .05 = .65$. Since this is not 0, A and B are not mutually exclusive.

$P(A \cap C) = 0$. Since this is 0, A and C are mutually exclusive.

$P(A \cap D) = .05$. Since this is not 0, A and D are not mutually exclusive.

$P(B \cap C) = 0$. Since this is 0, B and C are mutually exclusive.

$P(B \cap D) = .05$. Since this is not 0, B and D are not mutually exclusive.

$P(C \cap D) = 0$. Since this is 0, C and D are mutually exclusive.

3.35   a.   The analyst makes an early forecast and is only concerned with accuracy is the event $(A \cap B)$.

b.   The analyst is not only concerned with accuracy is the event A^c .

c.   The analyst is from a small brokerage firm or makes an early forecast is the event $C \cup B$.

d.   The analyst makes a late forecast and is not only concerned with accuracy is the event $B^c \cap A^c$.

3.37   a.   Define the following events:

   L: {Legs only}
   W: {Wheels only}
   B: {Both legs and wheels}
   N: {Neither legs nor wheels}

   The sample points are: L, W, B, and N

b.   From the given data:

$$P(L) = \frac{63}{106} = .594 \qquad P(W) = \frac{20}{106} = .189 \qquad P(B) = \frac{8}{106} = .075 \qquad P(N) = \frac{15}{106} = .142$$

c. $P(\text{Wheels}) = P(W \text{ or } B) = P(W) + P(B) = .189 + .075 = .264$

d. $P(\text{Legs}) = P(L \text{ or } B) = P(L) + P(B) = .594 + .075 = .669$

e. $P(\text{Either legs or wheels}) = 1 - P(N) = 1 - .142 = .858$

3.39   Define the following events:

A: {oil structure is active}
I: {oil structure is inactive}
C: {oil structure is caisson}
W: {oil structure is well protector}
F: {oil structure is fixed platform}

a.   The simple events are all combinations of structure type and activity type. The simple events are:

AC, *AW*, AF, *IC*, *IW*, IF

b.   Reasonable probabilities would be the frequency divided by the sample size of 3,400. The probabilities are:

$P(AC) = 503/3,400 = .148$ $\qquad$ $P(AW) = 225/3,400 = .066$

$P(AF) = 1,447/3,400 = .426$ $\qquad$ $P(IC) = 598/3,400 = .176$

$P(IW) = 177/3,400 = .052$ $\qquad$ $P(IF) = 450/3,400 = .132$

c. $P(A) = P(AC) + P(AW) + P(AF) = .148 + .066 + .426 = .640$

d. $P(W) = P(AW) + P(IW) = .066 + .052 = .118$

e. $P(IC) = .176$

f. $P(I \cup F) = P(IC) + P(IW) + P(IF) + P(AF) = .176 + .052 + .132 + .426 = .786$

g. $P(C^c) = 1 - P(C) = 1 - (P(AC) + P(IC)) = 1 - (.148 + .176) = 1 - .324 = .676$

3.41   First, define the following events:

F: {Fully compensated}
P: {Partially compensated}
N: {Non-compensated}
R: {Left because of retirement}

From the text, we know

$$P(F) = \frac{127}{244}, \quad P(P) = \frac{45}{244}, \quad P(N) = \frac{72}{244}, \text{ and } P(R) = \frac{7+11+10}{244} = \frac{28}{244}$$

a. $P(F) = \dfrac{127}{244}$

b. $P(F \cap R) = \dfrac{7}{244}$

c. $P(F^c) = 1 - P(F) = 1 - \dfrac{127}{244} = \dfrac{117}{244}$

d. $P(F \cup R) = P(F) + P(R) - P(F \cap R) = \dfrac{127}{244} + \dfrac{28}{244} - \dfrac{7}{244} = \dfrac{148}{244}$

3.43   a. $P \cap S \cap A$. Products 6 and 7 are contained in this intersection.

b. $P(\text{possess all the desired characteristics}) = P(P \cap S \cap A) = P(6) + P(7) = \dfrac{1}{10} + \dfrac{1}{10} = \dfrac{1}{5}$

c. $A \cup S$

$P(A \cup S) = P(2) + P(3) + P(5) + P(6) + P(7) + P(8) + P(9) + P(10)$

$= \dfrac{1}{10} + \dfrac{1}{10} + \dfrac{1}{10} + \dfrac{1}{10} + \dfrac{1}{10} + \dfrac{1}{10} + \dfrac{1}{10} + \dfrac{1}{10} = \dfrac{8}{10} = \dfrac{4}{5}$

d. $P \cap S$

$P(P \cap S) = P(2) + P(6) + P(7) = \dfrac{1}{10} + \dfrac{1}{10} + \dfrac{1}{10} = \dfrac{3}{10}$

3.45   Define the following events:

M_1: {Model 1}
M_2: {Model 2}

a. $P(5) = \dfrac{85}{160} = .531$

b. $P(5 \cup 0) = P(5) + P(0) - P(5 \cap 0) = .531 + \dfrac{35}{160} - 0 = .531 + .219 = .75$

c. $P(M_2 \cap 0) = \dfrac{15}{160} = .094$

3.47   Define the following events:

A: {Air pressure is over-reported by 4 psi or more}
B: {Air pressure is over-reported by 6 psi or more}
C: {Air pressure is over-reported by 8 psi or more

a.   For gas station air pressure gauges that read 35 psi, $P(B) = .09$.

b.   For gas station air pressure gauges that read 55 psi, $P(C) = .09$.

c.   For gas station air pressure gauges that read 25 psi, $P(A^c) = 1 - P(A) = 1 - .16 = .84$.

d.   No. If air pressure is over-reported by 6 psi or more, then it is also over-reported by 4 psi or more. Thus, these 2 events are not mutually exclusive.

e.   The columns in the table are not mutually exclusive. All events in the last column (% Over-reported by 8 psi or more) are also part of the events in the first and second columns. All events in the second column are also part of the events in the first column. In addition, there is no column for the event 'Over-reported by less than 4 psi or not over-reported'.

3.49 a. $P(A \mid B) = \dfrac{P(A \cap B)}{P(B)} = \dfrac{.1}{.2} = .5$

b. $P(B \mid A) = \dfrac{P(A \cap B)}{P(A)} = \dfrac{.1}{.4} = .25$

c. Events A and B are said to be independent if $P(A \mid B) = P(A)$. In this case, $P(A \mid B) = .5$ and $P(A) = .4$. Thus, A and B are not independent.

3.51 a. If two events are independent, then $P(A \cap B) = P(A)P(B) = .4(.2) = .08$.

b. If two events are independent, then $P(A \mid B) = P(A) = .4$.

c. $P(A \cup B) = P(A) + P(B) - P(A \cap B) = .4 + .2 - .08 = .52$

3.53 a. $P(A) = P(E_1) + P(E_2) + P(E_3) = .2 + .3 + .3 = .8$

$P(B) = P(E_2) + P(E_3) + P(E_5) = .3 + .3 + .1 = .7$

$P(A \cap B) = P(E_2) + P(E_3) = .3 + .3 = .6$

b. $P(E_1 \mid A) = \dfrac{P(E_1 \cap A)}{P(A)} = \dfrac{P(E_1)}{P(A)} = \dfrac{.2}{.8} = .25$

$P(E_2 \mid A) = \dfrac{P(E_2 \cap A)}{P(A)} = \dfrac{P(E_2)}{P(A)} = \dfrac{.3}{.8} = .375$

$P(E_3 \mid A) = \dfrac{P(E_3 \cap A)}{P(A)} = \dfrac{P(E_3)}{P(A)} = \dfrac{.3}{.8} = .375$

The original sample point probabilities are in the proportion .2 to .3 to .3 or 2 to 3 to 3.

The conditional probabilities for these sample points are in the proportion .25 to .375 to .375 or 2 to 3 to 3.

c. (1) $P(B \mid A) = P(E_2 \mid A) + P(E_3 \mid A) = .375 + .375 = .75$ (from part **b**)

(2) $P(B \mid A) = \dfrac{P(A \cap B)}{P(A)} = \dfrac{.6}{.8} = .75$ (from part **a**)

The two methods do yield the same result.

d. If A and B are independent events, $P(B \mid A) = P(B)$. From part **c**, $P(B \mid A) = .75$. From part **a**, $P(B) = .7$. Since $.75 \neq .7$, A and B are not independent events.

3.55 a. $P(A) = P(E_1) + P(E_3) = .22 + .15 = .37$

b. $P(B) = P(E_2) + P(E_3) + P(E_4) = .31 + .15 + .22 = .68$

c. $P(A \cap B) = P(E_3) = .15$

d. $P(A\,|\,B) = \dfrac{P(A \cap B)}{P(B)} = \dfrac{.15}{.68} = .2206$

e. $P(B \cap C) = 0$

f. $P(C\,|\,B) = \dfrac{P(C \cap B)}{P(B)} = \dfrac{0}{.68} = 0$

g.   For pair *A* and *B*: *A* and *B* are not independent because $P(A\,|\,B) \neq P(A)$ or $.2206 \neq .37$.

   For pair *A* and *C*: $P(A \cap C) = P(E_1) = .22$ $P(C) = P(E_1) + P(E_5) = .22 + .10 = .32$

   $$P(A\,|\,C) = \frac{P(A \cap C)}{P(C)} = \frac{.22}{.32} = .6875$$

   A and *C* are not independent because $P(A\,|\,C) \neq P(A)$ or $.6875 \neq .37$.

   For pair *B* and *C*: *B* and *C* are not independent because $P(C\,|\,B) \neq P(C)$ or $0 \neq .32$.

3.57   a. $P(A \cap C) = 0 \Rightarrow A$ and *C* are mutually exclusive.

   $P(B \cap C) = 0 \Rightarrow B$ and *C* are mutually exclusive.

b. $P(A) = P(1) + P(2) + P(3) = .20 + .05 + .30 = .55$ $P(B) = P(3) + P(4) = .30 + .10 = .40$

   $P(C) = P(5) + P(6) = .10 + .25 = .35$ $P(A \cap B) = P(3) = .30$

   $$P(A\,|\,B) = \frac{P(A \cap B)}{P(B)} = \frac{.30}{.40} = .75$$

   A and *B* are independent if $P(A\,|\,B) = P(A)$. Since $P(A\,|\,B) = .75$ and $P(A) = .55$, *A* and *B* are not independent.

   Since *A* and *C* are mutually exclusive, they are not independent. Similarly, since *B* and *C* are mutually exclusive, they are not independent.

c.   Using the probabilities of sample points,
   $P(A \cup B) = P(1) + P(2) + P(3) + P(4) = .20 + .05 + .30 + .10 = .65$

   Using the additive rule,
   $P(A \cup B) = P(A) + P(B) - P(A \cap B) = .55 + .40 - .30 = .65$

   Using the probabilities of sample points,
   $P(A \cup C) = P(1) + P(2) + P(3) + P(5) + P(6) = .20 + .05 + .30 + .10 + .25 = .90$

Using the additive rule,
$$P(A \cup C) = P(A) + P(C) - P(A \cap C) = .55 + .35 - 0 = .90$$

3.59   Define the following events:

A: {Company is a banking/investment company}
B: {Company is based in United States}

From the problem, we know that $P(A \cap B) = \dfrac{4}{20} = .20$ and $P(B) = \dfrac{9}{20} = .45$

$$P(A \mid B) = \frac{P(A \cap B)}{P(B)} = \frac{.20}{.45} = .444 \; .$$

3.61   Define the following events:

A: {Internet user has wireless connection via mobile device}
B: {Internet user uses Twitter}

From the exercise, $P(A) = .54$ and $P(B \mid A) = .25$.

$$P(A \cap B) = P(B \mid A)P(A) = .25(.54) = .135$$

3.63   Define the following events:

F: {Worker is fully compensated}
P: {Worker is partially compensated}
N: {Worker is non-compensated}
R: {Worker retired}

From the exercise, $P(F) = 127 / 244 = .520$, $P(P) = 45 / 244 = .184$, $P(R \mid F) = 7 / 127 = .055$, $P(R \mid P) = 11 / 45 = .244$, and $P(R \mid N) = 10 / 72 = .139$.

a. $P(R \mid F) = 7 / 127 = .055$

b. $P(R \mid N) = 10 / 72 = .139$

c.   The two events are independent if $P(R \mid F) = P(R)$.

$$P(R) = \frac{7 + 11 + 10}{244} = \frac{28}{244} = .115 \text{ and } P(R \mid F) = 10 / 72 = .055 \; .$$ Since these are not equal, events R and F are not independent.

3.65   Define the following events:

I: {Invests in Market}
N: {No investment}

a. $P(I \mid IQ \geq 6) = \dfrac{P(I \cap \{IQ \geq 6\})}{P(IQ \geq 6)} = \dfrac{\dfrac{10,270 + 6,698 + 5,135 + 4,464}{158,044}}{\dfrac{31,943 + 17,958 + 12,145 + 9,531}{158,044}} = \dfrac{26,567}{71,577} = .371$

b. $P(I \mid IQ \le 5) = \dfrac{P(I \cap \{IQ \le 5\})}{P(IQ \le 5)} = \dfrac{\dfrac{44,651-26,567}{158,044}}{\dfrac{158,044-71,577}{158,044}} = \dfrac{18,084}{86,467} = .209$.

c.   Yes, it appears that investing in the stock market is dependent on IQ. If investing in the stock market and IQ were independent, then $P(I \mid IQ \le 5) = P(I \mid IQ \ge 6) = P(I)$. Since $P(I \mid IQ \le 5) \ne P(I \mid IQ \ge 6)$, then investing in the stock market and IQ are dependent.

3.67   Define the following events:

A: {Ambulance can travel to location A under 8 minutes}
B: {Ambulance can travel to location B under 8 minutes}
C: {Ambulance is busy}

We are given $P(A) = .58$, $P(B) = .42$, and $P(C) = .3$.

a. $P(A \cap C^c) = P(A \mid C^c)P(C^c) = .58(1-.3) = .406$

b. $P(B \mid C^c)P(C^c) = .42(1-.3) = .294$

3.69   Define the following events:

A: {Alarm A sounds alarm}
B: {Alarm B sounds alarm}
I: {Intruder}

a.   From the problem $P(A \mid I) = .9$, $P(B \mid I) = .95$, $P(A \mid I^c) = .2$ and $P(B \mid I^c) = .1$.

b.   Since the two systems are operating independently of each other,

$P(A \cap B \mid I) = P(A \mid I)P(B \mid I) = .9(.95) = .855$

c. $P(A \cap B \mid I^c) = P(A \mid I^c)P(B \mid I^c) = .2(.1) = .02$

d. $P(A \cup B \mid I) = P(A \mid I) + P(B \mid I) - P(A \cap B \mid I) = .9 + .95 - .855 = .995$

3.71   Define the following event:

A: {The specimen labeled "red snapper" was really red snapper}

a.   The probability that you are actually served red snapper the next time you order it at a restaurant is $P(A) = 1 - .77 = .23$

b.   P(at least one customer is actually served red snapper)
      = 1 − P(no customer is actually served red snapper)
      $= 1 - P(A^c \cap A^c \cap A^c \cap A^c \cap A^c) = 1 - P(A^c)P(A^c)P(A^c)P(A^c)P(A^c)$
      $= 1 - .77^5 = 1 - .271 = .729$

Note: In order to compute the above probability, we had to assume that the trials or events are independent. This assumption is likely to not be valid. If a restaurant served one customer a look-a-like variety, then it probably served the next one a look-a-like variety.

3.73   Define the following events:

A: {Patient receives PMI sheet}
B: {Patient was hospitalized}

$$P(A) = .20 , \qquad P(A \cap B) = .12 , \qquad P(B \mid A) = \frac{P(A \cap B)}{P(A)} = \frac{.12}{.20} = .60$$

3.75   a.   If the coin is balanced, then $P(H) = .5$ and $P(T) = .5$ on any trial. Also, we can assume that the results of any coin toss is independent of any other. Thus,

$$P(H \cap H \cap H \cap H \cap H \cap H \cap H \cap H \cap H \cap H)$$
$$= P(H)P(H)P(H)P(H)P(H)P(H)P(H)P(H)P(H)P(H)$$
$$= .5(.5)(.5)(.5)(.5)(.5)(.5)(.5)(.5) = .5^{10} = .0009766$$

$$P(H \cap H \cap T \cap T \cap H \cap T \cap T \cap H \cap H \cap H)$$
$$= P(H)P(H)P(T)P(T)P(H)P(T)P(T)P(H)P(H)P(H)$$
$$= .5(.5)(.5)(.5)(.5)(.5)(.5)(.5)(.5) = .5^{10} = .0009766$$

$$P(T \cap T \cap T \cap T \cap T \cap T \cap T \cap T \cap T \cap T)$$
$$= P(T)P(T)P(T)P(T)P(T)P(T)P(T)P(T)P(T)P(T)$$
$$= .5(.5)(.5)(.5)(.5)(.5)(.5)(.5)(.5) = .5^{10} = .0009766$$

b.   Define the following events:

A: {10 coin tosses result in all heads or all tails}
B: {10 coin tosses result in mix of heads and tails}

$$P(A) = P(H \cap H \cap H \cap H \cap H \cap H \cap H \cap H \cap H \cap H)$$
$$+ P(T \cap T \cap T \cap T \cap T \cap T \cap T \cap T \cap T \cap T)$$
$$= .0009766 + .0009766 = .0019532$$

c. $P(B) = 1 - P(A) = 1 - .0019532 = .9980468$

d.   From the above probabilities, the chances that either all heads or all tails occurred is extremely rare. Thus, if one of these sequences really occurred, it is most likely sequence #2.

3.77   a. $P(B_1 \cap A) = P(A \mid B_1)P(B_1) = .3(.75) = .225$

b. $P(B_2 \cap A) = P(A \mid B_2)P(B_2) = .5(.25) = .125$

c. $P(A) = P(B_1 \cap A) + P(B_2 \cap A) = .225 + .125 = .35$

d. $P(B_1 \mid A) = \dfrac{P(B_1 \cap A)}{P(A)} = \dfrac{.225}{.35} = .643$

e. $P(B_2 \mid A) = \dfrac{P(B_2 \cap A)}{P(A)} = \dfrac{.125}{.35} = .357$

3.79   If A is independent of B_1, B_2, and B_3, then $P(A \mid B_1) = P(A) = .4$.

Then $P(B_1 \mid A) = \dfrac{P(A \mid B_1)P(B_1)}{P(A)} = \dfrac{.4(.2)}{.4} = .2$

3.81   Define the following events:

E: {Expert makes the correct decision}
N: {Novice makes the correct decision}
M: {Matched condition}
E: {Similar distracter condition}
E: {Non-similar distracter condition}

a. $P(E^c \mid M) = 1 - .9212 = .0788$

b. $P(N^c \mid M) = 1 - .7455 = .2545$

c.   Since $P(N^c \mid M) = .2545 > P(E^c \mid M) = .0788$, it is more likely that the participant is a Novice.

3.83   a.   Converting the percentages to probabilities,

$P(275 - 300) = .52$, $P(305 - 325) = .39$, and $P(330 - 350) = .09$.

b.   Using Bayes Theorem,

$$P(275 - 300 \mid CC) = \frac{P(275 - 300 \cap CC)}{P(CC)}$$

$$= \frac{P(CC \mid 275 - 300)P(275 - 300)}{P(CC \mid 275 - 300)P(275 - 300) + P(CC \mid 305 - 325)P(305 - 325) + P(CC \mid 330 - 350)P(330 - 350)}$$

$$= \frac{.775(.52)}{.775(.52) + .77(.39) + .86(.09)} = \frac{.403}{.403 + .3003 + .0774} = \frac{.403}{.7807} = .516$$

3.85   Define the following events:

S: {Shale}
D: {Dolomite }
G: {Gamma ray reading > 60 }

From the exercise: $P(D) = \dfrac{476}{771} = .617$, $P(S) = \dfrac{295}{771} = .383$, $P(G \mid D) = \dfrac{34}{476} = .071$, and $P(G \mid S) = \dfrac{280}{295} = .949$.

$P(D \cap G) = P(G \mid D)P(D) = .071(.617) = .0438$ and

$P(G) = P(G \mid D)P(D) + P(G \mid S)P(S) = .071(.617) + .949(.383) = .0438 + .3635 = .4073$.

Thus, $P(D|G) = \dfrac{P(D \cap G)}{P(G)} = \dfrac{.0438}{.4073} = .1075$. Since this probability is so small, we would suggest that the area should not be mined.

3.87   Define the following event:

D: {Chip is defective}

From the Exercise, $P(S_1) = .15$, $P(S_2) = .05$, $P(S_3) = .10$, $P(S_4) = .20$, $P(S_5) = .12$, $P(S_6) = .20$, and $P(S_7) = .18$. Also, $P(D|S_1) = .001$, $P(D|S_2) = .0003$, $P(D|S_3) = .0007$, $P(D|S_4) = .006$, $P(D|S_5) = .0002$, $P(D|S_6) = .0002$, and $P(D|S_7) = .001$.

a.   We must find the probability of each supplier given a defective chip.

$$P(S_1|D) = \frac{P(S_1 \cap D)}{P(D)} =$$

$$\frac{P(D|S_1)P(S_1)}{P(D|S_1)P(S_1) + P(D|S_2)P(S_2) + P(D|S_3)P(S_3) + P(D|S_4)P(S_4) + P(D|S_5)P(S_5) + P(D|S_6)P(S_6) + P(D|S_7)P(S_7)}$$

$$= \frac{.001(.15)}{.001(.15) + .0003(.05) + .0007(.10) + .006(.20) + .0002(.12) + .0002(.02) + .001(.18)}$$

$$= \frac{.00015}{.00015 + .000015 + .00007 + .0012 + .000024 + .00004 + .00018} = \frac{.00015}{.001679} = .0893$$

$$P(S_2|D) = \frac{P(S_2 \cap D)}{P(D)} = \frac{P(D|S_2)P(S_2)}{P(D)} = \frac{.0003(.05)}{.001679} = \frac{.000015}{.001679} = .0089$$

$$P(S_3|D) = \frac{P(S_3 \cap D)}{P(D)} = \frac{P(D|S_3)P(S_3)}{P(D)} = \frac{.0007(.10)}{.001679} = \frac{.00007}{.001679} = .0417$$

$$P(S_4|D) = \frac{P(S_4 \cap D)}{P(D)} = \frac{P(D|S_4)P(S_4)}{P(D)} = \frac{.006(.20)}{.001679} = \frac{.0012}{.001679} = .7147$$

$$P(S_5|D) = \frac{P(S_5 \cap D)}{P(D)} = \frac{P(D|S_5)P(S_5)}{P(D)} = \frac{.0002(.12)}{.001679} = \frac{.000024}{.001679} = .0143$$

$$P(S_6|D) = \frac{P(S_6 \cap D)}{P(D)} = \frac{P(D|S_6)P(S_6)}{P(D)} = \frac{.0002(.20)}{.001679} = \frac{.00004}{.001679} = .0238$$

$$P(S_7|D) = \frac{P(S_7 \cap D)}{P(D)} = \frac{P(D|S_7)P(S_7)}{P(D)} = \frac{.001(.18)}{.001679} = \frac{.00018}{.001679} = .1072$$

Of these probabilities, .7147 is the largest. This implies that if a failure is observed, supplier number 4 was most likely responsible.

b.   If the seven suppliers all produce defective chips at the same rate of .0005, then $P(D|S_i) = .0005$ for all $i = 1, 2, 3, \ldots 7$ and $P(D) = .0005$.

For any supplier i, $P(S_i \cap D) = P(D \mid S_i)P(S_i) = .0005P(S_i)$ and

$$P(S_i \mid D) = \frac{P(S_i \cap D)}{P(D)} = \frac{P(D \mid S_i)P(S_i)}{.0005} = \frac{.0005P(S_i)}{.0005} = P(S_i)$$

Thus, if a defective is observed, then it most likely came from the supplier with the largest proportion of sales (probability). In this case, the most likely supplier would be either supplier 4 or supplier 6. Both of these have probabilities of .20.

3.89   a.   If $\dfrac{P(T \mid E)}{P(T^c \mid E)} < 1$, then $P(T \mid E) < P(T^c \mid E)$. Thus, the probability of more than two bullets given the

evidence is greater than the probability of two bullets given the evidence. This supports the theory of more than two bullets were used in the assassination of JFK.

b.   Using Bayes Theorem,

$$P(T \mid E) = \frac{P(T)P(E \mid T)}{P(T)P(E \mid T) + P(T^c)P(E \mid T^c)} \text{ and } P(T^c \mid E) = \frac{P(T^c)P(E \mid T^c)}{P(T)P(E \mid T) + P(T^c)P(E \mid T^c)}.$$

Thus, $\dfrac{P(T \mid E)}{P(T^c \mid E)} = \dfrac{\dfrac{P(T)P(E \mid T)}{P(T)P(E \mid T) + P(T^c)P(E \mid T^c)}}{\dfrac{P(T^c)P(E \mid T^c)}{P(T)P(E \mid T) + P(T^c)P(E \mid T^c)}} = \dfrac{P(T)P(E \mid T)}{P(T^c)P(E \mid T^c)}.$

3.91   a.   The two probability rules for a sample space are that the probability for any sample point is between 0 and 1 and that the sum of the probabilities of all the sample points is 1.

For this Exercise, all the probabilities of the sample points are between 0 and 1 and

$$\sum_{i=1}^{4} P(S_i) = P(S_1) + P(S_2) + P(S_3) + P(S_4) = .2 + .1 + .3 + .4 = 1.0$$

b. $P(A) = P(S_1) + P(S_4) = .2 + .4 = .6$

3.93   a.   If events A and B are mutually exclusive, then $P(A \cap B) = 0$.

$$P(A \mid B) = \frac{P(A \cap B)}{P(B)} = \frac{0}{.3} = 0$$

b.   No. If events A and B are independent, then $P(A \mid B) = P(A)$. However, from the Exercise we know $P(A) = .2$ and from part a, we know $P(A \mid B) = 0$. Thus, events A and B are not independent.

3.95 $P(A \cap B) = .4$, $P(A \mid B) = .8$

Since $P(A \mid B) = \dfrac{P(A \cap B)}{P(B)}$, substitute the given probabilities into the formula and solve for $P(B)$.

$$.8 = \frac{.4}{P(B)} \Rightarrow P(B) = \frac{.4}{.8} = .5$$

3.97   a. $P(A \cap B) = 0$

$P(B \cap C) = P(2) = .2$

$P(A \cup C) = P(1) + P(2) + P(3) + P(5) + P(6) = .3 + .2 + .1 + .1 + .2 = .9$

$P(A \cup B \cup C) = P(1) + P(2) + P(3) + P(4) + P(5) + P(6) = .3 + .2 + .1 + .1 + .1 + .2 = 1$

$P(B^c) = P(1) + P(3) + P(5) + P(6) = .3 + .1 + .1 + .2 = .7$

$P(A^c \cap B) = P(2) + P(4) = .2 + .1 = .3$

$$P(B \mid C) = \frac{P(B \cap C)}{P(C)} = \frac{P(2)}{P(2) + P(5) + P(6)} = \frac{.2}{.2 + .1 + .2} = \frac{.2}{.5} = .4$$

$$P(B \mid A) = \frac{P(B \cap A)}{P(A)} = \frac{0}{P(A)} = 0$$

b.   Since $P(A \cap B) = 0$, and $P(A)P(B) > 0$, these two would not be equal, implying A and B are not independent. However, A and B are mutually exclusive, since $P(A \cap B) = 0$.

c. $P(B) = P(2) + P(4) = .2 + .1 = .3$. But $P(B \mid C)$, calculated above, is .4. Since these are not equal, B and C are not independent. Since $P(B \cap C) = .2$, B and C are not mutually exclusive.

3.99   Define the following events:

E: {Industrial accident caused by faulty Engineering & Design}
P: {Industrial accident caused by faulty Procedures & Practices}
M: {Industrial accident caused by faulty Management & Oversight}
T: {Industrial accident caused by faulty Training & Communication}

a.   The sample points for this problem are: E, P, M, and T. Reasonable probabilities are:

$P(E) = 27 / 83 = .3253$, $P(P) = 24 / 83 = .2892$, $P(M) = 22 / 83 = .2651$, and $P(T) = 10 / 83 = .1205$

b. $P(E) = 27 / 83 = .3253$. Approximately 32.53% of all industrial accidents are caused by faulty Engineering and Design.

c. P(Industrial accident caused by something other than procedures & practices)
$= 1 - P(P^c) = 1 - .2892 = .7108$. Approximately 71.08% of all industrial accidents are caused by something other than faulty procedures & practices.

3.101   Define the event:

B: {Small business owned by non-Hispanic white female}

From the problem, $P(B) = .27$

The probability that a small business owned by a non-Hispanic white is male-owned is
$P(B^c) = 1 - P(B) = 1 - .27 = .73$.

3.103   a.   This statement is false. All probabilities are between 0 and 1 inclusive. One cannot have a probability of 4.

   b.   If we assume that the probabilities are the same as the percents (changed to proportions), then this is a true statement.

$$P(4 \text{ or } 5) = P(4) + P(5) = .6020 + .1837 = .7857$$

   c.   This statement is true. There were no observations with one star. Thus, $P(1) = 0$.

   d.   This statement is false. $P(2) = .0408$ and $P(5) = .1837$. $P(5) > P(2)$.

3.105   a. $B \cap C$

   b. A^c

   c. $C \cup B$

   d. $A \cap C^c$

3.107   Define the following events:

G: {regularly use the golf course}
T: {regularly use the tennis courts}

Given: $P(G) = .7$ and $P(T) = .5$

The event "uses neither facility" can be written as $G^c \cap T^c$ or $(G \cup T)^c$. We are given
$P(G^c \cap T^c) = P[(G \cup T)^c] = .05$. The complement of the event "uses neither facility" is the event "uses at least one of the two facilities" which can be written as $G \cup T$.

$$P(G \cup T) = 1 - P(G \cup T)^c = 1 - .05 = .95$$

From the additive rule, $P(G \cup T) = P(G) + P(T) - P(G \cap T) \Rightarrow .95 = .7 + .5 - P(G \cap T) \Rightarrow P(G \cap T) = .25$

a.   The Venn Diagram is:

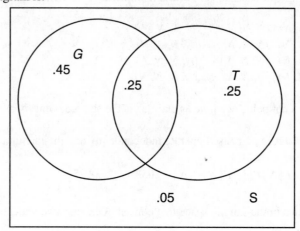

b. $P(G \cup T) = .95$ from above.

c. $P(G \cap T) = .25$ from above.

d. $P(G \mid T) = \dfrac{P(G \cap T)}{P(T)} = \dfrac{.25}{.5} = .5$

3.109   a. $P(A) = \dfrac{1,465}{2,143} = .684$

           b. $P(B) = \dfrac{265}{2,143} = .124$

           c.   No. There is one sample point that they have in common: Plaintiff trial win – reversed, Jury

           d. $P(A^c) = 1 - P(A) = 1 - .684 = .316$

           e. $P(A \cup B) = \dfrac{194 + 71 + 429 + 111 + 731}{2,143} = \dfrac{1,536}{2,143} = .717$

           f. $P(A \cap B) = \dfrac{194}{2,143} = .091$

3.111   Define the following events:

    A: {The watch is accurate}
    N: {The watch is not accurate}

    Assuming the manufacturer's claim is correct,

    $P(N) = .05$ and $P(A) = 1 - P(N) = 1 - .05 = .95$

The sample space for the purchase of four of the manufacturer's watches is listed below.

(A, A, A, A) (N, A, A, A) (A, N, N, A) (N, A, N, N)
(A, A, A, N) (A, A, N, N) (N, A, N, A) (N, N, A, N)
(A, A, N, A) (A, N, A, N) (N, N, A, A) (N, N, N, A)
(A, N, A, A) (N, A, A, N) (A, N, N, N) (N, N, N, N)

a.   All four watches not being accurate as claimed is the sample point *(N, N, N, N)*.

Assuming the watches purchased operate independently and the manufacturer's claim is correct,

$$P(N,N,N,N) = P(N)P(N)P(N)P(N) = .05^4 = .00000625$$

b.   The sample points in the sample space that consist of exactly two watches failing to meet the claim are listed below.

(A, A, N, N) (N, A, A, N)
(A, N, A, N) (N, A, N, A)
(A, N, N, A) (N, N, A, A)

The probability that exactly two of the four watches fail to meet the claim is the sum of the probabilities of these six sample points.

Assuming the watches purchased operate independently and the manufacturer's claim is correct,

$$P(A,A,N,N) = P(A)P(A)P(N)P(N) = .95(.95)(.05)(.05) = .00225625$$

All six of the sample points will have the same probability. Therefore, the probability that exactly two of the four watches fail to meet the claim when the manufacturer's claim is correct is

$$6(.00225625) = .0135$$

c.   The sample points in the sample space that consist of three of the four watches failing to meet the claim are listed below.

(A, N, N, N) (N, N, A, N)
(N, A, N, N) (N, N, N, A)

The probability that three of the four watches fail to meet the claim is the sum of the probabilities of the four sample points.

Assuming the watches purchased operate independently and the manufacturer's claim is correct,

$$P(A,N,N,N) = P(A)P(N)P(N)P(N) = .95(.05)(.05)(.05) = .00011875$$

All four of the sample points will have the same probability. Therefore, the probability that three of the four watches fail to meet the claim when the manufacturer's claim is correct is

$$4(.00011875) = .000475$$

If this event occurred, we would tend to doubt the validity of the manufacturer's claim since its probability of occurring is so small.

d.   All four watches tested failing to meet the claim is the sample point (N, N, N, N).

Assuming the watches purchased operate independently and the manufacturer's claim is correct,

$$P(N, N, N, N) = P(N)P(N)P(N)P(N) = .05(.05)(.05)(.05) = .00000625$$

Since the probability of observing this event is so small if the claim is true, we have strong evidence against the validity of the claim. However, we do not have conclusive proof that the claim is false. There is still a chance the event can occur (with probability .00000625) although it is extremely small.

3.113   Define the following events:

A: {Never smoked cigars}
B: {Former cigar smoker}
C: {Current cigar smoker}
D: {Died from cancer}
E: {Did not die from cancer}

a. $P(D \mid A) = \dfrac{P(D \cap A)}{P(A)} = \dfrac{782/137,243}{121,529/137,243} = \dfrac{782}{121,529} = .006$

b. $P(D \mid B) = \dfrac{P(D \cap B)}{P(B)} = \dfrac{91/137,243}{7,848/137,243} = \dfrac{91}{7,848} = .012$

c. $P(D \mid C) = \dfrac{P(D \cap C)}{P(C)} = \dfrac{141/137,243}{7,866/137,243} = \dfrac{141}{7,866} = .018$

3.115   Define the following events:

A: {Wheelchair user had an injurious fall}
B: {Wheelchair user had all five features installed in the home}
C: {Wheelchair user had no falls}
D: {Wheelchair user had none of the features installed in the home}

a. $P(A) = \dfrac{48}{306} = .157$

b. $P(B) = \dfrac{9}{306} = .029$

c. $P(C \cap D) = \dfrac{89}{306} = .291$

d. $P(A \mid B) = \dfrac{P(A \cap B)}{P(B)} = \dfrac{2/306}{9/306} = \dfrac{2}{9} = .222$

e. $\quad P(A \mid D) = \dfrac{P(A \cap D)}{P(D)} = \dfrac{20/306}{109/306} = \dfrac{20}{109} = .183$

3.117   Define the following events:

S_1: {Salesman makes sale on the first visit}
S_2: {Salesman makes a sale on the second visit}

$P(S_1) = .4 \qquad P(S_2 \mid S_1^c) = .65$

The sample points of the experiment are:

$S_1 \cap S_2^c, \ S_1^c \cap S_2, \ S_1^c \cap S_2^c$

The probability the salesman will make a sale is:

$P(S_1 \cap S_2^c) + P(S_1^c \cap S_2) = P(S_1) + P(S_2 \mid S_1^c) P(S_1^c) = .4 + .65(1 - .4) = .4 + .39 = .79$

3.119   a.   Suppose we let the four positions in a sample point represent in order (1) Raise a broad mix of crops, (2) Raise livestock, (3) Use chemicals sparingly, and (4) Use techniques for regenerating the soil, such as crop rotation. A farmer is either likely (L) to engage in an activity or unlikely (U). The possible classifications are:

*LLLL   LLLU   LLUL   LULL   ULLL   LLUU   LULU   LUUL   ULLU   ULUL   UULL
LUUU   ULUU   UULU   UUUL   UUUU*

b.   Since there are 16 classifications or sample points and all are equally likely, then each has a probability of 1/16.

$P(UUUU) = \dfrac{1}{16}$

c.   The probability that a farmer will be classified as likely on at least three criteria is

$P(LLLL) + P(LLLU) + P(LLUL) + P(LULL) + P(ULLL) = 5\left(\dfrac{1}{16}\right) = \dfrac{5}{16}.$

3.121   Define the following events:

O_1:   {Component #1 in System A operates properly}
O_2:   {Component #2 in System A operates properly}
O_3:   {Component #3 in System A operates properly}
A: {System A works properly}

$P(O_1) = 1 - P\left(O_1^c\right) = 1 - .12 = .88 \quad P(O_2) = 1 - P\left(O_2^c\right) = 1 - .09 = .91 \quad P(O_3) = 1 - P\left(O_3^c\right) = 1 - .11 = .89$

a. $P(A) = P(O_1 \cap O_2 \cap O_3) = P(O_1)P(O_2)P(O_3) = .88(.91)(.89) = .7127$
(since the three components operate independently)

b. $P(A^c) = 1 - P(A) = 1 - .7127 = .2873$
(see part **a**)

c. Define the following events:

C_1: {Component 1 in System B works properly}
C_2: {Component 2 in System B works properly}
D_3: {Component 3 in System B works properly}
D_4: {Component 4 in System B works properly}
C: {Subsystem C works properly}
D: {Subsystem D works properly}

The probability a component fails is .1, so the probability a component works properly is $1-.1=.9$.

Subsystem C works properly if both components 1 and 2 work properly.

$P(C) = P(C_1 \cap C_2) = P(C_1)P(C_2) = .9(.9) = .81$
(since the components operate independently)

Similarly, $P(D) = P(D_1 \cap D_2) = P(D_1)P(D_2) = .9(.9) = .81$

The system operates properly if either subsystem C or D operates properly.

The probability that System B operates properly is:

$P(C \cup D) = P(C) + P(D) - P(C \cap D) = P(C) + P(D) - P(C)P(D) = .81 + .81 - .81(.81) = .9639$

d. The probability exactly one subsystem fails in System B is:

$P(C \cap D^c) + P(C^c \cap D) = P(C)P(D^c) + P(C^c)P(D)$
$= .81(1-.81) + (1-.81)(.81) = .1539 + .1539 = .3078$

e. The probability that System B fails is the probability that both subsystems fail:

$P(C^c \cap D^c) = P(C^c)P(D^c) = (1-.81)(1-.81) = .0361$

f. The system operates correctly 99% of the time means it fails 1% of the time. The probability one subsystem fails is .19. The probability n subsystems fail is $.19^n$. Thus, we must find n such that

$(.19)^n \le .01 \Rightarrow n = 3$

3.123 The probability of a false positive is $P(A \mid B)$.

3.125 Define the following events:

A: {Press is correctly adjusted}
B: {Press is incorrectly adjusted}
D: {part is defective}

From the exercise, $P(A) = .90$, $P(D \mid A) = .05$, and. We also know that event B is the complement of event A. Thus, $P(B) = 1 - P(A) = 1 - .90 = .10$.

$$P(B \mid D) = \frac{P(B \cap D)}{P(D)} = \frac{P(D \mid B)P(B)}{P(D \mid B)P(B) + P(D \mid A)P(A)} = \frac{.50(.10)}{.50(.10) + .05(.90)} = \frac{.05}{.05 + .045} = \frac{.05}{.095} = .526$$

3.127   Define the flowing events:

A: {Dealer draws a blackjack}
B: {Player draws a blackjack}

a.   For the dealer to draw a blackjack, he needs to draw an ace and a face card. There are

$$\binom{4}{1} = \frac{4!}{1!(4-1)!} = \frac{4 \cdot 3 \cdot 2 \cdot 1}{1 \cdot 3 \cdot 2 \cdot 1} = 4 \text{ ways to draw an ace and}$$

$$\binom{12}{1} = \frac{12!}{1!(12-1)!} = \frac{12 \cdot 11 \cdot 10 \cdots 1}{1 \cdot 11 \cdot 10 \cdot 9 \cdots 1} = 12 \text{ ways to draw a face card (there are 12 face}$$

cards in the deck).

The total number of ways a dealer can draw a blackjack is $4 \cdot 12 = 48$.

The total number of ways a dealer can draw 2 cards is

$$\binom{52}{2} = \frac{52!}{2!(52-2)!} = \frac{52 \cdot 51 \cdot 50 \cdots 1}{2 \cdot 1 \cdot 50 \cdot 49 \cdot 48 \cdots 1} = 1326$$

Thus, the probability that the dealer draws a blackjack is $P(A) = \dfrac{48}{1326} = .0362$

b.   In order for the player to win with a blackjack, the player must draw a blackjack and the dealer does not. Using our notation, this is the event $B \cap A^C$. We need to find the probability that the player draws a blackjack $(P(B))$ and the probability that the dealer does not draw a blackjack given the player does $(P(A^c \mid B))$. Then, the probability that the player wins with a blackjack is $P(A^c \mid B)P(B)$.

The probability that the player draws a blackjack is the same as the probability that the dealer draws a blackjack, which is $P(B) = .0362$.

There are 5 scenarios where the dealer will not draw a blackjack given the player does. First, the dealer could draw an ace and not a face card. Next, the dealer could draw a face card and not an ace. Third, the dealer could draw two cards that are not aces or face cards. Fourth, the dealer could draw two aces, and finally, the dealer could draw two face cards.

The number of ways the dealer could draw an ace and not a face card given the player draws a blackjack is

$$\binom{3}{1}\binom{36}{1} = \frac{3!}{1!(3-1)!} \cdot \frac{36!}{1!(36-1)!} = \frac{3 \cdot 2 \cdot 1}{1 \cdot 2 \cdot 1} \cdot \frac{36 \cdot 35 \cdot 34 \cdots 1}{1 \cdot 35 \cdot 34 \cdot 33 \cdots 1} = 3(36) = 108$$

(Note: Given the player has drawn blackjack, there are only 3 aces left and 36 non-face cards.)

The number of ways the dealer could draw a face card and not an ace given the player draws a blackjack is

$$\binom{11}{1}\binom{36}{1} = \frac{11!}{1!(11-1)!} \cdot \frac{36!}{1!(36-1)!} = \frac{11 \cdot 10 \cdot 9 \cdots 1}{1 \cdot 10 \cdot 9 \cdot 8 \cdots 1} \cdot \frac{36 \cdot 35 \cdot 34 \cdots 1}{1 \cdot 35 \cdot 34 \cdot 33 \cdots 1} = 11(36) = 396$$

The number of ways the dealer could draw neither a face card nor an ace given the player draws a blackjack is

$$\binom{36}{2} = \frac{36!}{2!(36-2)!} = \frac{36 \cdot 35 \cdot 34 \cdots 1}{2 \cdot 1 \cdot 34 \cdot 33 \cdot 32 \cdots 1} = 630$$

The number of ways the dealer could draw two aces given the player draws a blackjack is

$$\binom{3}{2} = \frac{3!}{2!(3-2)!} = \frac{3 \cdot 2 \cdot 1}{2 \cdot 1 \cdot 1} = 3$$

The number of ways the dealer could draw two face cards given the player draws a blackjack is

$$\binom{11}{2} = \frac{11!}{2!(11-2)!} = \frac{11 \cdot 10 \cdot 9 \cdots 1}{2 \cdot 9 \cdot 8 \cdot 7 \cdots 1} = 55$$

The total number of ways the dealer can draw two cards given the player draws a blackjack is

$$\binom{50}{2} = \frac{50!}{2!(50-2)!} = \frac{50 \cdot 49 \cdot 48 \cdots 1}{2 \cdot 1 \cdot 48 \cdot 47 \cdot 46 \cdots 1} = 1225$$

The probability that the dealer does not draw a blackjack given the player draws a   blackjack is

$$P(A^c \mid B) = \frac{108 + 396 + 630 + 3 + 55}{1225} = \frac{1192}{1225} = .9731$$

Finally, the probability that the player wins with a blackjack is

$$P(B \cap A^c) = P(A^c \mid B)P(B) = .9731(.0362) = .0352$$

3.129   First, we will list all possible sample points for placing a car (C) and 2 goats (G) behind doors #1, #2, and #3. If the first position corresponds to door #1, the second position corresponds to door #2, and the third position corresponds to door #3, the sample space is:

(*C G G*) (*G C G*) (*G G C*)

Now, suppose you pick door #1. Initially, the probability that you will win the car is 1/3 – only one of the sample points has a car behind door #1.

The host will now open a door behind which is a goat. If you pick door #1 in the first sample point (*C G G*), the host will open either door #2 or door #3. Suppose he opens door #3 (it really does not matter). If you pick door #1 in the second sample point (*G C G*), the host will open door #3. If you pick door #1 in the third sample point (*G G C*), the host will open door #2. Now, the new sample space will be:

(*C G*) (*G C*) (*G C*)

where the first position corresponds to door #1 (the one you chose) and the second position corresponds to the door that was not opened by the host.

Now, if you keep door #1, the probability that you win the car is 1/3. However, if you switch to the remaining door, the probability that you win the car is now 2/3. Based on these probabilities, it is to your advantage to switch doors.

The above could be repeated by selecting door #2 initially or door #3 initially. In either of these cases, again, the probability of winning the car is 1/3 if you do not switch and 2/3 if you switch. Thus, Marilyn was correct.

Chapter 4
Random Variables
and Probability Distributions

4.1   a.   The number of newspapers sold by New York Times each month can take on a countable number of values. Thus, this is a discrete random variable.

        b.   The amount of ink used in printing the Sunday edition of the New York Times can take on an infinite number of different values. Thus, this is a continuous random variable.

        c.   The actual number of ounces in a one gallon bottle of laundry detergent can take on an infinite number of different values. Thus, this is a continuous random variable.

        d.   The number of defective parts in a shipment of nuts and bolts can take on a countable number of values. Thus, this is a discrete random variable.

        e.   The number of people collecting unemployment insurance each month can take on a countable number of values. Thus, this is a discrete random variable.

4.3   Since there are only a fixed number of outcomes to the experiment, the random variable, x, the number of stars in the rating, is discrete.

4.5   The variable x, total compensation in 2011 (in $ millions), is reported in whole number dollars. Since there are a countable number of possible outcomes, this variable is discrete.

4.7   An economist might be interested in the percentage of the work force that is unemployed, or the current inflation rate, both of which are continuous random variables.

4.9   The manager of a clothing store might be concerned with the number of employees on duty at a specific time of day, or the number of articles of a particular type of clothing that are on hand.

4.11   a. $p(22) = .25$

        b. $P(x = 20 \text{ or } x = 24) = P(x = 20) + P(x = 24) = .15 + .20 = .35$

        c. $P(x \le 23) = P(x = 20) + P(x = 21) + P(x = 22) + P(x = 23) = .15 + .10 + .25 + .30 = .80$

4.13   a.   We know $\sum p(x) = 1$. Thus, $p(2) + p(3) + p(5) + p(8) + p(10) = 1$
              $\Rightarrow p(5) = 1 - p(2) - p(3) - p(8) - p(10) = 1 - .15 - .10 - .25 - .25 = .25$

        b. $P(x = 2 \text{ or } x = 10) = P(x = 2) + P(x = 10) = .15 + .25 = .40$

        c. $P(x \le 8) = P(x = 2) + P(x = 3) + P(x = 5) + P(x = 8) = .15 + .10 + .25 + .25 = .75$

4.15   a.   When a die is tossed, the number of spots observed on the upturned face can be 1, 2, 3, 4, 5, or 6. Since the six sample points are equally likely, each one has a probability of 1/6.

The probability distribution of x may be summarized in tabular form:

x	1	2	3	4	5	6
$p(x)$	$\frac{1}{6}$	$\frac{1}{6}$	$\frac{1}{6}$	$\frac{1}{6}$	$\frac{1}{6}$	$\frac{1}{6}$

b.   The probability distribution of x may also be presented in graphical form:

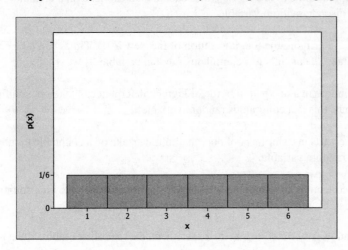

4.17   a. $\mu = E(x) = \sum xp(x) = -4(.02) + (-3)(.07) + (-2)(.10) + (-1)(.15) + 0(.3)$
$$+1(.18) + 2(.10) + 3(.06) + 4(.02)$$
$$= -.08 - .21 - .2 - .15 + 0 + .18 + .2 + .18 + .08 = 0$$

$\sigma^2 = E[(x-\mu)^2] = \sum (x-\mu)^2 p(x)$
$$= (-4-0)^2(.02) + (-3-0)^2(.07) + (-2-0)^2(.10)$$
$$+ (-1-0)^2(.15) + (0-0)^2(.30) + (1-0)^2(.18)$$
$$+ (2-0)^2(.10) + (3-0)^2(.06) + (4-0)^2(.02)$$
$$= .32 + .63 + .4 + .15 + 0 + .18 + .4 + .54 + .32 = 2.94$$

$\sigma = \sqrt{2.94} = 1.715$

b.   Using MINITAB, the graph is:

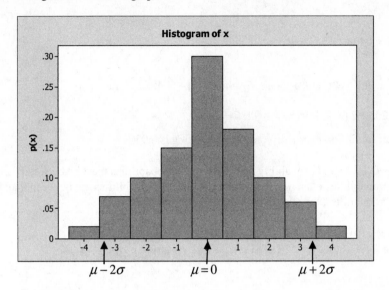

$$\mu \pm 2\sigma \Rightarrow 0 \pm 2(1.715) \Rightarrow 0 \pm 3.430 \Rightarrow (-3.430, 3.430)$$

c. $P(-3.430 < x < 3.430) = p(-3) + p(-2) + p(-1) + p(0) + p(1) + p(2) + p(3)$
$$= .07 + .10 + .15 + .30 + .18 + .10 + .06 = .96$$

4.19   a.   It would seem that the mean of both would be 1 since they both are symmetric distributions centered at 1.

b. $P(x)$ seems more variable since there appears to be greater probability for the two extreme values of 0 and 2 than there is in the distribution of y.

c.   For x: $\mu = E(x) = \sum xp(x) = 0(.3) + 1(.4) + 2(.3) + = 0 + .4 + .6 = 1$

$$\sigma^2 = E[(x - \mu)^2] = \sum (x - \mu)^2 p(x)$$
$$= (0 - 1)^2(.3) + (1 - 1)^2(.4) + (2 - 1)^2(.3) = .3 + 0 + .3 = .6$$

For y: $\mu = E(y) = \sum yp(y) = 0(.1) + 1(.8) + 2(.1) + = 0 + .8 + .2 = 1$

$$\sigma^2 = E[(y - \mu)^2] = \sum (y - \mu)^2 p(y)$$
$$= (0 - 1)^2(.1) + (1 - 1)^2(.8) + (2 - 1)^2(.1) = .1 + 0 + .1 = .2$$

The variance for x is larger than that for y.

4.21   a.   The probability distribution for x is found by converting the Percent column to a probability column by dividing the percents by 100. The probability distribution of x is:

x	$p(x)$
2	.0408
3	.1735
4	.6020
5	.1837

b. $P(x = 5) = p(5) = .1837$.

c. $P(x \leq 2) = p(2) = .0408$.

d. $\mu = E(x) = \sum_{i=1}^{4} x_i p(x_i) = 2(.0408) + 3(.1735) + 4(.6020) + 5(.1837)$

$= .0816 + .5205 + 2.4080 + .9185 = 3.9286 \approx 3.93$

The average star rating for a car's drivers-side star rating is 3.93.

4.23   a.   In order for this to be a valid probability distribution, all probabilities must be between 0 and 1 and the sum of all the probabilities must be 1. For this data, all the probabilities are between 0 and 1. If you sum all of the probabilities, the sum is 1.

b. $P(x \geq 10) = P(x = 10) + P(x = 11) + \cdots + P(x = 20)$

$= .02 + .02 + .02 + .02 + .01 + .01 + .01 + .01 + .01 + .005 + .005 = .14$

c.   The mean of x is

$\mu = E(x) = \sum xp(x) = 0(.17) + 1(.10) + 2(.11) + \cdots + 20(.005)$

$= 0 + .1 + .22 + .33 + \cdots + .1 = 4.655$

The variance of x is

$\sigma^2 = E(x - \mu)^2 = \sum(x - \mu)^2 p(x) = (0 - 4.655)^2(.17) + (1 - 4.655)^2(.1) + (2 - 4.655)^2(.11)$

$+ \cdots + (20 - 4.655)^2(.005)$

$= 3.6837 + 1.3359 + .7754 + \cdots + 1.1773 = 19.8560$

d.   From Chebyshev's Rule, we know that at least .75 of the observations will fall within 2 standard deviations of the mean. The standard deviation is $\sigma = \sqrt{19.8560} = 4.456$.

The interval is: $\mu \pm 2\sigma \Rightarrow 4.655 \pm 2(4.456) \Rightarrow 4.655 \pm 8.912 \Rightarrow (-4.257, 13.567)$.

4.25   a.   The possible values of x are 0, 2, 3, and 4.

b.   To find the probability distribution of x, we first find the frequency distribution of x. We then divide the frequencies by $n = 106$ to get the probabilities. The probability distribution of x is:

x	0	2	3	4
$f(x)$	35	58	5	8
$p(x)$	.3302	.5472	.0472	.0755

c. $\mu = E(x) = \sum xp(x) = 0(.3302) + 2(.5472) + 3(.0472) + 4(.0755) = 1.538$. For all social robots, the average number of legs on the robot is 1.538.

4.27   a.   The random variable x is a discrete random variable because it can take on only values 0, 1, 2, 3, 4, or 5 in this example.

b. $p(0) = \dfrac{5!(.35)^0 (.65)^{5-0}}{0!(5-0)!} = \dfrac{5 \cdot 4 \cdot 3 \cdot 2 \cdot 1(1)(.65)^5}{1 \cdot 5 \cdot 4 \cdot 3 \cdot 2 \cdot 1} = .65^5 = .1160$

$p(1) = \dfrac{5!(.35)^1 (.65)^{5-1}}{1!(5-1)!} = \dfrac{5 \cdot 4 \cdot 3 \cdot 2 \cdot 1(.35)^1 (.65)^4}{1 \cdot 4 \cdot 3 \cdot 2 \cdot 1} = 5(.35)(.65)^4 = .3124$

$p(2) = \dfrac{5!(.35)^2 (.65)^{5-2}}{2!(5-2)!} = \dfrac{5 \cdot 4 \cdot 3 \cdot 2 \cdot 1(.35)^2 (.65)^3}{2 \cdot 1 \cdot 3 \cdot 2 \cdot 1} = 10(.35)^2 (.65)^3 = .3364$

$p(3) = \dfrac{5!(.35)^3 (.65)^{5-3}}{3!(5-3)!} = \dfrac{5 \cdot 4 \cdot 3 \cdot 2 \cdot 1(.35)^3 (.65)^2}{3 \cdot 2 \cdot 1 \cdot 2 \cdot 1} = 10(.35)^3 (.65)^2 = .1811$

$p(4) = \dfrac{5!(.35)^4 (.65)^{5-4}}{4!(5-4)!} = \dfrac{5 \cdot 4 \cdot 3 \cdot 2 \cdot 1(.35)^4 (.65)^1}{4 \cdot 3 \cdot 2 \cdot 1 \cdot 1} = 5(.35)^4 (.65)^1 = .0488$

$p(5) = \dfrac{5!(.35)^5 (.65)^{5-5}}{5!(5-5)!} = \dfrac{5 \cdot 4 \cdot 3 \cdot 2 \cdot 1(.35)^5 (.65)^0}{5 \cdot 4 \cdot 3 \cdot 2 \cdot 1 \cdot 1} = (.35)^5 = .0053$

c. The two properties of discrete random variables are that $0 \le p(x) \le 1$ for all x and $\sum p(x) = 1$. From above, all probabilities are between 0 and 1 and

$$\sum p(x) = .1160 + .3124 + .3364 + .1811 + .0488 + .0053 = 1$$

d. $P(x \ge 4) = p(4) + p(5) = .0488 + .0053 = .0541$

4.29 a. $p(1) = .23(.77)^{1-1} = .23(.77)^0 = .23$. The probability that one would encounter a contaminated cartridge on the first trial is .23.

b. $p(5) = .23(.77)^{5-1} = .23(.77)^4 = .0809$. The probability that one would encounter a the first contaminated cartridge on the fifth trial is .0809.

c. $P(x \ge 2) = 1 - P(x \le 1) = 1 - P(x = 1) = 1 - .23 = .77$. The probability that the first contaminated cartridge is found on the second trial or later is .77.

4.31 a. $p(0) = \dfrac{\binom{20}{0}\binom{100-20}{3-0}}{\binom{100}{3}} = \dfrac{\dfrac{20!}{0!(20-0)!}\dfrac{80!}{3!(80-3)!}}{\dfrac{100!}{3!(100-3)!}} = \dfrac{\dfrac{20!}{0!20!}\dfrac{80!}{3!77!}}{\dfrac{100!}{3!97!}} = \dfrac{82,160}{161,700} = .508$

b. $p(1) = \dfrac{\binom{20}{1}\binom{100-20}{3-1}}{\binom{100}{3}} = \dfrac{\dfrac{20!}{1!(20-1)!}\dfrac{80!}{2!(80-2)!}}{\dfrac{100!}{3!(100-3)!}} = \dfrac{\dfrac{20!}{1!19!}\dfrac{80!}{2!78!}}{\dfrac{100!}{3!97!}} = \dfrac{63,200}{161,700} = .391$

c. $p(2) = \dfrac{\dbinom{20}{2}\dbinom{100-20}{3-2}}{\dbinom{100}{3}} = \dfrac{\dfrac{20!}{2!(20-2)!}\dfrac{80!}{1!(80-1)!}}{\dfrac{100!}{3!(100-3)!}} = \dfrac{\dfrac{20!}{2!18!}\dfrac{80!}{1!79!}}{\dfrac{100!}{3!97!}} = \dfrac{15,200}{161,700} = .094$

d. $p(3) = \dfrac{\dbinom{20}{3}\dbinom{100-20}{3-0}}{\dbinom{100}{3}} = \dfrac{\dfrac{20!}{3!(20-3)!}\dfrac{80!}{0!(80-0)!}}{\dfrac{100!}{3!(100-3)!}} = \dfrac{\dfrac{20!}{3!17!}\cdot 1}{\dfrac{100!}{3!97!}} = \dfrac{1,140}{161,700} = .007$

4.33   To find the probability distribution of x, we sum the probabilities associated with the same value of x. The probability distribution is:

x	8.5	9	9.5	10	10.5	11	12
$p(x)$	.462189	.288764	.141671	.069967	.025236	.011657	.000518

4.35   a.   Let x = the potential flood damages. Since we are assuming if it rains the business will incur damages and if it does not rain the business will not incur any damages, the probability distribution of x is:

x	0	300,000
$p(x)$	.7	.3

b.   The expected loss due to flood damage is

$$E(x) = \sum_{All\,x} xp(x) = 0(.7) + 300,000(.3) = 0 + 90,000 = \$90,000$$

4.37   a.   Since there are 20 possible outcomes that are all equally likely, the probability of any of the 20 numbers is 1/20. The probability distribution of x is:

$P(x=5) = 1/20 = .05$; $P(x=10) = 1/20 = .05$; etc.

x	5	10	15	20	25	30	35	40	45	50	55	60	65	70	75	80	85	90	95	100
$p(x)$	.05	.05	.05	.05	.05	.05	.05	.05	.05	.05	.05	.05	.05	.05	.05	.05	.05	.05	.05	.05

b. $E(x) = \sum xp(x) = 5(.05) + 10(.05) + 15(.05) + 20(.05) + 25(.05) + 30(.05) + 35(.05)$
$+ 40(.05) + 45(.05) + 50(.05) + 55(.05) + 60(.05) + 65(.05) + 70(.05) + 75(.05)$
$+ 80(.05) + 85(.05) + 90(.05) + 95(.05) + 100(.05) = 52.5$

c. $\sigma^2 = E(x-\mu)^2 = \sum(x-\mu)^2 p(x) = (5-52.5)^2(.05) + (10-52.5)^2(.05)$
$+ (15-52.5)^2(.05) + (20-52.5)^2(.05) + (25-52.5)^2(.05) + (30-52.5)^2(.05)$
$+ (35-52.5)^2(.05) + (40-52.5)^2(.05) + (45-52.5)^2(.05) + (50-52.5)^2(.05)$
$+ (55-52.5)^2(.05) + (60-52.5)^2(.05) + (65-52.5)^2(.05) + (70-52.5)^2(.05)$
$+ (75-52.5)^2(.05) + (80-52.5)^2(.05) + (85-52.5)^2(.05) + (90-52.5)^2(.05)$
$+ (95-52.5)^2(.05) + (100-52.5)^2(.05)$
$= 831.25$

$\sigma = \sqrt{831.25} = 28.83$

Since the uniform distribution is not mound-shaped, we will use Chebyshev's theorem to describe the data. We know that at least 8/9 of the observations will fall with 3 standard deviations of the mean and at least 3/4 of the observations will fall within 2 standard deviations of the mean. For this problem,

$\mu \pm 2\sigma \Rightarrow 52.5 \pm 2(28.83) \Rightarrow 52.5 \pm 57.66 \Rightarrow (-5.16, 110.16)$. Thus, at least 3/4 of the data will fall between −5.16 and 110.16. For our problem, all of the observations will fall within 2 standard deviations of the mean. Thus, x is just as likely to fall within any interval of equal length.

d. If a player spins the wheel twice, the total number of outcomes will be 20(20) = 400. The sample space is:

5, 5	10, 5	15, 5	20, 5	25, 5...	100, 5
5,10	10,10	15,10	20,10	25,10...	100,10
5,15	10,15	15,15	20,15	25,15...	100,15
.	.	.	.	.	.
.	.	.	.	.	.
.	.	.	.	.	.
5,100	10,100	15,100	20,100	25,100...	100,100

Each of these outcomes are equally likely, so each has a probability of 1/400 = .0025.

Now, let x equal the sum of the two numbers in each sample. There is one sample with a sum of 10, two samples with a sum of 15, three samples with a sum of 20, etc. If the sum of the two numbers exceeds 100, then x is zero. The probability distribution of x is:

x	$p(x)$	x	$p(x)$
0	.5250	55	.0250
10	.0025	60	.0275
15	.0050	65	.0300
20	.0075	70	.0325
25	.0100	75	.0350
30	.0125	80	.0375
35	.0150	85	.0400
40	.0175	90	.0425
45	.0200	95	.0450
50	.0225	100	.0475

e. We assumed that the wheel is fair, or that all outcomes are equally likely.

f. $\mu = E(x) = \sum xp(x) = 0(.5250) + 10(.0025) + 15(.0050) + 20(.0075) + \cdots + 100(.0475) = 33.25$

$\sigma^2 = E(x - \mu)^2 = \sum (x - \mu)^2 p(x) = (0 - 33.25)^2 (.5250) + (10 - 33.25)^2 (.0025)$
$\quad + (15 - 33.25)^2 (.0050) + (20 - 33.25)^2 (.0075) + \cdots + (100 - 33.25)^2 (.0475) = 1,471.3125$

$\sigma = \sqrt{1,471.3125} = 38.3577$

g. $P(x = 0) = .525$

h. Given that the player obtains a 20 on the first spin, the possible values for x (sum of the two spins) are 0 (player spins 85, 90, 95, or 100 on the second spin), 25, 30, ..., 100. To get an x of 25, the player would spin a 5 on the second spin. Similarly, the player would have to spin a 10 on the second spin order to get an x of 30, etc. Since all of the outcomes are equally likely on the second spin, the distribution of x is:

x	$p(x)$	x	$p(x)$
0	.20	65	.05
25	.05	70	.05
30	.05	75	.05
35	.05	80	.05
40	.05	85	.05
45	.05	90	.05
50	.05	95	.05
55	.05	100	.05
60	.05		

i. The probability that the players total score will exceed one dollar is the probability that x is zero.
$P(x = 0) = .20$

j. Given that the player obtains a 65 on the first spin, the possible values for x (sum of the two spins) are 0 (player spins 40, 45, 50, up to 100 on second spin), 70, 75, 80,..., 100. In order to get an x of 70, the player would spin a 5 on the second spin. Similarly, the player would have to spin a 10 on the second spin in order to get an x of 75, etc. Since all of the outcomes are equally likely on the second spin, the distribution of x is:

x	$p(x)$
0	.65
70	.05
75	.05
80	.05
85	.05
90	.05
95	.05
100	.05

The probability that the players total score will exceed one dollar is the probability that x is zero.
$P(x = 0) = .65$.

4.39 Let x = bookie's earnings per dollar wagered. Then x can take on values $1 (you lose) and $-5 (you win). The only way you win is if you pick 3 winners in 3 games. If the probability of picking 1 winner in 1 game is .5, then $P(www) = p(w)p(w)p(w) = .5(.5)(.5) = .125$ (assuming games are independent).

Thus, the probability distribution for x is:

x	$p(x)$
$1	.875
$-5	.125

$$E(x) = \sum xp(x)1(.875) - 5(.125) = .875 - .625 = \$.25$$

4.41 a. x is discrete. It can take on only six values.

b. This is a binomial distribution.

c. $p(0) = \binom{5}{0}(.7)^0(.3)^{5-0} = \frac{5!}{0!5!}(.7)^0(.3)^5 = \frac{5 \cdot 4 \cdot 3 \cdot 2 \cdot 1}{1 \cdot 5 \cdot 4 \cdot 3 \cdot 2 \cdot 1}(1)(.00243) = .00243$

$p(1) = \binom{5}{1}(.7)^1(.3)^{5-1} = \frac{5!}{1!4!}(.7)^1(.3)^4 = .02835$ $\qquad p(2) = \binom{5}{2}(.7)^2(.3)^{5-2} = \frac{5!}{2!3!}(.7)^2(.3)^3 = .1323$

$p(3) = \binom{5}{3}(.7)^3(.3)^{5-3} = \frac{5!}{3!2!}(.7)^3(.3)^2 = .3087$ $\qquad p(4) = \binom{5}{4}(.7)^4(.3)^{5-4} = \frac{5!}{4!1!}(.7)^4(.3)^1 = .36015$

$p(5) = \binom{5}{5}(.7)^5(.3)^{5-5} = \frac{5!}{5!0!}(.7)^5(.3)^0 = .16807$

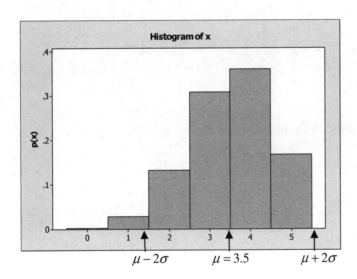

d. $\mu = np = 5(.7) = 3.5$ $\qquad\qquad \sigma = \sqrt{npq} = \sqrt{5(.7)(.3)} = 1.0247$

e. $\mu \pm 2\sigma \Rightarrow 3.5 \pm 2(1.0247) \Rightarrow 3.5 \pm 2.0494 \Rightarrow (1.4506, 5.5494)$

4.43 a. $P(x = 1) = \frac{5!}{1!4!}(.2)^1(.8)^4 = \frac{5 \cdot 4 \cdot 3 \cdot 2 \cdot 1}{(1)(4 \cdot 3 \cdot 2 \cdot 1)}(.2)^1(.8)^4 = 5(.2)^1(.8)^4 = .4096$

b. $P(x = 2) = \frac{4!}{2!2!}(.6)^2(.4)^2 = \frac{4 \cdot 3 \cdot 2 \cdot 1}{(2 \cdot 1)(2 \cdot 1)}(.6)^2(.4)^2 = 6(.6)^2(.4)^2 = .3456$

c. $P(x = 0) = \frac{3!}{0!3!}(.7)^0(.3)^3 = \frac{3 \cdot 2 \cdot 1}{(1)(3 \cdot 2 \cdot 1)}(.7)^0(.3)^3 = 1(.7)^0(.3)^3 = .027$

d. $P(x=3) = \dfrac{5!}{3!2!}(.1)^3(.9)^2 = \dfrac{5 \cdot 4 \cdot 3 \cdot 2 \cdot 1}{(3 \cdot 2 \cdot 1)(2 \cdot 1)}(.1)^3(.9)^2 = 10(.1)^3(.9)^2 = .0081$

e. $P(x=2) = \dfrac{4!}{2!2!}(.4)^2(.6)^2 = \dfrac{4 \cdot 3 \cdot 2 \cdot 1}{(2 \cdot 1)(2 \cdot 1)}(.4)^2(.6)^2 = 6(.4)^2(.6)^2 = .3456$

f. $P(x=1) = \dfrac{3!}{1!2!}(.9)^1(.1)^2 = \dfrac{3 \cdot 2 \cdot 1}{(1)(2 \cdot 1)}(.9)^1(.1)^2 = 3(.9)^1(.1)^2 = .027$

4.45   a. $\mu = np = 25(.5) = 12.5$

$\sigma^2 = np(1-p) = 25(.5)(.5) = 6.25$ and $\sigma = \sqrt{\sigma^2} = \sqrt{6.25} = 2.5$

b. $\mu = np = 80(.2) = 16$

$\sigma^2 = np(1-p) = 80(.2)(.8) = 12.8$ and $\sigma = \sqrt{\sigma^2} = \sqrt{12.8} = 3.578$

c. $\mu = np = 100(.6) = 60$

$\sigma^2 = np(1-p) = 100(.6)(.4) = 24$ and $\sigma = \sqrt{\sigma^2} = \sqrt{24} = 4.899$

d. $\mu = np = 70(.9) = 63$

$\sigma^2 = np(1-p) = 70(.9)(.1) = 6.3$ and $\sigma = \sqrt{\sigma^2} = \sqrt{6.3} = 2.510$

e. $\mu = np = 60(.8) = 48$

$\sigma^2 = np(1-p) = 60(.8)(.2) = 9.6$ and $\sigma = \sqrt{\sigma^2} = \sqrt{9.6} = 3.098$

f. $\mu = np = 1,000(.04) = 40$

$\sigma^2 = np(1-p) = 1,000(.04)(.96) = 38.4$ and $\sigma = \sqrt{\sigma^2} = \sqrt{38.4} = 6.197$

4.47   a.   Let S = adult who does not work while on summer vacation.

b.   To see if x is approximately a binomial random variable we check the characteristics:

1. n identical trials. Although the trials are not exactly identical, they are close. Taking a sample of reasonable size n from a very large population will result in trials being essentially identical.

2.   Two possible outcomes. The adults can either not work on their summer vacation or they can work on their summer vacation. S = adult does not work on summer vacation and F = adult does work on summer vacation.

3. $P(S)$ remains the same from trial to trial. If we sample without replacement, then $P(S)$ will change slightly from trial to trial. However, the differences are extremely small and will essentially be 0.

4. Trials are independent. Again, although the trials are not exactly independent, they are very close.

5. The random variable x = number of adults who work on their summer vacation in $n = 10$ trials.

Thus, x is very close to being a binomial. We will assume that it is a binomial random variable.

c. For this problem, $p = .35$.

d. Using MINITAB $n = 10$ and $p = .35$, the probability is:

Probability Density Function
```
Binomial with n = 10 and p = 0.35

x   P( X = x )
3    0.252220
```

Thus, $P(x = 3) = .2522$.

e. Using MINITAB $n = 10$ and $p = .35$, the probability is:

Cumulative Distribution Function
```
Binomial with n = 10 and p = 0.35

x   P( X <= x )
2    0.261607
```
Thus, $P(x \le 2) = P(x = 0) + P(x = 1) + P(x = 2) = .2616$.

4.49 a. To see if x is approximately a binomial random variable we check the characteristics:

1. n identical trials. Although the trials are not exactly identical, they are close. Taking a sample of size $n = 250$ from a very large population will result in trials being essentially identical.

2. Two possible outcomes. A U.S. adult has either used the internet and paid to download music or he/she has not. S = U.S. adult has used the internet and paid to download music and F = U.S. adult has not used the internet and/or has not paid to download music.

3. $P(S)$ remains the same from trial to trial. If we sample without replacement, then $P(S)$ will change slightly from trial to trial. However, the differences are extremely small and will essentially be 0.

4. Trials are independent. Again, although the trials are not exactly independent, they are very close.

5. The random variable x = number of U.S. adults who have used the internet and paid to download music in $n = 250$ trials.

Thus, x is very close to being a binomial. We will assume that it is a binomial random variable.

b. For this example, $p = .5$. Half of the adults in the U.S. have used the internet and have paid to download music.

c. $E(x) = \mu = np = 250(.5) = 125$

4.51   For this problem, let x = number of law librarians who are unsatisfied with their job. Then x is a binomial random variable with $n = 20$ and $p = 1 - .90 = .10$. Using a MINITAB with $n = 20$ and $p = .10$, the probability is

Cumulative Distribution Function
```
Binomial with n = 20 and p = 0.1

x   P( X <= x )
2     0.676927
```

Thus, $P(x \le 2) = .6769$.

4.53   a.   Let x = number of pairs correctly identified by an expert in 5 trials. Then x is a binomial random variable with $n = 5$ and $p = .92$. Using a MINITAB with $n = 5$ and $p = .92$, the probability is:

Probability Density Function
```
Binomial with n = 5 and p = 0.92

x   P( X = x )
5     0.659082
```

Thus, $P(x = 5) = .6591$.

b.   Let y = number of pairs correctly identified by a novice in 5 trials. Then y is a binomial random variable with $n = 5$ and $p = .75$. Using a MINITAB with $n = 5$ and $p = .75$, the probability is:

Probability Density Function
```
Binomial with n = 5 and p = 0.75

x   P( X = x )
5     0.237305
```

Thus, $P(x = 5) = .2373$.

4.55   Let x = number of major bridges in Denver that will have a rating of 4 or below in 2020 in 10 trials. Then x has an approximate binomial distribution with $n = 10$ and $p = .09$.

a. $P(x \ge 3) = 1 - P(x \le 2) = 1 - P(x = 0) - P(x = 1) - P(x = 2)$

$$= 1 - \binom{10}{0}.09^0(.91)^{10-0} - \binom{10}{1}.09^1(.91)^{10-1} - \binom{10}{2}.09^2(.91)^{10-2}$$

$$= 1 - \frac{10!}{0!10!}.09^0.91^{10} - \frac{10!}{1!9!}.09^1.91^9 - \frac{10!}{2!8!}.09^2.91^8 = 1 - .389 - .385 - .171 = .055$$

b.   Since the probability of seeing at least 3 bridges out of 10 with ratings of 4 or less is so small, we can conclude that the forecast of 9% of all major Denver bridges will have ratings of 4 or less in 2020 is too small. There would probably be more than 9%.

4.57   a. $\mu = E(x) = np = 800(.65) = 520$ $\sigma = \sqrt{npq} = \sqrt{800(.65)(.35)} = \sqrt{182} = 13.49$

b.   Half of the 800 food items would be 400. A value of $x = 400$ would have a z-score of:

$$z = \frac{x - \mu}{\sigma} = \frac{400 - 520}{13.49} = -8.90$$

Since the z-score associated with 400 items is so small (-8.90), it would be virtually impossible to observe less than half with any pesticides if the 65% value was correct.

4.59   a.   We must assume that the probability that a specific type of ball meets the requirements is always the same from trial to trial and the trials are independent. To use the binomial probability distribution, we need to know the probability that a specific type of golf ball meets the requirements.

   b.   For a binomial distribution, $\mu = np$ and $\sigma = \sqrt{npq}$.

   In this example, $n =$ two dozen $= 2(12) = 24$, $p = .10$, and $q = 1 - .10 = .90$.
   (Success here means the golf ball *does not* meet standards.)

   $\mu = np = 24(.10) = 2.4$ and $\sigma = \sqrt{npq} = \sqrt{24(.10)(.90)} = 1.47$

   c.   In this situation, $n = 24$, $p =$ Probability of success $=$ Probability golf ball *does* meet standards $= .90$, and $q = 1 - .90 = .10$.

   $E(y) = \mu = np = 24(.90) = 21.6$ and $\sigma = \sqrt{npq} = \sqrt{24(.10)(.90)} = 1.47$
   (Note that σ is the same as in part **b**.)

4.61   a.   The random variable x is discrete since it can assume a countable number of values (0, 1, 2, ...).

   b.   This is a Poisson probability distribution with $\lambda = 3$.

   c.   In order to graph the probability distribution, we need to know the probabilities for the possible values of x. Using MINITAB with $\lambda = 3$:

Probability Density Function
```
Poisson with mean = 3

   x    P( X = x )
   0     0.049787
   1     0.149361
   2     0.224042
   3     0.224042
   4     0.168031
   5     0.100819
   6     0.050409
   7     0.021604
   8     0.008102
   9     0.002701
  10     0.000810
```

Using MINITAB, the probability distribution of x in graphical form is:

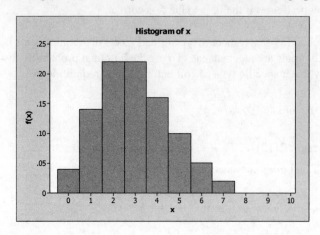

d. $\mu = \lambda = 3$

$\sigma^2 = \lambda = 3$ and $\sigma = \sqrt{3} = 1.7321$

4.63   a. $P(x=1) = \dfrac{\binom{r}{x}\binom{N-r}{n-x}}{\binom{N}{n}} = \dfrac{\binom{3}{1}\binom{5-3}{3-1}}{\binom{5}{3}} = \dfrac{\dfrac{3!}{1!2!}\dfrac{2!}{2!0!}}{\dfrac{5!}{3!2!}} = \dfrac{3(1)}{10} = .3$

b. $P(x=3) = \dfrac{\binom{r}{x}\binom{N-r}{n-x}}{\binom{N}{n}} = \dfrac{\binom{3}{3}\binom{9-3}{5-3}}{\binom{9}{5}} = \dfrac{\dfrac{3!}{3!0!}\dfrac{6!}{2!4!}}{\dfrac{9!}{5!4!}} = \dfrac{1(15)}{126} = .119$

c. $P(x=2) = \dfrac{\binom{r}{x}\binom{N-r}{n-x}}{\binom{N}{n}} = \dfrac{\binom{2}{2}\binom{4-2}{2-2}}{\binom{4}{2}} = \dfrac{\dfrac{2!}{2!0!}\dfrac{2!}{0!2!}}{\dfrac{4!}{2!2!}} = \dfrac{1(1)}{6} = .167$

d. $P(x=0) = \dfrac{\binom{r}{x}\binom{N-r}{n-x}}{\binom{N}{n}} = \dfrac{\binom{2}{0}\binom{4-2}{2-0}}{\binom{4}{2}} = \dfrac{\dfrac{2!}{0!2!}\dfrac{2!}{2!0!}}{\dfrac{4!}{2!2!}} = \dfrac{1(1)}{6} = .167$

4.65   a.   Using MINITAB with $\lambda = 1$, and the Poisson distribution, the probability is:

Cumulative Distribution Function
```
Poisson with mean = 1

x   P( X <= x )
2      0.919699
```

$P(x \le 2) = .919699$

b.   Using MINITAB with $\lambda = 2$, and the Poisson distribution, the probability is:

Cumulative Distribution Function
```
Poisson with mean = 2

x   P( X <= x )
2      0.676676
```

$P(x \le 2) = .676676$

c.   Using MINITAB with $\lambda = 3$, and the Poisson distribution, the probability is:

Cumulative Distribution Function
```
Poisson with mean = 3

x   P( X <= x )
2      0.423190
```

$P(x \le 2) = .42319$

d.   The probability decreases as λ increases. This is reasonable because λ is equal to the mean. As the mean increases, the probability that x is less than a particular value will decrease.

4.67   For this problem, $N = 100$, $n = 10$, and $x = 4$.

a.   If the sample is drawn without replacement, the hypergeometric distribution should be used. The hypergeometric distribution requires that sampling be done without replacement.

b.   If the sample is drawn with replacement, the binomial distribution should be used. The binomial distribution requires that sampling be done with replacement.

4.69   a.   The characteristics of a binomial random variable are:

1. n identical trials. We are selecting 10 robots from 106. On the first trial, we are selecting 1 robot out of 106. On the next trial, we are selecting 1 robot out of 105. On the 10th trial, we are selecting 1 robot out of 97. These trials are not identical.

2.   Two possible outcomes. A selected robot either has no legs or wheels or it has some legs or wheels. S = robot has no legs or wheels and F = robot has either legs and/or wheels. This condition is met

3. $P(S)$ remains the same from trial to trial. For this example the probability of success does not stay constant. On the first trial, there are 106 robots of which 15 have neither legs nor wheels. Thus, $P(S)$ on the first trial is 15/106. If a robot with neither legs nor wheels is selected on the first trial, then $P(S)$ on the second trial would be 14/105. If a robot with neither legs nor wheels is not selected on the first trial, then $P(S)$ on the second trial would be 15/105. The value of $P(S)$ is not constant from trial to trial. This condition is not met.

4.   Trials are independent. The trials are not independent. The type of robot selected on one trial affects the type of robot selected on the next trial. This condition is not met.

5.   The random variable x = number of robots selected that do not have legs or wheels in 10 trials.

The necessary conditions for a binomial random variable are not met.

Copyright © 2014 Pearson Education, Inc.

b.   The characteristics of a hypergeometric random variable are:

1. The experiment consists of randomly drawing n elements without replacement from a set of N elements, r of which are successes and $(N - r)$ of which are failures. For this example there are a total of $N = 106$ robots, of which $r = 15$ have neither legs nor wheels and $N - r = 106 - 15 = 95$ have some legs and/or wheels. We are selecting $n = 10$ robots.

2. The hypergeometric random variable x is the number of successes in the draw of n elements. For this example, $x =$ number of robots selected with no legs or wheels in 20 selections.

c. $\mu = \dfrac{nr}{N} = \dfrac{10(15)}{106} = 1.415$ and

$$\sigma = \sqrt{\dfrac{r(N-r)n(N-n)}{N^2(N-1)}} = \sqrt{\dfrac{15(106-15)10(106-10)}{106^2(106-1)}} = \sqrt{1.1107} = 1.0539$$

d. $P(x = 2) = \dfrac{\dbinom{15}{2}\dbinom{106-15}{10-2}}{\dbinom{106}{10}} = \dfrac{\dfrac{15!}{2!(15-2)!}\dfrac{91!}{8!(91-8)!}}{\dfrac{106!}{10!(106-10)!}} = \dfrac{105(8.49869x10^{12})}{3.18535x10^{13}} = .2801$

4.71   a.   With $\lambda = 4.5$, $P(x = 0) = \dfrac{4.5^0 e^{-4.5}}{0!} = 0.0111$

b. $P(x = 1) = \dfrac{4.5^1 e^{-4.5}}{1!} = 0.0500$

c. $\mu = E(x) = \lambda = 4.5$

$\sigma = \sqrt{\lambda} = \sqrt{4.5} = 2.12$

4.73   Let $x =$ number of "clean" cartridges selected in 5 trials. For this problem, $N = 158$, $n = 5$, and $r = 122$.

$$P(x = 5) = \dfrac{\dbinom{r}{x}\dbinom{N-r}{n-x}}{\dbinom{N}{n}} = \dfrac{\dbinom{122}{5}\dbinom{36}{0}}{\dbinom{158}{5}} = \dfrac{\dfrac{122!}{5!117!}\dfrac{36!}{0!36!}}{\dfrac{158!}{5!153!}} = .2693$$

4.75   Let $x =$ number of times "total visitors" is selected in 5 museums. For this exercise, x has a hypergeometric distribution with $N = 30$, $n = 5$, $r = 8$ and $x = 0$.

$$P(x = 0) = \dfrac{\dbinom{8}{0}\dbinom{30-8}{5-0}}{\dbinom{30}{5}} = \dfrac{\dfrac{8!}{0!(8-0)!}\dfrac{22!}{5!(22-5)!}}{\dfrac{30!}{5!(30-5)!}} = .1848$$

4.77   Let x = number of times cell phone accesses color code "b" in 7 handoffs. For this problem, x has a hypergeometric distribution with $N = 85$, $n = 7$, and $r = 40$.

$$P(x=2) = \frac{\binom{40}{2}\binom{85-40}{7-2}}{\binom{85}{7}} = \frac{\frac{40!}{2!(40-2)!}\frac{45!}{5!(45-5)!}}{\frac{85!}{7!(85-7)!}} = \frac{780(1,221,759)}{4,935,847,320} = .1931$$

4.79   Let x = number of flaws in a 4 meter length of wire. For this exercise, x has a Poisson distribution with $\lambda = .8$. The roll will be rejected if there is at least one flaw in the sample of a 4 meter length of wire.

$$P(x \geq 1) = 1 - P(x=0) = 1 - \frac{.8^0 e^{-.8}}{0!} = 1 - .4493 = .5507$$

We have to assume that the flaws are randomly distributed throughout the roll of wire and that the 4 meter sample of wire is representative of the entire roll.

4.81   a.   Using MINITAB with $\lambda = 10$,

Probability Density Function
Poisson with mean = 10

```
  x   P( X = x )
 24    0.0000732
```

$P(x = 24) = .0000732$

b.   Using MINITAB with $\lambda = 10$,

Probability Density Function
Poisson with mean = 10

```
  x   P( X = x )
 23    0.0001756
```

$P(x = 23) = .0001756$

c.   Yes, these probabilities are good approximations for the probability of "fire" and "theft". The researchers estimated these probabilities to be .0001, indicating that these would be extremely rare events. Our probabilities of .0001 and .0002 are very close to .0001.

4.83   Let x = number of females promoted in the 72 employees awarded promotion, where x is a hypergeometric random variable. From the problem, $N = 302$, $n = 72$, and $r = 73$. We need to find if observing 5 females who were promoted was fair.

$$E(x) = \mu = \frac{nr}{N} = \frac{72(73)}{302} = 17.40$$

If 72 employees are promoted, we would expect that about 17 would be females.

$$V(x) = \sigma^2 = \frac{r(N-r)n(N-n)}{N^2(N-1)} = \frac{73(302-73)72(302-72)}{302^2(302-1)} = 10.084$$

$$\sigma = \sqrt{10.084} = 3.176$$

Using Chebyshev's Theorem, we know that at least 8/9 of all observations will fall within 3 standard deviations of the mean. The interval from 3 standard deviations below the mean to 3 standard deviations above the mean is:

$$\mu \pm 3\sigma \Rightarrow 17.40 \pm 3(3.176) \Rightarrow 17.40 \pm 9.528 \Rightarrow (7.872, \ 26.928)$$

If there is no discrimination in promoting females, then we would expect between 8 and 26 females to be promoted within the group of 72 employees promoted. Since we observed only 5 females promoted, we would infer that females were not promoted fairly.

4.85   Using Table II, Appendix D:

a. $P(z > 1.46) = .5 - P(0 < z < 1.46) = .5 - .4279 = .0721$

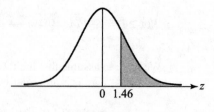

b. $P(z < -1.56) = .5 - P(-1.56 < z < 0) = .5 - .4406 = .0594$

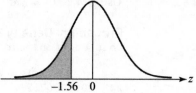

c. $P(.67 \leq z \leq 2.41) = P(0 < z \leq 2.41) - P(0 < z < .67)$
$$= .4920 - .2486 = .2434$$

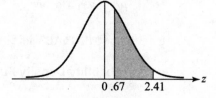

d. $P(-1.96 \leq z \leq -.33) = P(-1.96 \leq z < 0) - P(-.33 \leq z < 0)$
$$= .4750 - .1293 = .3457$$

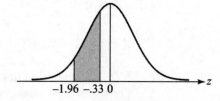

e. $P(z \geq 0) = .5$

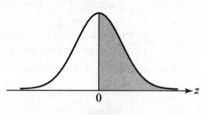

f. $P(-2.33 < z < 1.50) = P(-2.33 < z < 0) + P(0 < z < 1.50)$
$$= .4901 + .4332 = .9233$$

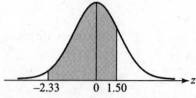

4.87   Using Table II, Appendix D:

a.

$$P(-1 \le z \le 1) = P(-1 \le z \le 0) + P(0 \le z \le 1)$$
$$= .3413 + .3413 = .6826$$

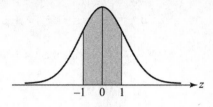

b.

$$P(-1.96 \le z \le 1.96) = P(-1.96 \le z \le 0) + P(0 \le z \le 1.96)$$
$$= .4750 + .4750 = .9500$$

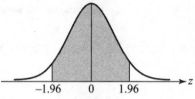

c.

$$P(-1.645 \le z \le 1.645) = P(-1.645 \le z \le 0) + P(0 \le z \le 1.645)$$
$$= .4500 + .4500 = .9000$$

(using interpolation)

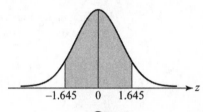

d.

$$P(-2 \le z \le 2) = P(-2 \le z \le 0) + P(0 \le z \le 2)$$
$$= .4772 + .4772 = .9544$$

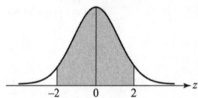

4.89   Using Table II of Appendix D:

a. $P(z \le z_0) = .2090$
$A = .5 - .2090 = .2910$
Looking up the area .2910 in the body of Table II
gives $z_0 = -.81$.   (z_0 is negative since the graph
shows z_0 is on the left side of 0.)

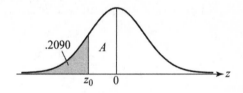

b. $P(z \le z_0) = .7090$
$$P(z \le z_0) = P(z \le 0) + P(0 \le z \le z_0)$$
$$= .5 + P(0 \le z \le z_0) = .7090$$

Therefore, $P(0 \le z \le z_0) = .7090 - .5 = .2090 = A$

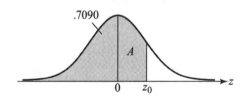

Looking up the area .2090 in the body of Table II gives $z_0 \approx .55$.

c. $P(-z_0 \le z \le z_0) = .8472$

$$P(-z_0 \le z \le z_0) = 2P(0 \le z \le z_0) = .8472$$

Therefore, $P(0 \le z \le z_0) = .8472 / 2 = .4236$.
Looking up the area .4236 in the body of Table II gives $z_0 = 1.43$.

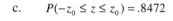

d. $P(-z_0 \leq z \leq z_0) = .1664$

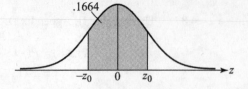

$P(-z_0 \leq z \leq z_0) = 2P(0 \leq z \leq z_0) = .1664$

Therefore, $P(0 \leq z \leq z_0) = .1664 / 2 = .0832$.

Looking up the area .0832 in the body of Table II gives $z_0 = .21$.

e. $P(z_0 \leq z \leq 0) = .4798$

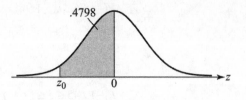

$P(z_0 \leq z \leq 0) = P(0 \leq z \leq -z_0)$

Looking up the area .4798 in the body of Table II gives
$z_0 = -2.05$.

f. $P(-1 < z < z_0) = .5328$

$P(-1 < z < z_0) = P(-1 < z < 0) + P(0 < z < z_0) = .5328$

$P(0 < z < 1) + P(0 < z < z_0) = .5328$

Thus, $P(0 < z < z_0) = .5328 - .3413 = .1915$

Looking up the area .1915 in the body of Table II gives $z_0 = .50$.

4.91   a. $z = \dfrac{x-\mu}{\sigma} = \dfrac{20-30}{4} = -2.50$

b. $z = \dfrac{x-\mu}{\sigma} = \dfrac{30-30}{4} = 0$

c. $z = \dfrac{x-\mu}{\sigma} = \dfrac{27.5-30}{4} = -0.625$

d. $z = \dfrac{x-\mu}{\sigma} = \dfrac{15-30}{4} = -3.75$

e. $z = \dfrac{x-\mu}{\sigma} = \dfrac{35-30}{4} = 1.25$

f. $z = \dfrac{x-\mu}{\sigma} = \dfrac{25-30}{4} = -1.25$

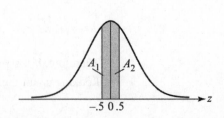

4.93   a.

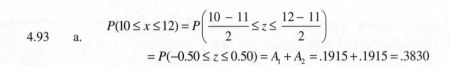

$$P(10 \leq x \leq 12) = P\left(\frac{10-11}{2} \leq z \leq \frac{12-11}{2}\right)$$

$$= P(-0.50 \leq z \leq 0.50) = A_1 + A_2 = .1915 + .1915 = .3830$$

b. $P(6 \le x \le 10) = P\left(\dfrac{6-11}{2} \le z \le \dfrac{10-11}{2}\right) = P(-2.50 \le z \le -0.50)$

$= P(-2.50 \le z \le 0) - P(-0.50 \le z \le 0) = .4938 - .1915 = .3023$

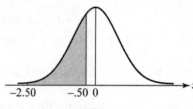

c. $P(13 \le x \le 16) = P\left(\dfrac{13-11}{2} \le z \le \dfrac{16-11}{2}\right) = P(1.00 \le z \le 2.50)$

$= P(0 \le z \le 2.50) - P(0 \le x \le 1.00) = .4938 - .3413 = .1525$

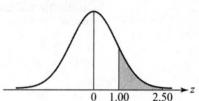

d. $P(7.8 \le x \le 12.6) = P\left(\dfrac{7.8-11}{2} \le z \le \dfrac{12.6-11}{2}\right)$

$= P(-1.60 \le z \le 0.80) = A_1 + A_2 = .4452 + .2881 = .7333$

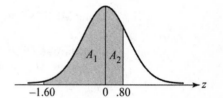

e. $P(x \ge 13.24) = P\left(z \ge \dfrac{13.24-11}{2}\right)$

$= P(z \ge 1.12) = A_2 = .5 - A_1 = .5000 - .3686 = .1314$

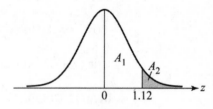

f. $P(x \ge 7.62) = P\left(z \ge \dfrac{7.62-11}{2}\right)$

$= P(z \ge -1.69) = A_1 + A_2 = .4545 + .5000 = .9545$

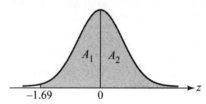

4.95   a.   In order to approximate the binomial distribution with the normal distribution, the interval $\mu \pm 3\sigma \Rightarrow np \pm 3\sqrt{npq}$ should lie in the range 0 to n.

When $n = 25$ and $p = .4$,
$np \pm 3\sqrt{npq} \Rightarrow 25(.4) \pm 3\sqrt{25(.4)(1-.4)} \Rightarrow 10 \pm 3\sqrt{6} \Rightarrow 10 \pm 7.3485 \Rightarrow (2.6515, 17.3485)$

Since the interval calculated does lie in the range 0 to 25, we can use the normal approximation.

b. $\mu = np = 25(.4) = 10$ and $\sigma^2 = npq = 25(.4)(.6) = 6$

c. $P(x \ge 9) = 1 - P(x \le 8) = 1 - .274 = .726$ (Table I, Appendix D)

d.
$$P(x \geq 9) \approx P\left(z \geq \frac{(9-.5)-10}{\sqrt{6}}\right)$$

$$= P(z \geq -.61) = .5000 + .2291 = .7291$$

(using Table II, Appendix D)

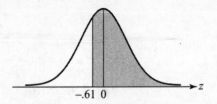

$-.61 \; 0$

4.97   a.   Using MINITAB with $\mu = 105.3$ and $\sigma = 8$, the probability is:

Cumulative Distribution Function
```
Normal with mean = 105.3 and standard deviation = 8

   x  P( X <= x )
120      0.966932
```

$$P(x > 120) = 1 - P(x \leq 120) = 1 - .966932 = .033068$$

b.   Using MINITAB with $\mu = 105.3$ and $\sigma = 8$, the probabilities are:

Cumulative Distribution Function
```
Normal with mean = 105.3 and standard deviation = 8

   x  P( X <= x )
110      0.721566
100      0.253825
```

$$P(100 < x < 110) = P(x < 110) - P(x \leq 100) = .721566 - .253825 = .467741$$

c.   Using MINITAB with $\mu = 105.3$ and $\sigma = 8$, the value of a is found:

Inverse Cumulative Distribution Function
```
Normal with mean = 105.3 and standard deviation = 8

P( X <= x )        x
      0.25   99.9041
```

Thus, $a = 99.9041$.

4.99   a.   Using MINITAB with $\mu = 59$ and $\sigma = 5$, the probability is:

Cumulative Distribution Function
```
Normal with mean = 59 and standard deviation = 5

  x  P( X <= x )
60      0.579260
```

$$P(x > 60) = 1 - P(x \leq 60) = 1 - .57926 = .42074$$

b.   Using MINITAB with $\mu = 43$ and $\sigma = 5$, the probability is:

Cumulative Distribution Function
```
Normal with mean = 43 and standard deviation = 5

  x  P( X <= x )
60      0.999663
```

$$P(x > 60) = 1 - P(x \le 60) = 1 - .999663 = .000337$$

4.101   a.   Let x = buy-side analyst's forecast error. Then x has an approximate normal distribution with $\mu = .85$ and $\sigma = 1.93$. Using Table II, Appendix D,

$$P(x > 2.00) = P\left(z > \frac{2.00 - .85}{1.93} \right) = P(z > .60) = .5 - .2257 = .2743$$

b.   Let y = sell-side analyst's forecast error. Then y has an approximate normal distribution with $\mu = -.05$ and $\sigma = .85$. Using Table II, Appendix D,

$$P(y > 2.00) = P\left(z > \frac{2.00 - (-.05)}{.85} \right) = P(z > 2.41) = .5 - .4920 = .0080$$

4.103   From Exercise 4.49, we determined that x is a binomial random variable with $n = 250$ and $p = .5$

a. $\mu = np = 250(.5) = 125$

b. $\sigma = \sqrt{npq} = \sqrt{250(.5)(.5)} = \sqrt{62.5} = 7.9057$

c. $z = \dfrac{x - \mu}{\sigma} = \dfrac{200 - 125}{7.9057} = 9.49$

d.   In order to approximate the binomial distribution with the normal distribution, the interval $\mu \pm 3\sigma \Rightarrow np \pm 3\sqrt{npq}$ should lie in the range 0 to n.

When $n = 250$ and $p = .5$, $np \pm 3\sqrt{npq} \Rightarrow 125 \pm 3(7.9057) \Rightarrow 125 \pm 23.7171 \Rightarrow (101.2829, 148.7171)$

Since the interval calculated does lie in the range 0 to 250, we can use the normal approximation.

Using MINITAB with $\mu = 125$ and $\sigma = 7.9057$, the approximate probability is:

Cumulative Distribution Function
```
Normal with mean = 125 and standard deviation = 7.9057

   x   P( X <= x )
200            1
```

$$P(x \le 200) = 1$$

4.105   If the goal keeper stands in the middle of the goal and can reach any ball within 9 feet, then the only way a player can score is if he/she shoots the ball within 3 feet of either goal post.

a.   If a player aims at the right goal post, then the player will score if x is between -3 and 0. Using Table II, Appendix D, we get $P(-3 < x < 0) = P\left(\dfrac{-3 - 0}{3} < z < \dfrac{0 - 0}{3} \right) = P(-1 < z < 0) = .3413$.

b.   If a player aims at the center of the goal, then the player will score if x is greater than 9 or less than -9. Using Table II, Appendix D, we get

$$P(x < -9) + P(x > 9) = P\left(z < \frac{-9-0}{3}\right) + P\left(z > \frac{9-0}{3}\right) = P(z < -3) + P(z > 3)$$

$$= (.5 - .4987) + (.5 - .4987) = .0026$$

c.   If a player aims halfway between the right goal post and the outer limit of the goal keeper's reach, then the player will score if x is between -1.5 and 1.5. Using Table II, Appendix D, we get

$$P(-1.5 < x < 1.5) = P\left(\frac{-1.5-0}{3} < z < \frac{1.5-0}{3}\right) = P(-.5 < z < .5) = .1915 + .1915 = .3830.$$

4.107   a.   Let x = rating. Then x has a normal distribution with $\mu = 50$ and $\sigma = 15$. Using Table II, Appendix D,

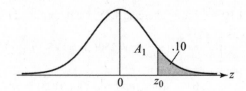

$P(x > x_0) = .10$. Find x_0.

$$P(x > x_o) = P\left(z > \frac{x_o - 50}{15}\right) = P(z > z_o) = .10$$

$A_1 = .5 - .10 = .4000$

Looking up area .4000 in Table II, $z_o = 1.28$

$$z_o = \frac{x_o - 50}{15} \Rightarrow 1.28 = \frac{x_o - 50}{15} \Rightarrow x_o = 50 + 1.28(15) = 69.2$$

b. $P(x > x_0) = .10 + .20 + .40 = .70$. Find x_0.

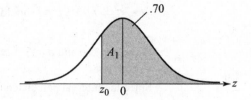

$$P(x > x_o) = P\left(z > \frac{x_o - 50}{15}\right) = P(z > z_o) = .70$$

$A_1 = .70 - .5 = .2000$

Looking up area .2000 in Table II, $z_o = -.52$

$$z_o = \frac{x_o - 50}{15} \Rightarrow -.52 = \frac{x_o - 50}{15} \Rightarrow x_o = 50 - .52(15) = 42.2$$

4.109   a.   Using Table II, Appendix D, and $\mu = 75$ and $\sigma = 7.5$,

$$P(x > 80) = P\left(z > \frac{80 - 75}{7.5}\right) = P(z > .67) = .5 - .2486 = .2514$$

Thus, 25.14% of the scores exceeded 80.

b. $P(x \le x_0) = .98$. Find x_0.

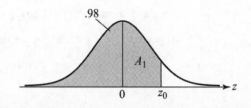

$$P(x \le x_0) = P\left(z \le \frac{x_0 - 75}{7.5}\right) = P(z \le z_0) = .98$$

$A_1 = .98 - .5 = .4800$

Looking up area .4800 in Table II, $z_o = 2.05$.

$$z_0 = \frac{x_0 - 75}{7.5} \Rightarrow 2.05 = \frac{x_0 - 75}{7.5} \Rightarrow x_0 = 90.375$$

4.111 Let x = number of additional Electoral College votes a candidate will win if he/she wins California's 55 votes. Then x has a normal distribution with $\mu = 241.5$ and $\sigma = 49.8$. In order to be elected, the candidate will have to win an additional $270 - 55 = 215$ votes or x has to be greater than or equal to 215. Using MINITAB with $\mu = 241.5$ and $\sigma = 49.8$, the probability is:

Cumulative Distribution Function
```
Normal with mean = 241.5 and standard deviation = 49.8

  x   P( X <= x )
215     0.297318
```

$$P(x \geq 215) = 1 - P(x < 215) = 1 - .297318 = .702682$$

The probability the candidate becomes the next president if he/she wins California is about .70.

4.113 b. Let v = number of credit card users out of 100 who carry Visa. Then v is a binomial random variable with $n = 100$ and $p_v = .50$.

$$E(v) = np_v = 100(.50) = 50.$$

Let d = number of credit card users out of 100 who carry Discover. Then d is a binomial random variable with $n = 100$ and $p_d = .09$.

$$E(d) = np_d = 100(.09) = 9.$$

c. To see if the normal approximation is valid, we use:

$$\mu \pm 3\sigma \Rightarrow np_v \pm 3\sqrt{np_v q_v} \Rightarrow 100(.5) \pm 3\sqrt{100(.5)(.5)} \Rightarrow 50 \pm 3(5)$$
$$\Rightarrow 50 \pm 15 \Rightarrow (35, \ 65)$$

Since the interval lies in the range 0 to 100, we can use the normal approximation to approximate the probability.

$$P(v \geq 50) \approx P\left(z \geq \frac{(50 - .5) - 50}{5}\right) = P(z \geq -.1) = .5 + .0398 = .5398$$

Let a = number of credit card users out of 100 who carry American Express. Then a is a binomial random variable with $n = 100$ and $p_a = .08$. To see if the normal approximation is valid, we use:

$$\mu \pm 3\sigma \Rightarrow np_a \pm 3\sqrt{np_a q_a} \Rightarrow 100(.08) \pm 3\sqrt{100(.08)(.92)} \Rightarrow 8 \pm 3(2.713)$$
$$\Rightarrow 8 \pm 8.139 \Rightarrow (-.139, \ 16.139)$$

Since the interval does not lie in the range 0 to 100, using the normal approximation to approximate the probability is risky.

$$P(a \geq 50) \approx P\left(z \geq \frac{(50 - .5) - 8}{2.713}\right) = P(z \geq 15.30) \approx .5 - .5 = 0$$

d.   In order for the normal approximation to be valid, $\mu \pm 3\sigma$ must lie in the interval $(0, n)$. This check was done in part **c** for both portions of the question. The normal approximation was justified for the first part but not the second.

4.115   We have to find the probability of observing $x = .7$ or anything more unusual given the two different values of μ.

Without receiving executive coaching: Using Table II, Appendix D with $\mu = .75$ and $\sigma = .085$,

$$P(x \le .7) = P\left(z \le \frac{.7 - .75}{.085} \right) = P(z \le -.59) = .5 - .2224 = .2776 .$$

After receiving executive coaching: Using Table II, Appendix D with $\mu = .52$ and $\sigma = .075$,

$$P(x \ge .7) = P\left(z \ge \frac{.7 - .52}{.075} \right) = P(z \ge 2.40) = .5 - .4918 = .0082 .$$

Since the probability of observing $x \le .7$ for those not receiving executive coaching is much larger than the probability of $x \ge .7$ for those receiving executive coaching, it is more likely that the leader did not receive executive coaching.

4.117   a.   The proportion of measurements that one would expect to fall in the interval $\mu \pm \sigma$ is about .68.

b.   The proportion of measurements that one would expect to fall in the interval $\mu \pm 2\sigma$ is about .95.

c.   The proportion of measurements that one would expect to fall in the interval $\mu \pm 3\sigma$ is about 1.00.

4.119   If the data are normally distributed, then the normal probability plot should be an approximate straight line. Of the three plots, only plot **c** implies that the data are normally distributed. The data points in plot **c** form an approximately straight line. In both plots **a** and **b**, the plots of the data points do not form a straight line.

4.121   a.   Using MINITAB, a histogram of the data is:

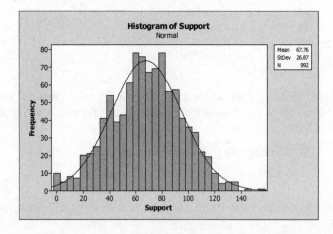

The data are fairly mound-shaped. This indicates that the data are probably from a normal distribution.

b.   Using MINITAB, the descriptive statistics are:

Descriptive Statistics: Support

Variable	N	Mean	StDev	Minimum	Q1	Median	Q3	Maximum
Support	992	67.755	26.871	0.000000000	49.000	68.000	86.000	155.000

If the data are normal, then approximately 68% of the observations should fall within 1 standard deviation of the mean. For this data, the interval is $\bar{x} \pm s \Rightarrow 67.755 \pm 26.871 \Rightarrow (40.884, 94.626)$.

There are 665 out of the 992 observations in this interval which is $665/992 = .670$ or 67%. This is very close to the 68%.

If the data are normal, then approximately 95% of the observations should fall within 2 standard deviations of the mean. For this data, the interval is
$\bar{x} \pm 2s \Rightarrow 67.755 \pm 2(26.871) \Rightarrow 67.755 \pm 53.742 \Rightarrow (14.013, 121.497)$. There are 946 out of the 992 observations in this interval which is $946/992 = .954$ or 95.4%. This is very close to the 95%.

If the data are normal, then approximately 100% of the observations should fall within 3 standard deviations of the mean. For this data, the interval is
$\bar{x} \pm 3s \Rightarrow 67.755 \pm 3(26.871) \Rightarrow 67.755 \pm 80.613 \Rightarrow (-12.858, 148.368)$. There are 991 out of the 992 observations in this interval which is $991/992 = .999$ or 99.9%. This is very close to the 100%.

Since these percents are very close to percentages for the normal distribution, this indicates that the data are probably from a normal distribution.

c.   The $IQR = Q_U - Q_L = 86 - 49 = 37$ and the standard deviation is $s = 26.871$. If the data are normal, then $\dfrac{IQR}{s} \approx 1.3$. For this data, $\dfrac{IQR}{s} = \dfrac{37}{26.871} = 1.377$. This is very close to 1.3. This indicates that the data probably come from a normal distribution.

d.   Using MINITAB, the normal probability plot is:

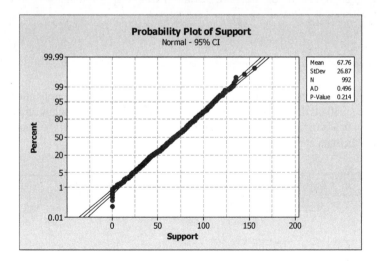

Except for the several 0's on the left of the plot, the data are very close to a straight line. This again indicates that the data probably come from a normal distribution.

4.123   a.   If the data are normal, then approximately 68% of the observations should fall within 1 standard deviation of the mean. For this data, the interval is $\bar{x} \pm s \Rightarrow 89.2906 \pm 3.1834 \Rightarrow (86.1072, 92.4740)$.

There are 34 out of the 50 observations in this interval which is $34/50 = .68$ or 68%. This is exactly the 68%.

If the data are normal, then approximately 95% of the observations should fall within 2 standard deviations of the mean. For this data, the interval is
$\bar{x} \pm 2s \Rightarrow 89.2906 \pm 2(3.1834) \Rightarrow 89.2906 \pm 6.3668 \Rightarrow (82.9238, 95.6574)$. There are 48 out of the 50 observations in this interval which is $48/50 = .96$ or 96%. This is very close to the 95%.

If the data are normal, then approximately 100% of the observations should fall within 3 standard deviations of the mean. For this data, the interval is
$\bar{x} \pm 3s \Rightarrow 89.2906 \pm 3(3.1934) \Rightarrow 89.2906 \pm 9.5502 \Rightarrow (79.7404, 98.8408)$. There are 50 out of the 50 observations in this interval which is $50/50 = 1.00$ or 100%. This is exactly the 100%.

Since these percents are very close to percentages for the normal distribution, this indicates that the data are approximately normal.

The $IQR = Q_U - Q_L = 91.88 - 87.2725 = 4.6075$ and the standard deviation is $s = 3.1834$. If the data are normal, then $\dfrac{IQR}{s} \approx 1.3$. For this data, $\dfrac{IQR}{s} = \dfrac{4.6075}{3.1834} = 1.447$. This is fairly close to 1.3. This indicates that the data are approximately normal.

   b.   The data on the plot are fairly close to a straight line. This indicates that the data are approximately normal.

4.125   The information given in the problem states that $\bar{x} = 4.71$, $s = 6.09$, $Q_L = 1$, and $Q_U = 6$. To be normal, the data have to be symmetric. If the data are symmetric, then the mean would equal the median and would be half way between the lower and upper quartile. Half way between the upper and lower quartiles is 3.5. The sample mean is 4.71, which is much larger than 3.5. This implies that the data may not be normal. In addition, the interquartile range divided by the standard deviation will be approximately 1.3 if the data are normal. For this data,

$$\frac{IQR}{s} = \frac{Q_U - Q_L}{s} = \frac{6-1}{6.09} = .82$$

The value of .82 is much smaller than the necessary 1.3 to be normal. Again, this is an indication that the data are not normal. Finally, the standard deviation is larger than the mean. Since one cannot have values of the variable in this case less than 0, a standard deviation larger than the mean indicates that the data are skewed to the right. This implies that the data are not normal.

4.127   We will look at the 4 methods for determining if the data are normal. First, we will look at a histogram of the data. Using MINITAB, the histogram of the driver's head injury rating is:

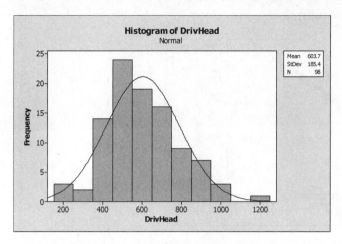

From the histogram, the data appear to be somewhat skewed to the right, but is fairly mound-shaped. This indicates that the data are approximately normal.

Next, we look at the intervals $\bar{x} \pm s$, $\bar{x} \pm 2s$, $\bar{x} \pm 3s$. If the proportions of observations falling in each interval are approximately .68, .95, and 1.00, then the data are approximately normal. Using MINITAB, the summary statistics are:

Descriptive Statistics: DrivHead

```
Variable    N    Mean   StDev   Minimum     Q1   Median     Q3   Maximum
DrivHead    98   603.7  185.4     216.0   475.0   605.0   724.3   1240.0
```

$\bar{x} \pm s \Rightarrow 603.7 \pm 185.4 \Rightarrow (418.3,\ 789.1)$ 68 of the 98 values fall in this interval. The proportion is .69. This is very close to the .68 we would expect if the data were normal.

$\bar{x} \pm 2s \Rightarrow 603.7 \pm 2(185.4) \Rightarrow 603.7 \pm 370.8 \Rightarrow (232.9,\ 974.5)$ 96 of the 98 values fall in this interval. The proportion is .98. This is a fair amount larger than the .95 we would expect if the data were normal.

$\bar{x} \pm 3s \Rightarrow 603.7 \pm 3(185.4) \Rightarrow 603.7 \pm 556.2 \Rightarrow (47.5,\ 1,159.9)$ 97 of the 98 values fall in this interval. The proportion is .99. This is fairly close to the 1.00 we would expect if the data were normal.

From this method, it appears that the data may be normal.

Next, we look at the ratio of the *IQR* to *s*. $IQR = Q_U - Q_L = 724.3 - 475.0 = 249.3$.

$\dfrac{IQR}{s} = \dfrac{249.3}{185.4} = 1.3$ This is equal to the 1.3 we would expect if the data were normal. This method indicates the data are approximately normal.

Finally, using MINITAB, the normal probability plot is:

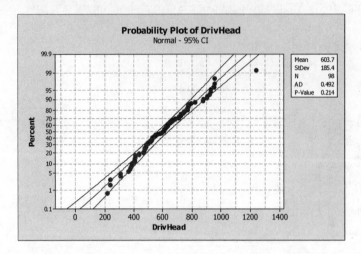

Since the data form a fairly straight line, the data are approximately normal.

From the 4 different methods, all indications are that the driver's head injury rating data are normal.

4.129   We will look at the 4 methods or determining if the 3 variables are normal.

Distance:
First, we will look at A histogram of the data. Using MINITAB, the histogram of the distance data is:

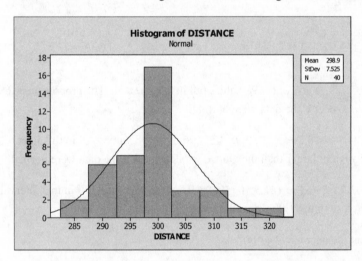

From the histogram, the distance data do not appear to have a normal distribution.

Next, we look at the intervals $\bar{x} \pm s$, $\bar{x} \pm 2s$, $\bar{x} \pm 3s$. If the proportions of observations falling in each interval are approximately .68, .95, and 1.00, then the data are approximately normal. Using MINITAB, the summary statistics are:

Descriptive Statistics: DISTANCE, ACCURACY, INDEX

Variable	N	Mean	StDev	Minimum	Q1	Median	Q3	Maximum
DISTANCE	40	298.95	7.53	283.20	294.60	299.05	302.00	318.90

$\bar{x} \pm s \Rightarrow 298.95 \pm 7.53 \Rightarrow (291.42, \ 306.48)$ 28 of the 40 values fall in this interval. The proportion is $28/40 = .70$. This is fairly close to the .68 we would expect if the data were normal.

$\bar{x} \pm 2s \Rightarrow 298.95 \pm 2(7.53) \Rightarrow 298.95 \pm 15.06 \Rightarrow (283.89, \ 314.01)$ 37 of the 40 values fall in this interval. The proportion is $37/40 = .925$. This is a fair amount below the .95 we would expect if the data were normal.

$\bar{x} \pm 3s \Rightarrow 298.95 \pm 3(7.53) \Rightarrow 298.95 \pm 22.59 \Rightarrow (276.36, \ 321.54)$ 40 of the 40 values fall in this interval. The proportion is $40/40 = 1.00$. This is equal to the 1.00 we would expect if the data were normal.

From this method, it appears that the distance data may not be normal.

Next, we look at the ratio of the *IQR* to *s*.

$IQR = Q_U - Q_L = 302 - 294.6 = 7.4$

$\dfrac{IQR}{s} = \dfrac{7.4}{7.53} = .983$. This is much smaller than the 1.3 we would expect if the data were normal. This method indicates the distance data may not be normal.

Finally, using MINITAB, the normal probability plot is:

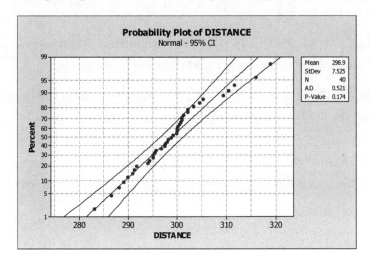

Since the data do not form a fairly straight line, the distance data may not be normal.

From the 4 different methods, all indications are that the distance data are not normal.

Accuracy:

First, we will look at a histogram of the data. Using MINITAB, the histogram of the accuracy data is:

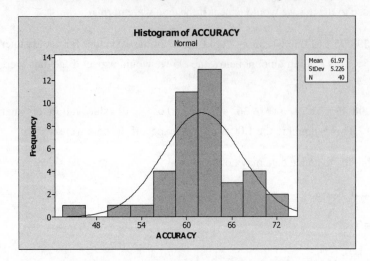

From the histogram, the accuracy data do not appear to have a normal distribution.

Descriptive Statistics: DISTANCE, ACCURACY, INDEX

```
Variable    N    Mean   StDev  Minimum      Q1  Median      Q3  Maximum
ACCURACY   40  61.970   5.226   45.400  59.400  61.950  64.075   73.000
```

$\bar{x} \pm s \Rightarrow 61.97 \pm 5.226 \Rightarrow (56.744, \ 67.196)$ 30 of the 40 values fall in this interval. The proportion is $30 / 40 = .75$. This is much greater than the .68 we would expect if the data were normal.

$\bar{x} \pm 2s \Rightarrow 61.97 \pm 2(5.226) \Rightarrow 61.97 \pm 10.452 \Rightarrow (51.518, \ 72.422)$ 37 of the 40 values fall in this interval. The proportion is $37 / 40 = .925$. This is a fair amount below the .95 we would expect if the data were normal.

$\bar{x} \pm 3s \Rightarrow 61.97 \pm 3(5.226) \Rightarrow 61.97 \pm 15.678 \Rightarrow (46.292, \ 77.648)$ 39 of the 40 values fall in this interval. The proportion is $39 / 40 = .975$. This is a fair amount lower than the 1.00 we would expect if the data were normal.

From this method, it appears that the accuracy data may not be normal.

Next, we look at the ratio of the IQR to s.

$IQR = Q_U - Q_L = 64.075 - 59.4 = 4.675$.

$\dfrac{IQR}{s} = \dfrac{4.675}{5.226} = .895$. This is much smaller than the 1.3 we would expect if the data were normal. This method indicates the accuracy data may not be normal.

Finally, using MINITAB, the normal probability plot is:

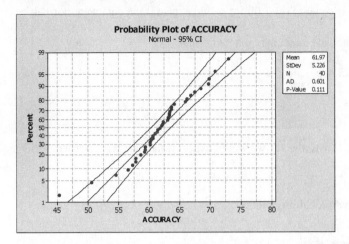

Since the data do not form a fairly straight line, the accuracy data may not be normal.

From the 4 different methods, all indications are that the accuracy data are not normal.

Index:
First, we will look at a histogram of the data. Using MINITAB, the histogram of the index data is:

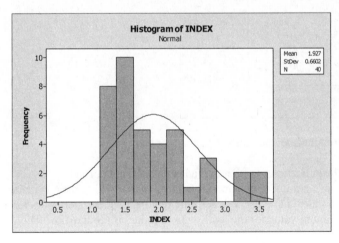

From the histogram, the index data do not appear to have a normal distribution.
Next, we look at the intervals $\bar{x} \pm s$, $\bar{x} \pm 2s$, $\bar{x} \pm 3s$. If the proportions of observations falling in each interval are approximately .68, .95, and 1.00, then the data are approximately normal. Using MINITAB, the summary statistics are:

Descriptive Statistics: DISTANCE, ACCURACY, INDEX

Variable	N	Mean	StDev	Minimum	Q1	Median	Q3	Maximum
INDEX	40	1.927	0.660	1.170	1.400	1.755	2.218	3.580

$\bar{x} \pm s \Rightarrow 1.927 \pm .660 \Rightarrow (1.267, \ 2.587)$ 30 of the 40 values fall in this interval. The proportion is
$30/40 = .75$. This is much greater than the .68 we would expect if the data were normal.
$\bar{x} \pm 2s \Rightarrow 1.927 \pm 2(.660) \Rightarrow 1.927 \pm 1.320 \Rightarrow (.607, \ 3.247)$ 37 of the 40 values fall in this interval. The
proportion is $37/40 = .925$. This is a fair amount below the .95 we would expect if the data were normal.

$\bar{x} \pm 3s \Rightarrow 1.927 \pm 3(.660) \Rightarrow 1.927 \pm 1.980 \Rightarrow (-.053, 3.907)$ 40 of the 40 values fall in this interval. The proportion is $40/40 = 1.000$. This is equal to the 1.00 we would expect if the data were normal.

From this method, it appears that the index data may not be normal.

Next, we look at the ratio of the *IQR* to *s*.

$IQR = Q_U - Q_L = 2.218 - 1.4 = .818$.

$\dfrac{IQR}{s} = \dfrac{.818}{.66} = 1.23$. This is fairly close to the 1.3 we would expect if the data were normal. This method indicates the index data may normal.

Finally, using MINITAB, the normal probability plot is:

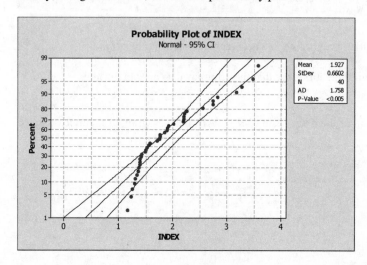

Since the data do not form a fairly straight line, the index data may not be normal.

From 3 of the 4 different methods, the indications are that the index data are not normal.

4.131   From Exercise 2.51, it states that the mean number of semester hours for those taking the CPA exam is 141.31 and the median is 140. It also states that most colleges only require 128 semester hours for an undergraduate degree. Thus, the minimum value for the total semester hours is around 128. The *z*-score associated with 128 is:

$$z = \frac{x - \mu}{\sigma} = \frac{128 - 141.31}{17.77} = -.75$$

If the data are normal, we know that about .34 of the observations are between the mean and 1 standard deviation below the mean. Thus, .16 of the observations are more than 1 standard deviation below the mean. With this distribution, that is impossible. Thus, the data are not normal. The mean is greater than the median, so we know that the data are skewed to the right.

4.133   a. $f(x) = \dfrac{1}{d - c}$ $(c \le x \le d)$

$$\frac{1}{d - c} = \frac{1}{45 - 20} = \frac{1}{25} = .04$$

So, $f(x) = \begin{cases} .04 & (20 \leq x \leq 45) \\ 0 & \text{otherwise} \end{cases}$

b. $\mu = \dfrac{c+d}{2} = \dfrac{20+45}{2} = \dfrac{65}{2} = 32.5$ $\qquad$ $\sigma = \dfrac{d-c}{\sqrt{12}} = \dfrac{45-20}{\sqrt{12}} = 7.22$

c. Using MINITAB, the graph is:

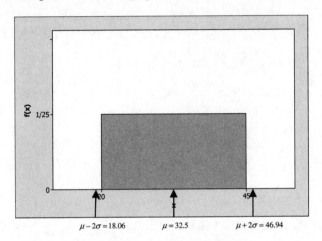

$\mu \pm 2\sigma \Rightarrow 32.5 \pm 2(7.22) \Rightarrow (18.06,\ 46.94)$

$P(18.06 < x < 46.94) = P(20 < x < 45) = (45-20).04 = 1$

4.135 $\quad P(x \geq a) = e^{-a/\theta} = e^{-a/1}$. Using a calculator:

a. $P(x>1) = e^{-1/1} = e^{-1} = .367879$

b. $P(x \leq 3) = 1 - P(x>3) = 1 - e^{-3/1} = 1 - e^{-3} = 1 - .049787 = .950213$

c. $P(x>1.5) = e^{-1.5/1} = e^{-1.5} = .223130$

d. $P(x \leq 5) = 1 - P(x>5) = 1 - e^{-5/1} = 1 - e^{-5} = 1 - .006738 = .993262$

4.137 $\quad f(x) = \dfrac{1}{d-c} = \dfrac{1}{200-100} = \dfrac{1}{100} = .01$

$f(x) = \begin{cases} .01 & (100 \leq x \leq 200) \\ 0 & \textit{otherwise} \end{cases}$

$\mu = \dfrac{c+d}{2} = \dfrac{100+200}{2} = \dfrac{300}{2} = 150$ $\qquad$ $\sigma = \dfrac{d-c}{\sqrt{12}} = \dfrac{200-100}{\sqrt{12}} = \dfrac{100}{\sqrt{12}} = 28.8675$

a. $\mu \pm 2\sigma \Rightarrow 150 \pm 2(28.8675) \Rightarrow 150 \pm 57.735 \Rightarrow (92.265,\ 207.735)$

$P(x < 92.265) + P(x > 207.735) = P(x < 100) + P(x > 200) = 0 + 0 = 0$

b. $\mu \pm 3\sigma \Rightarrow 150 \pm 3(28.8675) \Rightarrow 150 \pm 86.6025 \Rightarrow (63.3975,\ 236.6025)$

$P(63.3975 < x < 236.6025) = P(100 < x < 200) = (200 - 100)(.01) = 1$

c.   From **a**, $\mu \pm 2\sigma \Rightarrow (92.265,\ 207.735)$.

$P(92.265 < x < 207.735) = P(100 < x < 200) = (200 - 100)(.01) = 1$

4.139   For this problem, $f(x) = \dfrac{1}{3600 - 0} = \dfrac{1}{3600}$. Thus,

$$f(x) = \begin{cases} \dfrac{1}{3600} & 0 \le x \le 3600 \\[2mm] 0 & \text{otherwise} \end{cases}$$

The last 15 minutes would represent the last 15(60) = 900 seconds.

$$P(2700 < x < 3600) = (3600 - 2700)\dfrac{1}{3600} = \dfrac{900}{3600} = .25$$

4.141   a.   Let x = temperature with no bolt-on trace elements. Then x has a uniform distribution.

$$f(x) = \dfrac{1}{d - c} \quad (c \le x \le d)$$

$$\dfrac{1}{d - c} = \dfrac{1}{290 - 260} = \dfrac{1}{30}$$

Therefore, $f(x) = \begin{cases} \dfrac{1}{30} & (260 \le x \le 290) \\[2mm] 0 & \textit{otherwise} \end{cases}$

$$P(280 < x < 284) = (284 - 280)\dfrac{1}{30} = 4\left(\dfrac{1}{30}\right) = .133$$

Let y = temperature with bolt-on trace elements. Then y has a uniform distribution.

$$f(y) = \dfrac{1}{d - c} \quad (c \le y \le d)$$

$$\dfrac{1}{d - c} = \dfrac{1}{285 - 278} = \dfrac{1}{7}$$

Therefore, $f(y) = \begin{cases} \dfrac{1}{7} & (278 \le y \le 285) \\ 0 & otherwise \end{cases}$

$$P(280 < y < 284) = (284 - 280)\frac{1}{7} = 4\left(\frac{1}{7}\right) = .571$$

b. $P(x \le 268) = (268 - 260)\dfrac{1}{30} = 8\left(\dfrac{1}{30}\right) = .267$

$P(y \le 268) = (268 - 260)(0) = 0$

4.143   a. $P(x > 2) = e^{-2/2.5} = e^{-.8} = .449329$ (using a calculator)

b. $P(x < 5) = 1 - P(x \ge 5) = 1 - e^{-5/2.5} = 1 - e^{-2} = 1 - .135335 = .864665$ (using a calculator)

4.145   a.   For this problem, x has a uniform distribution on the interval from 0 to 1. Thus, $\mu = \dfrac{c+d}{2} = \dfrac{0+1}{2} = .5$.

b.   For this problem, $f(x) = \begin{cases} 1 & 0 \le x \le 1 \\ 0 & otherwise \end{cases}$ $P(x > .7) = (1 - .7)(1) = .3$

c.   With $n = 2$, the total possible connections is $\begin{pmatrix} 2 \\ 2 \end{pmatrix} = \dfrac{2!}{2!(2-2)!} = 1$. Thus, the density can be either 0 or 1.

Therefore, the uniform model would not be a good approximation for the distribution of network density.

4.147   a.   The amount dispensed by the beverage machine is a continuous random variable since it can take on any value between 6.5 and 7.5 ounces.

b.   Since the amount dispensed is random between 6.5 and 7.5 ounces, x is a uniform random variable.

$$f(x) = \frac{1}{d-c} \quad (c \le x \le d)$$

$$\frac{1}{d-c} = \frac{1}{7.5 - 6.5} = \frac{1}{1} = 1$$

Therefore, $f(x) = \begin{cases} 1 & (6.5 \le x \le 7.5) \\ 0 & otherwise \end{cases}$

The graph is as follows:

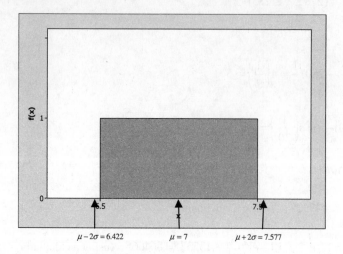

c.　$\mu = \dfrac{c+d}{2} = \dfrac{6.5+7.5}{2} = \dfrac{14}{2} = 7$

$\sigma = \dfrac{d-c}{\sqrt{12}} = \dfrac{7.5-6.5}{\sqrt{12}} = .2887$

$\mu \pm 2\sigma \Rightarrow 7 \pm 2(.2887) \Rightarrow 7 \pm .5774 \Rightarrow (6.422,\ 7.577)$

d.　$P(x \ge 7) = (7.5-7)(1) = .5$

e.　$P(x < 6) = 0$

f.　$P(6.5 \le x \le 7.25) = (7.25-6.5)(1) = .75$

g.　The probability that the next bottle filled will contain more than 7.25 ounces is:

$P(x > 7.25) = (7.5-7.25)(1) = .25$

The probability that the next 6 bottles filled will contain more than 7.25 ounces is:

$P[(x > 7.25) \cap (x > 7.25) \cap (x > 7.25) \cap (x > 7.25) \cap (x > 7.25) \cap (x > 7.25)]$
$= \left[P(x > 7.25)\right]^6 = .25^6 = .0002$

4.149　a.　Let x = product's lifetime at the end of its lifetime. Then x has an exponential distribution with $\mu = 500,000$.

$P(x < 700,000) = 1 - P(x \ge 700,000) = 1\ -e^{-700000/5000000} = 1 - e^{-1.4} = 1 - .246597 = .753403$

b.　Let y = product's lifetime during its normal life. Then y has a uniform distribution.

$f(y) = \dfrac{1}{d-c} \quad (c \le y \le d)$

$$\frac{1}{d-c} = \frac{1}{1,000,000-100,000} = \frac{1}{900,000}$$

Therefore, $f(y) = \begin{cases} \dfrac{1}{900,000} & (100,000 \le y \le 1,000,000) \\ 0 & \textit{otherwise} \end{cases}$

$$P(y < 700,000) = (700,000-100,000)\left(\frac{1}{900,000}\right) = .667$$

c. $P(x<830,000)=1-P(x\ge830,000)=1-e^{-830000/5000000}=1-e^{-1.66}=1-.190139=.809861$

(Using a calculator)

$$P(y < 830,000) = (830,000-100,000)\left(\frac{1}{900,000}\right) = .811$$

4.151 Let x = number of inches a gouge is from one end of the spindle. Then x has a uniform distribution with $f(x)$ as follows:

$$f(x) = \begin{cases} \dfrac{1}{d-c} = \dfrac{1}{18-0} = \dfrac{1}{18} & 0 \le x \le 18 \\ 0 & \textit{otherwise} \end{cases}$$

In order to get at least 14 consecutive inches without a gouge, the gouge must be within 4 inches of either end. Thus, we must find:

$$P(x<4)+P(x>14)=(4-0)(1/18)+(18-14)(1/18)=4/18+4/18=8/18=.4444$$

4.153 Let x be a random variable with an exponential distribution with mean θ. Let k = median of the distribution. Then $P(x > k) = .5$. We now need to find k.

$$P(x>k) = .5 \Rightarrow e^{-k/\theta} = .5 \Rightarrow -k/\theta = \ln(.5)$$
$$\Rightarrow k = -\theta\ln(.5) = .693147\theta$$

4.155 a. For $\theta = 250$, $P(x>a) = e^{-a/250}$

For $a = 300$ and $b = 200$, show $P(x>a+b) \ge P(x>a)P(x>b)$

$$P(x>300+200) = P(x>500) = e^{-500/250} = e^{-2} = .1353$$

$$P(x>300)P(x>200) = e^{-300/250}e^{-200/250} = e^{-1.2}e^{-.8} = .3012(.4493) = .1353$$

Since $P(x>300+200) = P(x>300)P(x>200)$, then $P(x>300+200) \ge P(x>300)P(x>200)$

Also, show $P(x>300+200) \le P(x>300)P(x>200)$. Since we already showed that $P(x>300+200) = P(x>300)P(x>200)$, then $P(x>300+200) \le P(x>300)P(x>200)$.

b. Let $a = 50$ and $b = 100$. Show $P(x > a+b) \leq P(x > a)P(x > b)$

$$P(x > 50+100) = P(x > 150) = e^{-150/250} = e^{-.6} = .5488$$

$$P(x > 50)P(x > 100) = e^{-50/250}e^{-100/250} = e^{-.2}e^{-.4} = .8187(.6703) = .5488$$

Since $P(x > 50+100) = P(x > 50)P(x > 100)$, then $P(x > 50+100) \geq P(x > 50)P(x > 100)$

Also, show $P(x > 50+100) \leq P(x > 50)P(x > 100)$. Since we already showed that $P(x > 50+100) = P(x > 50)P(x > 100)$, then $P(x > 50+100) \leq P(x > 50)P(x > 100)$.

c. Show $P(x > a+b) \geq P(x > a)P(x > b)$

$$P(x > a+b) = e^{-(a+b)/250} = e^{-a/250}e^{-b/250} = P(x > a)P(x > b)$$

4.157 $p(x) = \binom{n}{x} p^x q^{n-x} \quad x = 0, 1, 2, \dots, n$

a. $P(x=3) = p(3) = \binom{7}{3}.5^3.5^{7-3} = \frac{7!}{3!4!}.5^3.5^4 = 35(.125)(.0625) = .2734$

b. $P(x=3) = p(3) = \binom{4}{3}.8^3.2^{4-3} = \frac{4!}{3!1!}.8^3.2^1 = 4(.512)(.2) = .4096$

c. $P(x=1) = p(1) = \binom{15}{1}.1^1.9^{15-1} = \frac{15!}{1!14!}.1^1.9^{14} = 15(.1)(.228768) = .3432$

4.159 From Table I, Appendix D:

a. $P(x=14) = P(x \leq 14) - P(x \leq 13) = .584 - .392 = .192$

b. $P(x \leq 12) = .228$

c. $P(x > 12) = 1 - P(x \leq 12) = 1 - .228 = .772$

d. $P(9 \leq x \leq 18) = P(x \leq 18) - P(x \leq 8) = .992 - .005 = .987$

e. $P(8 < x < 18) = P(x \leq 17) - P(x \leq 8) = .965 - .005 = .960$

f. $\mu = np = 20(.7) = 14$, $\sigma^2 = npq = 20(.7)(.3) = 4.2$, $\sigma = \sqrt{4.2} = 2.049$

g. $\mu \pm 2\sigma \Rightarrow 14 \pm 2(2.049) \Rightarrow 14 \pm 4.098 \Rightarrow (9.902, 18.098)$

$P(9.902 < x < 18.098) = P(10 \leq x \leq 18) = P(x \leq 18) - P(x \leq 9) = .992 - .017 = .975$

4.161   a.   Poisson

      b.   Binomial

      c.   Binomial

4.163   a.   Discrete - The number of damaged inventory items is countable.

      b.   Continuous - The average monthly sales can take on any value within an acceptable limit.

      c.   Continuous - The number of square feet can take on any positive value.

      d.   Continuous - The length of time we must wait can take on any positive value.

4.165   a. $P(z \le 2.1) = A_1 + A_2 = .5 + .4821 = .9821$

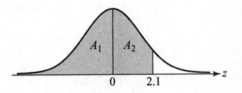

      b. $P(z \ge 2.1) = A_2 = .5 - A_1 = .5 - .4821 = .0179$

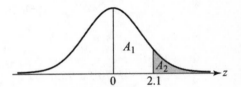

      c. $P(z \ge -1.65) = A_1 + A_2 = .4505 + .5000 = .9505$

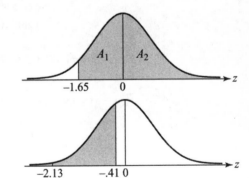

      d. $P(-2.13 \le z \le -.41) = P(-2.13 \le z \le 0) - P(-.41 \le z \le 0)$
$$= .4834 - .1591 = .3243$$

      e. $P(-1.45 \le z \le 2.15) = A_1 + A_2 = .4265 + .4842 = .9107$

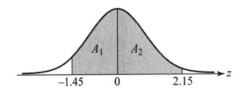

      f. $P(z \le -1.43) = A_1 = .5 - A_2 = .5000 - .4236 = .0764$

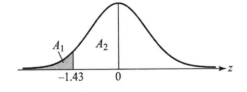

4.167   a.   For the probability density function, $f(x) = \dfrac{e^{-x/7}}{7}$, $x > 0$, x is an exponential random variable.

   b.   For the probability density function, $f(x) = \dfrac{1}{20}$, $5 < x < 25$, x is a uniform random variable.

   c.   For the probability function, $f(x) = \dfrac{e^{-.5[(x-10)/5]^2}}{5\sqrt{2\pi}}$, x is a normal random variable.

4.169   a. $P(x \le 80) = P\left(z \le \dfrac{80-75}{10}\right) = P(z \le .5) = .5 + .1915 = .6915$
         (Table II, Appendix D)

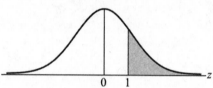

   b. $P(x \ge 85) = P\left(z \ge \dfrac{85-75}{10}\right) = P(z \ge 1) = .5 - .3413 = .1587$
         (Table II, Appendix D)

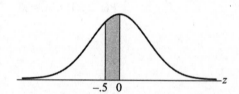

   c. $P(70 \le x \le 75) = P\left(\dfrac{70-75}{10} \le z \le \dfrac{75-75}{10}\right)$
         $= P(-.5 \le z \le 0) = P(0 \le z \le .5) = .1915$
         (Table II, Appendix D)

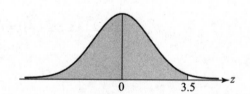

   d. $P(x > 80) = 1 - P(x \le 80) = 1 - .6915 = .3085$ (Refer to part **a**.)

   e. $P(x = 78) = 0$, since a single point does not have an area.

   f. $P(x \le 110) = P\left(z \le \dfrac{110-75}{10}\right) = P(z \le 3.5)$
         $= .5 + .49977 = .99977$
         (Table II, Appendix D)

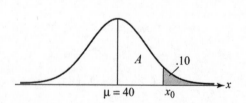

4.171 x is normal random variable with $\mu = 40$, $\sigma^2 = 36$, and $\sigma = 6$.

   a. $P(x \ge x_0) = .10$

        So, $A = .5 - .10 = .4000$. Looking up the area .4000
        In the body of Table II, Appendix D gives $z_0 = 1.28$.

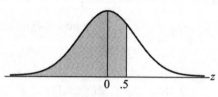

        To find x_0, substitute the values into the z-score formula:
        $$z_0 = \frac{x_0 - \mu}{\sigma} \Rightarrow 1.28 = \frac{x_0 - 40}{6} \Rightarrow x_0 = 1.28(6) + 40 = 47.68$$

b. $P(\mu \le x \le x_0) = .40$

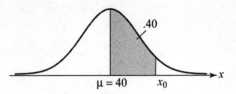

Looking up the area .4000 in the body of Table II, Appendix D gives $z_0 = 1.28$.

To find x_0, substitute the values into the z-score formula:

$$z_0 = \frac{x_0 - \mu}{\sigma} \Rightarrow 1.28 = \frac{x_0 - 40}{6} \Rightarrow x_0 = 1.28(6) + 40 = 47.68$$

c. $P(x < x_0) = .05$

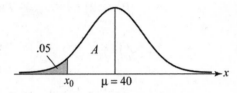

So, $A = .5000 - .0500 = .4500$.

Looking up the area .4500 in the body of Table II, Appendix D gives $z_0 = -1.645$. (.45 is halfway between .4495 and .4505; therefore, we average the z-scores)

$$\frac{1.64 + 1.65}{2} = 1.645$$

z_0 is negative since the graph shows z_0 is on the left side of 0.

To find x_0, substitute the values into the z-score formula:

$$z_0 = \frac{x_0 - \mu}{\sigma} \Rightarrow -1.645 = \frac{x_0 - 40}{6} \Rightarrow x_0 = -1.645(6) + 40 = 30.13$$

d. $P(x > x_0) = .40$

So, $A = .5000 - .4000 = .1000$.

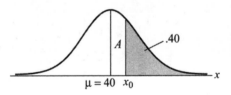

Looking up the area .1000 in the body of Table II, Appendix D gives $z_0 = .25$.

To find x_0, substitute the values into the z-score formula:

$$z_0 = \frac{x_0 - \mu}{\sigma} \Rightarrow .25 = \frac{x_0 - 40}{6} \Rightarrow x_0 = .25(6) + 40 = 41.5$$

e. $P(x_0 \le x < \mu) = .45$

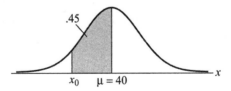

Looking up the area .4500 in the body of Table II, Appendix D gives $z_0 = -1.645$. (.45 is halfway between .4495 and .4505; therefore, we average the z-scores)

$$\frac{1.64 + 1.65}{2} = 1.645$$

z_0 is negative since the graph shows z_0 is on the left side of 0.

To find x_0, substitute the values into the z-score formula:

$$z_0 = \frac{x_0 - \mu}{\sigma} \Rightarrow -1.645 = \frac{x_0 - 40}{6} \Rightarrow x_0 = -1.645(6) + 40 = 30.13$$

4.173 a. $\displaystyle\sum_{i=1}^{6} p(x_i) = p(0) + p(1) + p(2) + p(3) + p(4) + p(5)$

$$= .0102 + .0768 + .2304 + .3456 + .2592 + .0778 = 1.0000$$

b. $P(x = 4) = .2592$

c. $P(x < 2) = P(x = 0) + P(x = 1) = .0102 + .0768 = .0870$

d. $P(x \geq 3) = P(x = 3) + P(x = 4) + P(x = 5) = .3456 + .2592 + .0778 = .6826$

e. $\displaystyle\mu = E(x) = \sum_{i=1}^{6} x_i p(x_i) = 0(.0102) + 1(.0768) + 2(.2304) + 3(.3456) + 4(.2592) + 5(.0778)$

$$= 0 + .0768 + .4608 + 1.0368 + 1.0368 + .3890 = 3.0002$$

On the average, 3 out of every 5 dentists will use nitrous oxide.

4.175 a. For this problem, $c = 0$ and $d = 1$. $\dfrac{1}{d - c} = \dfrac{1}{1 - 0} = 1$

$$f(x) = \begin{cases} 1 & (0 \leq x \leq 1) \\ 0 & \text{otherwise} \end{cases}$$

$$\mu = \frac{c + d}{2} = \frac{0 + 1}{2} = .5$$

$$\sigma^2 = \frac{(d - c)^2}{12} = \frac{(1 - 0)^2}{12} = \frac{1}{12} = .0833 \qquad \sigma = \sqrt{.0833} = .289$$

b. $P(.2 < x < .4) = (.4 - .2)(1) = .2$

c. $P(x > .995) = (1 - .995)(1) = .005$. Since the probability of observing a trajectory greater than .995 is so small, we would not expect to see a trajectory exceeding .995.

4.177 Let x = interarrival time between patients. Then x is an exponential random variable with a mean of 4 minutes.

a. $P(x < 1) = 1 - P(x \geq 1) = 1 - e^{-1/4} = 1 - e^{-.25} = 1 - .778801 = .221199$

b. Assuming that the interarrival times are independent,

$P(\text{next 4 interarrival times are all less than 1 minute})$

$$= \{P(x < 1)\}^4 = .221199^4 = .002394$$

c. $P(x > 10) = e^{-10/4} = e^{-2.5} = .082085$

4.179   a.   We will check the 5 characteristics of a binomial random variable.

1.   The experiment consists of $n = 20$ identical trials.
2.   There are only 2 possible outcomes for each trial. Let S = intruding object is detected and F = intruding object is not detected.
3.   The probability of success (S) is the same from trial to trial. For each trial, $p = P(S) = .8$ and $q = 1 - p = 1 - .8 = .2$.
4.   The trials are independent.
5.   The binomial random variable x is the number of intruding objects in the 20 trials that are detected.

Thus, x is a binomial random variable.

b.   For this experiment, $n = 20$ and $p = .8$.

c.   Using Table I, Appendix D, with $n = 20$ and $p = .8$,

$$P(x = 15) = P(x \le 15) - P(x \le 14) = .370 - .196 = .174$$

d.   Using Table I, Appendix D, with $n = 20$ and $p = .8$,

$$P(x \ge 15) = 1 - P(x \le 14) = 1 - .196 = .804$$

e. $E(x) = np = 20(.8) = 16$. For every 20 intruding objects, SBIRS will detect an average of 16.

4.181   a.   Let x_1 = repair time for machine 1. Then x_1 has an exponential distribution with $\mu_1 = 1$ hour.

$$P(x_1 > 1) = e^{-1/1} = e^{-1} = .367879 \text{ (using a calculator)}$$

b.   Let x_2 = repair time for machine 2. Then x_2 has an exponential distribution with $\mu_2 = 2$ hours.

$$P(x_2 > 1) = e^{-1/2} = e^{-.5} = .606531 \text{ (using a calculator)}$$

c.   Let x_3 = repair time for machine 3. Then x_3 has an exponential distribution with $\mu_3 = .5$ hours.

$$P(x_3 > 1) = e^{-1/.5} = e^{-2} = .135335 \text{ (using a calculator)}$$

Since the mean repair time for machine 4 is the same as for machine 3, $P(x_4 > 1) = P(x_3 > 1) = .135335$.

d.   The only way that the repair time for the entire system will not exceed 1 hour is if all four machines are repaired in less than 1 hour. Thus, the probability that the repair time for the entire system exceeds 1 hour is:

P(Repair time entire system exceeds 1 hour)
$$= 1 - P\big((x_1 \le 1) \cap (x_2 \le 1) \cap (x_3 \le 1) \cap (x_4 \le 1)\big) = 1 - P(x_1 \le 1)P(x_2 \le 1)P(x_3 \le 1)P(x_4 \le 1)$$
$$= 1 - (1 - .367879)(1 - .606531)(1 - .135335)(1 - .135335)$$
$$= 1 - (.632121)(.393469)(.864665)(.864665) = 1 - .185954 = .814046$$

4.183   a.   For $N = 209$, $r = 10$, and $n = 8$, $E(x) = \dfrac{nr}{N} = \dfrac{10(8)}{209} = .383$

b. $P(x = 4) = \dfrac{\dbinom{8}{4}\dbinom{209-8}{10-4}}{\dbinom{209}{10}} = \dfrac{\dfrac{8!}{4!(8-4)!} \cdot \dfrac{201!}{6!(201-6)!}}{\dfrac{209!}{10!(209-10)!}} = .0002$

4. 185   Using MINITAB, the histogram with the normal distribution overlaid is:

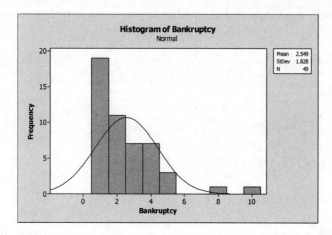

The data are skewed to the right, and do not appear to be normally distributed.

Using MINITAB, the descriptive statistics are:

Descriptive Statistics: Bankruptcy

Variable	N	Mean	StDev	Minimum	Q1	Median	Q3	Maximum
Bankruptcy	49	2.549	1.828	1.000	1.350	1.700	3.500	10.100

$\bar{x} \pm s \Rightarrow 2.549 \pm 1.828 \Rightarrow (0.721,\ 4.377)$

$\bar{x} \pm 2s \Rightarrow 2.549 \pm 2(1.828) \Rightarrow 2.549 \pm 3.656 \Rightarrow (-1.107,\ 6.205)$

$\bar{x} \pm 3s \Rightarrow 2.549 \pm 3(1.828) \Rightarrow 2.549 \pm 5.484 \Rightarrow (-2.935,\ 8.033)$

Of the 49 measurements, 44 are in the interval (0.721, 4.377). The proportion is $44/49 = .898$. This is much larger than the proportion (.68) stated by the Empirical Rule.

Of the 49 measurements, 47 are in the interval (−1.107, 6.205). The proportion is $47/49 = .959$. This is close to the proportion (.95) stated by the Empirical Rule.

Of the 49 measurements, 48 are in the interval (−2.935, 8.033). The proportion is $48/49 = .980$. This is smaller than the proportion (1.00) stated by the Empirical Rule.

This would imply that the data are not normal.

$IQR = Q_U - Q_L = 3.500 - 1.350 = 2.15$. $\dfrac{IQR}{s} = \dfrac{2.15}{1.828} = 1.176$. If the data are normally distributed, this

ratio should be close to 1.3. Since 1.176 is smaller than 1.3, this indicates that the data may not be normal.

Using MINITAB, the normal probability plot is:

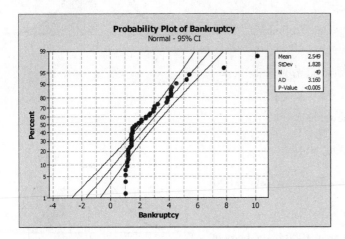

Since this plot is not a straight line, the data are not normal.

All four checks indicate that the data are not normal.

4.187   Let x equal the difference between the actual weight and recorded weight (the error of measurement). The random variable x is normally distributed with $\mu = 592$ and $\sigma = 628$.

a.   We want to find the probability that the weigh-in-motion equipment understates the actual weight of the truck. This would be true if the error of measurement is positive.

$$P(x > 0) = P\left(z > \frac{0 - 592}{628}\right) = P(z > -.94)$$
$$= .5000 + .3264 = .8264$$

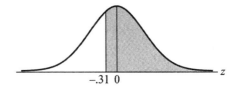

b. P(overstate the weight) $= 1 - P$(understate the weight)
$$= 1 - .8264 = .1736$$
(Refer to part **a**.)

For 100 measurements, approximately $100(.1736) = 17.36$ or 17 times the weight would be overstated.

c. $$P(x > 400) = P\left(z > \frac{400 - 592}{628}\right) = P(z > -.31)$$
$$= .5000 + .1217 = .6217$$

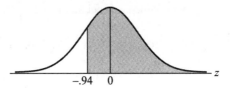

d. We want P(understate the weight) = .5

To understate the weight, $x > 0$. Thus, we want to find μ so that $P(x > 0) = .5$

$$P(x > 0) = P\left(z > \frac{0-\mu}{628}\right) = .5$$

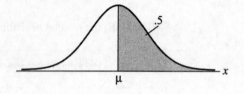

From Table II, Appendix D, $z_0 = 0$. To find μ, substitute into the z-score formula:

$$z_0 = \frac{x_0 - \mu}{\sigma} \Rightarrow 0 = \frac{0-\mu}{628} \Rightarrow \mu = 0$$

Thus, the mean error should be set at 0.

We want P(understate the weight) = .4

To understate the weight, $x > 0$. Thus, we want to find μ so that $P(x > 0) = .4$.

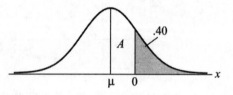

$A = .5 - .40 = .1$. Look up the area .1000 in the body of Table II, Appendix D, $z_0 = .25$.

To find μ, substitute into the z-score formula:

$$z_0 = \frac{x_0 - \mu}{\sigma} \Rightarrow .25 = \frac{0-\mu}{628} \Rightarrow \mu = 0 - (.25)628 = -157$$

4.189 a. $\mu = np = 25(.05) = 1.25$ $\sigma = \sqrt{npq} = \sqrt{25(.05)(.95)} = 1.09$

Since μ is not an integer, x could not equal its expected value.

b. The event is $(x \geq 5)$. From Table I with $n = 25$ and $p = .05$:

$$P(x \geq 5) = 1 - P(x \leq 4) = 1 - .993 = .007$$

c. Since the probability obtained in part **b** is so small, it is unlikely that 5% applies to this agency. The percentage is probably greater than 5%.

4.191 Let x = number of grants awarded to the north side in 140 trials. The random variable x has a hypergeometric distribution with $N = 743$, $n = 140$, and $r = 601$.

a. $\mu = E(x) = \dfrac{nr}{N} = \dfrac{140(601)}{743} = 113.24$

$$\sigma^2 = \frac{r(N-r)n(N-n)}{N^2(N-1)} = \frac{601(743-601)140(743-140)}{743^2(743-1)} = 17.5884$$

$$\sigma = \sqrt{17.5884} = 4.194$$

b. If the grants were awarded at random, we would expect approximately 113 to be awarded to the north side. We observed 140. The *z*-score associated with 140 is:

$$z = \frac{x - \mu}{\sigma} = \frac{140 - 113.24}{4.194} = 6.38$$

Because this *z*-score is so large, it would be extremely unlikely to observe all 140 grants to the north side if they are randomly selected. Thus, we would conclude that the grants were not randomly selected.

4.193   a. The properties of valid probability distributions are:

$$\sum p(x) = 1 \text{ and } 0 \le p(x) \le 1 \text{ for all } x.$$

For ARC a_1: $0 \le p(x) \le 1$ for all x and $\sum p(x) = .05 + .10 + .25 + .60 = 1.00$
Thus, this is a valid probability distribution.

For ARC a_2: $0 \le p(x) \le 1$ for all x and $\sum p(x) = .10 + .30 + .60 + 0 = 1.00$
Thus, this is a valid probability distribution.

For ARC a_3: $0 \le p(x) \le 1$ for all x and $\sum p(x) = .05 + .25 + .70 + 0 = 1.00$
Thus, this is a valid probability distribution.

For ARC a_4: $0 \le p(x) \le 1$ for all x and $\sum p(x) = .90 + .10 + 0 + 0 = 1.00$
Thus, this is a valid probability distribution.

b. For **Arc a_1**, $P(x > 1) = P(x = 2) + P(x = 3) = .25 + .6 = .85$

c. For **Arc a_2**, $P(x > 1) = P(x = 2) = .60$
For **Arc a_3**, $P(x > 1) = P(x = 2) = .70$
For **Arc a_4**, $P(x > 1) = 0$

d. For Arc a_1,
$$E(x) = \sum xp(x) = 0(.05) + 1(.10) + 2(.25) + 3(.60) = 0 + .10 + .50 + 1.80 = 2.40$$

The average capacity of Arc a_1 is 2.40.

For Arc a_2,
$$E(x) = \sum xp(x) = 0(.10) + 1(.30) + 2(.60) = 0 + .30 + 1.20 = 1.50$$

The average capacity of Arc a_2 is 1.50.

For Arc a_3,
$$E(x) = \sum xp(x) = 0(.05) + 1(.25) + 2(.70) + = 0 + .25 + 1.40 = 1.65$$

The average capacity of Arc a_3 is 1.65.

For Arc a_4,
$$E(x) = \sum xp(x) = 0(.90) + 1(.10) = 0 + .10 = .10$$

The average capacity of Arc a_4 is 0.10.

e.   For **Arc a_1**,
$$\sigma^2 = E\left[(x-\mu)\right]^2 = \sum (x-\mu)^2 \, p(x)$$
$$= (0-2.4)^2(.05) + (1-2.4)^2(.10) + (2-2.4)^2(.25) + (3-2.4)^2(.60)$$
$$= (-2.4)^2(.05) + (-1.4)^2(.10) + (-.4)^2(.25) + (.6)^2(.60)$$
$$= .288 + .196 + .04 + .216 = .74$$

$$\sigma = \sqrt{.74} = .86$$

We would expect most observations to fall within 2 standard deviations of the mean or
$2.40 \pm 2(.86) \Rightarrow 2.40 \pm 1.72 \Rightarrow (.68, \, 4.12)$

For **Arc a_2**,
$$\sigma^2 = E\left[(x-\mu)\right]^2 = \sum (x-\mu)^2 \, p(x)$$
$$= (0-1.5)^2(.10) + (1-1.5)^2(.30) + (2-1.5)^2(.60)$$
$$= (-1.5)^2(.10) + (-.5)^2(.30) + (.5)^2(.60) = .225 + .075 + .15 = .45$$

$$\sigma = \sqrt{.45} = .67$$

We would expect most observations to fall within 2 standard deviations of the mean or
$1.50 \pm 2(.67) \Rightarrow 1.50 \pm 1.34 \Rightarrow (.16, \, 2.84)$

For **Arc a_3**,
$$\sigma^2 = E\left[(x-\mu)\right]^2 = \sum (x-\mu)^2 \, p(x)$$
$$= (0-1.65)^2(.05) + (1-1.65)^2(.25) + (2-1.65)^2(.70)$$
$$= (-1.65)^2(.05) + (-.65)^2(.25) + (.35)^2(.70) = .136125 + .105625 + .08575 = .3275$$

$$\sigma = \sqrt{.3275} = .57$$

We would expect most observations to fall within 2 standard deviations of the mean or
$1.65 \pm 2(.57) \Rightarrow 1.65 \pm 1.14 \Rightarrow (.51, 2.79)$

For **Arc a_4**,
$$\sigma^2 = E\left[(x-\mu)\right]^2 = \sum (x-\mu)^2 \, p(x) = (0-.1)^2(.90) + (1-.1)^2(.10)$$
$$= (-.1)^2(.90) + (.9)^2(.10) = .009 + .081 = .090$$

$$\sigma = \sqrt{.09} = .30$$

We would expect most observations to fall within 2 standard deviations of the mean or
$.10 \pm 2(.30) \Rightarrow .10 \pm .60 \Rightarrow (-.50, .70)$

4.195   a.   Using MINITAB with $\lambda = 5$,

Cumulative Distribution Function
```
Poisson with mean = 5

x  P( X <= x )
2    0.124652
```

$$P(x < 3) = P(x \leq 2) = .125$$

b. $E(x) = \lambda = 5$. The average number of calls blocked during the peak hour of video conferencing call time is 5.

4.197   Let x = number of defective CDs in $n = 1,600$ trials. Then x is a binomial random variable with $n = 1,600$ and $p = .006$.

$$E(x) = \mu = np = 1,600(.006) = 9.6.$$

$$\sigma = \sqrt{\sigma^2} = \sqrt{npq} = \sqrt{1,600(.006)(.994)} = \sqrt{9.5424} = 3.089$$

To see if the normal approximation is appropriate, we use:

$$\mu \pm 3\sigma \Rightarrow 9.6 \pm 3(3.089) \Rightarrow 9.6 \pm 9.267 \Rightarrow (0.333, \ 18.867)$$

Since the interval lies in the range of 0 to 1,600, the normal approximation is appropriate.

$$P(x \geq 12) \approx P\left(z \geq \frac{11.5 - 9.6}{3.089}\right) = P(z \geq 0.62) = .5 - .2324 = .2676$$

(Using Table II, Appendix D)

Since this probability is fairly large, it would not be unusual to see 12 or more defectives in a sample of 1,600 if 99.4% were defect-free. Thus, there would be no evidence to cast doubt on the manufacturer's claim.

4.199   a.   The contract will be profitable if total cost, x, is less than $1,000,000.

$$P(x < 1,000,000) = P\left(z < \frac{1,000,000 - 850,000}{170,000}\right) = P(z < .88) = .5 + .3106 = .8106$$

b.   The contract will result in a loss if total cost, x, exceeds 1,000,000.

$$P(x > 1,000,000) = 1 - P(x < 1,000,000) = 1 - .8106 = .1894$$

c. $P(x < R) = .99$. Find R.

$$P(x < R) = P\left(z < \frac{R - 850,000}{170,000}\right) = P(z < z_0) = .99$$

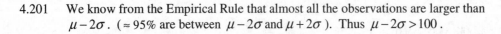

$A_1 = .99 - .5 = .4900$

Looking up the area .4900 in Table II, $z_0 = 2.33$

$$z_0 = \frac{R - 850,000}{170,000} \Rightarrow 2.33 = \frac{R - 850,000}{170,000}$$
$$\Rightarrow R = 2.33(170,000) + 850,000 = \$1,246,100$$

4.201   We know from the Empirical Rule that almost all the observations are larger than
$\mu - 2\sigma$. ($\approx 95\%$ are between $\mu - 2\sigma$ and $\mu + 2\sigma$). Thus $\mu - 2\sigma > 100$.

For the binomial, $\mu = np = n(.4)$ and $\sigma = \sqrt{npq} = \sqrt{n(.4)(.6)} = \sqrt{.24n}$

$\mu - 2\sigma > 100 \Rightarrow .4n - 2\sqrt{.24n} > 100 \Rightarrow .4n - .98\sqrt{n} - 100 > 0$

Solving for $\sqrt{n}$, we get:
$$\sqrt{n} = \frac{.98 \pm \sqrt{.98^2 - 4(.4)(-100)}}{2(.4)} = \frac{.98 \pm 12.687}{.8}$$
$$\Rightarrow \sqrt{n} = 17.084 \Rightarrow n = 17.084^2 = 291.9 \approx 292$$

4.203   Let x = load. Then x has a normal distribution with $\mu = 20,000$. We are given $P(10 < x < 30) = .95$. We
want to find σ .

$$P(10,000 < x < 30,000) = .95 \Rightarrow (z_1 < z < z_2) = .95 \Rightarrow (z_1 < z < 0) = P(0 < z < z_2) = .95/2 = .4750$$

Looking up area .4750 in Table II, Appendix D, $z_2 = 1.96$ and $z_1 = -1.96$.

$$z_2 = \frac{x - 30}{\sigma} = \frac{30,000 - 20,000}{\sigma} = 1.96 \Rightarrow \sigma = \frac{10,000}{1.96} = 5,102$$

4.205   a.   Using Table II, Appendix D.

For $\sigma = 1$:

$P(-1 < x < 1) + P(4 < x < 6) + P(9 < x < 11)$
$$= P\left(\frac{-1 - 5}{1} < z < \frac{1 - 5}{1}\right) + P\left(\frac{4 - 5}{1} < z < \frac{6 - 5}{1}\right) + P\left(\frac{9 - 5}{1} < z < \frac{11 - 5}{1}\right)$$
$$= P(-6 < z < -4) + P(-1 < z < 1) + P(4 < z < 6) = 0 + .3413 + .3413 + 0 = .6826$$

For $\sigma = 2$:

$$P(-1 < x < 1) + P(4 < x < 6) + P(9 < x < 11)$$

$$= P\left(\frac{-1-5}{2} < z < \frac{1-5}{2}\right) + P\left(\frac{4-5}{2} < z < \frac{6-5}{2}\right) + P\left(\frac{9-5}{2} < z < \frac{11-5}{2}\right)$$

$$= P(-3 < z < -2) + P(-.5 < z < .5) + P(2 < z < 3)$$

$$= (.4987 - .4772) + (.1915 + .1915) + (.4987 - .4772) = .4260$$

For $\sigma = 4$:

$$P(-1 < x < 1) + P(4 < x < 6) + P(9 < x < 11)$$

$$= P\left(\frac{-1-5}{4} < z < \frac{1-5}{4}\right) + P\left(\frac{4-5}{4} < z < \frac{6-5}{4}\right) + P\left(\frac{9-5}{4} < z < \frac{11-5}{4}\right)$$

$$= P(-1.5 < z < -1) + P(-.25 < z < .25) + P(1 < z < 1.5)$$

$$= (.4332 - .3413) + (.0948 + .0948) + (.4332 - .3413) = .3734$$

b. For $\sigma = 1$, 764 of the 1100 flechettes hit a target. The proportion is 764/1100 = .6945. This is a little higher than the probability that was computed in part *a*.

   For $\sigma = 2$, 462 of the 1100 flechettes hit a target. The proportion is 462/1100 = .42. This is very close to the probability that was computed in part *a*.

   For $\sigma = 4$, 408 of the 1100 flechettes hit a target. The proportion is 408/1100 = .3709. Again, this is very close to the probability that was computed in part *a*.

c. If the Army wants to maximize the chance of hitting the target that the prototype gun us aimed at, then σ should be set at 1. The probability of hitting the target is .6826.

   If the Army wants to hit multiple targets with a single shot of the weapon, then σ should be set at 2. The probability of hitting at least one of the targets is .4260.

Chapter 5
Sampling Distributions

5.1   a–b.   The different samples of $n = 2$ with replacement and their means are:

Possible Samples	$\bar{x}$	Possible Samples	$\bar{x}$
0, 0	0	4, 0	2
0, 2	1	4, 2	3
0, 4	2	4, 4	4
0, 6	3	4, 6	5
2, 0	1	6, 0	3
2, 2	2	6, 2	4
2, 4	3	6, 4	5
2, 6	4	6, 6	6

     c.   Since each sample is equally likely, the probability of any 1 being selected is $\dfrac{1}{4}\left(\dfrac{1}{4}\right) = \dfrac{1}{16}$

     d.

$$P(\bar{x} = 0) = \frac{1}{16}$$

$$P(\bar{x} = 1) = \frac{1}{16} + \frac{1}{16} = \frac{2}{16}$$

$$P(\bar{x} = 2) = \frac{1}{16} + \frac{1}{16} + \frac{1}{16} = \frac{3}{16}$$

$$P(\bar{x} = 3) = \frac{1}{16} + \frac{1}{16} + \frac{1}{16} + \frac{1}{16} = \frac{4}{16}$$

$$P(\bar{x} = 4) = \frac{1}{16} + \frac{1}{16} + \frac{1}{16} = \frac{3}{16}$$

$$P(\bar{x} = 5) = \frac{1}{16} + \frac{1}{16} = \frac{2}{16}$$

$$P(\bar{x} = 6) = \frac{1}{16}$$

$\bar{x}$	$p(\bar{x})$
0	1/16
1	2/16
2	3/16
3	4/16
4	3/16
5	2/16
6	1/16

     e.   Using MINITAB, the graph is:

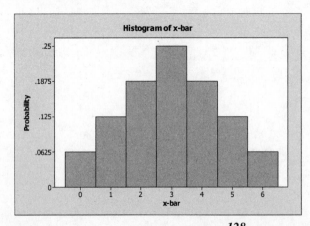

5.3   If the observations are independent of each other, then

$$P(1, 1) = p(1)\,p(1) = .2(.2) = .04 \qquad P(1, 2) = p(1)\,p(2) = .2(.3) = .06$$
$$P(1, 3) = p(1)\,p(3) = .2(.2) = .04$$

      etc.

a.

Possible Sample	$\bar{x}$	$p(\bar{x})$	Possible Samples	$\bar{x}$	$p(\bar{x})$
1, 1	1	.04	3, 4	3.5	.04
1, 2	1.5	.06	3, 5	4	.02
1, 3	2	.04	4, 1	2.5	.04
1, 4	2.5	.04	4, 2	3	.06
1, 5	3	.02	4, 3	3.5	.04
2, 1	1.5	.06	4, 4	4	.04
2, 2	2	.09	4, 5	4.5	.02
2, 3	2.5	.06	5, 1	3	.02
2, 4	3	.06	5, 2	3.5	.03
2, 5	3.5	.03	5, 3	4	.02
3, 1	2	.04	5, 4	4.5	.02
3, 2	2.5	.06	5, 5	5	.01
3, 3	3	.04			

Summing the probabilities, the probability distribution of is:

$\bar{x}$	$p(\bar{x})$
1	.04
1.5	.12
2	.17
2.5	.20
3	.20
3.5	.14
4	.08
4.5	.04
5	.01

b.   Using MINITAB, the graph is:

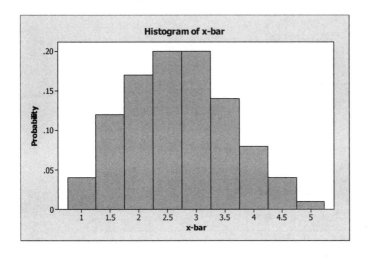

c. $P(\bar{x} \geq 4.5) = .04 + .01 = .05$

d.   No. The probability of observing $\bar{x} = 4.5$ or larger is small (.05).

5.5   a.   For a sample of size $n = 2$, the sample mean and sample median are exactly the same. Thus, the sampling distribution of the sample median is the same as that for the sample mean (see Exercise 5.3**a**).

        b.   The probability histogram for the sample median is identical to that for the sample mean (see Exercise 5.3**b**).

5.7   a.   Answers will vary. A statistical package was used to generate 500 samples of size 25 from a uniform distribution on the interval from 00 to 99. The sample mean was computed for each sample of size 25. Using MINITAB, a histogram of the sample means is:

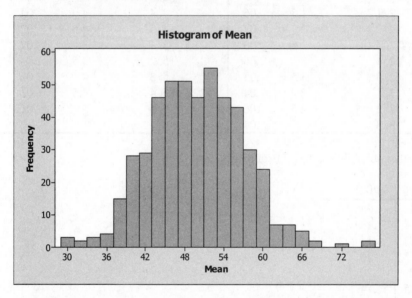

        b.   The sample variances were computed for each of the 500 samples of size 25 used in part **a**. Using MINITAB, a histogram of the sample variances is:

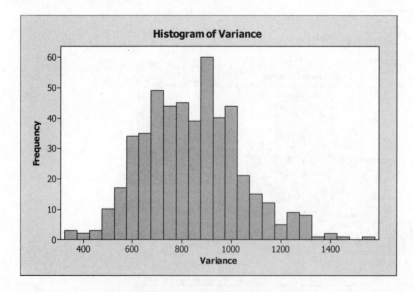

5.9   a. $\mu = \sum xp(x) = 2\left(\dfrac{1}{3}\right) + 4\left(\dfrac{1}{3}\right) + 9\left(\dfrac{1}{3}\right) = \dfrac{15}{3} = 5$

b.   The possible samples of size $n=3$, the sample means, and the probabilities are:

Possible Samples	$\bar{x}$	$p(\bar{x})$	m	Possible Samples	$\bar{x}$	$p(\bar{x})$	m
2, 2, 2	2	1/27	2	4, 4, 4	4	1/27	4
2, 2, 4	8/3	1/27	2	4, 4, 9	17/3	1/27	4
2, 2, 9	13/3	1/27	2	4, 9, 2	5	1/27	4
2, 4, 2	8/3	1/27	2	4, 9, 4	17/3	1/27	4
2, 4, 4	10/3	1/27	4	4, 9, 9	22/3	1/27	9
2, 4, 9	5	1/27	4	9, 2, 2	13/3	1/27	2
2, 9, 2	13/3	1/27	2	9, 2, 4	5	1/27	4
2, 9, 4	5	1/27	4	9, 2, 9	20/3	1/27	9
2, 9, 9	20/3	1/27	9	9, 4, 2	5	1/27	4
4, 2, 2	8/3	1/27	2	9, 4, 4	17/3	1/27	4
4, 2, 4	10/3	1/27	4	9, 4, 9	22/3	1/27	9
4, 2, 9	5	1/27	4	9, 9, 2	20/3	1/27	9
4, 4, 2	10/3	1/27	4	9, 9, 4	22/3	1/27	9
				9, 9, 9	9	1/27	9

The sampling distribution of $\bar{x}$ is:

$\bar{x}$	$p(\bar{x})$
2	1/27
8/3	3/27
10/3	3/27
4	1/27
13/3	3/27
5	6/27
17/3	3/27
20/3	3/27
22/3	3/27
9	1/27
	27/27

$$E(\bar{x}) = \sum \bar{x}p(\bar{x}) = 2\left(\frac{1}{27}\right) + \frac{8}{3}\left(\frac{3}{27}\right) + \frac{10}{3}\left(\frac{3}{27}\right) + 4\left(\frac{1}{27}\right) + \frac{13}{3}\left(\frac{3}{27}\right)$$

$$+ 5\left(\frac{6}{27}\right) + \frac{17}{3}\left(\frac{3}{27}\right) + \frac{20}{3}\left(\frac{3}{27}\right) + \frac{22}{3}\left(\frac{3}{27}\right) + 9\left(\frac{1}{27}\right)$$

$$= \frac{2}{27} + \frac{8}{27} + \frac{10}{27} + \frac{4}{27} + \frac{13}{27} + \frac{30}{27} + \frac{17}{27} + \frac{20}{27} + \frac{22}{27} + \frac{9}{27} = \frac{135}{27} = 5$$

Since $\mu = 5$ in part **a**, and $E(\bar{x}) = \mu = 5$, $\bar{x}$ is an unbiased estimator of μ.

c. The median was calculated for each sample and is shown in the table in part **b**. The sampling distribution of m is:

m	$p(m)$
2	7/27
4	13/27
9	7/27
	27/27

$$E(m) = \sum mp(m) = 2\left(\frac{7}{27}\right) + 4\left(\frac{13}{27}\right) + 9\left(\frac{7}{27}\right) = \frac{14}{27} + \frac{52}{27} + \frac{63}{27} = \frac{129}{27} = 4.778$$

The $E(m) = 4.778 \neq \mu = 5$. Thus, m is a biased estimator of μ.

d. Use the sample mean, $\bar{x}$. It is an unbiased estimator.

5.11 Answers will vary. MINITAB was used to generate 500 samples of size $n = 25$ observations from a uniform population from 1 to 50. The first 10 samples along with the sample means and medians are shown in the table below:

Sample	Observations																									Mean	Median
1	28	27	11	19	50	30	47	26	9	33	50	15	21	41	31	41	35	32	32	17	6	32	39	34	21	29.08	31
2	8	4	32	32	3	45	18	9	40	3	42	21	44	50	42	14	24	10	36	6	15	47	26	48	28	25.88	26
3	6	20	27	1	50	14	21	37	46	23	1	34	42	47	24	46	8	29	18	28	40	39	49	33	23	28.24	28
4	45	12	26	13	40	17	11	43	8	35	20	8	44	48	13	46	49	17	47	27	5	45	9	21	36	27.4	26
5	40	38	25	37	47	2	17	40	32	6	22	30	23	2	18	22	14	6	22	3	43	47	16	35	35	24.88	23
6	17	8	43	27	21	5	18	45	31	15	2	38	22	18	7	9	3	35	23	45	24	39	38	35	37	24.20	23
7	40	1	22	29	6	8	22	20	36	18	45	16	29	9	6	3	49	34	24	40	27	5	49	11	30	23.16	22
8	25	3	44	34	29	6	33	32	43	6	43	24	49	14	37	8	46	44	1	12	36	18	30	25	4	25.84	29
9	7	33	36	41	30	13	17	19	14	36	20	39	41	20	15	38	12	37	14	9	19	2	37	15	8	22.88	19
10	4	46	49	49	45	49	24	3	25	22	27	28	23	17	14	6	35	5	20	34	4	41	9	15	3	23.88	23

Using MINITAB, side-by side histograms of the means and medians of the 500 samples are:

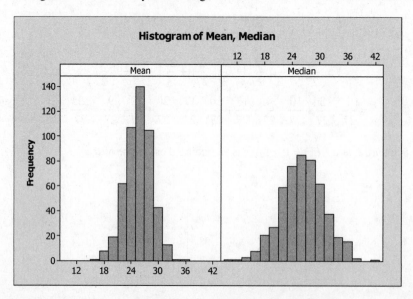

a.   Yes, it appears that $\bar{x}$ and the median are unbiased estimators of the population mean. The centers of both distributions above appear to be around 25 to 26. In fact, the mean of the sampling distribution of $\bar{x}$ is 25.65 and the mean of the sampling distribution of the median is 25.73.

b.   The sampling distribution of the median has greater variation because it is more spread out than the sampling distribution of $\bar{x}$.

5.13   a.   Refer to the solution to Exercise 5.3. The values of s^2 and the corresponding probabilities are listed below:

$$s^2 = \frac{\sum x^2 - \dfrac{\left(\sum x\right)^2}{n}}{n-1}$$

For sample 1, 1; $s^2 = \dfrac{2 - \dfrac{2^2}{2}}{1} = 0$ For sample 1, 2: $s^2 = \dfrac{5 - \dfrac{3^2}{2}}{1} = .5$

The rest of the values are calculated and shown:

s^2	$p(s^2)$	s^2	$p(s^2)$
0.0	.04	0.5	.04
0.5	.06	2.0	.02
2.0	.04	4.5	.04
4.5	.04	2.0	.06
8.0	.02	0.5	.04
0.5	.06	0.0	.04
0.0	.09	0.5	.02
0.5	.06	8.0	.02
2.0	.06	4.5	.03
4.5	.03	2.0	.02
2.0	.04	0.5	.02
0.5	.06	0.0	.01
0.0	.04		

The sampling distribution of s^2 is:

s^2	$p(s^2)$
0.0	.22
0.5	.36
2.0	.24
4.5	.14
8.0	.04

b. $\sigma^2 = \sum (x - \mu)^2 p(x) = (1 - 2.7)^2 (.2) + (2 - 2.7)^2 (.3) + (3 - 2.7)^2 (.2)$
$$+ (4 - 2.7)^2 (.2) + (5 - 2.7)^2 (.1) = 1.61$$

c. $E(s^2) = \sum s^2 p(s^2) = 0(.22) + .5(.36) + 2(.24) + 4.5(.14) + 8(.04) = 1.61$

d.   The sampling distribution of s is listed below, where $s = \sqrt{s^2}$:

s	$p(s)$
0.000	.22
0.707	.36
1.414	.24
2.121	.14
2.828	.04

e. $E(s) = \sum sp(s) = 0(.22) + .707(.36) + 1.41(.24) + 2.1212(.14) + 2.828(.04) = 1.00394$

Since $E(s) = 1.00394$ is not equal to $\sigma = \sqrt{\sigma^2} = \sqrt{1.61} = 1.269$, s is a biased estimator of σ.

5.15   The sampling distribution is approximately normal only if the sample size is sufficiently large or if the population being sampled from is normal.

5.17   a. $\mu_{\bar{x}} = \mu = 100, \ \sigma_{\bar{x}} = \dfrac{\sigma}{\sqrt{n}} = \dfrac{\sqrt{100}}{\sqrt{4}} = 5$

b. $\mu_{\bar{x}} = \mu = 100, \ \sigma_{\bar{x}} = \dfrac{\sigma}{\sqrt{n}} = \dfrac{\sqrt{100}}{\sqrt{25}} = 2$

c. $\mu_{\bar{x}} = \mu = 100, \ \sigma_{\bar{x}} = \dfrac{\sigma}{\sqrt{n}} = \dfrac{\sqrt{100}}{\sqrt{100}} = 1$

d. $\mu_{\bar{x}} = \mu = 100, \ \sigma_{\bar{x}} = \dfrac{\sigma}{\sqrt{n}} = \dfrac{\sqrt{100}}{\sqrt{50}} = 1.414$

e. $\mu_{\bar{x}} = \mu = 100, \ \sigma_{\bar{x}} = \dfrac{\sigma}{\sqrt{n}} = \dfrac{\sqrt{100}}{\sqrt{500}} = .447$

f. $\mu_{\bar{x}} = \mu = 100, \ \sigma_{\bar{x}} = \dfrac{\sigma}{\sqrt{n}} = \dfrac{\sqrt{100}}{\sqrt{1000}} = .316$

5.19   In Exercise 5.18, it was determined that the mean and standard deviation of the sampling distribution of the sample mean are 20 and 2 respectively. Using Table II, Appendix D:

a. $P(\bar{x} < 16) = P\left(z < \dfrac{16 - 20}{2}\right) = P(z < -2) = .5 - .4772 = .0228$

b. $P(\bar{x} > 23) = P\left(z > \dfrac{23 - 20}{2}\right) = P(z > 1.50) = .5 - .4332 = .0668$

c. $P(\bar{x} > 25) = P\left(z > \dfrac{25 - 20}{2}\right) = P(z > 2.5) = .5 - .4938 = .0062$

d. $P(16 < \bar{x} < 22) = P\left(\dfrac{16-20}{2} < z < \dfrac{22-20}{2}\right) = P(-2 < z < 1) = .4772 + .3413 = .8185$

e. $P(\bar{x} < 14) = P\left(z < \dfrac{14-20}{2}\right) = P(z < -3) = .5 - .4987 = .0013$

5.21   By the Central Limit Theorem, the sampling distribution of $\bar{x}$ is approximately normal with $\mu_{\bar{x}} = \mu = 30$ and $\sigma_{\bar{x}} = \sigma/\sqrt{n} = 16/\sqrt{100} = 1.6$. Using Table II, Appendix D:

a. $P(\bar{x} \geq 28) = P\left(z \geq \dfrac{28-30}{1.6}\right) = P(z \geq -1.25) = .5 + .3944 = .8944$

b. $P(22.1 \leq \bar{x} \leq 26.8) = P\left(\dfrac{22.1-30}{1.6} \leq z \leq \dfrac{26.8-30}{1.6}\right) = P(-4.94 \leq z \leq -2) = .5 - .4772 = .0228$

c. $P(\bar{x} \leq 28.2) = P\left(z \leq \dfrac{28.2-30}{1.6}\right) = P(z \leq -1.13) = .5 - .3708 = .1292$

d. $P(\bar{x} \geq 27.0) = P\left(z \geq \dfrac{27.0-30}{1.6}\right) = P(z \geq -1.88) = .5 + .4699 = .9699$

5.23   a.   From Exercise 2.33, the population of interarrival times is skewed to the right.

b.   The population mean and standard deviation are:

$$\mu = \frac{\sum x}{N} = \frac{25{,}504.845}{267} = 95.52$$

$$\sigma^2 = \frac{\sum x^2 - \dfrac{\left(\sum x\right)^2}{N}}{N} = \frac{4{,}665{,}241.665 - \dfrac{\left(25{,}504.845\right)^2}{267}}{267} = 8{,}348.025727$$

$$\sigma = \sqrt{8{,}348.025727} = 91.3675$$

c.   By the Central Limit Theorem, the sampling distribution of $\bar{x}$ will be approximately normal. Theoretically, $\mu_{\bar{x}} = \mu = 95.52$ and $\sigma_{\bar{x}} = \dfrac{\sigma}{\sqrt{n}} = \dfrac{91.3675}{\sqrt{40}} = 14.4465$.

d. $P(\bar{x} < 90) = P\left(z < \dfrac{90-95.52}{14.4465}\right) = P(z < -.38) = .5 - .1480 = .3520$ (using Table II, Appendix D.)

e &f.   Answers will vary. A statistical package was used to randomly select 40 interarrival times from the Phishing data set and $\bar{x}$ was computed. This was repeated 50 times to simulate 50 students selecting 40 interarrival times and computing $\bar{x}$.

Using MINITAB, a histogram of the 50 $\bar{x}$ values is:

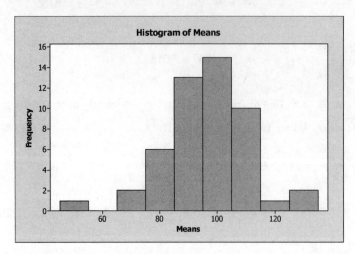

This shape is somewhat normal.

g. Using MINITAB, the mean and standard deviation of these 50 means is:

Descriptive Statistics: Means

```
Variable    N    Mean  StDev  Minimum     Q1  Median      Q3  Maximum
Means      50   96.09  14.08    52.73  86.36   95.65  105.23   130.23
```

The mean of these 50 means is 96.09. This is very close to $\mu_{\bar{x}} = 95.52$ found in part c. The standard

deviation of these 50 means is 14.08. This is also very close to $\sigma_{\bar{x}} = \dfrac{\sigma}{\sqrt{n}} = \dfrac{91.54}{\sqrt{40}} = 14.4465$ found in

part c.

5.25   a. $\mu_{\bar{x}} = \mu = 68$. The average value of sample mean level of support is 68.

b. $\sigma_{\bar{x}} = \dfrac{\sigma}{\sqrt{n}} = \dfrac{27}{\sqrt{45}} = 4.0249$ The standard deviation of the distribution of the sample means is 4.0249.

c.   Because the sample size is large ($n = 45 > 30$), the Central Limit Theorem says that the sampling
distribution of $\bar{x}$ is approximately normal.

d. $P(\bar{x} > 65) = P\left(z > \dfrac{65 - 68}{4.0249} \right) = P(z > -.75) = .5 + .2734 = .7734$ (using Table II, Appendix D)

5.27   By the Central Limit Theorem, the sampling distribution of $\bar{x}$ is approximately normal with

$\mu_{\bar{x}} = \mu = 105.3$ and $\sigma_{\bar{x}} = \dfrac{\sigma}{\sqrt{n}} = \dfrac{8}{\sqrt{64}} = 1$.

$P(\bar{x} < 103) = P\left(z < \dfrac{103 - 105.3}{1} \right) = P(z < -2.3) = .5 - .4893 = .0107$ (using Table II, Appendix D)

5.29   a.   By the Central Limit Theorem, the sampling distribution of $\bar{x}$ is approximately normal with a mean $\mu_{\bar{x}} = \mu = .53$ and standard deviation $\sigma_{\bar{x}} = \dfrac{\sigma}{\sqrt{n}} = \dfrac{.193}{\sqrt{50}} = .0273$.

b. $P(\bar{x} > .58) = P\left(z > \dfrac{.58 - .53}{.0273}\right) = P(z > 1.83) = .5 - .4664 = .0336$

c.   If Before Tensioning: $\mu_{\bar{x}} = \mu = .53$

$P(\bar{x} \geq .59) = P\left(z \geq \dfrac{.59 - .53}{.0273}\right) = P(z \geq 2.20) = .5 - .4861 = .0139$

If After Tensioning: $\mu_{\bar{x}} = \mu = .58$

$P(\bar{x} \geq .59) = P\left(z \geq \dfrac{.59 - .58}{.0273}\right) = P(z \geq 0.37) = .5 - .1443 = .3557$

Since the probability of getting a maximum differential of .59 or more Before Tensioning is so small, it would be very unlikely that the measurements were obtained Before Tensioning. However, since the probability of getting a maximum differential of .59 or more After Tensioning is not small, it would not be unusual that the measurements were obtained after tensioning. Thus, most likely, the measurements were obtained After Tensioning.

5.31   a.   By the Central Limit Theorem, the sampling distribution of $\bar{x}$ is approximately normal with $\mu_{\bar{x}} = \mu = 6$ and $\sigma_{\bar{x}} = \dfrac{\sigma}{\sqrt{n}} = \dfrac{10}{\sqrt{326}} = .5538$.

$P(\bar{x} > 7.5) = P\left(z > \dfrac{7.5 - 6}{.5538}\right) = P(z > 2.71) = .5 - .4966 = .0034$

(Using Table II, Appendix D)

b.   We first need to find the probability of observing the current data or anything more unusual if the true mean is 6.

$P(\bar{x} \geq 300) = P\left(z \geq \dfrac{300 - 6}{.5538}\right) = P(z \geq 530.88) \approx .5 - .5 = 0$

Since the probability of observing a sample mean of 300 ppb or higher is essentially 0 if the true mean is 6 ppb, we would infer that the true mean PFOA concentration for the population of people who live near DuPont's Teflon facility is not 6 ppb but higher than 6 ppb.

5.33   By the Central Limit Theorem, the sampling distribution of $\bar{x}$ is approximately normal with $\mu_{\bar{x}} = \mu = 40$ and $\sigma_{\bar{x}} = \dfrac{\sigma}{\sqrt{n}} = \dfrac{5}{\sqrt{100}} = .5$.

$P(\bar{x} \geq 42) = P\left(z \geq \dfrac{42 - 40}{.5}\right) = P(z > 4) \approx .5 - .5 = 0$ (using Table II, Appendix D)

Since this probability is so small, it is very unlikely that the sample was selected from the population of convicted drug dealers.

5.35   For $n = 50$, we can use the Central Limit Theorem to decide the shape of the distribution of the sample mean bacterial counts. For the handrubbing sample, the sampling distribution of $\bar{x}$ is approximately normal with a mean of $\mu_{\bar{x}} = 35$ and standard deviation $\dfrac{\sigma}{\sqrt{n}} = \dfrac{59}{\sqrt{50}} = 8.344$. For the handwashing sample, the sampling distribution of $\bar{x}$ is approximately normal with a mean of $\mu_{\bar{x}} = 69$ and standard deviation $\dfrac{\sigma}{\sqrt{n}} = \dfrac{106}{\sqrt{50}} = 14.991$.

For Handrubbing:

$$P(\bar{x} < 30 \mid \mu = 35) = P\left(z < \frac{30 - 35}{8.344} \right) = P(z < -.60) = .5 - .2257 = .2743 \ \text{(using Table II, Appendix D)}$$

For Handwashing:

$$P(\bar{x} < 30 \mid \mu = 69) = P\left(z < \frac{30 - 69}{14.991} \right) = P(z < -2.60) = .5 - .4953 = .0047 \ \text{(using Table II, Appendix D)}$$

Since the probability of getting a sample mean of less than 30 for the handrubbing is not small compared with that for the handwashing, the sample of workers probably came from the handrubbing group.

5.37   a. $\mu_{\hat{p}} = p = .1$ and $\sigma_{\hat{p}} = \sqrt{\dfrac{p(1-p)}{n}} = \sqrt{\dfrac{.1(1-.1)}{500}} = .0134$

     b. $\mu_{\hat{p}} = p = .5$ and $\sigma_{\hat{p}} = \sqrt{\dfrac{p(1-p)}{n}} = \sqrt{\dfrac{.5(1-.5)}{500}} = .0224$

     c. $\mu_{\hat{p}} = p = .7$ and $\sigma_{\hat{p}} = \sqrt{\dfrac{p(1-p)}{n}} = \sqrt{\dfrac{.7(1-.7)}{500}} = .0205$

5.39   a. $E(\hat{p}) = \mu_{\hat{p}} = p = .85$ and $\sigma_{\hat{p}} = \sqrt{\dfrac{p(1-p)}{n}} = \sqrt{\dfrac{.85(1-.85)}{250}} = .0226$

     b.   The sampling distribution of $\hat{p}$ will be approximately normal since the sample size is sufficiently large.

     c. $P(\hat{p} < .9) = P\left(z < \dfrac{.9 - .85}{\sqrt{\dfrac{.85(1-.85)}{250}}} \right) = P(z < 2.21) = .5 + .4864 = .9864 \ \text{(using Table II, Appendix D)}$

5.41   a.   Answers will vary. Using a statistical package, 500 samples of size 10 were generated from the population of (0,1). The histogram of the 500 sample proportions is:

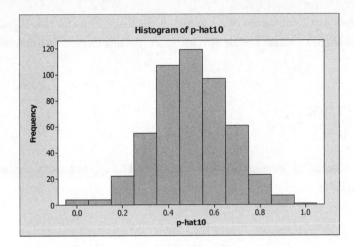

b.   Using a statistical package, 500 samples of size 25 were generated from the population of (0,1). The histogram of the 500 sample proportions is:

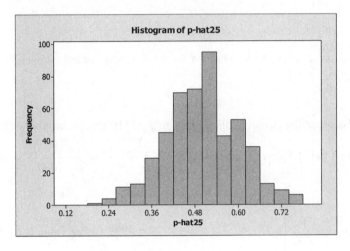

c.   Using a statistical package, 500 samples of size 100 were generated from the population of (0,1). The histogram of the 500 sample proportions is:

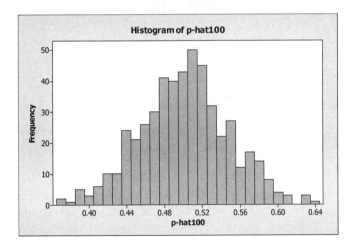

d.   As the sample size increases, the spread of the values of $\hat{p}$ decreases. In the graph in part a, the spread of the values of $\hat{p}$ is from 0 to 1. In the graph in part b, the spread of the values of $\hat{p}$ is from

.20 to .76. In the graph in part c, the spread of the values of $\hat{p}$ is from .37 to .64. In all graphs, the distributions are mound-shaped. As the sample size increases, the distribution becomes more peaked.

5.43   a. $\mu_{\hat{p}} = p = .67$

b. $\sigma_{\hat{p}} = \sqrt{\dfrac{p(1-p)}{n}} = \sqrt{\dfrac{.67(1-.67)}{1000}} = .0149$

c.   By the Central Limit Theorem, the sampling distribution of $\hat{p}$ will be approximately normal since the sample size is sufficiently large.

d. $P(\hat{p} < .75) = P\left(z < \dfrac{.75 - .67}{\sqrt{\dfrac{.67(1-.67)}{1000}}} \right) = P(z < 5.38) = .5 + .5 = 1$ (using Table II, Appendix D)

e. $P(\hat{p} > .5) = P\left(z > \dfrac{.5 - .67}{\sqrt{\dfrac{.67(1-.67)}{1000}}} \right) = P(z > -11.43) = .5 + .5 = 1$ (using Table II, Appendix D)

5.45   a.   By the Central Limit Theorem, the sampling distribution of $\hat{p}$ will be approximately normal since the sample size is sufficiently large, with $\mu_{\hat{p}} = p = .03$ and $\sigma_{\hat{p}} = \sqrt{\dfrac{p(1-p)}{n}} = \sqrt{\dfrac{.03(1-.03)}{1000}} = .0054$.

b. $P(\hat{p} < .05) = P\left(z < \dfrac{.05 - .03}{\sqrt{\dfrac{.03(1-.03)}{1000}}} \right) = P(z < 3.71) = .5 + .4999 = .9999$ (using Table II, Appendix D)

c. $P(\hat{p} > .025) = P\left(z > \dfrac{.025 - .03}{\sqrt{\dfrac{.03(1-.03)}{1000}}} \right) = P(z > -.93) = .5 + .3238 = .8238$ (using Table II, Appendix D)

5.47   a.   By the Central Limit Theorem, the sampling distribution of $\hat{p}$ will be approximately normal since the sample size is sufficiently large, with $\mu_{\hat{p}} = p = .4$ and $\sigma_{\hat{p}} = \sqrt{\dfrac{p(1-p)}{n}} = \sqrt{\dfrac{.4(1-.4)}{50}} = .0693$.

$P\left(\hat{p} > .6\right) = P\left(z > \dfrac{.6 - .4}{\sqrt{\dfrac{.4(1-.4)}{50}}} \right) = P(z > 2.89) = .5 - .4981 = .0019$ (using Table II, Appendix D)

b. Since the probability of observing a value of $\hat{p}$ larger than .6 is so small ($p = .0019$) and we observed a value of $\hat{p} = .62$, we would conclude that the true proportion of adult cell phone owners who download an "app" is not .4 but something larger than .4.

c. If the value of $\hat{p} = .62$ was obtained at a convention for the International Association for the Wireless Telecommunications Industry, then it is probably not representative of the population of all adult cell phone owners. Those who attend such a convention would tend to be more "tech" savvy than the population of all adult cell phone owners. The value of $\hat{p} = .62$ would be larger than what we would expect from the general population.

5.49 a. $E(\hat{p}) = \mu_{\hat{p}} = p = .92$

b. By the Central Limit Theorem, the sampling distribution of $\hat{p}$ will be approximately normal since the sample size is sufficiently large, with $\mu_{\hat{p}} = p = .92$ and $\sigma_{\hat{p}} = \sqrt{\dfrac{p(1-p)}{n}} = \sqrt{\dfrac{.92(1-.92)}{1000}} = .0086$.

$$P\left(\hat{p} < \frac{900}{1000}\right) = P(\hat{p} < .9) = P\left(z < \frac{.9 - .92}{\sqrt{\dfrac{.92(1-.92)}{1000}}}\right) = P(z < -2.33) = .5 - .4901 = .0099$$

(using Table II, Appendix D)

5.51 a. "The sampling distribution of the sample statistic A" is the probability distribution of the variable A.

b. "A" is an unbiased estimator of α if the mean of the sampling distribution of A is α.

c. If both A and B are unbiased estimators of α, then the statistic whose standard deviation is smaller is a better estimator of α.

d. No. The Central Limit Theorem applies only to the sample mean. If A is the sample mean, $\bar{x}$, and n is sufficiently large, then the Central Limit Theorem will apply. However, both A and B cannot be sample means. Thus, we cannot apply the Central Limit Theorem to both A and B.

5.53 By the Central Limit Theorem, the sampling distribution of $\bar{x}$ is approximately normal.

$$\mu_{\bar{x}} = \mu = 19.6 \,, \ \sigma_{\bar{x}} = \frac{3.2}{\sqrt{68}} = .388$$

a. $P(\bar{x} \le 19.6) = P\left(z \le \dfrac{19.6 - 19.6}{.388}\right) = P(z \le 0) = .5$ (Using Table II, Appendix D)

b. $P(\bar{x} \le 19) = P\left(z \le \dfrac{19 - 19.6}{.388}\right) = P(z \le -1.55) = .5 - .4394 = .0606$ (Using Table II, Appendix D)

c. $P(\bar{x} \ge 20.1) = P\left(z \ge \dfrac{20.1 - 19.6}{.388}\right) = P(z \ge 1.29) = .5 - .4015 = .0985$ (Using Table II, Appendix D)

d. $P(19.2 \le \bar{x} \le 20.6) = P\left(\dfrac{19.2 - 19.6}{.388} < z < \dfrac{20.6 - 19.6}{.388}\right)$

$$= P(-1.03 \le z \le 2.58) = .3485 + .4951 = .8436 \quad \text{(Using Table II, Appendix D)}$$

5.55   By the Central Limit Theorem, the sampling distribution of $\hat{p}$ will be approximately normal since the

sample size is sufficiently large with $\mu_{\hat{p}} = p = .8$ and $\sigma_{\hat{p}} = \sqrt{\dfrac{p(1-p)}{n}} = \sqrt{\dfrac{.8(1-.8)}{300}} = .0231$.

a. $P(\hat{p} < .83) = P\left(z < \dfrac{.83 - .8}{\sqrt{\dfrac{.8(1-.8)}{300}}} \right) = P(z < 1.30) = .5 + .4032 = .9032$ (using Table II, Appendix D)

b. $P(\hat{p} > .75) = P\left(z > \dfrac{.75 - .8}{\sqrt{\dfrac{.8(1-.8)}{300}}} \right) = P(z > -2.17) = .5 + .4850 = .9850$ (using Table II, Appendix D)

c. $P(.79 < \hat{p} < .81) = P\left(\dfrac{.79 - .8}{\sqrt{\dfrac{.8(1-.8)}{300}}} < z < \dfrac{.81 - .8}{\sqrt{\dfrac{.8(1-.8)}{300}}} \right) = P(-.43 < z < .43) = .1664 + .1664 = .3328$

         (using Table II, Appendix D)

5.57   Answers will vary. One hundred samples of size $n = 2$ were selected from a uniform distribution on the
         interval from 0 to 10. The process was repeated for samples of size $n = 5$, $n = 10$, $n = 30$, and $n = 50$. For
         each sample, the value of $\bar{x}$ was computed. Using MINITAB, the histograms for each set of 100 $\bar{x}$'s were
         constructed:

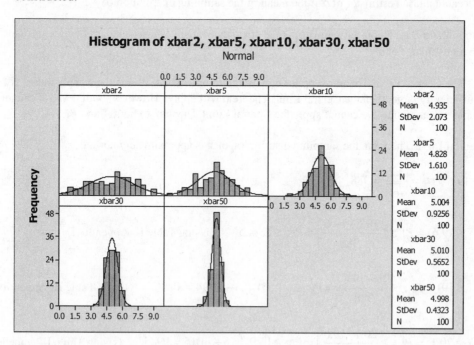

For small sizes of n, the sampling distributions of $\bar{x}$ are somewhat normal. As n increases, the sampling
distributions of $\bar{x}$ become more normal.

5.59   Given: $\mu = 100$ and $\sigma = 10$

n	1	5	10	20	30	40	50
$\dfrac{\sigma}{\sqrt{n}}$	10	4.472	3.162	2.236	1.826	1.581	1.414

The graph of $\dfrac{\sigma}{\sqrt{n}}$ against n is given here:

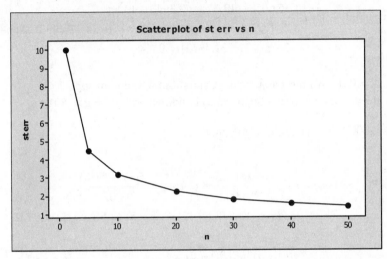

5.61   By the Central Limit Theorem, the sampling distribution of $\bar{x}$ is approximately normal with $\mu_{\bar{x}} = \mu = 19$

and $\sigma_{\bar{x}} = \dfrac{\sigma}{\sqrt{n}} = \dfrac{65}{\sqrt{100}} = 6.5$.

$$P(\bar{x} < 10) = P\left(z < \frac{10-19}{6.5}\right) = P(z < -1.38) = .5 - .4162 = .0838 \text{ (using Table II, Appendix D)}$$

5.63   a. $E(\hat{p}) = \mu_{\hat{p}} = p = .60$

b. $\sigma_{\hat{p}} = \sqrt{\dfrac{p(1-p)}{n}} = \sqrt{\dfrac{.6(1-.6)}{75}} = .0566$

c.   By the Central Limit Theorem, the sampling distribution of $\hat{p}$ will be approximately normal since the sample size is sufficiently large.

d. $P(\hat{p} > .70) = P\left(z > \dfrac{.70 - .6}{\sqrt{\dfrac{.6(1-.6)}{75}}}\right) = P(z > 1.77) = .5 - .4616 = .0384 \text{ (using Table II, Appendix D)}$

5.65   a.   By the Central Limit Theorem, the sampling distribution of $\bar{x}$ is approximately normal with $\mu_{\bar{x}} = \mu$ and $\sigma_{\bar{x}} = \sigma / \sqrt{n} = \sigma / \sqrt{50}$.

b. $\mu_{\bar{x}} = \mu = 40$ and $\sigma_{\bar{x}} = \sigma / \sqrt{50} = 12 / \sqrt{50} = 1.6971$.

$$P(\bar{x} \geq 44) = P\left(z \geq \frac{44 - 40}{1.6971} \right) = P(z \geq 2.36) = .5 - .4909 = .0091 \text{ (using Table II, Appendix D)}$$

c. $\mu \pm 2\sigma / \sqrt{n} \Rightarrow 40 \pm 2(1.6971) \Rightarrow 40 \pm 3.3942 \Rightarrow (36.6058,\ 43.3942)$

$$P(36.6058 \leq \bar{x} \leq 43.3942) = P\left(\frac{36.6058 - 40}{1.6971} \leq z \leq \frac{43.3942 - 40}{1.6971} \right) \text{ (using Table II, Appendix D)}$$
$$= P(-2 \leq z \leq 2) = 2(.4772) = .9544$$

5.67 From Exercise 5.66, $\sigma = .001$. We must assume the Central Limit Theorem applies (n is only 25). Thus, the distribution of $\bar{x}$ is approximately normal with $\mu_{\bar{x}} = \mu = .501$

and $\sigma_{\bar{x}} = \dfrac{\sigma}{\sqrt{n}} = \dfrac{.001}{\sqrt{25}} = .0002$. Using Table II, Appendix D,

$$P(\bar{x} < .4994) + P(\bar{x} > .5006) = P\left(z < \frac{.4994 - .501}{.0002} \right) + P\left(z > \frac{.5006 - .501}{.0002} \right)$$
$$= P(z < -8) + P(z > -2) = (.5 - .5) + (.5 + .4772) = .9772$$

5.69 a. $E(\hat{p}) = \mu_{\hat{p}} = p = .2$ and $\sigma_{\hat{p}} = \sqrt{\dfrac{p(1-p)}{n}} = \sqrt{\dfrac{.2(1-.2)}{250}} = .0253$

b. $E(\hat{p}) \pm 2\sigma_{\hat{p}} \Rightarrow .2 \pm 2(.0253) \Rightarrow .2 \pm .0506 \Rightarrow (.1494,\ .2506)$

c. By the Central Limit Theorem, the sampling distribution of $\hat{p}$ will be approximately normal since the sample size is sufficiently large. Thus,

$$P(.1494 \leq \hat{p} \leq .2506) = P\left(\frac{.1494 - .2}{.0253} \leq z \leq \frac{.2506 - .2}{.0253} \right) = P(-2 \leq z \leq 2) = .4772 + .4772 = .9544$$

5.71 a. Let p_1 = probability of an error = $1/100 = .01$ and p_2 = probability of an error resulting in a significant problem = $1/500 = .002$.

Let $\hat{p}_1$ = proportion of errors. Then $E(\hat{p}_1) = \mu_{\hat{p}_1} = p_1 = .01$.

Let $\hat{p}_2$ = proportion of significant errors. Then $E(\hat{p}_2) = \mu_{\hat{p}_2} = p_2 = .002$.

b. Since the distribution of $\hat{p}_2$ will be approximately normal by the Central Limit Theorem, we would expect the proportion of significant errors to fall within 2 standard deviations of the expected value. The interval would be:

$$\hat{p}_2 \pm 2\sigma_{\hat{p}_2} \Rightarrow .002 \pm 2\sqrt{\frac{.002(1-.002)}{60,000}} \Rightarrow .002 \pm .00036 \Rightarrow (.00164,\ .00236)$$

5.73   a.   If x is an exponential random variable, then $\mu = E(x) = \theta = 60$. The standard deviation of x is
$\sigma = \theta = 60$.

Then, $E(\overline{x}) = \mu_{\overline{x}} = \mu = 60$; $V(\overline{x}) = \sigma_{\overline{x}}^2 = \dfrac{\sigma^2}{n} = \dfrac{60^2}{100} = 36$

     b.   Because the sample size is fairly large, the Central Limit Theorem says that the sampling distribution of $\overline{x}$ is approximately normal.

     c. $P(\overline{x} \leq 30) = P\left(z \leq \dfrac{30-60}{\sqrt{36}} \right) = P(z \leq -5.0) \approx .5 - .5 = 0$ (using Table II, Appendix D)

5.75   Answers will vary. We are to assume that the fecal bacteria concentrations of water specimens follow an approximate normal distribution. Now, suppose that the distribution of the fecal bacteria concentration at a beach is normal with a true mean of 360 and with a standard deviation of 40. If only a single sample was selected, then the probability of getting an observation at the 400 level or higher would be:

$$P(x \geq 400) = P\left(z \geq \frac{400-360}{40} \right) = P(z \geq 1) = .5 - .3413 = .1587 \text{ (using Table II, Appendix D)}$$

Thus, even if the water is safe, the beach would be closed approximately 15.87% of the time.

On the other hand, if the mean was 440 and the standard deviation was still 40, then the probability of getting a single observation less than the 400 level would be:

$$P(x \leq 400) = P\left(z \leq \frac{400-440}{40} \right) = P(z \leq -1) = .5 - .3413 = .1587 \text{ (using Table II, Appendix D)}$$

Thus, the beach would remain open approximately 15.78% of the time when it should be closed.

Now, suppose we took a random sample of 64 water specimens. The sampling distribution of $\overline{x}$ is approximately normal by the Central Limit Theorem with $\mu_{\overline{x}} = \mu$ and $\sigma_{\overline{x}} = \dfrac{\sigma}{\sqrt{n}} = \dfrac{40}{\sqrt{64}} = 5$.

If $\mu = 360$, $P(\overline{x} \geq 400) = P\left(z \leq \dfrac{400-360}{5} \right) = P(z \geq 8) \approx .5 - .5 = 0$. Thus, the beach would never be shut down if the water was actually safe if we took samples of size 64.

If $\mu = 440$, $P(\overline{x} \leq 400) = P\left(z \leq \dfrac{400-440}{5} \right) = P(z \leq -8) \approx .5 - .5 = 0$. Thus, the beach would never be left open if the water was actually unsafe if we took samples of size 64.

The single sample standard can lead to unsafe decisions or inconvenient decisions, but is much easier to collect than samples of size 64.

Chapter 6
Inferences Based on a Single Sample:
Estimation with Confidence Intervals

6.1 a. For $\alpha = .10$, $\alpha/2 = .10/2 = .05$. $z_{\alpha/2} = z_{.05}$ is the z-score with .05 of the area to the right of it. The area between 0 and $z_{.05}$ is $.5 - .05 = .4500$. Using Table II, Appendix D, $z_{.05} = 1.645$.

  b. For $\alpha = .01$, $\alpha/2 = .01/2 = .005$. $z_{\alpha/2} = z_{.005}$ is the z-score with .005 of the area to the right of it. The area between 0 and $z_{.005}$ is $.5 - .005 = .4950$. Using Table II, Appendix D, $z_{.005} = 2.575$.

  c. For $\alpha = .05$, $\alpha/2 = .05/2 = .025$. $z_{\alpha/2} = z_{.025}$ is the z-score with .025 of the area to the right of it. The area between 0 and $z_{.025}$ is $.5 - .025 = .4750$. Using Table II, Appendix D, $z_{.025} = 1.96$.

  d. For $\alpha = .20$, $\alpha/2 = .20/2 = .10$. $z_{\alpha/2} = z_{.10}$ is the z-score with .10 of the area to the right of it. The area between 0 and $z_{.10}$ is $.5 - .10 = .4000$. Using Table II, Appendix D, $z_{.10} = 1.28$.

6.3 a. For confidence coefficient .95, $\alpha = .05$ and $\alpha/2 = .05/2 = .025$. From Table II, Appendix D, $z_{.025} = 1.96$. The confidence interval is:

$$\bar{x} \pm z_{.025} \frac{\sigma}{\sqrt{n}} \Rightarrow 28 \pm 1.96 \frac{\sqrt{12}}{\sqrt{75}} \Rightarrow 28 \pm .784 \Rightarrow (27.216,\ 28.784)$$

  b. $$\bar{x} \pm z_{.025} \frac{\sigma}{\sqrt{n}} \Rightarrow 102 \pm 1.96 \frac{\sqrt{22}}{\sqrt{200}} \Rightarrow 102 \pm .65 \Rightarrow (101.35,\ 102.65)$$

  c. $$\bar{x} \pm z_{.025} \frac{\sigma}{\sqrt{n}} \Rightarrow 15 \pm 1.96 \frac{.3}{\sqrt{100}} \Rightarrow 15 \pm .0588 \Rightarrow (14.9412,\ 15.0588)$$

  d. $$\bar{x} \pm z_{.025} \frac{\sigma}{\sqrt{n}} \Rightarrow 4.05 \pm 1.96 \frac{.83}{\sqrt{100}} \Rightarrow 4.05 \pm .163 \Rightarrow (3.887,\ 4.213)$$

  e. No. Since the sample size in each part was large (n ranged from 75 to 200), the Central Limit Theorem indicates that the sampling distribution of $\bar{x}$ is approximately normal.

6.5 a. For confidence coefficient .95, $\alpha = .05$ and $\alpha/2 = .05/2 = .025$. From Table II, Appendix D, $z_{.025} = 1.96$. The confidence interval is:

$$\bar{x} \pm z_{\alpha/2} \frac{s}{\sqrt{n}} \Rightarrow 26.2 \pm 1.96 \frac{4.1}{\sqrt{70}} \Rightarrow 26.2 \pm .96 \Rightarrow (25.24, 27.16)$$

  b. The confidence coefficient of .95 means that in repeated sampling, 95% of all confidence intervals constructed will include μ.

c. For confidence coefficient .99, $\alpha = .01$ and $\alpha/2 = .01/2 = .005$. From Table II, Appendix D, $z_{.005} = 2.58$. The confidence interval is:

$$\bar{x} \pm z_{\alpha/2}\frac{s}{\sqrt{n}} \Rightarrow 26.2 \pm 2.58\frac{4.1}{\sqrt{70}} \Rightarrow 26.2 \pm 1.26 \Rightarrow (24.94, 27.46)$$

d. As the confidence coefficient increases, the width of the confidence interval also increases.

e. Yes. Since the sample size is 70, the Central Limit Theorem applies. This ensures the distribution of $\bar{x}$ is normal, regardless of the original distribution.

6.7 A point estimator is a single value used to estimate the parameter, μ. An interval estimator is two values, an upper and lower bound, which define an interval with which we attempt to enclose the parameter, μ. An interval estimate also has a measure of confidence associated with it.

6.9 Yes. As long as the sample size is sufficiently large, the Central Limit Theorem says the distribution of $\bar{x}$ is approximately normal regardless of the original distribution.

6.11 a. The point estimate of μ is $\bar{x} = 3.11$.

b. For confidence coefficient .98, $\alpha = .02$ and $\alpha/2 = .02/2 = .01$. From Table II, Appendix D, $z_{.01} = 2.33$. The confidence interval is:

$$\bar{x} \pm z_{.01}\frac{\sigma}{\sqrt{n}} \Rightarrow 3.11 \pm 2.33\frac{.66}{\sqrt{307}} \Rightarrow 3.11 \pm .088 \Rightarrow (3.022, 3.198)$$

c. This statement is incorrect. Once the interval is constructed, there is no probability involved. The true mean is either in the interval or it is not. A better statement would be: "We are 98% confident that the true mean GPA will be between 3.022 and 3.198.

d. Since the sample size is so large ($n = 307$), the Central Limit Theorem applies. Thus, it does not matter whether the distributions of grades is skewed or not.

6.13 For confidence coefficient .90, $\alpha = .10$ and $\alpha/2 = .10/2 = .05$. From Table II, Appendix D, $z_{.05} = 1.645$. The 90% confidence interval is:

$$\bar{x} \pm z_{.05}\frac{s}{\sqrt{n}} \Rightarrow 6,563 \pm 1.645\frac{2,484}{\sqrt{1,751}} \Rightarrow 6,563 \pm 97.65 \Rightarrow (6,465.35, \ 6,660.65)$$

We are 90% confident that the true mean expenses per full-time equivalent employee of all U.S. Army hospitals is between $6,465.35 and $6,660.65.

6.15 a. Using MINITAB, the descriptive statistics are:

Descriptive Statistics: Wheels
```
Variable    N    Mean   StDev  Minimum     Q1  Median     Q3  Maximum
Wheels     28   3.214   1.371    1.000  2.000   3.000  4.000    8.000
```

For confidence coefficient .99, $\alpha=.01$ and $\alpha/2=.01/2=.005$. From Table II, Appendix D, $z_{.005}=2.58$. The confidence interval is:

$$\bar{x}\pm z_{.005}\frac{\sigma}{\sqrt{n}}\Rightarrow 67.755\pm 2.58\frac{1.371}{\sqrt{28}}\Rightarrow 3.214\pm.668\Rightarrow(2.546,\ 3.882)$$

b.   We are 99% confident that the true mean number of wheels used on all social robots is between 2.546 and 3.882.

c.   99% of all similarly constructed confidence intervals will contain the true mean.

6.17   a.   The target parameter is the population mean 20118 salary of these 500 CEOs who participated in the *Forbes'* survey, μ.

b.   Answers will vary. Using MINITAB, a sample of 50 CEOs was selected. The ranks of the 50 selected are:

9, 10, 14, 18, 19, 22, 25, 32, 38, 45, 49, 50, 55, 60, 66, 69, 77, 96, 104, 106, 115, 147, 152, 167, 192, 197, 209, 213, 229, 241, 245, 261, 268, 292, 305, 309, 325, 337, 342, 358, 364, 370, 376, 384, 405, 417, 423, 433, 470, 482.

c.   Using MINITAB, the descriptive statistics are:

Descriptive Statistics: Pay ($mil)

Variable	N	Mean	StDev	Minimum	Q1	Median	Q3	Maximum
Pay ($mil)	50	12.40	10.34	0.940	4.20	7.18	19.47	37.90

The sample mean is $\bar{x}=12.40$ and the sample standard deviation is $s=10.34$.

d.   Using MINITAB, the descriptive statistics for the entire data set is:

Descriptive Statistics: Pay ($mil)

Variable	N	Mean	StDev	Minimum	Q1	Median	Q3	Maximum
Pay ($mil)	478	9.247	9.842	0.000000000	3.413	6.100	11.346	101.965

From the above, the standard deviation of the population is $9.842 million.

e.   For confidence coefficient .99, $\alpha=.01$ and $\alpha/2=.01/2=.005$. From Table II, Appendix D, $z_{.005}=2.58$. The confidence interval is:

$$\bar{x}\pm z_{.005}\frac{\sigma}{\sqrt{n}}\Rightarrow 12.40\pm 2.58\frac{9.84}{\sqrt{50}}\Rightarrow 12.40\pm 3.59\Rightarrow(8.81,\ 15.99)$$

f.   We are 99% confident that the true mean salary of all 500 CEOs in the *Forbes'* survey is between $8.81 million and $15.99 million.

g.   From part d, the true mean salary of all 500 CEOs is $9.247 million. This value does fall within the 99% confidence interval that we found in part e.

6.19   a.   An estimate of the true mean Mach rating score of all purchasing managers is $\bar{x}=99.6$.

b. For confidence coefficient .95, $\alpha = .05$ and $\alpha / 2 = .05 / 2 = .025$. From Table II, Appendix D, $z_{.025} = 1.96$. The 95% confidence interval is:

$$\bar{x} \pm z_{\alpha/2} \frac{s}{\sqrt{n}} \Rightarrow 99.6 \pm 1.96 \frac{12.6}{\sqrt{122}} \Rightarrow 99.6 \pm 2.24 \Rightarrow (97.36, \ 101.84)$$

c. We are 95% confident that the true Mach rating score of all purchasing managers is between 97.36 and 101.84.

d. Yes, there is evidence to dispute this claim. We are 95% confident that the true mean Mach rating score is between 97.36 and 101.84. It would be very unlikely that the true means Mach scores is as low as 85.

6.21 To answer the question, we will first form 90% confidence intervals for each of the 2 SAT scores.

For confidence coefficient .90, $\alpha = .10$ and $\alpha / 2 = .10 / 2 = .05$. From Table II, Appendix D, $z_{.05} = 1.645$. The confidence interval for SAT-Mathematics scores is:

$$\bar{x} \pm z_{\alpha/2} \frac{s}{\sqrt{n}} \Rightarrow 19 \pm 1.645 \frac{65}{\sqrt{265}} \Rightarrow 19 \pm 6.57 \Rightarrow (12.43, \ 25.57)$$

We are 90% confident that the mean change in SAT-Mathematics score is between 12.43 and 25.57 points.

The confidence interval for SAT-Verbal scores is:

$$\bar{x} \pm z_{\alpha/2} \frac{s}{\sqrt{n}} \Rightarrow 7 \pm 1.645 \frac{49}{\sqrt{265}} \Rightarrow 7 \pm 4.95 \Rightarrow (2.05, \ 11.95)$$

We are 90% confident that the mean change in SAT-Verbal score is between 2.05 and 11.95 points.

The SAT-Mathematics test would be the most likely of the two to have 15 as the mean change in score. This value of 15 is in the 90% confidence interval for the mean change in SAT-Mathematics score. However, 15 does not fall in the 90% confidence interval for the mean SAT-Verbal test.

6.23 a. For confidence coefficient .80, $\alpha = .20$ and $\alpha / 2 = .20 / 2 = .10$. From Table II, Appendix D, $z_{.05} = 1.28$. From Table III, with df $= n - 1 = 5 - 1 = 4$, $t_{.10} = 1.533$.

b. For confidence coefficient .90, $\alpha = .10$ and $\alpha / 2 = .10 / 2 = .05$. From Table II, Appendix D, $z_{.05} = 1.645$. From Table III, with df $= n - 1 = 5 - 1 = 4$, $t_{.05} = 2.132$.

c. For confidence coefficient .95, $\alpha = .05$ and $\alpha / 2 = .05 / 2 = .025$. From Table II, Appendix D, $z_{.025} = 1.96$. From Table III, with df $= n - 1 = 5 - 1 = 4$, $t_{.025} = 2.776$.

d. For confidence coefficient .98, $\alpha = .02$ and $\alpha / 2 = .02 / 2 = .01$. From Table II, Appendix D, $z_{.01} = 2.33$. From Table III, with df $= n - 1 = 5 - 1 = 4$, $t_{.01} = 3.747$.

e. For confidence coefficient .99, $\alpha = .01$ and $\alpha / 2 = .01 / 2 = .005$. From Table II, Appendix D, $z_{.005} = 2.575$. From Table III, with df $= n - 1 = 5 - 1 = 4$, $t_{.005} = 4.604$.

f.   Both the t- and z-distributions are symmetric around 0 and mound-shaped. The t-distribution is more spread out than the z-distribution.

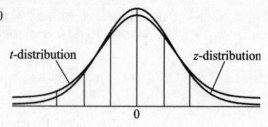

t-distribution z-distribution

6.25   a. $P(-t_0 < t < t_0) = .95$ where df = 10

Because of symmetry, the statement can be written

$$P(0 < t < t_0) = .475 \text{ where df} = 10$$

$$\Rightarrow P(t \geq t_0) = .025 \Rightarrow t_0 = 2.228$$

b. $P(t \leq -t_0 \text{ or } t \geq t_0) = .05$ where df = 10

$$\Rightarrow 2P(t \geq t_0) = .05 \Rightarrow P(t \geq t_0) = .025 \Rightarrow t_0 = 2.228$$

c. $P(t \leq t_0) = .05$ where df = 10

Because of symmetry, the statement can be written

$$\Rightarrow P(t \geq -t_0) = .05 \Rightarrow t_0 = -1.812$$

d. $P(t \leq -t_0 \text{ or } t \geq t_0) = .10$ where df = 20

$$\Rightarrow 2P(t \geq t_0) = .10 \Rightarrow P(t \geq t_0) = .05 \Rightarrow t_0 = 1.725$$

e. $P(t \leq -t_0 \text{ or } t \geq t_0) = .01$ where df = 5

$$\Rightarrow 2P(t \geq t_0) = .01 \Rightarrow P(t \geq t_0) = .005 \Rightarrow t_0 = 4.032$$

6.27   First, we must compute $\bar{x}$ and s.

$$\bar{x} = \frac{\sum x}{n} = \frac{30}{6} = 5, \quad s^2 = \frac{\sum x^2 - \frac{(\sum x)^2}{n}}{n-1} = \frac{176 - \frac{(30)^2}{6}}{6-1} = \frac{26}{5} = 5.2, \quad s = \sqrt{5.2} = 2.2804$$

a.   For confidence coefficient .90, $\alpha = .10$ and $\alpha/2 = .10/2 = .05$. From Table III, Appendix D, with df $= n - 1 = 6 - 1 = 5$, $t_{.05} = 2.015$. The 90% confidence interval is:

$$\bar{x} \pm t_{.05} \frac{s}{\sqrt{n}} \Rightarrow 5 \pm 2.015 \frac{2.2804}{\sqrt{6}} \Rightarrow 5 \pm 1.88 \Rightarrow (3.12, \ 6.88)$$

b.   For confidence coefficient .95, $\alpha = .05$ and $\alpha/2 = .05/2 = .025$. From Table III, Appendix D, with df $= n - 1 = 6 - 1 = 5$, $t_{.025} = 2.571$. The 95% confidence interval is:

$$\bar{x} \pm t_{.025} \frac{s}{\sqrt{n}} \Rightarrow 5 \pm 2.571 \frac{2.2804}{\sqrt{6}} \Rightarrow 5 \pm 2.39 \Rightarrow (2.61, \ 7.39)$$

d.   For confidence coefficient .99, $\alpha = .01$ and $\alpha/2 = .01/2 = .005$. From Table III, Appendix D, with df $= n - 1 = 6 - 1 = 5$, $t_{.005} = 4.032$. The 99% confidence interval is:

$$\overline{x} \pm t_{.005} \frac{s}{\sqrt{n}} \Rightarrow 5 \pm 4.032 \frac{2.2804}{\sqrt{6}} \Rightarrow 5 \pm 3.75 \Rightarrow (1.25, \ 8.75)$$

d.　a)　For confidence coefficient .90, $\alpha = .10$ and $\alpha / 2 = .10 / 2 = .05$. From Table III, Appendix D, with $df = n - 1 = 25 - 1 = 24$, $t_{.05} = 1.711$. The 90% confidence interval is:

$$\overline{x} \pm t_{.05} \frac{s}{\sqrt{n}} \Rightarrow 5 \pm 1.711 \frac{2.2804}{\sqrt{25}} \Rightarrow 5 \pm .78 \Rightarrow (4.22, \ 5.78)$$

　　b)　For confidence coefficient .95, $\alpha = .05$ and $\alpha / 2 = .05 / 2 = .025$. From Table III, Appendix D, with $df = n - 1 = 25 - 1 = 24$, $t_{.025} = 2.064$. The 95% confidence interval is:

$$\overline{x} \pm t_{.025} \frac{s}{\sqrt{n}} \Rightarrow 5 \pm 2.064 \frac{2.2804}{\sqrt{25}} \Rightarrow 5 \pm .94 \Rightarrow (4.06, \ 5.94)$$

　　c)　For confidence coefficient .99, $\alpha = .01$ and $\alpha / 2 = .01 / 2 = .005$. From Table III, Appendix D, with $df = n - 1 = 25 - 1 = 24$, $t_{.005} = 2.797$. The 99% confidence interval is:

$$\overline{x} \pm t_{.005} \frac{s}{\sqrt{n}} \Rightarrow 5 \pm 2.797 \frac{2.2804}{\sqrt{25}} \Rightarrow 5 \pm 1.28 \Rightarrow (3.72, \ 6.28)$$

Increasing the sample size decreases the width of the confidence interval.

6.29　a.　The target parameter is $\mu =$ mean trap spacing for the population of red spiny lobster fishermen fishing in Baja California Sur, Mexico.

　　b.　Using MINITAB, the descriptive statistics are:

Descriptive Statistics: Trap

Variable	N	Mean	StDev	Minimum	Q1	Median	Q3	Maximum
Trap	7	89.86	11.63	70.00	82.00	93.00	99.00	105.00

The point estimate of μ is $\overline{x} = 89.86$.

　　c.　For this problem, the sample size is $n = 7$. For a small sample size, the Central Limit Theorem does not apply. Therefore, we do not know what the sampling distribution of $\overline{x}$ is.

　　d.　For confidence coefficient .95, $\alpha = .05$ and $\alpha / 2 = .05 / 2 = .025$. From Table III, Appendix D, with $df = n - 1 = 7 - 1 = 6$, $t_{.025} = 2.447$. The 95% confidence interval is:

$$\overline{x} \pm t_{.025} \frac{s}{\sqrt{n}} \Rightarrow 89.86 \pm 2.447 \frac{11.63}{\sqrt{7}} \Rightarrow 89.86 \pm 10.756 \Rightarrow (79.104, \ 100.616)$$

　　e.　We are 95% confident that the true mean trap spacing for the population of red spiny lobster fishermen fishing in Baja California Sur, Mexico is between 79.104 and 100.616 meters.

　　f.　We must assume that the population of trap spacings is normally distributed and that the sample is a random sample.

6.31   For confidence coefficient .90, $\alpha = .10$ and $\alpha/2 = .10/2 = .05$. From Table III, Appendix D, with df $= n-1 = 25-1 = 24$, $t_{.05} = 1.711$. The 90% confidence interval is:

$$\bar{x} \pm t_{.05}\frac{s}{\sqrt{n}} \Rightarrow 75.4 \pm 1.711\frac{10.9}{\sqrt{25}} \Rightarrow 75.4 \pm 3.73 \Rightarrow (71.67, \; 79.13)$$

We are 90% confident that the true mean breaking strength of the white wood is between 71.67 and 79.13.

6.33   a.   The 95% confidence interval for the mean surface roughness of coated interior pipe is (1.63580, 2.12620).

    b.   No. Since 2.5 does not fall in the 95% confidence interval, it would be very unlikely that the average surface roughness would be as high as 2.5 micrometers.

6.35   a.   Using MINITAB, the descriptive statistics are:

Descriptive Statistics: Skid

Variable	N	Mean	StDev	Minimum	Q1	Median	Q3	Maximum
Skid	20	358.5	117.8	141.0	276.0	367.5	438.0	574.0

For confidence coefficient .95, $\alpha = .05$ and $\alpha/2 = .05/2 = .025$. From Table III, Appendix D, with df $= n-1 = 20-1 = 19$, $t_{.025} = 2.093$. The 95% confidence interval is:

$$\bar{x} \pm t_{.05}\frac{s}{\sqrt{n}} \Rightarrow 358.5 \pm 2.093\frac{117.8}{\sqrt{20}} \Rightarrow 358.5 \pm 55.13 \Rightarrow (303.37, \; 413.63)$$

    b.   We are 95% confident that the mean skidding distance is between 303.37 and 413.63 meters.

    c.   In order for the inference to be valid, the skidding distances must be from a normal distribution. We will use the four methods to check for normality. First, we will look at a histogram of the data.

Using MINITAB, the histogram of the data is:

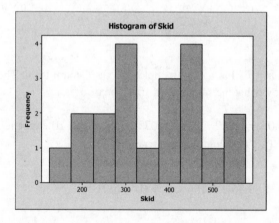

From the histogram, the data appear to be fairly mound-shaped. This indicates that the data may be normal.

Next, we look at the intervals $\bar{x} \pm s$, $\bar{x} \pm 2s$, $\bar{x} \pm 3s$. If the proportions of observations falling in each interval are approximately .68, .95, and 1.00, then the data are approximately normal.

$\bar{x} \pm s \Rightarrow 358.5 \pm 117.8 \Rightarrow (240.7, \ 476.3)$ 14 of the 20 values fall in this interval. The proportion is .70. This is very close to the .68 we would expect if the data were normal.

$\bar{x} \pm 2s \Rightarrow 358.5 \pm 2(117.8) \Rightarrow 358.5 \pm 235.6 \Rightarrow (122.9, \ 594.1)$ 20 of the 20 values fall in this interval. The proportion is 1.00. This is a larger than the .95 we would expect if the data were normal.

$\bar{x} \pm 3s \Rightarrow 358.5 \pm 3(117.8) \Rightarrow 358.5 \pm 353.4 \Rightarrow (5.1, \ 711.9)$ 20 of the 20 values fall in this interval. The proportion is 1.00. This is exactly the 1.00 we would expect if the data were normal.

From this method, it appears that the data may be normal.

Next, we look at the ratio of the *IQR* to *s*. $IQR = Q_U - Q_L = 438 - 276 = 162$.

$\dfrac{IQR}{s} = \dfrac{162}{117.8} = 1.37$ This is fairly close to the 1.3 we would expect if the data were normal. This method indicates the data may be normal.

Finally, using MINITAB, the normal probability plot is:

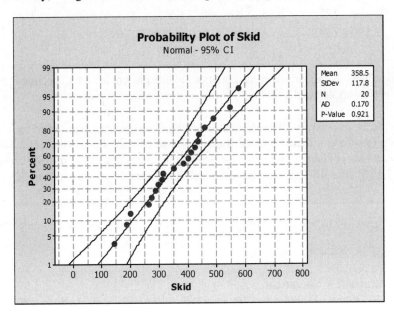

Since the data form a fairly straight line, the data may be normal.

From above, all the methods indicate the data may be normal. It appears that the assumption that the data come from a normal distribution is probably valid.

e. No. A distance of 425 meters falls above the 95% confidence interval that was computed in part **a**. It would be very unlikely to observe a mean skidding distance of at least 425 meters.

6.37   a.   Using MINITAB, the descriptive statistics are:

Descriptive Statistics: Diox Amt

Variable	Crude	N	Mean	StDev	Minimum	Q1	Median	Q3	Maximum
Diox Amt	No	10	2.590	1.542	0.100	1.125	2.850	4.000	4.000
	Yes	6	0.517	0.407	0.200	0.200	0.450	0.700	1.300

For confidence coefficient .95, $\alpha = .05$ and $\alpha/2 = .05/2 = .025$. From Table III, Appendix D, with $df = n-1 = 6-1 = 5$, $t_{.025} = 2.571$. The 90% confidence interval is:

$$\bar{x} \pm t_{.025}\frac{s}{\sqrt{n}} \Rightarrow .517 \pm 2.571\frac{.407}{\sqrt{6}} \Rightarrow .517 \pm .427 \Rightarrow (.090, .944)$$

We are 95% confident that the true mean amount of dioxide present in water specimens that contain oil is between .090 and .944mg/l.

     b.   For confidence coefficient .95, $\alpha = .05$ and $\alpha/2 = .05/2 = .025$. From Table III, Appendix D, with $df = n-1 = 10-1 = 9$, $t_{.025} = 2.262$. The 90% confidence interval is:

$$\bar{x} \pm t_{.025}\frac{s}{\sqrt{n}} \Rightarrow 2.590 \pm 2.262\frac{1.542}{\sqrt{10}} \Rightarrow 2.590 \pm 1.103 \Rightarrow (1.487, 3.693)$$

We are 95% confident that the true mean amount of dioxide present in water specimens that do not contain oil is between 1.487 and 3.693mg/l.

     c.   Since the confidence interval for the mean amount of dioxide present in water specimens that contain oil is entirely below the confidence interval for the mean amount of dioxide present in water specimens that do not contain oil, we can conclude that the mean amount of dioxide present in water containing oil is significantly less than the mean amount of dioxide present in water not containing oil.

6.39   a.   The population from which the sample was drawn is the Forbes 212 Biggest Private companies.

     b.   Using MINITAB, the descriptive statistics are:

Descriptive Statistics: Revenue

Variable	N	Mean	StDev	Minimum	Q1	Median	Q3	Maximum
Revenue	15	5.39	4.86	2.01	2.33	2.80	6.99	17.77

For confidence coefficient .98, $\alpha = .02$ and $\alpha/2 = .02/2 = .01$. From Table III, Appendix D, with $df = n-1 = 15-1 = 14$, $t_{.01} = 2.624$. The 98% confidence interval is:

$$\bar{x} \pm t_{.01}\frac{s}{\sqrt{n}} \Rightarrow 5.39 \pm 2.624\frac{4.86}{\sqrt{15}} \Rightarrow 5.39 \pm 3.293 \Rightarrow (2.097, 8.683)$$

     c.   We are 98% confident that the mean revenue is between $2.097 and $8.683 billion.

     d.   The population must be normally distributed in order for the procedure used in part **b** to be valid.

     e.   Yes. The value of $5.0 billion dollars falls in the 98% confidence interval computed in part **b.** Therefore, we should believe the claim.

6.41   The sample size is large enough if both $n\hat{p} \geq 15$ and $n\hat{q} \geq 15$.

    a.   When $n = 400$, $\hat{p} = .10$: $n\hat{p} = 400(.10) = 40$ and $n\hat{q} = 400(.90) = 360$

        Since both numbers are greater than or equal to 15, the sample size is sufficiently large to conclude the normal approximation is reasonable.

    b.   When $n = 50$, $\hat{p} = .10$: $n\hat{p} = 50(.10) = 5$ and $n\hat{q} = 50(.90) = 45$

        Since $n\hat{p}$ is less than 15, the sample size is not large enough to conclude the normal approximation is reasonable.

    c.   When $n = 20$, $\hat{p} = .5$: $n\hat{p} = 20(.5) = 10$ and $n\hat{q} = 20(.5) = 10$

        Since both numbers are less than 15, the sample size is not large enough to conclude the normal approximation is reasonable.

    d.   When $n = 20$, $\hat{p} = .3$: $n\hat{p} = 20(.3) = 6$ and $n\hat{q} = 20(.7) = 14$

        Since both numbers are less than 15, the sample size is not large enough to conclude the normal approximation is reasonable.

6.43   a.   The sample size is large enough if both $n\hat{p} \geq 15$ and $n\hat{q} \geq 15$.

        $n\hat{p} = 225(.46) = 103.5$ and $n\hat{q} = 225(.54) = 121.5$

        Since both numbers are greater than or equal to 15, the sample size is sufficiently large to conclude the normal approximation is reasonable.

    b.   For confidence coefficient .95, $\alpha = .05$ and $\alpha / 2 = .05 / 2 = .025$. From Table II, Appendix D, $z_{.025} = 1.96$. The 95% confidence interval is:

$$\hat{p} \pm z_{.025}\sqrt{\frac{pq}{n}} \Rightarrow \hat{p} \pm 1.96\sqrt{\frac{\hat{p}\hat{q}}{n}} \Rightarrow .46 \pm 1.96\sqrt{\frac{.46(.54)}{225}} \Rightarrow .46 \pm .065 \Rightarrow (.395, .525)$$

    c.   We are 95% confident the true value of p falls between .395 and .525.

    d.   "95% confidence interval" means that if repeated samples of size 225 were selected from the population and 95% confidence intervals formed, 95% of all confidence intervals will contain the true value of p.

6.45   a. $\hat{p} = \dfrac{x}{n} = \dfrac{818}{2,045} = .4$

    b.   By the Central Limit Theorem, the sampling distribution of $\hat{p}$ is approximately normal with $\mu_{\hat{p}} = p$

        and $\sigma_{\hat{p}} = \sqrt{\dfrac{pq}{n}}$ if n is sufficiently large. The sample size is sufficiently large if $n\hat{p} \geq 15$ and $n\hat{q} \geq 15$.

        For this exercise, $n\hat{p} = 2,045(.4) = 818$ and $n\hat{q} = 2,045(.6) = 1,227$. Since both values are greater than 15, the sample size is sufficiently large.

    c.   For confidence coefficient .95, $\alpha = .05$ and $\alpha / 2 = .05 / 2 = .025$. From Table II, Appendix D, $z_{.025} = 1.96$. The confidence interval is:

$$\hat{p} \pm z_{.025} \sqrt{\frac{\hat{p}\hat{q}}{n}} \Rightarrow .4 \pm 1.96 \sqrt{\frac{.4(.6)}{2,045}} \Rightarrow .4 \pm .021 \Rightarrow (.379, .421)$$

d. We are 95% confident that the true proportion of Arlington, Texas homes with market values that are overestimated by more than 10% by Zillow is between .379 and .421.

e. No, the claim is not believable. The 95% confidence interval constructed in part c does not contain .3. Thus, .3 is not a likely value for p.

6.47   a. The population of interest is all American adults.

b. The sample is the 1,000 adults surveyed.

c. The parameter of interest is the proportion of all American adults who think Starbucks coffee is overpriced, p.

d. The sample size is large enough if both $n\hat{p} \geq 15$ and $n\hat{q} \geq 15$.

$n\hat{p} = 1,000(.73) = 730$ and $n\hat{q} = 1,000(.27) = 270$

Since both numbers are greater than or equal to 15, the sample size is sufficiently large to conclude the normal approximation is reasonable.

For confidence coefficient .95, $\alpha = .05$ and $\alpha/2 = .05/2 = .025$. From Table II, Appendix D, $z_{.025} = 1.96$. The 95% confidence interval is:

$$\hat{p} \pm z_{\alpha/2} \sqrt{\frac{pq}{n}} \Rightarrow \hat{p} \pm z_{\alpha/2} \sqrt{\frac{\hat{p}\hat{q}}{n}} \Rightarrow .73 \pm 1.96 \sqrt{\frac{.73(.27)}{1000}} \Rightarrow .73 \pm .028 \Rightarrow (.702, .758)$$

We are 95% confident that the true proportion of all American adults who say Starbucks coffee is overpriced is between .702 and .758.

6.49   a. $\hat{p} = \dfrac{x}{n} = \dfrac{1,298}{2,163} = .60$

b. For confidence coefficient .95, $\alpha = .05$ and $\alpha/2 = .05/2 = .025$. From Table II, Appendix D, $z_{.025} = 1.96$. The confidence interval is:

$$\hat{p} \pm z_{.025} \sqrt{\frac{\hat{p}\hat{q}}{n}} \Rightarrow .60 \pm 1.96 \sqrt{\frac{.60(.40)}{2,163}} \Rightarrow .60 \pm .02 \Rightarrow (.58, .62)$$

c. We are 95% confident that the true proportion of all drivers who are using a cell phone while operating a motor passenger vehicle is between .58 and .62.

6.51 $\hat{p} = \dfrac{x}{n} = \dfrac{144}{351} = .41$

For confidence coefficient .90, $\alpha = .10$ and $\alpha/2 = .10/2 = .05$. From Table II, Appendix D, $z_{.05} = 1.645$. The confidence interval is:

$$\hat{p} \pm z_{.05} \sqrt{\frac{\hat{p}\hat{q}}{n}} \Rightarrow .41 \pm 1.645 \sqrt{\frac{.41(.59)}{351}} \Rightarrow .41 \pm .043 \Rightarrow (.367, .453)$$

We are 90% confident that the true probability of unauthorized use of computer systems at an organization is between .367 and .453. If we were to take repeated samples and form similar confidence intervals, 90% of the confidence intervals would contain the true probability.

6.53   Of the 2,778 sampled firms, 748 announced one or more acquisitions during the year 2000. Thus,

$$\hat{p} = \frac{x}{n} = \frac{748}{2,778} = .269$$

The sample size is large enough if both $n\hat{p} \geq 15$ and $n\hat{q} \geq 15$.

$$n\hat{p} = 2,778(.269) = 747 \text{ and } n\hat{q} = 2,778(.731) = 2,031$$

Since both numbers are greater than or equal to 15, the sample size is sufficiently large to conclude the normal approximation is reasonable.

For confidence coefficient .90, $\alpha = .10$ and $\alpha/2 = .10/2 = .05$. From Table II, Appendix D, $z_{.05} = 1.645$. The 90% confidence interval is:

$$\hat{p} \pm z_{\alpha/2} \sqrt{\frac{pq}{n}} \Rightarrow \hat{p} \pm 1.645 \sqrt{\frac{\hat{p}\hat{q}}{n}} \Rightarrow .269 \pm 1.645 \sqrt{\frac{.269(.731)}{2,778}} \Rightarrow .269 \pm .014 \Rightarrow (.255, \ .283)$$

We are 90% confident that the true proportion of all firms that announced one or more acquisitions during the year 2000 is between .255 and .283. Changing these to percentages, the results would be 25.5% and 28.3%.

6.55   a.   In order for the large-sample estimation method to be valid, $n\hat{p} \geq 15$ and $n\hat{q} \geq 15$. For this exercise,

$$\hat{p} = \frac{x}{n} = \frac{1}{333} = .003 \ , \ n\hat{p} = 333(.003) = .999 \ , \text{ and } n\hat{q} = 333(.997) = 332.001. \text{ Since one of these}$$

values is less than 15, the large-sample estimation method is not valid.

b. $\tilde{p} = \dfrac{x+2}{n+4} = \dfrac{1+2}{333+4} = \dfrac{3}{337} = .009$

For confidence coefficient .95, $\alpha = .05$ and $\alpha/2 = .05/2 = .025$. From Table II, Appendix D, $z_{.025} = 1.96$. The confidence interval is:

$$\tilde{p} \pm z_{.025} \sqrt{\frac{\tilde{p}\tilde{q}}{n+4}} \Rightarrow .009 \pm 1.96 \sqrt{\frac{.009(.991)}{333+4}} \Rightarrow .009 \pm .010 \Rightarrow (-.001, .019)$$

We are 95% confident that the true proportion of all mountain casualties that require a femoral shaft splint is between 0 and .019. (We know the proportion cannot be negative, so the lower end point must be 0.)

6.57   a.   The parameter of interest is p, the proportion of all fillets that are red snapper.

b.   The estimate of p is $\hat{p} = \dfrac{x}{n} = \dfrac{22-17}{22} = .23$

The sample size is large enough if both $n\hat{p} \geq 15$ and $n\hat{q} \geq 15$.

$$n\hat{p} = 22(.23) = 5 \text{ and } n\hat{q} = 22(.77) = 17$$

Since $n\hat{p}$ is less than 15, the sample size is not large enough to conclude the normal approximation is reasonable.

c.   We will use Wilson's adjustment to form the confidence interval.

Using Wilson's adjustment, the point estimate of the true proportion of all fillets that are not red snapper is

$$\tilde{p} = \frac{x+2}{n+4} = \frac{5+2}{22+4} = \frac{7}{26} = .269$$

For confidence coefficient .95, $\alpha = .05$ and $\alpha/2 = .05/2 = .025$. From Table II, Appendix D, $z_{.025} = 1.96$. Wilson's adjusted 95% confidence interval is:

$$\tilde{p} \pm z_{\alpha/2}\sqrt{\frac{\tilde{p}\tilde{q}}{n}} \Rightarrow .269 \pm 1.96\sqrt{\frac{.269(.731)}{22+4}} \Rightarrow .269 \pm .170 \Rightarrow (.099, \ .439)$$

d.   We are 95% confident that the true proportion of all fillets that are red snapper is between .099 and .439.

6.59 $\hat{p} = \dfrac{x}{n} = \dfrac{282,200}{332,000} = .85$

Suppose we form a 95% confidence interval for the true proportion of first class mail within the same city that is delivered on time between Dec. 10 and Mar. 3. For confidence coefficient .95, $\alpha = .05$ and $\alpha/2 = .05/2 = .025$. From Table II, Appendix D, $z_{.025} = 1.96$. The confidence interval is:

$$\hat{p} \pm z_{.025}\sqrt{\frac{\hat{p}\hat{q}}{n}} \Rightarrow .85 \pm 1.96\sqrt{\frac{.85(.15)}{332,000}} \Rightarrow .85 \pm .001 \Rightarrow (.849, .851)$$

We are 95% confident that the true proportion of first class mail within the same city that is delivered on time between Dec. 10 and Mar. 3 is between .849 and .851 or between 84.9% and 85.1%. This interval does not contain the reported 95% of first class mailed delivered on time. It appears that the performance of the USPS is below the standard during this time period.

6.61   a.   An estimate of σ is obtained from: range $\approx 4s \Rightarrow s \approx \dfrac{\text{range}}{4} = \dfrac{34-30}{4} = 1$

To compute the necessary sample size, use $n = \left(\dfrac{z_{\alpha/2}\sigma}{ME}\right)^2$ where $\alpha = .10$ and $\alpha/2 = .10/2 = .05$. From Table II, Appendix D, $z_{.05} = 1.645$.

Thus, $n = \left(\dfrac{1.645(1)}{.2}\right)^2 = 67.65 \approx 68$

b. A less conservative estimate of σ is obtained from range $\approx 6s \Rightarrow s \approx \dfrac{\text{range}}{6} = \dfrac{34-30}{6} = .6667$

Thus, $n = \left(\dfrac{z_{\alpha/2}\sigma}{ME} \right)^2 = \left(\dfrac{1.645(.6667)}{.2} \right)^2 = 30.07 \approx 31$

6.63 For confidence coefficient .90, $\alpha = .10$ and $\alpha/2 = .10/2 = .05$. From Table II, Appendix D, $z_{.05} = 1.645$.

We know $\hat{p}$ is in the middle of the interval, so $\hat{p} = \dfrac{.54 + .26}{2} = .4$

The confidence interval is $\hat{p} \pm z_{.05}\sqrt{\dfrac{\hat{p}\hat{q}}{n}} \Rightarrow .4 \pm 1.645\sqrt{\dfrac{.4(.6)}{n}}$

We know $.4 - 1.645\sqrt{\dfrac{.4(.6)}{n}} = .26$

$\Rightarrow .4 - \dfrac{.8059}{\sqrt{n}} = .26 \Rightarrow .4 - .26 = \dfrac{.8059}{\sqrt{n}} \Rightarrow \sqrt{n} = \dfrac{.8059}{.14} = 5.756 \Rightarrow n = 5.756^2 = 33.1 \approx 34$

6.65 a. The width of a confidence interval is $W = 2(ME) = 2z_{\alpha/2}\dfrac{\sigma}{\sqrt{n}}$

For confidence coefficient .95, $\alpha = .05$ and $\alpha/2 = .05/2 = .025$. From Table II, Appendix D, $z_{.025} = 1.96$.

For $n = 16$, $W = 2z_{\alpha/2}\dfrac{\sigma}{\sqrt{n}} = 2(1.96)\dfrac{1}{\sqrt{16}} = 0.98$

For $n = 25$, $W = 2z_{\alpha/2}\dfrac{\sigma}{\sqrt{n}} = 2(1.96)\dfrac{1}{\sqrt{25}} = 0.784$

For $n = 49$, $W = 2z_{\alpha/2}\dfrac{\sigma}{\sqrt{n}} = 2(1.96)\dfrac{1}{\sqrt{49}} = 0.56$

For $n = 100$, $W = 2z_{\alpha/2}\dfrac{\sigma}{\sqrt{n}} = 2(1.96)\dfrac{1}{\sqrt{100}} = 0.392$

For $n = 400$, $W = 2z_{\alpha/2}\dfrac{\sigma}{\sqrt{n}} = 2(1.96)\dfrac{1}{\sqrt{400}} = 0.196$

b.

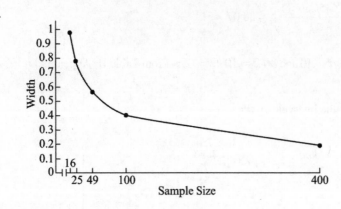

6.67   From Exercise 6.29, the standard deviation is 11.63. If the width of the interval is 5, then $ME = 5/2 = 2.5$.
For confidence coefficient .95, $\alpha = .05$ and $\alpha/2 = .05/2 = .025$. From Table II, Appendix D, $z_{.025} = 1.96$.

$$n = \left(\frac{z_{\alpha/2}\sigma}{ME}\right)^2 = \left(\frac{1.96(11.63)}{2.5}\right)^2 = 83.14 \approx 84$$

6.69   For confidence coefficient .90, $\alpha = .10$ and $\alpha/2 = .10/2 = .05$. From Table II, Appendix D, $z_{.05} = 1.645$.

$$n = \left(\frac{z_{\alpha/2}\sigma}{ME}\right)^2 = \left(\frac{1.645(10.9)}{4}\right)^2 = 20.09 \approx 21.$$ Thus, we would need a sample of size 21.

6.71   For confidence coefficient .90, $\alpha = .10$ and $\alpha/2 = .10/2 = .05$. From Table II, Appendix D, $z_{.05} = 1.645$.
Since we have no estimate given for the value of p, we will use .5. The sample size is:

$$n = \frac{z_{\alpha/2}^2 pq}{(ME)^2} = \frac{1.645^2(.5)(.5)}{.02^2} = 1,691.3 \approx 1,692$$

6.73   For confidence coefficient .99, $\alpha = .01$ and $\alpha/2 = .01/2 = .005$. From Table II, Appendix D, $z_{.005} = 2.575$.
From the previous estimate, we will use $\hat{p} = 1/3$ to estimate p.

$$n = \frac{z_{\alpha/2}^2 pq}{(ME)^2} = \frac{2.575^2(1/3)(2/3)}{.01^2} = 14,734.7 \approx 14,735$$

6.75   To compute the needed sample size, use $n = \left(\frac{z_{\alpha/2}\sigma}{ME}\right)^2$ where $\alpha = .05$ and $\alpha/2 = .05/2 = .025$. From Table
II, Appendix D, $z_{.025} = 1.96$.

Thus, for $s = 10$, $n = \left(\frac{1.96(10)}{3}\right)^2 = 42.68 \approx 43$

$$\text{For } s = 20, \ n = \left(\frac{1.96(20)}{3}\right)^2 = 170.72 \approx 171$$

$$\text{For } s = 30, \ n = \left(\frac{1.96(30)}{3}\right)^2 = 384.16 \approx 385$$

6.77   The bound is $ME = .05$. For confidence coefficient .99, $\alpha = .01$ and $\alpha/2 = .01/2 = .005$. From Table II, Appendix D, $z_{.005} = 2.575$.

We estimate p with $\hat{p} = 11/27 = .407$. Thus, $n = \dfrac{\left(z_{\alpha/2}\right)^2 pq}{(ME)^2} = \dfrac{2.575^2 (.407)(.593)}{.05^2} = 640.1 \approx 641$

The necessary sample size would be 641. The sample was not large enough.

6.79   a.   Percentage sampled $= \dfrac{n}{N}(100\%) = \dfrac{1000}{2500}(100\%) = 40\%$

Finite population correction factor: $\sqrt{\dfrac{N-n}{N}} = \sqrt{\dfrac{2500-1000}{2500}} = \sqrt{.6} = .7746$

b.   Percentage sampled $= \dfrac{n}{N}(100\%) = \dfrac{1000}{5000}(100\%) = 20\%$

Finite population correction factor: $\sqrt{\dfrac{N-n}{N}} = \sqrt{\dfrac{5000-1000}{5000}} = \sqrt{.8} = .8944$

c.   Percentage sampled $= \dfrac{n}{N}(100\%) = \dfrac{1000}{10,000}(100\%) = 10\%$

Finite population correction factor: $\sqrt{\dfrac{N-n}{N}} = \sqrt{\dfrac{10,000-1000}{10,000}} = \sqrt{.9} = .9487$

d.   Percentage sampled $= \dfrac{n}{N}(100\%) = \dfrac{1000}{100,000}(100\%) = 1\%$

Finite population correction factor: $\sqrt{\dfrac{N-n}{N}} = \sqrt{\dfrac{100,000-1000}{100,000}} = \sqrt{.99} = .995$

6.81   a. $\hat{\sigma}_{\bar{x}} = \dfrac{s}{\sqrt{n}}\sqrt{\dfrac{N-n}{N}} = \dfrac{50}{\sqrt{2000}}\sqrt{\dfrac{10,000-2000}{10,000}} = 1.00$

b. $\hat{\sigma}_{\bar{x}} = \dfrac{50}{\sqrt{4000}}\sqrt{\dfrac{10,000-4000}{10,000}} = .6124$

c. $\hat{\sigma}_{\bar{x}} = \dfrac{50}{\sqrt{10,000}}\sqrt{\dfrac{10,000-10,000}{10,000}} = 0$

d.   As n increases, $\sigma_{\bar{x}}$ decreases.

e.   We are computing the standard error of $\bar{x}$. If the entire population is sampled, then $\bar{x} = \mu$. There is no sampling error, so $\sigma_{\bar{x}} = 0$.

6.83   The approximate 95% confidence interval for p is

$$\hat{p} \pm 2\hat{\sigma}_{\hat{p}} \Rightarrow \hat{p} \pm 2\sqrt{\frac{\hat{p}(1 - \hat{p})}{n}}\sqrt{\frac{N - n}{N}} \Rightarrow .42 \pm 2\sqrt{\frac{.42(.58)}{1600}}\sqrt{\frac{6000 - 1600}{6000}} \Rightarrow .42 \pm .021 \Rightarrow (.399, .441)$$

6.85   a. $\bar{x} = \dfrac{\sum x}{n} = \dfrac{1081}{30} = 36.03$ $s^2 = \dfrac{\sum x^2 - \dfrac{(\sum x)^2}{n}}{n-1} = \dfrac{41,747 - \dfrac{1,081^2}{30}}{30-1} = 96.3782$

The approximate 95% confidence interval is:

$$\bar{x} \pm 2\hat{\sigma}_{\bar{x}} \Rightarrow \bar{x} \pm 2\frac{s}{\sqrt{n}}\sqrt{\frac{N-n}{N}} \Rightarrow 36.03 \pm 2\frac{\sqrt{96.3782}}{\sqrt{30}}\sqrt{\frac{300-30}{300}} \Rightarrow 36.03 \pm 3.40 \Rightarrow (32.63, \ 39.43)$$

b. $\hat{p} = \dfrac{x}{n} = \dfrac{21}{30} = .7$

The approximate 95% confidence interval is:

$$\hat{p} \pm 2\hat{\sigma}_{\hat{p}} \Rightarrow \hat{p} \pm 2\sqrt{\frac{\hat{p}(1 - \hat{p})}{n}}\sqrt{\frac{N - n}{N}} \Rightarrow .7 \pm 2\sqrt{\frac{.7(.3)}{30}}\sqrt{\frac{300-30}{300}} \Rightarrow .7 \pm .159 \Rightarrow (.541, .859)$$

6.87   a.   First, we must estimate p: $\hat{p} = \dfrac{x}{n} = \dfrac{759}{1,355} = .560$

For confidence coefficient .95, $\alpha = .05$ and $\alpha/2 = .05/2 = .025$. From Table II, Appendix D, $z_{.025} = 1.96$. Since $n/N = 1,355/1,696 = .799 > .05$, we must use the finite population correction factor. The 95% confidence interval is:

$$\hat{p} \pm z_{.025}\sqrt{\frac{\hat{p}\hat{q}}{n}\left(\frac{N-n}{N}\right)} \Rightarrow .560 \pm 1.96\sqrt{\frac{.560(.440)}{1,355}\left(\frac{1,696-1,355}{1,696}\right)} \Rightarrow .560 \pm .012 \Rightarrow (.548, .572)$$

b.   We used the finite correction factor because the sample size was very large compared to the population size.

c.   We are 95% confident that the true proportion of active NFL players who select a professional coach as the most influential in their career is between .548 and .572.

6.89   a.   First, we must calculate the sample mean:

$$\bar{x} = \frac{\sum\limits_{i=1}^{15} f_i x_i}{n} = \frac{3(108) + 2(55) + 1(500) + \cdots + 19(100)}{100} = \frac{15,646}{100} = 156.46$$

The point estimate of the mean value of the parts inventory is $\bar{x} = 156.46$.

b. The sample variance and standard deviation are:

$$s^2 = \frac{\displaystyle\sum_{i=1}^{15} f_i x_i^2 - \frac{\left(\sum f_i x_i\right)^2}{n}}{n-1} = \frac{3(108)^2 + 2(55)^2 + \cdots + 19(100)^2 - \frac{15,646^2}{100}}{100-1}$$

$$= \frac{6,776,336 - \dfrac{15,646^2}{100}}{99} = 43,720.83677$$

$$s = \sqrt{s^2} = \sqrt{43,720.83677} = 209.10$$

The estimated standard error is $\hat{\sigma}_{\bar{x}} = \dfrac{s}{\sqrt{n}}\sqrt{\dfrac{N-n}{N}} = \dfrac{209.10}{\sqrt{100}}\sqrt{\dfrac{500-100}{500}} = 18.7025$

c. The approximate 95% confidence interval is:

$$\bar{x} \pm 2\hat{\sigma}_{\bar{x}} \Rightarrow \bar{x} \pm 2\left(\frac{s}{\sqrt{n}}\right)\sqrt{\frac{N-n}{N}} \Rightarrow 156.46 \pm 2(18.7025) \Rightarrow 156.46 \pm 37.405 \Rightarrow (119.055,\ 193.865)$$

We are 95% confident that the mean value of the parts inventory is between $119.06 and $193.87.

d. Since the interval in part **c** does not include $300, the value of $300 is not a reasonable value for the mean value of the parts inventory.

6.91 $\hat{p} = \dfrac{x}{n} = \dfrac{15}{175} = .086$

The standard error of $\hat{p}$ is $\hat{\sigma}_{\hat{p}} = \sqrt{\dfrac{\hat{p}(1-\hat{p})}{n}\left(\dfrac{N-n}{N}\right)} = \sqrt{\dfrac{.086(1-.086)}{175}\left(\dfrac{3000-175}{3000}\right)} = .0206$

An approximate 95% confidence interval for p is $\hat{p} \pm 2\hat{\sigma}_{\hat{p}} \Rightarrow .086 \pm 2(.0206) \Rightarrow .086 \pm .041 \Rightarrow (.045,\ .127)$

Since .07 falls in the 95% confidence interval, it is not an uncommon value. Thus, there is no evidence that more than 7% of the corn-related products in this state have to be removed from shelves and warehouses.

6.93 a. For confidence level .90, $\alpha = .10$ and $\alpha/2 = .10/2 = .05$. Using Table IV, Appendix D, with $df = n-1 = 50-1 = 49$, $\chi^2_{.05,49} \approx 67.5048$ and $\chi^2_{.95,49} \approx 34.7642$. The 90% confidence interval is:

$$\frac{(n-1)s^2}{\chi^2_{.05}} \le \sigma^2 \le \frac{(n-1)s^2}{\chi^2_{.95}} \Rightarrow \frac{(50-1)2.5^2}{67.5048} \le \sigma^2 \le \frac{(50-1)2.5^2}{34.7642} \Rightarrow 4.537 \le \sigma^2 \le 8.809$$

b. For confidence level .90, $\alpha = .10$ and $\alpha/2 = .10/2 = .05$. Using Table IV, Appendix D, with $df = n-1 = 15-1 = 14$, $\chi^2_{.05,14} = 23.6848$ and $\chi^2_{.95,14} = 6.57063$. The 90% confidence interval is:

$$\frac{(n-1)s^2}{\chi^2_{.05}} \le \sigma^2 \le \frac{(n-1)s^2}{\chi^2_{.95}} \Rightarrow \frac{(15-1).02^2}{23.6848} \le \sigma^2 \le \frac{(15-1).02^2}{6.57063} \Rightarrow .00024 \le \sigma^2 \le .00085$$

c.   For confidence level .90, $\alpha = .10$ and $\alpha/2 = .10/2 = .05$. Using Table IV, Appendix D, with df $= n-1 = 22-1 = 21$, $\chi^2_{.05,21} = 32.6705$ and $\chi^2_{.95,21} = 11.5913$. The 90% confidence interval is:

$$\frac{(n-1)s^2}{\chi^2_{.05}} \leq \sigma^2 \leq \frac{(n-1)s^2}{\chi^2_{.95}} \Rightarrow \frac{(22-1)31.6^2}{32.6705} \leq \sigma^2 \leq \frac{(22-1)31.6^2}{11.5913} \Rightarrow 641.86 \leq \sigma^2 \leq 1,809.09$$

d.   For confidence level .90, $\alpha = .10$ and $\alpha/2 = .10/2 = .05$. Using Table IV, Appendix D, with df $= n-1 = 5-1 = 4$, $\chi^2_{.05,4} = 9.48773$ and $\chi^2_{.95,4} = .710721$. The 90% confidence interval is:

$$\frac{(n-1)s^2}{\chi^2_{.05}} \leq \sigma^2 \leq \frac{(n-1)s^2}{\chi^2_{.95}} \Rightarrow \frac{(5-1)1.5^2}{9.48773} \leq \sigma^2 \leq \frac{(5-1)1.5^2}{.710721} \Rightarrow .94859 \leq \sigma^2 \leq 12.6632$$

6.95   Using MINITAB, the descriptive statistics are:

Descriptive Statistics: x
```
Variable   N   Mean   StDev   Minimum    Q1   Median    Q3   Maximum
x          6   6.17   3.31    2.00     2.75    6.50    8.75    11.00
```

For confidence level .95, $\alpha = .05$ and $\alpha/2 = .05/2 = .025$. Using Table IV, Appendix D, with df $= n-1 = 6-1 = 5$, $\chi^2_{.025,5} = 12.8325$ and $\chi^2_{.975,5} = .831211$. The 95% confidence interval is:

$$\frac{(n-1)s^2}{\chi^2_{.025}} \leq \sigma^2 \leq \frac{(n-1)s^2}{\chi^2_{.975}} \Rightarrow \frac{(6-1)3.31^2}{12.8325} \leq \sigma^2 \leq \frac{(6-1)3.31^2}{.831211} \Rightarrow 4.269 \leq \sigma^2 \leq 65.904$$

6.97   a.   To find the confidence interval for σ, we first find the confidence interval for σ^2 and then take the square root of the endpoints. For confidence level .95, $\alpha = .05$ and $\alpha/2 = .05/2 = .025$. Using Table IV, Appendix D, with df $= n-1 = 55-1 = 54$, $\chi^2_{.025,54} \approx 71.4202$ and $\chi^2_{.975,54} \approx 32.3574$. The 95% confidence interval is:

$$\frac{(n-1)s^2}{\chi^2_{.025}} \leq \sigma^2 \leq \frac{(n-1)s^2}{\chi^2_{.975}} \Rightarrow \frac{(55-1)(.15)^2}{71.4202} \leq \sigma^2 \leq \frac{(55-1)(.15)^2}{32.3574} \Rightarrow .0170 \leq \sigma^2 \leq .0375$$

The 95% confidence interval for σ is: $\sqrt{.0170} \leq \sigma \leq \sqrt{.0375} \Rightarrow 0.130 \leq \sigma \leq 0.194$

We are 95% confident that the true standard deviation of the facial WHR values for all CEOs at publically traded Fortune 500 firms is between .130 and .194.

b. In order for the interval to be valid, the distribution of WHR values should be approximately normally distributed. The distribution should look like:

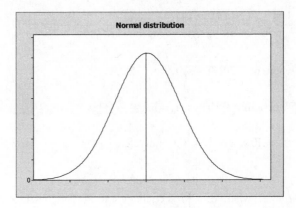

6.99   To find the confidence interval for σ, we first find the confidence interval for σ^2 and then take the square root of the endpoints. For confidence level .95, $\alpha = .05$ and $\alpha / 2 = .05 / 2 = .025$. Using Table IV, Appendix D, with df $= n-1 = 12-1 = 11$, $\chi^2_{.025,11} = 21.9200$ and $\chi^2_{.975,11} = 3.81575$. The 95% confidence interval is:

$$\frac{(n-1)s^2}{\chi^2_{.025}} \le \sigma^2 \le \frac{(n-1)s^2}{\chi^2_{.975}} \Rightarrow \frac{(12-1)(4,487)^2}{21.9200} \le \sigma^2 \le \frac{(12-1)(4,487)^2}{3.81575} \Rightarrow 10,103,323.86 \le \sigma^2 \le 58,039,666.91$$

The 95% confidence interval for σ is: $\sqrt{10,103,323.86} \le \sigma \le \sqrt{58,039,666.91} \Rightarrow 3,178.57 \le \sigma \le 7,618.38$

We are 95% confident that the true standard deviation of radon levels in tombs in the Valley of Kings is between 3,178.57 and 7,618.38 Bq/m^3.

6.101   Using MINITAB, the descriptive statistics are:

Descriptive Statistics: Drug
```
Variable   N     Mean   StDev   Variance   Minimum   Median   Maximum
Drug       50   89.291   3.183    10.134     81.790   89.375    94.830
```

For confidence level .99, $\alpha = .01$ and $\alpha / 2 = .01 / 2 = .005$. From Table IV, Appendix D, with df $= n-1 = 50-1 = 49$, $\chi^2_{.005,49} \approx 79.4900$ and $\chi^2_{.995,49} \approx 27.9907$. The 99% confidence interval is:

$$\frac{(n-1)s^2}{\chi^2_{.005}} \le \sigma^2 \le \frac{(n-1)s^2}{\chi^2_{.995}} \Rightarrow \frac{(50-1)(10.134)}{79.4900} \le \sigma^2 \le \frac{(50-1)(10.134)}{27.9907} \Rightarrow 6.247 \le \sigma^2 \le 17.740$$

We are 99% confident that the true population variation in drug concentrations for the new method is between 6.247 and 17.740.

6.103   Using MINITAB, the descriptive statistics are:

Descriptive Statistics: Spacing
```
Variable   N    Mean   StDev   Variance   Minimum   Median   Maximum
Spacing    7   89.86   11.63    135.14      70.00    93.00    105.00
```

For confidence level .99, $\alpha = .01$ and $\alpha / 2 = .01 / 2 = .005$. Using Table IV, Appendix D, with df $= n - 1 = 7 - 1 = 6$, $\chi^2_{.005,6} = 18.5476$ and $\chi^2_{.995,6} = .675727$. The 99% confidence interval is:

$$\frac{(n-1)s^2}{\chi^2_{.005}} \leq \sigma^2 \leq \frac{(n-1)s^2}{\chi^2_{.995}} \Rightarrow \frac{(7-1)(135.14)}{18.5476} \leq \sigma^2 \leq \frac{(7-1)(135.14)}{.675727} \Rightarrow 43.717 \leq \sigma^2 \leq 1,199.952$$

6.105 a. $P(t \leq t_0) = .05$ where df $= 20$. Thus, $t_0 = -1.725$.

     b. $P(t \geq t_0) = .005$ where df $= 9$. Thus, $t_0 = 3.250$.

     c. $P(t \leq -t_0 \text{ or } t \geq t_0) = .10$ where df $= 8$ is equivalent to $P(t \geq t_0) = .10 / 2 = .05$ where df $= 8$. Thus, $t_0 = 1.860$.

     d. $P(t \leq -t_0 \text{ or } t \geq t_0) = .01$ where df $= 17$ is equivalent to $P(t \geq t_0) = .01 / 2 = .005$ where df $= 17$. Thus, $t_0 = 2.898$.

6.107 a.   For confidence coefficient .99, $\alpha = .01$ and $\alpha / 2 = .01 / 2 = .005$. From Table II, Appendix D, $z_{.005} = 2.575$. The confidence interval is:

$$\bar{x} \pm z_{.005} \frac{s}{\sqrt{n}} \Rightarrow 32.5 \pm 2.575 \frac{30}{\sqrt{225}} \Rightarrow 32.5 \pm 5.15 \Rightarrow (27.35,\ 37.65)$$

     b.   The sample size is $n = \left(\frac{z_{\alpha/2}\sigma}{ME}\right)^2 = \left(\frac{2.575(30)}{.5}\right)^2 = 23,870.25 \approx 23,871$.

     c.   For confidence level .99, $\alpha = .01$ and $\alpha / 2 = .01 / 2 = .005$. Using MINITAB with df $= n - 1 = 225 - 1 = 224$, $\chi^2_{.005,224} = 282.268$ and $\chi^2_{.995,224} = 173.238$. The 99% confidence interval is:

$$\frac{(n-1)s^2}{\chi^2_{.005}} \leq \sigma^2 \leq \frac{(n-1)s^2}{\chi^2_{.995}} \Rightarrow \frac{(225-1)(30)^2}{282.268} \leq \sigma^2 \leq \frac{(225-1)(30)^2}{173.238} \Rightarrow 714.215 \leq \sigma^2 \leq 1,163.717$$

     d.   "99% confidence" means that if repeated samples of size 225 were selected from the population and 99% confidence intervals constructed for the population mean, then 99% of all the intervals constructed will contain the population mean.

6.109 a.   Using Table IV, Appendix D, with df $= n - 1 = 10 - 1 = 9$, $\chi^2_{.025,9} = 19.0228$ and $\chi^2_{.975,9} = 2.70039$.

     b.   Using Table IV, Appendix D, with df $= n - 1 = 20 - 1 = 19$, $\chi^2_{.025,19} = 32.8523$ and $\chi^2_{.975,19} = 8.90655$.

     c.   Using Table IV, Appendix D, with df $= n - 1 = 50 - 1 = 49$, $\chi^2_{.005,49} \approx 79.4900$ and $\chi^2_{.995,49} = 27.9907$.

6.111 The parameters of interest for the problems are:

     (1)   The question requires a categorical response. One parameter of interest might be the proportion, p, of all Americans over 18 years of age who think their health is generally very good or excellent.

    (2)   A parameter of interest might be the mean number of days, μ, in the previous 30 days that all Americans over 18 years of age felt that their physical health was not good because of injury or illness.

    (3)   A parameter of interest might be the mean number of days, μ, in the previous 30 days that all Americans over 18 years of age felt that their mental health was not good because of stress, depression, or problems with emotions.

    (4)   A parameter of interest might be the mean number of days, μ, in the previous 30 days that all Americans over 18 years of age felt that their physical or mental health prevented them from performing their usual activities.

6.113   a.   The point estimate of p is $\hat{p} = .11$.

    b.   The sample size is large enough if both $n\hat{p} \geq 15$ and $n\hat{q} \geq 15$.

$$n\hat{p} = 150(.11) = 16.5 \text{ and } n\hat{q} = 150(.89) = 133.5$$

Since both numbers are greater than or equal to 15, the sample size is sufficiently large to conclude the normal approximation is reasonable.

For confidence coefficient .95, $\alpha = .05$ and $\alpha/2 = .05/2 = .025$. From Table II, Appendix D, $z_{.025} = 1.96$. The confidence interval is:

$$\hat{p} \pm z_{.025}\sqrt{\frac{\hat{p}\hat{q}}{n}} \Rightarrow .11 \pm 1.96\sqrt{\frac{.11(.89)}{150}} \Rightarrow .11 \pm .05 \Rightarrow (.06, \ .16)$$

    c.   We are 95% confident that the true proportion of MSDSs that are satisfactorily completed is between .06 and .16.

6.115   For confidence coefficient .95, $\alpha = .05$ and $\alpha/2 = .05/2 = .025$. From Table II, Appendix D, $z_{.025} = 1.96$. For this study,

$$n = \left(\frac{z_{\alpha/2}\sigma}{ME}\right)^2 = \left(\frac{1.96(5)}{1}\right)^2 = 96.04 \approx 97 \quad \text{The sample size needed is 97.}$$

6.117   First, we must estimate p: $\hat{p} = \dfrac{x}{n} = \dfrac{50}{72} = .694$. The 95% confidence interval is:

$$\hat{p} \pm 2\sqrt{\frac{\hat{p}\hat{q}}{n}\left(\frac{N-n}{N}\right)} \Rightarrow .694 \pm 2\sqrt{\frac{.694(.306)}{72}\left(\frac{251-72}{251}\right)} \Rightarrow .694 \pm .092 \Rightarrow (.602, \ .786)$$

We are 95% confident that the true proportion of all New Jersey Governor's Council business members that have employees with substance abuse problems is between .602 and .786.

6.119   a.   For confidence coefficient .99, $\alpha = .01$ and $\alpha / 2 = .01 / 2 = .005$. From Table II, Appendix D, $z_{.005} = 2.58$. The 99% confidence interval is:

$$\bar{x} \pm z_{\alpha/2} \frac{s}{\sqrt{n}} \Rightarrow 4.25 \pm 2.58 \frac{12.02}{\sqrt{56}} \Rightarrow 4.25 \pm 4.14 \Rightarrow (0.11, \ 8.39)$$

   b.   We are 99% confident that the true mean number of blogs/forums per site of all Fortune 500 firms that provide blogs and forums for marketing tools is between 0.11 and 8.39.

   c.   No. Since our sample size is 56, the sampling distribution of $\bar{x}$ is approximately normal by the Central Limit Theorem.

6.121   There are a total of 96 channel catfish in the sample. The point estimate of p is $\hat{p} = \frac{x}{n} = \frac{96}{144} = .667$.

The sample size is large enough if both $n\hat{p} \geq 15$ and $n\hat{q} \geq 15$.

$$n\hat{p} = 144(.667) = 96 \text{ and } n\hat{q} = 144(.333) = 48$$

Since both numbers are greater than or equal to 15, the sample size is sufficiently large to conclude the normal approximation is reasonable.

For confidence coefficient .90, $\alpha = .10$ and $\alpha / 2 = .10 / 2 = .05$. From Table II, Appendix D, $z_{.05} = 1.645$. The confidence interval is:

$$\hat{p} \pm z_{.05} \sqrt{\frac{\hat{p}\hat{q}}{n}} \Rightarrow .667 \pm 1.645 \sqrt{\frac{.667(.333)}{144}} \Rightarrow .667 \pm .065 \Rightarrow (.602, \ .732)$$

We are 90% confident that the true proportion of channel catfish in the population is between .602 and .732.

6.123   a.   For confidence coefficient .99, $\alpha = .01$ and $\alpha / 2 = .01 / 2 = .005$. From Table III, Appendix D, with $df = n - 1 = 3 - 1 = 2$, $t_{.005} = 9.925$. The confidence interval is:

$$\bar{x} \pm t_{.005} \frac{s}{\sqrt{n}} \Rightarrow 49.3 \pm 9.925 \frac{1.5}{\sqrt{3}} \Rightarrow 49.3 \pm 8.60 \Rightarrow (40.70, \ 57.90)$$

   b.   We are 99% confident that the mean percentage of B(a)p removed from all soil specimens using the poison is between 40.70% and 57.90%.

   c.   We must assume that the distribution of the percentages of B(a)p removed from all soil specimens using the poison is normal.

   d.   Since the 99% confidence interval for the mean percent removed contains 50%, this would be a very possible value.

   e.   For confidence level .90, $\alpha = .10$ and $\alpha / 2 = .10 / 2 = .05$. Using Table IV, Appendix D, with $df = n - 1 = 3 - 1 = 2$, $\chi^2_{.05,2} = 5.99147$ and $\chi^2_{.95,2} = .102587$. The 90% confidence interval is:

$$\frac{(n-1)s^2}{\chi^2_{.05}} \leq \sigma^2 \leq \frac{(n-1)s^2}{\chi^2_{.95}} \Rightarrow \frac{(3-1)(1.5)^2}{5.99147} \leq \sigma^2 \leq \frac{(3-1)(1.5)^2}{.102587} \Rightarrow .751 \leq \sigma^2 \leq 43.865$$

We are 90% confident that the true population variance in the percentages of B(z)p removed is between .751 and 43.865.

6.125   a.   Using MINITAB, the descriptive statistics are:

Descriptive Statistics: IQ25, IQ60
```
Variable   N    Mean   Median   StDev   Minimum   Maximum     Q1      Q3
IQ25      36   66.83   66.50   14.36    41.00     94.00    54.25   80.00
IQ60      36   45.31   45.00   12.70    22.00     73.00    36.25   58.00
```

For confidence coefficient .99, $\alpha = .01$ and $\alpha/2 = .01/2 = .005$. From Table II, Appendix D, $z_{.005} = 2.58$. The confidence interval is:

$$\bar{x} \pm z_{.005}\frac{s}{\sqrt{n}} \Rightarrow 66.83 \pm 2.58\frac{14.36}{\sqrt{36}} \Rightarrow 66.83 \pm 6.17 \Rightarrow (60.66, \;\; 73.00)$$

We are 99% confident that the mean raw IQ score for all 25-year-olds is between 60.66 and 73.00.

   b.   We must assume that the sample is random, the observations are independent, and the sample size is sufficiently large.

   c.   For confidence coefficient .95, $\alpha = .05$ and $\alpha/2 = .05/2 = .025$. From Table II, Appendix D, $z_{.025} = 1.96$. The confidence interval is:

$$\bar{x} \pm z_{\alpha/2}\frac{s}{\sqrt{n}} \Rightarrow 45.31 \pm 1.96\frac{12.7}{\sqrt{36}} \Rightarrow 45.31 \pm 4.15 \Rightarrow (41.16, \;\; 49.46)$$

We are 95% confident that the mean raw IQ score for all 60-year-olds is between 41.16 and 49.46.

6.127   a.   The point estimate of p is $\hat{p} = \dfrac{x}{n} = \dfrac{52}{60} = .867$.

   b.   For confidence coefficient .95, $\alpha = .05$ and $\alpha/2 = .05/2 = .025$. From Table II, Appendix D, $z_{.025} = 1.96$. The confidence interval is:

$$\hat{p} \pm z_{.025}\sqrt{\frac{\hat{p}\hat{q}}{n}} \Rightarrow .867 \pm 1.96\sqrt{\frac{.867(.133)}{60}} \Rightarrow .867 \pm .086 \Rightarrow (.781, \;\; .953)$$

   c.   We are 95% confident that the true proportion of Wal-Mart stores in California that have more than 2 inaccurately priced items per 100 scanned is between .781 and .953.

   d.   If 99% of the California Wal-Mart stores are in compliance, then only 1% or .01 would not be. However, we found the 95% confidence interval for the proportion that are not in compliance is between .781 and .953. The value of .01 is not in this interval. Thus, it is not a likely value. This claim is not believable.

   e.   The sample size is large enough if both $n\hat{p} \geq 15$ and $n\hat{q} \geq 15$.

$n\hat{p} = 60(.867) = 52$ and $n\hat{q} = 60(.133) = 8$

Since $n\hat{q}$ is less than 15, the sample size is not large enough to conclude the normal approximation is reasonable. Thus, the confidence interval constructed in part b may not be valid. Any inference based on this interval is questionable.

f.   From above, the value of $\hat{p}$ is .867. For confidence coefficient .90, $\alpha = .10$ and $\alpha / 2 = .10 / 2 = .05$. From Table II, Appendix D, $z_{.05} = 1.645$.

$$n = \frac{z_{\alpha/2}^2 pq}{(ME)^2} = \frac{1.645^2(.867)(.133)}{.05^2} = 124.8 \approx 125$$

6.129   a.   Of the 24 observations, 20 were 2 weeks of vacation $\Rightarrow \hat{p} = 20 / 24 = .833$.

For confidence coefficient .95, $\alpha = .05$ and $\alpha / 2 = .05 / 2 = .025$. From Table II, Appendix D, $z_{.025} = 1.96$. The confidence interval is:

$$\hat{p} \pm z_{.025} \sqrt{\frac{\hat{p}\hat{q}}{n}} \Rightarrow .833 \pm 1.96 \sqrt{\frac{.833(.167)}{24}} \Rightarrow .833 \pm .149 \Rightarrow (.684, .982)$$

b.   The sample size is large enough if both $n\hat{p} \geq 15$ and $n\hat{q} \geq 15$.

$$n\hat{p} = 24(.833) = 20 \text{ and } n\hat{q} = 24(.167) = 4$$

Since $n\hat{q}$ is less than 15, the sample size is not sufficiently large to conclude the normal approximation is reasonable. The validity of the confidence interval is in question.

c.   The bound is $ME = .02$. For confidence coefficient .95, $\alpha = .05$ and $\alpha / 2 = .05 / 2 = .025$. From Table II, Appendix D, $z_{.025} = 1.96$. Thus,

$$n = \frac{(z_{\alpha/2})^2 pq}{(ME)^2} = \frac{1.96^2 (.833)(.167)}{.02^2} = 1,336.02 \approx 1,337$$

Thus, we would need a sample size of 1,337.

6.131   For confidence coefficient .95, $\alpha = .05$ and $\alpha / 2 = .05 / 2 = .025$. From Table II, Appendix D, $z_{.025} = 1.96$. From Exercise 6.130, a good approximation for p is .094. Also, $ME = .02$.

The sample size is $n = \dfrac{(z_{\alpha/2})^2 pq}{(ME)^2} = \dfrac{(1.96)^2(.094)(.906)}{.02^2} = 817.9 \approx 818$

You would need to take $n = 818$ samples.

6.133   Sampling error has to do with chance. In a population, there is variation – not all observations are the same. The sampling error has to do with the variation within a sample. By chance, one might get a sample that overestimates the mean just because all the observations in the sample happen to be high. Nonsampling error has to do with errors that have nothing to do with the sampling. These errors could be due to misunderstanding the question being asked, asking a question that the respondent does not know how to answer, etc.

6.135   a.   Answers will vary. Using a computer package, the 100 selected invoices are:

3590 1453 3726 2844 1767 1259 1091 1795 4431 4565 4586 1020 2135 1078 2659
4694 2572 4559 4601 965 4553 1052 3448 574 1360 3803 2247 1164 1862 2385
1255 4966 658 4007 4743 3746 3029 3723 3950 346 4744 312 4325 602 3137
4662 217 949 4580 4126 1794 2912   67 2514 3544 1596 2344 1603 3744 1886
 151 4258 183 1869 4509 4572 3875   34 3781 4993 1284 2177 4290   13 2717
1216 2052 4881 2220 3883 287 2977 3459 4639 2272 3620 4646 1544 919 3820
 121 2373 4684 2025 2254 4018 2304 3503 1634 2470

The observation numbers ending in 0 are highlighted above.

   b. $\hat{p} = \dfrac{x}{n} = \dfrac{10}{100} = .10$

For confidence coefficient .90, $\alpha = .10$ and $\alpha/2 = .10/2 = .05$. From Table II, Appendix D, $z_{.05} = 1.645$. The confidence interval is:

$$\hat{p} \pm z_{.05}\sqrt{\frac{\hat{p}\hat{q}}{n}} \Rightarrow .10 \pm 1.645\sqrt{\frac{.10(.90)}{100}} \Rightarrow .10 \pm .049 \Rightarrow (.051, .149)$$

   c.   Our sample proportion was $\hat{p} = .10$ which is equal to the true proportion. The confidence interval does contain .10.

6.137   a.   As long as the sample is random (and thus representative), a reliable estimate of the mean weight of all the scallops can be obtained.

   b.   The government is using only the sample mean to make a decision. Rather than using a point estimate, they should probably use a confidence interval to estimate the true mean weight of the scallops so they can include a measure of reliability.

   a.   We will form a 95% confidence interval for the mean weight of the scallops. Using MINITAB, the descriptive statistics are:

Descriptive Statistics: Weight

Variable	N	Mean	StDev	Minimum	Q1	Median	Q3	Maximum
Weight	18	0.9317	0.0753	0.8400	0.8800	0.9100	9800	1.1400

For confidence coefficient .95, $\alpha = .05$ and $\alpha/2 = .05/2 = .025$. From Table III, Appendix A, with df = $n - 1 = 18 - 1 = 17$, $t_{.025} = 2.110$. The 95% confidence interval is:

$$\bar{x} \pm t_{.025}\frac{s}{\sqrt{n}} \Rightarrow .932 \pm 2.110\frac{.0753}{\sqrt{18}} \Rightarrow .932 \pm .037 \Rightarrow (.895, .969)$$

We are 95% confident that the true mean weight of the scallops is between .8943 and .9691. Recall that the weights have been scaled so that a mean weight of 1 corresponds to 1/36 of a pound. Since the above confidence interval does not include 1, we have sufficient evidence to indicate that the minimum weight restriction was violated.

Chapter 7
Inferences Based on a Single Sample:
Tests of Hypothesis

7.1 The null hypothesis is the "status quo" hypothesis, while the alternative hypothesis is the research hypothesis.

7.3 The "level of significance" of a test is α. This is the probability that the test statistic will fall in the rejection region when the null hypothesis is true.

7.5 The four possible results are:
1. Rejecting the null hypothesis when it is true. This would be a Type I error.
2. Accepting the null hypothesis when it is true. This would be a correct decision.
3. Rejecting the null hypothesis when it is false. This would be a correct decision.
4. Accepting the null hypothesis when it is false. This would be a Type II error.

7.7 When you reject the null hypothesis in favor of the alternative hypothesis, this does not prove the alternative hypothesis is correct. We are $100(1-\alpha)\%$ confident that there is sufficient evidence to conclude that the alternative hypothesis is correct.

If we were to repeatedly draw samples from the population and perform the test each time, approximately $100(1-\alpha)\%$ of the tests performed would yield the correct decision.

7.9 a. Let p = proportion of college presidents who believe that their online education courses are as good as or superior to courses that utilize traditional face-to-face instruction. The null hypothesis would be:

$$H_0 : p = .68$$

b. The rejection region requires $\alpha / 2 = .01 / 2 = .005$ in each tail if the z-distribution. From Table II, Appendix D, $z_{.005} = 2.575$. The rejection region for a two-tailed test is $z < -2.575$ or $z > 2.575$.

7.11 Let p = student loan default rate in this year. To see if the student loan default rate is less than .07, we test:

$$H_0 : p = .07$$
$$H_a : p < .07$$

7.13 Let μ = mean caloric content of Virginia school lunches. To test the claim that after the testing period ended, the average caloric content dropped, we test:

$$H_0 : \mu = 863$$
$$H_a : \mu < 863$$

7.15 a. Since the company must give proof the drug is safe, the null hypothesis would be the drug is unsafe. The alternative hypothesis would be the drug is safe.

b. A Type I error would be concluding the drug is safe when it is not safe. A Type II error would be concluding the drug is not safe when it is. α is the probability of concluding the drug is safe when it is not. β is the probability of concluding the drug is not safe when it is.

c.   In this problem, it would be more important for α to be small. We would want the probability of concluding the drug is safe when it is not to be as small as possible.

7.17   a.   A Type I error is rejecting the null hypothesis when it is true. In a murder trial, we would be concluding that the accused is guilty when, in fact, he/she is innocent.

A Type II error is accepting the null hypothesis when it is false. In this case, we would be concluding that the accused is innocent when, in fact, he/she is guilty.

b.   Both errors are serious. However, if an innocent person is found guilty of murder and is put to death, there is no way to correct the error. On the other hand, if a guilty person is set free, he/she could murder again.

c.   In a jury trial, α is assumed to be smaller than β. The only way to convict the accused is for a unanimous decision of guilt. Thus, the probability of convicting an innocent person is set to be small.

d.   In order to get a unanimous vote to convict, there has to be overwhelming evidence of guilt. The probability of getting a unanimous vote of guilt if the person is really innocent will be very small.

e.   If a jury is prejudiced against a guilty verdict, the value of α will decrease. The probability of convicting an innocent person will be even smaller if the jury if prejudiced against a guilty verdict.

f.   If a jury is prejudiced against a guilty verdict, the value of β will increase. The probability of declaring a guilty person innocent will be larger if the jury is prejudiced against a guilty verdict.

7.19   a. $p = P(z \geq 1.20) = .5 - .3849 = .1151$

b. $p = P(z \leq -1.20) = .5 - .3849 = .1151$

c.   The $\bar{x}$ is $p = P(z \leq -1.20) + P(z \geq 1.20) = 2(.1151) = .2302$

7.21   a.   Since the p-value $= .10$ is greater than $\alpha = .05$, H_0 is not rejected.

b.   Since the p-value $= .05$ is less than $\alpha = .10$, H_0 is rejected.

c.   Since the p-value $= .001$ is less than $\alpha = .01$, H_0 is rejected.

d.   Since the p-value $= .05$ is greater than $\alpha = .025$, H_0 is not rejected.

e.   Since the p-value $= .45$ is greater than $\alpha = .10$, H_0 is not rejected.

7.23 p-value $= p = P(z \geq 2.17) = .5 - P(0 < z < 2.17) = .5 - .4850 = .0150$ (using Table II, Appendix D)

The probability of observing a test statistic of 2.17 or anything more unusual if the true mean is 100 is .0150. Since this probability is so small, there is evidence that the true mean is greater than 100.

7.25 p-value $= p = P(z \geq 2.17) + P(z \leq -2.17) = 2(.5 - .4850) = 2(.0150) = .0300$ (using Table II, Appendix D)

7.27   The smallest value of α for which the null hypothesis would be rejected is just greater than .06.

7.29   a.   The decision rule is to reject H_0 if $\overline{x} > 270$. Recall that $z = \dfrac{\overline{x} - \mu_0}{\sigma_{\overline{x}}}$.

Therefore, reject H_0 if $\overline{x} > 270$ can be written as reject H_0 if $z > \dfrac{\overline{x} - \mu_0}{\sigma_{\overline{x}}} = \dfrac{270 - 255}{63/\sqrt{81}} = 2.14$.

The decision rule in terms of z is to reject H_0 if $z > 2.14$.

b. $P(z > 2.14) = .5 - P(0 < z < 2.14) = .5 - .4838 = .0162$

7.31   a. $H_0 : \mu = .36$
$H_a : \mu < .36$

The test statistic is $z = \dfrac{\overline{x} - \mu_0}{\sigma_{\overline{x}}} \approx \dfrac{.323 - .36}{\sqrt{.034}/\sqrt{64}} = -1.61$

The rejection region requires $\alpha = .10$ in the lower tail of the z-distribution. From Table II, Appendix D, $z_{.10} = 1.28$. The rejection region is $z < -1.28$.

Since the observed value of the test statistic falls in the rejection region $(z = -1.61 < -1.28)$, H_0 is rejected. There is sufficient evidence to indicate the mean is less than .36 at $\alpha = .10$.

b. $H_0 : \mu = .36$
$H_a : \mu \neq .36$

The test statistic is $z = -1.61$ (see part **a**).

The rejection region requires $\alpha/2 = .10/2 = .05$ in the each tail of the z-distribution. From Table II, Appendix D, $z_{.05} = 1.645$. The rejection region is $z < -1.645$ or $z > 1.645$.

Since the observed value of the test statistic does not fall in the rejection region $(z = -1.61 < -1.645)$, H_0 is not rejected. There is insufficient evidence to indicate the mean is different from .36 at $\alpha = .10$.

7.33   a.   Let μ = true mean willingness to eat the brand of sliced apples. To determine if the true mean willingness to eat the brand of sliced apples exceeds 3, we test:

$H_0 : \mu = 3$
$H_a : \mu > 3$

The test statistic is $z = \dfrac{\overline{x} - \mu_0}{\dfrac{\sigma}{\sqrt{n}}} = \dfrac{3.69 - 3}{\dfrac{2.44}{\sqrt{408}}} = 5.71$.

The rejection region requires $\alpha = .05$ in the upper tail of the z-distribution. From Table II, Appendix D, $z_{.05} = 1.645$. The rejection region is $z > 1.645$.

Since the observed value of the test statistic falls in the rejection region $(z = 5.71 > 1.645)$, H_0 is rejected. There is sufficient evidence to indicate that the true mean willingness to eat the brand of sliced apples exceeds 3 at $\alpha = .05$.

b. Even though the willingness to eat scores are not normally distributed, the test in part a is valid. Because the sample size is so large $(n = 408)$, the Central Limit Theorem applies.

7.35   Let μ = true mean facial width-to-height ratio. To determine if the true mean facial width-to-height ratio differs from 2.2, we test:

$$H_0 : \mu = 2.2$$
$$H_a : \mu \neq 2.2$$

The test statistic is $z = \dfrac{\bar{x} - \mu_0}{\dfrac{\sigma}{\sqrt{n}}} = \dfrac{1.96 - 2.2}{\dfrac{.15}{\sqrt{55}}} = -11.87$.

The p-value is $p = P(z \leq -11.87) + P(z \geq 11.87) \approx 0 + 0 = 0$.

Since the p-value is so small $(p \approx 0)$, H_0 will be rejected for any reasonable value of α. There is sufficient evidence to indicate the true mean facial width-to-height ratio differs from 2.2 for $\alpha > .001$.

7.37   a. Let μ = true mean weight of golf tees. To determine if the process is not operating satisfactorily, we test:

$$H_0 : \mu = .250$$
$$H_a : \mu \neq .250$$

b. Using MINITAB, the descriptive statistics are:

Descriptive Statistics: Tees

Variable	N	Mean	Median	StDev	Minimum	Maximum	Q1	Q3
Tees	40	0.25248	0.25300	0.00223	0.24700	0.25600	0.25100	0.25400

Thus, $\bar{x} = .25248$ and $s = .00223$.

c. The test statistic is $z = \dfrac{\bar{x} - \mu_0}{\sigma_{\bar{x}}} \approx \dfrac{.25248 - .250}{.00223 / \sqrt{40}} = 7.03$.

d. The p-value is $p = P(z \leq -7.03) + P(z \geq 7.03) \approx 0 + 0 = 0$.

e. The rejection region requires $\alpha / 2 = .01 / 2 = .005$ in each tail of the z-distribution. From Table II, Appendix D, $z_{.005} = 2.575$. The rejection region is $z < -2.575$ or $z > 2.575$.

f. Since the observed value of the test statistic falls in the rejection region $(z = 7.03 > 2.575)$, H_0 is rejected. There is sufficient evidence to indicate the process is performing in an unsatisfactory manner at $\alpha = .01$.

g. α is the probability of a Type I error. A Type I error, in this case, is to say the process is unsatisfactory when, in fact, it is satisfactory. The risk, then, is to the producer since he will be spending time and money to repair a process that is not in error.

β is the probability of a Type II error. A Type II error, in this case, is to say the process is satisfactory when it, in fact, is not. This is the consumer's risk since he could unknowingly purchase a defective product.

7.39   a.   Let μ = mean estimated time to read the report. To determine if the students, on average, overestimate the time it takes to read the report, we test:

$$H_0 : \mu = 48$$
$$H_a : \mu > 48$$

The test statistic is $z = \dfrac{\bar{x} - \mu_0}{\sigma_{\bar{x}}} \approx \dfrac{60 - 48}{41/\sqrt{40}} = 1.85$.

The p-value is $p = P(z \geq 1.85) = .5 - .4678 = .0322$ (using Table II, Appendix D)

Since the p-value is less than α $(p = .0322 < .10)$, H_0 is rejected. There is sufficient evidence to indicate the students, on average, overestimate the time it takes to read the report at $\alpha = .10$.

b.   Let μ = mean estimated number of pages of the report read. To determine if the students, on average, underestimate the number of report pages read, we test:

$$H_0 : \mu = 32$$
$$H_a : \mu < 32$$

The test statistic is $z = \dfrac{\bar{x} - \mu_0}{\sigma_{\bar{x}}} \approx \dfrac{28 - 32}{14/\sqrt{42}} = -1.85$.

The p-value is $p = P(z \leq -1.85) = .5 - .4678 = .0322$ (using Table II, Appendix D)

Since the p-value is less than α $(p = .0322 < .10)$, H_0 is rejected. There is sufficient evidence to indicate the students, on average, underestimate the number of report pages read at $\alpha = .10$.

c.   No. In both tests, the sample sizes are greater than 30. Thus, the Central Limit Theorem will apply. The distribution of $\bar{x}$ is approximately normal regardless of the population distribution.

7.41   To determine if the mean point-spread error is different from 0, we test:

$$H_0 : \mu = 0$$
$$H_a : \mu \neq 0$$

The test statistic is $z = \dfrac{\bar{x} - \mu_0}{\sigma_{\bar{x}}} \approx \dfrac{-1.6 - 0}{13.3/\sqrt{240}} = -1.86$

The rejection region requires $\alpha/2 = .01/2 = .005$ in each tail of the z-distribution. From Table II, Appendix D, $z_{.005} = 2.575$. The rejection region is $z < -2.575$ or $z > 2.575$.

Since the observed value of the test statistic does not fall in the rejection region $(z = -1.86 \not< -2.575)$, H_0 is not rejected. There is insufficient evidence to indicate that the true mean point-spread error is different from 0 at $\alpha = .01$.

7.43 a. To determine if the true mean forecast error for buy-side analysts is positive, we test:

$$H_0 : \mu = 0$$
$$H_a : \mu > 0$$

The test statistic is $z = \dfrac{\bar{x} - \mu_o}{\sigma_{\bar{x}}} \approx \dfrac{.85 - 0}{1.93/\sqrt{3,526}} = 26.15$.

The observed p-value of the test is $p = P(z > 26.15) \approx 0$ (Using Table II, Appendix D)

Since the p-value is less than α $(p \approx 0 < .01)$, H_0 is rejected. There is sufficient evidence to indicate that the true mean forecast error for buy-side analysts is positive at $\alpha = .01$. This means that the buy-side analysts are overestimating earnings.

b. To determine if the true mean forecast error for sell-side analysts is negative; we test:

$$H_0 : \mu = 0$$
$$H_a : \mu < 0$$

The test statistic is $z = \dfrac{\bar{x} - \mu_o}{\sigma_{\bar{x}}} \approx \dfrac{-.05 - 0}{.85/\sqrt{58,562}} = -14.24$.

The observed p-value of the test is $p = P(z < -14.24) \approx 0$ (using Table II, Appendix D)

Since the p-value is less than α $(p \approx 0 < .01)$, H_0 is rejected. There is sufficient evidence to indicate that the true mean forecast error for sell-side analysts is negative at $\alpha = .01$. This means that the sell-side analysts are underestimating earnings.

7.45 a. To determine if CEOs at all California small firms generally agree with the statement, we test:

$$H_0 : \mu = 3.5$$
$$H_a : \mu > 3.5$$

The test statistic is $z = \dfrac{\bar{x} - \mu_o}{\sigma_{\bar{x}}} \approx \dfrac{3.85 - 3.5}{1.5/\sqrt{137}} = 2.73$

The rejection region requires $\alpha = .05$ in the upper tail of the z-distribution. From Table II, Appendix D, $z_{.05} = 1.645$. The rejection region is $z > 1.645$.

Since the observed value of the test statistics falls in the rejection region $(z = 2.73 > 1.645)$, H_0 is rejected. There is sufficient evidence to indicate CEOs at all California small firms generally agree with the statement (true mean scale score exceeds 3.5) at $\alpha = .05$.

b.   Although the sample mean of 3.85 is far enough away from 3.5 to statistically conclude the population mean score is greater than 3.5, a score of 3.85 may not be practically different from 3.5 to make any difference.

c.   No. Since the sample size $(n = 137)$ is greater than 30, the Central Limit Theorem applies. The distribution of $\bar{x}$ is approximately normal regardless of the population distribution.

7.47   a.   We should use the t-distribution in testing a hypothesis about a population mean if the sample size is small, the population being sampled from is normal, and the variance of the population is unknown.

b.   Both distributions are mound-shaped and symmetric. The t-distribution is flatter than the z-distribution.

7.49   a.   The rejection region requires $\alpha/2 = .05/2 = .025$ in each tail of the t-distribution with $df = n-1 = 14-1 = 13$. From Table III, Appendix D, $t_{.025} = 2.160$. The rejection region is $t < -2.160$ or $t > 2.160$.

b.   The rejection region requires $\alpha = .01$ in the upper tail of the t-distribution with $df = n-1 = 24-1 = 23$. From Table III, Appendix D, $t_{.01} = 2.500$. The rejection region is $t > 2.500$.

c.   The rejection region requires $\alpha = .10$ in the upper tail of the t-distribution with $df = n-1 = 9-1 = 8$. From Table III, Appendix D, $t_{.10} = 1.397$. The rejection region is $t > 1.397$.

d.   The rejection region requires $\alpha = .01$ in the lower tail of the t-distribution with $df = n-1 = 12-1 = 11$. From Table III, Appendix D, $t_{.01} = 2.718$. The rejection region is $t < -2.718$.

e.   The rejection region requires $\alpha/2 = .10/2 = .05$ in each tail of the t-distribution with $df = n-1 = 20-1 = 19$. From Table III, Appendix D, $t_{.05} = 1.729$. The rejection region is $t < -1.729$ or $t > 1.729$.

f.   The rejection region requires $\alpha = .05$ in the lower tail of the t-distribution with $df = n-1 = 4-1 = 3$. From Table III, Appendix D, $t_{.05} = 2.353$. The rejection region is $t < -2.353$.

7.51   a.   We must assume that a random sample was drawn from a normal population.

b.   The hypotheses are:

$$H_0 : \mu = 1,000$$
$$H_a : \mu > 1,000$$

The test statistic is $t = 1.89$ and the p-value is $p = .038$.

Since the p-value is so small, there is evidence to reject H_0. There is evidence to indicate the mean is greater than 1000 for $\alpha > .038$.

c.   The hypotheses are:

$$H_0 : \mu = 1,000$$
$$H_a : \mu \neq 1,000$$

The test statistic is $t = 1.89$ and the p-value is $2(.038) = .076$.

There is no evidence to reject H_0 for $\alpha = .05$. There is insufficient evidence to indicate the mean is different than 1000 for $\alpha = .05$.

There is evidence to reject H_0 for $\alpha > .076$. There is evidence to indicate the mean is different than 1000 for $\alpha > .076$.

7.53   To determine if the mean level of radon exposure in the tombs is less than 6,000 Bq/m^3, we test:

$$H_0: \mu = 6,000$$
$$H_a: \mu < 6,000$$

From the printout, the test statistic is $t = -1.82$.

Since this is a one-tailed test, the p-value is $p = .096 / 2 = .0480$.

Since the p-value is less than α ($p = .048 < .10$), H_0 is rejected. There is sufficient evidence to indicate the mean level of radon exposure is less than 6,000 Bq/m^3 at $\alpha = .10$.

7.55   a.   To determine if the mean surface roughness of coated interior pipe differs from 2 micrometers, we test:

$$H_0: \mu = 2$$
$$H_a: \mu \neq 2$$

b.   From the printout, the test statistic is $t = -1.02$.

c.   The rejection region requires $\alpha / 2 = .05 / 2 = .025$ in each tail of the t-distribution with $df = n - 1 = 20 - 1 = 19$. From Table III, Appendix D, $t_{.025} = 2.093$. The rejection region is $t < -2.093$ or $t > 2.093$.

d.   Since the observed value of the test statistic does not fall in the rejection region ($t = -1.02 \not< -2.093$), H_0 is not rejected. There is insufficient evidence to indicate the true mean surface roughness of coated interior pipe differs from 2 micrometers at $\alpha = .05$.

e.   The p-value is $p = .322$. Since the p-value is not less than $\alpha = .05$, H_0 is not rejected. There is insufficient evidence to indicate the true mean surface roughness of coated interior pipe differs from 2 micrometers at $\alpha = .05$.

f.   From Exercise 6.33, we found the 95% confidence interval for the mean surface roughness of coated interior pipe to be (1.636, 2.126). Since the hypothesized value of μ ($\mu = 2$) falls in the confidence interval, it is a likely value. We cannot reject it. The confidence interval and the test of hypothesis lead to the same conclusion because the critical values for the 2 techniques are the same.

7.57   a.   Let μ = mean daily amount of distilled water collected by the new system. To determine if the mean daily amount of distilled water collected by the new system is greater than 1.4, we test:

$$H_0: \mu = 1.4$$
$$H_a: \mu > 1.4$$

b. For this problem, $\alpha =$ probability of concluding the mean daily amount of distilled water collected by the new system is greater than 1.4 when, in fact, the mean daily amount of distilled water collected by the new system is not greater than 1.4. Since $\alpha = .10$, this means that H_0 will be rejected when it is true about 10% of the time.

c. Using MINITAB, the descriptive statistics are:

Descriptive Statistics: Water

```
Variable  N   Mean  StDev  Minimum    Q1  Median    Q3  Maximum
Water     3  5.243  0.192    5.070  5.070  5.210  5.450   5.450
```

$\bar{x} = 5.243$ and $s = .192$.

d. The test statistic is $t = \dfrac{\bar{x} - \mu_0}{s/\sqrt{n}} = \dfrac{5.243 - 1.4}{.192/\sqrt{3}} = 34.67$.

e. Using MINITAB:

One-Sample T: Water
```
Test of mu = 1.4 vs > 1.4
                                            95%
                                           Lower
Variable  N     Mean     StDev  SE Mean    Bound      T      P
Water     3  5.24333   0.19218  0.11096  4.91935  34.64  0.000
```

The p-value is $p = 0.000$.

f. Since the p-value is less than α ($p = .000 < .10$), H_0 is rejected. There is sufficient evidence to indicate daily amount of distilled water collected by the new system is greater than 1.4 at $\alpha = .10$.

7.59 Using MINITAB, the descriptive statistics are:

One-Sample T: Skid
```
Test of mu = 425 vs < 425
                                               95%
                                             Upper
Variable   N     Mean    StDev  SE Mean     Bound      T      P
Skid      20  358.450  117.817   26.345   404.004  -2.53  0.010
```

To determine if the mean skidding distance is less than 425 meters, we test:

$$H_0 : \mu = 425$$
$$H_a : \mu < 425$$

The test statistics is $t = \dfrac{\bar{x} - \mu_o}{s/\sqrt{n}} = \dfrac{358.45 - 425}{117.817/\sqrt{20}} = -2.53$.

The rejection region requires $\alpha = .10$ in the lower tail of the t-distribution with. From Table III, Appendix D, $t_{.10} = 1.328$. The rejection region is $t < -1.328$.

Since the observed value of the test statistic falls in the rejection region $(t = -2.53 < -1.328)$, H_0 is rejected. There is sufficient evidence to indicate the true mean skidding distance is less than 425 meters at $\alpha = .10$. There is sufficient evidence to refute the claim.

7.61   To determine if the true mean crack intensity of the Mississippi highway exceeds the AASHTO recommended maximum, we test:

$$H_0 : \mu = .100$$
$$H_a : \mu > .100$$

The test statistic is $t = \dfrac{\bar{x} - \mu_0}{s / \sqrt{n}} = \dfrac{.210 - .100}{\sqrt{.011} / \sqrt{8}} = 2.97$

The rejection region requires $\alpha = .01$ in the upper tail of the t-distribution with df $= n - 1 = 8 - 1 = 7$. From Table III, Appendix D, $t_{.01} = 2.998$. The rejection region is $t > 2.998$.

Since the observed value of the test statistic does not fall in the rejection region $(t = 2.97 \not> 2.998)$, H_0 is not rejected. There is insufficient evidence to indicate that the true mean crack intensity of the Mississippi highway exceeds the AASHTO recommended maximum at $\alpha = .01$.

7.63   Using MINITAB, the descriptive statistics for the 2 plants are:

Descriptive Statistics: AL1, AL2

```
Variable  N     Mean      StDev    Minimum   Q1   Median   Q3   Maximum
AL1       2   0.00750   0.00354   0.00500    *   0.00750   *   0.01000
AL2       2   0.0700    0.0283    0.0500     *   0.0700    *   0.0900
```

To determine if **plant 1** is violating the OSHA standard, we test:

$$H_0 : \mu = .004$$
$$H_a : \mu > .004$$

The test statistic is $t = \dfrac{\bar{x} - \mu_o}{s / \sqrt{n}} = \dfrac{.0075 - .004}{.00354 / \sqrt{2}} = 1.40$

Since no α level was given, we will use $\alpha = .10$. The rejection region requires $\alpha = .10$ in the upper tail of the t-distribution with df $= n - 1 = 2 - 1 = 1$. From Table III, Appendix D, $t_{.10} = 3.078$. The rejection region is $t > 3.078$.

Since the observed value of the test statistic does not fall in the rejection region $(t = 1.40 \not> 3.078)$, H_0 is not rejected. There is insufficient evidence to indicate the OSHA standard is violated by plant 1 at $\alpha = .10$.

To determine if **plant 2** is violating the OSHA standard, we test:

$$H_0 : \mu = .004$$
$$H_a : \mu > .004$$

The test statistic is $t = \dfrac{\bar{x} - \mu_o}{s / \sqrt{n}} = \dfrac{.07 - .004}{.0283 / \sqrt{2}} = 3.30$

Since no α level was given, we will use $\alpha = .10$. The rejection region requires $\alpha = .10$ in the upper tail of the t-distribution with df $= n - 1 = 2 - 1 = 1$. From Table III, Appendix D, $t_{.10} = 3.078$. The rejection region is $t > 3.078$.

Since the observed value of the test statistic falls in the rejection region $t = 3.30 > 3.078)$, H_0 is rejected. There is sufficient evidence to indicate the OSHA standard is violated by plant 2 at $\alpha = .10$.

7.65   a. $z = \dfrac{\hat{p} - p_0}{\sqrt{\dfrac{p_0 q_0}{n}}} = \dfrac{.83 - .9}{\sqrt{\dfrac{.9(.1)}{100}}} = -2.33$

         b.   The denominator in Exercise 7.64 is $\sqrt{\dfrac{.7(.3)}{100}} = .0458$ as compared to $\sqrt{\dfrac{.9(.1)}{100}} = .03$ in part **a**. Since the denominator in this problem is smaller, the absolute value of z is larger.

         c.   The rejection region requires $\alpha = .05$ in the lower tail of the z-distribution. From Table II, Appendix D, $z_{.05} = 1.645$. The rejection region is $z < -1.645$.

                Since the observed value of the test statistic falls in the rejection region $(z = -2.33 < -1.645)$, H_0 is rejected. There is sufficient evidence to indicate the population proportion is less than .9 at $\alpha = .05$.

         d.   The p-value $= p = P(z \leq -2.33) = .5 - .4901 = .0099$ (from Table II, Appendix D). Since the p-value is less than $\alpha = .05$, H_0 is rejected.

7.67   From Exercise 6.44, $n = 50$ and since p is the proportion of consumers who do not like the snack food, $\hat{p}$ will be:

$$\hat{p} = \frac{\text{Number of 0's in sample}}{n} = \frac{29}{50} = .58$$

First, check to see if the normal approximation will be adequate:

$$np_0 = 50(.5) = 25 \qquad\qquad nq_0 = 50(.5) = 25$$

Since both $np_0 \geq 15$ and $nq_0 \geq 15$, the normal distribution will be adequate.

     a. $\begin{aligned} H_0 &: p = .5 \\ H_a &: p > .5 \end{aligned}$

                The test statistic is $z = \dfrac{\hat{p} - p_0}{\sigma_{\hat{p}}} = \dfrac{\hat{p} - p_0}{\sqrt{\dfrac{p_0 q_0}{n}}} = \dfrac{.58 - .5}{\sqrt{\dfrac{.5(1 - .5)}{50}}} = 1.13$.

                The rejection region requires $\alpha = .10$ in the upper tail of the z-distribution. From Table II, Appendix D, $z_{.10} = 1.28$. The rejection region is $z > 1.28$.

Since the observed value of the test statistic does not fall in the rejection region ($z=1.13 \not> 1.28$), H_0 is not rejected. There is insufficient evidence to indicate the proportion of customers who do not like the snack food is greater than .5 at $\alpha = .10$.

b. $p-\text{value} = p = P(z \geq 1.13) = .5 - .3708 = .1292$ (using Table II, Appendix D)

7.69   a. $\hat{p} = \dfrac{x}{n} = \dfrac{506}{755} = .67$

b. To determine if the true proportion of all internet-using adults who have paid to download music exceeds .7, we test:

$H_0 : p = .7$

$H_a : p > .7$

c. The test statistic is $z = \dfrac{\hat{p} - p_0}{\sigma_{\hat{p}}} = \dfrac{\hat{p} - p_0}{\sqrt{\dfrac{p_0 q_0}{n}}} = \dfrac{.67 - .7}{\sqrt{\dfrac{.7(1-.7)}{755}}} = -1.80$.

d. The rejection region requires $\alpha = .01$ in the upper tail of the z-distribution. From Table II, Appendix D, $z_{.01} = 2.33$. The rejection region is $z > 2.33$.

e. $p-\text{value} = p = P(z \geq -1.80) = .5 + .4641 = .9641$ (using Table II, Appendix D)

f. Since the observed value of the test statistic does not fall in the rejection region ($t = -1.80 \not> 2.33$), H_0 is not rejected. There is insufficient evidence to indicate the true proportion of all internet-using adults who have paid to download music exceeds .7 at $\alpha = .01$.

g. Since the p-value is not less than α ($p = .9641 \not< .01$), H_0 is not rejected. There is insufficient evidence to indicate the true proportion of all internet-using adults who have paid to download music exceeds .7 at $\alpha = .01$.

7.71   To determine if the sample provides sufficient evidence to indicate that the true percentage of all firms that announced one or more acquisitions during the year 2000 is less than 30%, we test:

$H_0 : p = .30$

$H_a : p < .30$

The point estimate is $\hat{p} = \dfrac{x}{n} = \dfrac{748}{2,778} = .269$

The test statistic is $z = \dfrac{\hat{p} - p_o}{\sqrt{\dfrac{p_o q_o}{n}}} = \dfrac{.269 - .30}{\sqrt{\dfrac{.30(.70)}{2,778}}} = -3.57$

The rejection region requires $\alpha = .05$ in the lower tail of the z-distribution. From Table II, Appendix D, $z_{.05} = 1.645$. The rejection region is $z < -1.645$.

Since the observed value of the test statistic falls in the rejection region $(z = -3.57 < -1.645)$, H_0 is rejected. There is sufficient evidence to indicate that the true percentage of all firms that announced one or more acquisitions during the year 2000 is less than 30% at $\alpha = .05$.

7.73   a.   To determine whether the true proportion of toothpaste brands with the ADA seal verifying effective decay prevention is less than .5, we test:

$$H_0 : p = .5$$
$$H_a : p < .5$$

b.   From the printout, the p-value is $p = .231$.

c.   Since the observed p-value is greater than α $(p = .231 > .10)$, H_0 is not rejected. There is insufficient evidence to indicate the true proportion of toothpaste brands with the ADA seal verifying effective decay prevention is less than .5 at $\alpha = .10$.

7.75 $\hat{p} = \dfrac{x}{n} = \dfrac{417 + 77}{845} = .585$

To determine if fewer than 60% of the coffee growers in southern Mexico are either certified or transitioning to become certified, we test:

$$H_0 : p = .60$$
$$H_a : p < .60$$

The test statistic is $z = \dfrac{\hat{p} - p_0}{\sigma_{\hat{p}}} = \dfrac{\hat{p} - p_0}{\sqrt{\dfrac{p_0 q_0}{n}}} = \dfrac{.585 - .60}{\sqrt{\dfrac{.60(1 - .60)}{845}}} = -.89$.

The rejection region requires $\alpha = .05$ in the lower tail of the z-distribution. From Table II, Appendix D, $z_{.05} = 1.645$. The rejection region is $z < -1.645$.

Since the observed value of the test statistic does not fall in the rejection region $(z = -.89 \not< -1.645)$, H_0 is not rejected. There is insufficient evidence to indicate that fewer than 60% of the coffee growers in southern Mexico are either certified or transitioning to become certified at $\alpha = .05$.

7.77   a.   Le p = proportion of middle-aged women who exhibit skin improvement after using the cream. For this problem, $\hat{p} = \dfrac{x}{n} = \dfrac{24}{33} = .727$.

First we check to see if the normal approximation is adequate:
$np_0 = 33(.6) = 19.8$ $nq_0 = 33(.4) = 13.2$

Since $nq_0 = 13.2$ is less than 15, the assumption of normality may not be valid. We will go ahead and perform the test.

To determine if the cream will improve the skin of more than 60% of middle-aged women, we test:

$H_0: p = .60$

$H_a: p > .60$

The test statistic is $z = \dfrac{\hat{p} - p_0}{\sqrt{\dfrac{p_0 q_0}{n}}} = \dfrac{.727 - .60}{\sqrt{\dfrac{.60(.40)}{33}}} = 1.49$

The rejection region requires $\alpha = .05$ in the upper tail of the z-distribution. From Table II, Appendix D, $z_{.05} = 1.645$. The rejection region is $z > 1.645$.

Since the observed value of the test statistic does not fall in the rejection region $(z = 1.49 \not> 1.645)$, H_0 is not rejected. There is insufficient evidence to indicate the cream will improve the skin of more than 60% of middle-aged women at $\alpha = .05$.

b.   The p-value is $p = P(z \geq 1.49) = (.5 - .4319) = .0681$. (Using Table II, Appendix D.) Since the p-value is greater than α $(p = .0681 > .05)$, H_0 is not rejected. There is insufficient evidence to indicate the cream will improve the skin of more than 60% of middle-aged women at $\alpha = .05$.

7.79   Answers will vary. The target population will be all households in the United States that have televisions. The experimental unit will be an individual household in the United States with a television. The variable to be measured is whether or not the household has a DVR. Let $p =$ proportion of be all households in the United States that have televisions that also have DVR's. The hypotheses of interest are:

$H_0: p = .41$

$H_a: p \neq .41$

The test statistic is $z = \dfrac{\hat{p} - p_0}{\sigma_{\hat{p}}} = \dfrac{\hat{p} - p_0}{\sqrt{\dfrac{p_0 q_0}{n}}} = \dfrac{\hat{p} - .41}{\sqrt{\dfrac{.41(1 - .41)}{n}}}$.

One could take a random number generator to generate 500 random telephone numbers to call to obtain a random sample.

7.81   To minimize the probability of a Type I error, we will select $\alpha = .01$.

First, check to see if the normal approximation is adequate:

$np_0 = 100(.5) = 50$ $nq_0 = 100(.5) = 50$

Since both $np_0 \geq .15$ and $nq_0 \geq .15$, the normal distribution will be adequate

$\hat{p} = \dfrac{x}{n} = \dfrac{56}{100} = .56$

To determine if more than half of all Diet Coke drinkers prefer Diet Pepsi, we test:

$H_0: p = .5$

$H_a: p > .5$

The test statistic is $z = \dfrac{\hat{p} - p_0}{\sqrt{\dfrac{p_0 q_0}{n}}} = \dfrac{.56 - .5}{\sqrt{\dfrac{.5(.5)}{100}}} = 1.20$

The rejection region requires $\alpha = .01$ in the upper tail of the z-distribution. From Table II, Appendix D, $z_{.01} = 2.33$. The rejection region is $z > 2.33$.

Since the observed value of the test statistic does not fall in the rejection region $(z = 1.20 \ngtr 2.33)$, H_0 is not rejected. There is insufficient evidence to indicate that more than half of all Diet Coke drinkers prefer Diet Pepsi at $\alpha = .01$.

Since H_0 was not rejected, there is no evidence that Diet Coke drinkers prefer Diet Pepsi.

7.83   a.   df $= n - 1 = 16 - 1 = 15$; reject H_0 if $\chi^2 < 6.26214$ or $\chi^2 > 27.4884$

        b.   df $= n - 1 = 23 - 1 = 22$; reject H_0 if $\chi^2 > 40.2894$

        c.   df $= n - 1 = 15 - 1 = 14$; reject H_0 if $\chi^2 > 21.0642$

        d.   df $= n - 1 = 13 - 1 = 12$; reject H_0 if $\chi^2 < 3.57056$

        e.   df $= n - 1 = 7 - 1 = 6$; reject H_0 if $\chi^2 < 1.63539$ or $\chi^2 > 12.5916$

        f.   df $= n - 1 = 25 - 1 = 24$; reject H_0 if $\chi^2 < 13.8484$

7.85   a. $\begin{aligned} H_0 &: \sigma^2 = 1 \\ H_a &: \sigma^2 > 1 \end{aligned}$

The test statistic is $\chi^2 = \dfrac{(n-1)s^2}{\sigma_0^2} = \dfrac{(100-1)4.84}{1} = 479.16$

The rejection region requires $\alpha = .05$ in the upper tail of the χ^2 distribution with df $= n - 1 = 100 - 1 = 99$. From Table IV, Appendix D, $\chi_{.05}^2 \approx 124.342$. The rejection region is $\chi^2 > 124.342$.

Since the observed value of the test statistic falls in the rejection region $(\chi^2 = 479.16 > 124.342)$, H_0 is rejected. There is sufficient evidence to indicate the variance is larger than 1 at $\alpha = .05$.

        b.   In part **b** of Exercise 7.84, the test statistic was $\chi^2 = 29.04$. The conclusion was to reject H_0 as it was in this problem.

7.87   a.   To determine whether the population of institutional investors perform consistently, we test:

$$H_0 : \sigma^2 = 10^2 = 100$$
$$H_a : \sigma^2 < 100$$

b. The rejection region requires $\alpha = .05$ in the lower tail of the χ^2 distribution with $df = n-1 = 200-1 = 199$. Using MINITAB, we get:

Inverse Cumulative Distribution Function
```
Chi-Square with 199 DF

P( X <= x )        x
      0.05   167.361
```

The rejection region is $\chi^2 < 167.361$.

c. For this problem, $\alpha = .05$. The probability of concluding the standard deviation is less than 10 when, in fact, it is equal to 10 is .05. If this test was repeated a large number of times, approximately 5% of the time we would conclude the standard deviation was less than 10 when it really was 10.

d. From the printout, $\chi^2 = 154.81$ and the p-value is $p = .009$.

e. Since the p-value is less than α ($p = .009 < .05$), H_0 is rejected. There is sufficient evidence to indicate the standard deviation is less than 10% at $\alpha = .05$.

f. We must assume that a random sample was selected from the target population and the population sampled from is approximately normal.

7.89 a. Let $\sigma^2 = $ weight variance of tees. To determine if the weight variance differs from .000004 (injection mold process is out-of-control), we test:

$$H_0 : \sigma^2 = .000004$$
$$H_a : \sigma^2 \neq .000004$$

b. Using MINITAB, the descriptive statistics are:

Descriptive Statistics: Tees

Variable	N	Mean	Median	StDev	Minimum	Maximum	Q1	Q3
Tees	40	0.25248	0.25300	0.00223	0.24700	0.25600	0.25100	0.25400

The test statistic is $\chi^2 = \dfrac{(n-1)s^2}{\sigma_0^2} = \dfrac{(40-1)(.00223)^2}{.000004} = 48.49$

The rejection region requires $\alpha / 2 = .01 / 2 = .005$ in each tail of the χ^2 distribution with $df = n-1 = 40-1 = 39$. From Table IV, Appendix D, $\chi^2_{.005} \approx 66.7659$ and $\chi^2_{.995} \approx 20.7065$. The rejection region is $\chi^2 > 66.7659$ or $\chi^2 < 20.7065$.

Since the observed value of the test statistic does not fall in the rejection region ($\chi^2 = 49.49 \not> 66.7659$ and $\chi^2 = 49.49 \not< 20.7065$), H_0 is not rejected. There is insufficient evidence to indicate the injection mold process is out-of-control at $\alpha = .01$.

c.   We must assume that the distributions of the weights of tees is approximately normal. Using MINITAB, a histogram of the data is:

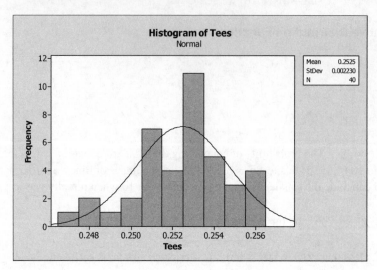

The data look fairly mound-shaped, so the assumption of normality seems to be reasonably satisfied.

7.91   To determine whether the true conduction time standard deviation is less than 7 seconds (variance less than 49), we test:

$$H_0 : \sigma^2 = 7^2$$
$$H_a : \sigma^2 < 7^2$$

The test statistic is $\chi^2 = \dfrac{(n-1)s^2}{\sigma_0^2} = \dfrac{(18-1)6.3^2}{7^2} = 13.77$.

The rejection region requires $\alpha = .01$ in the lower tail of the χ^2 distribution with df $= n-1 = 18-1 = 17$. From Table IV, Appendix D, $\chi^2_{.99} = 6.40776$. The rejection region is $\chi^2 < 6.40776$.

Since the observed value of the test statistic does not fall in the rejection region $(\chi^2 = 13.77 \not< 6.40776)$, H_0 is not rejected. There is insufficient evidence to indicate the true conduction time standard deviation is less than 7 seconds at $\alpha = .01$. Thus, the prototype system does not satisfy this requirement.

7.93   To determine if the diameters of the ball bearings are more variable when produced by the new process, test:

$$H_0 : \sigma^2 = .00156$$
$$H_a : \sigma^2 > .00156$$

The test statistic is $\chi^2 = \dfrac{(n-1)s^2}{\sigma_0^2} = \dfrac{99(.00211)}{.00156} = 133.90$

The rejection region requires use of the upper tail of the χ^2 distribution with $df = n-1 = 100-1 = 99$. We will use df $= 100 \approx 99$ due to the limitations of the table. From Table IV, Appendix D,

$\chi_{.025}^2 = 129.561 < 133.90 < 135.807 = \chi_{.010}^2$. The p-value of the test is between .010 and .025. The decision made depends on the desired α. For $\alpha < .010$, there is not enough evidence to show that the variance in the diameters is greater than .00156. For $\alpha \geq .025$, there is enough evidence to show that the variance in the diameters is greater than .00156.

7.95   a.   Since the sample mean of 3.85 is not that far from the value of 3.5, a large standard deviation would indicate that the value 3.85 is not very many standard deviations from 3.5.

        b.   The rejection region requires $\alpha = .01$ in the upper tail of the z-distribution. From Table II, Appendix D, $z_{.01} = 2.33$. The rejection region is $z > 2.33$.

The test statistic is $z = \dfrac{\bar{x} - \mu_o}{\sigma_{\bar{x}}} = \dfrac{3.85 - 3.5}{\sigma / \sqrt{137}}$

To reject H_0, $z > 2.33$. Thus, we need to find σ so $z > 2.33$.

$z = \dfrac{3.85 - 3.5}{\sigma / \sqrt{137}} > 2.33 \Rightarrow 3.85 - 3.5 > 2.33 \dfrac{\sigma}{\sqrt{137}} \Rightarrow .35 > .199065\sigma \Rightarrow 1.758 > \sigma$

Thus, the largest value of σ for which we will reject H_0 is 1.758.

        c.   To determine if $\sigma < 1.758$, we test:

$H_0: \sigma^2 = 1.758^2$

$H_a: \sigma^2 < 1.758^2$

The test statistic is $\chi^2 = \dfrac{(n-1)s^2}{\sigma_o^2} = \dfrac{(137-1)1.5^2}{1.758^2} = 99.011$.

The rejection region requires $\alpha = .01$ in the lower tail of the χ^2 distribution with $df = n - 1 = 137 - 1 = 136$. Since there are no values in the table with $df > 100$, we will use MINITAB to compute the p-value of the test statistic.

Cumulative Distribution Function
```
Chi-Square with 136 DF

        x   P( X <= x )
   99.011     0.0072496
```

Since the p-value is less than α ($p = 0.0072496 < \alpha = .01$), H_0 is rejected. There is sufficient evidence to indicate the standard deviation of the scores is less than 1.758 at $\alpha = .01$.

7.97   a.   By the Central Limit Theorem, the sampling distribution of $\bar{x}$ is approximately normal with

$\mu_{\bar{x}} = \mu = 500$ and $\sigma_{\bar{x}} = \dfrac{\sigma}{\sqrt{n}} = \dfrac{100}{\sqrt{25}} = 20$.

b. $\bar{x}_0 = \mu_0 + z_\alpha \sigma_{\bar{x}} = \mu_0 + z_\alpha \dfrac{\sigma}{\sqrt{n}}$ where $z_\alpha = z_{.05} = 1.645$ from Table

II, Appendix D.

Thus, $\bar{x}_0 = 500 + 1.645(20) = 532.9$

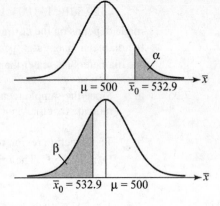

c.   The sampling distribution of $\bar{x}$ is approximately normal by the Central Limit Theorem with $\bar{x} = \mu = 550$ and

$\sigma_{\bar{x}} = \dfrac{\sigma}{\sqrt{n}} = \dfrac{100}{\sqrt{25}} = 20$.

d. $\beta = P(\bar{x}_0 < 532.9)$ when $\mu = 550) = P\left(z < \dfrac{532.9 - 550}{100/\sqrt{25}} \right) = P(z < -.86) = .5 - .3051 = .1949$

e. $Power = 1 - \beta = 1 - .1949 = .8051$

7.99   a.   The sampling distribution of $\bar{x}$ will be approximately normal (by the Central Limit Theorem) with

$\mu_{\bar{x}} = \mu = 75$ and $\sigma_{\bar{x}} = \dfrac{\sigma}{\sqrt{n}} = \dfrac{15}{\sqrt{49}} = 2.143$.

b.   The sampling distribution of $\bar{x}$ will be approximately normal (by the Central Limit Theorem) with

$\mu_{\bar{x}} = \mu = 70$ and $\sigma_{\bar{x}} = \dfrac{\sigma}{\sqrt{n}} = \dfrac{15}{\sqrt{49}} = 2.143$.

c.   First, find $\bar{x}_0 = \mu_0 - z_\alpha \sigma_{\bar{x}} = \mu_0 - z_\alpha \dfrac{\sigma}{\sqrt{n}}$ where $z_{.10} = 1.28$ from Table II, Appendix D.

Thus, $\bar{x}_0 = 75 - 1.28 \dfrac{15}{\sqrt{49}} = 72.257$

Now, find $\beta = P(\bar{x}_0 > 72.257$ when $\mu = 70) = P\left(z > \dfrac{72.257 - 70}{15/\sqrt{49}} \right) = P(z > 1.05) = .5 - .3531 = .1469$

d. $Power = 1 - \beta = 1 - .1469 = .8531$

7.101   a.   First, the sample is sufficiently large if both $np_0 \geq 15$ and $nq_0 \geq 15$.

$np_0 = 100(.7) = 70$ and $nq_0 \geq 100(1 - .7) = 30$.

Since both $np_0 \geq 15$ and $nq_0 \geq 15$, the normal distribution will be adequate.

Thus, the sampling distribution of $\hat{p}$ will be approximately normal with $E(\hat{p}) = p = .7$ and

$\sigma_{\hat{p}} = \sqrt{\dfrac{p_0 q_0}{n}} = \sqrt{\dfrac{.7(.3)}{100}} = .0458$.

b.   The sampling distribution of $\hat{p}$ will be approximately normal with $E(\hat{p}) = p = .65$ and

$\sigma_{\hat{p}} = \sqrt{\dfrac{p_0 q_0}{n}} = \sqrt{\dfrac{.65(.35)}{100}} = .0477$.

c. First, find $\hat{p}_{0,L} = p_0 - z_{\alpha/2}\sigma_{\hat{p}} = p_0 - z_{\alpha/2}\sqrt{\dfrac{p_0 q_0}{n}}$

where $z_{.05/2} = z_{.025} = 1.96$ from Table II, Appendix D.

Thus, $\hat{p}_{0,L} = .7 - 1.96\sqrt{\dfrac{.7(.3)}{100}} = .610$

$\hat{p}_{0,U} = p_0 + z_{\alpha/2}\sigma_{\hat{p}} = p_0 + z_{\alpha/2}\sqrt{\dfrac{p_0 q_0}{n}} = .7 + 1.96\sqrt{\dfrac{.7(.3)}{100}} = .790$

Now, find $\beta = P(.610 < \hat{p} < .79$ when $p = .65)$

$= P\left(\dfrac{.610 - .65}{\sqrt{\dfrac{.65(.35)}{100}}} < z < \dfrac{.79 - .65}{\sqrt{\dfrac{.65(.35)}{100}}}\right) = P(-.84 < z < 2.94) = .2995 + .4984 = .7979$

d. $\beta = P(.610 < \hat{p} < .79$ when $p = .71)$

$= P\left(\dfrac{.610 - .71}{\sqrt{\dfrac{.71(.29)}{100}}} < z < \dfrac{.79 - .71}{\sqrt{\dfrac{.71(.29)}{100}}}\right) = P(-2.20 < z < 1.76) = .4861 + .4608 = .9469$

7.103 a. We have failed to reject H_0 when it is not true. This is a Type II error.

To compute β, first find:

$\bar{x}_0 = \mu_0 - z_\alpha \sigma_{\bar{x}} = \mu_0 - z_\alpha \dfrac{\sigma}{\sqrt{n}}$ where $z_{.05} = 1.645$ from Table II, Appendix D.

Thus, $\bar{x}_0 = 5.0 - 1.645\dfrac{.01}{\sqrt{100}} = 4.998355$

Then find:

$\beta = P(\bar{x}_0 > 4.998355$ when $\mu = 4.9975) = P\left(z > \dfrac{4.998355 - 4.9975}{.01/\sqrt{100}}\right)$

$= P(z > .86) = .5 - .3051 = .1949$

b. We have rejected H_0 when it is true. This is a Type I error. The probability of a Type I error is $\alpha = .05$.

c. A departure of .0025 below 5.0 is $\mu = 4.9975$. Using **a**, $\beta = .1949$ when $\mu = 4.9975$. The power of the test is $1 - \beta = 1 - .1949 = .8051$.

7.105.   To compute the power, we must first set up the rejection region in terms of $\hat{p}$. The rejection region requires $\alpha / 2 = .01 / 2 = .005$ in each tail of the z-distribution. From Table II, Appendix D, $z_{.005} = 2.575$. The rejection region is $z > -2.575$ or $z > 2.575$.

Thus, $\hat{p}_{0,L} = p_0 - z_{\alpha/2}\sigma_{\hat{p}} = p_0 - z_{\alpha/2}\sqrt{\dfrac{p_0 q_0}{n}} = .5 - 2.575\sqrt{\dfrac{.5(.5)}{121}} = .5 - .117 = .383$ and

$$\hat{p}_{0,U} = p_0 + z_{\alpha/2}\sigma_{\hat{p}} = p_0 + z_{\alpha/2}\sqrt{\dfrac{p_0 q_0}{n}} = .5 + 2.575\sqrt{\dfrac{.5(.5)}{121}} = .5 + .117 = .617 .$$

$$Power = P(\hat{p} < .383 \text{ or } \hat{p} > .617 \mid p_0 = .65) = P\left(z < \dfrac{\hat{p} - p_0}{\sigma_{\hat{p}}}\right) + P\left(z > \dfrac{\hat{p} - p_0}{\sigma_{\hat{p}}}\right)$$

$$= P\left(z < \dfrac{.383 - .65}{\sqrt{\dfrac{.65(.35)}{121}}}\right) + P\left(z > \dfrac{.617 - .65}{\sqrt{\dfrac{.65(.35)}{121}}}\right) = P(z < -6.16) + P(z > -.76) = (.5 - .5) + (.5 + .2764) = .7764$$

7.107   First, find $\bar{x}_0$ such that $P(\bar{x} < \bar{x}_0) = .05$.

$$P(\bar{x} < \bar{x}_0) = P\left(z < \dfrac{\bar{x}_0 - 10}{1.2 / \sqrt{48}}\right) = P(z < z_0) = .05 .$$

From Table II, Appendix D, $z_0 = -1.645$.

Thus, $z_0 = \dfrac{\bar{x}_0 - 10}{1.2 / \sqrt{48}} \Rightarrow \bar{x}_0 = -1.645(.173) + 10 = 9.715$

The probability of a Type II error is:

$$\beta = P(\bar{x} \geq 9.715 \mid \mu = 9.5) = P\left(z \geq \dfrac{9.715 - 9.5}{1.2 / \sqrt{48}}\right) = P(z \geq 1.24) = .5 - .3925 = .1075$$

7.109   The smaller the p-value associated with a test of hypothesis, the stronger the support for the **alternative** hypothesis. The p-value is the probability of observing your test statistic or anything more unusual, given the null hypothesis is true. If this value is small, it would be very unusual to observe this test statistic if the null hypothesis were true. Thus, it would indicate the alternative hypothesis is true.

7.111   There is not a direct relationship between α and β. That is, if α is known, it does not mean β is known because β depends on the value of the parameter in the alternative hypothesis and the sample size. However, as α decreases, β increases for a fixed value of the parameter and a fixed sample size. Thus, if α is very small, β will tend to be large.

7.113   a. $H_0 : \mu = 80$
$H_a : \mu < 80$

The test statistic is $t = \dfrac{\bar{x} - \mu_0}{s / \sqrt{n}} = \dfrac{72.6 - 80}{\sqrt{19.4} / \sqrt{20}} = -7.51$

The rejection region requires $\alpha = .05$ in the lower tail of the *t*-distribution with df $= n-1 = 20-1 = 19$. From Table III, Appendix D, $t_{.05} = 1.729$. The rejection region is $t < -1.729$.

Since the observed value of the test statistic falls in the rejection region $(t = -7.51 < -1.729)$, H_0 is rejected. There is sufficient evidence to indicate that the mean is less than 80 at $\alpha = .05$.

b.
$H_0 : \mu = 80$
$H_a : \mu \neq 80$

The test statistic is $t = \dfrac{\bar{x} - \mu_0}{s / \sqrt{n}} = \dfrac{72.6 - 80}{\sqrt{19.4} / \sqrt{20}} = -7.51$

The rejection region requires $\alpha / 2 = .01 / 2 = .005$ in each tail of the *t*-distribution with df $= n-1 = 20-1 = 19$. From Table III, Appendix D, $t_{.005} = 2.861$. The rejection region is $t < -2.861$ or $t > 2.861$.

Since the observed value of the test statistic falls in the rejection region $(t = -7.51 < -2.861)$, H_0 is rejected. There is sufficient evidence to indicate that the mean is different from 80 at $\alpha = .01$.

7.115   a.
$H_0 : p = .35$
$H_a : p < .35$

The test statistic is $z = \dfrac{\hat{p} - p_0}{\sqrt{\dfrac{p_0 q_0}{n}}} = \dfrac{.29 - .35}{\sqrt{\dfrac{.35(.65)}{200}}} = -1.78$

The rejection region requires $\alpha = .05$ in the lower tail of the *z*-distribution. From Table II, Appendix D, $z_{.05} = 1.645$. The rejection region is $z < -1.645$.

Since the observed value of the test statistic falls in the rejection region $(z = -1.78 < -1.645)$, H_0 is rejected. There is sufficient evidence to indicate $p < .35$ at $\alpha = .05$.

b.
$H_0 : p = .35$
$H_a : p \neq .35$

The test statistic is $z = -1.78$ (from **a**).

The rejection region requires $\alpha / 2 = .05 / 2 = .025$ in each tail of the *z*-distribution. From Table II, Appendix D, $z_{.025} = 1.96$. The rejection region is $z < -1.96$ or $z > 1.96$.

Since the observed value of the test statistic does not fall in the rejection region $(z = -1.78 \not< -1.96)$, H_0 is not rejected. There is insufficient evidence to indicate p is different from .35 at $\alpha = .05$.

7.117   a.
$H_0 : \sigma^2 = 30$
$H_a : \sigma^2 > 30$

The test statistic is $\chi^2 = \dfrac{(n-1)s^2}{\sigma_0^2} = \dfrac{(41-1)(6.9)^2}{30} = 63.48$

The rejection region requires $\alpha = .05$ in the upper tail of the χ^2 distribution with $df = n - 1 = 41 - 1 = 40$. From Table IV, Appendix D, $\chi^2_{.05} = 55.7585$. The rejection region is $\chi^2 > 55.7585$.

Since the observed value of the test statistic falls in the rejection region ($\chi^2 = 63.48 > 55.7585$), H_0 is rejected. There is sufficient evidence to indicate the variance is larger than 30 at $\alpha = .05$.

b.
$$H_0 : \sigma^2 = 30$$
$$H_a : \sigma^2 \neq 30$$

The test statistic is $\chi^2 = 63.48$ (from part a).

The rejection region requires $\alpha / 2 = .05 / 2 = .025$ in each tail of the χ^2 distribution with $df = n - 1 = 41 - 1 = 40$. From Table IV, Appendix D, $\chi^2_{.025} = 59.3417$ and $\chi^2_{.975} = 24.4331$. The rejection region is $\chi^2 < 24.4331$ or $\chi^2 > 59.3417$.

Since the observed value of the test statistic falls in the rejection region ($\chi^2 = 63.48 > 59.3417$), H_0 is rejected. There is sufficient evidence to indicate the variance is not 30 at $\alpha = .05$.

7.119   a.   The rejection region requires $\alpha / 2 = .01 / 2 = .005$ in each tail of the χ^2 distribution with $df = n - 1 = 46 - 1 = 45$. Using MINITAB,

Inverse Cumulative Distribution Function

```
Chi-Square with 45 DF

P( X <= x )          x
     0.005   24.3110
```

Inverse Cumulative Distribution Function

```
Chi-Square with 45 DF

P( X <= x )          x
     0.995   73.1661
```

The rejection region is $\chi^2 < 24.3110$ or $\chi^2 > 73.1661$.

b.   The test statistic is $\chi^2 = \dfrac{(n-1)s^2}{\sigma_o^2} = \dfrac{(46-1)11.9^2}{100} = 63.7245$.

c.   Since the observed value of the test statistic does not fall in the rejection region ($\chi^2 = 63.7245 \not< 24.3110$ *and* $\chi^2 = 63.7245 \not> 73.1661$), H_0 is not rejected. There is insufficient evidence to indicate the variance is different from 100 at $\alpha = .01$.

7.121   a.   To determine if the average high technology stock is riskier than the market as a whole, we test:

$$H_0 : \mu = 1$$
$$H_a : \mu > 1$$

b.   The test statistic is $t = \dfrac{\bar{x} - \mu_0}{s / \sqrt{n}}$

The rejection region requires $\alpha = .10$ in the upper tail of the t-distribution with df $= n - 1 = 15 - 1 = 14$. From Table III, Appendix D, $t_{.10} = 1.345$. The rejection region is $t > 1.345$.

c.   We must assume the population of beta coefficients of technology stocks is normally distributed.

d.   The test statistic is $t = \dfrac{\bar{x} - \mu_0}{s / \sqrt{n}} = \dfrac{1.23 - 1}{.37 / \sqrt{15}} = 2.41$

Since the observed value of the test statistic falls in the rejection region $(t = 2.41 > 1.345)$, H_0 is rejected. There is sufficient evidence to indicate the mean high technology stock is riskier than the market as a whole at $\alpha = .10$.

e.   From Table III, Appendix D, with df $= n - 1 = 15 - 1 = 14$, $.01 < P(t \geq 2.41) < .025$. Thus, $.01 < p$-value $< .025$. The probability of observing this test statistic, $t = 2.41$, or anything more unusual is between .01 and .025. Since this probability is small, there is evidence to indicate the null hypothesis is false for $\alpha = .05$.

f.   To determine if the variance of the stock beta values differs from .15, we test:

$$H_0 : \sigma^2 = .15$$
$$H_a : \sigma^2 \neq .15$$

The test statistic is $\chi^2 = \dfrac{(n-1)s^2}{\sigma_o^2} = \dfrac{(15-1).37^2}{.15} = 12.7773$.

The rejection region requires $\alpha / 2 = .05 / 2 = .025$ in each tail of the χ^2 distribution with df $= n - 1 = 15 - 1 = 14$. From Table IV, Appendix D, $\chi^2_{.975} = 5.62872$ and $\chi^2_{.025} = 26.1190$. The rejection region is $\chi^2 < 5.62872$ or $\chi^2 > 26.1190$.

Since the observed value of the test statistic does not fall in the rejection region $(\chi^2 = 12.7773 \nless 5.62875$ and $\chi^2 = 12.7773 \ngtr 26.1190)$, H_0 is not rejected. There is insufficient evidence to indicate the variance of the stock beta values differs from .15 at $\alpha = .05$.

7.123   a.   Let $p =$ proportion of time the camera correctly detects liars. The null hypothesis would be:

$$H_0 : p = .75$$

b.   A Type I error would be to conclude the camera cannot correctly identify liars 75% of the time when, in fact, it can. A Type II error would be to conclude the camera can correctly identify liars 75% of the time when, in fact, it cannot.

7.125   Some preliminary calculations are:

$$\bar{x} = \frac{\sum x}{n} = \frac{667.3}{7} = 95.33 \qquad s^2 = \frac{\sum x^2 - \frac{(\sum x)^2}{n}}{n-1} = \frac{63,867.99 - \frac{(667.3)^2}{7}}{7-1} = 42.539$$

$$s = \sqrt{42.539} = 6.5222$$

a.   To determine if the true mean cost-of-living index for Southeastern cities is different than the mean national cost-of-living index of 100, we test:

$$H_0 : \mu = 100$$
$$H_a : \mu \neq 100$$

b.   Since the sample size is so small, we must assume that the population being sampled is normal. In addition, we must assume that the sample is random.

c.   The test statistic is $t = \dfrac{\bar{x} - \mu_0}{s/\sqrt{n}} = \dfrac{95.33 - 100}{6.5222/\sqrt{7}} = -1.89$

The rejection region requires $\alpha/2 = .05/2 = .025$ in each tail of the t-distribution. From Table III, Appendix D, with df $= n-1 = 7-1 = 6$, $t_{.025} = 2.447$. The rejection region is $t < -2.447$ or $t > 2.447$.

Since the observed value of the test statistic does not fall in the rejection region ($t = -1.89 \not< -2.447$), H_0 is not rejected. There is insufficient evidence to indicate the true mean cost-of-living index for Southeastern cities is different than the mean national cost-of-living index of 100 at $\alpha = .05$.

d.   The observed significance level is p-value $= p = P(t \leq -1.89) + P(t \geq 1.89)$. Since we did not reject H_0 in part c, we know that the p-value must be greater than .05. Using MINITAB,

Cumulative Distribution Function
```
Student's t distribution with 6 DF

     x  P( X <= x )
 -1.89    0.0538261
```

Thus, the p-value is $p = 2(.0538261) = .1076522$.

7.127   a.   The hypotheses would be:

H_0: Individual does not have the disease
H_a: Individual does have the disease

b.   A Type I error would be: Conclude the individual has the disease when in fact he/she does not. This would be a false positive test.

A Type II error would be: Conclude the individual does not have the disease when in fact he/she does. This would be a false negative test.

c. If the disease is serious, either error would be grave. Arguments could be made for either error being more grave. However, I believe a Type II error would be more grave: Concluding the individual does not have the disease when he/she does. This person would not receive critical treatment, and may suffer very serious consequences. Thus, it is more important to minimize β.

7.129 To determine if the true standard deviation of the point-spread errors exceed 15 (variance exceeds 225), we test:

$$H_0 : \sigma^2 = 225$$
$$H_a : \sigma^2 > 225$$

The test statistic is $\chi^2 = \dfrac{(n-1)s^2}{\sigma_0^2} = \dfrac{(240-1)13.3^2}{225} = 187.896$

The rejection region requires α in the upper tail of the χ^2 distribution with df $= n-1 = 240-1 = 239$. The maximum value of df in Table IV is 100. Thus, we cannot find the rejection region using Table IV. Using a statistical package, the *p*-value associated with $\chi^2 = 187.896$ is $p = .9938$.

Since the *p*-value is so large, there is no evidence to reject H_0. There is insufficient evidence to indicate that the true standard deviation of the point-spread errors exceeds 15 for any reasonable value of α.

Since the observed standard deviation (13.3) is less than the hypothesized value of the standard deviation (15) under H_0, there is no way H_0 will be rejected for any reasonable value of α.

7.131 a. First, check to see if *n* is large enough:

$$np_0 = 132(.5) = 66 \quad nq_0 = 132(.5) = 66$$

Since both $np_0 \geq 15$ and $nq_0 \geq 15$, the normal distribution will be adequate.

To determine if there is evidence to reject the claim that no more than half of all manufacturers are dissatisfied with their trade promotion spending, we test:

$$H_0 : p = .5$$
$$H_a : p > .5$$

The test statistic is $z = \dfrac{\hat{p} - p_0}{\sqrt{\dfrac{p_0 q_0}{n}}} = \dfrac{.36 - .5}{\sqrt{\dfrac{.5(.5)}{132}}} = -3.22$

The rejection region requires $\alpha = .02$ in the upper tail of the *z*-distribution. From Table II, Appendix D, $z_{.02} = 2.05$. The rejection region is $z > 2.05$.

Since the observed value of the test statistic does not fall in the rejection region ($z = -3.22 \not> 2.05$), H_0 is not rejected. There is insufficient evidence to reject the claim that no more than half of all manufacturers are dissatisfied with their trade promotion spending at $\alpha = .02$.

b. The observed significance level is *p*-value $= P(z \geq -3.22) \approx .5 + .5 = 1$. Since this *p*-value is so large, H_0 will not be rejected for any reasonable value of α.

c. First, we must define the rejection region in terms of $\hat{p}$.

$$\hat{p} = p_0 + z_\alpha \sigma_{\hat{p}} = .5 + 2.05\sqrt{\frac{.5(.5)}{132}} = .589$$

$$\beta = P(\hat{p} < .589 \mid p = .55) = P\left(z < \frac{.589 - .55}{\sqrt{\frac{.55(.45)}{132}}}\right) = P(z < .90) = .5 + .3159 = .8159$$

7.133 a. A Type II error is concluding the percentage of shoplifters turned over to police is 50% when in fact, the percentage is higher than 50%.

b. First, calculate the value of $\hat{p}$ that corresponds to the border between the acceptance region and the rejection region.

$$P(\hat{p} > p_o) = P(z > z_o) = .05. \quad \text{From Table II, Appendix D, } z_0 = 1.645$$

$$\hat{p}_0 = p_o + 1.645\sigma_{\hat{p}} = .5 + 1.645\sqrt{\frac{.5(.5)}{40}} = .5 + .1300 = .6300$$

$$\beta = P(\hat{p} \le .6300 \text{ when } p = .55) = P\left(z \le \frac{.6300 - .55}{\sqrt{\frac{.55(.45)}{40}}}\right) = P(z \le 1.02) = .5 + .3461 = .8461$$

c. If n increases, the probability of a Type II error would decrease.

First, calculate the value of $\hat{p}_0$ that corresponds to the border between the acceptance region and the rejection region.

$$P(\hat{p} > p_o) = P(z > z_o) = .05. \quad \text{From Table II, Appendix D, } z_0 = 1.645$$

$$\hat{p}_0 = p_o + 1.645\sigma_{\hat{p}} = .5 + 1.645\sqrt{\frac{.5(.5)}{100}} = .5 + .082 = .582$$

$$\beta = P(\hat{p} \le .582 \text{ when } p = .55) = P\left(z \le \frac{.582 - .55}{\sqrt{\frac{.55(.45)}{100}}}\right) = P(z \le 0.64) = .5 + .2389 = .7389$$

7.135 a. To determine if the production process should be halted, we test:

$$H_0 : \mu = 3$$
$$H_a : \mu > 3$$

where μ = mean amount of vinyl chloride in the air.

The test statistic is $z = \dfrac{\bar{x} - \mu_0}{\sigma_{\bar{x}}} = \dfrac{3.1 - 3}{.5/\sqrt{50}} = 1.41$

The rejection region requires $\alpha = .01$ in the upper tail of the z-distribution. From Table II, Appendix D, $z_{.01} = 2.33$. The rejection region is $z > 2.33$.

Since the observed value of the test statistic does not fall in the rejection region, $(z = 1.41 \not> 2.33)$, H_0 is not rejected. There is insufficient evidence to indicate the mean amount of vinyl chloride in the air is more than 3 parts per million at $\alpha = .01$. Do not halt the manufacturing process.

b. As plant manager, I do not want to shut down the plant unnecessarily. Therefore, I want $\alpha = P(\text{shut down plant when } \mu = 3)$ to be small.

c. The p-value is $p = P(z \geq 1.41) = .5 - .4207 = .0793$. Since the p-value is not less than $\alpha = .01$, H_0 is not rejected.

7.137   a. No, it increases the risk of falsely rejecting H_0, i.e., closing the plant unnecessarily.

b. First, find $\bar{x}_0$ such that $P(\bar{x} > \bar{x}_0) = P(z > z_0) = .05$.

From Table II, Appendix D, $z_0 = 1.645$

$$z = \frac{\bar{x}_0 - \mu}{\sigma/\sqrt{n}} \Rightarrow 1.645 = \frac{\bar{x}_0 - 3}{.5/\sqrt{50}} \Rightarrow \bar{x}_0 = 3.116$$

Then, compute:

$$\beta = P(\bar{x}_0 \leq 3.116 \text{ when } \mu = 3.1) = P\left(z \leq \frac{3.116 - 3.1}{.5/\sqrt{50}}\right) = P(z \leq .23) = .5 + .0910 = .5910$$

$$Power = 1 - \beta = 1 - .5910 = .4090$$

c. The power of the test increases as α increases.

7.139   a. To determine if the GSR for all scholarship athletes at Division I institutions differs from 60%, we test:
$$H_0: p = .60$$
$$H_a: p \neq .60$$

The point estimate is $\hat{p} = \dfrac{x}{n} = \dfrac{315}{500} = .63$

The test statistic is $z = \dfrac{\hat{p} - p_o}{\sqrt{\dfrac{p_o q_o}{n}}} = \dfrac{.63 - .60}{\sqrt{\dfrac{.60(.40)}{500}}} = 1.37$

The rejection region requires $\alpha/2 = .01/2 = .005$ in each tail of the z-distribution. From Table II, Appendix D, $z_{.005} = 2.58$. The rejection region is $z < -2.58$ or $z > 2.58$.

Since the observed value does not fall in the rejection region $(z = 1.37 \not> 2.58)$, H_0 is not rejected. There is insufficient evidence to conclude that the GSR for all scholarship athletes at Division I institution differs from 60% at $\alpha = .01$.

b. To determine if the GSR for all male basketball players at Division I institutions differs from 58%, we test:

$$H_0 : p = .58$$
$$H_a : p \neq .58$$

The point estimate is $\hat{p} = \dfrac{x}{n} = \dfrac{84}{200} = .42$

The test statistic is $z = \dfrac{\hat{p} - p_o}{\sqrt{\dfrac{p_o q_o}{n}}} = \dfrac{.42 - .58}{\sqrt{\dfrac{.58(.42)}{200}}} = -4.58$

The rejection region requires $\alpha/2 = .01/2 = .005$ in each tail of the z-distribution. From Table II, Appendix D, $z_{.005} = 2.58$. The rejection region is $z < -2.58$ or $z > 2.58$.

Since the observed value falls in the rejection region $(z = -4.58 < -2.58)$, H_0 is rejected. There is sufficient evidence to conclude that the GSR for all male basketball players at Division I institutions differs from 58% $\alpha = .01$.

7.141 Let μ = mean lacunarity measurement for all grassland pixels. To determine if the area sampled is grassland, we test:

$$H_0 : \mu = 220$$
$$H_a : \mu \neq 220$$

The test statistic is $z = \dfrac{\bar{x} - \mu_o}{\sigma_{\bar{x}}} \approx \dfrac{225 - 220}{20 / \sqrt{100}} = 2.50$.

The rejection region requires $\alpha / 2 = .01 / 2 = .005$ in each tail of the z-distribution. From Table II, Appendix D, $z_{.005} = 2.58$. The rejection region is $z < -2.58$ or $z > 2.58$.

Since the observed value of the test statistic does not fall in the rejection region $(z = 2.50 \not> 2.58)$, H_0 is not rejected. There is insufficient evidence to conclude that the area sampled is not grassland at $\alpha = .01$.

7.143 a. To determine whether the true mean rating for this instructor-related factor exceeds 4, we test:

$$H_0 : \mu = 4$$
$$H_a : \mu > 4$$

The test statistic is $z = \dfrac{\bar{x} - \mu_0}{\sigma_{\bar{x}}} \approx \dfrac{4.7 - 4}{1.62 / \sqrt{40}} = 2.73$

The rejection region requires $\alpha = .05$ in the upper tail of the z-distribution. From Table II, Appendix D, $z_{.05} = 1.645$. The rejection region is $z > 1.645$.

Since the observed value of the test statistic falls in the rejection region $(z=2.73 > 1.645)$, H_0 is rejected. There is sufficient evidence to indicate that the true mean rating for this instructor-related factor exceeds 4 at $\alpha = .05$.

b.   If the sample size is large enough, one could almost always reject H_0. Thus, we might be able to detect very small differences if the sample size is large enough. This would be statistical significance. However, even though statistical significance is found, it does not necessarily mean that there is practical significance. A statistical significance can sometimes be found between the hypothesized value of a mean and the estimated value of the mean, but, in practice, this difference would mean nothing. This would be practical significance.

c.   Since the sample size is sufficiently large $(n = 40)$, the Central Limit Theorem indicates that the sampling distribution of $\bar{x}$ is approximately normal. Also, since the sample size is large, s is a good estimator of σ. Thus, the analysis used is appropriate.

7.145   Using MINITAB, the descriptive statistics are:

Descriptive Statistics: Candy

```
Variable  N    Mean   StDev  Minimum    Q1    Median     Q3  Maximum
Candy     5  22.000  2.000   20.000  20.500   21.000  24.000   25.000
```

To give the benefit of the doubt to the students we will use a small value of α. (We do not want to reject H_0 when it is true to favor the students.) Thus, we will use $\alpha = .001$.

We must also assume that the sample comes from a normal distribution. To determine if the mean number of candies exceeds 15, we test:

$$H_0 : \mu = 15$$
$$H_a : \mu > 15$$

The test statistic is $z = \dfrac{\bar{x} - \mu_o}{\sigma / \sqrt{n}} = \dfrac{22 - 15}{2 / \sqrt{5}} = 7.83$

The rejection region requires $\alpha = .001$ in the upper tail of the z-distribution. From Table II, Appendix D, $z_{.001} = 3.08$. The rejection region is $z > 3.08$.

Since the observed value of the test statistic falls in the rejection region $(z = 7.83 > 3.08)$, H_0 is rejected. There is sufficient evidence to indicate the mean number of candies exceeds 15 at $\alpha = .001$.

Chapter 8
Inferences Based on Two Samples: Confidence Intervals and Tests of Hypotheses

8.1   a. $\mu_1 \pm 2\sigma_{\bar{x}_1} \Rightarrow \mu_1 \pm 2\dfrac{\sigma_1}{\sqrt{n_1}} \Rightarrow 150 \pm 2\dfrac{\sqrt{900}}{\sqrt{100}} \Rightarrow 150 \pm 6 \Rightarrow (144,\ 156)$

      b. $\mu_2 \pm 2\sigma_{\bar{x}_2} \Rightarrow \mu_2 \pm 2\dfrac{\sigma_2}{\sqrt{n_2}} \Rightarrow 150 \pm 2\dfrac{\sqrt{1600}}{\sqrt{100}} \Rightarrow 150 \pm 8 \Rightarrow (142,\ 158)$

      c. $\mu_{\bar{x}_1 - \bar{x}_2} = \mu_1 - \mu_2 = 150 - 150 = 0$ $\sigma_{\bar{x}_1 - \bar{x}_2} = \sqrt{\dfrac{\sigma_1^2}{n_1} + \dfrac{\sigma_2^2}{n_2}} = \sqrt{\dfrac{900}{100} + \dfrac{1600}{100}} = \sqrt{\dfrac{2500}{100}} = 5$

      d. $(\mu_1 - \mu_2) \pm 2\sqrt{\dfrac{\sigma_1^2}{n_1} + \dfrac{\sigma_2^2}{n_2}} \Rightarrow (150 - 150) \pm 2\sqrt{\dfrac{900}{100} + \dfrac{1600}{100}} \Rightarrow 0 \pm 10 \Rightarrow (-10,\ 10)$

      e.   The variability of the difference between the sample means is greater than the variability of the individual sample means.

8.3   a.   For confidence coefficient .95, $\alpha = .05$ and $\alpha/2 = .05/2 = .025$. From Table II, Appendix D, $z_{.025} = 1.96$. The confidence interval is:

$$(\bar{x}_1 - \bar{x}_2) \pm z_{.025}\sqrt{\dfrac{\sigma_1^2}{n_1} + \dfrac{\sigma_2^2}{n_2}} \Rightarrow (5,275 - 5,240) \pm 1.96\sqrt{\dfrac{150^2}{400} + \dfrac{200^2}{400}} \Rightarrow 35 \pm 24.5 \Rightarrow (10.5,\ 59.5)$$

      We are 95% confident that the difference between the population means is between 10.5 and 59.5.

      b.   The test statistic is $z = \dfrac{(\bar{x}_1 - \bar{x}_2) - (\mu_1 - \mu_2)}{\sqrt{\dfrac{\sigma_1^2}{n_1} + \dfrac{\sigma_2^2}{n_2}}} = \dfrac{(5,275 - 5,240) - 0}{\sqrt{\dfrac{150^2}{400} + \dfrac{200^2}{400}}} = 2.8$

      The p-value is $p = P(z \le -2.8) + P(z \ge 2.8) = 2P(z \ge 2.8) = 2(.5 - .4974) = 2(.0026) = .0052$

      Since the p-value is so small, there is evidence to reject H_0. There is evidence to indicate the two population means are different for $\alpha > .0052$.

      c.   The p-value would be half of the p-value in part **b**. The p-value $= p = P(z \ge 2.8) = .5 - .4974 = .0026$.

      Since the p-value is so small, there is evidence to reject H_0. There is evidence to indicate the mean for population 1 is larger than the mean for population 2 for $\alpha > .0026$.

d. The test statistic is $z = \dfrac{(\bar{x}_1 - \bar{x}_2) - (\mu_1 - \mu_2)}{\sqrt{\dfrac{\sigma_1^2}{n_1} + \dfrac{\sigma_2^2}{n_2}}} = \dfrac{(5,275 - 5,240) - 25}{\sqrt{\dfrac{150^2}{400} + \dfrac{200^2}{400}}} = .8$

The *p*-value of the test is $p = P(z \leq -.8) + P(z \geq .8) = 2P(z \geq .8) = 2(.5 - .2881) = 2(.2119) = .4238$

Since the *p*-value is so large, there is no evidence to reject H_0. There is no evidence to indicate that the difference in the 2 population means is different from 25 for $\alpha \leq .10$.

e. We must assume that we have two independent random samples.

8.5 a. No. Both populations must be normal.

b. No. Both populations variances must be equal.

c. No. Both populations must be normal.

d. Yes.

e. No. Both populations must be normal.

8.7 Some preliminary calculations are:

$\bar{x}_1 = \dfrac{\sum x_1}{n_1} = \dfrac{11.8}{5} = 2.36$ $s_1^2 = \dfrac{\sum x_1^2 - \dfrac{\left(\sum x_1\right)^2}{n_1}}{n_1 - 1} = \dfrac{30.78 - \dfrac{(11.8)^2}{5}}{5 - 1} = .733$

$\bar{x}_2 = \dfrac{\sum x_2}{n_2} = \dfrac{14.4}{4} = 3.6$ $s_2^2 = \dfrac{\sum x_2^2 - \dfrac{\left(\sum x_2\right)^2}{n_2}}{n_2 - 1} = \dfrac{53.1 - \dfrac{(14.4)^2}{4}}{4 - 1} = .42$

a. $s_p^2 = \dfrac{(n_1 - 1)s_1^2 + (n_2 - 1)s_2^2}{n_1 + n_2 - 2} = \dfrac{(5-1).773 + (4-1).42}{5 + 4 - 2} = \dfrac{4.192}{7} = .5989$

b. $H_0 : \mu_1 - \mu_2 = 0$
$H_a : \mu_1 - \mu_2 < 0$

The test statistic is $t = \dfrac{(\bar{x}_1 - \bar{x}_2) - D_0}{\sqrt{s_p^2 \left(\dfrac{1}{n_1} + \dfrac{1}{n_2}\right)}} = \dfrac{(2.36 - 3.6) - 0}{\sqrt{.5989 \left(\dfrac{1}{5} + \dfrac{1}{4}\right)}} = \dfrac{-1.24}{.5191} = -2.39$

The rejection region *requires* $\alpha = .10$ in the lower tail of the *t*-distribution with df $= n_1 + n_2 - 2 = 5 + 4 - 2 = 7$. From Table III, Appendix D, $t_{.10} = 1.415$. The rejection region is $t < -1.415$.

Since the test statistic falls in the rejection region $(t = -2.39 < -1.415)$, H_0 is rejected. There is sufficient evidence to indicate that $\mu_2 > \mu_1$ at $\alpha = .10$.

c.   A small sample confidence interval is needed because $n_1 = 5 < 30$ and $n_2 = 4 < 30$.

For confidence coefficient .90, $\alpha = .10$ and $\alpha / 2 = .10 / 2 = .05$. From Table III, Appendix D, with $df = n_1 + n_2 - 2 = 5 + 4 - 2 = 7$, $t_{.05} = 1.895$. The 90% confidence interval for $(\mu_1 - \mu_2)$ is:

$$(\bar{x}_1 - x_2) \pm t_{.05} \sqrt{s_p^2 \left(\frac{1}{n_1} + \frac{1}{n_2} \right)} \Rightarrow (2.36 - 3.6) \pm 1.895 \sqrt{.5989 \left(\frac{1}{5} + \frac{1}{4} \right)} \Rightarrow -1.24 \pm .98 \Rightarrow (-2.22, -0.26)$$

d.   The confidence interval in part **c** provides more information about $(\mu_1 - \mu_2)$ than the test of hypothesis in part **b**. The test in part **b** only tells us that μ_2 is greater than μ_1. However, the confidence interval estimates what the difference is between μ_1 and μ_2.

8.9   a.   The p-value $= p = .1150$. Since the p-value is not small, there is no evidence to reject H_0 for $\alpha \leq .10$. There is insufficient evidence to indicate the two population means differ for $\alpha \leq .10$.

b.   If the alternative hypothesis had been one-tailed, the p-value would be half of the value for the two-tailed test. Here, p-value $= .1150 / 2 = .0575$.

There is no evidence to reject H_0 for $\alpha = .05$. There is insufficient evidence to indicate the mean for population 1 is less than the mean for population 2 at $\alpha = .05$.

There is evidence to reject H_0 for $\alpha > .0575$. There is sufficient evidence to indicate the mean for population 1 is less than the mean for population 2 at $\alpha > .0575$.

8.11   a. $s_p^2 = \dfrac{(n_1 - 1)s_1^2 + (n_2 - 1)s_2^2}{n_1 + n_2 - 2} = \dfrac{(17 - 1)3.4^2 + (12 - 1)4.8^2}{17 + 12 - 2} = 16.237$

$H_0 : \mu_1 - \mu_2 = 0$
$H_a : \mu_1 - \mu_2 \neq 0$

The test statistic is $t = \dfrac{(\bar{x}_1 - \bar{x}_2) - 0}{\sqrt{s_p^2 \left(\frac{1}{n_1} + \frac{1}{n_2} \right)}} = \dfrac{(5.4 - 7.9) - 0}{\sqrt{16.237 \left(\frac{1}{17} + \frac{1}{12} \right)}} = -1.646$

Since no α was given, we will use $\alpha = .05$. The rejection region requires $\alpha / 2 = .05 / 2 = .025$ in each tail of the t-distribution with $df = n_1 + n_2 - 2 = 17 + 12 - 2 = 27$. From Table III, Appendix D, $t_{.025} = 2.052$. The rejection region is $t < -2.052$ or $t > 2.052$.

Since the observed value of the test statistic does not fall in the rejection region ($t = -1.646 \not< -2.052$), H_0 is not rejected. There is insufficient evidence to indicate $\mu_1 - \mu_2$ is different from 0 at $\alpha = .05$.

b. For confidence coefficient .95, $\alpha = .05$ and $\alpha / 2 = .05 / 2 = .025$. From Table III, Appendix D, with $df = n_1 + n_2 - 2 = 17 + 12 - 2 = 27$, $t_{.025} = 2.052$. The confidence interval is:

$$(\bar{x}_1 - \bar{x}_2) \pm t_{.025} \sqrt{s_p^2 \left(\frac{1}{n_1} + \frac{1}{n_2} \right)} \Rightarrow (5.4 - 7.9) - 2.052 \sqrt{16.237 \left(\frac{1}{17} + \frac{1}{12} \right)} \Rightarrow -2.50 \pm 3.12 \Rightarrow (-5.62, \ 0.62)$$

8.13 a. $s_p^2 = \dfrac{(n_1 - 1)s_1^2 + (n_2 - 1)s_2^2}{n_1 + n_2 - 2} = \dfrac{(25 - 1)10.41^2 + (25 - 1)7.12^2}{25 + 25 - 2} = \dfrac{3,817.5}{48} = 79.53125$

For confidence coefficient .95, $\alpha = .05$ and $\alpha / 2 = .05 / 2 = .025$. Using MINITAB with $df = n_1 + n_2 - 2 = 25 + 25 - 2 = 48$, $t_{.025} = 2.011$. The 95% confidence interval for $(\mu_1 - \mu_2)$ is:

$$(\bar{x}_1 - \bar{x}_2) \pm t_{\alpha/2} \sqrt{s_p^2 \left(\frac{1}{n_1} + \frac{1}{n_2} \right)} \Rightarrow (25.08 - 19.38) \pm 2.011 \sqrt{79.53125 \left(\frac{1}{25} + \frac{1}{25} \right)}$$

$$\Rightarrow 5.7 \pm 5.073 \Rightarrow (.627, \ 10.773)$$

b. Since 0 does not fall in the 95% confidence interval, there is evidence to indicate there is a difference in the mean response times between the two groups. Since the interval contains only positive numbers, it indicates that the mean response time for the group of students whose last names begin with the letters R-Z is shorter than the mean response time for the group of students whose last names begin with the letters A-I. This supports the researchers' *last name effect* theory.

8.15 a. Let $\mu_1 =$ mean number of items recalled by those in the video only group and $\mu_2 =$ mean number of items recalled by those in the audio and video group. To determine if the mean number of items recalled by the two groups is the same, we test:

$H_0 : \mu_1 - \mu_2 = 0$
$H_a : \mu_1 - \mu_2 \neq 0$

b. $s_p^2 = \dfrac{(n_1 - 1)s_1^2 + (n_2 - 1)s_2^2}{n_1 + n_2 - 2} = \dfrac{(20 - 1)1.98^2 + (20 - 1)2.13^2}{20 + 20 - 2} = 4.22865$

The test statistic is $t = \dfrac{(\bar{x}_1 - \bar{x}_2) - D_o}{\sqrt{s_p^2 \left(\frac{1}{n_1} + \frac{1}{n_2} \right)}} = \dfrac{(3.70 - 3.30) - 0}{\sqrt{4.22865 \left(\frac{1}{20} + \frac{1}{20} \right)}} = \dfrac{0.4}{.65028} = 0.62$

c. The rejection region requires $\alpha / 2 = .10 / 2 = .05$ in each tail of the t-distribution with $df = n_1 + n_2 - 2 = 20 + 20 - 2 = 38$. From Table III, Appendix D, $t_{.05} \approx 1.684$. The rejection region is $t < -1.684$ or $t > 1.684$.

d. Since the observed value of the test statistic does not fall in the rejection region $(t = 0.62 \not> 1.684)$, H_0 is not rejected. There is insufficient evidence to indicate a difference in the mean number of items recalled by the two groups at $\alpha = .10$.

e. The p-value is $p = .542$. This is the probability of observing our test statistic or anything more unusual if H_0 is true. Since the p-value is not less than $\alpha = .10$, there is no evidence to reject H_0.

There is insufficient evidence to indicate a difference in the mean number of items recalled by the two groups at $\alpha = .10$.

f. We must assume:

1. Both populations are normal
2. Random and independent samples
3. $\sigma_1^2 = \sigma_2^2$

8.17 a. Let μ_1 =mean forecast error of buy-side analysts and μ_2 =mean forecast error of sell-side analysts. For confidence coefficient 0.95, $\alpha = .05$ and $\alpha / 2 = .05 / 2 = .025$. From Table II, Appendix D, $z_{.025} = 1.96$. The 95% confidence interval is:

$$(\overline{x}_1 - \overline{x}_2) \pm z_{.025}\sqrt{\frac{\sigma_1^2}{n_1} + \frac{\sigma_2^2}{n_2}} \Rightarrow (.85 - (-.05)) \pm 1.96\sqrt{\frac{1.93^2}{3,526} + \frac{.85^2}{58,562}} \Rightarrow .90 \pm .064 \Rightarrow (.836, .964)$$

We are 95% confident that the difference in the mean forecast error of buy-side analysts and sell-side analysts is between .836 and .964.

b. Based on 95% confidence interval in part **a**, the buy-side analysts has the greater mean forecast error because our interval contains positive numbers.

c. The assumptions about the underlying populations of forecast errors that are necessary for the validity of the inference are:

1. The samples are randomly and independently sampled.
2. The sample sizes are sufficiently large.

8.19 a. The descriptive statistics are:

Descriptive Statistics: Text-line, Witness-line, Intersection

```
Variable        N    Mean   Median   StDev   Minimum  Maximum     Q1      Q3
Text-line       3  0.3830   0.3740  0.0531   0.3350   0.4400  0.3350  0.4400
Witness-line    6  0.3042   0.2955  0.1015   0.1880   0.4390  0.2045  0.4075
Intersection    5  0.3290   0.3190  0.0443   0.2850   0.3930  0.2900  0.3730
```

Let μ_1 =mean zinc measurement for the text-line, μ_2 =mean zinc measurement for the witness-line, and μ_3 =mean zinc measurement for the intersection.

$$s_p^2 = \frac{(n_1 - 1)s_1^2 + (n_3 - 1)s_3^2}{n_1 + n_3 - 2} = \frac{(3-1).0531^2 + (5-1).0443^2}{3 + 5 - 2} = .00225$$

For $\alpha = .05$, $\alpha / 2 = .05 / 2 = .025$. Using Table III, Appendix D, with df $= n_1 + n_2 - 2 = 3 + 5 - 2 = 6$, $t_{.025} = 2.447$. The 95% confidence interval is:

$$(\overline{x}_1 - \overline{x}_3) \pm t_{\alpha/2}\sqrt{s_p^2\left(\frac{1}{n_1} + \frac{1}{n_3}\right)} \Rightarrow (.3830 - .3290) \pm 2.447\sqrt{.00225\left(\frac{1}{3} + \frac{1}{5}\right)}$$

$$\Rightarrow 0.0540 \pm .0848 \Rightarrow (-0.0308, 0.1388)$$

We are 95% confident that the difference in mean zinc level between text-line and intersection is between −0.0308 and 0.1388.

To determine if there is a difference in the mean zinc measurement between text-line and intersection, we test:

$$H_0 : \mu_1 - \mu_3 = 0$$
$$H_a : \mu_1 - \mu_3 \neq 0$$

The test statistic is $t = \dfrac{(\bar{x}_1 - \bar{x}_3) - D_o}{\sqrt{s_p^2\left(\dfrac{1}{n_1} + \dfrac{1}{n_3}\right)}} = \dfrac{(.3830 - .3290) - 0}{\sqrt{.00225\left(\dfrac{1}{3} + \dfrac{1}{5}\right)}} = 1.56$

The rejection region requires $\alpha / 2 = .05 / 2 = .025$ in each tail of the t-distribution with df $= n_1 + n_2 - 2 = 3 + 5 - 2 = 6$. From Table III, Appendix D, $t_{.025} = 2.447$. The rejection region is $t < -2.447$ or $t > 2.447$.

Since the observed value of the test statistic does not fall in the rejection region $(t = 1.56 \not> 2.447)$, H_0 is not rejected. There is insufficient evidence to indicate a difference in the mean zinc measurement between text-line and intersection at $\alpha = .05$.

b. $\quad s_p^2 = \dfrac{(n_2 - 1)s_2^2 + (n_3 - 1)s_3^2}{n_2 + n_3 - 2} = \dfrac{(6 - 1).1015^2 + (5 - 1).0443^2}{6 + 5 - 2} = .006596$

For $\alpha = .05$, $\alpha / 2 = .05 / 2 = .025$. Using Table III, Appendix D, with df $= n_1 + n_2 - 2 = 6 + 5 - 2 = 9$, $t_{.025} = 2.262$. The 95% confidence interval is:

$$(\bar{x}_2 - \bar{x}_3) \pm t_{\alpha/2}\sqrt{s_p^2\left(\dfrac{1}{n_2} + \dfrac{1}{n_3}\right)} \Rightarrow (.3042 - .3290) \pm 2.262\sqrt{.006596\left(\dfrac{1}{6} + \dfrac{1}{5}\right)}$$
$$\Rightarrow -.0248 \pm .1112 \Rightarrow (-.1361, \ .0864)$$

We are 95% confident that the difference in mean zinc level between witness-line and intersection is between −0.1361 and 0.0864.

To determine if the difference in mean zinc measurement between the witness-line and the intersection, we test:

$$H_0 : \mu_2 - \mu_3 = 0$$
$$H_a : \mu_2 - \mu_3 \neq 0$$

The test statistic is $t = \dfrac{(\bar{x}_2 - \bar{x}_3) - D_o}{\sqrt{s_p^2\left(\dfrac{1}{n_2} + \dfrac{1}{n_3}\right)}} = \dfrac{(.3042 - .3290) - 0}{\sqrt{.006596\left(\dfrac{1}{6} + \dfrac{1}{5}\right)}} = -.50$

The rejection region requires $\alpha / 2 = .05 / 2 = .025$ in each tail of the t-distribution. From Table III, Appendix D, with df $= n_1 + n_2 - 2 = 6 + 5 - 2 = 9$, $t_{.025} = 2.262$. The rejection region is $t < -2.262$ or $t > 2.262$.

Since the observed value of the test statistic does not fall in the rejection region $(t = -.50 \not< -2.262)$, H_0 is not rejected. There is insufficient evidence to indicate a difference in mean zinc measurement between witness-line and intersection at $\alpha = .05$.

c. If we order the sample means, the largest is Text-line, the next largest is intersection and the smallest is witness-line. In parts **a** and **b**, we found that text-line is not different from the intersection and that the witness-line is not different from the intersection. However, we cannot make any decisions about the difference between the witness-line and the text-line.

d. In order for the above inferences to be valid, we must assume:

1. The three samples are randomly selected in an independent manner from the three target populations.

2. All three sampled populations have distributions that are approximately normal.

3. All three population variances are equal (i.e. $\sigma_1^2 = \sigma_2^2 = \sigma_3^2$)

8.21 Using MINITAB, the descriptive statistics are:

Descriptive Statistics: Control, Rude

Variable	N	Mean	StDev	Minimum	Q1	Median	Q3	Maximum
Rude	45	8.511	3.992	0.000	5.500	9.000	11.000	18.000
Control	53	11.81	7.38	0.00	5.50	12.00	17.50	30.00

Let $\mu_1 = $ mean performance level of students in the rudeness group and $\mu_2 = $ mean performance level of students in the control group. To determine if the true performance level for students in the rudeness condition is lower than the true mean performance level for students in the control group, we test:

$$H_0 : \mu_1 - \mu_2 = 0$$
$$H_a : \mu_1 - \mu_2 < 0$$

The test statistic is $z = \dfrac{(\bar{x}_1 - \bar{x}_2) - 0}{\sqrt{\dfrac{\sigma_1^2}{n_1} + \dfrac{\sigma_2^2}{n_2}}} \approx \dfrac{(8.511 - 11.81) - 0}{\sqrt{\dfrac{3.922^2}{45} + \dfrac{7.38^2}{53}}} = -2.81$

The rejection region requires $\alpha = .01$ in the lower tail of the z-distribution. From Table II, Appendix D, $z_{.01} = 2.33$. The rejection region is $z < -2.33$.

Since the observed value of the test statistic falls in the rejection region $(z = -2.81 < -2.33)$, H_0 is rejected. There is sufficient evidence to indicate the true mean performance level for students in the rudeness condition is lower than the true mean performance level for students in the control group at $\alpha = .01$.

8.23 Using MINITAB, the descriptive statistics are:

Descriptive Statistics: Honey, DM

Variable	N	Mean	StDev	Minimum	Q1	Median	Q3	Maximum
Honey	35	10.714	2.855	4.000	9.000	11.000	12.000	16.000
DM	33	8.333	3.256	3.000	6.000	9.000	11.500	15.000

Let μ_1 = mean improvement in total cough symptoms score for children receiving the Honey dosage and μ_2 = mean improvement in total cough symptoms score for children receiving the DM dosage. To test if honey may be a preferable treatment for the cough and sleep difficulty associated with childhood upper respiratory tract infection, we test:

$$H_0 : \mu_1 - \mu_2 = 0$$
$$H_a : \mu_1 - \mu_2 > 0$$

The test statistic is $z = \dfrac{(\bar{x}_1 - \bar{x}_2) - 0}{\sqrt{\dfrac{\sigma_1^2}{n_1} + \dfrac{\sigma_2^2}{n_2}}} \approx \dfrac{(10.714 - 8.333) - 0}{\sqrt{\dfrac{2.855^2}{35} + \dfrac{3.256^2}{33}}} = 3.20$

Since no α was given, we will use $\alpha = .05$. The rejection region requires $\alpha = .05$ in the upper tail of the z-distribution. From Table II, Appendix D, $z_{.05} = 1.645$. The rejection region is $z > 1.645$.

Since the observed value of the test statistic falls in the rejection region ($z = 3.20 > 1.645$), H_0 is rejected. There is sufficient evidence to indicate that honey may be a preferable treatment for the cough and sleep difficulty associated with childhood upper respiratory tract infection at $\alpha = .05$.

8.25   a.   We cannot provide a measure of reliability because we have no measure of the variability or variance of the data.

        b.   We would need the variances of the two samples.

        c.   Let μ_1 = mean age for self-employed immigrants and μ_2 = mean age for the wage-earning immigrants. To determine if the mean age for self-employed immigrants is less than the mean age for wage-earning immigrants, we test:

$$H_0 : \mu_1 - \mu_2 = 0$$
$$H_a : \mu_1 - \mu_2 < 0$$

The rejection region requires $\alpha = .01$ in the lower tail of the z-distribution. From Table II, Appendix D, $z_{.01} = 2.33$. The rejection region is $z < -2.33$.

d. We use the following to solve for σ:

$$z = \frac{(\bar{x}_1 - \bar{x}_2) - (\mu_1 - \mu_2)}{\sqrt{\dfrac{\sigma_1^2}{n_1} + \dfrac{\sigma_2^2}{n_2}}} = \frac{(44.88 - 46.79) - 0}{\sqrt{\dfrac{\sigma^2}{870} + \dfrac{\sigma^2}{84,875}}} \le -2.33$$

$$\Rightarrow -1.91 \le \sigma \sqrt{\frac{1}{870} + \frac{1}{84,875}}(-2.33) \Rightarrow \sigma \le 24.056$$

e. The true value of σ is likely to be smaller than 24.056. This standard deviation would be too large for the ages of people.

8.27   a. The rejection region requires $\alpha = .05$ in the upper tail of the t-distribution with $df = n_d - 1 = 12 - 1 = 11$. From Table III, Appendix D, $t_{.05} = 1.796$. The rejection region is $t > 1.796$.

b. From Table III, with $df = n_d - 1 = 24 - 1 = 23$, $t_{.10} = 1.319$. The rejection region is $t > 1.319$.

c. From Table III, with $df = n_d - 1 = 4 - 1 = 3$, $t_{.025} = 3.182$. The rejection region is $t > 3.182$.

d. Using Minitab, with $df = n_d - 1 = 80 - 1 = 79$, $t_{.01} = 2.374$. The rejection region is $t > 2.374$.

8.29   Let $\mu_1 =$ mean of population 1 and $\mu_2 =$ mean of population 2.

a. $H_0 : \mu_d = 0$
    $H_a : \mu_d < 0$ where $\mu_d = \mu_1 - \mu_2$

b. Some preliminary calculations are:

Pair	Population 1	Population 2	Difference, d
1	19	24	−5
2	25	27	−2
3	31	36	−5
4	52	53	−1
5	49	55	−6
6	34	34	0
7	59	66	−7
8	47	51	−4
9	17	20	−3
10	51	55	−4

$$\bar{d} = \frac{\sum_{i=1}^{n_d} d_i}{n_d} = \frac{-37}{10} = -3.7 \qquad s_d^2 = \frac{\sum_{i=1}^{n_d} d_i^2 - \dfrac{\left(\sum_{i=1}^{n_d} d_i\right)^2}{n_d}}{n_d - 1} = \frac{181 - \dfrac{(-37)^2}{10}}{10 - 1} = 4.9$$

The test statistic is $t = \dfrac{\bar{d}}{s_d/\sqrt{n_d}} = \dfrac{-3.7}{\sqrt{4.9}\big/\sqrt{10}} = -5.29$

The rejection region requires $\alpha = .10$ in the lower tail of the t-distribution with df $= n_d - 1 = 10 - 1 = 9$. From Table III, Appendix D, $t_{.10} = 1.383$. The rejection region is $t < -1.383$.

Since the observed value of the test statistic falls in the rejection region $(t = -5.29 < -1.383)$, H_0 is rejected. There is sufficient evidence to indicate the mean of population 1 is less than the mean for population 2 at $\alpha = .10$.

    c.   For confidence coefficient .90, $\alpha = .10$ and $\alpha/2 = .10/2 = .05$. From Table III, Appendix D, with df $= n_d - 1 = 10 - 1 = 9$, $t_{.05} = 1.833$. The 90% confidence interval is:

$$\bar{d} \pm t_{\alpha/2}\frac{s_d}{\sqrt{n_d}} \Rightarrow -3.7 \pm 1.833\frac{\sqrt{4.9}}{\sqrt{10}} \Rightarrow -3.7 \pm 1.28 \Rightarrow (-4.98,\ -2.42)$$

We are 90% confident that the difference in the two population means is between –4.98 and –2.42.

    d.   We must assume that the population of differences is normal, and the sample of differences is randomly selected.

8.31   a.   Let $\mu_1 =$ mean starting BMI and $\mu_2 =$ mean ending BMI. To determine if the mean BMI at the end of the camp is less than the mean BMI at the start of camp, we test:

$$\begin{aligned} H_0 &: \mu_d = 0 \\ H_a &: \mu_d > 0 \end{aligned} \quad \text{where } \mu_d = \mu_1 - \mu_2$$

    b.   The data should be analyzed as a paired-difference t-test. Each camper had his/her BMI measured at the start of the camp and at the end. Therefore, these two sets of BMI's are not independent.

    c.   The test statistic is $z = \dfrac{(\bar{x}_1 - \bar{x}_2) - (\mu_1 - \mu_2)}{\sqrt{\dfrac{\sigma_1^2}{n_1} + \dfrac{\sigma_2^2}{n_2}}} = \dfrac{(34.9 - 31.6) - 0}{\sqrt{\dfrac{6.9^2}{76} + \dfrac{6.2^2}{76}}} = 3.10$.

    d.   The test statistic is $z = \dfrac{\bar{d}}{\sigma_d/\sqrt{n_d}} = \dfrac{3.3}{1.5/\sqrt{76}} = 19.18$.

    e.   The test statistic using the paired-difference formula is much larger than the test statistic using the independent samples formula. The test statistic for the paired-difference provides more evidence to support the alternative hypothesis.

    f.   Since the p-value is less than α $(p < .0001 < .01)$, H_0 is rejected. There is sufficient evidence to indicate the mean BMI at the end of camp is less than the mean BMI at the start of camp.

    g.   No, the differences in the BMI values do not have to be normally distributed. The sample size is $n = 76$. Thus, the Central Limit Theorem applies and says that the sampling distribution of $\bar{d}$ will be approximately normally distributed.

h.   For confidence coefficient .99, $\alpha = .01$ and $\alpha/2 = .01/2 = .005$. From Table II, Appendix D, $z_{.005} = 2.58$. The 99% confidence interval is:

$$\bar{d} \pm z_{\alpha/2}\frac{\sigma_d}{\sqrt{n_d}} \Rightarrow 3.3 \pm 2.58\frac{1.5}{\sqrt{76}} \Rightarrow 3.3 \pm .444 \Rightarrow (2.856,\ 3.744)$$

We are 99% confident that the true difference in the mean BMI scores between the start of camp and the end of camp is between 2.857 and 3.743.

8.33   a.   Since the data were collected as "twin holes," it needs to be analyzed as paired differences.

b.   The differences are calculated by finding the difference between the first hole and the second hole.

Location	1st hole	2nd hole	Difference
1	5.5	5.7	-0.2
2	11.0	11.2	-0.2
3	5.9	6.0	-0.1
4	8.2	5.6	2.6
5	10.0	9.3	0.7
6	7.9	7.0	0.9
7	10.1	8.4	1.7
8	7.4	9.0	-1.6
9	7.0	6.0	1.0
10	9.2	8.1	1.1
11	8.3	10.0	-1.7
12	8.6	8.1	0.5
13	10.5	10.4	0.1
14	5.5	7.0	-1.5
15	10.0	11.2	-1.2

c. $\bar{d} = \dfrac{\sum_1^{n_d} d_i}{n_d} = \dfrac{2.1}{15} = 0.14 \qquad s_d^2 = \dfrac{\sum_1^{n_d} d_i^2 - \dfrac{\left(\sum_1^{n_d} d_i\right)^2}{n_d}}{n_d - 1} = \dfrac{22.65 - \dfrac{(2.1)^2}{15}}{15 - 1} = 1.597 \qquad s_d = \sqrt{1.597} = 1.2637$.

d.   For confidence coefficient .90, $\alpha = .10$ and $\alpha/2 = .10/2 = .05$. From Table III, Appendix D with df $= n_d - 1 = 15 - 1 = 14$, $t_{.05} = 1.761$. The 90% confidence interval is:

$$\bar{d} \pm t_{\alpha/2}\frac{s_d}{\sqrt{n_d}} \Rightarrow .14 \pm 1.761\frac{1.2637}{\sqrt{15}} \Rightarrow .14 \pm .575 \Rightarrow (-.435,\ .715)$$

e.   We are 90% confident that the true difference in the mean THM measurements between the 1st and 2nd hole is between -.435 and .715.

Yes, the geologists can conclude that there is no evidence of a difference in the true mean THM measurements between the original holes and their twin holes because 0 falls in the interval at $\alpha = .10$.

8.35   a.   The data should be analyzed using a paired-difference experiment because that is how the data were collected. Response rates were observed twice from each survey using the "not selling" introduction method and the standard introduction method. Since the two sets of data are not independent, they cannot be analyzed using independent samples.

b.   Some preliminary calculations are:

$$s_p^2 = \frac{(n_1 - 1)s_1^2 + (n_2 - 1)s_2^2}{n_1 + n_2 - 2} = \frac{(29-1)(.12)^2 + (29-1)(.11)^2}{29 + 29 - 2} = .01325$$

Let μ_1 = mean response rate for those using the "not selling" introduction and μ_2 = mean response rate for those using the standard introduction. Using the independent-samples t-test to determine if the mean response rate for "not selling" is higher than that for the standard introduction, we test:

$$H_0 : \mu_1 - \mu_2 = 0$$
$$H_a : \mu_1 - \mu_2 > 0$$

The test statistic is $t = \dfrac{(\bar{x}_1 - \bar{x}_2) - 0}{\sqrt{s_p^2 \left(\dfrac{1}{n_1} + \dfrac{1}{n_2} \right)}} = \dfrac{(.262 - .246) - 0}{\sqrt{.01325 \left(\dfrac{1}{29} + \dfrac{1}{29} \right)}} = .53$

The rejection region requires $\alpha = .05$ in the upper tail of the t-distribution with $df = n_1 + n_2 - 2 = 29 + 29 - 2 = 56$. From Table III, Appendix D, $t_{.05} \approx 1.671$. The rejection region is $t > 1.671$.

Since the observed value of the test statistic does not fall in the rejection region $(t = .53 \not> 1.671)$, H_0 is not rejected. There is insufficient evidence to indicate the mean response rate for "not selling" is higher than that for the standard introduction at $\alpha = .05$.

c.   Since p-value is less than $\alpha = .05$ $(p = .001 < .05)$, H_0 is rejected. There is sufficient evidence to indicate the mean response rate for "not selling" is higher than that for the standard introduction at $\alpha = .05$.

d.   The two inferences in parts **b** and **c** have different results because using the independent samples t-test is not appropriate for this study. The paired-difference design is better. There is much variation in response rates from survey to survey. By using the paired difference design, we can eliminate the survey to survey differences.

8.37   Some preliminary calculations are:

Operator	Difference (Before - After)
1	5
2	3
3	9
4	7
5	2
6	-2
7	-1
8	11
9	0
10	5

$$\bar{d} = \frac{\sum d}{n_d} = \frac{39}{10} = 3.9 \qquad s_d^2 = \frac{\sum d^2 - \frac{(\sum d)^2}{n_E}}{n_d - 1} = \frac{319 - \frac{39^2}{10}}{10-1} = 18.5444 \qquad s_d = \sqrt{18.5444} = 4.3063$$

a.   To determine if the new napping policy reduced the mean number of customer complaints, we test:

$$H_0 : \mu_d = 0$$
$$H_a : \mu_d > 0$$

The test statistic is $t = \dfrac{\bar{d} - 0}{\dfrac{s_d}{\sqrt{n_d}}} = \dfrac{3.9 - 0}{\dfrac{4.3063}{\sqrt{10}}} = 2.864$

The rejection region requires $\alpha = .05$ in the upper tail of the t-distribution with df $= n_d - 1 = 10 - 1 = 9$. From Table III, Appendix D, $t_{.05} = 1.833$. The rejection region is $t > 1.833$.

Since the observed value of the test statistic falls in the rejection region $(t = 2.864 > 1.833)$, H_0 is rejected. There is sufficient evidence to indicate the new napping policy reduced the mean number of customer complaints at $\alpha = .05$.

b.   In order for the above test to be valid, we must assume that

1. The population of differences is normal
2. The differences are randomly selected

c.   Variables that were not controlled that could lead to an invalid conclusion include time of day agents worked, day of the week agents worked, and how much sleep the agents got before working, among others.

8.39   Some preliminary calculations are:

Circuit	Standard Method	Huffman-coding Method	Difference
1	.80	.78	.02
2	.80	.80	.00
3	.83	.86	-.03
4	.53	.53	.00
5	.50	.51	-.01
6	.96	.68	.28
7	.99	.82	.17
8	.98	.72	.26
9	.81	.45	.36
10	.95	.79	.16
11	.99	.77	.22

$$\bar{d} = \frac{\sum_{1}^{n_d} d_i}{n_d} = \frac{1.43}{11} = 0.13 \qquad s_d^2 = \frac{\sum_{1}^{n_d} d_i^2 - \frac{\left(\sum_{1}^{n_d} d_i\right)^2}{n_d}}{n_d - 1} = \frac{0.3799 - \frac{(1.43)^2}{11}}{11 - 1} = 0.0194 \qquad s_d = \sqrt{0.0194} = 0.1393$$

For confidence coefficient .95, $\alpha = .05$ and $\alpha/2 = .05/2 = .025$. From Table III, Appendix D, with $df = n_d - 1 = 11 - 1 = 10$, $t_{.025} = 2.228$. The 95% confidence interval is:

$$\bar{d} \pm t_{.025} \frac{s_d}{\sqrt{n}} \Rightarrow .13 \pm 2.228 \frac{.1393}{\sqrt{11}} \Rightarrow .13 \pm .094 \Rightarrow (0.036, \ 0.224)$$

We are 95% confident that the true difference in mean compression ratio between the standard method and the Huffman-based coding method is between 0.036 and 0.224. Since 0 is not contained in the interval, we can conclude there is a difference in mean compression ratios between the two methods. Since the values of the confidence interval are positive, we can conclude that the mean compression ratio for the Huffman-based method is smaller than the standard method.

8.41   Using MINITAB, the descriptive statistics are:

Descriptive Statistics: Male, Female, Diff

```
Variable   N    Mean   Median   StDev   Minimum   Maximum     Q1      Q3
Male      19   5.895   6.000   2.378    3.000    12.000   4.000   8.000
Female    19   5.526   5.000   2.458    3.000    12.000   4.000   7.000
Diff      19   0.368   1.000   3.515   -5.000     7.000  -3.000   3.000
```

Let μ_1 = mean number of swims by male rat pups and μ_2 = mean number of swims by female rat pups. Then $\mu_d = \mu_1 - \mu_2$. To determine if there is a difference in the mean number of swims required by male and female rat pups, we test:

$$H_0 : \mu_d = 0$$
$$H_a : \mu_d \neq 0$$

The test statistic is $t = \dfrac{\bar{d} - D_o}{\dfrac{s_d}{\sqrt{n_d}}} = \dfrac{.368 - 0}{\dfrac{3.515}{\sqrt{19}}} = 0.46$

The rejection region requires $\alpha/2 = .10/2 = .05$ in each tail of the t-distribution with df $= n_d - 1 = 19 - 1 = 18$. From Table III, Appendix D, $t_{.05} = 1.734$. The rejection region is $t < -1.734$ or $t > 1.734$.

Since the observed value of the test statistic does not fall in the rejection region $(t = .46 \not> 1.734)$, H_0 is not rejected. There is insufficient evidence to indicate that there is a difference in the mean number of swims required by male and female rat pups at $\alpha = .10$ (using Minitab, the p-value $\approx .653$).

Since the sample size is not large, we must assume that the population of differences is normally distributed and that the sample of differences is random. There is no indication that the sample differences are not from a random sample. However, because the number of swims is discrete, the differences are probably not normal.

8.43   a.   From the exercise, we know that x_1 and x_2 are binomial random variables with the number of trials equal to n_1 and n_2. From Chapter 7, we know that for large n, the distribution of $\hat{p}_1 = \dfrac{x_1}{n_1}$ is approximately normal. Since x_1 is simply $\hat{p}_1$ multiplied by a constant, x_1 will also have an approximate normal distribution. Similarly, the distribution of $\hat{p}_2 = \dfrac{x_2}{n_2}$ is approximately normal, and thus, the distribution of x_2 is approximately normal.

   b.   The Central Limit Theorem is necessary to find the sampling distributions of $\hat{p}_1$ and $\hat{p}_2$ when n_1 and n_2 are large. Once we have established that both $\hat{p}_1$ and $\hat{p}_2$ have normal distributions, then the distribution of their difference will also be normal.

8.45   From Section 6.4, it was given that the distribution of $\hat{p}$ is approximately normal if $n\hat{p} \geq 15$ and $n\hat{q} \geq 15$.

   a. $n_1 \hat{p}_1 = 12(.42) = 5.04 < 15$ and $n_1 \hat{q}_1 = 12(.58) = 6.96 < 15$
         $n_2 \hat{p}_2 = 14(.57) = 7.98 < 15$ and $n_2 \hat{q}_2 = 14(.43) = 6.02 < 15$
         Thus, the sample sizes are not large enough to conclude the sampling distribution of $(\hat{p}_1 - \hat{p}_2)$ is approximately normal.

   b. $n_1 \hat{p}_1 = 12(.92) = 11.04 < 15$ and $n_1 \hat{q}_1 = 12(.08) = 0.96 < 15$
         $n_2 \hat{p}_2 = 14(.86) = 12.04 < 15$ and $n_2 \hat{q}_2 = 14(.14) = 1.96 < 15$
         Thus, the sample sizes are not large enough to conclude the sampling distribution of $(\hat{p}_1 - \hat{p}_2)$ is approximately normal.

c. $n_1\hat{p}_1 = 30(.70) = 21 > 15$ and $n_1\hat{q}_1 = 30(.30) = 9 < 15$

$n_2\hat{p}_2 = 30(.73) = 21.9 > 15$ and $n_2\hat{q}_2 = 30(.27) = 8.1 < 15$

Thus, the sample sizes are not large enough to conclude the sampling distribution of $(\hat{p}_1 - \hat{p}_2)$ is approximately normal.

d. $n_1\hat{p}_1 = 100(.93) = 93 > 15$ and $n_1\hat{q}_1 = 100(.07) = 7 < 15$

$n_2\hat{p}_2 = 250(.97) = 242.5 > 15$ and $n_2\hat{q}_2 = 250(.03) = 7.5 < 15$

Thus, the sample sizes are not large enough to conclude the sampling distribution of $(\hat{p}_1 - \hat{p}_2)$ is approximately normal.

e. $n_1\hat{p}_1 = 125(.08) = 10 < 15$ and $n_1\hat{q}_1 = 125(.92) = 115 > 15$

$n_2\hat{p}_2 = 200(.12) = 24 > 15$ and $n_2\hat{q}_2 = 200(.88) = 176 > 15$

Thus, the sample sizes are not large enough to conclude the sampling distribution of $(\hat{p}_1 - \hat{p}_2)$ is approximately normal.

8.47   a. $H_0: p_1 - p_2 = 0$

$H_a: p_1 - p_2 > 0$

Will need to calculate the following:

$$\hat{p}_1 = \frac{320}{800} = .40 \qquad \hat{p}_2 = \frac{400}{800} = .50 \qquad \hat{p} = \frac{320 + 400}{800 + 800} = .45$$

The test statistic is $z = \dfrac{(\hat{p}_1 - \hat{p}_2) - 0}{\sqrt{\hat{p}\hat{q}\left(\dfrac{1}{n_1} + \dfrac{1}{n_2}\right)}} = \dfrac{(.40 - .50) - 0}{\sqrt{(.45)(.55)\left(\dfrac{1}{800} + \dfrac{1}{800}\right)}} = -4.02$

The rejection region requires $\alpha = .05$ in the upper tail of the z-distribution. From Table II, Appendix D, $z_{.05} = 1.645$. The rejection region is $z > 1.645$.

Since the observed value of the test statistic does not fall in the rejection region $(z = -4.02 \not> 1.645)$, H_0 is not rejected. There is insufficient evidence to indicate that $p_1 > p_2$ the proportions are unequal at $\alpha = .05$.

b. $H_0: p_1 - p_2 = 0$

$H_a: p_1 - p_2 \neq 0$

The test statistic is $z = -4.02$.

The rejection region requires $\alpha / 2 = .01 / 2 = .005$ in each tail of the z-distribution. From Table II, Appendix D, $z_{.005} = 2.58$. The rejection region is $z < -2.58$ or $z > 2.58$.

Since the observed value of the test statistic falls in the rejection region $(z = -4.02 < -2.58)$, H_0 is rejected. There is sufficient evidence to indicate that the proportions are unequal at $\alpha = .01$.

c. $H_0 : p_1 - p_2 = 0$
$H_a : p_1 - p_2 < 0$

Test statistic as above $z = -4.02$.

The rejection region requires $\alpha = .01$ in the lower tail of the z-distribution. From Table II, Appendix D, $z_{.01} = 2.33$. The rejection region is $z < -2.33$.

Since the observed value of the test statistic falls in the rejection region $(z = -4.02 < -2.33)$, H_0 is rejected. There is sufficient evidence to indicate that $p_1 < p_2$ at $\alpha = .01$.

d.   For confidence coefficient .90, $\alpha = .10$ and $\alpha / 2 = .10 / 2 = .05$. From Table II, Appendix D, $z_{.05} = 1.645$. The confidence interval is:

$$(\hat{p}_1 - \hat{p}_2) \pm z_{.05} \sqrt{\frac{\hat{p}_1 \hat{q}_1}{n_1} + \frac{\hat{p}_2 \hat{p}_2}{n_2}} \Rightarrow (.4 - .5) \pm 1.645 \sqrt{\frac{(.4)(.6)}{800} + \frac{(.5)(.5)}{800}} \Rightarrow -.10 \pm .04 \Rightarrow (-.14, -.06)$$

We are 90% confident that the difference between p_1 and p_2 is between $-.14$ and $-.06$.

8.49   a. $\hat{p}_1 = \frac{x_1}{n_1} = \frac{29}{189} = .153$

b. $\hat{p}_2 = \frac{x_2}{n_2} = \frac{32}{149} = .215$

c.   For confidence coefficient .90, $\alpha = .10$ and $\alpha / 2 = .10 / 2 = .05$. From Table II, Appendix D, $z_{.05} = 1.645$. The 90% confidence interval is:

$$(\hat{p}_1 - \hat{p}_2) \pm z_{\alpha/2} \sqrt{\frac{\hat{p}_1 \hat{q}_1}{n_1} + \frac{\hat{p}_2 \hat{q}_2}{n_2}} \Rightarrow (.153 - .215) \pm 1.645 \sqrt{\frac{.153(.847)}{189} + \frac{.215(.785)}{149}}$$
$$\Rightarrow -.062 \pm .070 \Rightarrow (-.132, \quad .008)$$

d.   We are 90% confident that the difference in the proportion of bidders who fall prey to the winner's curse between super-experienced bidders and less-experienced bidders is between $-.132$ and $.008$. Since this interval contains 0, there is no evidence to indicate that there is a difference in the proportion of bidders who fall prey to the winner's curse between super-experienced bidders and less-experienced bidders.

8.51   a.   Let p_1 = proportion of producers who are willing to offer windrowing services to the biomass market in Missouri and p_2 = proportion of producers who are willing to offer windrowing services to the biomass market in Illinois. The parameter of interest is $p_1 - p_2$.

b.   To determine if the proportion of producers who are willing to offer windrowing services differs between Missouri and Illinois, we test:

$H_0 : p_1 - p_2 = 0$
$H_a : p_1 - p_2 \neq 0$

c. The test statistic is $z = -2.67$.

d. The rejection region requires $\alpha/2 = .01/2 = .005$ in each tail of the z-distribution. From Table II, Appendix D, $z_{.005} = 2.58$. The rejection region is $z < -2.58$ and $z > 2.58$.

e. The p-value is $p = .008$.

f. Since the observed value of the test statistic falls in the rejection region ($z = -2.67 < -2.58$), H_0 is rejected. There is sufficient evidence to indicate that the proportion of producers who are willing to offer windrowing services differs between Missouri and Illinois at $\alpha = .01$.

Since the p-value is less than α ($p = .008 < .01$), H_0 is rejected. This is the same conclusion as above.

8.53 a. The first population of interest is all hospital patients admitted in January. The second population of interest is all hospital patients admitted in May.

b. $\hat{p}_1 = \dfrac{x_1}{n_1} = \dfrac{32}{192} = .167$ $\quad$ $\hat{p}_2 = \dfrac{x_2}{n_2} = \dfrac{34}{403} = .084$

The point estimate for the difference in malaria admission rates in January and May is $\hat{p}_1 - \hat{p}_2 = .167 - .084 = .083$.

c. For confidence coefficient .90, $\alpha = .10$ and $\alpha/2 = .10/2 = .05$. From Table II, Appendix D, $z_{.05} = 1.645$. The 90% confidence interval is:

$$(\hat{p}_1 - \hat{p}_2) \pm z_{.05}\sqrt{\frac{\hat{p}_1\hat{q}_1}{n_1} + \frac{\hat{p}_2\hat{q}_2}{n_2}} \Rightarrow (.167 - .084) \pm 1.645\sqrt{\frac{.167(.833)}{192} + \frac{.084(.916)}{403}}$$
$$\Rightarrow .083 \pm .050 \Rightarrow (.033, .133)$$

d. Since 0 is not contained in the confidence interval, we can conclude that a difference exists in the true malaria admission rates in January and May.

8.55 Let p_1 = proportion of salmonella in the region's water and p_2 = proportion of salmonella in the region's wildlife.

Some preliminary calculations are:

$$\hat{p}_1 = \frac{x_1}{n_1} = \frac{18}{252} = .071 \qquad \hat{p}_2 = \frac{x_2}{n_2} = \frac{20}{476} = .042 \qquad \hat{p} = \frac{x_1 + x_2}{n_1 + n_2} = \frac{18 + 20}{252 + 476} = \frac{38}{728} = .052$$

To determine if the prevalence of salmonella in the region's water differs from the prevalence of salmonella in the region's wildlife, we test:

$$H_0 : p_1 - p_2 = 0$$
$$H_a : p_1 - p_2 \neq 0$$

The test statistic is $z = \dfrac{(\hat{p}_1 - \hat{p}_2) - 0}{\sqrt{\hat{p}\hat{q}\left(\dfrac{1}{n_1} + \dfrac{1}{n_2}\right)}} = \dfrac{.071 - .042}{\sqrt{.052(.948)\left(\dfrac{1}{252} + \dfrac{1}{476}\right)}} = 1.68$

The rejection region requires $\alpha / 2 = .01 / 2 = .005$ in each tail of the z-distribution. From Table II, Appendix D, $z_{.005} = 2.58$. The rejection region is $z < -2.58$ and $z > 2.58$.

Since the observed value of the test statistic does not fall in the rejection region $(z = 1.68 \not> 2.58)$, H_0 is not rejected. There is insufficient evidence to indicate the prevalence of salmonella in the region's water differs from the prevalence of salmonella in the region's wildlife at $\alpha = .01$.

8.57   Let $p_1 =$ proportion of African American MBA students who begin their career as entrepreneurs and $p_2 =$ proportion of white MBA students who begin their career as entrepreneurs.

Some preliminary calculations:

$\hat{p}_1 = \dfrac{x_1}{n_1} = \dfrac{209}{1,304} = .1603 \qquad\qquad \hat{q}_1 = 1 - \hat{p}_1 = 1 - .1603 = .8397$

$\hat{p}_2 = \dfrac{x_2}{n_2} = \dfrac{356}{7,120} = .05 \qquad\qquad \hat{q}_2 = 1 - \hat{p}_2 = 1 - .05 = .95$

$\hat{p} = \dfrac{x_1 + x_2}{n_1 + n_2} = \dfrac{209 + 356}{1,304 + 7,120} = .0671 \qquad \hat{q} = 1 - \hat{p} = 1 - .0671 = .9329$

To determine if African American MBA students are more likely to begin their careers as an entrepreneur than white MAB students, we test:

$H_0 : p_1 - p_2 = 0$

$H_a : p_1 - p_2 > 0$

The test statistic is $z = \dfrac{(\hat{p}_1 - \hat{p}_2) - 0}{\sqrt{\hat{p}\hat{q}\left(\dfrac{1}{n_1} + \dfrac{1}{n_2}\right)}} = \dfrac{.1603 - .05}{\sqrt{.0671(.9329)\left(\dfrac{1}{1,304} + \dfrac{1}{7,120}\right)}} = 14.64$

Since no α was given, we will use $\alpha = .05$. The rejection region requires $\alpha = .05$ in the upper tail of the z-distribution. From Table II, Appendix D, $z_{.05} = 1.645$. The rejection region is $z > 1.645$.

Since the observed value of the test statistic falls in the rejection region $(z = 14.64 > 1.645)$, H_0 is rejected. There is sufficient evidence to indicate that the proportion of African American MBA students who begin their career as entrepreneurs is significantly greater than the proportion of white MBA students who begin their career as entrepreneurs.

8.59   a.   Let $p_1 =$ proportion of women who have food cravings and $p_2 =$ proportion of men who have food cravings.

We know that $\hat{p}_1 = .97$ and $\hat{p}_2 = .67$. We know that $n_1 p_1 > 15$ and $n_1 q_1 > 15$ in order for the test to be valid. Thus, $n_1(.97) > 15 \Rightarrow n_1 > 15 / .97 \approx 16$ and $n_1(.03) > 15 \Rightarrow n_1 > 15 / .03 = 500$.

Also, $n_2 p_2 > 15$ and $n_2 q_2 > 15$. Thus, $n_2 (.67) > 15 \Rightarrow n_2 > 15/.97 \approx 23$ and
$n_2 (.33) > 15 \Rightarrow n_2 > 15/.33 \approx 46$.

Thus, $n_1 > 500$ and $n_2 > 46$.

b.   This study involved 1,000 McMaster University students. It is very dangerous to generalize the results of this study to the general adult population of North America. The sample of students used may not be representative of the population of interest.

8.61   a.   For confidence coefficient .99, $\alpha = .01$ and $\alpha / 2 = .01 / 2 = .005$. From Table II, Appendix D,
$z_{.005} = 2.58$.

$$n_1 = n_2 = \frac{(z_{\alpha/2})^2 (p_1 q_1 + p_2 q_2)}{(ME)^2} = \frac{2.58^2 (.4(1-.4) + .7(1-.7))}{.01^2} = \frac{2.99538}{.0001} = 29,953.8 \approx 29,954$$

b.   For confidence coefficient .90, $\alpha = .10$ and $\alpha / 2 = .10 / 2 = .05$. From Table II, Appendix D,
$z_{.05} = 1.645$. Since we have no prior information about the proportions, we use $p_1 = p_2 = .5$ to get a conservative estimate. For a width of .05, the margin of error is .025.

$$n_1 = n_2 = \frac{(z_{\alpha/2})^2 (p_1 q_1 + p_2 q_2)}{(ME)^2} = \frac{(1.645)^2 (.5(1-.5) + .5(1-.5))}{.025^2} = 2164.82 \Rightarrow 2165$$

c.   From part **b**, $z_{.05} = 1.645$.

$$n_1 = n_2 = \frac{(z_{\alpha/2})^2 (p_1 q_1 + p_2 q_2)}{(ME)^2} = \frac{(1.645)^2 (.2(1-.2) + .3(1-.3))}{.03^2} = \frac{1.00123}{.0009} = 1112.48 \approx 1113$$

8.63 $n_1 = n_2 = \dfrac{(z_{\alpha/2})^2 (\sigma_1^2 + \sigma_2^2)}{ME^2}$

For confidence coefficient .95, $\alpha = .05$ and $\alpha / 2 = .05 / 2 = .025$. From Table II, Appendix D, $z_{.025} = 1.96$.

$$n_1 = n_2 = \frac{1.96^2 (14 + 14)}{1.8^2} = 33.2 \approx 34$$

8.65   For confidence coefficient .95, $\alpha = .05$ and $\alpha / 2 = .05 / 2 = .025$. From Table II, Appendix D, $z_{.025} = 1.96$.

$$n_1 = n_2 = \frac{(z_{\alpha/2})^2 (\sigma_1^2 + \sigma_2^2)}{ME^2} = \frac{(1.96)^2 (9^2 + 9^2)}{2^2} = 155.6 \approx 156$$

8.67   For confidence coefficient .90, $\alpha = .10$ and $\alpha / 2 = .10 / 2 = .05$. From Table II, Appendix D, $z_{.05} = 1.645$. If we assume that we do not know the return rates, we will use .5 for both.

$$n_1 = n_2 = \frac{(z_{.05})^2 (p_1 q_1 + p_2 q_2)}{ME^2} = \frac{1.645^2 (.5(.5) + .5(.5))}{.01^2} = 13,530.1 \approx 13,531$$

8.69   For confidence coefficient .95, $\alpha = .05$ and $\alpha/2 = .05/2 = .025$. From Table II, Appendix D, $z_{.025} = 1.96$.

$$n_1 = n_2 = \frac{(z_{\alpha/2})^2(\sigma_1^2 + \sigma_2^2)}{ME^2} = \frac{1.96^2(15^2 + 15^2)}{1^2} = 1728.72 \approx 1729$$

8.71   a.   For confidence coefficient .95, $\alpha = .05$ and $\alpha/2 = .05/2 = .025$. From Table II, Appendix D, $z_{.025} = 1.96$. From Exercise 8.56, $\hat{p}_1 = .184$ and $\hat{p}_2 = .177$.

$$n_1 = n_2 = \frac{(z_{\alpha/2})^2(p_1 q_1 + p_2 q_2)}{(ME)^2} = \frac{1.96^2(.184(.816) + .177(.823))}{.015^2} = 5,050.7 \approx 5,051$$

    b.   The study would involve $5,051 \times 2 = 10,102$ patients. A study this large would be extremely time consuming and expensive.

    c.   Since a difference of .015 is so small, the practical significance detecting a 0.015 difference may not be very worthwhile. A difference of .015 is so close to 0, that it might not make any difference.

8.73   a.   With $v_1 = 9$ and $v_2 = 6$, $F_{.05} = 4.10$.

    b.   With $v_1 = 18$ and $v_2 = 14$, $F_{.01} \approx 3.57$. (Since $v_1 = 18$ is not given, we estimate the value between those for $v_1 = 15$ and $v_1 = 20$.)

    c.   With $v_1 = 11$ and $v_2 = 4$, $F_{.025} \approx 8.80$. (Since $v_1 = 11$ is not given, we estimate the value by averaging those given for $v_1 = 10$ and $v_1 = 12$.)

    d.   With $v_1 = 20$ and $v_2 = 5$, $F_{.10} = 3.21$.

8.75   a.   Reject H_0 if $F > F_{.10} = 1.74$. (From Table V, Appendix D, with $v_1 = 30$ and $v_2 = 20$.)

    b.   Reject H_0 if $F > F_{.05} = 2.04$. (From Table VI, Appendix D, with $v_1 = 30$ and $v_2 = 20$.)

    c.   Reject H_0 if $F > F_{.025} = 2.35$. (From Table VII.)

    d.   Reject H_0 if $F > F_{.01} = 2.78$. (From Table VIII.)

8.77   a.   The rejection region requires $\alpha = .05$ in the upper tail of the F-distribution with $v_1 = n_1 - 1 = 25 - 1 = 24$ and $v_2 = n_2 - 1 = 20 - 1 = 19$. From Table VI, Appendix D, $F_{.05} = 2.11$. The rejection region is $F > 2.11$ (if $s_1^2 > s_2^2$).

    b.   The rejection region requires $\alpha = .05$ in the upper tail of the F-distribution with $v_1 = n_2 - 1 = 15 - 1 = 14$ and $v_2 = n_1 - 1 = 10 - 1 = 9$. From Table VI, Appendix D, $F_{.05} \approx 3.01$. The rejection region is $F > 3.01$ (if $s_2^2 > s_1^2$).

c. The rejection region requires $\alpha / 2 = .10 / 2 = .05$ in the upper tail of the F-distribution. If $s_1^2 > s_2^2$, $\nu_1 = n_1 - 1 = 21 - 1 = 20$ and $\nu_2 = n_2 - 1 = 31 - 1 = 30$. From Table VI, Appendix D, $F_{.05} = 1.93$. The rejection region is $F > 1.93$. If $s_1^2 < s_2^2$, $\nu_1 = n_2 - 1 = 30$ and $\nu_2 = n_1 - 1 = 20$. From Table VI, $F_{.05} = 2.04$. The rejection region is $F > 2.04$.

d. The rejection region requires $\alpha = .01$ in the upper tail of the F-distribution with $\nu_1 = n_2 - 1 = 41 - 1 = 40$ and $\nu_2 = n_1 - 1 = 31 - 1 = 30$. From Table VIII, Appendix D, $F_{.01} = 2.30$. The rejection region is $F > 2.30$ (if $s_2^2 > s_1^2$).

e. The rejection region requires $\alpha = .05$ and $\alpha / 2 = .05 / 2 = .025$ in the upper tail of the F-distribution. If $s_1^2 > s_2^2$, $\nu_1 = n_1 - 1 = 7 - 1 = 6$ and $\nu_2 = n_2 - 1 = 16 - 1 = 15$. From Table VII, Appendix D, $F_{.025} = 3.41$. The rejection region is $F > 3.41$. If $s_1^2 < s_2^2$, $\nu_1 = n_2 - 1 = 15$ and $\nu_2 = n_1 - 1 = 6$. From Table VII, Appendix D, $F_{.025} = 5.27$. The rejection region is $F > 5.27$.

8.79   a. Using MINITAB, the descriptive statistics are:

Descriptive Statistics: Sample 1, Sample 2

```
Variable   N   Mean   Median   StDev   Minimum   Maximum     Q1     Q3
Sample 1   6   2.417  2.400    1.436    0.700     4.400   1.075  3.650
Sample 2   5   4.36   3.70     2.97     1.40      8.90    1.84   7.20
```

To determine if the variance for population 2 is greater than that for population 1, we test:

$$H_0 : \sigma_1^2 = \sigma_2^2$$
$$H_a : \sigma_1^2 < \sigma_2^2$$

The test statistic is $F = \dfrac{s_2^2}{s_1^2} = \dfrac{2.97^2}{1.436^2} = 4.28$

The rejection region requires $\alpha = .05$ in the upper tail of the F-distribution with $\nu_1 = n_2 - 1 = 5 - 1 = 4$ and $\nu_2 = n_1 - 1 = 6 - 1 = 5$. From Table VI, Appendix D, $F_{.05} = 5.19$. The rejection region is $F > 5.19$.

Since the observed value of the test statistic does not fall in the rejection region $(F = 4.29 \not> 5.19)$, H_0 is not rejected. There is insufficient evidence to indicate the variance for population 2 is greater than that for population 1 at $\alpha = .05$.

b. The p-value is $p = P(F \geq 4.28)$. From Tables V and VI, with $\nu_1 = 4$ and $\nu_2 = 5$,

$.05 < p = P(F \geq 4.28) < .10$

There is no evidence to reject H_0 for $\alpha = .05$ but there is evidence to reject H_0 for $\alpha = .10$.

8.81   Let σ_1^2 = variance of the number of ads recalled by children in the video only group and σ_2^2 = variance of the number of ads recalled by children in the A/V group.

a.   To determine if the group variances are equal, we test:

$$H_0 : \sigma_1^2 = \sigma_2^2$$
$$H_a : \sigma_1^2 \neq \sigma_2^2$$

b.   The test statistic is: $F = \dfrac{\text{larger sample variance}}{\text{smaller sample variance}} = \dfrac{s_2^2}{s_1^2} = \dfrac{2.13^2}{1.98^2} = 1.157$

c.   The rejection region requires $\alpha / 2 = .10 / 2 = .05$ in the upper tail of the F-distribution with $v_1 = n_2 - 1 = 20 - 1 = 19$ and $v_2 = n_1 - 1 = 20 - 1 = 19$. From the Table VI, Appendix D, $F_{.05} \approx 2.16$. The rejection region is $F > 2.16$.

d.   Since the observed value of the test statistic does not fall in the rejection region $(F = 1.157 \not> 2.16)$, H_0 is not rejected. There is insufficient evidence to indicate the variances of the number of ads recalled by the children in the video-only group and the A/V group differ at $\alpha = .10$.

e.   Since we could not reject H_0 that the variances were equal, it indicates that the assumption of equal variances is probably valid. The inference about the population means is probably valid.

8.83   Let σ_1^2 = variance at site 1 and σ_2^2 = variance of site 2. To determine if the variances at the two locations differ, we test:

$$H_0 : \sigma_1^2 = \sigma_2^2$$
$$H_a : \sigma_1^2 \neq \sigma_2^2$$

From the printout, the test statistic is $F = .844$ and the p-value is $p = .681$.

Since the p-value is not less than α $(p = .681 \not< .05)$, H_0 is not rejected. There is insufficient evidence to indicate the variances at the two locations differ at $\alpha = .05$.

8.85   Using MINITAB, the descriptive statistics are:

Descriptive Statistics: Novice, Experienced

Variable	N	Mean	Median	StDev	Minimum	Maximum	Q1	Q3
Novice	12	32.83	32.00	8.64	20.00	48.00	26.75	39.00
Experien	12	20.58	19.50	5.74	10.00	31.00	17.25	24.75

a.   Let σ_1^2 = variance in inspection errors for novice inspectors and σ_2^2 = variance in inspection errors for experienced inspectors. Since we wish to determine if the data support the belief that the variance is lower for experienced inspectors than for novice inspectors, we test:

$$H_0 : \sigma_1^2 = \sigma_2^2$$
$$H_a : \sigma_1^2 > \sigma_2^2$$

The test statistic is $F = \dfrac{\text{Larger sample variance}}{\text{Smaller sample variance}} = \dfrac{s_1^2}{s_2^2} = \dfrac{8.64^2}{5.74^2} = 2.27$

The rejection region requires $\alpha = .05$ in the upper tail of the F-distribution with $\nu_1 = n_1 - 1 = 12 - 1 = 11$ and $\nu_2 = n_2 - 1 = 12 - 1 = 11$. Using MINITAB:

Inverse Cumulative Distribution Function

```
F distribution with 11 DF in numerator and 11 DF in denominator

P( X <= x )          x
  0.95   2.81793
```

The rejection region is $F > 2.82$.

Since the observed value of the test statistic does not fall in the rejection region $(F = 2.27 \not> 2.82)$, H_0 is not rejected. The sample data do not support her belief at $\alpha = .05$.

b. Using MINITAB:

Cumulative Distribution Function

```
F distribution with 11 DF in numerator and 11 DF in denominator

   x   P( X <= x )
2.27     0.905144
```

The p-value $= P(F \geq 2.27) = 1 - P(F < 2.27) = 1 - .905) = .095$.

8.87   a. Let σ_1^2 = variance of the order-to-delivery times for the Persian Gulf War and σ_2^2 = variance of the order-to-delivery times for Bosnia.

Descriptive Statistics: Gulf, Bosnia

```
Variable   N    Mean   Median    StDev  Minimum  Maximum     Q1     Q3
Gulf       9   25.24    27.50  10.5204     9.10    41.20  15.30  32.15
Bosnia     9    7.38     6.50   3.6537     3.00    15.10   5.25   9.20
```

To determine if the variances of the order-to-delivery times for the Persian Gulf and Bosnia shipments are equal, we test:

$$H_0 : \frac{\sigma_1^2}{\sigma_2^2} = 1$$

$$H_a : \frac{\sigma_1^2}{\sigma_2^2} \neq 1$$

The test statistic is $F = \dfrac{\text{Larger sample variance}}{\text{Smaller sample variance}} = \dfrac{s_1^2}{s_2^2} = \dfrac{10.5204^2}{3.6537^2} = 8.29$

The rejection region requires $\alpha / 2 = .05 / 2 = .025$ in the upper tail of the F-distribution with $\nu_1 = n_1 - 1 = 9 - 1 = 8$ and $\nu_2 = n_2 - 1 = 9 - 1 = 8$. From Table VII, Appendix D, $F_{.025} = 4.43$. The rejection region is $F > 4.43$.

Since the observed value of the test statistic falls in the rejection region $(F = 8.29 > 4.43)$, H_0 is rejected. There is sufficient evidence to indicate the variances of the order-to-delivery times for the Persian Gulf and Bosnia shipments differ at $\alpha = .05$.

b.   No. One assumption necessary for the small sample confidence interval for $(\mu_1 - \mu_2)$ is that $\sigma_1^2 = \sigma_2^2$. For this problem, there is evidence to indicate that $\sigma_1^2 \neq \sigma_2^2$.

8.89   a.   The 2 samples are randomly selected in an independent manner from the two populations. The sample sizes, n_1 and n_2, are large enough so that $\bar{x}_1$ and $\bar{x}_2$ each have approximately normal sampling distributions and so that s_1^2 and s_2^2 provide good approximations to σ_1^2 and σ_2^2. This will be true if $n_1 \geq 30$ and $n_2 \geq 30$.

b.   1.   Both sampled populations have relative frequency distributions that are approximately normal.
2.   The population variances are equal.
3.   The samples are randomly and independently selected from the populations.

c.   1.   The relative frequency distribution of the population of differences is normal.
2.   The sample of differences are randomly selected from the population of differences.

d.   The two samples are independent random samples from binomial distributions. Both samples should be large enough so that the normal distribution provides an adequate approximation to the sampling distributions of $\hat{p}_1$ and $\hat{p}_2$.

e.   The two samples are independent random samples from populations which are normally distributed.

8.91   a. $s_p^2 = \dfrac{(n_1 - 1)s_1^2 + (n_1 - 1)s_2^2}{n_1 + n_2 - 2} = \dfrac{11(74.2) + 13(60.5)}{12 + 14 - 2} = 66.7792$

$$H_0 : \mu_1 - \mu_2 = 0$$
$$H_a : \mu_1 - \mu_2 > 0$$

The test statistic is $t = \dfrac{(\bar{x}_1 - \bar{x}_2) - 0}{\sqrt{s_p^2 \left(\dfrac{1}{n_1} + \dfrac{1}{n_2} \right)}} = \dfrac{(17.8 - 15.3) - 0}{\sqrt{66.7792 \left(\dfrac{1}{12} + \dfrac{1}{14} \right)}} = .78$

The rejection region requires $\alpha = .05$ in the upper tail of the t-distribution with $\mathrm{df} = n_1 + n_2 - 2 = 12 + 14 - 2 = 24$. From Table III, Appendix D, $t_{.05} = 1.711$. The rejection region is $t > 1.711$.

Since the observed value of the test statistic does not fall in the rejection region $(t = 0.78 \not> 1.711)$, H_0 is not rejected. There is insufficient evidence to indicate that $\mu_1 > \mu_2$ at $\alpha = .05$.

b.   For confidence coefficient .99, $\alpha = .01$ and $\alpha/2 = .01/2 = .005$. From Table III, Appendix D, with df $= n_1 + n_2 - 2 = 12 + 14 - 2 = 24$, $t_{.005} = 2.797$. The confidence interval is:

$$(\bar{x}_1 - \bar{x}_2) \pm t_{.005} \sqrt{s_p^2 \left(\frac{1}{n_1} + \frac{1}{n_2} \right)} \Rightarrow (17.8 - 15.3) \pm 2.797 \sqrt{66.7792 \left(\frac{1}{12} + \frac{1}{14} \right)}$$

$$\Rightarrow 2.50 \pm 8.99 \Rightarrow (-6.49, 11.49)$$

c.   For confidence coefficient .99, $\alpha = .01$ and $\alpha/2 = .01/2 = .005$. From Table II, Appendix D, $z_{.005} = 2.58$.

$$n_1 = n_2 = \frac{(z_{\alpha/2})(\sigma_1^2 + \sigma_2^2)}{(ME)^2} = \frac{(2.58)^2(74.2 + 60.5)}{2^2} = 224.15 \approx 225$$

8.93   a.   For confidence coefficient .90, $\alpha = .10$ and $\alpha/2 = .10/2 = .05$. From Table II, Appendix D, $z_{.05} = 1.645$. The confidence interval is:

$$(\bar{x}_1 - \bar{x}_2) \pm z_{.05} \sqrt{\frac{s_1^2}{n_1} + \frac{s_2^2}{n_2}} \Rightarrow (12.2 - 8.3) \pm 1.645 \sqrt{\frac{2.1}{135} + \frac{3.0}{148}}$$

$$\Rightarrow 3.90 \pm .31 \Rightarrow (3.59, 4.21)$$

b. $H_0 : \mu_1 - \mu_2 = 0$
$H_a : \mu_1 - \mu_2 \neq 0$

The test statistic is $z = \dfrac{(\bar{x}_1 - \bar{x}_2)}{\sqrt{\dfrac{s_1^2}{n_1} + \dfrac{s_2^2}{n_2}}} = \dfrac{(12.2 - 8.3) - 0}{\sqrt{\dfrac{2.1}{135} + \dfrac{3.0}{148}}} = 20.60$

The rejection region requires $\alpha/2 = .01/2 = .005$ in each tail of the z-distribution. From Table II, Appendix D, $z_{.005} = 2.58$. The rejection region is $z < -2.58$ or $z > 2.58$.

Since the observed value of the test statistic falls in the rejection region $(z = 20.60 > 2.58)$, H_0 is rejected. There is sufficient evidence to indicate that $\mu_1 \neq \mu_2$ at $\alpha = .01$.

c.   For confidence coefficient .90, $\alpha = .10$ and $\alpha/2 = .10/2 = .05$. From Table II, Appendix D, $z_{.05} = 1.645$.

$$n_1 = n_2 = \frac{(z_{\alpha/2})(\sigma_1^2 + \sigma_2^2)}{(ME)^2} = \frac{(1.645)^2(2.1 + 3.0)}{.2^2} = 345.02 \approx 346$$

8.95   a.   Let μ_1 = average size of the right temporal lobe of the brain for the short-recovery group and μ_2 = average size of the right temporal lobe of the brain for the long-recovery group.

The target parameter is $\mu_1 - \mu_2$. We must assume that the two samples are random and independent, the two populations being sampled from are approximately normal, and the two population variances are equal.

b.   Let p_1 = proportion of athletes who have a good self-image of their body and p_2 = proportion of non-athletes who have a good self-image of their body.

The target parameter for this comparison is $p_1 - p_2$. We must assume that the two samples are random and independent and that the sample sizes are sufficiently large.

c.   Let μ_1 = average weight of eggs produced by a sample of chickens on regular feed and

μ_2 = average weight of eggs produced by a sample of chickens fed a diet supplemented by corn oil.

Let $\mu_d = \mu_1 - \mu_2$ = average difference in weight between eggs produced by the chickens on regular feed and then on a diet supplemented with corn oil.

The target parameter is μ_d. We must assume that we have a random sample of differences and that the population of differences is approximately normal if the sample size is small. If the sample size of differences is greater than 30, we do not need to assume that the population of differences is normal.

8.97   a.   Let μ_1 = mean score for males and μ_2 = mean score for females. For confidence coefficient .90, $\alpha = .10$ and $\alpha / 2 = .10 / 2 = .05$. From Table II, Appendix D, $z_{.05} = 1.645$. The 90% confidence interval is:

$$(\bar{x}_1 - \bar{x}_2) \pm z_{\alpha/2} \sqrt{\frac{\sigma_1^2}{n_1} + \frac{\sigma_2^2}{n_2}} \Rightarrow (39.08 - 38.79) \pm 1.645 \sqrt{\frac{6.73^2}{127} + \frac{6.94^2}{114}}$$

$$\Rightarrow 0.29 \pm 1.452 \Rightarrow (-1.162, \ 1.742)$$

We are 90% confident that the difference in mean service-rating scores between males and females is between -1.162 and 1.742.

b.   To determine if the service-rating score variances differ by gender, we test:

$$H_0 : \sigma_1^2 = \sigma_2^2$$
$$H_a : \sigma_1^2 \neq \sigma_2^2$$

The test statistic is $F = \dfrac{\text{larger sample variance}}{\text{smaller sample variance}} = \dfrac{s_2^2}{s_1^2} = \dfrac{6.94^2}{6.73^2} = 1.06$

The rejection region requires $\alpha / 2 = .10 / 2 = .05$ in the upper tail of the F-distribution with numerator df $= v_2 = n_2 - 1 = 114 - 1 = 113$ and denominator df $= v_1 = n_1 - 1 = 127 - 1 = 126$. Using MINITAB, we get:

Inverse Cumulative Distribution Function
```
F distribution with 113 DF in numerator and 126 DF in denominator

P( X <= x )          x
     0.95   1.35141
```

$F_{.05} = 1.35$. The rejection region is $F > 1.35$.

Since the observed value of the test statistic does not fall in the rejection region $(F = 1.06 \not> 1.35)$, H_0 is not rejected. There is insufficient evidence to indicate the service-rating score variances differ by gender at $\alpha = .10$.

c. Since we did not reject H_0 in part b, the confidence interval in part a is valid. Because 0 falls in the 90% confidence interval, we are 90% confident that there is no difference in the mean service-rating scores between males and females.

8.99 a. Yes. The sample mean of the virtual-reality group is 10.67 points higher than the sample mean of the simple user interface group.

b. Let μ_1 = mean improvement score for the virtual-reality group and μ_2 = mean improvement score for the simple user interface group.

To determine if the mean improvement scores for the virtual-reality group is higher than that for the simple user interface group, we test:

$$H_0 : \mu_1 - \mu_2 = 0$$
$$H_a : \mu_1 - \mu_2 > 0$$

The test statistic is $z = \dfrac{(\bar{x}_1 - \bar{x}_2) - D_o}{\sqrt{\left(\dfrac{\sigma_1^2}{n_1} + \dfrac{\sigma_2^2}{n_2}\right)}} = \dfrac{(43.15 - 32.48) - 0}{\sqrt{\left(\dfrac{12.57^2}{45} + \dfrac{9.26^2}{45}\right)}} = \dfrac{10.67}{2.3274} = 4.58$

The rejection region requires $\alpha = .05$ in the upper tail of the z-distribution. From Table II, Appendix D, $z_{.05} = 1.645$. The rejection region is $z > 1.645$.

Since the observed value of the test statistic falls in the rejection region $(z = 4.58 > 1.645)$, H_0 is rejected. There is sufficient evidence to indicate the mean improvement scores for the virtual-reality group is higher than that for the simple user interface group $\alpha = .05$.

8.101 a. The data should be analyzed as a paired difference experiment because each actor who won an Academy Award was paired with another actor with similar characteristics who did not win the award.

b. Let μ_1 = mean life expectancy of Academy Award winners and μ_2 = mean life expectancy of non-Academy Award winners. Let $\mu_d = \mu_1 - \mu_2$. To compare the mean life expectancies of Academy Award winners and non-winners, we test:

$$H_0 : \mu_d = 0$$
$$H_a : \mu_d \neq 0$$

c. Since the p-value was so small, there is sufficient evidence to indicate the mean life expectancies of the Academy Award winners and non-winners are different for any value of $\alpha > .003$. Since the sample mean life expectancy of Academy Award winners is greater than that for non-winners, we can conclude that Academy Award winners have a longer mean life expectancy than non-winners.

8.103 a. Let μ_1 = mean response by noontime watchers and μ_2 = mean response by non-noontime watchers.

To determine if the mean response differs for noontime and non-noontime watchers, we test:

$$H_0 : \mu_1 - \mu_2 = 0$$
$$H_a : \mu_1 - \mu_2 \neq 0$$

b.   Since the p-value ($p = .02$) is less than $\alpha = .05$, H_0 is rejected. There is sufficient evidence to indicate the mean response differs for noontime and non-noontime watchers at $\alpha = .05$.

c.   Since the p-value ($p = .02$) is greater than $\alpha = .01$, H_0 is not rejected. There is insufficient evidence to indicate the mean response differs for noontime and non-noontime watchers at $\alpha = .01$.

d.   Since the two sample means are so close together, there appears to be no "practical" difference between the two means. Even if there is a statistically significant difference between the two means, there is no practical difference.

8.105   a.   Let p_1 = proportion of employed individuals who had a routine checkup in the past year and p_2 = proportion of unemployed individuals who had a routine checkup in the past year. The researchers are interested in whether there is a difference in these two proportions, so the parameter of interest is $p_1 - p_2$.

b.   To determine if there is a difference in the proportions of employed and unemployed individuals who had a routine checkup in the past year, we test:

$$H_0 : p_1 - p_2 = 0$$
$$H_a : p_1 - p_2 \neq 0$$

c.   Some preliminary calculations are:

$$\hat{p}_1 = \frac{x_1}{n_1} = \frac{642}{1,140} = .563 \qquad \hat{p}_2 = \frac{x_2}{n_2} = \frac{740}{1,106} = .669$$

$$\hat{p} = \frac{x_1 + x_2}{n_1 + n_2} = \frac{642 + 740}{1,140 + 1,106} = \frac{1,382}{2,246} = .615 \qquad \hat{q} = 1 - \hat{p} = 1 - .615 = .385$$

The test statistic is $z = \dfrac{(\hat{p}_1 - \hat{p}_2) - 0}{\sqrt{\hat{p}\hat{q}\left(\dfrac{1}{n_1} + \dfrac{1}{n_2}\right)}} = \dfrac{(.563 - .669) - 0}{\sqrt{.615(.385)\left(\dfrac{1}{1,140} + \dfrac{1}{1,106}\right)}} = -5.16$

d.   The rejection region requires $\alpha / 2 = .01 / 2 = .005$ in each tail of the z-distribution. From Table II, Appendix D, $z_{.005} = 2.58$. The rejection region is $z < -2.58$ or $z > 2.58$.

e.   The p-value is $p = P(z \leq -5.16) + P(z \geq 5.16) \approx (.5 - .5) + (.5 - .5) = 0$. This agrees with what was reported.

f.   Since the observed value of the test statistic falls in the rejection region ($z = -5.16 < -2.58$), H_0 is rejected. There is sufficient evidence to indicate a difference in the proportion of employed and unemployed individuals who had routine checkups in the past year at $\alpha = .01$.

8.107   a.   The two populations of interest are all male cell phone users and all female cell phone users.

b. The estimate of the proportion of men who sometimes do not drive safely while talking or texting on a cell phone is $\hat{p}_1 = .32$. The estimate of the proportion of women is $\hat{p}_2 = .25$.

c. For confidence coefficient .90, $\alpha = .10$ and $\alpha/2 = .10/2 = .05$. From Table II, Appendix D, $z_{.05} = 1.645$. A 90% confidence interval for the difference between the proportions of men and women who sometimes do not drive safely while talking or texting on a cell phone is:

$$(\hat{p}_1 - \hat{p}_2) \pm z_{.05}\sqrt{\frac{\hat{p}_1\hat{q}_1}{n_1} + \frac{\hat{p}_2\hat{q}_2}{n_2}} \Rightarrow (.32 - .25) \pm 1.645\sqrt{\frac{.32(.68)}{643} + \frac{.25(.75)}{643}} \Rightarrow .07 \pm .041 \Rightarrow (.029, \ .111)$$

d. Since the interval does not contain 0, then there is a sufficient evidence to indicate that there is a difference between the proportions of men and women who sometimes do not drive safely while talking or texting on a cell phone. Also, the interval contains all positive values so we can conclude that men are more likely than women to sometimes not drive safely while talking or texting on a cell phone.

e. The estimate of the proportion of men who used their cell phone in an emergency is $\hat{p}_1 = .71$. The estimate of the proportion of women is $\hat{p}_2 = .77$.

f. Let $p_1 = $ proportion of men who used their cell phone in an emergency and $p_2 = $ the proportion of women who used their cell phone in an emergency.

Some preliminary calculations are:

$$\hat{p}_1 = \frac{x_1}{n_1} \Rightarrow x_1 = n_1\hat{p}_1 = 643(.71) = 456.53 \qquad \hat{p}_2 = \frac{x_2}{n_2} \Rightarrow x_2 = n_2\hat{p}_2 = 643(.77) = 495.11$$

$$\hat{p} = \frac{x_1 + x_2}{n_1 + n_2} = \frac{456.53 + 495.11}{643 + 643} = .74 \qquad \hat{q} = 1 - \hat{p} = 1 - .74 = .26$$

To determine whether the proportions of men and women who used their cell phones in an emergency differ, we test:

$$H_0 : p_1 - p_2 = 0$$
$$H_a : p_1 - p_2 \neq 0$$

The test statistic is $z = \dfrac{(\hat{p}_1 - \hat{p}_2) - 0}{\sqrt{\hat{p}\hat{q}\left(\dfrac{1}{n_1} + \dfrac{1}{n_2}\right)}} = \dfrac{(.71 - .77) - 0}{\sqrt{.74(.26)\left(\dfrac{1}{643} + \dfrac{1}{643}\right)}} = -2.45$.

The rejection region requires $\alpha/2 = .10/2 = .05$ in each tail of the z-distribution. From Table II, Appendix D, $z_{.05} = 1.645$. The rejection region is $z < -1.645$ or $z > 1.645$.

Since the observed value of the test statistic falls in the rejection region $(z = -2.45 < -1.645)$, H_0 is rejected. There is sufficient evidence to indicate the proportions of men and women who used their cell phone in an emergency differ at $\alpha = .10$.

8.109   a.   Using MINITAB, the descriptive statistics are:

Descriptive Statistics: Purchasers, Nonpurchasers

```
Variable    N    Mean   Median   StDev   Minimum Maximum     Q1      Q3
Purchase   20   39.80    38.00   10.04    23.00   59.00   32.25   48.75
Nonpurch   20   47.20    52.00   13.62    22.00   66.00   33.50   58.75
```

$$s_p^2 = \frac{(n_1-1)s_1^2 + (n_2-1)s_2^2}{n_1+n_2-2} = \frac{(20-1)13.62^2 + (20-1)10.04^2}{20+20-2} = 143.153$$

Let $\mu_1 =$ mean age of nonpurchasers and $\mu_2 =$ mean age of purchasers.

To determine if there is a difference in the mean age of purchasers and nonpurchasers, we test:

$$H_0: \mu_1 - \mu_2 = 0$$
$$H_a: \mu_1 - \mu_2 \neq 0$$

The test statistic is $t = \dfrac{(\bar{x}_1 - \bar{x}_2)-0}{\sqrt{s_p^2\left(\dfrac{1}{n_1}+\dfrac{1}{n_2}\right)}} = \dfrac{(47.20-39.80)-0}{\sqrt{143.153\left(\dfrac{1}{20}+\dfrac{1}{20}\right)}} = 1.956$

The rejection region requires $\alpha/2 = .10/2 = .05$ in each tail of the t-distribution with $df = n_1 + n_2 - 2 = 20+20-2 = 38$. From Table III, Appendix D, $t_{.05} \approx 1.684$. The rejection region is $t < -1.684$ or $t > 1.684$.

Since the observed value of the test statistic falls in the rejection region $(t = 1.956 > 1.684)$, H_0 is rejected. There is sufficient evidence to indicate the mean age of purchasers and nonpurchasers differ at $\alpha = .10$.

b.   The necessary assumptions are:

1.   Both sampled populations are approximately normal.
2.   The population variances are equal.
3.   The samples are randomly and independently sampled.

c.   The p-value is $p = P(t \leq -1.956) + P(t \geq 1.956) = (.5-.4748)+(.5-.4748) = .0504$. The probability of observing a test statistic of this value or more unusual if H_0 is true is .0504. Since this value is less than $\alpha = .10$, H_0 is rejected. There is sufficient evidence to indicate there is a difference in the mean age of purchasers and nonpurchasers.

d. For confidence coefficient .90, $\alpha = .10$ and $\alpha / 2 = .10 / 2 = .05$. From Table III, Appendix D, with df $= 38$, $t_{.05} \approx 1.684$. The confidence interval is:

$$(\bar{x}_2 - \bar{x}_1) \pm t_{.05} \sqrt{s_p^2 \left(\frac{1}{n_1} + \frac{1}{n_2} \right)} \Rightarrow (39.8 - 47.2) \pm 1.684 \sqrt{143.153 \left(\frac{1}{20} + \frac{1}{20} \right)}$$

$$\Rightarrow -7.4 \pm 6.37 \Rightarrow (-13.77, -1.03)$$

We are 90% confident that the difference in mean ages between purchasers and nonpurchasers is between -13.77 and -1.03.

8.111   a. Let $p_1 =$ proportion of African-American drivers searched by the LAPD and $p_2 =$ proportion of white drivers searched by the LAPD.

Some preliminary calculations are:

$$\hat{p}_1 = \frac{x_1}{n_1} = \frac{12,016}{61,688} = .195 \qquad \hat{p}_2 = \frac{x_2}{n_2} = \frac{5,312}{106,892} = .050$$

$$\hat{p} = \frac{x_1 + x_2}{n_1 + n_2} = \frac{12,016 + 5,312}{61,688 + 106,892} = \frac{17,328}{168,580} = .103$$

To determine if the proportions of African-American and white drivers searched differs, we test:

$$H_0 : p_1 - p_2 = 0$$
$$H_a : p_1 - p_2 \neq 0$$

The test statistic is $z = \dfrac{(\hat{p}_1 - \hat{p}_2) - 0}{\sqrt{\hat{p}\hat{q} \left(\frac{1}{n_1} + \frac{1}{n_2} \right)}} = \dfrac{.195 - .050}{\sqrt{.103(.897) \left(\frac{1}{61,688} + \frac{1}{106,892} \right)}} = 94.35$

The rejection region requires $\alpha / 2 = .05 / 2 = .025$ in each tail of the z-distribution. From Table II, Appendix D, $z_{.025} = 1.96$. The rejection region is $z < -1.96$ or $z < -1.96$.

Since the observed value of the test statistic falls in the rejection region $(z = 94.35 > 1.96)$, H_0 is rejected. There is sufficient evidence to indicate the proportions of African-American drivers and white drivers searched differs at $\alpha = .05$.

b. Let $p_1 =$ proportion of "hits" for African-American drivers searched by the LAPD and $p_2 =$ proportion of "hits" for white drivers searched by the LAPD.

Some preliminary calculations are:

$$\hat{p}_1 = \frac{x_1}{n_1} = \frac{5,134}{12,016} = .427 \qquad\qquad \hat{p}_2 = \frac{x_2}{n_2} = \frac{3,006}{5,312} = .566$$

$$\hat{p} = \frac{x_1 + x_2}{n_1 + n_2} = \frac{5,134 + 3,006}{12,016 + 5,312} = \frac{8,140}{17,328} = .470$$

For confidence coefficient .95, $\alpha = .05$ and $\alpha/2 = .05/2 = .025$. From Table II, Appendix D, $z_{.025} = 1.96$. The 95% confidence interval is:

$$(\hat{p}_1 - \hat{p}_2) \pm z_{.025}\sqrt{\frac{\hat{p}_1\hat{q}_1}{n_1} + \frac{\hat{p}_2\hat{q}_2}{n_2}} \Rightarrow (.427 - .566) \pm 1.96\sqrt{\frac{.427(.573)}{12,016} + \frac{.566(.434)}{5,312}}$$

$$\Rightarrow -.139 \pm .016 \Rightarrow (-.155, \; -.123)$$

We are 95% confident that the difference in "hit" rates between African-American drivers and white drivers searched by the LAPD is between $-.155$ and $-.123$.

8.113   For probability .95, $\alpha = .05$ and $\alpha/2 = .05/2 = .025$. From Table II, Appendix D, $z_{.025} = 1.96$. Since we have no prior information about the proportions, we use $p_1 = p_2 = .5$ to get a conservative estimate.

$$n_1 = n_2 = \frac{(z_{\alpha/2})^2(p_1q_1 + p_2q_2)}{ME^2} = \frac{(1.96)^2(.5(1-.5) + .5(1-.5))}{.02^2} = \frac{1.9208}{.0004} = 4,802$$

8.115   Some preliminary calculations are:

$$s_1^2 = \frac{\sum x_1^2 - \frac{\left(\sum x_1\right)^2}{n_1}}{n_1 - 1} = \frac{10,251 - \frac{225^2}{5}}{5-1} = \frac{126}{4} = 31.5$$

$$s_2^2 = \frac{\sum x_2^2 - \frac{\left(\sum x_2\right)^2}{n_2}}{n_2 - 1} = \frac{10,351 - \frac{227^2}{5}}{5-1} = \frac{45.2}{4} = 11.3$$

Let σ_1^2 = variance for instrument A and σ_2^2 = variance for instrument B. Since we wish to determine if there is a difference in the precision of the two machines, we test:

$$H_0 : \sigma_1^2 = \sigma_2^2$$
$$H_a : \sigma_1^2 \neq \sigma_2^2$$

The test statistic is $F = \dfrac{\text{Larger sample variance}}{\text{Smaller sample variance}} = \dfrac{s_1^2}{s_2^2} = \dfrac{31.5}{11.3} = 2.79$

The rejection region requires $\alpha/2 = .10/2 = .05$ in the upper tail of the F-distribution with $v_1 = n_1 - 1 = 5 - 1 = 4$ and $v_2 = n_2 - 1 = 5 - 1 = 4$. From Table VI, Appendix D, $F_{.05} = 6.39$. The rejection region is $F > 6.39$.

Since the observed value of the test statistic does not fall in the rejection region $(F = 2.79 \not> 6.39)$, H_0 is not rejected. There is insufficient evidence of a difference in the precision of the two instruments at $\alpha = .10$.

8.117 a. Let μ_{C1} = mean relational intimacy score for the CMC group on the first meeting and μ_{C3} = mean relational intimacy score for the CMC group on the third meeting. Let μ_{Cd} = difference in mean relational intimacy score between the first and third meetings for the CMC group. To determine if the mean relational intimacy score will increase between the first and third meetings, we test:

$$H_0 : \mu_{Cd} = 0$$
$$H_a : \mu_{Cd} < 0$$

     b. The researchers used the paired t-test because the same individuals participated in each of the three meeting sessions. Thus, the samples would not be independent.

     c. Since the p-value is so small ($p = .003$), H_0 would be rejected. There is sufficient evidence to indicate that the mean relational intimacy score for participants in the CMC group increased from the first to the third meeting for any value of $\alpha > .003$.

     d. Let μ_{F1} = mean relational intimacy score for the FTF group on the first meeting and μ_{F3} = mean relational intimacy score for the FTF group on the third meeting. Let μ_{Fd} = difference in mean relational intimacy score between the first and third meetings for the FTF group. To determine if the mean relational intimacy score will change between the first and third meetings, we test:

$$H_0 : \mu_{Fd} = 0$$
$$H_a : \mu_{Fd} \neq 0$$

     e. Since the p-value is not small ($p = .39$), H_0 would be not be rejected. There is insufficient evidence to indicate that the mean relational intimacy score for participants in the FTF group changed from the first to the third meeting for any value of $\alpha < .39$.

8.119 **Attitude towards the Advertisement**:

The p-value is $p = .091$. There is no evidence to reject H_0 for $\alpha = .05$. There is no evidence to indicate the first ad will be more effective when shown to males for $\alpha = .05$. There is evidence to reject H_0 for $\alpha = .10$. There is evidence to indicate the first ad will be more effective when shown to males for $\alpha = .10$.

Attitude toward Brand of Soft Drink:

The p-value is $p = .032$. There is evidence to reject H_0 for $\alpha > .032$. There is evidence to indicate the first ad will be more effective when shown to males for $\alpha > .032$.

Intention to Purchase the Soft Drink:

The p-value is $p = .050$. There is no evidence to reject H_0 for $\alpha = .05$. There is no evidence to indicate the first ad will be more effective when shown to males for $\alpha = .05$. There is evidence to reject H_0 for $\alpha > .050$. There is evidence to indicate the first ad will be more effective when shown to males for $\alpha > .050$.

No, I do not agree with the author's hypothesis. The results agree with the author's hypothesis for only the attitude toward the Brand using $\alpha = .05$. If we want to use $\alpha = .10$, then the author's hypotheses are all supported.

8.121   a.   Let p_1 = proportion of 9th grade boys who gambled weekly or daily in 1992 and p_2 = proportion of 9th grade boys who gambled weekly or daily in 1998. The researchers are interested in whether there is a difference in these two proportions, so the parameter of interest is $p_1 - p_2$.

Some preliminary calculations are:

$$\hat{p}_1 = \frac{x_1}{n_1} = \frac{4,684}{21,484} = .218 \qquad \hat{p}_2 = \frac{x_2}{n_2} = \frac{5,313}{23,199} = .229$$

$$\hat{p} = \frac{x_1 + x_2}{n_1 + n_2} = \frac{4,684 + 5,313}{21,484 + 23,199} = \frac{9,997}{44,683} = .224 \qquad \hat{q} = 1 - \hat{p} = 1 - .224 = .776$$

To determine if there is a difference in the proportions of 9th grade boys who gambled weekly or daily in 1992 and 1998, we test:

$$H_0 : p_1 - p_2 = 0$$
$$H_a : p_1 - p_2 \neq 0$$

The test statistic is $z = \dfrac{(\hat{p}_1 - \hat{p}_2) - 0}{\sqrt{\hat{p}\hat{q}\left(\dfrac{1}{n_1} + \dfrac{1}{n_2}\right)}} = \dfrac{(.218 - .229) - 0}{\sqrt{.224(.776)\left(\dfrac{1}{21,484} + \dfrac{1}{23,199}\right)}} = -2.79$

The rejection region requires $\alpha / 2 = .01 / 2 = .005$ in each tail of the z-distribution. From Table II, Appendix D, $z_{.005} = 2.58$. The rejection region is $z < -2.58$ or $z > 2.58$.

Since the observed value of the test statistic falls in the rejection region $(z = -2.79 < -2.58)$, H_0 is rejected. There is sufficient evidence to indicate a difference in the proportions of 9th grade boys who gambled weekly or daily in 1992 and 1998 at $\alpha = .01$.

b.   Yes. If samples sizes are large enough, differences can almost always be found. Suppose we compute a 99% confidence interval. For confidence coefficient .99, $\alpha = .01$ and $\alpha / 2 = .01 / 2 = .005$. From Table II, Appendix D, $z_{.005} = 2.58$. The 99% confidence interval is:

$$(\hat{p}_1 - \hat{p}_2) \pm z_{\alpha/2}\sqrt{\frac{\hat{p}_1\hat{q}_1}{n_1} + \frac{\hat{p}_2\hat{q}_2}{n_2}} \Rightarrow (.218 - .229) \pm 2.58\sqrt{\frac{.218(.782)}{21,484} + \frac{.229(.771)}{23,199}}$$

$$\Rightarrow -.011 \pm .010 \Rightarrow (-.021, \ -.001)$$

We are 99% confident that the difference in the proportions of 9th grade boys who gambled weekly or daily in 1992 and 1998 is between $-.021$ and $-.001$.

8.123   Let μ_1 = mean output for Design 1, μ_2 = mean output for Design 2, and $\mu_d = \mu_1 - \mu_2$.

Some preliminary calculations are:

Working Days	Difference (Design 1 - Design 2)
8/16	−53
8/17	−271
8/18	−206
8/19	−266
8/20	−213
8/23	−183
8/24	−118
8/25	−87

$$\bar{d} = \frac{\sum d}{n_d} = \frac{-1,397}{8} = -174.625 \qquad s_d^2 = \frac{\sum d^2 - \dfrac{\left(\sum d\right)^2}{n_d}}{n_d - 1} = \frac{289,793 - \dfrac{(-1,397)^2}{8}}{8-1} = 6,548.839$$

$$s_d = \sqrt{s_d^2} = \sqrt{6,548.839} = 80.925$$

To determine if Design 2 is superior to Design 1, we test:

$$H_0: \mu_d = 0$$
$$H_a: \mu_d < 0$$

The test statistic is $t = \dfrac{\bar{d} - \mu_o}{s_d / \sqrt{n_d}} = \dfrac{-174.625 - 0}{80.925 / \sqrt{8}} = -6.103$

Since no α value was given, we will use $\alpha = .05$. The rejection region requires $\alpha = .05$ in the lower tail of the t-distribution with df $= n_d - 1 = 8 - 1 = 7$. From Table III, Appendix D, $t_{.05} = 1.895$. The rejection region is $t < -1.895$.

Since the observed value of the test statistic falls in the rejection region $(t = -6.103 < -1.895)$, H_0 is rejected. There is sufficient evidence to indicate Design 2 is superior to Design 1 at $\alpha = .05$.

For confidence coefficient .95, $\alpha = .05$ and $\alpha/2 = .05/2 = .025$. From Table III, Appendix D, with df $= n_d - 1 = 8 - 1 = 7$, $t_{.025} = 2.365$. A 95% confidence interval for μ_d is:

$$\bar{d} \pm t_{.025} \frac{s_d}{\sqrt{n_d}} \Rightarrow -174.625 \pm 2.365 \frac{80.925}{\sqrt{8}} \Rightarrow -174.625 \pm 67.666 \Rightarrow (-242.29, \ -106.96)$$

Since this interval does not contain 0, there is evidence to indicate Design 2 is superior to Design 1.

Chapter 9
Design of Experiments and
Analysis of Variance

9.1   Since only one factor is utilized, the treatments are the four levels (A, B, C, D) of the qualitative factor.

9.3   One has no control over the levels of the factors in an observational experiment. One does have control of the levels of the factors in a designed experiment.

9.5   a.   This is an observational experiment. The economist has no control over the factor levels or unemployment rates.

        b.   This is a designed experiment. The manager chooses only three different incentive programs to compare, and randomly assigns an incentive program to each of nine plants.

        c.   This is an observational experiment. Even though the marketer chooses the publication, he has no control over who responds to the ads.

        d.   This is an observational experiment. The load on the facility's generators is only observed, not controlled.

        e.   This is an observational experiment. One has no control over the distance of the haul, the goods hauled, or the price of diesel fuel.

9.7   a.   The experimental units are the firms with CPAs.

        b.   The response variable is the firm's likelihood of reporting sustainability policies.

        c.   There are two factors – firm size and firm type.

        d.   There are two levels of firm size – large and small. There are two levels of firm type – public and private.

        e.   The treatments are the combinations of the factor levels. There are $2 \times 2 = 4$ treatments – large/public, large/private, small/public, and small/private.

9.9   a.   The study is designed because the experimental units (study participants) were randomly assigned to the treatments (gift givers and gift receivers).

        b.   The experimental units are the study participants. The response variable is the level of appreciation measured on a scale from 1 to 7. There is one factor – role. There are two levels of role and thus, two treatments. The treatments are gift giver or gift receiver.

9.11   a.   There are 2 factors in this problem, each with 2 levels. Thus, there are a total of $2 \times 2 = 4$ treatments.

        b.   The 4 treatments are: (Within-store, home), (Within-store, in store), (Between-store, home), and (Between-store, in store).

9.13   a.   The experimental units for this study are the students in the introductory psychology class.

        b.   The study is a designed experiment because the students are randomly assigned to a particular study group.

        c.   There are 2 factors in this problem: Class standing and study group.

        d.   Class standing has 3 levels: Low, Medium, and High. Study group has 2 levels: practice test and review.

        e.   There are a total of $3 \times 2 = 6$ treatments. They are: (Low, Review), (Low, Practice exam), (Medium, Review), (Medium, Practice exam), (High, Review), and (High, Practice exam).

        f.   The response variable is the final exam score.

9.15   a.   From Table VI with $v_1 = 4$ and $v_2 = 4$, $F_{.05} = 6.39$.

        b.   From Table VIII with $v_1 = 4$ and $v_2 = 4$, $F_{.01} = 15.98$.

        c.   From Table V with $v_1 = 30$ and $v_2 = 40$, $F_{.10} = 1.54$.

        d.   From Table VII with $v_1 = 15$ and $v_2 = 12$, $F_{.025} = 3.18$.

9.17   a.   In the second dot diagram **#2**, the difference between the sample means is small relative to the variability within the sample observations. In the first dot diagram **#1**, the values in each of the samples are grouped together with a range of 4, while in the second diagram **#2**, the range of values is 8.

        b.   For diagram **#1**,

$$\bar{x}_1 = \frac{\sum x_1}{n} = \frac{7+8+9+9+10+11}{6} = \frac{54}{6} = 9 \qquad \bar{x}_2 = \frac{\sum x_2}{n} = \frac{12+13+14+14+15+16}{6} = \frac{84}{6} = 14$$

For diagram **#2**,

$$\bar{x}_1 = \frac{\sum x_1}{n} = \frac{5+5+7+11+13+13}{6} = \frac{54}{6} = 9 \qquad \bar{x}_2 = \frac{\sum x_2}{n} = \frac{10+10+12+16+18+18}{6} = \frac{84}{6} = 14$$

        c.   For diagram **#1**,

$$SST = \sum_{i=1}^{2} n_i (\bar{x}_i - \bar{x})^2 = 6(9-11.5)^2 + 6(14-11.5)^2 = 75 \qquad \left(\bar{x} = \frac{\sum x}{n} = \frac{54+84}{12} = 11.5 \right)$$

For diagram **#2**,

$$SST = \sum_{i=1}^{2} n_i (\bar{x}_i - \bar{x})^2 = 6(9 - 11.5)^2 + 6(14 - 11.5)^2 = 75$$

d. For diagram **#1**,

$$s_1^2 = \frac{\sum x_1^2 - \frac{\left(\sum x_1\right)^2}{n_1}}{n_1 - 1} = \frac{496 - \frac{54^2}{6}}{6 - 1} = 2 \qquad s_2^2 = \frac{\sum x_2^2 - \frac{\left(\sum x_2\right)^2}{n_2}}{n_2 - 1} = \frac{1186 - \frac{84^2}{6}}{6 - 1} = 2$$

$$SSE = (n_1 - 1)s_1^2 + (n_2 - 1)s_2^2 = (6 - 1)2 + (6 - 1)2 = 20$$

For diagram **#2**,

$$s_1^2 = \frac{\sum x_1^2 - \frac{\left(\sum x_1\right)^2}{n_1}}{n_1 - 1} = \frac{558 - \frac{54^2}{6}}{6 - 1} = 14.4 \qquad s_2^2 = \frac{\sum x_2^2 - \frac{\left(\sum x_2\right)^2}{n_2}}{n_2 - 1} = \frac{1248 - \frac{84^2}{6}}{6 - 1} = 14.4$$

$$SSE = (n_1 - 1)s_1^2 + (n_2 - 1)s_2^2 = (6 - 1)14.4 + (6 - 1)14.4 = 144$$

e. For diagram **#1**, $SS(Total) = SST + SSE = 75 + 20 = 95$

$$SST \text{ is } \frac{SST}{SS(Total)} \times 100\% = \frac{75}{95} \times 100\% = 78.95\% \text{ of } SS(Total)$$

For diagram **#2**, $SS(Total) = SST + SSE = 75 + 144 = 219$

$$SST \text{ is } \frac{SST}{SS(Total)} \times 100\% = \frac{75}{219} \times 100\% = 34.25\% \text{ of } SS(Total)$$

f. For diagram **#1**, $MST = \dfrac{SST}{k-1} = \dfrac{75}{2-1} = 75$, $MSE = \dfrac{SSE}{n-k} = \dfrac{20}{12-2} = 2$, $F = \dfrac{MST}{MSE} = \dfrac{75}{2} = 37.5$

For diagram **#2**, $MST = \dfrac{SST}{k-1} = \dfrac{75}{2-1} = 75$, $MSE = \dfrac{SSE}{n-k} = \dfrac{144}{12-2} = 14.4$, $F = \dfrac{MST}{MSE} = \dfrac{75}{14.4} = 5.21$

g. The rejection region for both diagrams requires $\alpha = .05$ in the upper tail of the F-distribution with $v_1 = k - 1 = 2 - 1 = 1$ and $v_2 = n - k = 12 - 2 = 10$. From Table VI, Appendix D, $F_{.05} = 4.96$. The rejection region is $F > 4.96$.

For diagram **#1**, since the observed value of the test statistic falls in the rejection region $(F = 37.5 > 4.96)$, H_0 is rejected. There is sufficient evidence to indicate the samples were drawn from populations with different means at $\alpha = .05$.

For diagram **#2**, since the observed value of the test statistic falls in the rejection region $(F = 5.21 > 4.96)$, H_0 is rejected. There is sufficient evidence to indicate the samples were drawn from populations with different means at $\alpha = .05$.

h. We must assume both populations are normally distributed with common variances.

9.19   Refer to Exercise 9.17, the ANOVA table is:

For diagram **#1**:

Source	df	SS	MS	F
Treatment	1	75	75	37.5
Error	10	20	2	
Total	11	95		

For diagram **#2**:

Source	df	SS	MS	F
Treatment	1	75	75	5.21
Error	10	144	14.4	
Total	11	219		

9.21   a.   Using MINITAB, the results are:

One-way ANOVA: T1, T2, T3

```
Source  DF    SS    MS    F     P
Factor   2  12.30  6.15  2.93  0.105
Error    9  18.89  2.10
Total   11  31.19

S = 1.449   R-Sq = 39.44%   R-Sq(adj) = 25.98%
```

b. $H_0 : \mu_1 = \mu_2 = \mu_3$

H_a : At least two treatment means differ

The test statistic is $F = 2.931$ and the p-value is $p = .105$.

Since the p-value is not less than α ($p = .105 \not< .01$), H_0 is not rejected. There is insufficient evidence to indicate a difference in the treatment means at $\alpha = .01$.

9.23   a.   A completely randomized design was used for this study. The experimental units are the bus customers. The dependent variable is the performance score. There is one factor which is bus depot with 3 levels – Depot 1, Depot 2, and Depot 3. These factor levels are the treatments of the experiment.

b.   Yes. The p-value from the ANOVA F-test was $p = .0001$. For a 95% confidence level, $\alpha = .05$. Since the p-value is less than α ($p = .0001 < .05$), H_0 is rejected. There is sufficient evidence to indicate the mean customer performance scores differed across the three bus depots at $\alpha = .05$.

9.25   a.   To determine if the mean LUST discount percentages across the seven states differ, we test:

$H_0 : \mu_1 = \mu_2 = \cdots = \mu_7$

H_a : At least two treatment means differ

b.   From the ANOVA table, the test statistic is $F = 1.60$ and the p-value is $p = 0.174$.

Since the observed p-value is not less than α ($p = .174 \not< .10$), H_0 is not rejected. There is insufficient evidence to indicate a difference in the mean LUST discount percentages among the seven states at $\alpha = .10$.

9.27   To determine if the mean road rage score differs for the three income groups, we test:

$H_0 : \mu_1 = \mu_2 = \mu_3$
H_a : At least two treatment means differ

The test statistic is $F = 3.90$ and the p-value is $p < .01$. Since the p-value is less than $\alpha = .05$, H_0 is rejected. There is sufficient evidence to indicate the mean road rage score differs for the three income groups for $\alpha > .01$. Since the sample means increase as the income increases, it appears that road rage increases as income increases.

9.29   a.   This was a completely randomized design.

b.   The experimental units are the college students. The dependent variable is the attitude toward tanning score and the treatments are the 3 conditions (view product advertisement with models with a tan, view product advertisement with models with no tan, and view product advertisement with no model).

c.   Let μ_1 = mean attitude score for those viewing product advertisement with models with a tan, μ_2 = mean attitude score for those viewing product advertisement with models without a tan, and μ_3 = mean attitude score for those viewing product advertisement with no models. To determine if the treatment mean scores differ among the three groups, we test:

$H_0 : \mu_1 = \mu_2 = \mu_3$

d.   These are just sample means. To determine if the population means differ, we have to determine how many standard deviations are between these sample means. In addition, the next time an experiment was conducted, the sample means could change.

e.   The hypotheses are:

$H_0 : \mu_1 = \mu_2 = \mu_3$
H_a : At least two treatment means differ

The test statistic is $F = 3.60$ and the p-value is $p = .03$. Since the p-value is less than α ($p = .03 < .05$), H_0 is rejected. There is sufficient evidence to indicate a difference in the mean attitude scores among the three groups at $\alpha = .05$.

f.   We must assume that we have random samples from approximately normal populations with equal variances.

9.31   a.   To determine if the mean level of trust differs among the six treatments, we test:

$$H_0 : \mu_1 = \mu_2 = \cdots = \mu_6$$
$$H_a : \text{At least two treatment means differ}$$

      b.   The test statistic is $F = 2.21$.

The rejection region requires $\alpha = .05$ in the upper tail of the F-distribution with $v_1 = k - 1 = 6 - 1 = 5$ and $v_2 = n - k = 230 - 6 = 224$. Using MINITAB,

Inverse Cumulative Distribution Function

```
F distribution with 5 DF in numerator and 231 DF in denominator

P( X <= x )          x
       0.95   2.25436
```

The rejection region is $F > 2.25$.

Since the observed value of the test statistic does not fall in the rejection region $(F = 2.21 \ngtr 2.25)$, H_0 is not rejected. There is insufficient evidence to indicate that at least two mean trusts differ at $\alpha = .05$.

      c.   We must assume that all six samples are drawn from normal populations, the six population variances are the same, and that the samples are independent.

      d.   I would classify this experiment as designed. Each subject was randomly assigned to receive one of the six scenarios.

9.33   To determine if the mean THICKNESS differs among the 4 types of housing, we test:

$$H_0 : \mu_1 = \mu_2 = \mu_3 = \mu_4$$
$$H_a : \text{At least two treatment means differ}$$

The test statistic is $F = 11.74$ and the p-value is $p = 0.000$. Since the observed p-value ($p = 0.000$) is less than any reasonable value of α, H_0 is rejected. There is sufficient evidence to indicate a difference in the mean thickness among the four levels of housing for any reasonable value of α.

To determine if the mean WHIPPING CAPACITY differs among the 4 types of housing, we test:

$$H_0 : \mu_1 = \mu_2 = \mu_3 = \mu_4$$
$$H_a : \text{At least two treatment means differ}$$

The test statistic is $F = 31.36$ and the p-value is $p = 0.000$. Since the observed p-value ($p = 0.000$) is less than any reasonable value of α, H_0 is rejected. There is sufficient evidence to indicate a difference in the mean whipping capacity among the four levels of housing for any reasonable value of α.

To determine if the mean STRENGTH differs among the 4 types of housing, we test:

$H_0: \mu_1 = \mu_2 = \mu_3 = \mu_4$

H_a : At least two treatment means differ

The test statistic is $F = 1.70$ and the p-value is $p = 0.193$. Since the observed p-value ($p = 0.193$) is higher than any reasonable value of α, H_0 is not rejected. There is insufficient evidence to indicate a difference in the mean strength among the four levels of housing for any reasonable value of α.

Thus, the mean thickness and the mean percent overrun differ among the 4 housing systems.

9.35   The number of pairwise comparisons is equal to $k(k-1)/2$.

   a.   For $k = 3$, the number of comparisons is $3(3-1)/2 = 3$.

   b.   For $k = 5$, the number of comparisons is $5(5-1)/2 = 10$.

   c.   For $k = 4$, the number of comparisons is $4(4-1)/2 = 6$.

   d.   For $k = 10$, the number of comparisons is $10(10-1)/2 = 45$.

9.37   A comparisonwise error rate is the error rate (or the probability of declaring the means different when, in fact, they are not different, which is also the probability of a Type I error) for each individual comparison. That is, if each comparison is run using $\alpha = .05$, then the comparisonwise error rate is .05.

9.39 $(\mu_1 - \mu_2)$: $(2, 15)$ Since all values in the interval are positive, μ_1 is significantly greater than μ_2.

   $(\mu_1 - \mu_3)$: $(4, 7)$ Since all values in the interval are positive, μ_1 is significantly greater than μ_3.

   $(\mu_1 - \mu_4)$: $(-10, 3)$ Since 0 is in the interval, μ_1 is not significantly different from μ_4.
   However, since the center of the interval is less than 0, μ_4 is larger than μ_1.

   $(\mu_2 - \mu_3)$: $(-5, 11)$ Since 0 is in the interval, μ_2 is not significantly different from μ_3.
   However, since the center of the interval is greater than 0, μ_2 is larger than μ_3.

   $(\mu_2 - \mu_4)$: $(-12, -6)$ Since all values in the interval are negative, μ_4 is significantly greater than μ_2.

   $(\mu_3 - \mu_4)$: $(-8, -5)$ Since all values in the interval are negative, μ_4 is significantly greater than μ_3.

   Thus, the largest mean is μ_4 followed by μ_1, μ_2, and μ_3.

9.41   Since all confidence intervals contain only positive values, this indicates that there is evidence that all population means are different. The largest mean is for Depot 1, then next highest is Depot 2, and the lowest is Depot 3.

9.43   a.   Tukey's multiple comparison method is preferred over other methods because it controls experimental error at the chosen α level. It is more powerful than the other methods.

b. From the confidence interval comparing large-cap and medium-cap mutual funds, we find that 0 is in the interval. Thus, 0 is not an unusual value for the difference in the mean rates of return between large-cap and medium-cap mutual funds. This means we would not reject H_0. There is insufficient evidence of a difference in mean rates of return between large-cap and medium-cap mutual funds at $\alpha = .05$.

c. From the confidence interval comparing large-cap and small-cap mutual funds, we find that 0 is not in the interval. Thus, 0 is an unusual value for the difference in the mean rates of return between large-cap and small-cap mutual funds. This means we would reject H_0. There is sufficient evidence of a difference in mean rates of return between large-cap and small-cap mutual funds at $\alpha = .05$.

d. From the confidence interval comparing medium-cap and small-cap mutual funds, we find that 0 is in the interval. Thus, 0 is not an unusual value for the difference in the mean rates of return between medium-cap and small-cap mutual funds. This means we would not reject H_0. There is insufficient evidence of a difference in mean rates of return between medium-cap and small-cap mutual funds at $\alpha = .05$.

e. From the above, the mean rate of return for large-cap mutual funds is the largest, followed by medium-cap, followed by small-cap mutual funds. The mean rate of return for large-cap funds is significantly larger than that for small-cap funds. No other differences exist.

f. We are 95% confident of this decision.

9.45   a. The probability of declaring at least one pair of means different when they are not is .01.

b. There are a total of $\dfrac{k(k-1)}{2} = \dfrac{3(3-1)}{2} = 3$ pair-wise comparisons. They are:

"Under $30 thousand" to "Between $30 and $60 thousand"
"Under $30 thousand" to "Over $60 thousand"
"Between $30 and $60 thousand" to "Over $60 thousand"

c. Means for groups in homogeneous subsets are displayed in the table:

Income Group		Subsets	
	N	1	2
Under $30,000	379	4.60	
$30,000-$60,000	392		5.08
Over $60,000	267		5.15

d. Two of the comparisons in part b will yield confidence intervals that do not contain 0. They are:

"Under $30 thousand" to "Between $30 and $60 thousand"
"Under $30 thousand" to "Over $60 thousand"

9.47   The mean level of trust for the "no close" technique is significantly higher than that for "the visual close" and the "thermometer close" techniques. The mean level of trust for the "impending event" technique is significantly higher than that for the "thermometer close" technique. No other significant differences exist.

9.49   a. The confidence interval for $(\mu_{CAGE} - \mu_{BARN})$ is $(-.1250, -.0323)$. Since 0 is not contained in this interval, there is sufficient evidence of a difference in the mean shell thickness between cage and barn egg housing systems. Since this interval is negative, this implies that the thickness is larger for the barn egg housing system.

b.　The confidence interval for $(\mu_{CAGE} - \mu_{FREE})$ is $(-.1233, -.0307)$. Since 0 is not contained in this interval, there is sufficient evidence of a difference in the mean shell thickness between cage and free range egg housing systems. Since this interval is negative, this implies that the thickness is larger for the free range egg housing system.

c.　The confidence interval for $(\mu_{CAGE} - \mu_{ORGANIC})$ is $(-.1050, -.0123)$. Since 0 is not contained in this interval, there is sufficient evidence of a difference in the mean shell thickness between cage and organic egg housing systems. Since this interval is negative, this implies that the thickness is larger for the organic egg housing system.

d.　The confidence interval for $(\mu_{BARN} - \mu_{FREE})$ is $(-.0501, .0535)$. Since 0 is contained in this interval, there is insufficient evidence of a difference in the mean shell thickness between barn and free range egg housing systems. Since the center of the interval is greater than 0, the sample mean for barn is greater than that for free range.

e.　The confidence interval for $(\mu_{BARN} - \mu_{ORGANIC})$ is $(-.0318, .0718)$. Since 0 is contained in this interval, there is insufficient evidence of a difference in the mean shell thickness between barn and organic egg housing systems. Since the center of the interval is greater than 0, the sample mean for barn is greater than that for organic.

f.　The confidence interval for $(\mu_{FREE} - \mu_{ORGANIC})$ is $(-.0335, .0701)$. Since 0 is contained in this interval, there is insufficient evidence of a difference in the mean shell thickness between free range and organic egg housing systems. Since the center of the interval is greater than 0, the sample mean for free range is greater than that for organic.

g.　We rank the housing system means as follows:

Housing System:　Cage < <u>Organic < Free < Barn</u>

We are 95% confident that the mean shell thickness for the cage housing system is significantly less than the mean thickness for the other three housing systems. There is no significant difference in the mean shell thicknesses among the barn, free range and organic housing systems.

9.51　a.　$SSB = \displaystyle\sum_{i=1}^{b} \frac{B_i^2}{k} - CM$　where $CM = \dfrac{\left(\sum x_i\right)^2}{n} = \dfrac{49^2}{9} = 266.7778$

$SSB = \dfrac{17^2}{3} + \dfrac{15^2}{3} + \dfrac{17^2}{3} - 266.7778 = .8889$

$SSE = SS\,(Total) - SST - SSB = 30.2222 - 21.5555 - .8889 = 7.7778$

$MST = \dfrac{SST}{k-1} = \dfrac{21.5555}{2} = 10.7778$　　$MSB = \dfrac{SSB}{b-1} = \dfrac{.8889}{2} = .4445$

$MSE = \dfrac{SSE}{n-k-b+1} = \dfrac{7.7778}{4} = 1.9445$

$F_T = \dfrac{MST}{MSE} = \dfrac{10.7778}{1.9445} = 5.54$　　$F_B = \dfrac{MSB}{MSE} = \dfrac{.4445}{1.9445} = .23$

The ANOVA table is:

Source	df	SS	MS	F
Treatment	2	21.5555	10.7778	5.54
Block	2	.8889	.4445	.23
Error	4	7.7778	1.9445	
Total	8	30.2222		

b.
$H_0 : \mu_1 = \mu_2 = \mu_3$

$H_a :$ At least two treatment means differ

c. The test statistic is $F = \dfrac{MST}{MSE} = 5.54$

d. A Type I error would be concluding at least two treatment means differ when they do not.

A Type II error would be concluding all the treatment means are the same when at least two differ.

e. The rejection region requires $\alpha = .05$ in the upper tail of the F distribution with $v_1 = k - 1 = 3 - 1 = 2$ and $v_2 = n - k - b + 1 = 9 - 3 - 3 + 1 = 4$. From Table VI, Appendix A, $F_{.05} = 6.94$. The rejection region is $F > 6.94$.

Since the observed value of the test statistic does not fall in the rejection region $(F = 5.54 \not> 6.94)$, H_0 is not rejected. There is insufficient evidence to indicate at least two of the treatment means differ at $\alpha = .05$.

9.53 a. $SST = .2(500) = 100 \quad SSB = .3(500) = 150$

$SSE = SS\left(Total\right) - SST - SSB = 500 - 100 - 150 = 250$

$MST = \dfrac{SST}{k-1} = \dfrac{100}{4-1} = 33.3333 \qquad MSB = \dfrac{SSB}{b-1} = \dfrac{150}{9-1} = 18.75$

$MSE = \dfrac{SSE}{n-k-b+1} = \dfrac{250}{36-4-9+1} = \dfrac{250}{24} = 10.4167$

$F_T = \dfrac{MST}{MSE} = \dfrac{33.3333}{10.4167} = 3.20 \qquad F_B = \dfrac{MSB}{MSE} = \dfrac{18.75}{10.4167} = 1.80$

To determine if differences exist among the treatment means, we test:

$H_0 : \mu_1 = \mu_2 = \mu_3 = \mu_4$
$H_a :$ At least two treatment means differ

The test statistic is $F = 3.20$.

The rejection region requires $\alpha = .05$ in the upper tail of the F distribution with $v_1 = k - 1 = 4 - 1 = 3$ and $v_2 = n - k - b + 1 = 36 - 4 - 9 + 1 = 24$. From Table VI, Appendix D, $F_{.05} = 3.01$. The rejection region is $F > 3.01$.

Since the observed value of the test statistic falls in the rejection region $(F = 3.20 > 3.01)$, H_0 is rejected. There is sufficient evidence to indicate differences among the treatment means at $\alpha = .05$.

To determine if differences exist among the block means, we test:

$H_0 : \mu_1 = \mu_2 = \cdots = \mu_9$

H_a : At least two block means differ

The test statistic is $F = 1.80$.

The rejection region requires $\alpha = .05$ in the upper tail of the F distribution with $\nu_1 = b - 1 = 9 - 1 = 8$ and $\nu_2 = n - k - b + 1 = 36 - 4 - 9 + 1 = 24$. From Table VI, Appendix D, $F_{.05} = 2.36$. The rejection region is $F > 2.36$.

Since the observed value of the test statistic does not fall in the rejection region $(F = 1.80 \ngtr 2.36)$, H_0 is not rejected. There is insufficient evidence to indicate differences among the block means at $\alpha = .05$.

b. $SST = .5(500) = 250 \qquad SSB = .2(500) = 100$

$SSE = SS(Total) - SST - SSB = 500 - 250 - 100 = 150$

$$MST = \frac{SST}{k-1} = \frac{250}{4-1} = 83.3333 \qquad MSB = \frac{SSB}{b-1} = \frac{100}{9-1} = 12.5$$

$$MSE = \frac{SSE}{n-k-b+1} = \frac{150}{36-4-9+1} = 6.25$$

$$F_T = \frac{MST}{MSE} = \frac{83.3333}{6.25} = 13.33 \qquad F_B = \frac{MSB}{MSE} = \frac{12.5}{6.25} = 2$$

To determine if differences exist among the treatment means, we test:

$H_0 : \mu_1 = \mu_2 = \mu_3 = \mu_4$

H_a : At least two treatment means differ

The test statistic is $F = 13.33$.

The rejection region is $F > 3.01$ (same as above).

Since the observed value of the test statistic falls in the rejection region $(F = 13.33 > 3.01)$, H_0 is rejected. There is sufficient evidence to indicate differences exist among the treatment means at $\alpha = .05$.

To determine if differences exist among the block means, we test:

$H_0 : \mu_1 = \mu_2 = \cdots = \mu_9$

H_a : At least two block means differ

The test statistic is $F = 2.00$.

The rejection region is $F > 2.36$ (same as above).

Since the observed value of the test statistic does not fall in the rejection region $(F = 2.00 \ngtr 2.36)$, H_0

is not rejected. There is insufficient evidence to indicate differences exist among the block means at $\alpha = .05$.

c. $SST = .2(500) = 100$ $\qquad$ $SSB = .5(500) = 250$

$SSE = SS\,(Total) - SST - SSB = 500 - 100 - 250 = 150$

$$MST = \frac{SST}{k-1} = \frac{100}{4-1} = 33.3333 \qquad MSB = \frac{SSB}{b-1} = \frac{250}{9-1} = 31.25$$

$$MSE = \frac{SSE}{n-k-b+1} = \frac{150}{36-4-9+1} = 6.25$$

$$F_T = \frac{MST}{MSE} = \frac{33.3333}{6.25} = 5.33 \qquad F_B = \frac{MSB}{MSE} = \frac{31.25}{6.25} = 5.00$$

To determine if differences exist among the treatment means, we test:

$H_0 : \mu_1 = \mu_2 = \mu_3 = \mu_4$
H_a : At least two treatment means differ

The test statistic is $F = 5.33$.

The rejection region is $F > 3.01$ (same as above).

Since the observed value of the test statistic falls in the rejection region $(F = 5.33 > 3.01)$, H_0 is rejected. There is sufficient evidence to indicate differences exist among the treatment means at $\alpha = .05$.

To determine if differences exist among the block means, we test:

$H_0 : \mu_1 = \mu_2 = \cdots = \mu_9$
H_a : At least two block means differ

The test statistic is $F = 5.00$.

The rejection region is $F > 2.36$ (same as above).

Since the observed value of the test statistic falls in the rejection region $(F = 5.00 > 2.36)$, H_0 is rejected. There is sufficient evidence to indicate differences exist among the block means at $\alpha = .05$.

d. $SST = .4(500) = 200$ $\qquad$ $SSB = .4(500) = 200$

$SSE = SS\,(Total) - SST - SSB = 500 - 200 - 200 = 100$

$$MST = \frac{SST}{k-1} = \frac{200}{4-1} = 66.6667 \qquad MSB = \frac{SSB}{b-1} = \frac{200}{9-1} = 25$$

$$MSE = \frac{SSE}{n-k-b+1} = \frac{100}{36-4-9+1} = 4.1667$$

$$F_T = \frac{MST}{MSE} = \frac{66.6667}{4.1667} = 16.0 \qquad F_B = \frac{MSB}{MSE} = \frac{25}{4.1667} = 6.00$$

To determine if differences exist among the treatment means, we test:

$H_0: \mu_1 = \mu_2 = \mu_3 = \mu_4$

$H_a:$ At least two treatment means differ

The test statistic is $F = 16.0$.

The rejection region is $F > 3.01$ (same as above).

Since the observed value of the test statistic falls in the rejection region $(F = 16.0 > 3.01)$, H_0 is rejected. There is sufficient evidence to indicate differences among the treatment means at $\alpha = .05$.

To determine if differences exist among the block means, we test:

$H_0: \mu_1 = \mu_2 = \cdots = \mu_9$

$H_a:$ At least two block means differ

The test statistic is $F = 6.00$.

The rejection region is $F > 2.36$ (same as above).

Since the observed value of the test statistic falls in the rejection region $(F = 6.00 > 2.36)$, H_0 is rejected. There is sufficient evidence to indicate differences exist among the block means at $\alpha = .05$.

e. $SST = .2(500) = 100$ $SSB = .2(500) = 100$

$SSE = SS\left(Total\right) - SST - SSB = 500 - 100 - 100 = 300$

$MST = \dfrac{SST}{k-1} = \dfrac{100}{4-1} = 33.3333$ $MSB = \dfrac{SSB}{b-1} = \dfrac{100}{9-1} = 12.5$

$MSE = \dfrac{SSE}{n-k-b+1} = \dfrac{300}{36-4-9+1} = 12.5$

$F_T = \dfrac{MST}{MSE} = \dfrac{33.3333}{12.5} = 2.67$ $F_B = \dfrac{MSB}{MSE} = \dfrac{12.5}{12.5} = 1.00$

To determine if differences exist among the treatment means, we test:

$H_0: \mu_1 = \mu_2 = \mu_3 = \mu_4$

$H_a:$ At least two treatment means differ

The test statistic is $F = 2.67$.

The rejection region is $F > 3.01$ (same as above).

Since the observed value of the test statistic does not fall in the rejection region $(F = 2.67 \ngtr 3.01)$, H_0 is not rejected. There is insufficient evidence to indicate differences exist among the treatment means at $\alpha = .05$.

To determine if differences exist among the block means, we test:

$H_0: \mu_1 = \mu_2 = \cdots = \mu_9$

$H_a:$ At least two block means differ

The test statistic is $F = 1.00$.

The rejection region is $F > 2.36$ (same as above).

Since the observed value of the test statistic does not fall in the rejection region ($F = 1.00 \ngtr 2.36$), H_0 is not rejected. There is insufficient evidence to indicate differences among the block means at $\alpha = .05$.

9.55   a.   A randomized block design should be used to analyze the data because the same employees were measured at all three time periods. Thus, the blocks are the employees and the treatments are the three time periods.

        b.   There is still enough information in the table to make a conclusion because the *p*-values are given.

        c.   To determine if there are differences in the mean competence levels among the three time periods, we test:

$$H_0 : \mu_1 = \mu_2 = \mu_3$$
$$H_a : \text{At least two treatment means differ}$$

        d.   The *p*-value is $p = 0.001$. At a significance level $> .001$, we reject H_0. There is sufficient evidence to conclude that there is a difference in the mean competence levels among the three time periods for any value of $\alpha > .001$.

        e.   With 90% confidence, the mean competence before the training is significantly less than the mean competence 2-days after and 2-months after. There is no significant difference in the mean competence between 2-days after and 2-months after.

9.57   a.   The treatments were the 8 different activities.

        b.   The blocks were the 15 adults who participated in the study.

        c.   Since the *p*-value is less than $\alpha (p = .001 < .01)$, H_0 is rejected. There is sufficient evidence to indicate a difference in mean heart rate among the 8 activities at $\alpha = .01$.

        d.   The treadmill jogging had the highest mean heart rate. It was significantly greater than the mean heart rates of all the other activities. Brisk treadmill walking had the second highest mean heart rate. It was significantly less than the mean heart rate of treadmill jogging, but significantly greater than the mean heart rates of the other 6 activities. There was no significant difference in the mean heart rates among the treatments Wii aerobics, Wii muscle conditioning, Wii yoga, and Wii balance. The mean heart rates for these activities were significantly less than the mean heart rates for treadmill jogging and brisk treadmill walking, but greater than the mean heart rates of handheld gaming and rest. There was no significant difference in the mean heart rate between handheld gaming and rest. The mean heart rate for these two activities were significantly less than those for the other 6 activities.

9.59   a.   To compare the mean item scores, we test:

$$H_0 : \mu_1 = \mu_2 = \cdots = \mu_5$$
$$H_a : \text{At least 2 of the treatment means differs}$$

        b.   Each of the 11 items were reviewed by each of the 5 systematic reviews. Since all reviews were made on each item, the observations are not independent. Thus, the randomized block ANOVA is appropriate.

c.   The *p*-value for Review is $p = 0.319$. Since the *p*-value is not small, H_0 would not be rejected for any reasonable value of α. There is insufficient evidence to indicate a difference in the mean review scores among the 5 systematic reviews.

The *p*-value for Item is $p = 0.000$. Since the *p*-value is small, H_0 would be rejected for any reasonable value of α. There is sufficient evidence to indicate a difference in the mean scores among the 5 reviews.

d.   None of the means are significantly different because all means are connected with the letter "a". This agrees with the conclusion drawn in part c about the treatment Review.

e.   The experiment-wise error rate is .05. This means that the probability of declaring at least 2 means different when they are not different is .05.

9.61   Using MINITAB, the ANOVA table is:

Two-way ANOVA: Rate versus Week, Day

```
Analysis of Variance for Rate
Source          DF        SS        MS        F         P
Week             8     575.2      71.9      6.10     0.000
Day              4      94.2      23.5      2.00     0.118
Error           32     376.9      11.8
Total           44    1046.4
```

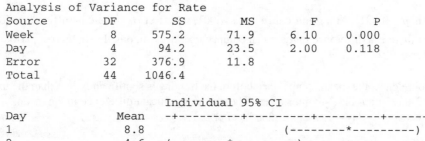

```
                        Individual 95% CI
Day            Mean    -+---------+---------+---------+---------+
1               8.8                         (--------*---------)
2               4.6     (---------*---------)
3               5.8          (--------*--------)
4               5.4        (--------*---------)
5               6.4          (---------*--------)
                       -+---------+---------+---------+---------+
                       2.5       5.0       7.5      10.0      12.5
```

To determine if there is a difference in mean rate of absenteeism among the 5 days of the week, we test:

$H_0 : \mu_1 = \mu_2 = \mu_3 = \mu_4 = \mu_5$

H_a : At least 2 of the treatment means differs

The test statistic is $F = 2.00$ and the *p*-value is $p = .118$.

Since the *p*-value is not small, H_0 is not rejected. There is insufficient evidence to indicate a difference in mean rate of absenteeism among the 5 days of the week for any value of $\alpha < .118$.

To test for the effectiveness of blocking, we test:

$H_0 : \mu_1 = \mu_2 = \cdots = \mu_9$

H_a : At least 2 of the block means differs

The test statistic is $F = 6.10$ and the *p*-value is $p = .000$.

Since the p-value is so small, H_0 is rejected. There is sufficient evidence to indicate blocking was effective at any reasonable value of α.

9.63   Using MINITAB, the ANOVA table is:

Two-way ANOVA: Corrosion versus Time, System

```
Source   DF      SS       MS       F      P
Time      2  63.1050  31.5525  337.06  0.000
System    3   9.5833   3.1944   34.12  0.000
Error     6   0.5617   0.0936
Total    11  73.2500

S = 0.3060   R-Sq = 99.23%   R-Sq(adj) = 98.59%


                       Individual 95% CIs For Mean Based on
                       Pooled StDev
System    Mean    ------+---------+---------+---------+---
1        9.0667       (----*-----)
2        9.7333            (-----*----)
3       11.0667                           (----*-----)
4        8.7333   (----*-----)
                  ------+---------+---------+---------+---
                     8.80      9.60     10.40     11.20
```

To determine if there is a difference in mean corrosion rates among the 4 systems, we test:

$H_0 : \mu_1 = \mu_2 = \mu_3 = \mu_4$

$H_a :$ At least 2 of the treatment means differs

The test statistic is $F = 34.12$ and the p-value is $p = .000$.

Since the p-value is so small, H_0 is rejected. There is sufficient evidence to indicate a difference in mean corrosion rates among the 4 systems at any reasonable value of α.

Using SAS, Tukey's multiple comparison results are:

```
          Tukey's Studentized Range (HSD) Test for CORROSION

NOTE: This test controls the Type I experimentwise error rate, but it generally has a higher
      Type II error rate than REGWQ.

                        Alpha                               0.05
                        Error Degrees of Freedom               6
                        Error Mean Square               0.093611
                        Critical Value of Studentized Range  4.89559
                        Minimum Significant Difference     0.8648


          Means with the same letter are not significantly different.


              Tukey Grouping         Mean      N    SYSTEM

                          A       11.0667       3    3

                          B        9.7333       3    2
                          B
                  C       B        9.0667       3    1
                  C
                  C                 8.7333       3    4
```

The mean corrosion rate for system 3 is significantly larger than all of the other mean corrosion rates. The mean corrosion rate of system 2 is significantly larger than the mean for system 4. If we want the system (epoxy coating) with the lowest corrosion rate, we would pick either system 1 or system 4. There is no significant difference between these two groups and they are in the lowest corrosion rate group.

9.65   a.   The ANOVA table is:

Source	df	SS	MS	F
A	2	.8	.4000	3.69
B	3	5.3	1.7667	16.31
AB	6	9.6	1.6000	14.77
Error	12	1.3	.1083	
Total	23	17.0		

df for A is $a - 1 = 3 - 1 = 2$ df for B is $b - 1 = 4 - 1 = 3$

df for AB is $(a-1)(b-1) = 2(3) = 6$ df for Error is $n - ab = 24 - 3(4) = 12$

df for Total is $n - 1 = 24 - 1 = 23$

$$SSE = SS\,(Total) - SST - SSB = 17.0 - .8 - 5.3 - 9.6 = 1.3 \qquad MSA = \frac{SSA}{a-1} = \frac{.8}{3-1} = .40$$

$$MSB = \frac{SSB}{b-1} = \frac{5.3}{4-1} = 1.7667 \qquad\qquad MSAB = \frac{SSAB}{(a-1)(b-1)} = \frac{9.6}{(3-1)(4-1)} = 1.60$$

$$MSE = \frac{SSE}{n-ab} = \frac{1.3}{24-3(4)} = .1083 \quad F_A = \frac{MSA}{MSE} = \frac{.4000}{.1083} = 3.69 \quad F_B = \frac{MSB}{MSE} = \frac{1.7667}{.1083} = 16.31$$

$$F_{AB} = \frac{MSAB}{MSE} = \frac{1.6000}{.1083} = 14.77$$

b.   Sum of Squares for Treatment $= SSA + SSB + SSAB = .8 = 5.3 + 2.6 = 15.7$

$$MST = \frac{SST}{ab-1} = \frac{15.7}{3(4)-1} = 1.4273 \qquad F_T = \frac{MST}{MSE} = \frac{1.4273}{.1083} = 13.18$$

To determine if the treatment means differ, we test:

$H_0 : \mu_1 = \mu_2 = \cdots = \mu_{12}$

H_a : At least 2 of the treatment means differs

The test statistic is $F = 13.18$.

The rejection region requires $\alpha = .05$ in the upper tail of the F-distribution with $v_1 = ab - 1 = 3(4) - 1 = 11$ and $v_2 = n - ab = 24 - 3(4) = 12$. From Table VI, Appendix D, $F_{.05} \approx 2.75$. The rejection region is $F > 2.75$.

Since the observed value of the test statistic falls in the rejection region $(F = 13.18 > 2.75)$, H_0 is rejected. There is sufficient evidence to indicate the treatment means differ at $\alpha = .05$.

c. Yes. We need to partition the Treatment Sum of Squares into the Main Effects and Interaction Sum of Squares. Then we test whether factors A and B interact. Depending on the conclusion of the test for interaction, we either test for main effects or compare the treatment means.

d. Two factors are said to interact if the effect of one factor on the dependent variable is not the same at different levels of the second factor. If the factors interact, then tests for main effects are not necessary. We need to compare the treatment means for one factor at each level of the second.

e. To determine if the factors interact, we test:

H_0: Factors A and B do not interact to affect the response mean
H_a: Factors A and B do interact to affect the response mean

The test statistic is $F = \dfrac{MS\,AB}{MSE} = 14.77$

The rejection region requires $\alpha = .05$ in the upper tail of the F-distribution with $v_1 = (a-1)(b-1) = (3-1)(4-1) = 6$ and $v_2 = n - ab = 24 - 3(4) = 12$. From Table VI, Appendix D, $F_{.05} = 3.00$. The rejection region is $F > 3.00$.

Since the observed value of the test statistic falls in the rejection region $(F = 14.77 > 3.00)$, H_0 is rejected. There is sufficient evidence to indicate the two factors interact to affect the response mean at $\alpha = .05$.

f. No. Testing for main effects is not warranted because interaction is present. Instead, we compare the treatment means of one factor at each level of the second factor.

9.67 a. The treatments are the combinations of the levels of factor A and the levels of factor B. There are $2 \times 3 = 6$ treatments. The treatment means are:

$$\bar{x}_{11} = \frac{\sum x_{11}}{2} = \frac{3.1 + 4.0}{2} = 3.55 \qquad \bar{x}_{12} = \frac{\sum x_{12}}{2} = \frac{4.6 + 4.2}{2} = 4.4 \qquad \bar{x}_{13} = \frac{\sum x_{13}}{2} = \frac{6.4 + 7.1}{2} = 6.75$$

$$\bar{x}_{21} = \frac{\sum x_{21}}{2} = \frac{5.9 + 5.3}{2} = 5.6 \qquad \bar{x}_{22} = \frac{\sum x_{22}}{2} = \frac{2.9 + 2.2}{2} = 2.55 \qquad \bar{x}_{23} = \frac{\sum x_{23}}{2} = \frac{3.3 + 2.5}{2} = 2.9$$

Using MNIITAB, the graph is:

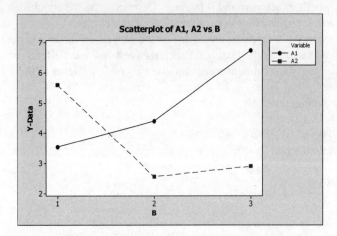

The treatment means appear to be different because the sample means are quite different. The factors appear to interact because the lines are not parallel.

b. $SST = SSA + SSB + SSAB = 4.4408 + 4.1267 + 18.0667 = 26.5742$

$$MST = \frac{SST}{ab-1} = \frac{26.5742}{2(3)-1} = 5.315 \qquad F_T = \frac{MST}{MSE} = \frac{5.315}{.246} = 21.62$$

To determine whether the treatment means differ, we test:

$H_0 : \mu_1 = \mu_2 = \cdots = \mu_6$
H_a : At least two treatment means differs

The test statistic is $F = \dfrac{MST}{MSE} = 21.62$

The rejection region requires $\alpha = .05$ in the upper tail of the F-distribution with $v_1 = ab - 1 = 2(3) - 1 = 5$ and $v_2 = n - ab = 12 - 2(3) = 6$. From Table VI, Appendix D, $F_{.05} = 4.39$. The rejection region is $F > 4.39$.

Since the observed value of the test statistic falls in the rejection region $(F = 21.62 > 4.39)$, H_0 is rejected. There is sufficient evidence to indicate that the treatment means differ at $\alpha = .05$. This supports the plot in **a**.

c. Yes. Since there are differences among the treatment means, we test for interaction. To determine whether the factors A and B interact, we test:

H_0: Factors A and B do not interact to affect the mean response
H_a: Factors A and B do interact to affect the mean response

The test statistic is $F = \dfrac{MSAB}{MSE} = \dfrac{9.0033}{.24583} = 36.62$

The rejection region requires $\alpha = .05$ in the upper tail of the F-distribution with

$v_1 = (a-1)(b-1) = (2-1)(3-1) = 2$ and $v_2 = n - ab = 12 - 2(3) = 6$. From Table VI, Appendix D, $F_{.05} = 5.14$. The rejection region is $F > 5.14$.

Since the observed value of the test statistic falls in the rejection region $(F = 36.62 > 5.14)$, H_0 is rejected. There is sufficient evidence to indicate that factors A and B interact to affect the response mean at $\alpha = .05$.

d. No. Because interaction is present, the tests for main effects are not warranted.

e. The results of the tests in parts **b** and **c** support the visual interpretation in part **a**.

9.69 a. $SSA = .2(1000) = 200$, $SSB = .1(1000) = 100$, $SSAB = .1(1000) = 100$

$SSE = SS(Total) - SSA - SSB - SSAB = 1000 - 200 - 100 - 100 = 600$

$SST = SSA + SSB + SSAB = 200 + 100 + 100 = 400$ $\qquad MSA = \dfrac{SSA}{a-1} = \dfrac{200}{3-1} = 100$

$MSB = \dfrac{SSB}{b-1} = \dfrac{100}{3-1} = 50$ $\qquad MSAB = \dfrac{SSAB}{(a-1)(b-1)} = \dfrac{100}{(3-1)(3-1)} = 25$

$MSE = \dfrac{SSE}{n-ab} = \dfrac{600}{27-3(3)} = 33.333$ $\qquad MST = \dfrac{SST}{ab-1} = \dfrac{400}{3(3)-1} = 50$

$F_A = \dfrac{MSA}{MSE} = \dfrac{100}{33.333} = 3.00$ $\qquad\qquad F_B = \dfrac{MSB}{MSE} = \dfrac{50}{33.333} = 1.50$

$F_{AB} = \dfrac{MSAB}{MSE} = \dfrac{25}{33.333} = .75$ $\qquad\qquad F_T = \dfrac{MST}{MSE} = \dfrac{50}{33.333} = 1.50$

Source	df	SS	MS	F
A	2	200	100	3.00
B	2	100	50	1.50
AB	4	100	25	.75
Error	18	600	33.333	
Total	26	1000		

To determine whether the treatment means differ, we test:

$H_0: \mu_1 = \mu_2 = \cdots = \mu_9$
H_a: At least two treatment means differs

The test statistic is $F = \dfrac{MST}{MSE} = 1.50$

Suppose $\alpha = .05$. The rejection region requires $\alpha = .05$ in the upper tail of the F-distribution with $v_1 = ab - 1 = 3(3) - 1 = 8$ and $v_2 = n - ab = 27 - 3(3) = 18$. From Table VI, Appendix D, $F_{.05} = 2.51$. The rejection region is $F > 2.51$.

Since the observed value of the test statistic does not fall in the rejection region ($F = 1.50 \not> 2.51$), H_0 is not rejected. There is insufficient evidence to indicate the treatment means differ at $\alpha = .05$. Since there are no treatment mean differences, we have nothing more to do.

b. $SSA = .1(1000) = 100$, $SSB = .1(1000) = 100$, $SSAB = .5(1000) = 500$

$$SSE = SS(Total) - SSA - SSB - SSAB = 1000 - 100 - 100 - 500 = 300$$

$$SST = SSA + SSB + SSAB = 100 + 100 + 500 = 700 \qquad MSA = \frac{SSA}{a-1} = \frac{100}{3-1} = 50$$

$$MSB = \frac{SSB}{b-1} = \frac{100}{3-1} = 50 \qquad\qquad MSAB = \frac{SSAB}{(a-1)(b-1)} = \frac{500}{(3-1)(3-1)} = 125$$

$$MSE = \frac{SSE}{n-ab} = \frac{300}{27-3(3)} = 16.667 \qquad MST = \frac{SST}{ab-1} = \frac{700}{9-1} = 87.5$$

$$F_A = \frac{MSA}{MSE} = \frac{50}{16.667} = 3.00 \qquad\qquad F_B = \frac{MSB}{MSE} = \frac{50}{16.667} = 3.00$$

$$F_{AB} = \frac{MSAB}{MSE} = \frac{125}{16.667} = 7.50 \qquad\qquad F_T = \frac{MST}{MSE} = \frac{87.5}{16.667} = 5.25$$

Source	df	SS	MS	F
A	2	100	50	3.00
B	2	100	50	3.00
AB	4	500	125	7.50
Error	18	300	16.667	
Total	26	1000		

To determine if the treatment means differ, we test:

$H_0 : \mu_1 = \mu_2 = \cdots = \mu_9$

H_a : At least two treatment means differs

The test statistic is $F = \dfrac{MST}{MSE} = 5.25$

The rejection region requires $\alpha = .05$ in the upper tail of the F-distribution with $v_1 = ab - 1 = 3(3) - 1 = 8$ and $v_2 = n - ab = 27 - 3(3) = 18$. From Table VI, Appendix D, $F_{.05} = 2.51$. The rejection region is $F > 2.51$.

Since the observed value of the test statistic falls in the rejection region ($F = 5.25 > 2.51$), H_0 is rejected. There is sufficient evidence to indicate the treatment means differ at $\alpha = .05$.

Since the treatment means differ, we next test for interaction between factors A and B. To determine if factors A and B interact, we test:

H_0: Factors A and B do not interact to affect the mean response
H_a: Factors A and B do interact to affect the mean response

The test statistic is $F = \dfrac{MSAB}{MSE} = 7.50$

The rejection region requires $\alpha = .05$ in the upper tail of the F-distribution with $v_1 = (a-1)(b-1) = (3-1)(3-1) = 4$ and $v_2 = n - ab = 27 - 3(3) = 18$. From Table VI, Appendix D, $F_{.05} = 2.93$. The rejection region is $F > 2.93$.

Since the observed value of the test statistic falls in the rejection region $(F = 7.50 > 2.93)$, H_0 is rejected. There is sufficient evidence to indicate the factors A and B interact at $\alpha = .05$. Since interaction is present, no tests for main effects are necessary.

c. $SSA = .4(1000) = 400$, $\quad SSB = .1(1000) = 100$, $\quad SSAB = .2(1000) = 200$

$SSE = SS(Total) - SSA - SSB - SSAB = 1000 - 400 - 100 - 200 = 300$

$SST = SSA + SSB + SSAB = 400 + 100 + 200 = 700 \qquad MSA = \dfrac{SSA}{a-1} = \dfrac{400}{3-1} = 50$

$MSB = \dfrac{SSB}{b-1} = \dfrac{100}{3-1} = 50 \qquad\qquad MSAB = \dfrac{MSAB}{(a-1)(b-1)} = \dfrac{200}{(3-1)(3-1)} = 50$

$MSE = \dfrac{SSE}{n-ab} = \dfrac{300}{27-3(3)} = 16.667 \qquad MST = \dfrac{SST}{ab-1} = \dfrac{700}{3(3)-1} = 87.5$

$F_A = \dfrac{MSA}{MSE} = \dfrac{200}{16.667} = 12.00 \qquad\qquad F_B = \dfrac{MSB}{MSE} = \dfrac{50}{16.667} = 3.00$

$F_{AB} = \dfrac{MSAB}{MSE} = \dfrac{50}{16.667} = 3.00 \qquad\qquad F_T = \dfrac{MST}{MSE} = \dfrac{87.5}{16.667} = 5.25$

Source	df	SS	MS	F
A	2	400	200	12.00
B	2	100	50	3.00
AB	4	200	50	3.00
Error	18	300	16.667	
Total	26	1000		

To determine if the treatment means differ, we test:

$H_0: \mu_1 = \mu_2 = \cdots = \mu_9$
$H_a:$ At least two treatment means differs

The test statistic is $F = \dfrac{MST}{MSE} = 5.25$

The rejection region requires $\alpha = .05$ in the upper tail of the F-distribution with $v_1 = ab - 1 = 3(3) - 1 = 8$ and $v_2 = n - ab = 27 - 3(3) = 18$. From Table VI, Appendix D, $F_{.05} = 2.51$. The rejection region is $F > 2.51$.

Since the observed value of the test statistic falls in the rejection region $(F = 5.25 > 2.51)$, H_0 is rejected. There is sufficient evidence to indicate the treatment means differ at $\alpha = .05$.

Since the treatment means differ, we next test for interaction between factors A and B. To determine if factors A and B interact, we test:

H_0: Factors A and B do not interact to affect the mean response
H_a: Factors A and B do interact to affect the mean response

The test statistic is $F = \dfrac{MSAB}{MSE} = 3.00$

The rejection region requires $\alpha = .05$ in the upper tail of the F-distribution with $v_1 = (a-1)(b-1) = (3-1)(3-1) = 4$ and $v_2 = n - ab = 27 - 3(3) = 18$. From Table VI, Appendix D, $F_{.05} = 2.93$. The rejection region is $F > 2.93$.

Since the observed value of the test statistic falls in the rejection region $(F = 3.00 > 2.93)$, H_0 is rejected. There is sufficient evidence to indicate the factors A and B interact at $\alpha = .05$. Since interaction is present, no tests for main effects are necessary.

d. $SSA = .4(1000) = 400, \quad SSB = .4(1000) = 400, \quad SSAB = .1(1000) = 100$

$SSE = SS\,(Total) - SSA - SSB - SSAB = 1000 - 400 - 400 - 100 = 100$

$SST = SSA + SSB + SSAB = 400 + 400 + 100 = 900 \qquad MSA = \dfrac{SSA}{a-1} = \dfrac{400}{3-1} = 200$

$MSB = \dfrac{SSB}{b-1} = \dfrac{400}{3-1} = 200 \qquad MSAB = \dfrac{SSAB}{(a-1)(b-1)} = \dfrac{100}{(3-1)(3-1)} = 25$

$MSE = \dfrac{SSE}{n-ab} = \dfrac{100}{27 - 3(3)} = 5.556 \qquad MST = \dfrac{SST}{ab-1} = \dfrac{900}{3(3)-1} = 112.5$

$F_A = \dfrac{MSA}{MSE} = \dfrac{200}{5.556} = 36.00 \qquad F_B = \dfrac{MSB}{MSE} = \dfrac{200}{5.556} = 36.00$

$F_{AB} = \dfrac{MSAB}{MSE} = \dfrac{25}{5.556} = 4.50 \qquad F_T = \dfrac{MST}{MSE} = \dfrac{112.5}{5.556} = 20.25$

Source	df	SS	MS	F
A	2	400	200	36.00
B	2	400	200	36.00
AB	4	100	25	4.50
Error	18	100	5.556	
Total	26	1000		

To determine if the treatment means differ, we test:

$H_0: \mu_1 = \mu_2 = \cdots = \mu_9$

$H_a:$ At least two treatment means differs

The test statistic is $F = \dfrac{MST}{MSE} = 20.25$

The rejection region requires $\alpha = .05$ in the upper tail of the F-distribution with $v_1 = ab - 1 = 3(3) - 1 = 8$ and $v_2 = n - ab = 27 - 3(3) = 18$. From Table VI, Appendix D, $F_{.05} = 2.51$. The rejection region is $F > 2.51$.

Since the observed value of the test statistic falls in the rejection region $(F = 20.25 > 2.51)$, H_0 is rejected. There is sufficient evidence to indicate the treatment means differ at $\alpha = .05$.

Since the treatment means differ, we next test for interaction between factors A and B. To determine if factors A and B interact, we test:

$H_0:$ Factors A and B do not interact to affect the mean response

$H_a:$ Factors A and B do interact to affect the mean response

The test statistic is $F = \dfrac{MSAB}{MSE} = 4.50$

The rejection region requires $\alpha = .05$ in the upper tail of the F-distribution with $v_1 = (a-1)(b-1) = (3-1)(3-1) = 4$ and $v_2 = n - ab = 27 - 3(3) = 18$. From Table VI, Appendix D, $F_{.05} = 2.93$. The rejection region is $F > 2.93$.

Since the observed value of the test statistic falls in the rejection region $(F = 4.50 > 2.93)$, H_0 is rejected. There is sufficient evidence to indicate the factors A and B interact at $\alpha = .05$. Since interaction is present, no tests for main effects are necessary.

9.71   a.   The two factors are type of statement and order of information. There are $2 \times 2 = 4$ treatments: concrete/statement first, concrete/behavior first, abstract/statement first, and abstract/behavior first.

      b.   This indicates that the effect of type of statement on the level of hypocrisy depends on the order of the information.

c.   Using MINITAB, a plot of the means is:

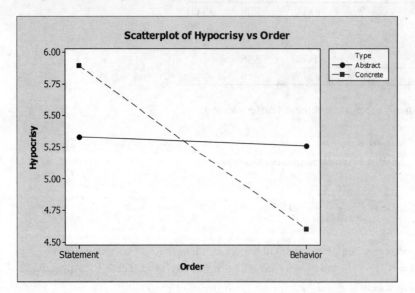

d.   Since the interaction between the type of statement and the order of information was significant, then the tests for main effects should not be performed. Multiple comparisons on some or all of the pairs of treatments should be performed next.

9.73   a.   If *justice reparation potential* and *producer need* interact, then the effect of *justice reparation potential* on intension depends on the level of *producer need*.

b.   To determine if interaction exists, we test:

H_0: *Justice reparation potential* and *producer need* do not interact
H_a: *Justice reparation potential* and *producer need* do interact

The test statistic is $F = 20.55$ and the *p*-value is $p = 0.000$. Since the *p*-value is less than $\alpha(p = 0.000 < .01)$, H_0 is rejected. There is sufficient evidence to indicate *reparation justice potential* and *producer need* interact to affect intension at $\alpha = .01$.

c.   No. Since the test for interaction was significant, then the tests for the main effects are not necessary.

d.   This plot indicates that for high *reparation justice potential*, as *producer need* changes from High to Moderate, the mean intension decreases. However, for low *reparation justice potential*, as *producer need* changes from High to Moderate, the mean intension increases. This indicates that the effect of *reparation justice potential* on intension depends on the level of *producer need*.

e.   Yes. This is exactly what the graph shows.

9.75   a. $df_{Order} = a - 1 = 2 - 1 = 1$, $df_{Menu} = b - 1 = 2 - 1 = 1$, $df_{OxM} = (a-1)(b-1) = (2-1)(2-1) = 1$,

$df_{Error} = n - ab = 180 - 2(2) = 176$

Source	df	*F*-value	*p*-value
Order	1	---	---
Menu	1	---	---
Order x Menu	1	11.25	<.001
Error	176		
Total	179		

b.   Since the *p*-value is less than $\alpha(p < 0.001 < .05)$, H_0 is rejected. There is sufficient evidence to indicate order and menu interact to affect the amount willing to pay at $\alpha = .05$.

c.   No, these results are not required to complete the analysis. Since the test for interaction was significant, there is no need to run the main effect tests.

d.   Using MINITAB, a graph of the means is:

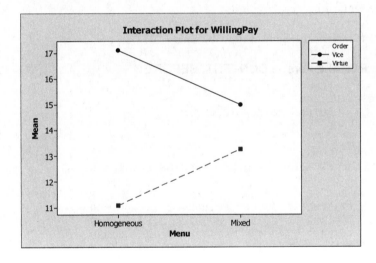

9.77   Yes. Using MINITAB, a plot of the data is:

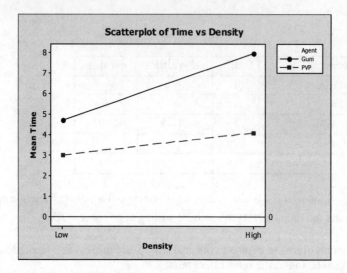

Since the lines are not parallel, this indicates interaction is present. The increase in mean time when density is increased from low to high for PVP is not as great as the increase in mean time when density is increased from low to high for GUM.

9.79   Using MINITAB, a complete factorial design was fit to the data:

General Linear Model: RECALL versus CONTENT, BEFORE

```
Factor    Type    Levels  Values
CONTENT   fixed      3    NEUTRAL, SEX, VIOLENT
BEFORE    fixed      2    NO, YES


Analysis of Variance for RECALL, using Adjusted SS for Tests

Source           DF    Seq SS    Adj SS   Adj MS      F      P
CONTENT           2   123.265   120.004   60.002  20.01  0.000
BEFORE            1     6.458     6.393    6.393   2.13  0.145
CONTENT*BEFORE    2     7.472     7.472    3.736   1.25  0.289
Error           318   953.421   953.421    2.998
Total           323  1090.617


S = 1.73153   R-Sq = 12.58%   R-Sq(adj) = 11.21%

Grouping Information Using Tukey Method and 95.0% Confidence

CONTENT     N   Mean  Grouping
NEUTRAL   108  3.167  A
VIOLENT   108  2.090    B
SEX       108  1.731    B

Means that do not share a letter are significantly different.
```

```
Grouping Information Using Tukey Method and 95.0% Confidence

BEFORE    N    Mean   Grouping
NO       162   2.470   A
YES      162   2.188   A
```

Means that do not share a letter are significantly different.

First, we test for the interaction term. To determine if content group and whether one had watched the commercial before interact to affect recall, we test:

H_0 : Content and whether one watched commercial before do not interact

H_a : Content and whether one watched commercial before do interact

The test statistic is $F = 1.25$ and the p-value is $p = .289$. Since the p-value is not small, H_0 is not rejected. There is no evidence to indicate content and whether the commercial was viewed before interact to affect recall for any reasonable value of α.

Next, we test for the main effects.

To determine if the mean recall differs among the content groups, we test:

H_0 : $\mu_1 = \mu_2 = \mu_3$

H_a : At least two means differ

The test statistic is $F = 20.01$ and the p-value is $p = .000$. Since the p-value is very small, H_0 is rejected. There is evidence to indicate the mean recall differs among the different content groups for any reasonable value of α.

Tukey's multiple comparison on the content means yielded the following. The mean recall for those in the neutral content group was significantly higher than the mean recall of the other 2 groups. No other differences existed.

To determine if the mean recall differs between whether one watched the ad before or not, we test:

H_0 : $\mu_1 = \mu_2$

H_a : $\mu_1 \neq \mu_2$

The test statistic is $F = 2.13$ and the p-value is $p = .145$. Since the p-value is not small, H_0 is not rejected. There is no evidence to indicate the mean recall differs between whether one watched the ad before or not for any reasonable value of α.

These results agree with the researchers' conclusions.

9.81   a.   Low Load, Ambiguous: $\text{Total}_1 = n_1\bar{x}_1 = 25(18) = 450$

High Load, Ambiguous: $\text{Total}_2 = n_2\bar{x}_2 = 25(6.1) = 152.5$

Low Load, Common: $\text{Total}_3 = n_3\bar{x}_3 = 25(7.8) = 195$

High Load, Common: $\text{Total}_4 = n_4\bar{x}_4 = 25(6.3) = 157.5$

b. $\text{CM} = \dfrac{(\text{sum of all observations})^2}{n} = \dfrac{(450+152.5+195+157.5)^2}{100} = \dfrac{955^2}{100} = 9{,}120.25$

c.   Low Load total is $450+195 = 645$. High Load total is $152.5+157.5 = 310$.

$$\text{SS}(Load) = \frac{\sum_{i=1}^{a} A_i^2}{br} - \text{CM} = \frac{645^2}{2(25)} + \frac{310^2}{2(25)} - 9{,}120.25 = 10{,}242.5 - 9{,}120.25 = 1{,}122.25$$

Ambiguous total is $450+152.5 = 602.5$.   Common total is $195+157.5 = 352.5$

$$\text{SS}(Name) = \frac{\sum_{j=1}^{b} B_j^2}{ar} - \text{CM} = \frac{602.5^2}{2(25)} + \frac{352.5^2}{2(25)} - 7{,}700.0625 = 9{,}745.25 - 9{,}120.25 = 625$$

$$\text{SS}(\text{Load} \times \text{Name}) = \frac{\sum_{i=1}^{a}\sum_{j=1}^{b} AB_{ij}^2}{r} - SS(\text{Load}) - SS(\text{Name}) - CM$$

$$= \frac{450^2}{25} + \frac{152.5^2}{25} + \frac{195^2}{25} + \frac{157.5^2}{25} - 1{,}122.25 - 625 - 9{,}120.25$$

$$= 11{,}543.5 - 1{,}122.25 - 625 - 9{,}120.25 = 676$$

d.   Low Load, Ambiguous: $s_1^2 = 15^2 = 225$ $(n_1-1)s_1^2 = (25-1)225 = 5{,}400$

High Load, Ambiguous: $s_2^2 = 9.5^2 = 90.25$ $(n_2-1)s_2^2 = (25-1)90.25 = 2{,}166$

Low Load, Common: $s_3^2 = 9.5^2 = 90.25$ $(n_3-1)s_3^2 = (25-1)90.25 = 2{,}166$

High Load, Common: $s_4^2 = 10^2 = 100$ $(n_4-1)s_4^2 = (25-1)100 = 2{,}400$

e. $SSE = (n_1-1)s_1^2 + (n_2-1)s_2^2 + (n_3-1)s_3^2 + (n_4-1)s_4^2 = 5{,}400 + 2{,}166 + 2{,}166 + 2{,}400 = 12{,}132$

f. $SS(Total) = SS(Load) + SS(Name) + SS(Load \ x \ Name) + SSE$
$$= 1{,}122.25 + 625 + 676 + 12{,}132 = 14{,}555.25$$

g. The ANOVA table is:

Source	df	SS	MS	F
Load	1	1,122.25	1,122.25	8.88
Name	1	625.00	625.00	4.95
Load x Name	1	676.00	676.00	5.35
Error	96	12,132.00	126.375	
Total	99	14,555.25		

h. Yes. We computed 5.35, which is almost the same as 5.34. The difference could be due to round-off error.

i. To determine if interaction between Load and Name is present, we test:

H_0: Load and Name do not interact
H_a: Load and Name class do interact

The test statistic is $F = 5.35$.

The rejection region requires $\alpha = .05$ in the upper tail of the F-distribution with $v_1 = (a-1)(b-1) = (2-1)(2-1) = 1$ and $v_2 = n - ab = 100 - 2(2) = 96$. From Table VI, Appendix D, $F_{.05} \approx 3.96$. The rejection region is $F > 3.96$.

Since the observed value of the test statistic falls in the rejection region $(F = 5.35 > 3.96)$, H_0 is rejected. There is sufficient evidence to indicate that Load and Name interact at $\alpha = .05$.

Using MINITAB, a graph of the results is:

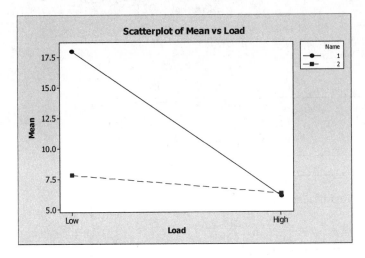

From the graph, the interaction is quite apparent. For Low load, the mean number of jelly beans taken for the ambiguous name is much higher than the mean number taken for the common name. However, for High load, there is essentially no difference in the mean number of jelly beans taken between the two names.

j. We must assume that:
1. The response distributions for each Load-Name combination (treatment) is normal.

2. The response variance is constant for all Load-Name combinations.

3. Random and independent samples of experimental units are associated with each Load-Name combination.

9.83 In a completely randomized design, independent random selection of treatments to be assigned to experimental units is required. In a randomized block design, the experimental units are first grouped into blocks such that within the blocks the experimental units are homogeneous and between the blocks the experimental units are heterogeneous. Once the experimental units are grouped into blocks, the treatments are randomly assigned to the experimental units within each block so that each treatment appears one time in each block.

9.85 When the overall level of significance of a multiple comparisons procedure is α, the level of significance for each comparison is less than α. This is because the comparisons within the experiment are not independent of each other.

9.87 a. $SST = SS(Tot) - SS(Block) - SSE = 22.31 - 10.688 - .288 = 11.334$

$$MST = \frac{SST}{k-1} = \frac{11.334}{4-1} = 3.778, \quad df = k-1 = 4-1 = 3$$

$$MS(Block) = \frac{SS(Block)}{b-1} = \frac{10.688}{5-1} = 2.672, \quad df = b-1 = 5-1 = 4$$

$$MSE = \frac{SSE}{n-k-b+1} = \frac{.288}{20-4-5+1} = .024, \quad df = n-k-b+1 = 20-4-5+1 = 12$$

$$F_T = \frac{MST}{MSE} = \frac{3.778}{.024} = 157.42 \qquad F_B = \frac{MS(Block)}{MSE} = \frac{2.672}{.024} = 111.33$$

The ANOVA Table is:

Source	df	SS	MS	F
Treatment	3	11.334	3.778	157.42
Block	4	10.688	2.672	111.33
Error	12	0.288	0.024	
Total	19	22.310		

b. To determine if there are differences among the treatment means, we test:

$H_0 : \mu_A = \mu_B = \mu_C = \mu_D$
H_a : At least two treatment means differ

The test statistic is $F = \frac{MST}{MSE} = 157.42$

The rejection region requires $\alpha = .05$ in the upper tail of the F-distribution with $v_1 = k-1 = 4-1 = 3$ and $v_2 = n-k-b+1 = 20-4-5+1 = 12$. From Table VI, Appendix D, $F_{.05} = 3.49$. The rejection region is $F > 3.49$.

Since the observed value of the test statistic falls in the rejection region $(F = 157.42 > 3.49)$, H_0 is rejected. There is sufficient evidence to indicate differences among the treatment means at $\alpha = .05$.

c. Since there is evidence of differences among the treatment means, we need to compare the treatment means. The number of pairwise comparisons is $\dfrac{k(k-1)}{2} = \dfrac{4(4-1)}{2} = 6$.

d. To determine if there are differences among the block means, we test:

H_0: All block means are the same
H_a: At least two block means differ

The test statistic is $F = \dfrac{MS(Block)}{MSE} = 111.33$

The rejection region requires $\alpha = .05$ in the upper tail of the F distribution with $v_1 = b - 1 = 5 - 1 = 4$ and $v_2 = n - k - b + 1 = 20 - 4 - 5 + 1 = 12$. From Table VI, Appendix D, $F_{.05} = 3.26$. The rejection region is $F > 3.26$.

Since the observed value of the test statistic falls in the rejection region $(F = 111.33 > 3.26)$, H_0 is rejected. There is sufficient evidence that the block means differ at $\alpha = .05$.

9.89   a. A completely randomized design was used.

b. There are 4 treatments: 3 robots/colony, 6 robots/colony, 9 robots/colony, and 12 robots/colony.

c. To determine if there were differences in the mean energy expended (per robot) among the 4 colony sizes, we test:

$H_0 : \mu_1 = \mu_2 = \mu_3 = \mu_4$
$H_a :$ At least two means differ

d. Since the p-value is less than $\alpha(p < .001 < .05)$, H_0 is rejected. There is sufficient evidence to indicate differences in mean energy expended per robot among the 4 colony sizes at $\alpha = .05$.

e. The total number of comparisons conducted is $c = \dfrac{k(k-1)}{2} = \dfrac{4(4-1)}{2} = 6$.

f. The mean energy expended by robots in the 12 robot colony is significantly smaller than the mean energy expended by robots in any of the other size colonies. There are no differences in the mean energy expended by robots in the 3 robot colony, the 6 robot colony, and the 9 robot colony.

9.91   a. This is a complete 2×2 factorial design. The 2 factors are Color and Question. There are two levels of color – Blue and Red. There are two levels of question – difficult and simple. The 4 treatments are: blue/difficult, blue/simple, red/difficult, red/simple.

b. Since the p-value is so small $(p < .03)$, H_0 is rejected. There is a significant interaction between color and question. The effect of color on the mean score is different at each level of question.

c.   Using MINITAB, the graph is:

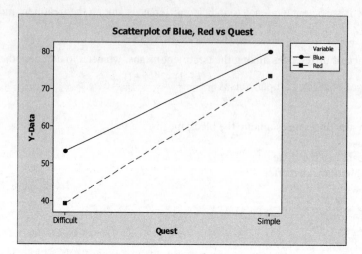

Since the lines are not parallel, it indicates that there is significant interaction between color and question.

9.93   a.   The experimental design used in this example was a randomized block design.

        b.   The experimental units in this problem are the electronic commerce and internet-based companies. The response variable is the rate of return for the stock of the companies. The treatments are the 4 categories of companies: e-companies, internet software and service, internet hardware, and internet communication. The blocks are the 3 age categories: 1 year-old, 3 year-old, and 5 year-old.

9.95   a.   To determine if leadership style affects behavior of subordinates, we test:

$$H_0 : \mu_1 = \mu_2 = \mu_3 = \mu_4$$
$$H_a : \text{At least two treatment means differ}$$

The test statistic is $F = 30.4$.

The rejection region requires $\alpha = .05$ in the upper tail of the F-distribution with $v_1 = ab - 1 = 2(2) - 1 = 3$ and $v_2 = n - ab = 257 - 2(2) = 253$. From Table VI, Appendix D, $F_{.05} \approx 2.60$. The rejection region is $F > 2.60$.

Since the observed value of the test statistic falls in the rejection region $(F = 30.4 > 2.60)$, H_0 is rejected. There is sufficient evidence to indicate that leadership style affects behavior of subordinates at $\alpha = .05$.

        b.   From the table, the mean response for High control, low consideration is significantly higher than that for any other three treatments. The mean response for Low control, low consideration is significantly higher than that for High control, high consideration and for Low control, high consideration. No other significant differences exist.

c.   The assumptions for Bonferroni's method are the same as those for the ANOVA. Thus, we must assume that:

   i.   The populations sampled from are normal.
   ii. The population variances are the same.
   iii. The samples are independent.

9.97   a.   This is a complete 6×6 factorial design.

   b.   There are 2 factors – Coagulant and pH level. There are 6 levels of coagulant: 5, 10, 20, 50, 100, and 200 mg / liter. There are 6 levels of pH: 4.0, 5.0, 6.0, 7.0, 8.0, and 9.0.

   There are $6 \times 6 = 36$ treatments. In the pairs, let the coagulant level be the first number and pH level the second. The 36 treatments are:

(5, 4.0)	(5, 5.0)	(5, 6.0)	(5, 7.0)	(5, 8.0)	(5, 9.0)
(10, 4.0)	(10, 5.0)	(10, 6.0)	(10, 7.0)	(10, 8.0)	(10, 9.0)
(20, 4.0)	(20, 5.0)	(20, 6.0)	(20, 7.0)	(20, 8.0)	(20, 9.0)
(50, 4.0)	(50, 5.0)	(50, 6.0)	(50, 7.0)	(50, 8.0)	(50, 9.0)
(100, 4.0)	(100, 5.0)	(100, 6.0)	(100, 7.0)	(100, 8.0)	(100, 9.0)
(200, 4.0)	(200, 5.0)	(200, 6.0)	(200, 7.0)	(200, 8.0)	(200, 9.0)

9.99   a.   There is one factor in this problem which is Group. There are 5 treatments in this problem, corresponding to the 5 levels of Group: Casualties, Survivors, Implementers/casualties, Implementers/survivors, and Formulators. The response variable is the ethics score. The experimental units are the employees enrolled in an Executive MBA program.

   b.   To determine if there are any differences among the mean ethics scores for the five groups, we test:

   $$H_0 : \mu_1 = \mu_2 = \mu_3 = \mu_4 = \mu_5$$
   $$H_a : \text{At least two means differ}$$

   c.   The test statistic is $F = 9.85$ and the p-value is $p = .000$. Since the p-value (0.000) is less than any reasonable significance level α, H_0 is rejected. There is sufficient evidence to indicate a difference in the mean ethics scores among the five groups of employees for any reasonable value of α.

d.   We will check the assumptions of normality and equal variances. Using MINITAB, the histograms are:

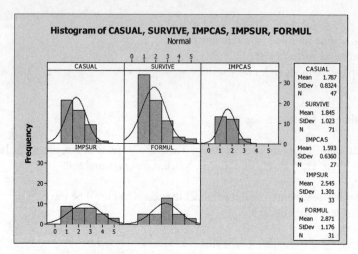

The data for some of the 5 groups do not look particularly mound-shaped, so the assumption of normality is probably not valid.

Using MINITAB, the boxplots are:

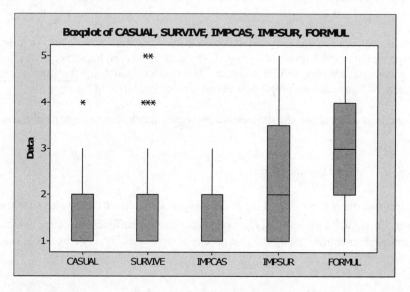

The spreads of responses do not appear to be about the same. The groups Implementers/survivors and Formulators have more variability than the other three groups. Thus, the assumption of constant variance is probably not valid.

The assumptions required for the ANOVA *F*-test do not appear to be reasonably satisfied.

e.   The Bonferroni method is preferred over other multiple comparisons methods because it does not require equal sample sizes. The five groups of employees do not have the same sample sizes. In addition, it is more powerful than Scheffe's method.

f.   The number of pairwise comparisons for this analysis is $c = \dfrac{k(k-1)}{2} = \dfrac{5(5-1)}{2} = \dfrac{20}{2} = 10$.

g.   The mean ethics scores for both Groups 4 and 5 are significantly higher than the mean ethics scores for Groups 1, 2, and 3. There is no difference in the mean ethics scores between Group 4 and Group 5. There is no difference in the mean ethics scores among Groups 1, 2 and 3.

9.101   a.   The response is the quality of the steel ingot.

   b.   There are two factors: temperature and pressure. They are quantitative factors since they are numerical.

   c.   The treatments are the $3 \times 5 = 15$ factor-level combinations of temperature and pressure.

   d.   The steel ingots are the experimental units.

9.103   a.   We will select size as the quantitative variable and color as the qualitative variable. To determine if the mean size of diamonds differ among the 6 colors, we test:

$H_0 : \mu_1 = \mu_2 = \mu_3 = \mu_4 = \mu_5 = \mu_6$
$H_a :$ At least two means differ

   b.   Using MINITAB, the ANOVA table is:

One-way ANOVA: Carats versus Color

```
Analysis of Variance for Carats
Source      DF        SS        MS         F        P
Color        5    0.7963    0.1593      2.11    0.064
Error      302   22.7907    0.0755
Total      307   23.5869
                                   Individual 95% CIs For Mean
                                   Based on Pooled StDev
Level        N      Mean     StDev   ----------+---------+---------+------
D           16    0.6381    0.3195   (-------------*------------)
E           44    0.6232    0.2677      (-------*-------)
F           82    0.5929    0.2648    (-----*-----)
G           65    0.5808    0.2792   (------*------)
H           61    0.6734    0.2643              (------*------)
I           40    0.7310    0.2918                 (-------*--------)
                                   ----------+---------+---------+------
Pooled StDev =    0.2747               0.60      0.70      0.80
```

The test statistic is $F = 2.11$ and the p-value is $p = .064$.

Since the p-value is less than $\alpha\,(p = .064 < .10)$, H_0 is rejected. There is sufficient evidence to indicate the mean sizes of diamonds differ among the 6 colors at $\alpha = .10$.

b.   We will check the assumptions of normality and equal variances. Using MINITAB, the histograms are:

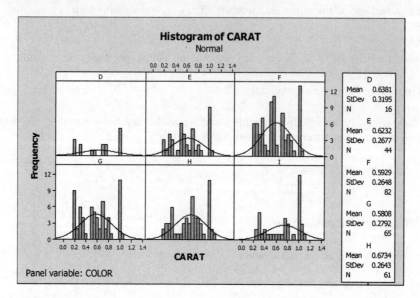

The data for the 6 colors do not look particularly mound-shaped, so the assumption of normality is probably not valid. However, departures from this assumption often do not invalidate the ANOVA results.

Using MINITAB, the box plots are:

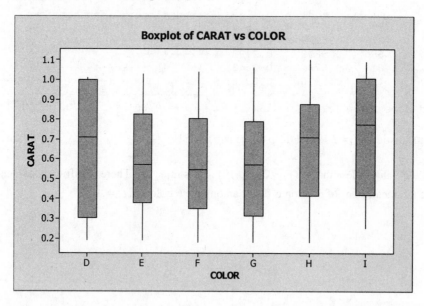

The spreads of all the colors appear to be about the same, so the assumption of constant variance is probably valid.

d. Using MINITAB, the Tukey confidence intervals are:

```
Tukey 95% Simultaneous Confidence Intervals
All Pairwise Comparisons among Levels of COLOR

Individual confidence level = 99.53%


COLOR = D subtracted from:

COLOR    Lower    Center    Upper    ---------+---------+---------+---------+
E       -0.2435  -0.0149   0.2136       (-------------*-------------)
F       -0.2591  -0.0452   0.1688      (------------*-------------)
G       -0.2758  -0.0574   0.1611     (------------*-------------)
H       -0.1846   0.0353   0.2552        (-------------*-------------)
I       -0.1387   0.0929   0.3244           (--------------*-------------)
                                     ---------+---------+---------+---------+
                                          -0.16      0.00      0.16      0.32


COLOR = E subtracted from:

COLOR    Lower    Center    Upper    ---------+---------+---------+---------+
F       -0.1765  -0.0303   0.1160         (--------*--------)
G       -0.1952  -0.0424   0.1104        (--------*---------)
H       -0.1046   0.0503   0.2051           (---------*---------)
I       -0.0632   0.1078   0.2788             (---------*---------)
                                     ---------+---------+---------+---------+
                                          -0.16      0.00      0.16      0.32


COLOR = F subtracted from:

COLOR    Lower    Center    Upper    ---------+---------+---------+---------+
G       -0.1422  -0.0122   0.1178          (-------*-------)
H       -0.0518   0.0805   0.2129             (-------*-------)
I       -0.0129   0.1381   0.2890              (---------*--------)
                                     ---------+---------+---------+---------+
                                          -0.16      0.00      0.16      0.32


COLOR = G subtracted from:

COLOR    Lower   Center   Upper    ---------+---------+---------+---------+
H       -0.0469  0.0927  0.2322             (--------*--------)
I       -0.0071  0.1502  0.3075              (--------*---------)
                                   ---------+---------+---------+---------+
                                        -0.16      0.00      0.16      0.32


COLOR = H subtracted from:

COLOR    Lower   Center   Upper    ---------+---------+---------+---------+
I       -0.1017  0.0576  0.2168            (---------*---------)
                                   ---------+---------+---------+---------+
                                        -0.16      0.00      0.16      0.32
```

All of the confidence intervals contain 0. Thus, at 95% confidence, there is no evidence that the mean sizes of the diamonds are different among the different colors. This disagrees with the test of hypothesis because the test was run using $\alpha = .10$.

9.105 a. The treatments are the $3 \times 3 = 9$ combinations of PES and Trust. The nine treatments are: (BC, Low), (PC, Low), (NA, Low), (BC, Med), (PC, Med), (NA, Med), (BC, High), (PC, High), and (NA, High).

b. $df(\text{Trust}) - 1 = 3 - 1 = 2$;

$$SSE = SSTot - SS(PES) - SS(Trust) - SSPT = 301.55 - 4.35 - 15.20 - 3.50 = 278.50$$

$$MS(PES) = \frac{SS(PES)}{df(PES)} = \frac{4.35}{2} = 2.175 \qquad MS(Trust) = \frac{SS(Trust)}{df(Trust)} = \frac{15.20}{2} = 7.600$$

$$MS(PT) = \frac{SS(PT)}{df(PT)} = \frac{3.50}{4} = .875 \qquad MSE = \frac{SSE}{df(Error)} = \frac{278.50}{191} = 1.458$$

$$F_{PES} = \frac{MS(PES)}{MSE} = \frac{2.175}{1.458} = 1.49 \qquad F_{Trust} = \frac{MS(Trust)}{MSE} = \frac{7.600}{1.458} = 5.21$$

$$F_{PT} = \frac{MS(PT)}{MSE} = \frac{.875}{1.458} = .600$$

The ANOVA table is:

Source	df	SS	MS	F
PES	2	4.35	2.175	1.49
Trust	2	15.20	7.600	5.21
PES × Trust	4	3.50	.875	0.60
Error	191	278.50	1.458	
Total	199	301.55		

c.   To determine if PES and Trust interact, we test:

H_0: PES and Trust do not interact to affect the mean tension
H_a: PES and Trust do interact to affect the mean tension

The test statistic is $F = 0.60$.

The rejection region requires $\alpha = .05$ in the upper tail of the F-distribution with $v_1 = (a-1)(b-1) = (3-1)(3-1) = 4$ and $v_2 = n - ab = 215 - 3(3) = 191$. From Table VI, Appendix D, $F_{.05} \approx 2.37$. The rejection region is $F > 2.37$.

Since the observed value of the test statistic does not fall in the rejection region $(F = 0.60 \not> 2.37)$, H_0 is not rejected. There is insufficient evidence to indicate that PES and Trust interact at $\alpha = .05$.

d. The plot of the treatment means is:

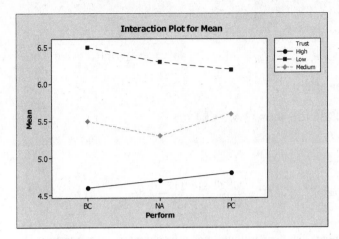

The three lines corresponding to the Trust levels are almost parallel. This indicates that PES and Trust do not interact. This agrees with the result in part **c**.

e. Since the interaction is not significant, the tests for the main effects should be run.

9.107 a. This is a 2×2 factorial experiment.

b. The two factors are the tent type (treated or untreated) and location (inside or outside). There are $2 \times 2 = 4$ treatments. The four treatments are (treated, inside), (treated, outside), (untreated, inside), and (untreated, outside).

c. The response variable is the number of mosquito bites received in a 20 minute interval.

d. There is sufficient evidence to indicate interaction is present. This indicates that the effect of the tent type on the number of mosquito bites depends on whether the person is inside or outside.

9.109 Using MINITAB, the ANOVA Table is:

ANOVA: Rating versus Prep, Standing

```
Factor     Type  Levels  Values
Prep       fixed      2  PRACTICE REVIEW
Standing   fixed      3  HI  LOW MED

Analysis of Variance for Rating

Source           DF        SS        MS      F       P
Prep              1    54.735    54.735  14.40   0.000
Standing          2    16.500     8.250   2.17   0.118
Prep*Standing     2    13.470     6.735   1.77   0.174
Error           126   478.955     3.801
Total           131   563.659


S = 1.94967   R-Sq = 15.03%   R-Sq(adj) = 11.66%


Tukey 95.0% Simultaneous Confidence Intervals
Response Variable Rating
All Pairwise Comparisons among Levels of Prep
```

```
Prep = PRACTICE subtracted from:

Prep        Lower     Center    Upper    ---+---------+---------+---------+---
REVIEW      -1.960    -1.288    -0.6162  (-----------*----------)
                                         ---+---------+---------+---------+---
                                          -1.80     -1.20     -0.60      0.00
```

First, we must test for treatment effects.

$$SST = SSP + SSS + SSPS = 54.735 + 16.500 + 13.470 = 84.705 \,.$$

The df $= 1 + 2 + 2 = 5$.

$$MST = \frac{SST}{ab-1} = \frac{84.705}{2(3)-1} = 16.941 \qquad F = \frac{MST}{MSE} = \frac{16.941}{3.801} = 4.46$$

To determine if there are differences in mean ratings among the 6 treatments, we test:

H_0: All treatment means are the same
H_a: At least two treatment means differ

The test statistic is $F = 4.46$.

Since no α was given, we will use $\alpha = .05$. The rejection region requires $\alpha = .05$ in the upper tail of the F distribution with $v_1 = ab - 1 = 2(3) - 1 = 5$ and $v_2 = n - ab = 132 - 2(3) = 126$. From Table VI, Appendix D, $F_{.05} \approx 2.29$. The rejection region is $F > 2.29$.

Since the observed value of the test statistic falls in the rejection region $(F = 4.46 > 2.29)$, H_0 is rejected. There is sufficient evidence that differences exist among the treatment means at $\alpha = .05$. Since differences exist, we now test for the interaction effect between Preparation and Class Standing.

To determine if Preparation and Class Standing interact, we test:

H_0: Preparation and Class Standing do not interact
H_a: Preparation and Class Standing do interact

The test statistic is $F = 1.77$ and the p-value is $p = .174$.

Since the p-value is greater than α $(p = .174 > .05)$, H_0 is not rejected. There is insufficient evidence that Preparation and Class Standing interact at $\alpha = .05$. Since the interaction does not exist, we test for the main effects of Preparation and Class standing.

To determine if there are differences in the mean rating between the three levels of Class standing, we test:

$H_0 : \mu_L = \mu_M = \mu_H$
H_a : At leaset two treatment means differ

The test statistics is $F = 2.17$ and the p-value is $p = 0.118$.

Since the p-value is greater than α $(p = .118 > .05)$, H_0 is not rejected. There is insufficient evidence that the mean ratings differ among the 3 levels of Class Standing at $\alpha = .05$.

To determine if there are differences in the mean rating between the two levels of Preparation, we test:

$H_0 : \mu_P = \mu_R$

$H_a : \mu_P \neq \mu_R$

The test statistics is $F = 14.40$ and the p-value is $p = 0.000$.

Since the p-value is less than α ($p = .000 < .05$), H_0 is rejected. There is sufficient evidence that the mean ratings differ between the two levels of preparation at $\alpha = .05$.

There are only 2 levels of Preparation. The mean rating for Practice is higher than the mean rating Review.

Chapter 10
Categorical Data Analysis

10.1   a.   The rejection region requires $\alpha = .05$ in the upper tail of the χ^2 distribution with $df = k - 1 = 3 - 1 = 2$. From Table IV, Appendix D, $\chi^2_{.05} = 5.99147$. The rejection region is $\chi^2 > 5.99147$.

       b.   The rejection region requires $\alpha = .10$ in the upper tail of the χ^2 distribution with $df = k - 1 = 5 - 1 = 4$. From Table IV, Appendix D, $\chi^2_{.10} = 7.77944$. The rejection region is $\chi^2 > 7.77944$.

       c.   The rejection region requires $\alpha = .01$ in the upper tail of the χ^2 distribution with $df = k - 1 = 4 - 1 = 3$. From Table IV, Appendix D, $\chi^2_{.01} = 11.3449$. The rejection region is $\chi^2 > 11.3449$.

10.3   The sample size n will be large enough so that, for every cell, the expected cell count, E_i, will be equal to 5 or more.

10.5   Some preliminary calculations are:

If the probabilities are the same, $p_{1,0} = p_{2,0} = p_{3,0} = p_{4,0} = .25$

$$E_1 = np_{1,0} = 205(.25) = 51.25 = E_2 = E_3 = E_4$$

       a.   To determine if the multinomial probabilities differ, we test:

$$H_0 : p_1 = p_2 = p_3 = p_4 = .25$$
$$H_a : \text{At lease one of the probabilities differs from .25}$$

The test statistic is

$$\chi^2 = \sum \frac{[n_i - E_i]^2}{E_i} = \frac{(43 - 51.25)^2}{51.25} + \frac{(56 - 51.25)^2}{51.25} + \frac{(59 - 51.25)^2}{51.25} + \frac{(47 - 51.25)^2}{51.25} = 3.293$$

The rejection region requires $\alpha = .05$ in the upper tail of the χ^2 distribution with $df = k - 1 = 4 - 1 = 3$. From Table IV, Appendix D, $\chi^2_{.05} = 7.81473$. The rejection region is $\chi^2 > 7.81473$.

Since the observed value of the test statistic does not fall in the rejection region $(\chi^2 = 3.293 \not> 7.81473)$, H_0 is not rejected. There is insufficient evidence to indicate the multinomial probabilities differ at $\alpha = .05$.

       b.   The Type I error is concluding the multinomial probabilities differ when, in fact, they do not.

The Type II error is concluding the multinomial probabilities are equal, when, in fact, they are not.

c.   For confidence coefficient .95, $\alpha = .05$ and $\alpha/2 = .05/2 = .025$. From Table II, Appendix D, $z_{.025} = 1.96$.

$\hat{p}_3 = 59/205 = .288$

The confidence interval is:

$$\hat{p}_3 \pm z_{.025}\sqrt{\frac{\hat{p}\hat{q}}{n}} \Rightarrow .288 \pm 1.96\sqrt{\frac{.288(.712)}{205}} \Rightarrow .288 \pm .062 \Rightarrow (.226,\ .350)$$

10.7   a.   Let p_1 = proportion using total visitors, p_2 = proportion using paying visitors, p_3 = proportion using big shows, p_4 = proportion using funds raised, and p_5 = proportion using members.

To determine if one performance measure is used more often than any of the others, we test:

$H_0: p_1 = p_2 = p_3 = p_4 = p_5 = .20$
H_a : At least one of the probabilities differs from the hypothesized value

From the printout, the test statistic is $\chi^2 = 1.66667$ and the *p*-value is $p = 0.797$.

Since the *p*-value is not less than $\alpha (p = .797 \not< .10)$, H_0 is not rejected. There is insufficient evidence to indicate that one performance measure is used more often than any of the others at $\alpha = .10$.

b.   For confidence coefficient .90, $\alpha = .10$ and $\alpha/2 = .10/2 = .05$. From Table II, Appendix D, $z_{.05} = 1.645$.

$\hat{p}_1 = 8/30 = .267$

The confidence interval is:

$$\hat{p}_1 \pm z_{.05}\sqrt{\frac{\hat{p}\hat{q}}{n}} \Rightarrow .267 \pm 1.645\sqrt{\frac{.267(.733)}{30}} \Rightarrow .267 \pm .133 \Rightarrow (.134,\ .400)$$

We are 90% confident that the proportion of museums world-wide that use total visitors as their performance measure is between .134 and .400.

10.9   a.   Since there are 10 income groups, we would expect 10% or $1,072(.10) = 107.2$ givers in each of the income categories.

b.   The null hypothesis for testing whether the true proportions of charitable givers in each income group are the same is:

$H_0: p_1 = p_2 = \cdots = p_{10} = .10$

c.   Some preliminary calculations are: $E_1 = E_2 = \cdots = E_{10} = np_{i,0} = 1,072(.10) = 107.2$

$$\chi^2 = \sum \frac{[n_i - E_i]^2}{E_i} = \frac{(42 - 107.2)^2}{107.2} + \frac{(93 - 107.2)^2}{107.2} + \dots + \frac{(127 - 107.2)^2}{107.2} = 93.15$$

d.   The rejection region requires $\alpha = .10$ in the upper tail of the χ^2 distribution with df $= k-1 = 10-1 = 9$. From Table IV, Appendix D, $\chi^2_{.10} = 14.6837$. The rejection region is $\chi^2 > 14.6837$.

e.   Since the observed value of the test statistic falls in the rejection region ($\chi^2 = 93.15 > 14.6837$), H_0 is rejected. There is sufficient evidence to indicate that the true proportions of charitable givers in each income group are not all the same at $\alpha = .10$.

10.11   Let $p_1 =$ proportion users using both hands/both thumbs, $p_2 =$ proportion of users using right hand/right thumb, $p_3 =$ proportion of users suing left hand/left thumb, $p_4 =$ proportion of users using both hands/right index finger, $p_5 =$ proportion of users using left hand/right index finger and $p_6 =$ proportion of users using other. Some preliminary calculations: $E_1 = E_2 = E_3 = E_4 = E_5 = E_6 = np_{i,0} = 859(1/6) = 143.167$.

To determine if the proportions of mobile device users in the six texting style categories differ, we test:

$H_0 : p_1 = p_2 = p_3 = p_4 = p_5 = p_6 = 1/6$
H_a : At least one of the probabilities differs from the hypothesized value

The test statistic is

$$\chi^2 = \sum \frac{[n_i - E_i]^2}{E_i} = \frac{(396-143.167)^2}{143.167} + \frac{(311-143.167)^2}{143.167} + \frac{(70-143.167)^2}{143.167} + \frac{(39-143.167)^2}{143.167}$$
$$+ \frac{(18-143.167)^2}{143.167} + \frac{(25-143.167)^2}{143.167} = 756.436$$

The rejection region requires $\alpha = .10$ in the upper tail of the χ^2 distribution with df $= k-1 = 6-1 = 5$. From Table IV, Appendix D, $\chi^2_{.10} = 9.23635$. The rejection region is $\chi^2 > 9.23635$.

Since the observed value of the test statistic falls in the rejection region ($\chi^2 = 756.436 > 9.23635$), H_0 is rejected. There is sufficient evidence to indicate that the proportions of mobile device users in the six texting style categories differ at $\alpha = .10$.

10.13   a.   The data come from a multinomial experiment because there are several possible categorical responses to the question.

b.   To determine if the multinomial probabilities agree with the theory, we test:

$H_0 : p_1 = .50, \; p_2 = p_3 = p_4 = p_5 = .10, \; p_6 = p_7 = .05$

c.   Using MINITAB, the results are:

Chi-Square Goodness-of-Fit Test for Observed Counts in Variable: C1

Category	Observed	Test Proportion	Expected	Contribution to Chi-Sq
1	869	0.50	1059.50	34.252
2	339	0.10	211.90	76.236
3	338	0.10	211.90	75.041
4	127	0.10	211.90	34.016
5	85	0.10	211.90	75.996
6	128	0.05	105.95	4.589
7	233	0.05	105.95	152.352

N	DF	Chi-Sq	P-Value
2119	6	452.483	0.000

To determine if the multinomial probabilities agree with the theory, we test:

$$H_0 : p_1 = .50, \ p_2 = p_3 = p_4 = p_5 = .10, \ p_6 = p_7 = .05$$

H_a : At least one of the probabilities differs from its hypothesized value

The test statistic is $\chi^2 = 452.843$ and the p-value is $p = 0.000$. Since the p-value is less that $\alpha = .01$, H_0 is rejected. There is sufficient evidence to indicate that at least one of the proportions differs from its hypothesized value at $\alpha = .01$.

10.15   Let p_1 = proportion of mail only users, p_2 = proportion of Internet only users, and p_3 = proportion of both mail and Internet. Some preliminary calculations:

$$E_1 = E_2 = E_3 = np_{1,0} = 440(1/3) = 146.667$$

To determine if the professor's beliefs are correct, we test:

$H_0 : p_1 = p_2 = p_3 = 1/3$

H_a : At least one of the probabilities differs from the hypothesized value

The test statistic is

$$\chi^2 = \sum \frac{[n_i - E_i]^2}{E_i} = \frac{(262-146.667)^2}{146.667} + \frac{(43-146.667)^2}{146.667} + \frac{(135-146.667)^2}{146.667} = 164.895$$

The rejection region requires $\alpha = .01$ in the upper tail of the χ^2 distribution with df $= k - 1 = 3 - 1 = 2$. From Table IV, Appendix D, $\chi^2_{.01} = 9.21034$. The rejection region is $\chi^2 > 9.21034$.

Since the observed value of the test statistic falls in the rejection region ($\chi^2 = 164.895 > 9.21034$), H_0 is rejected. There is sufficient evidence to indicate that the proportions mail only, Internet only, and both mail and Internet users differ at $\alpha = .01$.

10.17 To determine if the number of overweight trucks per week is distributed over the 7 days of the week in direct proportion to the volume of truck traffic, we test:

H_0: $p_1 = .191, p_2 = .198, p_3 = .187, p_4 = .180, p_5 = .155, p_6 = .043, p_7 = .046$
H_a: At least one of the probabilities differs from the hypothesized value

$$E_1 = np_{1,0} = 414(.191) = 79.074 \qquad E_2 = np_{2,0} = 414(.198) = 81.972 \qquad E_3 = np_{3,0} = 414(.187) = 77.418$$

$$E_4 = np_{4,0} = 414(.180) = 74.520 \qquad E_5 = np_{2,0} = 414(.155) = 64.170 \qquad E_6 = np_{3,0} = 414(.043) = 17.802$$

$$E_7 = np_{3,0} = 414(.046) = 19.044$$

The test statistic is

$$\chi^2 = \sum \frac{[n_i - E_i]^2}{E_i} = \frac{(90-79.074)^2}{79.074} + \frac{(82-81.972)^2}{81.972} + \frac{(72-77.418)^2}{77.418} + \frac{(70-74.520)^2}{74.520}$$

$$+ \frac{(51-64.170)^2}{64.170} + \frac{(18-17.802)^2}{17.802} + \frac{(31-19.044)^2}{19.044} = 12.374$$

The rejection region requires $\alpha = .05$ in the upper tail of the χ^2 distribution with df $= k-1 = 7-1 = 6$. From Table IV, Appendix D, $\chi^2_{.05} = 12.5916$. The rejection region is $\chi^2 > 12.5916$.

Since the observed value of the test statistic does not fall in the rejection region ($\chi^2 = 12.374 \not> 12.5916$), H_0 is not rejected. There is insufficient evidence to indicate the number of overweight trucks per week is distributed over the 7 days of the week is not in direct proportion to the volume of truck traffic at $\alpha = .05$.

10.19 a.   df $= (r-1)(c-1) = (5-1)(5-1) = 16$. From Table IV, Appendix D, $\chi^2_{.05} = 26.2962$. The rejection region is $\chi^2 > 26.2962$.

b.   df $= (r-1)(c-1) = (3-1)(6-1) = 10$. From Table IV, Appendix D, $\chi^2_{.10} = 15.9871$. The rejection region is $\chi^2 > 15.9871$.

c.   df $= (r-1)(c-1) = (2-1)(3-1) = 2$. From Table IV, Appendix D, $\chi^2_{.01} = 9.21034$. The rejection region is $\chi^2 > 9.21034$.

10.21 a.   To convert the frequencies to percentages, divide the numbers in each column by the column total and multiply by 100. Also, divide the row totals by the overall total and multiply by 100. The column totals are 25, 64, and 78, while the row totals are 96 and 71. The overall sample size is 165. The table of percentages are:

		Column		
	1	2	3	
Row 1	$\frac{9}{25} \times 100 = 36\%$	$\frac{34}{64} \times 100 = 53.1\%$	$\frac{53}{78} \times 100 = 67.9\%$	$\frac{96}{167} \times 100 = 57.5\%$
2	$\frac{16}{25} \times 100 = 64\%$	$\frac{30}{64} \times 100 = 46.9\%$	$\frac{25}{78} \times 100 = 32.1\%$	$\frac{71}{167} \times 100 = 42.5\%$

b.   Using MINITAB, the graph is:

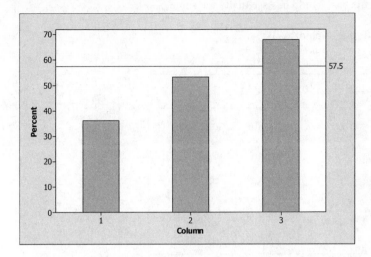

c.   If the rows and columns are independent, the row percentages in each column would be close to the row total percentages. This pattern is not evident in the plot, implying the rows and columns are not independent. In Exercise 10.20, we did not have enough evidence to say the rows and columns were not independent. If the sample sizes were bigger, we would have been able to reject H_0.

10.23   a-b.   To convert the frequencies to percentages, divide the numbers in each column by the column total and multiply by 100. Also, divide the row totals by the overall total and multiply by 100.

	B_1	B_2	B_3	Totals
A_1	$\dfrac{40}{134} \times 100 = 29.9\%$	$\dfrac{72}{163} \times 100 = 44.2\%$	$\dfrac{42}{142} \times 100 = 29.6\%$	$\dfrac{154}{439} \times 100 = 35.1\%$
A_2	$\dfrac{63}{134} \times 100 = 47.0\%$	$\dfrac{53}{163} \times 100 = 32.5\%$	$\dfrac{70}{142} \times 100 = 49.3\%$	$\dfrac{186}{439} \times 100 = 42.4\%$
A_3	$\dfrac{31}{134} \times 100 = 23.1\%$	$\dfrac{38}{163} \times 100 = 23.3\%$	$\dfrac{30}{142} \times 100 = 21.1\%$	$\dfrac{99}{439} \times 100 = 22.6\%$

(Header spanning: **B** over B_1, B_2, B_3; **Row** label on left for A_1, A_2, A_3)

c.   Using MINITAB, the graph of A_1 is:

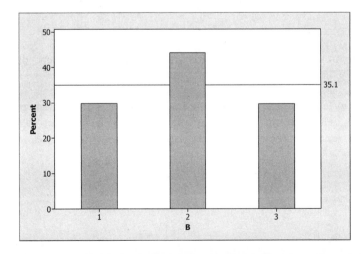

The graph supports the conclusion that the rows and columns are not independent. If they were, then the height of all the bars would be essentially the same.

d.   Using MINITAB, the graph of A_2 is:

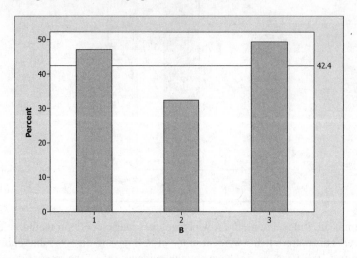

The graph supports the conclusion that the rows and columns are not independent. If they were, then the height of all the bars would be essentially the same.

e.   Using MINITAB, the graph of A_3 is:

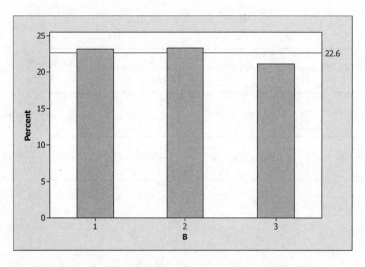

The graph does not support the conclusion that the rows and columns are not independent. All the bars would be essentially the same.

10.25   a.   Yes, it appears that the male and female tourists differ in their responses to purchasing photographs, postcards, and paintings. The values in the "Always" and "Rarely or Never" categories are quite different. The percentages are insufficient to draw a conclusion because the sample sizes must be taken into account.

b. The counts are found by changing the percentages to proportions and multiplying the proportions by the sample sizes in each gender. The counts are:

	Male Tourist	Female Tourist	Total
Always	240	476	716
Often	405	527	932
Occasionally	525	493	1018
Rarely or Never	330	204	534
Total	1500	1700	3200

c. To determine whether male and female tourists differ in their responses to purchasing photographs, postcards, or paintings, we test:

H_0 : Gender and purchasing are independent

H_a : Gender and purchasing are dependent

d. The test statistic is $\chi^2 = 112.433$ and the p-value is $p = .000$.

e. Since the p-value is less than $\alpha(p = .000 < .01)$, H_0 is rejected. There is sufficient evidence to indicate male and female tourists differ in their responses to purchasing photographs, postcards, or paintings at $\alpha = .01$.

10.27 a. To compare the two proportions, we could use either a test of hypothesis or a confidence interval. I will use a 95% confidence interval.

Some preliminary calculations are:

$$\hat{p}_{M1} = \frac{x_{M1}}{n_M} = \frac{29}{103} = .282 \qquad\qquad \hat{p}_{F1} = \frac{x_{F1}}{n_F} = \frac{89}{174} = .511$$

For confidence coefficient .95, $\alpha = .05$ and $\alpha / 2 = .05 / 2 = .025$. From Table II, Appendix D, $z_{.025} = 1.96$. The 95% confidence interval is:

$$\left(\hat{p}_{M1} - \hat{p}_{F1} \right) \pm z_{.025} \sqrt{\frac{\hat{p}_{M1}\hat{q}_{M1}}{n_M} + \frac{\hat{p}_{F1}\hat{q}_{F1}}{n_F}} \Rightarrow (.282 - .511) \pm 1.96 \sqrt{\frac{.282(.718)}{103} + \frac{.511(.489)}{174}}$$
$$\Rightarrow -.229 \pm .114 \Rightarrow (-.343, \ -.115)$$

We are 95% confident that the difference in the proportions of male and female professionals who believe their salaries are too low is between $-.343$ and $-.115$. Since 0 is not in this interval, there is evidence that the two proportions are different.

b. Some preliminary calculations are:

$$\hat{p}_{M2} = \frac{x_{M2}}{n_M} = \frac{58}{103} = .563 \qquad\qquad \hat{p}_{F2} = \frac{x_{F2}}{n_F} = \frac{64}{174} = .368$$

For confidence coefficient .95, $\alpha = .05$ and $\alpha / 2 = .05 / 2 = .025$. From Table II, Appendix D, $z_{.025} = 1.96$. The 95% confidence interval is:

$$\left(\hat{p}_{M2} - \hat{p}_{F2}\right) \pm z_{.025}\sqrt{\frac{\hat{p}_{M2}\hat{q}_{M2}}{n_M} + \frac{\hat{p}_{F2}\hat{q}_{F2}}{n_F}} \Rightarrow (.563 - .368) \pm 1.96\sqrt{\frac{.563(.437)}{103} + \frac{.368(.632)}{174}}$$

$$\Rightarrow .195 \pm .120 \Rightarrow (.075,\ .315)$$

We are 95% confident that the difference in the proportions of male and female professionals who believe their salaries are equitable/fair is between .075 and .315. Since 0 is not in this interval, there is evidence that the two proportions are different.

c.   Some preliminary calculations are:

$$\hat{p}_{M3} = \frac{x_{M3}}{n_M} = \frac{16}{103} = .155 \qquad\qquad \hat{p}_{F3} = \frac{x_{F3}}{n_F} = \frac{21}{174} = .121$$

For confidence coefficient .95, $\alpha = .05$ and $\alpha/2 = .05/2 = .025$. From Table II, Appendix D, $z_{.025} = 1.96$. The 95% confidence interval is:

$$\left(\hat{p}_{M3} - \hat{p}_{F3}\right) \pm z_{.025}\sqrt{\frac{\hat{p}_{M3}\hat{q}_{M3}}{n_M} + \frac{\hat{p}_{F3}\hat{q}_{F3}}{n_F}} \Rightarrow (.155 - .121) \pm 1.96\sqrt{\frac{.155(.845)}{103} + \frac{.121(.879)}{174}}$$

$$\Rightarrow .034 \pm .085 \Rightarrow (-.051,\ .119)$$

We are 95% confident that the difference in the proportions of male and female professionals who believe they are well paid is between −.051 and .119. Since 0 is in this interval, there is no evidence that the two proportions are different.

d.   Yes. Since there were differences between the proportions of males and females on 2 of the 3 levels, there is evidence that the opinions of males and females are different.

e.   Some preliminary calculations are:

$$\hat{E}_{11} = \frac{R_1 C_1}{n} = \frac{118(103)}{277} = 43.877 \qquad\qquad \hat{E}_{12} = \frac{R_1 C_2}{n} = \frac{118(174)}{277} = 74.123$$

$$\hat{E}_{21} = \frac{R_2 C_1}{n} = \frac{122(103)}{277} = 45.365 \qquad\qquad \hat{E}_{22} = \frac{R_2 C_2}{n} = \frac{122(174)}{277} = 76.635$$

$$\hat{E}_{31} = \frac{R_3 C_1}{n} = \frac{37(103)}{277} = 13.758 \qquad\qquad \hat{E}_{33} = \frac{R_3 C_3}{n} = \frac{37(174)}{277} = 23.242$$

To determine if the opinion on the fairness of a travel professional's salary differ for males and females, we test:

H_0: Opinion and Gender are independent
H_a: Opinion and Gender are dependent

The test statistic is

$$\chi^2 = \sum\sum \frac{\left[n_{ij} - \hat{E}_{ij}\right]^2}{\hat{E}_{ij}} = \frac{(29 - 43.877)^2}{43.877} + \frac{(89 - 74.123)^2}{74.123} + \frac{(58 - 45.365)^2}{45.365}$$

$$+ \frac{(64 - 76.635)^2}{76.635} + \frac{(16 - 13.758)^2}{13.758} + \frac{(21 - 23.242)^2}{23.242} = 14.214$$

The rejection region requires $\alpha = .10$ in the upper tail of the χ^2 distribution with $df = (r-1)(c-1) = (3-1)(2-1) = 2$. From Table IV, Appendix D, $\chi^2_{.10} = 4.60517$. The rejection region is $\chi^2 > 4.60517$.

Since the observed value of the test statistic falls in the rejection region $(\chi^2 = 14.214 > 4.60517)$, H_0 is rejected. There is sufficient evidence to indicate that the opinions on the fairness of a travel professional's salary differ for males and females at $\alpha = .10$.

f.   For confidence coefficient .90, $\alpha = .10$ and $\alpha/2 = .10/2 = .05$. From Table II, Appendix D, $z_{.05} = 1.645$. The 90% confidence interval is:

$$\left(\hat{p}_{M1} - \hat{p}_{F1}\right) \pm z_{.05}\sqrt{\frac{\hat{p}_{M1}\hat{q}_{M1}}{n_M} + \frac{\hat{p}_{F1}\hat{q}_{F1}}{n_F}} \Rightarrow (.282 - .511) \pm 1.645\sqrt{\frac{.282(.718)}{103} + \frac{.511(.489)}{174}}$$

$$\Rightarrow -.229 \pm .096 \Rightarrow (-.325, \ -.133)$$

We are 90% confident that the difference in the proportions of male and female professionals who believe their salaries are too low is between -.325 and -.133. Since 0 is not in this interval, there is evidence that the two proportions are different.

10.29   Using MINITAB, the contingency table analysis is:

Tabulated statistics: Position, Nationality

```
Using frequencies in Fr

Rows: Position    Columns: Nationality

          1     2     3     4    All

1        126    75    35    93    329
2         72    36    10    27    145
3         30     9     4     6     49
4        372   180    51   174    777
All      600   300   100   300   1300

Cell Contents:        Count

Pearson Chi-Square = 21.242, DF = 9, P-Value = 0.012
Likelihood Ratio Chi-Square = 21.327, DF = 9, P-Value = 0.011
```

To determine if a firm's position on off-shoring depends on the firm's nationality, we test:

   H_0 : Position and Nationality are independent

   H_a : Position and Nationality are dependent

From the printout, the test statistic is $\chi^2 = 21.242$ and the p-value is $p = .012$. Since the p-value is less than α ($p = .012 < .05$), H_0 is rejected. There is sufficient evidence to indicate a firm's position on off-shoring depends on the firm's nationality at $\alpha = .05$.

10.31   Some preliminary calculations are:

$$\hat{E}_{11} = \frac{R_1 C_1}{n} = \frac{396(335)}{859} = 154.435 \qquad \hat{E}_{21} = \frac{R_2 C_1}{n} = \frac{311(335)}{859} = 121.286 \qquad \hat{E}_{31} = \frac{R_3 C_1}{n} = \frac{70(335)}{859} = 27.299$$

$$\hat{E}_{41} = \frac{R_4 C_1}{n} = \frac{39(335)}{859} = 15.210 \qquad \hat{E}_{51} = \frac{R_5 C_1}{n} = \frac{18(335)}{859} = 7.020 \qquad \hat{E}_{61} = \frac{R_6 C_1}{n} = \frac{25(335)}{859} = 9.750$$

$$\hat{E}_{12} = \frac{R_1 C_2}{n} = \frac{396(524)}{859} = 241.565 \qquad \hat{E}_{22} = \frac{R_2 C_2}{n} = \frac{311(524)}{859} = 189.714 \qquad \hat{E}_{32} = \frac{R_3 C_2}{n} = \frac{70(524)}{859} = 42.701$$

$$\hat{E}_{42} = \frac{R_4 C_2}{n} = \frac{39(524)}{859} = 23.790 \qquad \hat{E}_{52} = \frac{R_5 C_2}{n} = \frac{18(524)}{859} = 10.980 \qquad \hat{E}_{62} = \frac{R_6 C_2}{n} = \frac{25(524)}{859} = 15.250$$

To determine if the proportions of mobile device users in the six texting style categories depend on whether a male or female are texting, we test:

H_0 : Texting style and sex are independent

H_a : Texting style and sex are dependent

The test statistic is:

$$\chi^2 = \sum\sum \frac{\left[n_{ij} - \hat{E}_{ij} \right]^2}{\hat{E}_{ij}} = \frac{(161-154.435)^2}{154.435} + \frac{(235-241.565)^2}{241.565} + \cdots + \frac{(14-15.250)^2}{15.250} = 4.209$$

The rejection region requires $\alpha = .10$ in the upper tail of the χ^2 distribution with $df = (r-1)(c-1) = (6-1)(2-1) = 5$. From Table IV, Appendix D, $\chi^2_{.10} = 9.23635$. The rejection region is $\chi^2 > 9.23635$.

Since the observed value of the test statistic does not fall in the rejection region ($\chi^2 = 4.209 \not> 9.23635$), H_0 is not rejected. There is insufficient evidence to indicate the proportions of mobile device users in the six texting style categories depend on whether a male or female are texting at $\alpha = .10$.

10.33   Some preliminary calculations are:

$$\hat{E}_{11} = \frac{R_1 C_1}{n} = \frac{32(32)}{96} = 10.667 \qquad \hat{E}_{21} = \frac{R_2 C_1}{n} = \frac{32(32)}{96} = 10.667 \qquad \hat{E}_{31} = \frac{R_3 C_1}{n} = \frac{32(32)}{96} = 10.667$$

$$\hat{E}_{12} = \frac{R_1 C_2}{n} = \frac{32(64)}{96} = 21.333 \qquad \hat{E}_{22} = \frac{R_2 C_2}{n} = \frac{32(64)}{96} = 21.333 \qquad \hat{E}_{32} = \frac{R_3 C_2}{n} = \frac{32(64)}{96} = 21.333$$

To determine if the proportion of subjects who selected menus consistent with the theory depends on goal condition, we test:

H_0: Goal condition and Consistent with theory are independent
H_a: Goal condition and Consistent with theory are dependent

The test statistic is

$$\chi^2 = \sum\sum \frac{\left[n_{ij} - \hat{E}_{ij}\right]^2}{\hat{E}_{ij}} = \frac{(15-10.667)^2}{10.667} + \frac{(17-21.333)^2}{21.333} + \frac{(14-10.667)^2}{10.667} + \frac{(18-21.333)^2}{21.333}$$

$$+ \frac{(3-10.667)^2}{10.667} + \frac{(29-21.333)^2}{21.333} = 12.469$$

The rejection region requires $\alpha = .01$ in the upper tail of the χ^2 distribution with $df = (r-1)(c-1) = (3-1)(2-1) = 2$. From Table IV, Appendix D, $\chi^2_{.01} = 9.21034$. The rejection region is $\chi^2 > 9.21034$.

Since the observed value of the test statistic falls in the rejection region $(\chi^2 = 12.469 > 9.21034)$, H_0 is rejected. There is sufficient evidence to indicate that the proportion of subjects who selected menus consistent with the theory depends on goal condition at $\alpha = .01$.

10.35   Using MINITAB, the results are:

Tabulated statistics: Instruction, Strategy

```
Rows: Instruction   Columns: Strategy

              Guess    Other     TTBC      All

Cue               5        6       13       24
              20.83    25.00    54.17   100.00
              35.71    35.29    76.47    50.00

Pattern           9       11        4       24
              37.50    45.83    16.67   100.00
              64.29    64.71    23.53    50.00

All              14       17       17       48
              29.17    35.42    35.42   100.00
             100.00   100.00   100.00   100.00

Cell Contents:        Count
                      % of Row
                      % of Column

Pearson Chi-Square = 7.378, DF = 2, P-Value = 0.025
Likelihood Ratio Chi-Square = 7.668, DF = 2, P-Value = 0.022
```

To determine if the choice of heuristic strategy depends on type of instruction, we test:

H_0: Heuristic strategy and type of instruction are independent
H_a: Heuristic strategy and type of instruction are dependent

From the printout, the test statistic is $\chi^2 = 7.378$ and the *p*-value is $p = .025$.
Since the *p*-value is less than α ($p = .025 < .05$), H_0 is rejected. There is sufficient evidence to indicate the choice of heuristic strategy depends on type of instruction at $\alpha = .05$.

Since the *p*-value is not less than α ($p = .025 \not< .01$), H_0 is not rejected. There is insufficient evidence to indicate the choice of heuristic strategy depends on type of instruction at $\alpha = .01$.

10.37   a.   To determine if the vaccine is effective in treating the MN strain of HIV, we test:

H_0: Vaccine status and MN strain are independent
H_a: Vaccine status and MN strain are dependent

From the printout the test statistic is $\chi^2 = 4.411$ and the p-value is $p = 0.036$. Since the p-value is less than α ($p = .036 < .05$), H_0 is rejected. There is sufficient evidence to indicate that the vaccine is effective in treating the MN strain of HIV at $\alpha = .05$.

   b.   We must assume that we have a random sample from the population of interest. We cannot really check this assumption. The second assumption is that all expected cell counts will be 5 or more. In this case, since there are only 7 observations in the second row, there is no way that the expected cell counts in that row will both be 5 or more (the sum of the expected cell counts in the row must sum to the observed row total).

   c.
$$\frac{\binom{7}{2}\binom{31}{22}}{\binom{38}{24}} = \frac{\dfrac{7!}{2!(7-2)!}\dfrac{31!}{22!(31-22)!}}{\dfrac{38!}{24!(38-24)!}} = \frac{\dfrac{7\cdot6\cdots1}{2\cdot5\cdot4\cdot3\cdot2\cdot1}\dfrac{31\cdot30\cdots1}{22\cdot21\cdots1\cdot9\cdot8\cdots1}}{\dfrac{38\cdot37\cdots1}{24\cdot23\cdots1\cdot14\cdot13\cdots1}} = .04378$$

   d.   If vaccine status and MN are independent, then the proportion of those in each group that are positive should be very similar. In these two additional tables, the proportion of positive results for the unvaccinated group is increasing and the proportion of positive results for the vaccinated group is decreasing.

Table 1:

$$\frac{\binom{7}{1}\binom{31}{23}}{\binom{38}{24}} = \frac{\dfrac{7!}{1!(7-1)!}\dfrac{31!}{23!(31-23)!}}{\dfrac{38!}{24!(38-24)!}} = \frac{\dfrac{7\cdot6\cdots1}{1\cdot6\cdot5\cdot4\cdot3\cdot2\cdot1}\dfrac{31\cdot30\cdots1}{23\cdot22\cdots1\cdot8\cdot7\cdots1}}{\dfrac{38\cdot37\cdots1}{24\cdot23\cdots1\cdot14\cdot13\cdots1}} = .00571$$

Table 2:

$$\frac{\binom{7}{0}\binom{31}{24}}{\binom{38}{24}} = \frac{\dfrac{7!}{0!(7-0)!}\dfrac{31!}{24!(31-24)!}}{\dfrac{38!}{24!(38-24)!}} = \frac{\dfrac{7\cdot6\cdots1}{1\cdot7\cdot6\cdot5\cdot4\cdot3\cdot2\cdot1}\dfrac{31\cdot30\cdots1}{24\cdot23\cdots1\cdot7\cdot6\cdots1}}{\dfrac{38\cdot37\cdots1}{24\cdot23\cdots1\cdot14\cdot13\cdots1}} = .00027$$

   e.   The p-value is $04378 + .00571 + .00027 = .04976$. Since the p-value is less than α ($p = .04976 < .05$), H_0 is rejected. There is sufficient evidence to indicate that the vaccine is effective in treating the MN strain of HIV at $\alpha = .05$.

10.39   a.   If all the categories are equally likely, then $p_{1,0} = p_{2,0} = p_{3,0} = p_{4,0} = p_{5,0} = .2$.

$$E_1 = E_2 = E_3 = E_4 = E_5 = np_{i,0} = 150(.20) = 30$$

To determine if the categories are not equally likely, we test:

$H_0 : p_1 = p_2 = p_3 = p_4 = p_5 = .2$
$H_a :$ At lease one of the probabilities differs from .2

The test statistic is $\chi^2 = \sum \dfrac{[n_i - E_i]^2}{E_i} = \dfrac{(28-30)^2}{30} + \dfrac{(35-30)^2}{30} + \dfrac{(33-30)^2}{30} + \dfrac{(25-30)^2}{30} = 2.133$

The rejection region requires $\alpha = .10$ in the upper tail of the χ^2 distribution with df $= k - 1 = 5 - 1 = 4$. From Table IV, Appendix D, $\chi^2_{.10} = 7.77944$. The rejection region is $\chi^2 > 7.77944$.

Since the observed value of the test statistic does not fall in the rejection region $(\chi^2 = 2.133 \not> 7.77944)$, H_0 is not rejected. There is insufficient evidence to indicate the categories are not equally likely at $\alpha = .10$.

b. $\hat{p}_2 = \dfrac{35}{150} = .233$

For confidence coefficient .90, $\alpha = .10$ and $\alpha / 2 = .10 / 2 = .05$. From Table II, Appendix D, $z_{.05} = 1.645$. The confidence interval is:

$$\hat{p}_2 \pm z_{.05}\sqrt{\dfrac{\hat{p}_2\hat{q}_2}{n_2}} \Rightarrow .233 \pm 1.645\sqrt{\dfrac{.233(.767)}{150}} \Rightarrow .233 \pm .057 \Rightarrow (.176, \ .290)$$

10.41   a. The qualitative variable in this exercise is what "Made in the USA" means. There are 4 levels or categories for this variable: 100% of labor and materials are produced in the US, 75-99% of labor and materials are produced in the US, 50-74% of labor and materials are produced in the US, and less than 50% of labor and materials are produced in the US.

b. The consumer advocate group hypothesized that $p_1 = 1/2 = .5$, $p_2 = 1/4 = .25$, $p_3 = 1/5 = .20$, and $p_4 = .05$.

c. To determine if the consumer advocate group's claim is correct, we test:

$H_0 : p_1 = .5, \ p_2 = .25, \ p_3 = .20$ and $p_4 = .05$
$H_a :$ At lease one of the probabilities differs from its hypothesized value

d. Some preliminary calculations are:

$n = 64 + 20 + 18 + 4 = 106$.

$E_1 = np_{1,0} = 106(.50) = 53$; $E_2 = np_{2,0} = 106(.25) = 26.5$;

$E_3 = np_{3,0} = 106(.20) = 21.2$; $E_4 = np_{4,0} = 106(.05) = 5.3$

$\chi^2 = \sum \dfrac{[n_i - E_i]^2}{E_i} = \dfrac{(64-53)^2}{53} + \dfrac{(20-26.5)^2}{26.5} + \dfrac{(18-21.2)^2}{21.2} + \dfrac{(4-5.3)^2}{5.3} = 4.68$

e. The rejection region requires $\alpha = .10$ in the upper tail of the χ^2 distribution with df $= k - 1 = 4 - 1 = 3$. From Table IV, Appendix D, $\chi^2_{.10} = 6.25139$. The rejection region is $\chi^2 > 6.25139$.

f. Since the observed value of the test statistic does not fall in the rejection region $(\chi^2 = 4.68 \ngtr 6.25139)$, H_0 is not rejected. There is insufficient evidence to indicate the consumer advocate group's claim is incorrect at $\alpha = .10$.

g. $\hat{p}_1 = \dfrac{n_1}{n} = \dfrac{64}{106} = .604$

For confidence coefficient .90, $\alpha = .10$ and $\alpha/2 = .10/2 = .05$. From Table II, Appendix D, $z_{.05} = 1.645$. The 90% confidence interval is:

$$\hat{p}_1 \pm z_{.05}\sqrt{\frac{\hat{p}_1(1 - \hat{p}_1)}{n}} \Rightarrow .604 \pm 1.645\sqrt{\frac{.604(.396)}{106}} \Rightarrow .604 \pm .078 \Rightarrow (.526, \ .682)$$

We are 90% confident that the proportion of all consumers who believe "Made in the USA" means "100%" of labor and material are produced in the US" is between .526 and .682.

10.43 a. Some preliminary calculations are:

$\hat{p}_{C1} = \dfrac{x_{C1}}{n_1} = \dfrac{175}{6,222} = .028$ $\hat{p}_{C2} = \dfrac{x_{C2}}{n_2} = \dfrac{236}{4,692} = .050$ $\hat{p}_{C3} = \dfrac{x_{C3}}{n_3} = \dfrac{319}{7,140} = .045$

$\hat{p}_{C4} = \dfrac{x_{C4}}{n_4} = \dfrac{231}{6,120} = .038$ $\hat{p}_{C5} = \dfrac{x_{C5}}{n_5} = \dfrac{480}{10,353} = .046$ $\hat{p}_{C6} = \dfrac{x_{C6}}{n_6} = \dfrac{187}{4794} = .039$

The proportions range from .028 to .050. Since .050 is about twice as big as .028, there may be evidence to conclude some of the proportions are different.

b. Some preliminary calculations are:

$\hat{E}_{11} = \dfrac{R_1 C_1}{n} = \dfrac{6,222(37,693)}{39,321} = 5,964.39$ $\hat{E}_{12} = \dfrac{R_1 C_2}{n} = \dfrac{6,222(1628)}{39,321} = 257.61$

$\hat{E}_{21} = \dfrac{R_2 C_1}{n} = \dfrac{4,692(37,693)}{39,321} = 4497.74$ $\hat{E}_{22} = \dfrac{R_2 C_2}{n} = \dfrac{4,692(1,628)}{39,321} = 194.26$

$\hat{E}_{31} = \dfrac{R_3 C_1}{n} = \dfrac{7,140(37,693)}{39,321} = 6,844.38$ $\hat{E}_{32} = \dfrac{R_3 C_2}{n} = \dfrac{7,140(1,628)}{39,321} = 295.62$

$\hat{E}_{41} = \dfrac{R_4 C_1}{n} = \dfrac{6,120(37,693)}{39,321} = 5,866.61$ $\hat{E}_{42} = \dfrac{R_4 C_2}{n} = \dfrac{6,120(1,628)}{39,321} = 253.39$

$\hat{E}_{51} = \dfrac{R_5 C_1}{n} = \dfrac{10,353(37,693)}{39,321} = 9,924.36$ $\hat{E}_{52} = \dfrac{R_5 C_2}{n} = \dfrac{10,353(1,628)}{39,321} = 428.64$

$\hat{E}_{61} = \dfrac{R_6 C_1}{n} = \dfrac{4,794(37,693)}{39,321} = 4,595.51$ $\hat{E}_{62} = \dfrac{R_6 C_2}{n} = \dfrac{4,794(1,628)}{39,321} = 198.49$

To determine if the proportions of censored measurements differ for the six tractor lines, we test:

H_0: Tractor lines and Censored measurements are independent

H_a: Tractor lines and Censored measurements are dependent

The test statistic is

$$\chi^2 = \sum\sum \frac{\left[n_{ij} - \hat{E}_{ij}\right]^2}{\hat{E}_{ij}} = \frac{(6047 - 5964.39)^2}{5964.39} + \frac{(175 - 257.61)^2}{257.61} + \frac{(4456 - 4497.74)^2}{4497.74}$$

$$+ \cdots + \frac{(187 - 198.49)^2}{198.49} = 48.0978$$

The rejection region requires $\alpha = .01$ in the upper tail of the χ^2 distribution with

$df = (r-1)(c-1) = (6-1)(2-1) = 5$. From Table IV, Appendix D, $\chi^2_{.01} = 15.0863$. The rejection

region is $\chi^2 > 15.0863$.

Since the observed value of the test statistic falls in the rejection region ($\chi^2 = 48.0978 > 15.0863$),

H_0 is rejected. There is sufficient evidence to indicate that the proportions of censored measurements

differ for the six tractor lines at $\alpha = .01$.

c.   Even though there are differences in the proportions of censored data among the 6 tractor lines, these

proportions range from .028 to .050. In practice, there is very little difference between .028 and .050.

10.45   a.   Some preliminary calculations are:

$E_1 = np_{1,0} = 400(.30) = 120 \quad E_2 = np_{2,0} = 400(.20) = 80 \quad E_3 = np_{3,0} = 400(.20) = 80$

$E_4 = np_{4,0} = 400(.10) = 40 \quad E_5 = np_{5,0} = 400(.10) = 40 \quad E_6 = np_{6,0} = 400(.10) = 40$

b.   The test statistic is

$$\chi^2 = \sum \frac{[n_i - E_i]^2}{E_i} = \frac{(100 - 120)^2}{120} + \frac{(75 - 80)^2}{80} + \frac{(85 - 80)^2}{80} + \frac{(50 - 40)^2}{40}$$

$$+ \frac{(40 - 40)^2}{40} + \frac{(50 - 40)^2}{40} = 8.958$$

c.   To determine if the true percentages of the colors produced differ from the manufacturer's stated

percentages, we test:

$H_0 : p_1 = .30, \; p_2 = .20, \; p_3 = .20, \; p_4 = .10, \; p_5 = .10, \; \text{and} \; p_6 = .10$

H_a : At least one of the probabilities differs from the hypothesized value

The test statistic is $\chi^2 = 8.958$.

The rejection region requires $\alpha = .05$ in the upper tail of the χ^2 distribution with $df = k - 1 = 6 - 1 = 5$.

From Table IV, Appendix D, $\chi^2_{.05} = 11.0705$. The rejection region is $\chi^2 > 11.0705$.

Since the observed value of the test statistic does not fall in the rejection region $(\chi^2 = 8.958 \not> 11.0705)$, H_0 is not rejected. There is insufficient evidence to indicate the true percentages of the colors produced differ from the manufacturer's stated percentages at $\alpha = .05$.

10.47   a.   Some preliminary calculations are:

$$\hat{E}_{11} = \frac{R_1 C_1}{n} = \frac{53(35)}{70} = 26.5 \qquad \hat{E}_{12} = \frac{R_1 C_2}{n} = \frac{53(35)}{70} = 26.5$$

$$\hat{E}_{21} = \frac{R_2 C_1}{n} = \frac{17(35)}{70} = 8.5 \qquad \hat{E}_{22} = \frac{R_2 C_2}{n} = \frac{17(35)}{70} = 8.5$$

To determine if the severity of the ethical issue influenced whether the issue was identified or not by the auditors, we test:

H_0: Severity of ethical issue and identification are independent
H_a: Severity of ethical issue and identification are dependent

The test statistic is

$$\chi^2 = \sum\sum \frac{\left[n_{ij} - \hat{E}_{ij}\right]^2}{\hat{E}_{ij}} = \frac{(27 - 26.5)^2}{26.5} + \frac{(26 - 26.5)^2}{26.5} + \frac{(8 - 8.5)^2}{8.5} + \frac{(9 - 8.5)^2}{8.5} = .078$$

The rejection region requires $\alpha = .05$ in the upper tail of the χ^2 distribution with df $= (r-1)(c-1) = (2-1)(2-1) = 1$. From Table IV, Appendix D, $\chi^2_{.05} = 3.84146$. The rejection region is $\chi^2 > 3.84146$.

Since the observed value of the test statistic does not fall in the rejection region $(\chi^2 = .078 \not> 3.84146)$, H_0 is not rejected. There is insufficient evidence to indicate that the severity of the ethical issue influenced whether the issue was identified or not by the auditors at $\alpha = .05$.

b.   No. If there were 0 in the bottom cell of the column, then the expected count for that cell will be less than 5. One of the assumptions necessary for the test statistic to have a χ^2 distribution will not hold.

c.   Suppose we change the numbers in the table to be as follows:

	Severity of Ethical Issue	
	Moderate	Severe
Ethical Issue Identified	32	21
Ethical Issue Not Identified	3	14

Since the row and column totals are the same, the expected cell counts are the same as above.

The test statistic is

$$\chi^2 = \sum\sum \frac{\left[n_{ij} - \hat{E}_{ij}\right]^2}{\hat{E}_{ij}} = \frac{(32 - 26.5)^2}{26.5} + \frac{(21 - 26.5)^2}{26.5} + \frac{(3 - 8.5)^2}{8.5} + \frac{(14 - 8.5)^2}{8.5} = 9.401$$

Now the test statistic would fall in the rejection region.

10.49   Some preliminary calculations are: $E_1 = E_2 = E_3 = E_4 = np_{1,0} = 83(.25) = 20.75$

To determine if there are differences in the percentages of incidents in the four cause categories, we test:

$H_0 : p_1 = p_2 = p_3 = p_4 = .25$

$H_a :$ At lease one of the probabilities differs from its hypothesized value

The test statistic is

$$\chi^2 = \sum \frac{[n_i - E_i]^2}{E_i} = \frac{(27 - 20.75)^2}{20.75} + \frac{(24 - 20.75)^2}{20.75} + \frac{(22 - 20.75)^2}{20.75} + \frac{(10 - 20.75)^2}{20.75} = 8.036$$

The rejection region requires $\alpha = .05$ in the upper tail of the χ^2 distribution with df $= k - 1 = 4 - 1 = 3$. From Table IV, Appendix D, $\chi^2_{.05} = 7.81473$. The rejection region is $\chi^2 > 7.81473$.

Since the observed value of the test statistic falls in the rejection region $(\chi^2 = 8.036 > 7.81473)$, H_0 is rejected. There is sufficient evidence to indicate there are differences in the percentages of incidents in the four cause categories at $\alpha = .05$.

10.51　a.　The contingency table is:

		Committee		
		Acceptable	**Rejected**	**Totals**
Inspector	**Acceptable**	101	23	124
	Rejected	10	19	29
	Totals	111	42	153

　b.　Yes. To plot the percentages, first convert frequencies to percentages by dividing the numbers in each column by the column total and multiplying by 100. Also, divide the row totals by the overall total and multiply by 100.

		Acceptable	**Rejected**	**Totals**
Inspector	**Acceptable**	$\frac{101}{111} \times 100 = 90.99\%$	$\frac{23}{42} \times 100 = 54.76\%$	$\frac{124}{153} \times 100 = 81.05\%$
	Rejected	$\frac{10}{111} \times 100 = 9.01\%$	$\frac{19}{42} \times 100 = 45.23\%$	$\frac{29}{153} \times 100 = 18.95\%$

Using MINITAB, the graph of the data is:

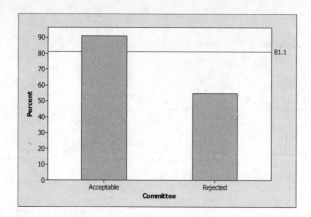

Since the heights of the bars are not similar, it appears there is a relationship.

c.   Some preliminary calculations are:

$$\hat{E}_{11} = \frac{R_1 C_1}{n_1} = \frac{124(111)}{153} = 89.691 \qquad \hat{E}_{21} = \frac{R_1 C_2}{n_1} = \frac{124(42)}{153} = 34.039$$

$$\hat{E}_{21} = \frac{R_2 C_1}{n_1} = \frac{29(111)}{153} = 21.039 \qquad \hat{E}_{22} = \frac{R_2 C_2}{n_1} = \frac{29(42)}{153} = 7.961$$

To determine if the inspector's classifications and the committee's classifications are related, we test:

H_0: The inspector's and committee's classification are independent
H_a: The inspector's and committee's classifications are dependent

The test statistic is

$$\chi^2 = \sum \sum \frac{\left[n_{ij} - \hat{E}_{ij}\right]^2}{\hat{E}_{ij}} = \frac{(101 - 89.961)^2}{89.961} + \frac{(23 - 34.039)^2}{34.039} + \frac{(10 - 21.039)^2}{21.039} + \frac{(19 - 7.961)^2}{7.961} = 26.034$$

The rejection region requires $\alpha = .05$ in the upper tail of the χ^2 distribution with $df = (r-1)(c-1) = (2-1)(2-1) = 1$. From Table IV, Appendix D, $\chi^2_{.05} = 3.84146$. The rejection region is $\chi^2 > 3.84146$.

Since the observed value of the test statistic falls in the rejection region $(\chi^2 = 26.034 > 3.84146)$, H_0 is rejected. There is sufficient evidence to indicate the inspector's and committee's classifications are related at $\alpha = .05$. This indicates that the inspector and committee tend to make the same decisions.

10.53 a. The contingency table is:

	Flight Response		
Altitude	**Low**	**High**	**Totals**
< 300	85	105	190
300-600	77	121	198
≥ 600	17	59	76
Totals	179	285	464

b. Some preliminary calculations are:

$$\hat{E}_{11} = \frac{R_1 C_1}{n} = \frac{190(179)}{464} = 73.297 \qquad \hat{E}_{12} = \frac{R_1 C_2}{n} = \frac{190(285)}{464} = 116.703$$

$$\hat{E}_{21} = \frac{R_2 C_1}{n} = \frac{198(179)}{464} = 76.384 \qquad \hat{E}_{22} = \frac{R_2 C_2}{n} = \frac{198(285)}{464} = 121.616$$

$$\hat{E}_{31} = \frac{R_3 C_1}{n} = \frac{76(179)}{464} = 29.319 \qquad \hat{E}_{32} = \frac{R_3 C_2}{n} = \frac{76(285)}{464} = 46.681$$

To determine if flight response of the geese depends on the altitude of the helicopter, we test:

H_0: Flight response and Altitude of helicopter are independent
H_a: Flight response and Altitude of helicopter are dependent

The test statistic is

$$\chi^2 = \sum\sum \frac{\left[n_{ij} - \hat{E}_{ij}\right]^2}{\hat{E}_{ij}} = \frac{(85 - 73.297)^2}{73.297} + \frac{(105 - 116.703)^2}{116.703} + \frac{(77 - 76.384)^2}{76.384}$$

$$+ \frac{(121 - 121.616)^2}{121.616} + \frac{(17 - 29.319)^2}{29.319} + \frac{(59 - 46.681)^2}{46.681} = 11.477$$

The rejection region requires $\alpha = .01$ in the upper tail of the χ^2 distribution with df $= (r-1)(c-1) = (3-1)(2-1) = 2$. From Table IV, Appendix D, $\chi^2_{.01} = 9.21034$. The rejection region is $\chi^2 > 9.21034$.

Since the observed value of the test statistic falls in the rejection region ($\chi^2 = 11.477 > 9.21034$), H_0 is rejected. There is sufficient evidence to indicate that the flight response of the geese depends on the altitude of the helicopter at $\alpha = .01$.

c. The contingency table is:

	Flight Response		
Lateral Distance	**Low**	**High**	**Totals**
< 1000	37	243	280
1000-2000	68	37	105
2000-3000	44	4	48
≥ 3000	30	1	31
Totals	179	285	464

d.   Some preliminary calculations are:

$$\hat{E}_{11} = \frac{R_1 C_1}{n} = \frac{280(179)}{464} = 108.017 \qquad \hat{E}_{12} = \frac{R_1 C_2}{n} = \frac{280(285)}{464} = 171.983$$

$$\hat{E}_{21} = \frac{R_2 C_1}{n} = \frac{105(179)}{464} = 40.506 \qquad \hat{E}_{22} = \frac{R_2 C_2}{n} = \frac{105(285)}{464} = 64.494$$

$$\hat{E}_{31} = \frac{R_3 C_1}{n} = \frac{48(179)}{464} = 18.517 \qquad \hat{E}_{32} = \frac{R_3 C_2}{n} = \frac{48(285)}{464} = 29.483$$

$$\hat{E}_{41} = \frac{R_4 C_1}{n} = \frac{31(179)}{464} = 11.959 \qquad \hat{E}_{42} = \frac{R_4 C_2}{n} = \frac{31(285)}{464} = 19.041$$

To determine if flight response of the geese depends on the lateral distance of the helicopter, we test:

H_0: Flight response and Lateral distance of the helicopter are independent
H_a: Flight response and Lateral distance of the helicopter are dependent

The test statistic is

$$\chi^2 = \sum\sum \frac{\left[n_{ij} - \hat{E}_{ij}\right]^2}{\hat{E}_{ij}} = \frac{(37-108.017)^2}{108.017} + \frac{(243-171.983)^2}{171.983} + \frac{(68-40.506)^2}{40.506} + \frac{(37-64.494)^2}{64.494}$$

$$+ \frac{(44-18.517)^2}{18.517} + \frac{(4-29.494)^2}{29.494} + \frac{(30-11.959)^2}{11.959} + \frac{(1-19.041)^2}{19.041} = 207.814$$

The rejection region requires $\alpha = .01$ in the upper tail of the χ^2 distribution with

$df = (r-1)(c-1) = (4-1)(2-1) = 3$. From Table IV, Appendix D, $\chi^2_{.01} = 11.3449$. The rejection region is $\chi^2 > 11.3449$.

Since the observed value of the test statistic falls in the rejection region $(\chi^2 = 207.814 > 11.3449)$, H_0 is rejected. There is sufficient evidence to indicate that the flight response of the geese depends on the lateral distance of the helicopter at $\alpha = .01$.

e. Using SAS, the contingency table for altitude by response with the column percents is:

```
                    Table of ALTGRP by RESPONSE

          ALTGRP      RESPONSE

          Frequency|
          Percent  |
          Row Pct  |
          Col Pct  |LOW     |HIGH    |  Total
          ---------+--------+--------+
          <300     |     85 |    105 |    190
                   |  18.32 |  22.63 |  40.95
                   |  44.74 |  55.26 |
                   |  47.49 |  36.84 |
          ---------+--------+--------+
          300-600  |     77 |    121 |    198
                   |  16.59 |  26.08 |  42.67
                   |  38.89 |  61.11 |
                   |  43.02 |  42.46 |
          ---------+--------+--------+
          600+     |     17 |     59 |     76
                   |   3.66 |  12.72 |  16.38
                   |  22.37 |  77.63 |
                   |   9.50 |  20.70 |
          ---------+--------+--------+
          Total         179      285      464
                       38.58    61.42   100.00

          Statistics for Table of ALTGRP by RESPONSE

          Statistic                    DF     Value     Prob
          ------------------------------------------------------
          Chi-Square                    2    11.4770   0.0032
          Likelihood Ratio Chi-Square   2    12.1040   0.0024
          Mantel-Haenszel Chi-Square    1    10.2104   0.0014
          Phi Coefficient                    0.1573
          Contingency Coefficient            0.1554
          Cramer's V                         0.1573
                      Sample Size = 464
```

From the row percents, it appears that the lower the plane, the lower the response. For altitude <300m, 55.26% of the geese had a high response. For altitude 300-600m, 61.11% of the geese had a high response. For altitude 600+m, 77.63% of the geese had a high response. Thus, instead of setting a minimum altitude for the planes, we need to set a maximum altitude. For this data, the lowest response is at an altitude of < 300 meters.

Using SAS, the contingency table for lateral distance by response with the column   percents is:

```
                     The FREQ Procedure

                 Table of LATGRP by RESPONSE

        LATGRP        RESPONSE

        Frequency |
        Percent   |
        Row Pct   |
        Col Pct   |LOW      |HIGH     |  Total
        ----------+---------+---------+
        <1000     |      37 |     243 |    280
                  |    7.97 |   52.37 |  60.34
                  |   13.21 |   86.79 |
                  |   20.67 |   85.26 |
        ----------+---------+---------+
        1000-2000 |      68 |      37 |    105
                  |   14.66 |    7.97 |  22.63
                  |   64.76 |   35.24 |
                  |   37.99 |   12.98 |
        ----------+---------+---------+
        2000-3000 |      44 |       4 |     48
                  |    9.48 |    0.86 |  10.34
                  |   91.67 |    8.33 |
                  |   24.58 |    1.40 |
        ----------+---------+---------+
        3000+     |      30 |       1 |     31
                  |    6.47 |    0.22 |   6.68
                  |   96.77 |    3.23 |
                  |   16.76 |    0.35 |
        ----------+---------+---------+
        Total            179       284      464
                       38.58     61.42   100.00

        Statistics for Table of LATGRP by RESPONSE

        Statistic                     DF      Value      Prob
        ------------------------------------------------------
        Chi-Square                     3    207.0812    <.0001
        Likelihood Ratio Chi-Square    3    227.5212    <.0001
        Mantel-Haenszel Chi-Square     1    189.2843    <.0001
        Phi Coefficient                       0.6692
        Contingency Coefficient               0.5562
        Cramer's V                            0.6692

                   Sample Size = 464
```

From the row percents, it appears that the greater the lateral distance, the lower the response. For a lateral distance of 3000+m only 3.23% of the geese had a high response. Thus, the further away the plane is laterally, the lower the response. For this data, the lowest response is when the plane is further than 3000 meters.

Thus, the recommendation would be a maximum height of 300 m and a minimum lateral distance of 3000 m.

10.55   a. $\chi^2 = \sum \dfrac{[n_i - E_i]^2}{E_i} = \dfrac{(26-23)^2}{23} + \dfrac{(146-136)^2}{136} + \dfrac{(361-341)^2}{341} + \dfrac{(143-136)^2}{136} + \dfrac{(13-23)^2}{23} = 9.647$

         b.   From Table IV, Appendix D, with df $= 5$, $\chi^2_{.05} = 11.0705$

         c.   No. Since the observed value of the test statistics does not fall in the rejection region $(\chi^2 = 9.647 \not> 11.0705)$, H_0 is not rejected. There is insufficient evidence to indicate the salary distribution is non-normal for $\alpha = .05$.

d.   The p-value is $p = P(\chi^2 \geq 9.647)$. Using MINITAB,

Cumulative Distribution Function

```
Chi-Square with 5 DF

    x  P( X <= x )
9.647     0.914122
```

The p-value is $p = P(\chi^2 \geq 9.647) = 1 - .914122 = .085878$.

10.57   Using SAS, the output is:

```
                    The FREQ Procedure

                 Table of CANDIDATE by TIME

      CANDIDATE      TIME
```

Frequency Col Pct	1	2	3	4	5	6	Total
SMITH	208 52.53	208 55.32	451 55.34	392 55.92	351 56.16	410 55.33	2020
COPPIN	55 13.89	51 13.56	109 13.37	98 13.98	88 14.08	104 14.04	505
MONTES	133 33.59	117 31.12	255 31.29	211 30.10	186 29.76	227 30.63	1129
Total	396	376	815	701	625	741	3654

```
           Statistics for Table of CANDIDATE by TIME
```

Statistic	DF	Value	Prob
Chi-Square	10	2.2839	0.9937
Likelihood Ratio Chi-Square	10	2.2722	0.9938
Mantel-Haenszel Chi-Square	1	0.9851	0.3209
Phi Coefficient		0.0250	
Contingency Coefficient		0.0250	
Cramer's V		0.0177	

```
                   Sample Size = 3654
```

To determine if candidates received votes independent of time period, we test:

H_0: Voting and Time period are independent
H_a: Voting and Time period are dependent

The test statistic is $\chi^2 = 2.2839$.

Since no value of α was given, we will use $\alpha = .05$. The rejection region requires $\alpha = .05$ in the upper tail of the χ^2 distribution with $\text{df} = (r-1)(c-1) = (3-1)(6-1) = 10$. From Table IV, Appendix D, $\chi^2_{.05} = 18.3070$. The rejection region is $\chi^2 > 18.3070$.

Since the observed value of the test statistic does not fall in the rejection region $(\chi^2 = 2.2839 \not> 18.3070)$, H_0 is not rejected. There is insufficient evidence to indicate Voting and Time period are dependent at $\alpha = .05$. Thus, we can conclude that voting and time period are independent. This means that regardless of time period, the percentage of votes received by each candidate is the same. In the table created by SAS, the bottom number in each cell is the column percent. This is the percent of votes received by the candidate in each time period. An inspection of these percents indicates that candidate Smith received approximately 55.3% of the votes each time period, candidate Coppin received approximately 13.8% of the vote, and candidate Montes received approximately 30.9% of the vote. All of this indicates that the election was rigged.

Chapter 11
Simple Linear Regression

11.1 a.
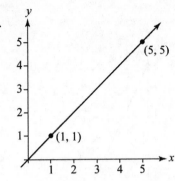

b.
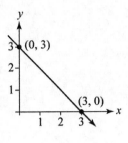

c.
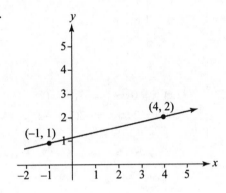

d.
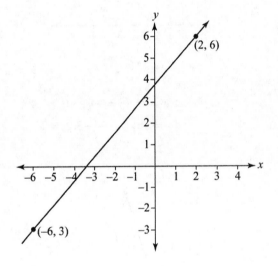

11.3   The two equations are: $4 = \beta_0 + \beta_1(-2)$ and $6 = \beta_0 + \beta_1(4)$

Subtracting the first equation from the second, we get

$$
\begin{aligned}
6 &= \beta_0 + 4\beta_1 \\
-(4 &= \beta_0 - 2\beta_1) \\
\hline
2 &= 6\beta_1 \Rightarrow \beta_1 = \frac{1}{3}
\end{aligned}
$$

Substituting $\beta_1 = \dfrac{1}{3}$ into the first equation, we get:

$$
4 = \beta_0 + \frac{1}{3}(-2) \Rightarrow \beta_0 = 4 + \frac{2}{3} = \frac{14}{3}
$$

The equation for the line is $y = \dfrac{14}{3} + \dfrac{1}{3}x$.

11.5   To graph a line, we need two points. Pick two values for x, and find the corresponding y values by substituting the values of x into the equation.

a.   Let $x = 0 \Rightarrow y = 4 + (0) = 4$

and $x = 2 \Rightarrow y = 4 + (2) = 6$

b.   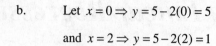Let $x = 0 \Rightarrow y = 5 - 2(0) = 5$

and $x = 2 \Rightarrow y = 5 - 2(2) = 1$

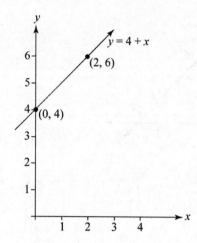

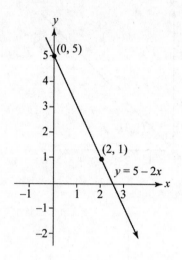

c.   Let $x = 0 \Rightarrow y = -4 + 3(0) = -4$

and $x = 2 \Rightarrow y = -4 + 3(2) = 2$

d.   Let $x = 0 \Rightarrow y = -2(0) = 0$

and $x = 2 \Rightarrow y = -2(2) = -4$

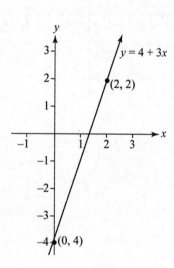

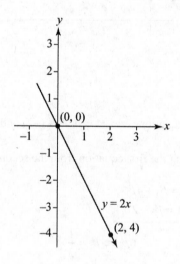

e.   Let $x = 0 \Rightarrow y = 0$
and $x = 2 \Rightarrow y = 2$

f.   Let $x = 0 \Rightarrow y = .5 + 1.5(0) = .5$
and $x = 2 \Rightarrow y = .5 + 1.5(2) = 3.5$

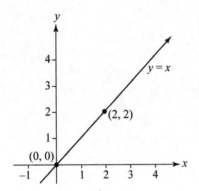

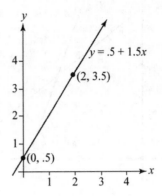

11.7   A deterministic model does not allow for random error or variation, whereas a probabilistic model does. An example where a deterministic model would be appropriate is:

Let y = cost of a 2×4 piece of lumber and
x = length (in feet)

The model would be $y = \beta_1 x$. There should be no variation in price for the same length of wood.

An example where a probabilistic model would be appropriate is:

Let y = sales per month of a commodity and
x = amount of money spent advertising

The model would be $y = \beta_0 + \beta_1 x + \varepsilon$. The sales per month will probably vary even if the amount of money spent on advertising remains the same.

11.9   No. The random error component, ε, allows the values of the variable to fall above or below the line.

11.11   From Exercise 11.10, $\hat{\beta}_0 = 7.10$ and $\hat{\beta}_1 = -.78$.

The fitted line is $\hat{y} = 7.10 - .78x$. To obtain values for $\hat{y}$, we substitute values of x into the equation and solve for $\hat{y}$.

a.

x	y	$\hat{y} = 7.10 - .78x$	$(y - \hat{y})$	$(y - \hat{y})^2$
7	2	1.64	.36	.1296
4	4	3.98	.02	.0004
6	2	2.42	−.42	.1764
2	5	5.54	−.54	.2916
1	7	6.32	.68	.4624
1	6	6.32	−.32	.1024
3	5	4.76	.24	.0576
			$\sum(y - \hat{y}) = 0.02$	$SSE = \sum(y - \hat{y})^2 = 1.2204$

b.

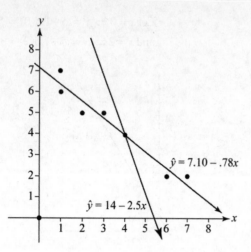

$\hat{y} = 7.10 - .78x$

$\hat{y} = 14 - 2.5x$

c.

x	y	$\hat{y} = 14 - 2.5x$	$(y - \hat{y})$	$(y - \hat{y})^2$
7	2	−3.5	5.5	30.25
4	4	4	0	0
6	2	−1	3	9
2	5	9	−4	16
1	7	11.5	−4.5	20.25
1	6	11.5	−5.5	30.25
3	5	6.5	−1.5	2.25
			$\sum (y - \hat{y}) = -7$	$SSE = 108.00$

11.13   a.   Using MINITAB, the scattergram of the data is:

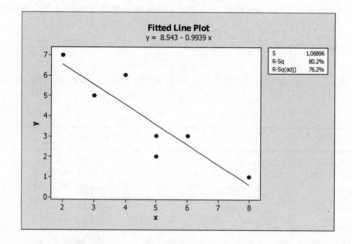

b.   Looking at the scattergram, x and y appear to have a negative linear relationship.

c.   Some preliminary calculations are:

$$\sum x = 33 \qquad \sum y = 27 \qquad \sum xy = 104 \qquad \sum x^2 = 179$$

$$SS_{xy} = \sum xy - \frac{(\sum x)(\sum y)}{n} = 104 - \frac{(33)(27)}{7} = -23.2857143$$

$$SS_{xx} = \sum x^2 - \frac{(\sum x)^2}{n} = 179 - \frac{(33)^2}{7} = 23.4285714$$

$$\hat{\beta}_1 = \frac{SS_{xy}}{SS_{xx}} = \frac{-23.2857143}{23.4285714} = -.99390244$$

$$\bar{x} = \frac{\sum x}{7} = \frac{33}{7} = 4.714285714 \qquad \bar{y} = \frac{\sum y}{7} = \frac{27}{7} = 3.857142857$$

$$\hat{\beta}_0 = \bar{y} - \hat{\beta}_1\bar{x} = 3.857142857 - (-.99390244)(4.714285714) = 8.542682931 \approx 8.5427$$

The least squares line is $\hat{y} = 8.5427 - .9939x$.

    d.   The least squares line is plotted in part **a**. It appears to fit the data well.

11.15   a.   The straight-line model would be: $y = \beta_0 + \beta_1 x + \varepsilon$

    b.   From the printout, the least squares line is: $\hat{y} = -97.414 + 1.188x$.

    c.   Since range of observed values for the 2001 Math SAT scores (*x*) does not include 0, the *y*-intercept has no meaning.

    d.   The slope of the least squares line is $\hat{\beta}_1 = 1.188$. In terms of this problem, for each additional point increase in the 2001 Math SAT score, the mean 2011 Math SAT score is estimated to increase by 1.188. This interpretation is meaningful for values of *x* within the observed range. The observed range of *x* is 474 to 603.

11.17   a.   Some preliminary calculations are:

$$\sum x = 5.45 \quad \sum y = 239 \quad \sum xy = 237.1 \quad \sum x^2 = 5.5075 \quad \sum y^2 = 10,255$$

$$\bar{x} = \frac{\sum x}{n} = \frac{5.45}{6} = .908333333 \qquad \bar{y} = \frac{\sum y}{n} = \frac{239}{6} = 39.83333333$$

$$SS_{xy} = \sum xy - \frac{(\sum x)(\sum y)}{n} = 237.1 - \frac{5.45(239)}{6} = 237.1 - 217.09166667 = 20.0083333$$

$$SS_{xx} = \sum x^2 - \frac{(\sum x)^2}{n} = 5.5075 - \frac{(5.45)^2}{6} = 5.5075 - 4.950416667 = .5570833333$$

$$\hat{\beta}_1 = \frac{SS_{xy}}{SS_{xx}} = \frac{20.0083333}{.5570833333} = 35.91623038 \approx 35.92$$

$$\hat{\beta}_o = \bar{y} - \hat{\beta}_1\bar{x} = 39.8333333 - 35.91623038(.90833333) = 7.20942408 \approx 7.21$$

The least squares line is $\hat{y} = 7.21 + 35.92x$.

b.   Since 0 is not in the observed range of x (Surface Area to Volume), $\hat{\beta}_o$ has not meaning. $\hat{\beta}_1 = 35.92$. For each unit change in Surface Area to Volume, the mean Drug Release Rate is estimated to increase by 35.92.

c.   For $x = .50$, $\hat{y} = 7.21 + 35.92(.50) = 25.17$

d.   The reliability of the estimate in part c is in question. The value of x, .50, is outside the observed range of x. We have no idea what the relationship between y and x is outside the observed range.

11.19   a.   Using MINITAB, the results are:

Regression Analysis: MillionaireBirths versus TotalBirths

```
The regression equation is
MillionaireBirths = - 14.1 + 0.628 TotalBirths


Predictor        Coef   SE Coef       T      P
Constant      -14.138     8.121   -1.74  0.157
TotalBirths    0.6277    0.2435    2.58  0.061


S = 3.32256   R-Sq = 62.4%   R-Sq(adj) = 53.0%


Analysis of Variance

Source           DF       SS      MS      F      P
Regression        1    73.34   73.34   6.64  0.061
Residual Error    4    44.16   11.04
Total             5   117.50
```

The least squares prediction equation is $\hat{y} = -14.138 + .6277x$.

b. $\hat{\beta}_0 = -14.138$. Since 0 is not in the observed range of total US births, $\hat{\beta}_0$ has no meaning.

$\hat{\beta}_1 = .6277$. For each additional one million births, the mean number of software millionaire birthdays is estimated to increase by .6277.

c.   For $x = 35$, $\hat{y} = -14.138 + .6277(35) = 7.8315$.

d.   Using MINITAB, the results are:

Regression Analysis: MillionaireBirths versus CEOBirths

```
The regression equation is
MillionaireBirths = 2.72 + 0.306 CEOBirths

Predictor     Coef   SE Coef      T      P
Constant    2.7227    0.8513   3.20  0.033
CEOBirths   0.30626   0.04592  6.67  0.003

S = 1.55683   R-Sq = 91.7%   R-Sq(adj) = 89.7%

Analysis of Variance

Source           DF      SS      MS      F      P
Regression        1  107.81  107.81  44.48  0.003
Residual Error    4    9.69    2.42
Total             5  117.50
```

The least squares prediction equation is $\hat{y} = 2.7227 + .3063x$.

e. $\hat{\beta}_0 = 2.7227$. The estimate of the mean number of software millionaire birthdays is 2.7227 when the number of CEO birthdays is 0.

$\hat{\beta}_1 = .3063$. For each additional CEO birthday, the mean number of software millionaire birthdays is estimated to increase by .3063.

f.   For $x = 10$, $\hat{y} = 2.7227 + .3063(10) = 5.7857$.

11.21   a.   The straight line model would be: $E(y) = \beta_0 + \beta_1 x$

b.   Some preliminary calculations are:

$$\sum x = 11,958 \quad \sum y = 2,478.8 \quad \sum xy = 739,647.16 \quad \sum x^2 = 3,577,052.56 \quad \sum y^2 = 154,676.28$$

$$\bar{x} = \frac{\sum x}{n} = \frac{11,958}{40} = 298.95 \qquad \bar{y} = \frac{\sum y}{n} = \frac{2,478.8}{40} = 61.97$$

$$SS_{xy} = \sum xy - \frac{\left(\sum x\right)\left(\sum y\right)}{n} = 739,647.16 - \frac{11,958(2,478.8)}{40} = -1,390.1$$

$$SS_{xx} = \sum x^2 - \frac{\left(\sum x\right)^2}{n} = 3,577,052.56 - \frac{11,958^2}{40} = 2,208.46$$

$$\hat{\beta}_1 = \frac{SS_{xy}}{SS_{xx}} = \frac{-1,390.1}{2,208.46} = -0.629443141 \approx -0.629$$

$$\hat{\beta}_0 = \bar{y} - \hat{\beta}_1\bar{x} = 61.97 - (-0.629443141)(298.95) = 250.142027 \approx 250.14$$

The least squares line is $\hat{y} = 250.14 - 0.629x$.

c.   Since 0 is not in the observed range of x (distance), $\hat{\beta}_0$ has no meaning.

d. $\hat{\beta}_1 = -0.629$. For each additional yard in a golfer's average driving distance, the mean driving accuracy is estimated to decrease by 0.629%.

e.   The estimate of the slope will help determine if the golfer's concern is valid since it tells us the change in driving accuracy per unit change in driving distance.

11.23   Some preliminary calculations are:

$$\sum x = 6,980.65 \qquad \sum y = 576.3 \qquad \sum xy = 396,603.225 \qquad \sum x^2 = 4,933,198.773 \qquad \sum y^2 = 35,626.09$$

$$\bar{x} = \frac{\sum x}{n} = \frac{6,980.65}{23} = 303.5065 \qquad\qquad \bar{y} = \frac{\sum y}{n} = \frac{576.3}{23} = 25.0565$$

$$SS_{xy} = \sum xy - \frac{\left(\sum x\right)\left(\sum y\right)}{n} = 396,603.225 - \frac{6,980.65(576.3)}{23} = 221,692.4165$$

$$SS_{xx} = \sum x^2 - \frac{\left(\sum x\right)^2}{n} = 4,933,198.773 - \frac{6,980.65^2}{23} = 2,814,525.972$$

$$\hat{\beta}_1 = \frac{SS_{xy}}{SS_{xx}} = \frac{221,692.4165}{2,814,525.972} = 0.07876723 \approx 0.0788$$

$$\hat{\beta}_0 = \bar{y} - \hat{\beta}_1\bar{x} = 25.0565 - (.07876723)(303.5065) = 1.1501335 \approx 1.1501$$

The fitted regression line is $\hat{y} = 1.1501 + .0788x$. We would estimate that the movie's opening weekend revenue would increase by $(.0788)(100) = 7.88$ million dollars as the tweet rate increases by 100.

11.25   a.   We will select Average Salary as the dependent variable and Mean GMAT as the independent variable.

b.   Some preliminary calculations are:

$$\sum x = 6,944 \qquad \sum y = 1,080,288 \qquad \sum xy = 751,698,490 \qquad \sum x^2 = 4,824,680 \qquad \sum y^2 = 118,151,669,430$$

$$\bar{x} = \frac{\sum x}{n} = \frac{6,944}{10} = 694.4 \qquad\qquad \bar{y} = \frac{\sum y}{n} = \frac{1,080,288}{10} = 108,028.8$$

$$SS_{xy} = \sum xy - \frac{\left(\sum x\right)\left(\sum y\right)}{n} = 751,698,490 - \frac{6,944(1,080,288)}{10}$$
$$= 751,698,490 - 75,015,987.2 = 1,546,502.8$$

$$SS_{xx} = \sum x^2 - \frac{\left(\sum x\right)^2}{n} = 4,824,680 - \frac{(6,944)^2}{10} = 4,824,680 - 4,821,913.6 = 2,766.4$$

$$\hat{\beta}_1 = \frac{SS_{xy}}{SS_{xx}} = \frac{1,546,502.8}{2,766.4} = 559.0307981 \approx 559.031$$

$$\hat{\beta}_o = \bar{y} - \hat{\beta}_1 \bar{x} = 108,028.8 - (559.0307981)(694.4) = -280,162.1862 \approx -280,162.186$$

The fitted regression line is: $\hat{y} = -280,162.186 + 559.031x$

$\hat{\beta}_o = -280,162.186$.   Since 0 is not in the range of observed values of the variable Mean GMAT, the y-intercept has no meaning.

$\hat{\beta}_1 = -0.271$.   For each additional point increase in the mean GMAT score, the mean value of Average Salary is estimated to increase by $\$559.031$.

11.27   The graph in **b** would have the smallest s^2 because the width of the data points is the smallest.

11.29   a. $s^2 = \dfrac{SSE}{n-2} = \dfrac{8.34}{26-2} = .3475$

b.   We would expect most of the observations to be within $2s = 2\sqrt{.3475} \approx 1.179$ of the least squares line.

11.31   a. $s^2 = \dfrac{SSE}{n-2} = \dfrac{1.04}{28-2} = .04$ and $s = \sqrt{.04} = .2$

b.   We would expect most of the observations to be within $2s$ or of the $2(.2) = .4$ units of the fitted regression line.

11.33   a.   From part **a** of Exercise 11.17, $SS_{xy} = 20.00833333$, $\sum y = 239$, $\sum y^2 = 10,255$, and $\hat{\beta}_1 = 35.91623038$.

$$SS_{yy} = \sum y^2 - \frac{\left(\sum y\right)^2}{n} = 10,255 - \frac{(239)^2}{6} = 10,255 - 9520.166667 = 734.8333333$$

$$SSE = SS_{yy} - \hat{\beta}_1 SS_{xy} = 734.833333 - 35.91623068(20.00833333) = 16.2094179$$

$$s^2 = MSE = \frac{SSE}{n-2} = \frac{16.2094179}{6-2} = 4.052354475 \text{ and } s = \sqrt{4.052354475} = 2.01$$

b. $s = 2.01$. We would expect approximately 95% of the observed values of y (Drug release rate) to fall within $2s$ or $2(2.01) = 4.02$ units of their least squares predicted values.

11.35   a.   Using MINITAB, the results are:

Regression Analysis: MillionaireBirths versus TotalBirths

```
The regression equation is
MillionaireBirths = - 14.1 + 0.628 TotalBirths


Predictor        Coef   SE Coef       T      P
Constant      -14.138     8.121   -1.74  0.157
TotalBirths    0.6277    0.2435    2.58  0.061


S = 3.32256   R-Sq = 62.4%   R-Sq(adj) = 53.0%


Analysis of Variance

Source          DF      SS     MS      F      P
Regression       1   73.34  73.34   6.64  0.061
Residual Error   4   44.16  11.04
Total            5  117.50
```

From the printout, $SSE = 44.16$, $s^2 = MSE = 11.04$, and $s = 3.32256$.

b.   Using MINITAB, the results are:

Regression Analysis: MillionaireBirths versus CEOBirths

```
The regression equation is
MillionaireBirths = 2.72 + 0.306 CEOBirths


Predictor       Coef   SE Coef       T      P
Constant      2.7227    0.8513    3.20  0.033
CEOBirths    0.30626   0.04592    6.67  0.003


S = 1.55683   R-Sq = 91.7%   R-Sq(adj) = 89.7%


Analysis of Variance

Source          DF       SS      MS       F      P
Regression       1   107.81  107.81   44.48  0.003
Residual Error   4     9.69    2.42
Total            5   117.50
```

From the printout, $SSE = 9.69$, $s^2 = MSE = 2.42$, and $s = 1.55683$.

c.   The model containing CEO birthdays will have smaller errors of prediction because the value of s for that model ($s = 1.55683$) is smaller than the value of s for the other model ($s = 3.32256$).

11.37   a.   From Exercise 11.22, $SS_{xy} = -130.44167$, $\hat{\beta}_1 = -.002310625$, $\sum y = 135.8$, and $\sum y^2 = 769.72$.

$$SS_{yy} = \sum y^2 - \frac{\left(\sum y\right)^2}{n} = 769.72 - \frac{(135.8)^2}{24} = 769.72 - 768.4016667 = 1.3183333$$

$$SSE = SS_{yy} - \hat{\beta}_1 SS_{xy} = 1.3183333 - (-.002310625)(-130.44167) = 1.016931516 \approx 1.017$$

$$s^2 = MSE = \frac{SSE}{n-2} = \frac{1.016931516}{24-2} = 0.046224159 \approx .0462 \text{ and } s = \sqrt{0.046224159} = 0.215$$

   b. s^2 is measured in square units. It is very difficult to explain something measured in square units.

   c. $s = 0.215$. We would expect approximately 95% of the observed values of y (sweetness index) to fall within $2s$ or $2(0.215) = 0.43$ units of their least squares predicted values.

11.39   a.   From Exercise 11.24, $SS_{xy} = -3,882.3686$, $\sum y = 3,781.1$, $\sum y^2 = 651,612.45$, and
$\hat{\beta}_1 = -0.305444503$.

$$SS_{yy} = \sum y^2 - \frac{\left(\sum y\right)^2}{n} = 651,612.45 - \frac{(3,781.1)^2}{22} = 651,612.45 - 649,850.7823 = 1,761.6677$$

$$SSE = SS_{yy} - \hat{\beta}_1 SS_{xy} = 1,761.6677 - (-.305444503(-3,882.3686)) = 575.8195525$$

$$s^2 = MSE = \frac{SSE}{n-2} = \frac{575.8195525}{22-2} = 28.79097763 \text{ and } s = \sqrt{28.79097763} = 5.37$$

$s = 5.37$. We would expect approximately 95% of the observed values of y (FCAT-Math scores) to fall within $2s$ or $2(5.37) = 10.74$ units of their least squares predicted values.

   b.   From Exercise 11.24, $SS_{xy} = -3,442.16$, $\sum y = 3,764.2$, $\sum y^2 = 645,221.16$, and $\hat{\beta}_1 = -0.270811187$.

$$SS_{yy} = \sum y^2 - \frac{\left(\sum y\right)^2}{n} = 645,221.16 - \frac{(3,764.2)^2}{22} = 645,221.16 - 644,054.62 = 1,166.54$$

$$SSE = SS_{yy} - \hat{\beta}_1 SS_{xy} = 1,166.54 - (-.270811187)(-3,442.16) = 234.3645646$$

$$s^2 = MSE = \frac{SSE}{n-2} = \frac{234.3645646}{22-2} = 11.71822823 \text{ and } s = \sqrt{11.71822823} = 3.42$$

$s = 3.42$. We would expect approximately 95% of the observed values of y (FCAT-Reading scores) to fall within $2s$ or $2(3.42) = 6.84$ units of their least squares predicted values.

   c.   The sample standard deviation for predicting FCAT-Math scores is $s = 5.37$. The sample standard deviation for predicting FCAT-Reading scores is $s = 3.42$. Since the standard deviation for predicting FCAT-Reading scores is smaller than the standard deviation for predicting FCAT-Math scores, we can more accurately predict the FCAT-Reading scores.

11.41   a.   For confidence coefficient .95, $\alpha = .05$ and $\alpha/2 = .05/2 = .025$. From Table III, Appendix D, with df $= n - 2 = 10 - 2 = 8$, $t_{.025} = 2.306$. The 95% confidence interval for β_1 is:

$$\hat{\beta}_1 \pm t_{.025} s_{\hat{\beta}_1} \Rightarrow \hat{\beta}_1 \pm t_{.025} \frac{s}{\sqrt{SS_{xx}}} \Rightarrow 31 \pm 2.306 \frac{3}{\sqrt{35}} \Rightarrow 31 \pm 1.17 \Rightarrow (29.83, \ 32.17)$$

For confidence coefficient .90, $\alpha = .10$ and $\alpha/2 = .10/2 = .05$. From Table III, Appendix D, with df $= 8$, $t_{.05} = 1.860$. The 90% confidence interval for β_1 is:

$$\hat{\beta}_1 \pm t_{.05} s_{\hat{\beta}_1} \Rightarrow 31 \pm 1.860 \frac{3}{\sqrt{35}} \Rightarrow 31 \pm .94 \Rightarrow (30.06, \ 31.94)$$

b. $s^2 = \dfrac{SSE}{n-2} = \dfrac{1960}{14-2} = 163.33$, $s = \sqrt{s^2} = 12.7802$

For confidence coefficient, .95, $\alpha = .05$ and $\alpha/2 = .05/2 = .025$. From Table III, Appendix D, with df $= n - 2 = 14 - 2 = 12$, $t_{.025} = 2.179$. The 95% confidence interval for β_1 is:

$$\hat{\beta}_1 \pm t_{.025} s_{\hat{\beta}_1} \Rightarrow \hat{\beta}_1 \pm t_{.025} \frac{s}{\sqrt{SS_{xx}}} \Rightarrow 64 \pm 2.179 \frac{12.7802}{\sqrt{30}} \Rightarrow 64 \pm 5.08 \Rightarrow (58.92, \ 69.08)$$

For confidence coefficient .90, $\alpha = .10$ and $\alpha/2 = .10/2 = .05$. From Table III, Appendix D, with df $= 12$, $t_{.05} = 1.782$. The 90% confidence interval for β_1 is:

$$\hat{\beta}_1 \pm t_{.05} s_{\hat{\beta}_1} \Rightarrow 64 \pm 1.782 \frac{12.7802}{\sqrt{30}} \Rightarrow 64 \pm 4.16 \Rightarrow (59.84, \ 68.16).$$

c. $s^2 = \dfrac{SSE}{n-2} = \dfrac{146}{20-2} = 8.1111$, $s = \sqrt{s^2} = 2.848$.

For confidence coefficient .95, $\alpha = .05$ and $\alpha/2 = .05/2 = .025$. From Table III, Appendix D, with df $= n - 2 = 20 - 2 = 18$, $t_{.025} = 2.101$. The 95% confidence interval for β_1 is:

$$\hat{\beta}_1 \pm t_{.025} s_{\hat{\beta}_1} \Rightarrow \hat{\beta}_1 \pm t_{.025} \frac{s}{\sqrt{SS_{xx}}} \Rightarrow -8.4 \pm 2.101 \frac{2.848}{\sqrt{64}} \Rightarrow -8.4 \pm .75 \Rightarrow (-9.15, \ -7.65)$$

For confidence coefficient .90, $\alpha = .10$ and $\alpha/2 = .10/2 = .05$. From Table III, Appendix D, with df $= 18$, $t_{.05} = 1.734$. The 90% confidence interval for β_1 is:

$$\hat{\beta}_1 \pm t_{.05} s_{\hat{\beta}_1} \Rightarrow -8.4 \pm 1.734 \frac{2.848}{\sqrt{64}} \Rightarrow -8.4 \pm .62 \Rightarrow (-9.02, \ -7.78)$$

11.43   From Exercise 11.42, $\hat{\beta}_1 = .82$, $s = 1.1922$, $SS_{xx} = 28$, and $n = 7$.

For confidence coefficient .80, $\alpha = .20$ and $\alpha / 2 = .20 / 2 = .10$. From Table III, Appendix D, with df $= n - 2 = 7 - 2 = 5$, $t_{.10} = 1.476$. The 80% confidence interval for β_1 is:

$$\hat{\beta}_1 \pm t_{.10} s_{\hat{\beta}_1} \Rightarrow .82 \pm 1.476 \frac{1.1922}{\sqrt{28}} \Rightarrow .82 \pm 1.476(.2253) \Rightarrow .82 \pm .33 \Rightarrow (.49, \ 1.15)$$

For confidence coefficient .98, $\alpha = .02$ and $\alpha / 2 = .02 / 2 = .01$. From Table III, Appendix D, with df $= 5$, $t_{.01} = 3.365$. The 98% confidence interval for β_1 is:

$$\hat{\beta}_1 \pm t_{.01} s_{\hat{\beta}_1} \Rightarrow .82 \pm 3.365 \frac{1.1922}{\sqrt{28}} \Rightarrow .82 \pm 3.365(.2253) \Rightarrow .82 \pm .76 \Rightarrow (.06, \ 1.58)$$

11.45   a.   To determine if the average state Math SAT score in 2011 has a positive relationship with the average state Math SAT score in 2001, we test:

$$H_0 : \beta_1 = 0$$
$$H_a : \beta_1 > 0$$

   b.   From the printout in Exercise 11.15, the p-value is $p = 0.000$. This is the p-value for a 2-tailed test. The p-value for this one-tailed test is $0.000/2 = 0.000$. Since the p-value is less than $\alpha = .05$, H_0 is rejected. There is sufficient evidence to indicate the average state Math SAT score in 2011 has a positive relationship with the average state Math SAT score in 2001 at $\alpha = .05$.

   c.   For confidence coefficient .95, $\alpha = .05$ and $\alpha / 2 = .05 / 2 = .025$. From Table III, Appendix D, with df $= n - 2 = 51 - 2 = 49$, $t_{.025} \approx 2.011$. The 95% confidence interval is:

$$\hat{\beta}_1 \pm t_{.025} s_{\hat{\beta}_1} \Rightarrow 1.188 \pm 2.011(.050) \Rightarrow 1.188 \pm .101 \Rightarrow (1.087, \ 1.289)$$

We are 95% confident that for each additional point on the 2001 average state Math SAT score, the increase in the mean 2011 average state Math SAT score is between 1.087 and 1.289.

11.47   a.   The sign of β_1 should be positive. As the number of daughters increase, the AAUW score should be higher.

   b.   For confidence coefficient .95, $\alpha = .05$ and $\alpha / 2 = .05 / 2 = .025$. From Table II, Appendix D, $z_{.025} = 1.96$. The 95% confidence interval is:

$$\hat{\beta}_1 \pm z_{.025} s_{\hat{\beta}_1} \Rightarrow .27 \pm 1.96(.74) \Rightarrow .27 \pm 1.4504 \Rightarrow (-1.1804, \ 1.7204)$$

   c.   Since 0 falls in the confidence interval found in part a, there is no evidence to reject H_0. There is insufficient evidence to indicate the number of daughters is linearly related to the AAUW score at $\alpha = .05$.

11.49   First, we must compute s^2. From Exercise 11.17, $SS_{xy} = 20.00833333$,

$SS_{xx} = 0.5570833333$, $\sum y = 239$, $\sum y^2 = 10,255$, and $\hat{\beta}_1 = 35.91623038$.

$$SS_{yy} = \sum y^2 - \frac{(\sum y)^2}{n} = 10,255 - \frac{(239)^2}{6} = 10,255 - 9,520.1666667 = 734.8333333$$

$$SSE = SS_{yy} - \hat{\beta}_1 SS_{xy} = 734.83333333 - (35.91623038)(20.008333333) = 16.2094236$$

$$s^2 = MSE = \frac{SSE}{n-2} = \frac{16.2094326}{6-2} = 4.0523559 \text{ and } s = \sqrt{4.0523559} = 2.0130$$

$$s_{\hat{\beta}_1} = \frac{\sqrt{MSE}}{\sqrt{SS_{xx}}} = \frac{\sqrt{4.0523559}}{\sqrt{0.55708333}} = 2.6971$$

For confidence coefficient .90, $\alpha = .10$ and $\alpha / 2 = .10 / 2 = .05$. From Table III, Appendix D, with $df = n - 2 = 6 - 2 = 4$, $t_{.05} = 2.132$. The 90% confidence interval is:

$$\hat{\beta}_1 \pm t_{.05} s_{\hat{\beta}_1} \Rightarrow 35.916 \pm 2.132(2.6971) \Rightarrow 35.916 \pm 5.7502 \Rightarrow (30.17, \ 41.67)$$

We are 90% confident that for each additional unit increase in Surface Area to Volume, the increase in the Drug release rate is between 30.17 and 41.67.

11.51   a.   From Exercise 11.19 a, $\hat{\beta}_1 = .6277$ and $s_{\hat{\beta}_1} = .2435$.

For confidence coefficient .95, $\alpha = .05$ and $\alpha / 2 = .05 / 2 = .025$. From Table III, Appendix D, with $df = n - 2 = 6 - 2 = 4$, $t_{.025} = 2.776$. The confidence interval is:

$$\hat{\beta}_1 \pm t_{.025} s_{\hat{\beta}_1} \Rightarrow .6277 \pm 2.776(.2435) \Rightarrow .6277 \pm .6760 \Rightarrow (-.0483, \ 1.3037)$$

We are 95% confident that for each additional one million US births, the mean number of software millionaire birthdays will change from -.0483 to 1.3037. Since 0 is in this interval, there is no evidence of a linear relationship between total US births and the number of software millionaire birthdays.

b.   From Exercise 11.19 d, $\hat{\beta}_1 = .3063$ and $s_{\hat{\beta}_1} = .0459$.

For confidence coefficient .95, $\alpha = .05$ and $\alpha / 2 = .05 / 2 = .025$. From Table III, Appendix D, with $df = n - 2 = 6 - 2 = 4$, $t_{.025} = 2.776$. The confidence interval is:

$$\hat{\beta}_1 \pm t_{.025} s_{\hat{\beta}_1} \Rightarrow .3063 \pm 2.776(.0459) \Rightarrow .3063 \pm .1274 \Rightarrow (.1789, \ .4337)$$

We are 95% confident that for each CEO birthdays, the mean number of software millionaire birthdays will increase from .1789 to .4337. Since 0 is not in this interval, there is evidence of a linear relationship between the number of CEO birthdays and the number of software millionaire birthdays.

c.   No, you cannot conclude that the number of software millionaires born in a decade is linearly related to the total number of people born in the U.S. because 0 is contained in the 95% confidence interval for β_1.

Yes, you can conclude that the number of software millionaires born in a decade is linearly related to the number of CEOs born in a decade because 0 is not contained in the 95% confidence interval for β_1.

11.53   a.   To determine if driving accuracy decreases linearly as driving distance increases, we test:

$$H_0 : \beta_1 = 0$$
$$H_a : \beta_1 < 0$$

b.   From Exercise 11.21:

$$\sum y = 2,478.8 \qquad \sum y^2 = 154,676.28 \qquad SS_{xy} = -1,390.1 \qquad SS_{xx} = 2,208.46 \qquad \hat{\beta}_1 = -0.629443141$$

$$SS_{yy} = \sum y^2 - \frac{\left(\sum y\right)^2}{n} = 154,676.28 - \frac{2,478.8^2}{40} = 1,065.044$$

$$SSE = SS_{yy} - \hat{\beta}_1 SS_{xy} = 1,065.044 - (-.629443141)(-1,390.1) = 190.0550891$$

$$s^2 = MSE = \frac{SSE}{n-2} = \frac{190.0550891}{40-2} = 5.001449713 \qquad\qquad s = \sqrt{5.001449713} = 2.23639212$$

$$s_{\hat{\beta}_1} = \frac{s}{\sqrt{SS_{xx}}} = \frac{2.23639212}{\sqrt{2,208.46}} = .04759$$

The test statistic is $t = \dfrac{\hat{\beta}_1}{s_{\hat{\beta}_1}} = \dfrac{-.6294}{.04759} = -13.23$.

Using Table III, with df $= n - 2 = 40 - 2 = 38$, the p-value is approximately 0.000.

c.   Since the p-value is less than $\alpha = .01$, H_0 is rejected. There is sufficient evidence to indicate driving accuracy decreases linearly as driving distance increases at $\alpha = .01$.

11.55   Some preliminary calculations are:

$$\sum x = 301,713 \qquad \sum y = 811 \qquad \sum xy = 27,261,248 \qquad \sum x^2 = 10,707,042,109 \qquad \sum y^2 = 73,235$$

$$\bar{x} = \frac{\sum x}{n} = \frac{301,713}{9} = 33,523.66667 \qquad\qquad \bar{y} = \frac{\sum y}{n} = \frac{811}{9} = 90.1111111$$

$$SS_{xy} = \sum xy - \frac{\left(\sum x\right)\left(\sum y\right)}{n} = 27,261,248 - \frac{301,713(811)}{9} = 27,261,248 - 27,187,693.67 = 73,554.33$$

$$SS_{xx} = \sum x^2 - \frac{\left(\sum x\right)^2}{n} = 10,707,042,109 - \frac{(301,713)^2}{9} = 10,707,042,109 - 10,114,526,041 = 592,516,068$$

$$SS_{yy} = \sum y^2 - \frac{\left(\sum y\right)^2}{n} = 73,235 - \frac{(811)^2}{9} = 73,235 - 73,080.111111 = 154.88889$$

$$\hat{\beta}_1 = \frac{SS_{xy}}{SS_{xx}} = \frac{73,554.33}{592,516,068} = 0.000124138 \approx 0.0001241$$

$$SSE = SS_{yy} - \hat{\beta}_1 SS_{xy} = 154.888889 - (.000124138)(73,554.33) = 145.7580026$$

$$s^2 = MSE = \frac{SSE}{n-2} = \frac{145.7580026}{9-2} = 20.8225718 \text{ and } s = \sqrt{20.8225718} = 4.5632$$

$$s_{\hat{\beta}_1} = \frac{\sqrt{MSE}}{\sqrt{SS_{xx}}} = \frac{\sqrt{20.8225718}}{\sqrt{592,516,068}} = 0.0001875$$

To determine if there is a positive linear relationship between the percentage of graduates with job offers and tuition costs, we test:

$$H_0 : \beta_1 = 0$$
$$H_a : \beta_1 > 0$$

The test statistic is $t = \dfrac{\hat{\beta}_1 - 0}{s_{\hat{\beta}_1}} = \dfrac{.0001243}{.0001875} = .66$

The rejection region requires $\alpha = .10$ in the upper tail of the t-distribution with df $= n - 2 = 9 - 2 = 7$. From Table III, Appendix D, $t_{.10} = 1.415$. The rejection region is $t > 1.415$.

Since the observed value of the test statistic does not fall in the rejection region $(t = .66 \not> 1.415)$, H_0 is not rejected. There is insufficient evidence to indicate a positive linear relationship between the percentage of graduates with job offers and tuition costs at $\alpha = .10$.

11.57   a.   Using MINITAB, the results are:

Regression Analysis: SLUGPCT versus ELEVATION

```
The regression equation is
SLUGPCT = 0.515 + 0.000021 ELEVATION

Predictor        Coef       SE Coef        T       P
Constant       0.515140    0.007954    64.76    0.000
ELEVATION    0.00002074  0.00000719     2.89    0.008

S = 0.0369803   R-Sq = 23.6%   R-Sq(adj) = 20.7%

Analysis of Variance

Source            DF        SS        MS      F      P
Regression         1    0.011390  0.011390   8.33   0.008
Residual Error    27    0.036924  0.001368
Total             28    0.048314
```

To determine if a positive linear relationship exists between elevation and slugging percentage, we test:

$$H_0 : \beta_1 = 0$$
$$H_a : \beta_1 > 0$$

The test statistic is $t = 2.89$ and the p-value is $p = .008 / 2 = .004$. Since the p-value is less than α ($p = .004 < .01$), H_0 is rejected. There is sufficient evidence to indicate that a positive linear relationship exists between elevation and slugging percentage at $\alpha = .01$.

b. The scatterplot for the data is:

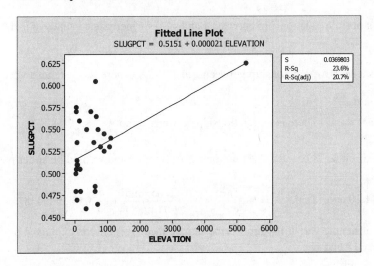

The data point for Denver is very far from the rest. This point looks to be an outlier. It is much different than all of the rest of the points.

c. Removing the data point for Denver, the Minitab output is:

Regression Analysis: SLUGPCT versus ELEVATION

```
The regression equation is
SLUGPCT = 0.515 + 0.000020 ELEVATION


Predictor        Coef      SE Coef       T       P
Constant      0.51537      0.01066   48.33   0.000
ELEVATION   0.00002012   0.00002034    0.99   0.332


S = 0.0376839   R-Sq = 3.6%   R-Sq(adj) = 0.0%

Analysis of Variance

Source          DF        SS        MS      F       P
Regression       1   0.001389   0.001389   0.98   0.332
Residual Error  26   0.036922   0.001420
Total           27   0.038311
```

To determine if a positive linear relationship exists between elevation and slugging percentage, we test:

$$H_0 : \beta_1 = 0$$
$$H_a : \beta_1 > 0$$

The test statistic is $t = .99$ and the p-value is $p = .332 / 2 = .166$. Since the p-value is not less than α ($p = .166 \not< .01$), H_0 is not rejected. There is insufficient evidence to indicate that a positive linear relationship exists between elevation and slugging percentage when Denver is removed form the data at $\alpha = .01$. Since there was a linear relationship with Denver in the data set and no linear relationship with Denver removed from the data set, it supports the "thin air" theory.

11.59   a.   If $r = .7$, there is a positive relationship between x and y. As x increases, y tends to increase. The slope is positive.

b.   If $r = -.7$, there is a negative relationship between x and y. As x increases, y tends to decrease. The slope is negative.

c.   If $r = 0$, there is a 0 slope. There is no relationship between x and y.

d.   If $r^2 = .64$, then r is either $.8$ or $-.8$. The relationship between x and y could be either positive or negative.

11.61   a.   From Exercises 11.10 and 11.30, $r^2 = 1 - \dfrac{SSE}{SS_{yy}} = 1 - \dfrac{1.22033896}{21.7142857} = 1 - .0562 = .9438$

94.38% of the total sample variability around the sample mean response is explained by the linear relationship between y and x.

b.   Some preliminary calculations are:

$$\sum x = 33 \qquad \sum y = 27 \qquad \sum xy = 104 \qquad \sum x^2 = 179 \qquad \sum y^2 = 133$$

$$SS_{xy} = \sum xy - \frac{\left(\sum x\right)\left(\sum y\right)}{n} = 104 - \frac{33(27)}{7} = -23.2857143$$

$$SS_{xx} = \sum x^2 - \frac{\left(\sum x\right)^2}{n} = 179 - \frac{33^2}{7} = 23.4285714$$

$$\hat{\beta}_1 = \frac{SS_{xy}}{SS_{xx}} = \frac{-23.2857143}{23.4285714} = -.99390244$$

$$SS_{yy} = \sum y^2 - \frac{\left(\sum y\right)^2}{n} = 133 - \frac{27^2}{7} = 28.8571429$$

$$SSE = SS_{yy} - \hat{\beta}_1 SS_{xy} = 28.8571429 - (-.99390244)(-23.2857143) = 5.71341462$$

$$r^2 = 1 - \frac{SSE}{SS_{yy}} = 1 - \frac{5.71341462}{28.8571429} = 1 - .1980 = .802$$

80.2% of the total sample variability around the sample mean response is explained by the linear relationship between y and x.

11.63   a. $r^2 = .18$. 18% of the total sample variability around the sample mean number of points scored by a team that has a first-down is explained by the linear relationship between the number of points scored by a team that has a first-down and the number of yards from the opposing goal line.

        b. $r = \sqrt{.18} = -.424$. The value of r will be negative because the sign of the estimate of β_1 is negative.

11.65   a.   The linear model would be: $E(y) = \beta_0 + \beta_1 x$

        b. $r = .68$. There is a moderate positive linear relationship between RMP and SET.

        c.   Since $r = .68$ is positive, the slope of the line will also be positive.

        d.   The p-value is $p = .001$. Since this value is so small, we would reject H_0. There is sufficient evidence of a linear relationship between RMP and SET for any value of $\alpha > .001$.

        e. $r^2 = .68^2 = .4624$. 46.24% of the total sample variability around the sample mean SET values is explained by the linear relationship between SET and RMP.

11.67   a. $r = .983$. There is a strong positive linear relationship between the number of females in managerial positions and the number of females with college degrees.

        b. $r = .074$. There is a very weak positive linear relationship between the number of females in managerial positions and the number of female high school graduates with no college degree.

        c. $r = .722$. There is a moderately strong positive linear relationship between the number of males in managerial positions and the number of males with college degrees.

        d. $r = .528$. There is a moderately weak positive linear relationship between the number of males in managerial positions and the number of male high school graduates with no college degree.

11.69   a.   From the printout in Exercise 11.19a, $r^2 = 62.4\%$. 62.4% of the total sample variability around the sample mean number of software millionaire birthdays is explained by the linear relationship between the number of software millionaire birthdays and the total number of U.S. births.

        b.   From the printout in Exercise 11.19d, $r^2 = 91.7\%$. 91.7% of the total sample variability around the sample mean number of software millionaire birthdays is explained by the linear relationship between the number of software millionaire birthdays and the number of CEO birthdays.

        c.   Yes. There is a very strong positive linear relationship between the number of sotware millionaire birthdays and the number of CEO birthdays. As the number of software millionaire birthdays increase, the number of CEO birthdays also increases.

11.71   Some preliminary calculations are:

$$\sum x = 6,167 \qquad \sum x^2 = 1,641,115 \qquad \sum xy = 34,764.5 \qquad \sum y = 135.8 \qquad \sum y^2 = 769.72$$

$$SS_{xy} = \sum xy - \frac{\sum x \sum y}{n} = 34,764.5 - \frac{6167(135.8)}{24} = -130.44167$$

$$SS_{xx} = \sum x^2 - \frac{\left(\sum x\right)^2}{n} = 1,641,115 - \frac{(6,167)^2}{24} = 56,452.95833$$

$$SS_{yy} = \sum y^2 - \frac{\left(\sum y\right)^2}{n} = 769.72 - \frac{135.8^2}{24} = 1.3183333$$

$$\hat{\beta}_1 = \frac{SS_{xy}}{SS_{xx}} = \frac{-130.44167}{56,452.95833} = -0.002310625$$

$$SSE = SS_{yy} - \hat{\beta}_1 SS_{xy} = 1.3183333 - (-0.002310625)(-130.44167) = 1.016931516$$

$$r^2 = \frac{SS_{yy} - SSE}{SS_{yy}} = \frac{1.3183333 - 1.016931516}{1.3183333} = .2286$$

22.86% of the total sample variability around the sample mean sweetness index is explained by the linear relationship between the sweetness index and the amount of water soluble pectin.

$$r = -\sqrt{.2286} = -.478 \quad \text{(The value of } r \text{ is negative because } \hat{\beta}_1 \text{ is negative.)}$$

Since this value is not close to one, there is a rather weak negative linear relationship between the sweetness index and the amount of water soluble pectin.

11.73   From Exercise 11.25, $SS_{xy} = 73,554.33$, $SS_{xx} = 592,516,068$, $SS_{yy} = 154.888889$,

$\hat{\beta}_1 = 0.000124138 \approx 0.0001241$, $\sum y = 811$ and $\sum x = 301,713$

$$r = \frac{SS_{xy}}{\sqrt{SS_{xx}}\sqrt{SS_{yy}}} = \frac{73,554.33}{\sqrt{592,516,068}\sqrt{154.888889}} = .243$$

There is a weak positive linear relationship between the percentage of graduates with job offers and the tuition cost.

$r^2 = .243^2 = .059$ Approximately 5.9% of the variability in the percentage of graduates with job offers around the sample mean is explained by the linear relationship between percentage of graduates with job offers and tuition cost.

$$\hat{\beta}_o = \bar{y} - \hat{\beta}_1 \bar{x} = \frac{811}{9} - (0.000124138)(\frac{301,713}{9}) = 85.94955018 \approx 85.9496$$

The fitted regression line is: $\hat{y} = 85.9496 + .0001241x$.

11.75 To determine whether average earnings and height are positively correlated for those in the different occupations, we test:

$$H_0 : \rho = 0$$
$$H_a : \rho > 0$$

The test statistic is $t = \dfrac{r\sqrt{n-2}}{\sqrt{1-r^2}}$

We will use $\alpha = .01$ for all tests. The rejection region requires $\alpha = .01$ in the upper tail of the *t*-distribution. Since all of the sample sizes are over 100, the rejection regions will all be approximately the same. Using $df = \infty$ and Table III, Appendix D, $t_{.01} \approx 2.33$. The rejection region is $t > 2.33$.

For Sales, the test statistic is $t = \dfrac{r\sqrt{n-2}}{\sqrt{1-r^2}} = \dfrac{.41\sqrt{117-2}}{\sqrt{1-.41^2}} = 4.82$

For Managers, the test statistic is $t = \dfrac{r\sqrt{n-2}}{\sqrt{1-r^2}} = \dfrac{.35\sqrt{455-2}}{\sqrt{1-.35^2}} = 7.95$

For Blue Collar Workers, the test statistic is $t = \dfrac{r\sqrt{n-2}}{\sqrt{1-r^2}} = \dfrac{.32\sqrt{349-2}}{\sqrt{1-.32^2}} = 6.29$

For Service Workers, the test statistic is $t = \dfrac{r\sqrt{n-2}}{\sqrt{1-r^2}} = \dfrac{.31\sqrt{265-2}}{\sqrt{1-.31^2}} = 5.29$

For Professional/Technical Workers, the test statistic is $t = \dfrac{r\sqrt{n-2}}{\sqrt{1-r^2}} = \dfrac{.30\sqrt{453-2}}{\sqrt{1-.30^2}} = 6.68$

For Clerical Workers, the test statistic is $t = \dfrac{r\sqrt{n-2}}{\sqrt{1-r^2}} = \dfrac{.25\sqrt{358-2}}{\sqrt{1-.25^2}} = 4.87$

For Crafts/Forepersons, the test statistic is $t = \dfrac{r\sqrt{n-2}}{\sqrt{1-r^2}} = \dfrac{.24\sqrt{250-2}}{\sqrt{1-.24^2}} = 3.89$

Since the observed value of the test statistic falls in the rejection region for all occupations, H_0 is rejected. There is sufficient evidence to indicate the average earnings and height for those in all occupations are positively correlated at $\alpha = .01$.

We cannot conclude that a person taller than oneself will earn a higher salary. These correlation coefficients indicate that although there is a significant correlation, the correlations are all fairly weak. There is a trend, but there is also much variation that is not explained.

11.77   a.,b.   The scattergram is:

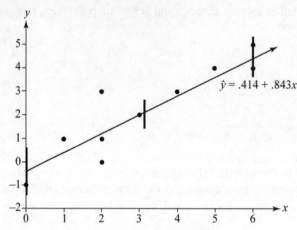

$\hat{y} = .414 + .843x$

c. $SSE = SS_{yy} - \hat{\beta}_1 SS_{xy} = 33.6 - .84318766(32.8) = 5.94344473$

$s^2 = \dfrac{SSE}{n-2} = \dfrac{5.94344473}{10-2} = .742930591$ $s = \sqrt{.742930591} = .8619$ $\bar{x} = \dfrac{31}{10} = 3.1$

The form of the confidence interval is $\hat{y} \pm t_{\alpha/2}\, s \sqrt{\dfrac{1}{n} + \dfrac{\left(x_p - \bar{x}\right)^2}{SS_{xx}}}$

For $x_p = 6$, $\hat{y} = -.414 + .843(6) = 4.64$

For confidence coefficient .95, $\alpha = .05$ and $\alpha/2 = .05/2 = .025$. From Table III, Appendix D, with df $= n - 2 = 10 - 2 = 8$, $t_{.025} = 2.306$. The confidence interval is:

$$4.64 \pm 2.306(.8619)\sqrt{\dfrac{1}{10} + \dfrac{(6 - 3.1)^2}{38.9}} \Rightarrow 4.64 \pm 1.12 \Rightarrow (3.52,\ 5.76)$$

d.   For $x_p = 3.2$, $\hat{y} = -.414 + .843(3.2) = 2.28$

The confidence interval is:

$$2.28 \pm 2.306(.8619)\sqrt{\dfrac{1}{10} + \dfrac{(3.2 - 3.1)^2}{38.9}} \Rightarrow 2.28 \pm .63 \Rightarrow (1.65,\ 2.91)$$

For $x_p = 0$, $\hat{y} = -.414 + .843(0) = -.41$

The confidence interval is:

$$-.41 \pm 2.306(.8619)\sqrt{\dfrac{1}{10} + \dfrac{(0 - 3.1)^2}{38.9}} \Rightarrow -.41 \pm 1.17 \Rightarrow (-1.58,\ .76)$$

e.   The width of the confidence interval for the mean value of y depends on the distance x_p is from $\bar{x}$. The width of the interval for $x_p = 3.2$ is the smallest because 3.2 is the closest to $\bar{x} = 3.1$. The width of the interval for $x_p = 0$ is the widest because 0 is the farthest from $\bar{x} = 3.1$.

11.79   a. $\hat{\beta}_1 = \dfrac{SS_{xy}}{SS_{xx}} = \dfrac{28}{32} = .875$ $\hat{\beta}_0 - \bar{y} - \hat{\beta}_1\bar{x} = 4 - .875(3) = 1.375$

The least squares line is $\hat{y} = 1.375 + .875x$.

b.   The least squares line is:

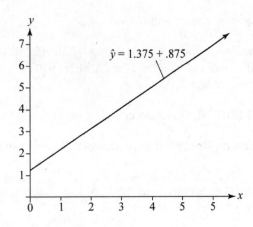

c. $SSE = SS_{yy} - \hat{\beta}_1 SS_{xy} = 26 - .875(28) = 1.5$

d. $s^2 = \dfrac{SSE}{n-2} = \dfrac{1.5}{10-2} = .1875$

e. $s = \sqrt{.1875} = .4330$

For $x_p = 2.5$, $\hat{y} = 1.375 + .875(2.5) = 3.5625$

For confidence coefficient .95, $\alpha = .05$ and $\alpha / 2 = .05 / 2 = .025$. From Table III, Appendix D, with $df = n - 2 = 10 - 2 = 8$, $t_{.025} = 2.306$. The confidence interval is:

$$\hat{y} \pm t_{\alpha/2}\, s\sqrt{\dfrac{1}{n} + \dfrac{\left(x_p - \bar{x}\right)^2}{SS_{xx}}} \Rightarrow 3.5625 \pm 2.306\left(.4330\right)\sqrt{\dfrac{1}{10} + \dfrac{(2.5-3)^2}{32}} \Rightarrow 3.5625 \pm .3279 \Rightarrow (3.2346,\ 3.8904)$$

f.   For $x_p = 4$, $\hat{y} = 1.375 + .875(4) = 4.875$

For confidence coefficient .95, $\alpha = .05$ and $\alpha / 2 = .05 / 2 = .025$. From Table III, Appendix D, with $df = n - 2 = 10 - 2 = 8$, $t_{.025} = 2.306$. The prediction interval is:

$$\hat{y} \pm t_{\alpha/2}\, s\sqrt{1 + \dfrac{1}{n} + \dfrac{\left(x_p - \bar{x}\right)^2}{SS_{xx}}} \Rightarrow 4.875 \pm 2.306\left(.4330\right)\sqrt{1 + \dfrac{1}{10} + \dfrac{(4-3)^2}{32}} \Rightarrow 4.875 \pm 1.062$$

$$\Rightarrow (3.813,\ 5.937)$$

11.81   a.   The 95% confidence interval for $E(y)$ is (4,783, 6,792). We are 95% confident that the true mean total catch is between 4,783 and 6,792 kilograms when the search function is 25.

b.   The 95% prediction interval for y is (2,643, 8,933). We are 95% confident that the true actual total catch is between 2,643 and 8,933 kilograms when the search function is 25.

11.83   Answers may vary. One possible answer is:

For run 1, the 90% confidence interval for $x = 220$ is (5.64898, 5.83848). We are 90% confident that the mean sweetness index of all orange juice samples will be between 5.64898 and 5.83848 parts per million when the pectin value is 220.

11.85   a.   Using MINITAB, the results are:

Regression Analysis: MillionaireBirths versus CEOBirths

```
The regression equation is
MillionaireBirths = 2.72 + 0.306 CEOBirths


Predictor      Coef   SE Coef      T       P
Constant     2.7227    0.8513   3.20   0.033
CEOBirths   0.30626   0.04592   6.67   0.003


S = 1.55683    R-Sq = 91.7%    R-Sq(adj) = 89.7%

Analysis of Variance

Source          DF      SS      MS       F      P
Regression       1  107.81  107.81   44.48  0.003
Residual Error   4    9.69    2.42
Total            5  117.50
```

Predicted Values for New Observations

```
New
Obs    Fit  SE Fit       95% CI            95% PI
  1  10.379   0.862  (7.987, 12.771)  (5.439, 15.320)
Values of Predictors for New Observations

New
Obs  CEOBirths
  1       25.0
```

The 95% prediction interval is (5.439, 15.320). We are 95% confident that the actual number of software millionaire birthdays in the decade will be between 5.439 and 15.320 when the number of CEO birthdays is 25.

b.   The sample mean number of CEO birthdays per decade is $\bar{x} = \dfrac{\sum x}{n} = \dfrac{74}{6} = 12.333$. The narrowest prediction interval is when the value of x used for the prediction is equal to $\bar{x}$. The further the value of x is from $\bar{x}$, the wider the prediction interval. Thus, the interval when $x = 11$ will be narrower than the interval when $x = 25$.

11.87   a.   From Exercises 11.26 and 11.58, $\hat{\beta}_0 = 5.221$, $\hat{\beta}_1 = -.114$, $SS_{xx} = 6,906.6087$, and $s = .8573$.

For $x_p = 15$, $\hat{y} = 5.2207 - .11402(15) = 3.5104$

For confidence coefficient .99, $\alpha = .01$ and $\alpha/2 = .01/2 = .005$. From Table III, Appendix D, with $df = n-2 = 23-2 = 21$, $t_{.005} = 2.831$. The confidence interval is:

$$\hat{y} \pm t_{\alpha/2}\, s\sqrt{\frac{1}{n} + \frac{(x_p - \bar{x})^2}{SS_{xx}}} \Rightarrow 3.5104 \pm 2.831(.8573)\sqrt{\frac{1}{23} + \frac{(15 - 22.8696)^2}{6,906.6087}} \Rightarrow 3.5104 \pm .5558$$
$$\Rightarrow (2.9546,\ 4.0662)$$

We are 99% confident that the mean mass of all spills will be between 2.9546 and 4.0662 when the elapsed time is 15 minutes.

b.   For $x_p = 15$, $\hat{y} = 5.2207 - .11402(15) = 3.5104$

For confidence coefficient .99, $\alpha = .01$ and $\alpha/2 = .01/2 = .005$. From Table III, Appendix D, with $df = n-2 = 23-2 = 21$, $t_{.005} = 2.831$. The prediction interval is:

$$\hat{y} \pm t_{\alpha/2}\, s\sqrt{1 + \frac{1}{n} + \frac{(x_p - \bar{x})^2}{SS_{xx}}} \Rightarrow 3.5104 \pm 2.831(.8573)\sqrt{1 + \frac{1}{23} + \frac{(15 - 22.8696)^2}{6,906.6087}} \Rightarrow 3.5104 \pm 2.4898$$
$$\Rightarrow (1.0206,\ 6.0002)$$

We are 99% confident that the actual mass of a spill will be between 1.0206 and 6.0002 when the elapsed time is 15 minutes.

c.   The prediction interval for the actual value is larger than the confidence interval for the mean. This will always be true. The prediction interval for the actual value contains 2 errors. First, we must locate the true mean of the distribution. Once this mean is located, the actual values of the variables can still vary around this mean. There is variance in locating the mean and then variance of the actual observations around the mean.

11.89   a.   Using MINITAB, the results of the regression analysis are:

Regression Analysis: QuitRate versus AvgWage

```
The regression equation is
QuitRate = 4.86 - 0.347 AvgWage

Predictor        Coef      SE Coef         T        P
Constant       4.8615       0.5201      9.35    0.000
AvgWage       -0.34655      0.05866     -5.91    0.000

S = 0.4862      R-Sq = 72.9%      R-Sq(adj) = 70.8%

Analysis of Variance

Source            DF          SS          MS         F        P
Regression         1      8.2507      8.2507     34.90    0.000
Residual Error    13      3.0733      0.2364
Total             14     11.3240
```

To determine if the average hourly wage rate contributes information to predict quit rates, we test:

$$H_0 : \beta_1 = 0$$
$$H_a : \beta_1 \neq 0$$

The test statistic is $t = \dfrac{\hat{\beta}_1 - 0}{s_{\hat{\beta}_1}} = -5.91$ and the p-value is $p = 0.000$.

Since the p-value is less than α ($p = 0.000 < .05$), H_0 is rejected. There is sufficient evidence to indicate that the average hourly wage rate contributes information to predict quit ratio at $\alpha = .05$.

Since the slope is negative ($\hat{\beta}_1 = -.34655$), the model suggests that x and y have a negative relationship. As the average hourly wage rate increases, the quit rate tends to decrease.

b.   Some preliminary calculations are:

$$\sum x = 129.05 \qquad \sum x^2 = 1,178.9601 \qquad \bar{x} = \frac{\sum x}{n} = \frac{129.05}{15} = 8.6033 \qquad \hat{y} = 4.8615 - 0.34655(9) = 1.743$$

$$SS_{xx} = \sum x^2 - \frac{\left(\sum x\right)^2}{n} = 1,178.9601 - \frac{(129.05)^2}{15} = 68.699933$$

For confidence level .95, $\alpha = .05$ and $\alpha / 2 = .05 / 2 = .025$. From Table III, Appendix D, with $df = n - 2 = 15 - 2 = 13$, $t_{.025} = 2.160$. The 95% prediction interval is:

$$\hat{y} \pm t_{\alpha/2} s \sqrt{1 + \frac{1}{n} + \frac{\left(x_p - \bar{x}\right)^2}{SS_{xx}}} \Rightarrow 1.743 \pm 2.160(.4862)\sqrt{1 + \frac{1}{15} + \frac{(9 - 8.6033)^2}{68.699933}}$$

$$\Rightarrow 1.743 \pm 1.086 \Rightarrow (0.657, \ 2.829)$$

We are 95% confident that the actual quit rate when the average hourly wage is $9.00 is between 0.657 and 2.829.

c.   The 95% confidence interval is:

$$\hat{y} \pm t_{\alpha/2} s \sqrt{\frac{1}{n} + \frac{\left(x_p - \bar{x}\right)^2}{SS_{xx}}} \Rightarrow 1.743 \pm 2.160(.4862)\sqrt{\frac{1}{15} + \frac{(9 - 8.6033)^2}{68.699933}}$$

$$\Rightarrow 1.743 \pm 0.276 \Rightarrow (1.467, \ 2.019)$$

We are 95% confident that the mean quit rate when the average hourly wage is $9.00 is between 1.467 and 2.019.

11.91   **Step 1**: The hypothesized model is $y = \beta_0 + \beta_1 x + \varepsilon$.

Step 2: The estimates of the unknown parameters are $\hat{\beta}_0 = -32.35$ and $\hat{\beta}_1 = 4.82$.

Since 0 is not in the range of observed values of the monthly price of naphtha, $\hat{\beta}_0$ has no practical interpretation. For each additional unit increase in the monthly price of naphtha, the mean monthly price of recycled colored plastic bottles is estimated to increase by 4.82.

Step 3:   We assume that the error terms are normally and independently distributed with a mean of 0 and constant variance. Not enough information was provided in the exercise to estimate the variance of the error terms.

Step 4:   To determine if there is a linear relationship between the monthly price of recycled colored plastic bottles and the monthly price of naphtha, we test:

$$H_0 : \beta_1 = 0$$
$$H_a : \beta_1 \neq 0$$

The test statistic is $t = 16.60$.

The p-value is $P(t > 16.60) + P(t < -16.60)$ where the t-distribution has df $= n - 2 = 120 - 2 = 118$. Using MINITAB, $P(t > 16.60) + P(t < -16.60) = .000 + .000 = .000$.

Since the p-value is so small, H_0 is rejected for any reasonable value of α. There is sufficient evidence to indicate a linear relationship exists between the monthly price of recycled colored plastic bottles and the monthly price of naphtha.

$r^2 = .69$.   69% of the total sample variation of monthly prices of recycled colored plastic bottles around their sample mean is explained by the linear relationship between the monthly price of recycled colored plastic bottles and the monthly price of naphtha.

$r = .83$.   The correlation indicates a fairly strong positive linear relationship. This confirms our conclusion that monthly naphtha prices and monthly prices of recycled colored plastic bottles are positively linearly related.

11.93   Using MINITAB, a scattergram of the data is:

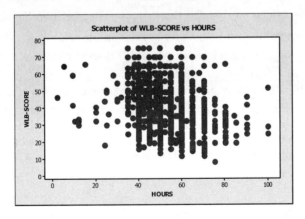

From the plot, it appears that there may be a negative linear relationship between WLB-scores and the average number of hours worked per week.

Using MINITAB, the results are:

Regression Analysis: WLB-SCORE versus HOURS

```
The regression equation is
WLB-SCORE = 62.5 - 0.347 HOURS


Predictor        Coef   SE Coef       T       P
Constant       62.499     1.414   44.22   0.000
HOURS        -0.34673   0.02761  -12.56   0.000


S = 12.2845   R-Sq = 7.0%   R-Sq(adj) = 7.0%


Analysis of Variance

Source            DF       SS      MS       F       P
Regression         1    23803   23803  157.73   0.000
Residual Error  2085   314647     151
Total           2086   338451
```

The fitted straight line model is: $\hat{y} = 62.499 - .34673x$. For each additional hour worked per week, the mean WLB-score is estimated to decrease by .34673.

To determine if the model is adequate, we test:

$$H_0 : \beta_1 = 0$$
$$H_a : \beta_1 \neq 0$$

From the printout, the test statistic is $t = -12.56$ and the p-value is $p = 0.000$. Since the p-value is so small, H_0 is rejected. There is sufficient evidence to indicate that there is a linear relationship between the average number of hours worked per week and the WLB-score for any reasonable value of α. Since $\hat{\beta}_1$ is negative, as the average number of hours worked per week increases, the WLB-score decreases.

From the printout, $r^2 = 7\%$ or .07. This means that only 7% of the sample variation of the WLB-scores around their means is explained by the linear relationship between the average number of hours worked per week and the WLB-scores. Even though the p-value for testing whether the model is adequate is extremely small, this model does not explain much of the variation. There is much variation in the WLB-scores that is not explained by the average number of hours worked per week.

11.95   a. $\hat{\beta}_1 = \dfrac{SS_{xy}}{SS_{xx}} = \dfrac{-88}{55} = -1.6$, $\hat{\beta}_0 = \bar{y} - \hat{\beta}_1\bar{x} = 35 - (-1.6)(1.3) = 37.08$

The least squares line is $\hat{y} = 37.08 - 1.6x$.

b.

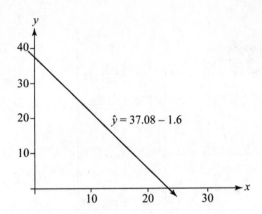

$$\hat{y} = 37.08 - 1.6$$

c. $$SSE = SS_{yy} - \hat{\beta_1}SS_{xy} = 198 - (-1.6)(-88) = 57.2$$

d. $$s^2 = \frac{SSE}{n-2} = \frac{57.2}{15-2} = 4.4$$

e. For confidence coefficient .90, $\alpha = .10$ and $\alpha/2 = .10/2 = .05$. From Table III, Appendix D, with df $= n - 2 = 15 - 2 = 13$, $t_{.05} = 1.771$. The 90% confidence interval for β_1 is:

$$\hat{y} \pm t_{\alpha/2}\frac{s}{\sqrt{SS_{xx}}} \Rightarrow -1.6 \pm 1.771\frac{\sqrt{4.4}}{\sqrt{55}} \Rightarrow -1.6 \pm .50 \Rightarrow (-2.10, -1.10)$$

We are 90% confident the change in the mean value of y for each unit change in x is between -2.10 and -1.10.

f. For $x_p = 15$, $\hat{y} = 37.08 - 1.6(15) = 13.08$

The 90% confidence interval is:

$$\hat{y} \pm t_{\alpha/2}\, s\sqrt{\frac{1}{n} + \frac{(x_p - \bar{x})^2}{SS_{xx}}} \Rightarrow 13.08 \pm 1.771(\sqrt{4.4})\sqrt{\frac{1}{15} + \frac{(15-1.3)^2}{55}} \Rightarrow 13.08 \pm 6.93 \Rightarrow (6.15,\ 20.01)$$

g. The 90% prediction interval is:

$$\hat{y} \pm t_{\alpha/2}\, s\sqrt{1 + \frac{1}{n} + \frac{(x_p - \bar{x})^2}{SS_{xx}}} \Rightarrow 13.08 \pm 1.771(\sqrt{4.4})\sqrt{1 + \frac{1}{15} + \frac{(15-1.3)^2}{55}} \Rightarrow 13.08 \pm 7.86$$
$$\Rightarrow (5.22,\ 20.94)$$

11.97 a. The value of r is .70. Since this number is somewhat close to 1, there is a moderate positive linear relationship between self-knowledge skill level and goal-setting ability.

b. Since the p-value is so small ($p = 0.001$), there is evidence to reject H_0. There is sufficient evidence to indicate a significant linear relationship between self-knowledge skill level and goal-setting ability for any value of $\alpha > .001$.

c. $r^2 = .70^2 = .49$. 49% of the total sample variability around the sample mean goal-setting ability is explained by the linear relationship between self-knowledge skill level and goal-setting ability.

11.99   a.   Using MINITAB, the scattergram is:

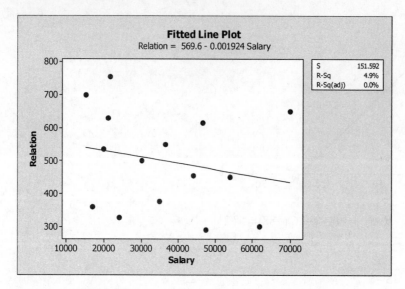

It appears as salary increases, the retaliation index decreases.

b. $\sum x = 544,100$ $\sum y = 7,497$ $\sum xy = 263,977,000$ $\sum x^2 = 23,876,290,000$

$\sum y^2 = 4,061,063$ $\bar{x} = \dfrac{\sum x}{n} = \dfrac{544,100}{15} = 36,273.333$ $\bar{y} = \dfrac{\sum y}{n} = \dfrac{7,497}{15} = 499.8$

$SS_{xy} = \sum xy - \dfrac{(\sum x)(\sum y)}{n} = 263,977,000 - \dfrac{(544,100)(7,497)}{15} = 263,977,000 - 271,941,180 = -7,964,180$

$SS_{xx} = \sum x^2 - \dfrac{(\sum x)^2}{n} = 23,876,290,000 - \dfrac{(544,100)^2}{15} = 23,876,290,000 - 19,736,320,670 = 4,139,969,330$

$\hat{\beta}_1 = \dfrac{SS_{xy}}{SS_{xx}} = \dfrac{-7,964,180}{4,139,969,330} = -.001923729 \approx -.00192$

$\hat{\beta}_0 = \bar{y} - \hat{\beta}_1 \bar{x} = 499.8 - (-.001923729)(36,273.333) = 499.8 + 69.78007144$
$$= 569.5800714 \approx 569.5801$$

The fitted regression line is $\hat{y} = 569.5801 - .00192x$.

c.   The least squares line supports the answer because the line has a negative slope.

d. $\hat{\beta}_0 = 569.58$ This has no meaning because $x = 0$ is not in the observed range.

e. $\hat{\beta}_1 = -.00192$ When the salary increases by \$1, the mean retaliation index is estimated to decrease by .00192. This is meaningful for the range of x from \$16,900 to \$70,000.

f. Some preliminary calculations are:

$$SS_{yy} = \sum y^2 - \frac{\left(\sum y\right)^2}{n} = 4,061,063 - \frac{7,497^2}{15} = 314,062.4$$

$$SSE = SS_{yy} - \hat{\beta}_1 SS_{xy} = 314,062.4 - (-.001923729)(-7,964,180) = 298,741.476$$

$$s^2 = MSE = \frac{SSE}{n-2} = \frac{298,741.476}{15-2} = 22,980.11354 \qquad s = \sqrt{22,980.11354} = 151.591931$$

$$s_{\hat{\beta}_1} = \frac{s}{\sqrt{SS_{xx}}} = \frac{151.591931}{\sqrt{4,139,969,330}} = .002356$$

To determine if the model is adequate, we test:

$$H_0 : \beta_1 = 0$$
$$H_a : \beta_1 \neq 0$$

The test statistic is $t = \dfrac{\hat{\beta}_1}{s_{\hat{\beta}_1}} = \dfrac{-.00192}{.002356} = -.82$.

The rejection region requires $\alpha/2 = .05/2 = .025$ in each tail of the t-distribution with df $= n-2 = 15-2 = 13$. From Table III, Appendix D, $t_{.025} = 2.160$. The rejection region is $t < -2.160$ or $t > 2.160$.

Since the observed value of the test statistic does not fall in the rejection region $(t = -.82 \not< -2.160)$, H_0 is not rejected. There is insufficient evidence to indicate that the model is adequate at $\alpha = .05$.

11.101 a. The straight-line model is $y = \beta_0 + \beta_1 x + \varepsilon$.

b. The least squares line is $\hat{y} = -2,298.3676 + 11,598.884x$.

c. Since 0 is not in the range of observed number of carats, $\hat{\beta}_0$ has no practical interpretation.

d. The 95% confidence interval is $(11,146.0846, \ 12,051.6834)$. We are 95% confident that for each additional carat, the mean asking price is estimated to increase from between \$11,146.0846 and \$12,051.6834.

e. The estimated standard deviation is $s = RMSE = 1,117.5642$. Most of the observed values of asking price will fall within approximately $2s$ or $2(1,117.5642) = 2,235.1284$ dollars of their respective predicted values.

f. To determine if a positive linear relationship exits between asking price and size, we test:

$$H_0 : \beta_1 = 0$$
$$H_a : \beta_1 > 0$$

g.   The *p*-value is $p < 0.0001$. Since the *p*-value is less than α ($p < .0001 < .05$), H_0 is rejected. There is sufficient evidence to indicate a positive linear relationship exists between asking price and size at $\alpha = .05$.

h. $r^2 = .8925$. 89.25% of the total sample variation in the asking prices around their sample mean is explained by the linear relationship between size and asking price.

i. $r = .9447$. Since this value is very close to 1, it indicates that there is a strong, positive linear relationship between size and asking price.

j.   The prediction interval is $(1,297.6366, \ 5,704.5322)$. We are 95% confident that the true asking price will fall between \$1,297.6366 and \$5,704.5322 when the size is .5 carats.

k.   The confidence interval is $(3,362.4670, \ 3,639.7018)$. We are 95% confident that the true mean asking price will fall between \$3,362.4670 and \$3,639.7018 when the size is .5 carats.

11.103   a.   Using MINITAB, the scattergram is:

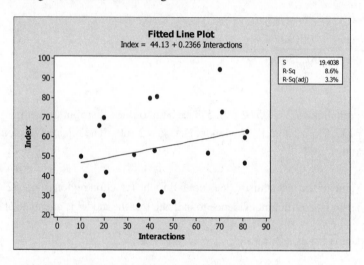

b.   Using MINITAB, the regression analysis is:

Regression Analysis: Index versus Interactions

```
The regression equation is
Index = 44.1 + 0.237 Interactions

Predictor        Coef       SE Coef          T          P
Constant       44.130         9.362       4.71      0.000
Interact       0.2366        0.1865       1.27      0.222

S = 19.40        R-Sq = 8.6%        R-Sq(adj) = 3.3%

Analysis of Variance

Source            DF            SS           MS          F          P
Regression         1         606.0        606.0       1.61      0.222
Residual Error    17        6400.6        376.5
Total             18        7006.6
```

From the printout, the least squares line is $\hat{y} = 44.13 + .2366x$.

c.   From the printout, $s = 19.40$.

The standard deviation s represents the spread of the manager success index about the least squares line. Approximately 95% of the manager success indexes should lie within $2s = 2(19.40) = 38.8$ units of the least squares line.

d.   Refer to the scattergram in part **a**. The number of interactions with outsiders might contribute some information in the prediction of managerial success, but it does not look like a very strong relationship.

e.   To determine if the number of interactions contributes information for the prediction of managerial success, we test:

$$H_0 : \beta_1 = 0$$
$$H_a : \beta_1 \neq 0$$

The test statistic is $t = \dfrac{\hat{\beta}_1 - 0}{s_{\hat{\beta}_1}} = 1.27$ .and the p-value is $p = .222$.

Since the p-value is not less than α ($p = .222 \not< .05$), H_0 is not rejected. There is insufficient evidence to indicate the number of interactions contributes information for the prediction of managerial success at $\alpha = .05$.

f.   For confidence coefficient .95, $\alpha = .05$ and $\alpha / 2 = .05 / 2 = .025$. From Table III, Appendix D, with df $= 17$, $t_{.025} = 2.110$. The 95% confidence interval is:

$$\hat{\beta}_1 \pm t_{.025} s_{\hat{\beta}_1} \Rightarrow .2366 \pm 2.110(.1865) \Rightarrow .2366 \pm .3935 \Rightarrow (-.1569,\ .6301)$$

We are 95% confident the change in the mean manager success index for each additional interaction with outsiders is between $-.1569$ and $.6301$.

g.   For confidence coefficient .90, $\alpha = .10$ and $\alpha / 2 = .10/2 = .05$. From Table III, Appendix D, with df $= n - 2 = 19 - 2 = 17$, $t_{.05} = 1.740$.

When $x_p = 55$, $\hat{y} = 44.13 + .2366(55) = 57.143$

The prediction interval is:

$$\hat{y} \pm t_{\alpha/2} s \sqrt{1 + \frac{1}{n} + \frac{(x_p - \bar{x})^2}{SS_{xx}}} \Rightarrow 57.143 \pm 1.74(19.40)\sqrt{1 + \frac{1}{19} + \frac{(55 - 44.1579)^2}{10,824.5263}}$$

$$\Rightarrow 57.143 \pm 34.811 \Rightarrow (22.332,\ 91.954)$$

h.   The number of interactions with outsiders in the study went from 10 to 82. The value 110 is not within this interval. We do not know if the relationship between x and y is the same outside the observed range. Also, the farther x_p lies from $\bar{x}$ the larger will be the error of prediction. The prediction interval for a particular value of y will be very wide when $x_p = 110$.

i.   The prediction interval for a manager's success index will be narrowest when the number of contacts with people outside her work unit is $\bar{x} = 44.1579\ (44)$.

11.105 a.   Using MINITAB, the scattergram is:

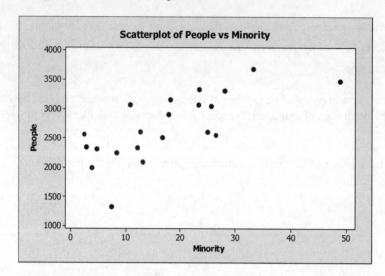

It appears from the plot that as the percentage of the population that is minority increases, the number of people per branch bank tends to increase.

b.   The value of β_1 will be positive. As one variable increases, the other tends to increase.

c. $\sum x = 363.8 \qquad \sum y = 56,560 \qquad \sum xy = 1,075,763 \qquad \sum x^2 = 9,020.86 \qquad \sum y^2 = 158,763,894$

$$\bar{x} = \frac{\sum x}{n} = \frac{363.8}{21} = 17.32380952 \qquad \bar{y} = \frac{\sum x}{n} = \frac{56,560}{21} = 2,693.33333$$

$$SS_{xy} = \sum xy - \frac{\left(\sum x\right)\left(\sum y\right)}{n} = 1,075,763 - \frac{363.8(56,560)}{21} = 1,075,763 - 979,834.6667$$
$$= 95,928.23333$$

$$SS_{xx} = \sum x^2 - \frac{\left(\sum x\right)^2}{n} = 9,020.86 - \frac{363.8^2}{21} = 9,020.86 - 6,302.401905 = 2,718.458095$$

$$\hat{\beta}_1 = \frac{SS_{xy}}{SS_{xx}} = \frac{95,928.23333}{2,718.458095} = 35.28773664 \approx 35.288$$

$$SS_{yy} = \sum y^2 - \frac{\left(\sum y\right)^2}{n} = 158,863,894 - \frac{56,560^2}{21} = 158,763,894 - 152,334,933.3 = 6,428,960.667$$

$$SSE = SS_{yy} - \hat{\beta}_1 SS_{xy} = 6,428,960.667 - 35.28773664\left(95,928.23333\right) = 3,043,870.433$$

$$s^2 = \frac{SSE}{n-2} = \frac{3,043,870.433}{21-2} = 160,203.707 \qquad s = \sqrt{s^2} = \sqrt{160,203.707} = 400.25455$$

To determine if the data support the charge made against the New Jersey banking community, we test:

$$H_0 : \beta_1 = 0$$
$$H_a : \beta_1 \neq 0$$

The test statistic is $t = \dfrac{\hat{\beta}_1 - 0}{s_{\hat{\beta}_1}} = \dfrac{35.288 - 0}{\dfrac{400.25455}{\sqrt{2{,}718.458095}}} = 4.60$

The rejection region requires $\alpha = .01$ in the upper tail of the t-distribution with $df = n - 2 = 21 - 2 = 19$. From Table III, Appendix D, $t_{.01} = 2.539$. The rejection region is $t > 2.539$.

Since the observed value of the test statistic falls in the rejection region $(t = 4.60 > 2.539)$, H_0 is rejected. There is sufficient evidence to support the charge made against the New Jersey banking community at $\alpha = .01$.

11.107 a.   Using MINITAB, the scattergram of the data is:

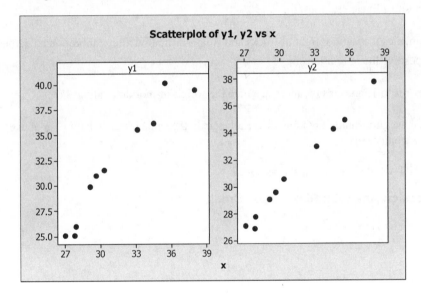

   b.   It appears that the weigh-in-motion reading after calibration adjustment is more highly correlated with the static weight of trucks than prior to calibration adjustment. The scattergram is closer to a straight line.

   c.   Some preliminary calculations are:

$$\sum x = 312.8 \qquad \sum x^2 = 9{,}911.42 \qquad \sum xy_1 = 10{,}201.41 \qquad \sum xy_2 = 9{,}859.84$$

$$\sum y_1 = 320.2 \qquad \sum y_1^2 = 10{,}543.68 \qquad \sum y_2 = 311.2 \qquad \sum y_2^2 = 9{,}809.52$$

$$SS_{xy_1} = \sum xy_1 - \frac{\sum x \sum y_1}{n} = 10{,}201.41 - \frac{312.8(320.2)}{10} = 185.554$$

$$SS_{xx} = \sum x^2 - \frac{\left(\sum x\right)^2}{n} = 9{,}911.42 - \frac{312.8^2}{10} = 127.036$$

$$SS_{y_1 y_1} = \sum y_1^2 - \frac{\left(\sum y_1\right)^2}{n} = 10{,}543.68 - \frac{320.2^2}{10} = 290.876$$

$$SS_{xy_2} = \sum xy_2 - \frac{\sum x \sum y_2}{n} = 9{,}859.84 - \frac{312.8(311.2)}{10} = 125.504$$

$$SS_{y_2 y_2} = \sum y_2^2 - \frac{\left(\sum y_2\right)^2}{n} = 9{,}809.52 - \frac{311.2^2}{10} = 124.976$$

$$r_1 = \frac{SS_{xy_1}}{\sqrt{SS_{xx}SS_{y_1 y_1}}} = \frac{185.554}{\sqrt{127.036(290.876)}} = .965 \qquad r_2 = \frac{SS_{xy_2}}{\sqrt{SS_{xx}SS_{y_2 y_2}}} = \frac{125.504}{\sqrt{127.036(124.976)}} = .996$$

$r_1 = .965$ implies the static weight of trucks and weigh-in-motion prior to calibration adjustment have a strong positive linear relationship.

$r_2 = .996$ implies the static weight of trucks and weigh-in-motion after calibration adjustment have a stronger positive linear relationship.

The closer r is to 1 indicates the more accurate the weigh-in-motion readings are.

d.   Yes. If the weigh-in-motion readings were all exactly the same distance below (or above) the actual readings, r would be 1.

11.109 a.   Using MINITAB, the regression analysis is:

Regression Analysis: Risk versus Credit

```
The regression equation is
Risk = 57.8 - 0.400 Credit

Predictor        Coef      SE Coef         T        P
Constant       57.755        6.128      9.43    0.000
Credit        -0.39961      0.09152     -4.37    0.000

S = 12.6777    R-Sq = 33.4%     R-Sq(adj) = 31.7%

Analysis of Variance

Source           DF          SS         MS        F        P
Regression        1      3064.4     3064.4    19.07    0.000
Residual Error   38      6107.5      160.7
Total            39      9171.9
```

To determine if country credit risk contributes information for the prediction of market volatility, we test:

$$H_0 : \beta_1 = 0$$
$$H_a : \beta_1 \neq 0$$

The test statistic is $t = \dfrac{\hat{\beta}_1 - 0}{s_{\hat{\beta}_1}} = -4.37$ and the p-value is $p = 0.000$.

Since the p-value is so small, there is strong evidence to indicate that country credit risk contributes information for the prediction of market volatility at $\alpha > .000$.

b. Using MINITAB, a scattergram of the data with the fitted regression line is:

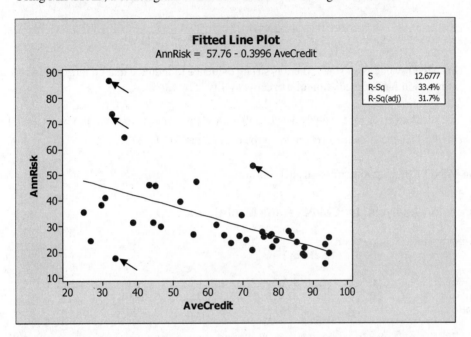

From the plot, there appears to be several outliers. Observations 1, 19, 34, and 36 have arrows pointing at them.

c. Eliminating those four data points and using MINITAB, the regression analysis is as follows:

Regression Analysis: Risk versus Credit

```
The regression equation is
Risk = 50.3 - 0.316 Credit
```

Predictor	Coef	Stdev	t-ratio	p
Constant	50.338	4.052	12.42	0.000
Credit	-0.31599	0.05883	-5.37	0.000

```
s = 7.46401      R-sq = 45.9%     R-sq(adj) = 44.3%
```

```
Analysis of Variance
```

SOURCE	DF	SS	MS	F	p
Regression	1	1607.4	1607.4	28.85	0.000
Error	34	1894.2	55.7		
Total	35	3501.6			

After eliminating the four data points, the regression analysis is very similar. The fitted regression line is: $\hat{y} = 50.338 - .31599x$

To determine if country credit risk contributes information for the prediction of market volatility, we test:

$$H_0 : \beta_1 = 0$$
$$H_a : \beta_1 \neq 0$$

The test statistic is $t = \dfrac{\hat{\beta}_1 - 0}{s_{\hat{\beta}_1}} = -5.37$ and the *p*-value is $p = 0.000$.

Since the *p*-value is so small, there is strong evidence to indicate that country credit risk contributes information for the prediction of market volatility at $\alpha > .000$.

The standard error for the analysis when the four data points have been removed ($s = 7.464$) is much smaller than the standard error with all the data points ($s = 12.6777$).

11.111   Using MINITAB, the two regression analyses are:

Regression Analysis: IndCosts versus MachHours

```
The regression equation is
Ind.Costs = 301 + 10.3 MachHours


Predictor      Coef      StDev        T        P
Constant      301.0      229.8      1.31    0.219
MachHour     10.312      3.124      3.30    0.008


S = 170.5      R-Sq = 52.1%      R-Sq(adj) = 47.4%


Analysis of Variance


Source          DF       SS         MS        F       P
Regression       1     316874     316874    10.90   0.008
Residual Error  10     290824      29082
Total           11     607698
```

Regression Analysis: IndCosts versus DirectHour

```
The regression equation is
Ind.Costs = 745 + 7.72 DirectHour


Predictor      Coef      StDev        T        P
Constant      744.7      217.6      3.42    0.007
DirectHo      7.716      5.396      1.43    0.183


S = 224.6      R-Sq = 17.0%      R-Sq(adj) = 8.7%


Analysis of Variance


Source          DF       SS         MS        F       P
Regression       1     103187     103187     2.05   0.183
Residual Error  10     504511      50451
Total           11     607698
```

From these two cost functions, the model containing Machine-Hours should be used to predict Indirect Manufacturing Labor Costs. There is a significant linear relationship between Indirect Manufacturing Labor Costs and Machine-Hours $(t = 3.30,\ p = 0.008)$. There is not a significant linear relationship between Indirect Manufacturing Labor Costs and Direct Manufacturing Labor-Hours $(t = 1.43,\ p = 0.183)$. The r^2 for the first model is .521 while the r^2 for the second model is .170. In addition, the standard deviation for the first model is 170.5 while the standard deviation for the second model is 224.6. All of these lead to the better model as the model containing Machine-Hours as the independent variable.

Chapter 12
Multiple Regression and Model Building

12.1   a. $E(y) = \beta_0 + \beta_1 x_1 + \beta_2 x_2$

        b. $E(y) = \beta_0 + \beta_1 x_1 + \beta_2 x_2 + \beta_3 x_3 + \beta_4 x_4$

        c. $E(y) = \beta_0 + \beta_1 x_1 + \beta_2 x_2 + \beta_3 x_3 + \beta_4 x_4 + \beta_5 x_5$

12.3   a.   We are given $\hat{\beta}_2 = 2.7$, $s_{\hat{\beta}_1} = 1.86$, and $n = 30$.

$$H_0 : \beta_2 = 0$$
$$H_a : \beta_2 \neq 0$$

The test statistic is $t = \dfrac{\hat{\beta}_2 - 0}{s_{\hat{\beta}_2}} = \dfrac{2.7}{1.86} = 1.45$

The rejection region requires $\alpha / 2 = .05 / 2 = .025$ in each tail of the t distribution with $df = n - (k+1) = 30 - (3+1) = 26$. From Table III, Appendix D, $t_{.025} = 2.056$. The rejection region is $t < -2.056$ or $t > 2.056$.

Since the observed value of the test statistic does not fall in the rejection region ($t = 1.45 \not> 2.056$), H_0 is not rejected. There is insufficient evidence to indicate $\beta_2 \neq 0$ at $\alpha = .05$.

        b.   We are given $\hat{\beta}_3 = .93$, $s_{\hat{\beta}_3} = .29$, and $n = 30$.

$$H_0 : \beta_3 = 0$$
$$H_a : \beta_3 \neq 0$$

The test statistic is $t = \dfrac{\hat{\beta}_3 - 0}{s_{\hat{\beta}_3}} = \dfrac{.93}{.29} = 3.21$

The rejection region is the same as part **a**, $t < -2.056$ or $t > 2.056$.

Since the observed value of the test statistic falls in the rejection region ($t = 3.21 > 2.056$), H_0 is rejected. There is sufficient evidence to indicate $\beta_3 \neq 0$ at $\alpha = .05$.

        c. $\hat{\beta}_3$ has a smaller estimated standard error than $\hat{\beta}_2$. Therefore, the test statistic is larger for $\hat{\beta}_3$ even though $\hat{\beta}_3$ is smaller than $\hat{\beta}_2$.

12.5   The number of degrees of freedom available for estimating σ^2 is $n - (k+1)$ where k is the number of independent variables in the regression model. Each additional independent variable placed in the model causes a corresponding decrease in the degrees of freedom.

12.7 a. Yes. Since $R^2 = .92$ is close to 1, this indicates the model provides a good fit. Without knowledge of the units of the dependent variable, the value of SSE cannot be used to determine how well the model fits.

b. $H_0 : \beta_1 = \beta_2 = \cdots = \beta_5 = 0$

H_a : At least one $\beta_i \neq 0$

The test statistic is $F = \dfrac{R^2 / k}{(1 - R^2) / [n - (k + 1)]} = \dfrac{.92 / 5}{(1 - .92) / [30 - (5 + 1)]} = 55.2$

The rejection region requires $\alpha = .05$ in the upper tail of the F distribution with $v_1 = k = 5$ and $v_2 = n - (k + 1) = 30 - (5 + 1) = 24$. From Table VI, Appendix D, $F_{.05} = 2.62$. The rejection region is $F > 2.62$.

Since the observed value of the test statistic falls in the rejection region $(F = 55.2 > 2.62)$, H_0 is rejected. There is sufficient evidence to indicate the model is useful in predicting y at $\alpha = .05$.

12.9 a. For $x_1 = 10$, $x_2 = 0$, and $x_3 = 1$, $\hat{y} = 52,484 + 2,941(10) + 16,880(0) + 11,108(1) = \$93,002$.

b. For $x_1 = 10$, $x_2 = 1$, and $x_3 = 0$, $\hat{y} = 52,484 + 2,941(10) + 16,880(1) + 11,108(0) = \$98,774$

c. $R_{adj}^2 = .32$. 32% of the sample variation in salary about its mean is explained by the model containing years of experience, PhD status, and manager status, adjusted for the sample size and the number of parameters in the model.

d. We are 95% confident that for each additional year of experience, the mean salary will increase anywhere from $2,700 to $3,200, holding PhD status and manager status constant.

e. We are 95% confident that those who hold a PhD, the mean salary will be anywhere from $11,500 to $22,300 higher than those who do not hold a PhD, holding years of experience and manager status constant.

f. We are 95% confident that those who are managers, the mean salary will be anywhere from $7,600 to $14,600 higher than those who are not managers, holding years of experience and PhD status constant.

12.11 a. To determine if the model is useful, we test:

$H_0 : \beta_1 = \beta_2 = \beta_3 = \beta_4 = 0$

H_a : At least one $\beta_i \neq 0$

From the problem, the test statistic is $F = 4.74$ and the p-value is $p < .01$. Since the p-value is less than α $(p < .01 < .05)$, H_0 is rejected. There is sufficient evidence to indicate the model is useful for predicting accountant's Mach scores at $\alpha = .05$.

b. $R^2 = .13$. 13% of the total sample variation of the accountant's Mach scores around their means is explained by the model containing age, gender, education, and income.

c.   To determine if income is a useful predictor of Mach score, we test:

$$H_0 : \beta_4 = 0$$
$$H_a : \beta_4 \neq 0$$

From the printout, $t = 0.52$ and the p-value is $p > .10$. Since the p-value is not less than α $(p > .10 \not< .05)$, H_0 is not rejected. There is insufficient evidence to indicate that income is a useful predictor of Mach score adjusted for age, gender, and education at $\alpha = .05$.

12.13   a.   The least squares prediction equation is: $\hat{y} = 1.81231 + 0.10875 x_1 + 0.00017 x_2$

b. $\hat{\beta}_o = 1.81231$. Since $x_1 = 0$ and $x_2 = 0$ are not in the observed range, $\hat{\beta}_o$ has no meaning.

$\hat{\beta}_1 = 0.10875$. For each additional mile of roadway length, the mean number of crashes per three years is estimated to increase by .10875 when average annual daily traffic is held constant.

$\hat{\beta}_2 = 0.00017$. For each additional unit increase in average annual daily traffic, the mean number of crashes per three years is estimated to increase by .00017 when miles of roadway length is held constant.

c.   For confidence coefficient $.99, \alpha = .01$ and $\alpha / 2 = .01 / 2 = .005$. From Table III, Appendix D, with $df = n - (k + 1) = 100 - (2 + 1) = 97$, $t_{.005} = 2.63$. The 99% confidence interval is:

$$\hat{\beta}_1 \pm t_{.005} s_{\hat{\beta}_1} \Rightarrow 0.10875 \pm 2.63(0.03166) \Rightarrow 0.10875 \pm 0.08327 \Rightarrow (0.02548, \ 0.19202)$$

We are 99% confident that the increase in the mean number of crashes per three years will be between 0.02548 and 0.19202 for each additional mile of roadway length, holding average annual daily traffic constant.

d.   The 99% confidence interval is:

$$\hat{\beta}_2 \pm t_{.005} s_{\hat{\beta}_2} \Rightarrow 0.00017 \pm 2.63(0.00003) \Rightarrow 0.00017 \pm 0.00008 \Rightarrow (0.00009, \ 0.00025)$$

We are 99% confident that the increase in the mean number of crashes per three years will be between 0.00009 and 0.00025 for each additional unit increase in average annual daily traffic, holding mile of roadway length constant.

e.   The least squares prediction equation is: $\hat{y} = 1.20785 + 0.06343 x_1 + 0.00056 x_2$

$\hat{\beta}_o = 1.20785$. Since $x_1 = 0$ and $x_2 = 0$ are not in the observed range, $\hat{\beta}_o$ has no meaning.

$\hat{\beta}_1 = 0.06343$. For each additional mile of roadway length, the mean number of crashes per three years is estimated to increase by 0.06343 when average annual daily traffic is held constant.

$\hat{\beta}_2 = 0.00056$. For each additional unit increase in average annual daily traffic, the mean number of crashes per three years is estimated to increase by 0.00056 when miles of roadway length is held constant.

The 99% confidence interval is:

$$\hat{\beta}_1 \pm t_{.005}s_{\hat{\beta}_1} \Rightarrow 0.06343 \pm 2.63(0.01809) \Rightarrow 0.06343 \pm 0.04758 \Rightarrow (0.01585, \ 0.11101)$$

We are 99% confident that the increase in the mean number of crashes per three years will be between 0.01585 and 0.11101 for each additional mile of roadway length, holding average annual daily traffic constant.

The 99% confidence interval is:

$$\hat{\beta}_2 \pm t_{.005}s_{\hat{\beta}_2} \Rightarrow 0.00056 \pm 2.63(0.00012) \Rightarrow 0.00056 \pm 0.00032 \Rightarrow (0.00024, \ 0.00088)$$

We are 99% confident that the increase in the mean number of crashes per three years will be between 0.00024 and 0.00088 for each additional unit increase in average annual daily traffic, holding mile of roadway length constant.

12.15 a. The first order model would be $E(y) = \beta_0 + \beta_1 x_1 + \beta_2 x_2 + \beta_3 x_3 + \beta_4 x_4$.

b. Since the p-value is less than α $(p = .005 < .01)$, H_0 is rejected. There is sufficient evidence to indicate that there is a negative linear relationship between change from routine and the number of years played golf, holding number of rounds of golf per year, total number of golf vacations, and average golf score constant.

c. The statement would be correct if the independent variables are not correlated. However, if the independent variables are correlated, then this interpretation would not necessarily hold.

d. To determine if the overall first-order regression model is adequate, we test:

$$H_0 : \beta_1 = \beta_2 = \beta_3 = \beta_4 = 0$$

e. For all dependent variables, the rejection region requires $\alpha = .01$ in the upper tail of the F-distribution with $v_1 = k = 4$ and $v_2 = n - (k+1) = 393 - (4+1) = 388$. From Table VIII, Appendix D, $F_{.01} \approx 3.32$. The rejection region is $F > 3.32$. Using MINITAB, $F_{.01,4,388} = 3.67$. The true rejection region is $F > 3.67$.

f. For **Thrill**: Since the observed value of the test statistic falls in the rejection region $(F = 5.56 > 3.67)$, H_0 is rejected. There is sufficient evidence to indicate at least one of the 4 independent variables is linearly related to Thrill at $\alpha = .01$.

For **Change from Routine**: Since the observed value of the test statistic does not fall in the rejection region $(F = 3.02 \not> 3.67)$, H_0 is not rejected. There is insufficient evidence to indicate at least one of the 4 independent variables is linearly related to Change from Routine at $\alpha = .01$.

For **Surprise**: Since the observed value of the test statistic does not fall in the rejection region $(F = 3.33 \not> 3.67)$, H_0 is not rejected. There is insufficient evidence to indicate at least one of the 4 independent variables is linearly related to Surprise at $\alpha = .01$.

g. For **Thrill**: Since the p-value is less than α $(p < .001 < .01)$, H_0 is rejected. There is sufficient evidence to indicate that at least one of the independent variables is linearly related to Thrill at $\alpha = .01$.

For **Change from Routine**: Since the p-value is not less than α $(p = .018 \not< .01)$, H_0 is not rejected. There is insufficient evidence to indicate that at least one of the independent variables is linearly related to Change from Routine at $\alpha = .01$.

For **Surprise**: Since the p-value is not less than α $(p = .011 \not< .01)$, H_0 is not rejected. There is insufficient evidence to indicate that at least one of the independent variables is linearly related to Surprise at $\alpha = .01$.

h.   For **Thrill**: $R^2 = .055$. 5.5% of the total variability around the mean thrill values can be explained by the model containing the 4 independent variables: x_1 = number of rounds of golf per year, x_2 = total number of golf vacations taken, x_3 = number of years played golf, and x_4 = average golf score.

For **Change from Routine**: $R^2 = .030$. 3.0% of the total variability around the mean change from routine values can be explained by the model containing the 4 independent variables: x_1 = number of rounds of golf per year, x_2 = total number of golf vacations taken, x_3 = number of years played golf, and x_4 = average golf score.

For **Surprise**: $R^2 = .023$. 2.3% of the total variability around the mean surprise values can be explained by the model containing the 4 independent variables: x_1 = number of rounds of golf per year, x_2 = total number of golf vacations taken, x_3 = number of years played golf, and x_4 = average golf score.

12.17   a.   Using MINITAB, the results of fitting the first-order model are:

Regression Analysis: DESIRE versus GENDER, SELFESTM, BODYSAT, IMPREAL

```
The regression equation is
DESIRE = 14.0 - 2.19 GENDER - 0.0479 SELFESTM - 0.322 BODYSAT + 0.493 IMPREAL

Predictor       Coef   SE Coef       T       P
Constant     14.0107    0.7753   18.07   0.000
GENDER       -2.1865    0.6766   -3.23   0.001
SELFESTM    -0.04794   0.03669   -1.31   0.193
BODYSAT      -0.3223    0.1435   -2.25   0.026
IMPREAL       0.4931    0.1274    3.87   0.000

S = 2.25087   R-Sq = 49.8%   R-Sq(adj) = 48.5%

Analysis of Variance

Source           DF       SS      MS       F       P
Regression        4   827.83  206.96   40.85   0.000
Residual Error  165   835.95    5.07
Total           169  1663.79


Source      DF   Seq SS
GENDER       1   674.64
SELFESTM     1    57.66
BODYSAT      1    19.62
IMPREAL      1    75.91
```

The least squares prediction equation is $\hat{y} = 14.0107 - 2.1865x_1 - .04794x_2 - .3223x_3 + .4931x_4$

b. $\hat{\beta}_0 = 14.0107$.   This has no meaning other than the y-intercept.

$\hat{\beta}_1 = -2.1865$.   The mean value of desire to have cosmetic surgery is estimated to be 2.1865 units lower for males than females, holding all other variables constant.

$\hat{\beta}_2 = -0.04794$.   For each unit increase in self-esteem, the mean value of desire to have cosmetic surgery is estimated to decrease by 0.04794 units, holding all other variables constant.

$\hat{\beta}_3 = -0.3223$.   For each unit increase in body satisfaction, then mean value of desire to have cosmetic surgery is estimated to decrease by .3223 units, holding all other variables constant.

$\hat{\beta}_4 = 0.4931$.   For each unit increase in impression of reality TV, the mean value of desire to have cosmetic surgery is estimated to increase by 0.4931 units, holding all other variables constant.

c.   To determine if the overall model is useful for predicting desire to have cosmetic surgery, we test:

$$H_0 : \beta_1 = \beta_2 = \beta_3 = \beta_4 = 0$$
$$H_a : \text{At least } 1 \beta_i \neq 0$$

From the printout, the test statistic is $F = 40.85$ and the p-value is $p = 0.000$.

Since the p-value is less than α $(p = 0.000 < .01)$, H_0 is rejected. There is sufficient evidence to indicate the overall model is useful for predicting desire to have cosmetic surgery at $\alpha = .01$.

d. R_a^2 is the preferred measure of model fit. From the printout, $R_a^2 = .485$. This indicates that 48.5% of the total sample variation in desire values is explained by the model containing gender, self-esteem, body satisfaction and impression of reality TV, adjusting for the sample size and the number of variables in the model.

e.   To determine if the desire to have cosmetic surgery decreases linearly as level of body satisfaction increases, we test:

$$H_0 : \beta_3 = 0$$
$$H_a : \beta_3 < 0$$

From the printout, the test statistic is $t = -2.25$ and the p-value is $p = .026 / 2 = .013$.

Since the p-value is less than α $(p = 0.013 < .05)$, H_0 is rejected. There is sufficient evidence to indicate the desire to have cosmetic surgery decreases linearly as level of body satisfaction increases, holding all other variables constant at $\alpha = .05$.

f.   For confidence coefficient .95, $\alpha = .05$ and $\alpha / 2 = .05 / 2 = .025$. From Table III, Appendix D, with $df = n - (k + 1) = 170 - (4 + 1) = 165$, $t_{.025} \approx 1.98$. The 95% confidence interval is

$$\hat{\beta}_4 \pm t_{.025} s_{\hat{\beta}_4} \Rightarrow .4931 \pm 1.98(.1274) \Rightarrow .4931 \pm .2523 \Rightarrow (.2408, .7454)$$

We are 95% confident that the increase in mean desire for cosmetic surgery is between .2408 and .7454 for each unit increase in impression of reality TV, holding all other variables constant.

12.19   a.   The 1st-order model is $E(y) = \beta_0 + \beta_1 x_1 + \beta_2 x_2 + \beta_3 x_3 + \beta_4 x_4 + \beta_5 x_5$.

b.   Using MINITAB, the results are:

Regression Analysis: HEATRATE versus RPM, INLET-TEMP, ...

```
The regression equation is
HEATRATE = 13614 + 0.0888 RPM - 9.20 INLET-TEMP + 14.4 EXH-TEMP
              + 0.4 CPRATIO - 0.848 AIRFLOW


Predictor       Coef    SE Coef       T       P
Constant     13614.5      870.0   15.65   0.000
RPM          0.08879    0.01391    6.38   0.000
INLET-TEMP    -9.201      1.499   -6.14   0.000
EXH-TEMP      14.394      3.461    4.16   0.000
CPRATIO         0.35      29.56    0.01   0.991
AIRFLOW      -0.8480     0.4421   -1.92   0.060


S = 458.828   R-Sq = 92.4%   R-Sq(adj) = 91.7%

Analysis of Variance

Source           DF          SS         MS       F       P
Regression        5   155055273   31011055  147.30   0.000
Residual Error   61    12841935     210524
Total            66   167897208

Source       DF     Seq SS
RPM           1  119598530
INLET-TEMP    1   26893467
EXH-TEMP      1    7784225
CPRATIO       1       4623
AIRFLOW       1     774427
```

The least squares prediction equation is:

$$\hat{y} = 13,614.5 + 0.08879 x_1 - 9.201 x_2 + 14.394 x_3 + 0.35 x_4 - 0.848 x_5$$

c. $\hat{\beta}_o = 13,614.5$. Since 0 is not within the range of all the independent variables, this value has no meaning.

$\hat{\beta}_1 = 0.08879$. For each unit increase in RPM, the mean heat rate is estimated to increase by .08879, holding all the other 4 variables constant.

$\hat{\beta}_2 = -9.201$. For each unit increase in inlet temperature, the mean heat rate is estimated to decrease by 9.201, holding all the other 4 variables constant.

$\hat{\beta}_3 = 14.394$. For each unit increase in exhaust temperature, the mean heat rate is estimated to increase by 14.394, holding all the other 4 variables constant.

$\hat{\beta}_4 = 0.35$. For each unit increase in cycle pressure ratio, the mean heat rate is estimated to increase by 0.35, holding all the other 4 variables constant.

$\hat{\beta}_5 = -0.8480$. For each unit increase in air flow rate, the mean heat rate is estimated to decrease by .848, holding all the other 4 variables constant.

d. From the printout, $s = 458.828$. We would expect to see most of the heat rate values within $2s = 2(458.828) = 917.656$ units of the least squares line.

e. To determine if at least one of the variables is useful in predicting the heat rate values, we test:

$$H_0 : \beta_1 = \beta_2 = \beta_3 = \beta_4 = \beta_5 = 0$$
$$H_a : \text{At least one } \beta_i \neq 0$$

The test statistic is $F = 147.30$ and the p-value is $p = .000$. Since the p-value is less than α $(p = .000 < .01)$, H_0 is rejected. There is sufficient evidence to indicate at least one of the variables is useful in predicting the heat rate values at $\alpha = .01$.

f. $R_a^2 = \text{R-Sq(adj)} = .917$. 91.7% of the total sample variance of the heat rate values is explained by the model containing the 5 independent variables, adjusted for the number of variable and the sample size.

g. To determine if there is evidence to indicate heat rate is linearly related to inlet temperature, we test:

$$H_0 : \beta_2 = 0$$
$$H_a : \beta_2 \neq 0$$

The test statistic is $t = -6.14$ and the p-value is $p = .000$. Since the p-value is less than α $(p = .000 < .01)$, H_0 is rejected. There is sufficient evidence to indicate heat rate is linearly related to inlet temperature, adjusted for the other 4 variables at $\alpha = .01$.

12.21 a. $R^2 = .362$. 36.2% of the variability in the AC scores can be explained by the model containing the variables self-esteem score, optimism score, and group cohesion score.

b. To test the utility of the model, we test:

$$H_0 : \beta_1 = \beta_2 = \beta_3 = 0$$
$$H_a : \text{At least one } \beta_i \neq 0$$

The test statistic is $F = \dfrac{R^2 / k}{(1-R^2)/[n-(k+1)]} = \dfrac{.362/3}{(1-.362)/[31-(3+1)]} = 5.11$

The rejection region requires $\alpha = .05$ in the upper tail of the F-distribution with $v_1 = k = 3$ and $v_2 = n - (k+1) = 31 - (3+1) = 27$. From Table VI, Appendix D, $F_{.05} = 2.96$. The rejection region is $F > 2.96$.

Since the observed value of the test statistic falls in the rejection region $(F = 5.11 > 2.96)$, H_0 is rejected. There is sufficient evidence that the model is useful in predicting AC score at $\alpha = .05$.

12.23   a.   **Model 1:**

$$H_0 : \beta_1 = 0$$
$$H_a : \beta_1 \neq 0$$

The test statistic is $t = \dfrac{\hat{\beta}_1 - 0}{s_{\hat{\beta}_1}} = \dfrac{.0354}{.0137} = 2.58$.

Since no α was given, we will use $\alpha = .05$. The rejection region requires $\alpha / 2 = .05 / 2 = .025$ in each tail of the t-distribution. From Table III, Appendix D, with df $= n - (k+1) = 29 - (1+1) = 27$, $t_{.025} = 2.052$. The rejection region is $t < -2.052$ or $t > 2.052$.

Since the observed value of the test statistic falls in the rejection region ($t = 2.58 > 2.052$), H_0 is rejected. There is sufficient evidence to indicate that there is a linear relationship between vintage year and the logarithm of price at $\alpha = .05$.

Model 2:

$$H_0 : \beta_1 = 0$$
$$H_a : \beta_1 \neq 0$$

The test statistic is $t = \dfrac{\hat{\beta}_1 - 0}{s_{\hat{\beta}_1}} = \dfrac{.0238}{.00717} = 3.32$

Since no α was given, we will use $\alpha = .05$. The rejection region requires $\alpha / 2 = .05 / 2 = .025$ in each tail of the t-distribution. From Table III, Appendix D, with df $= n - (k+1) = 29 - (4+1) = 24$, $t_{.025} = 2.064$. The rejection region is $t < -2.064$ or $t > 2.064$.

Since the observed value of the test statistic falls in the rejection region ($t = 3.32 > 2.064$), H_0 is rejected. There is sufficient evidence to indicate that there is a linear relationship between vintage year and the logarithm of price, adjusting for all other variables at $\alpha = .05$.

$$H_0 : \beta_2 = 0$$
$$H_a : \beta_2 \neq 0$$

The test statistic is $t = \dfrac{\hat{\beta}_2 - 0}{s_{\hat{\beta}_2}} = \dfrac{.616}{.0952} = 6.47$

The rejection region is $t < -2.064$ or $t > 2.064$.

Since the observed value of the test statistic falls in the rejection region ($t = 6.47 > 2.064$), H_0 is rejected. There is sufficient evidence to indicate that there is a linear relationship between average growing season temperature and the logarithm of price, adjusting for all other variables at $\alpha = .05$.

$$H_0 : \beta_3 = 0$$
$$H_a : \beta_3 \neq 0$$

The test statistic is $t = \dfrac{\hat{\beta}_3 - 0}{s_{\hat{\beta}_3}} = \dfrac{-.00386}{.00081} = -4.77$

The rejection region is $t < -2.064$ or $t > 2.064$.

Since the observed value of the test statistic falls in the rejection region $(t = -4.77 < -2.064)$, H_0 is rejected. There is sufficient evidence to indicate that there is a linear relationship between Sept./Aug. rainfall and the logarithm of price, adjusting for all other variables at $\alpha = .05$.

$$H_0 : \beta_4 = 0$$
$$H_a : \beta_4 \neq 0$$

The test statistic is $t = \dfrac{\hat{\beta}_4 - 0}{s_{\hat{\beta}_4}} = \dfrac{.0001173}{.000482} = 0.24$.

The rejection region is $t < -2.064$ or $t > 2.064$.

Since the observed value of the test statistic does not fall in the rejection region $(t = 0.24 \ngtr 2.064)$, H_0 is not rejected. There is insufficient evidence to indicate that there is a linear relationship between rainfall in months preceding vintage and the logarithm of price, adjusting for all other variables at $\alpha = .05$.

Model 3:

$$H_0 : \beta_1 = 0$$
$$H_a : \beta_1 \neq 0$$

The test statistic is $t = \dfrac{\hat{\beta}_1 - 0}{s_{\hat{\beta}_1}} = \dfrac{.0240}{.00747} = 3.21$

Since no α was given, we will use $\alpha = .05$. The rejection region requires $\alpha / 2 = .05 / 2 = .025$ in each tail of the t-distribution. From Table III, Appendix D, with df $= n - (k+1) = 29 - (5+1) = 23$, $t_{.025} = 2.069$. The rejection region is $t < -2.069$ or $t > 2.069$.

Since the observed value of the test statistic falls in the rejection region $(t = 3.21 > 2.069)$, H_0 is rejected. There is sufficient evidence to indicate that there is a linear relationship between vintage and the logarithm of price, adjusting for all other variables at $\alpha = .05$.

$$H_0 : \beta_2 = 0$$
$$H_a : \beta_2 \neq 0$$

The test statistic is $t = \dfrac{\hat{\beta}_2 - 0}{s_{\hat{\beta}_2}} = \dfrac{.608}{.116} = 5.24$.

The rejection region is $t < -2.069$ or $t > 2.069$.

Since the observed value of the test statistic falls in the rejection region $(t = 5.24 > 2.069)$, H_0 is rejected. There is sufficient evidence to indicate that there is a linear relationship between average growing season temperature and the logarithm of price, adjusting for all other variables at $\alpha = .05$.

$$H_0 : \beta_3 = 0$$
$$H_a : \beta_3 \neq 0$$

The test statistic is $t = \dfrac{\hat{\beta}_3 - 0}{s_{\hat{\beta}_3}} = \dfrac{-.00380}{.00095} = -4.00$

The rejection region is $t < -2.069$ or $t > 2.069$.

Since the observed value of the test statistic falls in the rejection region ($t = -4.00 < -2.069$), H_0 is rejected. There is sufficient evidence to indicate that there is a linear relationship between Sept./Aug. rainfall and the logarithm of price, adjusting for all other variables at $\alpha = .05$.

$H_0 : \beta_4 = 0$
$H_a : \beta_4 \neq 0$

The test statistic is $t = \dfrac{\hat{\beta}_4 - 0}{s_{\hat{\beta}_4}} = \dfrac{.00115}{.000505} = 2.28$

The rejection region is $t < -2.069$ or $t > 2.069$.

Since the observed value of the test statistic falls in the rejection region ($t = 2.28 > 2.069$), H_0 is rejected. There is sufficient evidence to indicate that there is a linear relationship between rainfall in months preceding vintage and the logarithm of price, adjusting for all other variables at $\alpha = .05$.

$H_0 : \beta_5 = 0$
$H_a : \beta_5 \neq 0$

The test statistic is $t = \dfrac{\hat{\beta}_5 - 0}{s_{\hat{\beta}_5}} = \dfrac{.00765}{.0565} = .014$.

The rejection region is $t < -2.069$ or $t > 2.069$.

Since the observed value of the test statistic does not fall in the rejection region ($t = .014 \not> 2.069$), H_0 is not rejected. There is insufficient evidence to indicate that there is a linear relationship between average September temperature and the logarithm of price, adjusting for all other variables at $\alpha = .05$.

b.   **Model 1:**

$\hat{\beta}_1 = .0354$, $e^{.0354} - 1 = .036$

We estimate that the mean price will increase by 3.6% for each additional year increase in x_1, vintage year.

Model 2:

$\hat{\beta}_1 = .0238$, $e^{.0238} - 1 = .024$

We estimate that the mean price will increase by 2.4% for each additional year increase in x_1, vintage year (with all other variables held constant).

$\hat{\beta}_2 = .616$, $e^{.616} - 1 = .852$

We estimate that the mean price will increase by 85.2% for each additional degree increase in x_2, average growing season temperature °C (with all other variables held constant).

$$\hat{\beta}_3 = -.00386, \ e^{-.00386} - 1 = -.004$$

We estimate that the mean price will decrease by .4% for each additional centimeter increase in x_3, Sept./Aug. rainfall in cm (with all other variables held constant).

$$\hat{\beta}_4 = .0001173, \ e^{.0001173} - 1 = .0001$$

We estimate that the mean price will increase by .01% for each additional centimeter increase in x_4, rainfall in months preceding vintage in cm (with all other variables held constant).

Model 3:

$$\hat{\beta}_1 = .0240, \ e^{.0240} - 1 = .024$$

We estimate that the mean price will increase by 2.4% for each additional year increase in x_1, vintage year (with all other variables held constant).

$$\hat{\beta}_2 = .608, \ e^{.608} - 1 = .837$$

We estimate that the mean price will increase by 83.7% for each additional degree increase in x_2, average growing season temperatures in °C (with all other variables held constant).

$$\hat{\beta}_3 = -.00380, \ e^{-.00380} - 1 = -.004$$

We estimate that the mean price will decrease by .4% for each additional centimeter increase in x_3, Sept./Aug. rainfall in cm, (with all other variables held constant).

$$\hat{\beta}_4 = .00115, \ e^{.00115} - 1 = .001$$

We estimate that the average mean price will increase by .1% for each additional centimeter increase in x_4, rainfall in months preceding vintage in cm (with all other variables held constant).

$$\hat{\beta}_5 = .00765, \ e^{.00765} - 1 = .008$$

We estimate that the average mean price will increase by .8% for each additional degree increase in x_5, average Sept. temperature in °C (with all other variables held constant).

c. I would recommend model 2. Model 1 has only 1 independent variable in the model and it is significant at $\alpha = .05$. The R^2 for this model is $R^2 = .212$ and $s = .575$. Model 2 has 4 independent variables in the model and all terms are significant at $\alpha = .05$ except one. This one variable is significant at $\alpha = .10$. This model has $R^2 = .828$ and $s = .287$. Comparing model 2 to model 1, the R^2 for model 2 is much larger than that for model 1 and the estimate of the standard deviation is much smaller. Model 3 contains all of the independent variables that model 2 has plus one additional variable. This additional variable is not significant at $\alpha = .10$. In addition, the R^2 for this new model is $R^2 = .828$, the same as for model 2. However, the estimate of the standard deviation of model 3 is now larger than that of model 2. This indicates that model 2 is better than model 3.

12.25   a.   For $x_1 = 1$, $x_2 = 10$, $x_3 = 5$, and $x_4 = 2$, $\hat{y} = 3.58 + .01(1) - .06(10) - .01(5) + .42(2) = 3.78$

         b.   For $x_1 = 0$, $x_2 = 8$, $x_3 = 10$, and $x_4 = 4$, $\hat{y} = 3.58 + .01(0) - .06(8) - .01(10) + .42(4) = 4.68$

12.27   a.   The confidence interval is $(13.42, 14.31)$. We are 95% confident that the mean desire to have cosmetic surgery is between 13.42 and 14.31 for females with a self-esteem of 24, body satisfaction of 3 and impression of reality TV of 4.

               The confidence interval is $(8.79, 10.89)$. We are 95% confident that the mean desire to have cosmetic surgery is between 8.79 and 10.89 for males with a self-esteem of 22, body satisfaction of 9 and impression of reality TV of 4.

12.29   a.   The 95% prediction interval is $(11,599.6, \ 13,665.5)$. We are 95% confident that the actual heat rate will be between 11,599.6 and 13.665.5 when the RPM is 7,500, the inlet temperature is 1,000, the exhaust temperature is 525, the cycle pressure ratio is 13.5 and the air flow rate is 10.

         b.   The 95% confidence interval is $(12,157.9, \ 13,107.1)$. We are 95% confident that the mean heat rate will be between 12,157.9 and 13,107.1 when the RPM is 7,500, the inlet temperature is 1,000, the exhaust temperature is 525, the cycle pressure ratio is 13.5 and the air flow rate is 10.

         c.   Yes. The confidence interval for the mean will always be smaller than the prediction interval for the actual value. This is because there are 2 error terms involved in predicting an actual value and only one error term involved in estimating the mean. First, we have the error in locating the mean of the distribution. Once the mean is located, the actual value can still vary around the mean, thus, the second error. There is only one error term involved when estimating the mean, which is the error in locating the mean.

12.31   a.   Using MINITAB, the results are:

Regression Analysis: Pay5Years versus Efficiency, Shares, Age

```
The regression equation is
Pay5Years = 130 + 0.169 Efficiency + 0.0259 Shares - 1.11 Age

103 cases used, 72 cases contain missing values

Predictor        Coef    SE Coef       T      P
Constant       130.22      45.77    2.84  0.005
Efficiency    0.16900    0.09077    1.86  0.066
Shares       0.025864   0.001509   17.14  0.000
Age           -1.1115     0.7572   -1.47  0.145

S = 50.8780    R-Sq = 75.2%    R-Sq(adj) = 74.4%

Analysis of Variance

Source            DF       SS      MS       F      P
Regression         3   777044  259015  100.06  0.000
Residual Error    99   256268    2589
Total            102  1033312

Source      DF  Seq SS
Efficiency   1    9722
Shares       1  761745
Age          1    5577
```

The least squares prediction equation is: $\hat{y} = 130.22 + .169x_1 + .0259x_2 - 1.1115x_3$

b. To determine if the model is adequate, we test:

$$H_0 : \beta_1 = \beta_2 = \beta_3 = 0$$
$$H_a : \text{At least } 1\,\beta_i \neq 0$$

From the printout, the test statistic is $F = 100.06$ and the p-value is $p = .000$.

Since the p-value is less than α ($p = .000 < .05$), H_0 is rejected. There is sufficient evidence to indicate the model is adequate at $\alpha = .05$.

c. Using MINITAB, the results are:

Predicted Values for New Observations

```
New
Obs    Fit   SE Fit      95% CI            95% PI
  1   96.55    8.35   (79.99, 113.10)   (-5.76, 198.85)
```

```
Values of Predictors for New Observations
```

```
New
Obs   Efficiency   Shares   Age
  1         173      103    59.0
```

The 95% prediction interval for the 5-year pay of a CEO with $x_1 = 173$, $x_2 = \$102.9$ million, and $x_3 = 59$ is $(-5.76, 198.85)$. We are 95% confident that the actual 5-year pay of a CEO with the above values for the independent variables is between -5.76 and 198.85.

12.33 a. From MINITAB, the output is:

Regression Analysis: Man-Hours versus Capacity, Pressure, Type, Drum

```
The regression equation is
Man-Hours = - 3783 + 0.00875 Capacity + 1.93 Pressure + 3444 Type + 2093 Drum

Predictor       Coef      SE Coef        T        P
Constant        -3783        1205     -3.14    0.004
Capacity    0.0087490    0.0009035     9.68    0.000
Pressure       1.9265       0.6489     2.97    0.006
Type           3444.3        911.7     3.78    0.001
Drum           2093.4        305.6     6.85    0.000

S = 894.6      R-Sq = 90.3%     R-Sq(adj) = 89.0%

Analysis of Variance

Source           DF         SS         MS       F       P
Regression        4  230854854   57713714   72.11   0.000
Residual Error   31   24809761     800315
Total            35  255664615

Source       DF     Seq SS
Capacity      1  175007141
Pressure      1     490357
Type          1   17813091
Drum          1   37544266
```

```
Predicted Values for New Observations

New Obs     Fit     SE Fit      95.0% CI              95.0% PI
1          1936       239    (   1449,    2424)   (     48,    3825)

Values of Predictors for New Observations

New Obs  Capacity  Pressure     Type       Drum
1          150000       500     1.00   0.000000
```

The fitted regression line is $\hat{y} = -3,783 + 0.00875x_1 + 1.9265x_2 + 3,444.3x_3 + 2,093.4x_4$.

b.   To determine if the model is useful for predicting the number of man-hours needed, we test:

$$H_0 : \beta_1 = \beta_2 = \beta_3 = \beta_4 = 0$$
$$H_a : \text{At least one } \beta_i \neq 0$$

The test statistic is $F = 72.11$ and the p-value is $p = 0.000$. Since the p-value is less than α ($p = .000 < .01$), H_0 is rejected. There is sufficient evidence that the model is useful for predicting man-hours at $\alpha = .01$.

c.   The confidence interval is (14,49, 2,424).

With 95% confidence, we can conclude that the mean number of man-hours for all boilers with characteristics $x_1 = 150,000$, $x_2 = 500$, $x_3 = 1$, $x_4 = 0$ will fall between 1,449 hours and 2,424 hours.

12.35   a.   The response surface is a twisted surface in three-dimensional space.

b.   For $x_1 = 0$, $E(y) = 3 + 0 + 2x_2 - 0x_2 = 3 + 2x_2$
For $x_1 = 1$, $E(y) = 3 + 1 + 2x_2 - 1x_2 = 4 + x_2$
For $x_1 = 2$, $E(y) = 3 + 2 + 2x_2 - 2x_2 = 5$

The plot of the lines is

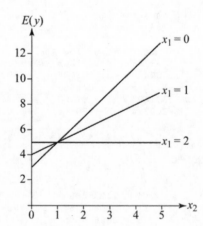

c.   The lines are not parallel because interaction between x_1 and x_2 is present. Interaction between x_1 and x_2 means that the effect of x_2 on y depends on what level x_1 takes on.

d.   For $x_1 = 0$, as x_2 increases from 0 to 5, $E(y)$ increases from 3 to 13.
For $x_1 = 1$, as x_2 increases from 0 to 5, $E(y)$ increases from 4 to 9.
For $x_1 = 2$, as x_2 increases from 0 to 5, $E(y) = 5$.

e.   For $x_1 = 2$ and $x_2 = 4$, $E(y) = 5$. For $x_1 = 0$ and $x_2 = 5$, $E(y) = 13$.

Thus, $E(y)$ changes from 5 to 13.

12.37   a.   The prediction equation is $\hat{y} = -2.55 + 3.82x_1 + 2.63x_2 - 1.29x_1x_2$

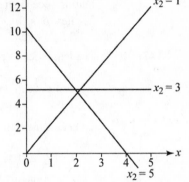

b.   The response surface is a twisted plane, since the equation contains an interaction term.

c.   For $x_2 = 1$, $\hat{y} = -2.55 + 3.82x_1 + 2.63(1) - 1.29x_1(1) = .08 + 2.53x_1$
For $x_2 = 3$, $\hat{y} = -2.55 + 3.82x_1 + 2.63(3) - 1.29x_1(3) = 5.34 - .05x_1$
For $x_2 = 5$, $\hat{y} = -2.55 + 3.82x_1 + 2.63(5) - 1.29x_1(5) = 10.6 - 2.63x_1$

d.   If x_1 and x_2 interact, the effect of x_1 on $\hat{y}$ is different at different levels of x_2. When $x_2 = 1$, as x_1 increases, $\hat{y}$ also increases. When $x_2 = 5$, as x_1 increases, $\hat{y}$ decreases.

e.   The hypotheses are:

$$H_0 : \beta_3 = 0$$
$$H_a : \beta_3 \neq 0$$

f.   The test statistic is $t = \dfrac{\hat{\beta}_3}{s_{\hat{\beta}_3}} = \dfrac{-1.285}{.159} = -8.06$

The rejection region requires $\alpha / 2 = .01 / 2 = .005$ in each tail of the t-distribution with $df = n - (k+1) = 15 - (3+1) = 11$. From Table III, Appendix D, $t_{.005} = 3.106$. The rejection region is $t < -3.106$ or $t > 3.106$.

Since the observed value of the test statistic falls in the rejection region $(t = -8.06 < -3.106)$, H_0 is rejected. There is sufficient evidence to indicate that x_1 and x_2 interact at $\alpha = .01$.

12.39   a.   The interaction model is $E(y) = \beta_0 + \beta_1 x_1 + \beta_2 x_2 + \beta_3 x_1 x_2$.

b.   For $x_2 = 2.5$, $E(y) = \beta_0 + \beta_1 x_1 + \beta_2(2.5) + \beta_3 x_1(2.5) = \beta_0 + 2.5\beta_2 + (\beta_1 + 2.5\beta_3)x_1$. The change in revenue for every 1-tweet increase in tweet rate is $(\beta_1 + 2.5\beta_3)$.

c.   For $x_2 = 5$, $E(y) = \beta_0 + \beta_1 x_1 + \beta_2(5) + \beta_3 x_1(5) = \beta_0 + 5\beta_2 + (\beta_1 + 5\beta_3)x_1$. The change in revenue for every 1-tweet increase in tweet rate is $(\beta_1 + 5\beta_3)$.

d.   For $x_1 = 100$, $E(y) = \beta_0 + \beta_1(100) + \beta_2 x_2 + \beta_3(100)x_2 = \beta_0 + 100\beta_1 + (\beta_2 + 100\beta_3)x_2$. The change in revenue for every 1-unit increase in PN-ratio is $(\beta_2 + 100\beta_3)$.

e.   To determine if tweet rate and PN-ratio interact, we test:

$$H_0 : \beta_3 = 0$$

12.41 a.   A regression model incorporating interaction between x_1 and x_2 would be:

$$E(y) = \beta_o + \beta_1 x_1 + \beta_2 x_2 + \beta_3 x_1 x_2$$

b.   If the slope of the relationship between number of defects (y) and turntable speed (x_1) is steeper for lower values of cutting blade speed, then the interaction term must be negative. As the value of cutting speed increases, the steepness gets smaller, thus, the interaction term must get smaller. This implies $\beta_3 < 0$.

12.43 a.   The least squares prediction equation is $\hat{y} = 11.779 - 1.972 x_1 + .585 x_4 - .553 x_1 x_4$.

b.   For $x_1 = 1$ and $x_4 = 5$, $\hat{y} = 11.779 - 1.972(1) + .585(5) - .553(1)(5) = 9.967$.

c.   To determine if the model is adequate, we test:

$$H_0 : \beta_1 = \beta_2 = \beta_3 = 0$$
$$H_a : \text{At least } 1 \beta_i \neq 0$$

The test statistic is $F = 45.086$ and the p-value is $p = .000$.

Since the p-value is less than α $(p = .000 < .10)$, H_0 is rejected. There is sufficient evidence to indicate the model is adequate in predicting desire to have cosmetic surgery at $\alpha = .10$.

d. $R_a^2 = .439$. 43.9% of the sample variation in the desire to have cosmetic surgery around its mean is explained by the model containing gender, impression of reality TV and the interaction of the two variables.

e. $s = 2.350$. Most of the observed values of desire will fall within $2s = 2(2.350) = 4.70$ units of their predicted values.

f.   To determine if gender and impression of reality TV interact, we test:

$$H_0 : \beta_3 = 0$$
$$H_a : \beta_3 \neq 0$$

The test statistic is $t = -2.004$ and the p-value is $p = .047$.

Since the p-value is less than α $(p = .047 < .10)$, H_0 is rejected. There is sufficient evidence to indicate gender and impression of reality TV interact to affect desire to have cosmetic surgery at $\alpha = .10$.

12.45 a.   Let $x_1 = $ latitude, $x_2 = $ longitude, and $x_3 = $ depth. The model is

$$E(y) = \beta_0 + \beta_1 x_1 + \beta_2 x_2 + \beta_3 x_3 + \beta_4 x_1 x_3 + \beta_5 x_2 x_3.$$

b. Using MINITAB, the results are:

Regression Analysis: ARSENIC versus LATITUDE, LONGITUDE, ...

```
The regression equation is
ARSENIC = 10845 - 1280 LATITUDE + 217 LONGITUDE - 1549 DEPTH-FT - 11.0 Lat_d
          + 20.0 Long_d


327 cases used, 1 cases contain missing values


Predictor     Coef   SE Coef      T       P
Constant     10845     67720    0.16   0.873
LATITUDE     -1280      1053   -1.22   0.225
LONGITUDE    217.4     814.5    0.27   0.790
DEPTH-FT   -1549.2     985.6   -1.57   0.117
Lat_D       -11.00     11.86   -0.93   0.355
Long_D       19.98     11.20    1.78   0.076


S = 103.072    R-Sq = 13.7%    R-Sq(adj) = 12.4%


Analysis of Variance

Source          DF        SS       MS       F       P
Regression       5    542303   108461   10.21   0.000
Residual Error 321   3410258    10624
Total          326   3952562


Source     DF   Seq SS
LATITUDE    1   132448
LONGITUDE   1   320144
DEPTH-FT    1    53179
Lat_D       1     2756
Long_D      1    33777
```

The least squares model is: $\hat{y} = 10,845 - 1,280x_1 + 217.4x_2 - 1,549.2x_3 - 11.00x_1x_3 + 19.98x_2x_3$

c. To determine if latitude and depth interact to affect arsenic level, we test:

$$H_0 : \beta_4 = 0$$
$$H_a : \beta_4 \neq 0$$

From the printout, the test statistic is $F = -.93$ and the p-value is $p = .355$. Since the p-value is not less than α ($p = .355 \not< .05$), H_0 is not rejected. There is insufficient evidence to indicate latitude and depth interact to affect arsenic level at $\alpha = .05$.

d. To determine if longitude and depth interact to affect arsenic level, we test:

$$H_0 : \beta_5 = 0$$
$$H_a : \beta_5 \neq 0$$

From the printout, the test statistic is $F = 1.78$ and the p-value is $p = .076$. Since the p-value is not less than α ($p = .076 \not< .05$), H_0 is not rejected. There is insufficient evidence to indicate longitude and depth interact to affect arsenic level at $\alpha = .05$.

e. Because the interactions are not significant, this means that the effect of latitude on the arsenic levels does not depend on the depth and the effect of longitude on the arsenic levels does not depend on the depth.

12.47 a. By including the interaction terms, it implies that the relationship between voltage and volume fraction of the disperse phase depends on the levels of salinity and surfactant concentration.

A possible sketch of the relationship is:

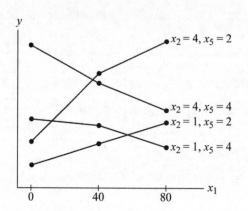

b. From MINITAB, the output is:

Regression Analysis: Voltage versus x1, x2, x5, x1x2, x1x5

```
The regression equation is
Voltage = 0.906 - 0.0228 x1 + 0.305 x2 + 0.275 x5 - 0.00280 x1x2
+ 0.00158 x1x5

Predictor          Coef      SE Coef          T         P
Constant         0.9057       0.2855       3.17     0.007
x1            -0.022753      0.008318      -2.74     0.017
x2              0.3047        0.2366       1.29     0.220
x5              0.2747        0.2270       1.21     0.248
x1x2          -0.002804      0.003790      -0.74     0.473
x1x5           0.001579      0.003947       0.40     0.696

S = 0.5047     R-Sq = 67.9%     R-Sq(adj) = 55.6%

Analysis of Variance

Source              DF           SS          MS         F        P
Regression           5       7.0103      1.4021      5.51    0.006
Residual Error      13       3.3107      0.2547
Total               18      10.3210

Source         DF      Seq SS
x1              1      1.4016
x2              1      1.9263
x5              1      3.5422
x1x2            1      0.0994
x1x5            1      0.0408
```

The fitted regression line is $\hat{y} = .906 - .0228x_1 + .305x_2 + .275x_5 - .0028x_1x_2 + .00158x_1x_5$.

To determine if the model is useful, we test:

$$H_0 : \beta_1 = \beta_2 = \beta_3 = \beta_4 = \beta_5 = 0$$
$$H_a : \text{At least } 1 \beta_i \neq 0$$

The test statistic is $F = 5.51$ and the p-value is $p = .006$.

Since the p-value is so small, H_0 is rejected. There is sufficient evidence to indicate the model is useful for predicting voltage at $\alpha > .006$.

$R^2 = .679$. Thus, 67.9% of the sample variation of voltage is explained by the model containing the three independent variables and two interaction terms.

The estimate of the standard deviation is $s = .5047$.

Comparing this model to that fit in Exercise 12.20, the model in Exercise 12.20 appears to fit the data better. The model in Exercise 12.20 has a higher R^2 (.771 vs .679) and a smaller estimate of the standard deviation (.4365 vs .5047).

c. $\hat{\beta}_0 = .906$. This is simply the estimate of the y-intercept.

$\hat{\beta}_1 = -.0228$. For each unit increase in disperse phase volume, we estimate that the mean voltage will decrease by .0228 units, holding salinity and surfactant concentration at 0.

$\hat{\beta}_2 = .305$. For each unit increase in salinity, we estimate that the mean voltage will increase by .305 units, holding disperse phase volume and surfactant concentration at 0.

$\hat{\beta}_3 = .275$. For each unit increase in surfactant concentration, we estimate that the mean voltage will increase by .275 units, holding disperse phase volume and salinity at 0.

$\hat{\beta}_4 = -.0028$. This estimates the difference in the slope of the relationship between voltage and disperse phase volume for each unit increase in salinity, holding surfactant concentration constant.

$\hat{\beta}_5 = .00158$. This estimates the difference in the slope of the relationship between voltage and disperse phase volume for each unit increase in surfactant concentration, holding salinity constant.

12.49 a. $E(y) = \beta_0 + \beta_1 x + \beta_2 x^2$

b. $E(y) = \beta_0 + \beta_1 x_1 + \beta_2 x_2 + \beta_3 x_1 x_2 + \beta_4 x_1^2 + \beta_5 x_2^2$

c. $E(y) = \beta_0 + \beta_1 x_1 + \beta_2 x_2 + \beta_3 x_3 + \beta_4 x_1 x_2 + \beta_5 x_1 x_3 + \beta_6 x_2 x_3 + \beta_7 x_1^2 + \beta_8 x_2^2 + \beta_9 x_3^2$

12.51 a. To determine if the model contributes information for predicting y, we test:

$$H_0 : \beta_1 = \beta_2 = 0$$
$$H_a : \text{At least one } \beta_i \neq 0$$

The test statistic is $F = \dfrac{R^2 / k}{(1-R^2)/[n-(k+1)]} = \dfrac{.91/2}{(1-.91)/[20-(2+1)]} = 85.94$.

The rejection region requires $\alpha = .05$ in the upper tail of the F-distribution, with $v_1 = k = 2$, and $v_2 = n - (k+1) = 20 - (2+1) = 17$. From Table VI, Appendix D, $F_{.05} = 3.59$. The rejection region is $F > 3.59$.

Since the observed value of the test statistic falls in the rejection region $(F = 85.94 > 3.59)$, H_0 is rejected. There is sufficient evidence that the model contributes information for predicting y at $\alpha = .05$.

b.   To determine if upward curvature exists, we test:

$$H_0 : \beta_2 = 0$$
$$H_a : \beta_2 > 0$$

c.   To determine if downward curvature exists, we test:

$$H_0 : \beta_2 = 0$$
$$H_a : \beta_2 < 0$$

12.53   a.   To determine if at least one of the parameters is nonzero, we test:

$$H_0 : \beta_1 = \beta_2 = \beta_3 = \beta_4 = \beta_5 = 0$$
$$H_a : \text{At least one } \beta_i \neq 0$$

The test statistic is $F = 25.93$ and the p-value is $p = 0.000$. Since the p-value is less than α $(p = 0.000 < .05)$, H_0 is rejected. There is sufficient evidence to indicate that at least one of the parameters β_1 , β_2 , β_3 , β_4 , and β_5 is nonzero at $\alpha = .05$.

b.
$$H_0 : \beta_4 = 0$$
$$H_a : \beta_4 \neq 0$$

The test statistic is $t = -10.74$ and the p-value is $p = 0.000$. Since the p-value is less than α $(p = 0.000 < .01)$, H_0 is rejected. There is sufficient evidence to indicate that $\beta_4 \neq 0$ at $\alpha = .01$.

c.
$$H_0 : \beta_5 = 0$$
$$H_a : \beta_5 \neq 0$$

The test statistic is $t = .60$ and the p-value is $p = .550$. Since the p-value is greater than α $(p = .550 \not< .01)$, H_0 is not rejected. There is insufficient evidence to indicate that $\beta_5 \neq 0$ at $\alpha = .01$.

d.   A possible graph may look like:

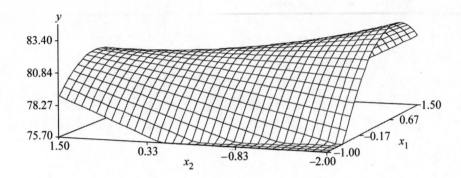

Notice that there is no curvature in the x_2 plane but there is curvature in the x_1 plane.

12.55   a. $\hat{\beta}_0 = 6.13$. Since 0 is not in the observed range (one cannot have the ball on the goal line), this has no meaning other than the y-intercept.

$\hat{\beta}_1 = .141$. Since the quadratic term is present in the model, this is no longer the slope of the line. It is simply a location parameter.

$\hat{\beta}_2 = -.0009$. Since this term is negative, it indicates that the shape of the relationship is mound-shaped, or concave downward. As the distance from the goal line increases, the predicted number of points scored will increase to some point and then start decreasing.

b. $R^2 = .226$. 22.6% of the sample variation in the number of points scored around their mean is explained by the quadratic relationship between the number of points scored and the number of yards from the opposing goal line.

c.   No. Even though the value of R^2 has increased, we do not know if the increase is statistically significant.

d.   To determine if the quadratic model is a better fit, we would test:

$$H_0 : \beta_2 = 0$$
$$H_a : \beta_2 \neq 0$$

12.57   a.   Using MINITAB, a scattergram of the data is:

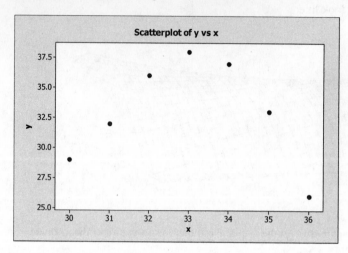

b.   If information were available only for $x = 30$, 31, 32, and 33, we would suggest a first-order model where $\beta_1 > 0$. If information was available only for $x = 33$, 34, 35, and 36, we would again suggest a first-order model where $\beta_1 < 0$. If all the information was available, we would suggest a second-order model.

12.59   a.   The complete 2nd order model is $E(y) = \beta_0 + \beta_1 x_1 + \beta_2 x_2 + \beta_3 x_1 x_2 + \beta_4 x_1^2 + \beta_5 x_2^2$.

b. $R^2 = .14$. 14% of the total variation in the efficiency scores is explained by the complete 2nd order model containing level of CEO leadership and level of congruence between the CEO and the VP.

c.   If the β-coefficient for the x_2^2 term is negative, then as the value of the level of congruence increases, the efficiency will increase at a decreasing rate to some point and then the efficiency will decrease at an increasing rate, holding level of CEO leadership constant.

d.   Since the p-value is less than α ($p = .02 < .05$), H_0 is rejected. There is sufficient evidence to indicate that the level of CEO leadership and the level of congruence between the CEO and the VP interact to affect efficiency. This means that the effect of CEO leadership on efficiency depends on the level of congruence between the CEO and the VP.

12.61   a.   A first order model is $E(y) = \beta_0 + \beta_1 x$.

b.   A second order model is $E(y) = \beta_0 + \beta_1 x + \beta_2 x^2$.

c.   Using MINITAB, a scattergram of these data is:

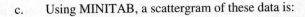
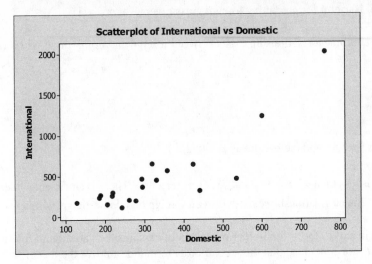

From the plot, it appears that the second order model might fit the data better. There appears to be an upward curve to the relationship.

d.   Using MINITAB, the output is:

Regression Analysis: International versus Domestic, Dsq

```
The regression equation is
International = 406 - 1.79 Domestic + 0.00499 Dsq

Predictor      Coef    SE Coef      T       P
Constant      406.4      222.7    1.82   0.087
Domestic     -1.793      1.192   -1.50   0.152
Dsq        0.004993   0.001364    3.66   0.002


S = 172.952   R-Sq = 87.1%    R-Sq(adj) = 85.5%

Analysis of Variance

Source          DF        SS        MS       F       P
Regression       2   3233145   1616572   54.04   0.000
Residual Error  16    478599     29912
Total           18   3711743


Source     DF    Seq SS
Domestic    1   2832374
Dsq         1    400771
```

To investigate the usefulness of the model, we test:

$$H_0 : \beta_1 = \beta_2 = 0$$
$$H_a : \text{At least } 1\beta_i \neq 0$$

The test statistic is $F = 54.04$ and the p-value is $p = 0.000$.

Since the *p*-value is less than α ($p = 0.000 < .05$), H_0 is rejected. There is sufficient evidence to indicate the model is useful for predicting foreign gross revenue at $\alpha = .05$.

To determine if a curvilinear relationship exists between foreign and domestic gross revenues, we test:

$$H_0 : \beta_2 = 0$$
$$H_a : \beta_2 \neq 0$$

The test statistic is $t = 3.66$ and the *p*-value is $p = .002$.

Since the *p*-value is less than α ($p = .002 < .05$), H_0 is rejected. There is sufficient evidence to indicate that a curvilinear relationship exists between foreign and domestic gross revenues at $\alpha = .05$.

e.   From the analysis in part **d**, the second-order model better explains the variation in foreign gross revenues. In part **d**, we concluded that the second-order term did improve the model.

12.63   a.   Using MINITAB, the scattergram of the data is:

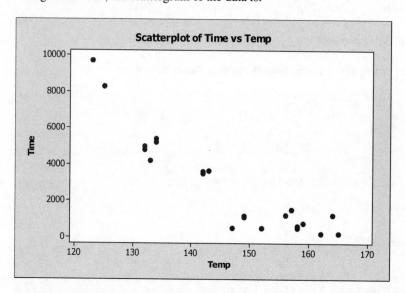

The relationship appears to be curvilinear. As temperature increases, the value of time tends to decrease but at a decreasing rate.

b.   Using MINITAB the results are:

Regression Analysis: Time versus Temp, Tempsq

```
The regression equation is
Time = 154243 - 1909 Temp + 5.93 Tempsq


Predictor       Coef   SE Coef        T       P
Constant      154243     21868     7.05   0.000
Temp         -1908.9     303.7    -6.29   0.000
Tempsq         5.929     1.048     5.66   0.000

S = 688.137    R-Sq = 94.2%    R-Sq(adj) = 93.5%
```

```
Analysis of Variance

Source              DF          SS          MS        F       P
Regression           2   144830280    72415140   152.93   0.000
Residual Error      19     8997107      473532
Total               21   153827386


Source   DF      Seq SS
Temp      1   129663987
Tempsq    1    15166293
```

The fitted regression line is $\hat{y} = 154,243 - 1,908.9x + 5.929x^2$.

c. To determine if there is an upward curvature in the relationship between failure time and solder temperature, we test:

$$H_0 : \beta_2 = 0$$
$$H_a : \beta_2 > 0$$

From the printout, the test statistic is $t = 5.66$ and the p-value is $p = 0.000$. Since the p-value is less than α ($p = 0.000 < .05$), H_0 is rejected. There is sufficient evidence to indicate an upward curvature in the relationship between failure time and solder temperature at $\alpha = .05$.

12.65 a. A scatterplot of the data is:

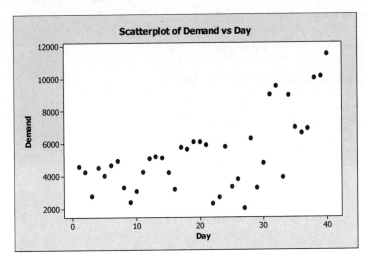

b. From the plot, it looks like a second-order model would fit the data better than a first-order model. There is little evidence that a third-order model would fit the data better than a second-order model.

c.   Using MINITAB, the output for fitting a first-order model is:

Regression Analysis: Demand versus Day

```
The regression equation is
Demand = 2802 + 123 Day

Predictor     Coef   SE Coef      T      P
Constant    2802.4     604.7   4.63  0.000
Day         122.95     25.70   4.78  0.000

S = 1876.57    R-Sq = 37.6%    R-Sq(adj) = 35.9%

Analysis of Variance

Source           DF          SS          MS      F      P
Regression        1    80572885    80572885  22.88  0.000
Residual Error   38   133817026     3521501
Total            39   214389911
```

To see if there is a significant linear relationship between day and demand, we test:

$$H_0 : \beta_1 = 0$$
$$H_a : \beta_1 \neq 0$$

The test statistic is $t = 4.78$ and the p-value is $p = .000$. Since the p-value is less than α ($p = .000 < .05$), H_0 is rejected. There is sufficient evidence to indicate that there is a linear relationship between day and demand at $\alpha = .05$.

d.   Using MINITAB, the output for fitting a second-order model is:

Regression Analysis: Demand versus Day, Day-sq

```
The regression equation is
Demand = 4944 - 183 Day + 7.46 Day-sq

Predictor     Coef   SE Coef      T      P
Constant    4944.2     829.6   5.96  0.000
Day        -183.03     93.32  -1.96  0.057
Day-sq       7.463     2.207   3.38  0.002

S = 1662.23    R-Sq = 52.3%    R-Sq(adj) = 49.7%

Analysis of Variance

Source           DF          SS          MS      F      P
Regression        2   112158325    56079162  20.30  0.000
Residual Error   37   102231587     2763016
Total            39   214389911

Source   DF    Seq SS
Day       1  80572885
Day-sq    1  31585440
```

To see if there is a significant quadratic relationship between day and demand, we test:

$$H_0: \beta_2 = 0$$
$$H_a: \beta_2 \neq 0$$

The test statistic is $t = 3.38$ and the p-value is $p = .002$. Since the p-value is less than α ($p = .002 < .05$), H_0 is rejected. There is sufficient evidence to indicate that there is a quadratic relationship between day and demand at $\alpha = .05$.

e. Since the quadratic term is significant in the second-order model in part **d**, the second order model is better.

12.67 The model is $E(y) = \beta_0 + \beta_1 x_1 + \beta_2 x_2$

where $\quad x_1 = \begin{cases} 1 & \text{if the variable is at level 2} \\ 0 & \text{otherwise} \end{cases}$ $\quad x_2 = \begin{cases} 1 & \text{if the variable is at level 3} \\ 0 & \text{otherwise} \end{cases}$

β_0 = mean value of y when qualitative variable is at level 1.
β_1 = difference in mean value of y between level 2 and level 1 of qualitative variable.
β_2 = difference in mean value of y between level 3 and level 1 of qualitative variable.

12.69 a. Level 1 implies $x_1 = x_2 = x_3 = 0$. $\hat{y} = 10.2 - 4(0) + 12(0) + 2(0) = 10.2$
Level 2 implies $x_1 = 1$ and $x_2 = x_3 = 0$. $\hat{y} = 10.2 - 4(1) + 12(0) + 2(0) = 6.2$
Level 3 implies $x_2 = 1$ and $x_1 = x_3 = 0$. $\hat{y} = 10.2 - 4(0) + 12(1) + 2(0) = 22.2$
Level 4 implies $x_3 = 1$ and $x_1 = x_2 = 0$. $\hat{y} = 10.2 - 4(0) + 12(0) + 2(1) = 12.2$

b. The hypotheses are:

$$H_0: \beta_1 = \beta_2 = \beta_3 = 0$$
$$H_a: \text{At least one } \beta_i \neq 0$$

12.71 a. Let $x_1 = \begin{cases} 1 \text{ if grape-picking method is manual} \\ 0 \text{ otherwise} \end{cases}$ $\quad$ Let $x_2 = \begin{cases} 1 \text{ if soil type is clay} \\ 0 \text{ otherwise} \end{cases}$

Let $x_3 = \begin{cases} 1 \text{ if soil type is gravel} \\ 0 \text{ otherwise} \end{cases}$ $\quad$ Let $x_4 = \begin{cases} 1 \text{ if slope orientation is East} \\ 0 \text{ otherwise} \end{cases}$

Let $x_5 = \begin{cases} 1 \text{ if slope orientation is South} \\ 0 \text{ otherwise} \end{cases}$ $\quad$ Let $x_6 = \begin{cases} 1 \text{ if slope orientation is West} \\ 0 \text{ otherwise} \end{cases}$

Let $x_7 = \begin{cases} 1 \text{ if slope orientation is Southeast} \\ 0 \text{ otherwise} \end{cases}$

b. The model is: $E(y) = \beta_0 + \beta_1 x_1$
β_0 = mean wine quality for grape-picking method automated
β_1 = difference in mean wine quality between grape-picking methods manual and automated

c. The model is: $E(y) = \beta_0 + \beta_1 x_2 + \beta_2 x_3$

β_0 = mean wine quality for soil type sand

β_1 = difference in mean wine quality between soil types clay and sand

β_2 = difference in mean wine quality between soil types gravel and sand

d. The model is: $E(y) = \beta_0 + \beta_1 x_4 + \beta_2 x_5 + \beta_3 x_6 + \beta_4 x_7$

β_0 = mean wine quality for slope orientation Southwest

β_1 = difference in mean wine quality between slope orientations East and Southwest

β_2 = difference in mean wine quality between slope orientations South and Southwest

β_3 = difference in mean wine quality between slope orientations West and Southwest

β_4 = difference in mean wine quality between slope orientations Southeast and Southwest

12.73   a.   Let $x = \begin{cases} 1 & \text{if developer} \\ 0 & \text{otherwise} \end{cases}$

Then the model would be: $E(y) = \beta_0 + \beta_1 x$

β_0 = mean accuracy for the project leader

β_1 = difference in mean accuracy between the developer and the project leader

b.   Let $x_1 = \begin{cases} 1 & \text{if low} \\ 0 & \text{otherwise} \end{cases}$ Let $x_2 = \begin{cases} 1 & \text{if medium} \\ 0 & \text{otherwise} \end{cases}$

Then the model would be: $E(y) = \beta_0 + \beta_1 x_1 + \beta_2 x_2$

β_0 = mean accuracy for the high task complexity

β_1 = difference in mean accuracy between low and high task complexity

β_2 = difference in mean accuracy between medium and high task complexity

c.   Let $x = \begin{cases} 1 & \text{if fixed price} \\ 0 & \text{otherwise} \end{cases}$

Then the model would be: $E(y) = \beta_0 + \beta_1 x$

β_0 = mean accuracy for the hourly rate

β_1 = difference in mean accuracy between the fixed price and the hourly rate

d.   Let $x_1 = \begin{cases} 1 & \text{if time-of-delivery} \\ 0 & \text{otherwise} \end{cases}$ Let $x_2 = \begin{cases} 1 & \text{if cost} \\ 0 & \text{otherwise} \end{cases}$

Then the model would be: $E(y) = \beta_0 + \beta_1 x_1 + \beta_2 x_2$

β_0 = mean accuracy for the quality

β_1 = difference in mean accuracy between time of delivery and quality

β_2 = difference in mean accuracy between cost and quality

12.75   a.   Let $x_1 = \begin{cases} 1 & \text{if blonde Caucasian} \\ 0 & \text{otherwise} \end{cases}$ Let $x_2 = \begin{cases} 1 & \text{if brunette Caucasian} \\ 0 & \text{otherwise} \end{cases}$

b.   The model would be: $E(y) = \beta_0 + \beta_1 x_1 + \beta_2 x_2$

c.   The mean for a blonde Caucasian solicitor would be $E(y) = \beta_0 + \beta_1(1) + \beta_2(0) = \beta_0 + \beta_1$.

d.   The difference in the mean level of contribution between a blode solicitor and a minority female solicitor is β_1.

e.   If the theory is correct, then β_0 (mean for minority female solicitors) will be positive, β_1 will be positive (mean for female Caucasian solicitors is greator than the means of the other groups), and β_2 will be close to 0 (no difference in the means for minority female solicitors and brunette Caucasian solicitors).

f.   Yes. The β-estimate for the dummy variable for blonde Caucasian solicitors should be positive and significantly different from 0. The β-estimate for the dummy variable for brunette Caucasian solicitors should be close to 0. In this case, it is not statistically different from 0.

12.77   a.   Since there are four groups, we need 3 dummy variables.

Let $x_1 = \begin{cases} 1 & \text{if large/private} \\ 0 & \text{otherwise} \end{cases}$ Let $x_2 = \begin{cases} 1 & \text{if small/public} \\ 0 & \text{otherwise} \end{cases}$ Let $x_3 = \begin{cases} 1 & \text{if small/private} \\ 0 & \text{otherwise} \end{cases}$

b.   The model is $E(y) = \beta_0 + \beta_1 x_1 + \beta_2 x_2 + \beta_3 x_3$.

$\beta_0 =$ mean likelihood of reporting sustainability policies for large/public firms.

$\beta_1 =$ difference in mean likelihood of reporting sustainability policies between large/private firms and large/public firms.

$\beta_2 =$ difference in mean likelihood of reporting sustainability policies between small/public firms and large/public firms.

$\beta_3 =$ difference in mean likelihood of reporting sustainability policies between small/private firms and large/public firms.

c.   Since the p-value is very small $(p < .001)$, H_0 would be rejected for any reasonable value of α. There is sufficient evidence to indicate a difference in the mean likelihood of reporting sustainability policies among the 4 groups.

d.   Since there are 2 levels of each of the 2 variables, we need to create 2 dummy variables.

Let $x_1 = \begin{cases} 1 & \text{if small} \\ 0 & \text{otherwise} \end{cases}$ Let $x_2 = \begin{cases} 1 & \text{if private} \\ 0 & \text{otherwise} \end{cases}$.

e.   The main effects model would be: $E(y) = \beta_0 + \beta_1 x_1 + \beta_2 x_2$.

f.   For large/public, $E(y) = \beta_0 + \beta_1(0) + \beta_2(0) = \beta_0$.

For large/private, $E(y) = \beta_0 + \beta_1(0) + \beta_2(1) = \beta_0 + \beta_2$.

For small/public, $E(y) = \beta_0 + \beta_1(1) + \beta_2(0) = \beta_0 + \beta_1$.

For small/private, $E(y) = \beta_0 + \beta_1(1) + \beta_2(1) = \beta_0 + \beta_1 + \beta_2$.

g.   For public firms, the difference between small and large firms is $(\beta_0 + \beta_1) - \beta_0 = \beta_1$.

For private firms, the difference between small and large firms is $(\beta_0 + \beta_1 + \beta_2) - (\beta_0 + \beta_2) = \beta_1$.

h.   The model is $E(y) = \beta_0 + \beta_1 x_1 + \beta_2 x_2 + \beta_3 x_1 x_2$.

i.   For large/public, $E(y) = \beta_0 + \beta_1(0) + \beta_2(0) + \beta_3(0)(0) = \beta_0$.

For large/private, $E(y) = \beta_0 + \beta_1(0) + \beta_2(1) + \beta_3(0)(1) = \beta_0 + \beta_2$.

For small/public, $E(y) = \beta_0 + \beta_1(1) + \beta_2(0) + \beta_3(1)(0) = \beta_0 + \beta_1$.

For small/private, $E(y) = \beta_0 + \beta_1(1) + \beta_2(1) + \beta_3(1)(1) = \beta_0 + \beta_1 + \beta_2 + \beta_3$.

j.   For public firms, the difference between small and large firms is $(\beta_0 + \beta_1) - \beta_0 = \beta_1$.

For private firms, the difference between small and large firms is
$(\beta_0 + \beta_1 + \beta_2 + \beta_3) - (\beta_0 + \beta_2) = \beta_1 + \beta_3$.

12.79   a.   Let $x = \begin{cases} 1 \text{ if Lotion/cream} \\ 0 \text{ otherwise} \end{cases}$ The model is $E(y) = \beta_0 + \beta_1 x$..

b.   From MINITAB, the output is:

Regression Analysis: Cost/Use versus Type

```
The regression equation is
Cost/Use = 0.778 + 0.109 Type
```

Predictor	Coef	SE Coef	T	P
Constant	0.7775	0.2975	2.61	0.023
Type	0.1092	0.4545	0.24	0.814

```
S = 0.8415     R-Sq = 0.5%     R-Sq(adj) = 0.0%
```

Analysis of Variance

Source	DF	SS	MS	F	P
Regression	1	0.0409	0.0409	0.06	0.814
Residual Error	12	8.4973	0.7081		
Total	13	8.5381			

The fitted model is $\hat{y} = 0.7775 + .1092x$.

c.   To determine whether repellent type is a useful predictor of cost-per-use, we test:

$$H_0 : \beta_1 = 0$$

d.   The alternative hypothesis is

$$H_a : \beta_1 \neq 0$$

The test statistic is $t = 0.24$ and the p-value is $p = .814$.

Since the p-value is not less than α ($p = .814 \not< .10$), H_0 is not rejected. There is insufficient evidence to indicate that repellent type is a useful predictor of cost-per-use at $\alpha = .10$.

e.   The dummy variable will be defined the same way and the model will look the same (just the dependent variable will be different).

From MINITAB, the output is:

Regression Analysis: MaxProt versus Type

```
The regression equation is
MaxProt = 7.56 - 1.65 Type
```

Predictor	Coef	SE Coef	T	P
Constant	7.563	2.339	3.23	0.007
Type	-1.646	3.574	-0.46	0.653

```
S = 6.617      R-Sq = 1.7%      R-Sq(adj) = 0.0%
```

Analysis of Variance

Source	DF	SS	MS	F	P
Regression	1	9.29	9.29	0.21	0.653
Residual Error	12	525.43	43.79		
Total	13	534.71			

The fitted model is $\hat{y} = 7.56 - 1.65x$.

To determine whether repellent type is a useful predictor of cost-per-use, we test:

$$H_0 : \beta_1 = 0$$
$$H_a : \beta_1 \neq 0$$

The test statistic is $t = -0.46$ and the p-value is $p = .653$.

Since the p-value is not less than α ($p = .653 \not< .10$), H_0 is not rejected. There is insufficient evidence to indicate that repellent type is a useful predictor of maximum number of hours of protection at $\alpha = .10$.

12.81   a.   Let $x_1 = \begin{cases} 1 & \text{if Group V} \\ 0 & \text{otherwise} \end{cases}$ Let $x_2 = \begin{cases} 1 & \text{if Group S} \\ 0 & \text{otherwise} \end{cases}$

The model would be: $E(y) = \beta_0 + \beta_1 x_1 + \beta_2 x_2$

b.   Using MINITAB, the results are:

Regression Analysis: Recall versus x1, x2

```
The regression equation is
Recall = 3.17 - 1.08 x1 - 1.45 x2


Predictor      Coef   SE Coef      T      P
Constant     3.1667    0.1670  18.96  0.000
x1          -1.0833    0.2362  -4.59  0.000
x2          -1.4537    0.2362  -6.15  0.000

S = 1.73596    R-Sq = 11.3%    R-Sq(adj) = 10.7%

Analysis of Variance

Source            DF       SS      MS      F      P
Regression         2  123.265  61.633  20.45  0.000
Residual Error   321  967.352   3.014
Total            323 1090.617

Source  DF    Seq SS
x1       1     9.150
x2       1   114.116
```

The least squares prediction equation is $\hat{y} = 3.1667 - 1.0833x_1 - 1.4537x_2$.

c.   To determine if the overall model is useful, we test:

$$H_0 : \beta_1 = \beta_2 = 0$$
$$H_a : \text{At least one } \beta_i \neq 0$$

The test statistic is $F = 20.45$ and the p-value is $p = .000$. Since the p-value is less than α ($p = .000 < .01$), H_0 is rejected. There is sufficient evidence to indicate the model is useful in predicting brand recall at $\alpha = .01$.

From the Chapter 9 SIA, the test statistic was $F = 20.45$ and the p-value was $p = .000$. These are identical to those above. The model is useful in predicting recall. This is the same as the conclusion that there is a difference in mean recall among the 3 groups.

d.   With the dummy variable coding in part **a**, β_0 is the mean recall for group N. Thus, the estimated mean recall for Group N is 3.1667 or 3.17. β_1 is the difference in mean recall between Group V and Group N. Thus, the mean recall for Group V is $\beta_0 + \beta_1$ and is estimated to be $3.1667 - 1.0833 = 2.0834$ or 2.08. β_2 is the difference in mean recall between Group S and Group N. Thus, the mean recall for Group S is $\beta_0 + \beta_2$ and is estimated to be $3.1667 - 1.4537 = 1.7130$ or 1.71.

12.83   a.   The complete second-order model is $E(y) = \beta_0 + \beta_1 x_1 + \beta_2 x_1^2$.

b.   The new model is $E(y) = \beta_0 + \beta_1 x_1 + \beta_2 x_1^2 + \beta_3 x_2 + \beta_4 x_3$

$$\text{where } x_2 = \begin{cases} 1 \text{ if level 2} \\ 0 \text{ otherwise} \end{cases} \quad x_3 = \begin{cases} 1 \text{ if level 3} \\ 0 \text{ otherwise} \end{cases}$$

c. The model with the interaction terms is:

$$E(y) = \beta_0 + \beta_1 x_1 + \beta_2 x_1^2 + \beta_3 x_2 + \beta_4 x_3 + \beta_5 x_1 x_2 + \beta_6 x_1 x_3 + \beta_7 x_1^2 x_2 + \beta_8 x_1^2 x_3$$

d. The response curves will have the same shape if none of the interaction terms are present or if $\beta_5 = \beta_6 = \beta_7 = \beta_8 = 0$.

e. The response curves will be parallel lines if the interaction terms as well as the second-order terms are absent or if $\beta_2 = \beta_5 = \beta_6 = \beta_7 = \beta_8 = 0$.

f. The response curves will be identical if no terms involving the qualitative variable are present or $\beta_3 = \beta_4 = \beta_5 = \beta_6 = \beta_7 = \beta_8 = 0$

12.85 a. For $x_2 = 0$ and $x_3 = 0$, $E(y) = \beta_0 + \beta_1 x_1 + \beta_2 x_1^2$

For $x_2 = 1$ and $x_3 = 0$,
$$E(y) = \beta_0 + \beta_1 x_1 + \beta_2 x_1^2 + \beta_3 + \beta_5 x_1 + \beta_7 x_1^2 = (\beta_0 + \beta_3) + (\beta_1 + \beta_5)x_1 + (\beta_2 + \beta_7)x_1^2$$

For $x_2 = 0$ and $x_3 = 1$,
$$E(y) = \beta_0 + \beta_1 x_1 + \beta_2 x_1^2 + \beta_4 + \beta_6 x_1 + \beta_8 x_1^2 = (\beta_0 + \beta_4) + (\beta_1 + \beta_6)x_1 + (\beta_2 + \beta_8)x_1^2$$

b. Foe level 1, $\hat{y} = 48.8 - 3.4x_1 + .07x_1^2$

For level 2, $\hat{y} = 48.8 - 3.4x_1 + .07x_1^2 - 2.4(1) + 3.7x_1(1) - .02x_1^2(1) = 46.4 + 0.3x_1 + .05x_1^2$

For level 3, $\hat{y} = 48.8 - 3.4x_1 + .07x_1^2 - 7.5(1) + 2.7x_1(1) - .04x_1^2(1) = 41.3 - 0.7x_1 + 0.03x_1^2$

The plots of the lines are:

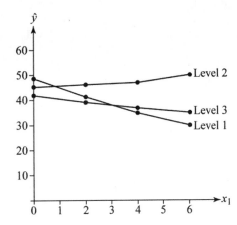

12.87 a. For female students, the equation is $\hat{y} = 11.78 - 1.97(0) + .58x_4 - .55(0)x_4 = 11.78 + .58x_4$. Thus, for females for each 1-point increase in impression of reality TV show, the mean desire is estimated to increase by .58.

b. For male students, the equation is $\hat{y} = 11.78 - 1.97(1) + .58x_4 - .55(1)x_4 = 9.81 + .03x_4$. Thus, for males for each 1-point increase in impression of reality TV show, the mean desire is estimated to increase by .03.

12.89   a.   To determine if the model is adequate, we test:

$$H_0: \beta_1 = \beta_2 = \cdots = \beta_{12} = 0$$
$$H_a: \text{At least one } \beta_i \neq 0$$

The test statistic is $F = 26.9$.

Using MINITAB with $v_1 = k = 12$ and $v_2 = n - (k + 1) = 148 - (12 + 1) = 135$,

Cumulative Distribution Function

```
F distribution with 12 DF in numerator and 135 DF in denominator

    x   P( X <= x )
26.9              1
```

The p-value associated with $F = 26.9$ is $p = 1 - 1 = 0$. Since the p-value is so small, H_0 is rejected. There is sufficient evidence to indicate the model is adequate for any reasonable value of α.

$R^2 = .705$. 70.5% of the total variation of the natural logarithm of card prices is explained by the model with the 12 variables in the model.

$R_a^2 = .681$. 68.1% of the total variation of the natural logarithm of card prices is explained by the model with the 12 variables in the model, adjusting for the sample size and the number of variables in the model.

Since these R^2 values are fairly large, it indicates that the model is pretty good.

b.   To determine if race contributes to the price, we test:

$$H_0: \beta_1 = 0$$
$$H_a: \beta_1 \neq 0$$

The test statistic is $t = -1.014$ and the p-value is $p = .312$. Since the p-value is so large, H_0 is not rejected. There is insufficient evidence to indicate race has an impact on the value of professional football player's rookie cards for any reasonable value of α, holding the other variables constant.

b.   To determine if card vintage contributes to the price, we test:

$$H_0: \beta_3 = 0$$
$$H_a: \beta_3 \neq 0$$

The test statistic is $t = -10.92$ and the p-value is $p = .000$. Since the p-value is so small, H_0 is rejected. There is sufficient evidence to indicate card vintage has an impact on the value of professional football player's rookie cards for any reasonable value of α, holding the other variables constant.

d.   The first order model is:

$$E(y) = \beta_0 + \beta_1 x_3 + \beta_2 x_5 + \beta_3 x_6 + \beta_4 x_7 + \beta_5 x_8 + \beta_6 x_9 + \beta_7 x_{10} + \beta_8 x_{11} + \beta_9 x_{12}$$
$$+ \beta_{10} x_5 x_3 + \beta_{11} x_6 x_3 + \beta_{12} x_7 x_3 + \beta_{13} x_8 x_3 + \beta_{14} x_9 x_3 + \beta_{15} x_{10} x_3 + \beta_{16} x_{11} x_3 + \beta_{17} x_{12} x_3$$

12.91   a.   Let $x_2 = \begin{cases} 1 \text{ if perceived organizational support is low} \\ 0 \text{ otherwise} \end{cases}$

$x_3 = \begin{cases} 1 \text{ if perceived organizational support is neutral} \\ 0 \text{ otherwise} \end{cases}$

   b.   The model would be $E(y) = \beta_0 + \beta_1 x_1 + \beta_2 x_2 + \beta_3 x_3$.

   c.   The model would be $E(y) = \beta_0 + \beta_1 x_1 + \beta_2 x_2 + \beta_3 x_3 + \beta_4 x_1 x_2 + \beta_5 x_1 x_3$.

   d.   If the effect of bullying on intention to leave is greater at the low level of POS than at the high level of POS, this indicates that POS and bullying interact. Thus, the model in part c supports these findings.

12.93   a.   Let $x_1 = \begin{cases} 1 \text{ if channel catfish} \\ 0 \text{ otherwise} \end{cases}$ $x_2 = \begin{cases} 1 \text{ if largemouth bass} \\ 0 \text{ otherwise} \end{cases}$

   b.   Let x_3 = weight. The model would be: $E(y) = \beta_0 + \beta_1 x_1 + \beta_2 x_2 + \beta_3 x_3$

   c.   The model would be: $E(y) = \beta_0 + \beta_1 x_1 + \beta_2 x_2 + \beta_3 x_3 + \beta_4 x_1 x_3 + \beta_4 x_2 x_3$

   d.   From MINITAB, the output is:

Regression Analysis: DDT versus x1, x2, Weight

```
The regression equation is
DDT = 3.1 + 26.5 x1 - 4.1 x2 + 0.0037 Weight
```

Predictor	Coef	SE Coef	T	P
Constant	3.13	38.89	0.08	0.936
x1	26.51	21.52	1.23	0.220
x2	-4.09	37.91	-0.11	0.914
Weight	0.00371	0.02598	0.14	0.887

```
S = 98.57      R-Sq = 1.7%      R-Sq(adj) = 0.0%
```

```
Analysis of Variance
```

Source	DF	SS	MS	F	P
Regression	3	23652	7884	0.81	0.490
Residual Error	140	1360351	9717		
Total	143	1384003			

Source	DF	Seq SS
x1	1	23041
x2	1	414
Weight	1	198

The least squares prediction equation is: $\hat{y} = 3.13 + 26.51 x_1 - 4.09 x_2 + 0.00371 x_3$

   e. $\hat{\beta}_3 = 0.00371$. For each additional gram of weight, the mean level of DDT is expected to increase by 0.00371 units, holding species constant.

f.   From MINITAB, the output is:

Regression Analysis: DDT versus x1, x2, Weight, x1Weight, x2Weight

```
The regression equation is
DDT = 3.5 + 25.6 x1 - 3.5 x2 + 0.0034 Weight + 0.0008 x1Weight
          - 0.0013 x2Weight

Predictor          Coef      SE Coef           T          P
Constant           3.50        54.69        0.06      0.949
x1                25.59        67.52        0.38      0.705
x2                -3.47        84.70       -0.04      0.967
Weight          0.00344      0.03843        0.09      0.929
x1Weight        0.00082      0.05459        0.02      0.988
x2Weight       -0.00129      0.09987       -0.01      0.990

S = 99.29        R-Sq = 1.7%        R-Sq(adj) = 0.0%

Analysis of Variance

Source            DF           SS          MS         F        P
Regression         5        23657        4731      0.48    0.791
Residual Error   138      1360346        9858
Total            143      1384003

Source       DF     Seq SS
x1            1      23041
x2            1        414
Weight        1        198
x1Weight      1          4
x2Weight      1          2
```

The least squares prediction equation is:

$$\hat{y} = 3.50 + 25.59x_1 - 3.47x_2 + 0.00344x_3 + 0.00082x_1x_3 - .00129x_2x_3$$

g.   For channel catfish, $x_1 = 1$ and $x_2 = 0$. The least squares line is

$$\hat{y} = 3.50 + 25.59(1) - 3.47(0) + 0.00344x_3 + 0.00082(1)x_3 - .00129(0)x_3 = 29.09 + .00426x_3$$

The estimated slope is .00426.

12.95   a.   Let x_1 = sales volume

$$x_2 = \begin{cases} 1 \text{ if NW} \\ 0 \text{ if not} \end{cases} \qquad x_3 = \begin{cases} 1 \text{ if S} \\ 0 \text{ if not} \end{cases} \qquad x_4 = \begin{cases} 1 \text{ if W} \\ 0 \text{ if not} \end{cases}$$

The complete second order model for the sales price of a single-family home is:

$$E(y) = \beta_0 + \beta_1 x_1 + \beta_2 x_1^2 + \beta_3 x_2 + \beta_4 x_3 + \beta_5 x_4 + \beta_6 x_1 x_2 + \beta_7 x_1 x_3 + \beta_8 x_1 x_4 + \beta_9 x_1^2 x_2 + \beta_{10} x_1^2 x_3 + \beta_{11} x_1^2 x_4$$

b.　For the West, $x_2 = 0$, $x_3 = 0$, and $x_4 = 1$. The equation would be:

$$E(y) = \beta_0 + \beta_1 x_1 + \beta_2 x_1^2 + \beta_3(0) + \beta_4(0) + \beta_5(1) + \beta_6 x_1(0) + \beta_7 x_1(0) + \beta_8 x_1(1)$$
$$+ \beta_9 x_1^2(0) + \beta_{10} x_1^2(0) + \beta_{11} x_1^2(1)$$
$$= \beta_0 + \beta_1 x_1 + \beta_2 x_1^2 + \beta_5 + \beta_8 x_1 + \beta_{11} x_1^2 = (\beta_0 + \beta_5) + (\beta_1 + \beta_8)x_1 + (\beta_2 + \beta_{11})x_1^2$$

c.　For the Northwest, $x_2 = 1$, $x_3 = 0$, and $x_4 = 0$. The equation would be:

$$E(y) = \beta_0 + \beta_1 x_1 + \beta_2 x_1^2 + \beta_3(1) + \beta_4(0) + \beta_5(0) + \beta_6 x_1(1) + \beta_7 x_1(0) + \beta_8 x_1(0)$$
$$+ \beta_9 x_1^2(1) + \beta_{10} x_1^2(0) + \beta_{11} x_1^2(0)$$
$$= \beta_0 + \beta_1 x_1 + \beta_2 x_1^2 + \beta_3 + \beta_6 x_1 + \beta_9 x_1^2 = (\beta_0 + \beta_3) + (\beta_1 + \beta_6)x_1 + (\beta_2 + \beta_9)x_1^2$$

d.　The parameters β_3, β_4, and β_5 allow for the y-intercepts of the 4 regions to be different. The parameters β_6, β_7, and β_8 allow for the peaks of the curves to be a different value of sales volume (x_1) for the four regions. The parameters β_9, β_{10}, and β_{11} allow for the shapes of the curves to be different for the four regions. Thus, all the parameters from β_3 through β_{11} allow for differences in mean sales prices among the four regions.

e.　Using MINITAB, the printout is:

Regression Analysis: Price versus X1, X1SQ, ...

```
The regression equation is
Price = 1904740 - 70.4 X1 + 0.000721 X1SQ + 159661 X2 + 5291908 X3 + 3663319 X4
        + 22.2 X1X2 - 23.9 X1X3 - 37 X1X4 - 0.000421 X1SQX2 - 0.000404 X1SQX3
        - 0.000181 X1SQX4
```

Predictor	Coef	SE Coef	T	P
Constant	1904740	1984278	0.96	0.351
X1	-70.44	72.09	-0.98	0.343
X1SQ	0.0007211	0.0006515	1.11	0.285
X2	159661	2069265	0.08	0.939
X3	5291908	4812586	1.10	0.288
X4	3663319	4478880	0.82	0.425
X1X2	22.25	73.74	0.30	0.767
X1X3	-23.86	92.09	-0.26	0.799
X1X4	-37.2	103.0	-0.36	0.723
X1SQX2	-0.0004210	0.0006589	-0.64	0.532
X1SQX3	-0.0004044	0.0006777	-0.60	0.559
X1SQX4	-0.0001810	0.0007333	-0.25	0.808

```
S = 24365.8   R-Sq = 85.0%   R-Sq(adj) = 74.6%
```

Analysis of Variance

Source	DF	SS	MS	F	P
Regression	11	53633628997	4875784454	8.21	0.000
Residual Error	16	9499097458	593693591		
Total	27	63132726455			

```
Source   DF      Seq SS
X1        1       3591326
X1SQ      1      64275360
X2        1   11338642654
X3        1   10081000583
X4        1     241539024
X1X2      1   18258475317
X1X3      1    5579187440
X1X4      1    7566169810
X1SQX2    1     138146367
X1SQX3    1     326425228
X1SQX4    1      36175888
```

To determine if the model is useful for predicting sales price, we test:

$$H_0 : \beta_1 = \beta_2 = \cdots = \beta_{11} = 0$$
$$H_a : \text{At least one } \beta_i \neq 0$$

The test statistic is $F = \dfrac{MS(Model)}{MSE} = 8.21$ and the p-value is $p = .000$. Since the p-value is less than α $(p = .000 < .01)$, H_0 is rejected. There is sufficient evidence to indicate the model is useful in predicting sales price at $\alpha = .01$.

12.97   The models in parts **a** and **b** are nested:

The complete model is $E(y) = \beta_0 + \beta_1 x_1 + \beta_2 x_2$.
The reduced model is $E(y) = \beta_0 + \beta_1 x_1$.

The models in parts **a** and **d** are nested.

The complete model is $E(y) = \beta_0 + \beta_1 x_1 + \beta_2 x_2 + \beta_3 x_1 x_2$.
The reduced model is $E(y) = \beta_0 + \beta_1 x_1 + \beta_2 x_2$.

The models in parts **a** and **e** are nested.

The complete model is $E(y) = \beta_0 + \beta_1 x_1 + \beta_2 x_2 + \beta_3 x_1 x_2 + \beta_4 x_1^2 + \beta_5 x_2^2$.
The reduced model is $E(y) = \beta_0 + \beta_1 x_1 + \beta_2 x_2$.

The models in parts **b** and **c** are nested.

The complete model is $E(y) = \beta_0 + \beta_1 x_1 + \beta_2 x_1^2$.
The reduced model is $E(y) = \beta_0 + \beta_1 x_1$.

The models in parts **b** and **d** are nested.

The complete model is $E(y) = \beta_0 + \beta_1 x_1 + \beta_2 x_2 + \beta_3 x_1 x_2$.
The reduced model is $E(y) = \beta_0 + \beta_1 x_1$.

The models in parts **b** and **e** are nested.

The complete model is $E(y) = \beta_0 + \beta_1 x_1 + \beta_2 x_2 + \beta_3 x_1 x_2 + \beta_4 x_1^2 + \beta_5 x_2^2$

The reduced model is $E(y) = \beta_0 + \beta_1 x_1$.

The models in parts **c** and **e** are nested.

The complete model is $E(y) = \beta_0 + \beta_1 x_1 + \beta_2 x_2 + \beta_3 x_1 x_2 + \beta_4 x_1^2 + \beta_5 x_2^2$

The reduced model is $E(y) = \beta_0 + \beta_1 x_1 + \beta_2 x_1^2$

The models in parts **d** and **e** are nested.

The complete model is $E(y) = \beta_0 + \beta_1 x_1 + \beta_2 x_2 + \beta_3 x_1 x_2 + \beta_4 x_1^2 + \beta_5 x_2^2$

The reduced model is $E(y) = \beta_0 + \beta_1 x_1 + \beta_2 x_2 + \beta_3 x_1 x_2$

12.99   a.   Including β_0, there are five β parameters in the complete model and three in the reduced model.

b.   The hypotheses are:

$$H_0 : \beta_3 = \beta_4 = 0$$
$$H_a : \text{At least one } \beta_i \neq 0, \ i = 3, 4$$

c.   The test statistic is $F = \dfrac{(SSE_R - SSE_C)/(k-g)}{SSE_C/[n-(k+1)]} = \dfrac{(160.44 - 152.66)/(4-2)}{152.66/[20-(4+1)]} = \dfrac{3.89}{10.1773} = .38$

The rejection region requires $\alpha = .05$ in the upper tail of the F-distribution with $v_1 = k - g = 4 - 2 = 2$ and $v_2 = n - (k+1) = 20 - (4+1) = 15$. From Table VI, Appendix D, $F_{.05} = 3.68$. The rejection region is $F > 3.68$.

Since the observed value of the test statistic does not fall in the rejection region $(F = .38 \not> 3.68)$, H_0 is not rejected. There is insufficient evidence to indicate the complete model is better than the reduced model at $\alpha = .05$.

12.101   a.   To determine whether the quadratic terms in the model are statistically useful for predicting relative optimism, we test:

$$H_0 : \beta_4 = \beta_5 = 0$$
$$H_a : \text{At least one } \beta_i \neq 0$$

b.   The complete model is $E(y) = \beta_0 + \beta_1 x_1 + \beta_2 x_2 + \beta_3 x_1 x_2 + \beta_4 x_1^2 + \beta_5 x_1 x_2^2$ and the reduced model is $E(y) = \beta_0 + \beta_1 x_1 + \beta_2 x_2 + \beta_3 x_1 x_2$.

b.   To determine whether the interaction terms in the model are statistically useful for predicting relative optimism, we test:

$$H_0 : \beta_3 = \beta_5 = 0$$
$$H_a : \text{At least one } \beta_i \neq 0$$

d.   The complete model is $E(y) = \beta_0 + \beta_1 x_1 + \beta_2 x_2 + \beta_3 x_1 x_2 + \beta_4 x_1^2 + \beta_5 x_1 x_2^2$ and the reduced model is $E(y) = \beta_0 + \beta_1 x_1 + \beta_2 x_2 + \beta_4 x_2^2$.

e.   To determine whether the dummy variable terms in the model are statistically useful for predicting relative optimism, we test:

$$H_0 : \beta_1 = \beta_3 = \beta_5 = 0$$
$$H_a : \text{At least one } \beta_i \neq 0$$

f.   The complete model is $E(y) = \beta_0 + \beta_1 x_1 + \beta_2 x_2 + \beta_3 x_1 x_2 + \beta_4 x_2^2 + \beta_5 x_1 x_2^2$ and the reduced model is $E(y) = \beta_0 + \beta_2 x_2 + \beta_4 x_2^2$.

12.103 a.   Let x_1 = cycle speed and x_2 = cycle pressure ratio. A complete second order model is:

$$E(y) = \beta_0 + \beta_1 x_1 + \beta_2 x_2 + \beta_3 x_1^2 + \beta_4 x_2^2 + \beta_5 x_1 x_2$$

b.   To determine whether the curvature terms in the complete 2nd –order model are useful for predicting heat rate, we test:

$$H_0 : \beta_3 = \beta_4 = 0$$
$$H_a : \text{At least one } \beta_i \neq 0$$

c.   The complete model is $E(y) = \beta_0 + \beta_1 x_1 + \beta_2 x_2 + \beta_3 x_1^2 + \beta_4 x_2^2 + \beta_5 x_1 x_2$

The reduced model is $E(y) = \beta_0 + \beta_1 x_1 + \beta_2 x_2 + \beta_5 x_1 x_2$

d.   From the printout, $SSE_R = 25,310,639$, $SSE_C = 19,370,350$, and $MSE_C = 317,547$.

e.   The test statistic is $F = \dfrac{(SSE_R - SSE_C)/(k-g)}{SSE_C/[n-(k+1)]} = \dfrac{(25,310,639 - 19,370,350)/(5-3)}{19,370,350/[67-(5+1)]} = 9.35$

f.   The rejection region requires $\alpha = .10$ in the upper tail of the F-distribution with $v_1 = k - g = 5 - 3 = 2$ and $v_2 = n - (k+1) = 67 - (5+1) = 61$. From Table V, Appendix D, $F_{.10} = 2.39$. The rejection region is $F > 2.39$.

g.   Since the observed value of the test statistic falls in the rejection region $(F = 9.35 > 2.39)$, H_0 is rejected. There is sufficient evidence to indicate at least one of the curvature terms in the complete 2nd –order model are useful for predicting heat rate at $\alpha = .10$.

12.105 a.   The model would be: $E(y) = \beta_0 + \beta_1 x_1 + \beta_2 x_2 + \beta_3 x_3 + \beta_4 x_4 + \beta_5 x_1 x_4 + \beta_6 x_2 x_4 + \beta_7 x_3 x_4$

b. Using MINITAB, the results are:

Regression Analysis: DESIRE versus GENDER, SELFESTM, ...

```
The regression equation is
DESIRE = 13.1 - 1.89 GENDER - 0.091 SELFESTM + 0.135 BODYSAT + 0.746 IMPREAL
        - 0.065 G_I + 0.0098 SE_I - 0.112 BS_I

Predictor      Coef   SE Coef      T      P
Constant     13.092     2.013   6.50  0.000
GENDER       -1.890     2.074  -0.91  0.363
SELFESTM    -0.0908    0.1176  -0.77  0.441
BODYSAT      0.1350    0.4749   0.28  0.777
IMPREAL      0.7460    0.4918   1.52  0.131
G_I         -0.0647    0.5110  -0.13  0.899
SE_I        0.00977   0.02808   0.35  0.728
BS_I        -0.1121    0.1160  -0.97  0.335


S = 2.23593   R-Sq = 51.3%   R-Sq(adj) = 49.2%


Analysis of Variance

Source            DF        SS      MS      F      P
Regression         7    853.89  121.98  24.40  0.000
Residual Error   162    809.90    5.00
Total            169   1663.79


Source      DF   Seq SS
GENDER       1   674.64
SELFESTM     1    57.66
BODYSAT      1    19.62
IMPREAL      1    75.91
G_I          1    20.36
SE_I         1     1.03
BS_I         1     4.67
```

To determine the overall utility of the model, we test:

$$H_0 : \beta_1 = \beta_2 = \beta_3 = \beta_4 = \beta_5 = \beta_6 = \beta_7 = 0$$
$$H_a : \text{At least } 1 \beta_i \neq 0$$

The test statistic is $F = 24.40$ and the p-value is $p = .000$. Since the p-value is so small, H_0 will be rejected for any reasonable value of α. There is sufficient evidence to indicate the model is useful for predicting desire to have cosmetic surgery.

c. To determine if impression of reality TV interacts with each of the other independent variables, the null hypothesis is:

$$H_0 : \beta_5 = \beta_6 = \beta_7 = 0$$

d. The reduced model is $E(y) = \beta_0 + \beta_1 x_1 + \beta_2 x_2 + \beta_3 x_3 + \beta_4 x_4$. This model was fit in Exercise 12.17. From this exercise, $SSE_R = 835.95$.

The test statistic is $F = \dfrac{(SSE_R - SSE_C)/(k-g)}{SSE_C/[n-(k+1)]} = \dfrac{(835.95 - 809.90)/(7-4)}{809.90/[170-(7+1)]} = 1.74$.

Since no α was given, we will use $\alpha = .05$. The rejection region requires $\alpha = .05$ in the upper tail of the F-distribution with $v_1 = k - g = 7 - 4 = 3$ and $v_2 = n - (k+1) = 170 - (7+1) = 162$. From Table VI, Appendix D, $F_{.05} \approx 2.68$. The rejection region is $F > 2.68$.

Since the observed value of the test statistic does not fall in the rejection region $(F = 1.74 \not> 2.68)$, H_0 is not rejected. There is insufficient evidence to indicate impression of reality TV interacts with each of the other independent variables at $\alpha = .05$.

12.107   a.   If the theory is correct, then the sign of β_3 should be positive.

b.   A possible graph might look like:

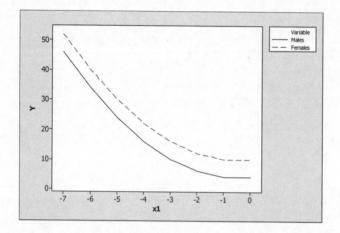

c.   The complete 2$^\text{nd}$-order model is $E(y) = \beta_0 + \beta_1 x_1 + \beta_2 x_1^2 + \beta_3 x_2 + \beta_4 x_1 x_2 + \beta_5 x_1^2 x_2$.

d.   A possible graph might look like:

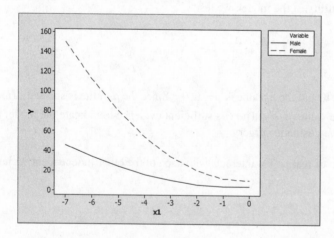

e.   To compare the two models, we test:

$H_0 : \beta_4 = \beta_5 = 0$
H_a : At least 1 $\beta_i \neq 0$

f. Using MINITAB, the results of fitting the model in part a are:

Regression Analysis: Income versus Agree, Agree-sq, Gender

```
The regression equation is
Income = - 21657 + 37155 Agree - 7056 Agree-sq + 25482 Gender

Predictor    Coef   SE Coef       T      P
Constant   -21657     31780   -0.68  0.497
Agree       37155     19257    1.93  0.057
Agree-sq    -7056      2903   -2.43  0.017
Gender      25482      1552   16.42  0.000

S = 7737.36   R-Sq = 76.5%   R-Sq(adj) = 75.8%

Analysis of Variance

Source            DF           SS          MS       F      P
Regression         3  18708663846  6236221282  104.17  0.000
Residual Error    96   5747214158    59866814
Total             99  24455878004

Source       DF      Seq SS
Agree         1  1896882849
Agree-sq      1   663015651
Gender        1 16148765346
```

Using MINITAB, the results of fitting the model in part c are:

Regression Analysis: Income versus Agree, Agree-sq, Gender, G_A, G_A-sq

```
The regression equation is
Income = - 9847 + 27248 Agree - 5169 Agree-sq + 42549 Gender - 4765 G_A
         - 128 G_A-sq

Predictor    Coef   SE Coef       T      P
Constant    -9847     45303   -0.22  0.828
Agree       27248     28743    0.95  0.346
Agree-sq    -5169      4520   -1.14  0.256
Gender      42549     71654    0.59  0.554
G_A         -4765     43177   -0.11  0.912
G_A-sq       -128      6474   -0.02  0.984

S = 7751.27   R-Sq = 76.9%   R-Sq(adj) = 75.7%

Analysis of Variance

Source            DF           SS          MS      F      P
Regression         5  18808157832  3761631566  62.61  0.000
Residual Error    94   5647720172    60082129
Total             99  24455878004

Source       DF      Seq SS
Agree         1  1896882849
Agree-sq      1   663015651
Gender        1 16148765346
G_A           1    99470471
G_A-sq        1       23515
```

The test statistic is $F = \dfrac{(SSE_R - SSE_C)/(k-g)}{SSE_C/[n-(k+1)]} = \dfrac{(5,747,214,158 - 5,647,720,172)/(5-3)}{5,647,720,172/[100-(5+1)]} = .83$.

The rejection region requires $\alpha = .10$ in the upper tail of the F-distribution with $v_1 = k - g = 5 - 3 = 2$ and $v_2 = n - (k+1) = 100 - (5+1) = 94$. From Table V, Appendix D, $F_{.10} \approx 2.37$. The rejection region is $F > 2.37$.

Since the observed value of the test statistic does not fall in the rejection region ($F = .83 \not> 2.37$), H_0 is not rejected. There is insufficient evidence to indicate the interaction terms improve the model at $\alpha = .10$.

12.109 a.   The model would be $E(y) = \beta_0 + \beta_1 x_1 + \beta_2 x_2 + \beta_3 x_3$.

b.   The model including the interaction terms is: $E(y) = \beta_0 + \beta_1 x_1 + \beta_2 x_2 + \beta_3 x_3 + \beta_4 x_1 x_2 + \beta_5 x_1 x_3$

c.   For AL, $x_2 = x_3 = 0$. The model would be:

$E(y) = \beta_0 + \beta_1 x_1 + \beta_2 (0) + \beta_3 (0) + \beta_4 x_1 (0) + \beta_5 x_1 (0) = \beta_0 + \beta_1 x_1$

The slope of the line is β_1.

For TDS-3A, $x_2 = 1$ and $x_3 = 0$. The model would be:

$E(y) = \beta_0 + \beta_1 x_1 + \beta_2 (1) + \beta_3 (0) + \beta_4 x_1 (1) + \beta_5 x_1 (0) = (\beta_0 + \beta_2) + (\beta_1 + \beta_4) x_1$

The slope of the line is $\beta_1 + \beta_4$.

For FE, $x_2 = 0$ and $x_3 = 1$. The model would be:

$E(y) = \beta_0 + \beta_1 x_1 + \beta_2 (0) + \beta_3 (1) + \beta_4 x_1 (0) + \beta_5 x_1 (1) = (\beta_0 + \beta_3) + (\beta_1 + \beta_5) x_1$

The slope of the line is $\beta_1 + \beta_5$.

d.   To test for the presence of temperature-waste type interaction, we would fit the complete model listed in part **b** and the reduced model found in part **a**. The hypotheses would be:

$H_0 : \beta_4 = \beta_5 = 0$

H_a : At least one $\beta_i \neq 0$

The test statistic would be $F = \dfrac{(SSE_R - SSE_C)/(k-g)}{SSE_C/[n-(k+1)]}$ where $k = 5$, $q = 3$, SSE_R is the SSE for the reduced model, and SSE_c is the SSE for the complete model.

12.111 a.   The best one-variable predictor of y is the one whose t statistic has the largest absolute value. The t statistics for each of the variables are:

Independent Variable	$t = \dfrac{\hat{\beta}_i}{s_{\hat{\beta}_i}}$
x_1	$t = 1.6 / .42 = 3.81$
x_2	$t = -.9 / .01 = -90$
x_3	$t = 3.4 / 1.14 = 2.98$
x_4	$t = 2.5 / 2.06 = 1.21$
x_5	$t = -4.4 / .73 = -6.03$
x_6	$t = .3 / .35 = .86$

The variable x_2 is the best one-variable predictor of y. The absolute value of the corresponding t score is 90. This is larger than any of the others.

b.   Yes. In the stepwise procedure, the first variable entered is the one which has the largest absolute value of t, provided the absolute value of the t falls in the rejection region.

c.   Once x_2 is entered, the next variable that is entered is the one that, in conjunction with x_2, has the largest absolute t value associated with it.

12.113 a.   In Step 1, all one-variable models are fit to the data. These models are of the form:

$$E(y) = \beta_0 + \beta_1 x_i$$

Since there are 7 independent variables, 7 models are fit. (Note: There are actually only 6 independent variables. One of the qualitative variables has three levels and thus two dummy variables. Some statistical packages will allow one to bunch these two variables together so that they are either both in or both out. In this answer, we are assuming that each x_i stands by itself.)

b.   In Step 2, all two-variable models are fit to the data, where the variable selected in Step 1, say x_1, is one of the variables. These models are of the form:

$$E(y) = \beta_0 + \beta_1 x_1 + \beta_2 x_i$$

Since there are 6 independent variables remaining, 6 models are fit.

c.   In Step 3, all three-variable models are fit to the data, where the variables selected in Step 2, say x_1 and x_2, are two of the variables. These models are of the form:

$$E(y) = \beta_0 + \beta_1 x_1 + \beta_2 x_2 + \beta_3 x_i$$

Since there are 5 independent variables remaining, 5 models are fit.

d.   The procedure stops adding independent variables when none of the remaining variables, when added to the model, have a p-value less than some predetermined value. This predetermined value is usually $\alpha = .05$.

e.   Two major drawbacks to using the final stepwise model as the "best" model are:

(1)   An extremely large number of single β parameter t-tests have been conducted. Thus, the probability is very high that one or more errors have been made in including or excluding variables.

(2)   Often the variables selected to be included in a stepwise regression do not include the high-order terms. Consequently, we may have initially omitted several important terms from the model.

12.115   a.   In step 1, there were 11 one-variable models fit to the data. Thus, there were 11 t-tests run.

b.   In step 2, there were 10 two-variable models fit to the data. Thus, there were 10 t-tests run.

c.   The Global F p-value = .001. Since this p-value is so small, there is evidence that the final model is useful for predicting TME. $R^2 = .988$. 98.8% of the total sample variation of TME about its mean is explained by the model containing AMAP and NDF.

d.   The stepwise procedure does not guarantee that the "best" model has been determined. It is possible that important variables were not located. In addition, 2nd order terms and interaction terms should be considered.

e.   The complete 2nd order model would be:

$$E(y) = \beta_0 + \beta_1(AMAP) + \beta_2(NDF) + \beta_3(AMAP)^2 + \beta_4(NDF)^2 + \beta_5(AMAP)(NDF)$$

f.   To determine if the terms in the model that allow for curvature are statistically significant, we test:

$$H_0 : \beta_3 = \beta_4 = \beta_5 = 0$$
$$H_a : \text{At least } 1 \beta_i \neq 0$$

We would compare the complete model (form part e) to the reduced model with just the main effects of AMAP and NDF using the test statistic $F = \dfrac{(SSE_R - SSE_C)/(k-g)}{SSE_C /[n-(k+1)]}$.

12.117   a.   In step 1, all 1 variable models are fit. Thus, there are a total of 11 models fit.

b.   In step 2, all two-variable models are fit, where 1 of the variables is the best one selected in step 1. Thus, a total of 10 two-variable models are fit.

c.   In the 11th step, only one model is fit – the model containing all the independent variables.

d.   The model would be $E(y) = \beta_0 + \beta_1 x_{11} + \beta_2 x_4 + \beta_3 x_2 + \beta_4 x_7 + \beta_5 x_{10} + \beta_6 x_1 + \beta_7 x_9 + \beta_8 x_3$.

e.   67.7% of the total sample variability of overall satisfaction is explained by the model containing the independent variables safety on bus, seat availability, dependability, travel time, convenience of route, safety at bus stops, hours of service, and frequency of service.

f.   Using stepwise regression does not guarantee that the best model will be found. There may be better combinations of the independent variables that are never found, because of the order in which the independent variables are entered into the model. In addition, there are no squared or interaction terms included. There is a high probability of making at least one Type 1 error.

12.119   Yes. x_2 and x_4 are highly correlated (.93), as well as x_4 and x_5 (.86). When highly correlated independent variables are present in a regression model, the results can be confusing. The researcher may want to include only one of the variables.

12.121   a.   For a basic wooden casket $(x_2 = 1)$ and funeral home in a restricted state $(x_1 = 1)$,
$\hat{y} = 1,432 + 793(1) - 252(1) + 261(1)(1) = 2,234$.

   b.   No, this would not be an outlier. The point \$2,200 is less than one standard deviation from its predicted value.

   c.   Yes. This data point is $z = \dfrac{2,500 - 2,200}{50} = 6$ standard deviations from its predicted value.

12.123   a.   The number of females in managerial positions is the dependent variable. The correlation between it and the independent variables does not imply multicollinearity.

   b.   Again, the number of females in managerial positions is the dependent variable. The correlation between it and the independent variables does not imply multicollinearity.

   c.   Since the absolute value of the correlation coefficient is .722, this would imply there is a moderate potential for multicollinearity.

   d.   Since the absolute value of the correlation coefficient is .528, this would imply there is a moderate potential for multicollinearity.

12.125   It is possible that company role of estimator and previous accuracy could be correlated with each other. This could indicate multicollinearity may be present.

12.127   Using MINITAB, the residual plots are:

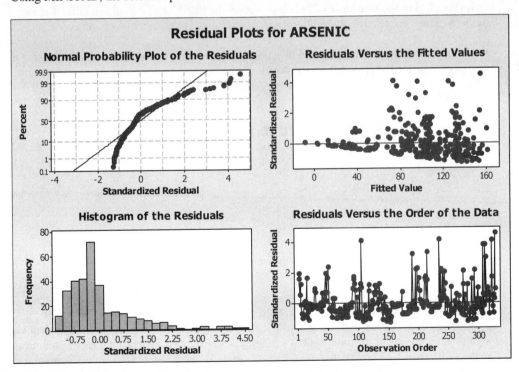

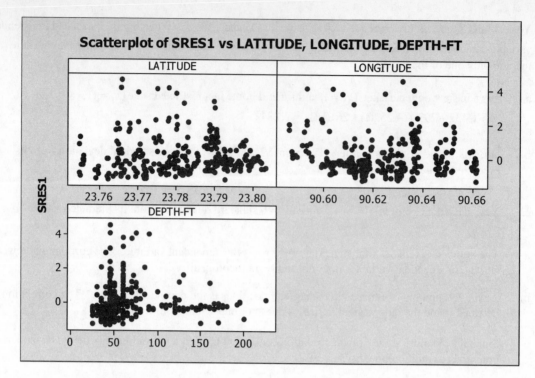

a. From the histogram of the standardized residuals, it appears that the mean of the residuals is close to 0. Thus, the assumption that the mean error is 0 appears to be met.

b. From the plot of the standardized residuals versus the fitted values, it appears that the spread of the residuals increases as the fitted values increase. Thus, it appears that the assumption of constant variance is violated.

c. From the plots of the standardized residuals versus the fitted values, it appears that there are some outliers. There are several observations with standardized residuals of 4 or more.

d. From the normal probability plot, the data do not form a straight line. Thus, it appears that the assumption of normal error terms is violated.

e. Using MINITAB, the correlations among the independent variables are:

Correlations: LATITUDE, LONGITUDE, DEPTH-FT

```
           LATITUDE  LONGITUDE
LONGITUDE     0.311
              0.000


DEPTH-FT      0.151     -0.328
              0.006      0.000


Cell Contents:  Pearson correlation
                P-Value
```

None of the pairwise correlations are large in absolute value, so there is no evidence of multicollinearity. In addition, the global test indicates that at least one of the independent variables is significant and each of the independent variables is statistically significant. This also indicates that multicollinearity does not exist.

12.129   a.   Using MINITAB, the results are:

Regression Analysis: Time versus Temp

```
The regression equation is
Time = 30856 - 192 Temp


Predictor      Coef   SE Coef       T      P
Constant      30856      2713   11.37  0.000
Temp        -191.57     18.49  -10.36  0.000


S = 1099.17    R-Sq = 84.3%    R-Sq(adj) = 83.5%


Analysis of Variance

Source            DF          SS         MS       F      P
Regression         1   129663987  129663987  107.32  0.000
Residual Error    20    24163399    1208170
Total             21   153827386
```

The fitted regression line is $\hat{y} = 30,856 - 191.57x$.

b.   For temperature = 149, $\hat{y} = 30,856 - 191.57(150) = 2,312.07$. There are 2 observations with a temperature of 149. The residuals for the microchips manufactured at a temperature of $149°$ C are $\hat{\varepsilon} = y - \hat{y} = 1,100 - 2,312.07 = -1,212.07$ and $\hat{\varepsilon} = y - \hat{y} = 1,150 - 2,312.07 = -1,162.07$.

c.   Using MINITAB, the plot of the residuals versus temperature is:

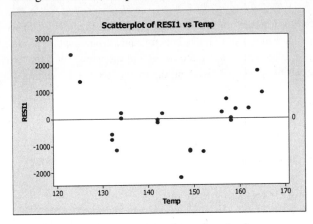

There appears to be a U-shaped trend to the data.

d.   Yes. Because there appears to be a U-shaped trend to the data, this indicates that there is a curvilinear relationship between temperature and time.

12.131   Using MINITAB, the residual plots are:

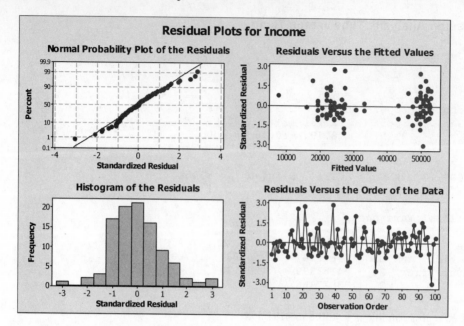

From the plot of the standardized residuals versus the fitted values, there is a slight increase in the spread of the residuals as the fitted values increase. There is some evidence of non-constant variance. All of the standardized residuals are less than 3 in absolute value, indicating there are no outliers. Looking at the normal probability plot and the histogram of the residuals, there is no evidence that the error terms are not normal. The data were not collected sequentially, so the plot of the residuals versus time is meaningless.

To correct the non-constant variance, one might transform the dependent variable.

12.133   In multiple regression, as in simple regression, the confidence interval for the mean value of y is narrower than the prediction interval of a particular value of y. This is because the variance when predicting a particular value of y contains both the variance in locating the mean and the variance of the actual values once the mean has been located. The variance when estimating the mean value is y contains only the variance in locating the mean.

12.135   a.   The least squares equation is $\hat{y} = 90.1 - 1.836x_1 + .285x_2$.

b. $R^2 = .916$. About 91.6% of the sample variability in the y's is explained by the model $E(y) = \beta_0 + \beta_1 x_1 + \beta_2 x_2$.

c.   To determine if the model is useful for predicting y, we test:

$$H_0 : \beta_1 = \beta_2 = 0$$
$$H_a : \text{At least one } \beta_i \neq 0$$

The test statistic is $F = \dfrac{MSR}{MSE} = \dfrac{7400}{114} = 64.91$ and the p-value is $p = .001$.

Since the p-value is less than α ($p = .001 < .05$), H_0 is rejected. There is sufficient evidence to indicate the model is useful for predicting y at $\alpha = .05$.

d.
$$H_0 : \beta_1 = 0$$
$$H_a : \beta_1 \neq 0$$

The test statistic is $t = \dfrac{\hat{\beta}_1}{s_{\hat{\beta}_1}} = \dfrac{-1.836}{.367} = -5.01$ and the p-value is $p = .001$.

Since the p-value is less than α $(p = .001 < .05)$, H_0 is rejected. There is sufficient evidence to indicate β_1 is not 0 at $\alpha = .05$.

e.
The standard deviation is $s = 10.68$. We would expect about 95% of the observations to fall within $2s = 2(10.68) = 21.36$ units of the fitted regression line.

12.137 $E(y) = \beta_0 + \beta_1 x_1 + \beta_2 x_2 + \beta_3 x_3$

where $x_1 = \begin{cases} 1 & \text{if level 2} \\ 0 & \text{otherwise} \end{cases}$ $\quad x_2 = \begin{cases} 1 & \text{if level 3} \\ 0 & \text{otherwise} \end{cases}$ $\quad x_3 = \begin{cases} 1 & \text{if level 4} \\ 0 & \text{otherwise} \end{cases}$

12.139 The stepwise regression method is used to try to find the best model to describe a process. It is a screening procedure that tries to select a small subset of independent variables from a large set of independent variables that will adequately predict the dependent variable. This method is useful in that it can eliminate some unimportant independent variables from consideration.

12.141 Even though $SSE = 0$, we cannot estimate σ^2 because there are no degrees of freedom corresponding to error. With three data points, there are only two degrees of freedom available. The degrees of freedom corresponding to the model is $k = 2$ and the degrees of freedom corresponding to error is $df = n - (k+1) = 3 - (2+1) = 0$. Without an estimate for σ^2, no inferences can be made.

12.143 a. A confidence interval for the difference of two population means, $(\mu_1 - \mu_2)$, could be used. Since both sample sizes are over 30, the large sample confidence interval is used (with independent samples).

b. Let $x = \begin{cases} 1 & \text{if public college} \\ 0 & \text{otherwise} \end{cases}$ $\qquad$ The model is $E(y) = \beta_0 + \beta_1 x_1$.

c. β_1 is the difference between the two population means. A point estimate for β_1 is $\hat{\beta}_1$. A confidence interval for β_1 could be used to estimate the difference in the two population means.

12.145 a. The type of juice extractor is qualitative. The size of the orange is quantitative.

b. The model is $E(y) = \beta_0 + \beta_1 x_1 + \beta_2 x_2$ where $x_1 = $ diameter of orange and $x_2 = \begin{cases} 1 & \text{if Brand B} \\ 0 & \text{if not} \end{cases}$

c. To allow the lines to differ, the interaction term is added: $E(y) = \beta_0 + \beta_1 x_1 + \beta_2 x_2 + \beta_3 x_1 x_2$

d.   For part **b**:

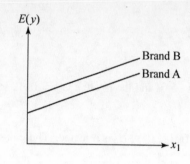

For part **c**:

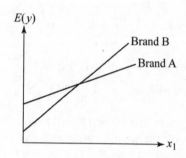

e.   To determine whether the model in part **c** provides more information for predicting yield than does the model in part **b**, we test:

$$H_0 : \beta_3 = 0$$
$$H_a : \beta_3 \neq 0$$

f.   The test statistic would be $F = \dfrac{(SSE_R - SSE_C)/(k-g)}{SSE_C /[n-(k+1)]}$.

To compute SSE_R: The model in part **b** is fit and SSE_R is the sum of squares for error.

To compute SSE_C: The model in part **c** is fit and SSE_C is the sum of squares for error.

$k - g = 3 - 2 = 1 =$ number of parameters in H_0

$n - (k+1) =$ degrees of freedom for error in the complete model

12.147   Variables that are highly correlated with each other are x_4 and x_5 $(r = -.84)$. When highly correlated independent variables are present in a regression model, the results can be confusing. Possible problems include:

1.   Global test indicates at least one independent variable is useful in the prediction of y, but none of the individual tests for the independent variables is significant.

2.   The signs of the estimated beta coefficients are opposite from what is expected.

12.149   a. $\hat{\beta}_0 = -.0304$. Since $x_1 = 0$ and $x_2 = 0$ would not be in the observed range, this is simply the y-intercept.

         $\hat{\beta}_1 = 2.006$. For each unit increase in the proportion of block with low-density residential areas, the mean population density is estimated to increase by 2.006, holding proportion of block with high-density residential areas constant. Since x_1 is a proportion, it is unlikely that it can increase by one unit. A better interpretation is: For each increase of .1 in the proportion of block with low-density residential areas, the mean population density is estimated to increase by .2006, holding proportion of block with high-density residential areas constant.

         $\hat{\beta}_2 = 5.006$. For each unit increase in the proportion of block with high-density residential areas, the mean population density is estimated to increase by 5.006, holding proportion of block with low-density residential areas constant. Since x_2 is a proportion, it is unlikely that it can increase by one unit. A better interpretation is: For each increase of .1 in the proportion of block with high-density residential areas, the mean population density is estimated to increase by .5006, holding proportion of block with low-density residential areas constant.

   b. $R^2 = .686$. 68.6% of the total sample variation of the population densities is explained by the linear relationship between population density and the independent variables proportion of block with low-density residential areas and the proportion of block with high-density residential areas.

   c.   To determine if the overall model is adequate, we test:

$$H_0 : \beta_1 = \beta_2 = 0$$
$$H_a : \text{At least one } \beta_i \neq 0$$

   d.   The test statistic is $F = \dfrac{R^2 / k}{(1-R^2)/[n-(k+1)]} = \dfrac{.686/2}{(1-.686)/[125-(2+1)]} = 133.27$.

   e.   The rejection region requires $\alpha = .01$ in the upper tail of the F-distribution with $v_1 = k = 2$ and $v_2 = n-(k+1) = 125-(2+1) = 122$. From Table VIII, Appendix D, $F_{.01} \approx 4.79$. The rejection region is $F > 4.79$.

         Since the observed value of the test statistic falls in the rejection region $(F = 133.27 > 4.79)$, H_0 is rejected. There is sufficient evidence to indicate the model is adequate at $\alpha = .01$.

12.151   The correlation coefficient between Importance and Replace is .2682. This correlation coefficient is fairly small and would not indicate a problem with multicollinearity between Importance and Replace. The correlation coefficient between Importance and Support is .6991. This correlation coefficient is fairly large and would indicate a potential problem with multicollinearity between Importance and Support. Probably only one of these variables should be included in the regression model. The correlation coefficient between Replace and Support is $-.0531$. This correlation coefficient is very small and would not indicate a problem with multicollinearity between Replace and Support. Thus, the model could probably include Replace and one of the variables Support or Importance.

12.153   a.   Let $x_2 = \begin{cases} 1 \text{ if intervention group} \\ 0 \text{ if otherwise} \end{cases}$

The first-order model would be $E(y) = \beta_0 + \beta_1 x_1 + \beta_2 x_2$.

b.   For the control group, $x_2 = 0$. The first-order model is $E(y) = \beta_0 + \beta_1 x_1 + \beta_2(0) = \beta_0 + \beta_1 x_1$.

For the intervention group, $x_2 = 1$. The first-order model is

$$E(y) = \beta_0 + \beta_1 x_1 + \beta_2(1) = (\beta_0 + \beta_2) + \beta_1 x_1.$$

In both models, the slope of the line is β_1.

c.   If pretest score and group interact, the first-order model would be

$$E(y) = \beta_0 + \beta_1 x_1 + \beta_2 x_2 + \beta_3 x_1 x_2.$$

d.   For the control group, $x_2 = 0$. The first-order model including the interaction is

$$E(y) = \beta_0 + \beta_1 x_1 + \beta_2(0) + \beta_3 x_1(0) = \beta_0 + \beta_1 x_1.$$

For the intervention group, $x_2 = 1$. The first-order model including the interaction is

$$E(y) = \beta_0 + \beta_1 x_1 + \beta_2(1) + \beta_3 x_1(1) = (\beta_0 + \beta_2) + (\beta_1 + \beta_3) x_1.$$

The slope of the model for the control group is β_1. The slope of the model for the intervention group is $\beta_1 + \beta_3$.

12.155   a.   Not necessarily. If Nickel was highly correlated with several other variables, then it might be better to keep Nickel and drop some of the other highly correlated variables.

b.   Using stepwise regression is a good start for selecting the best set of predictor variables. However, one should use caution when looking at the model selected using stepwise regression. Sometimes important variables are not selected to be entered into the model. Also, many t-tests have been run, thus inflating the Type I and Type II error rates. One must also consider using higher order terms in the model and interaction terms.

c.   No, further exploration should be used. One should consider using higher order terms for the variables (i.e. squared terms) and also interaction terms.

12.157 a.   Using MINITAB, the scattergram is:

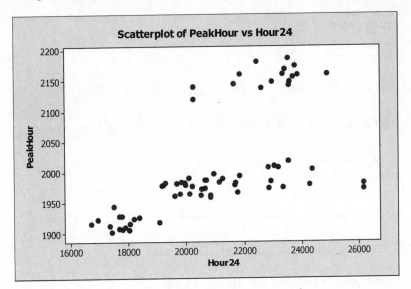

b.   Let $x_2 = \begin{cases} 1 \text{ if I-35W} \\ 0 \text{ if not} \end{cases}$

The complete second-order model would be $E(y) = \beta_0 + \beta_1 x_1 + \beta_2 x_1^2 + \beta_3 x_2 + \beta_4 x_1 x_2 + \beta_5 x_1^2 x_2$

c.   Using MINITAB, the printout is:

Regression Analysis: PeakHour versus x1, x1-sq, x2, x1x2, x1-sqx2

```
The regression equation is
PeakHour = 776 + 0.104 x1 - 0.000002 x1-sq + 232 x2 - 0.0091 x1x2
           + 0.000000 x1-sqx2


Predictor          Coef      SE Coef       T      P
Constant          776.4        144.5    5.37  0.000
x1              0.10418      0.01388    7.50  0.000
x1-sq       -0.00000223   0.00000033   -6.73  0.000
x2                  232         1094    0.21  0.833
x1x2           -0.00914      0.09829   -0.09  0.926
x1-sqx2      0.00000027   0.00000220    0.12  0.903


S = 15.5829   R-Sq = 97.2%   R-Sq(adj) = 97.0%


Analysis of Variance

Source           DF      SS       MS       F      P
Regression        5  555741   111148  457.73  0.000
Residual Error   66   16027      243
Total            71  571767
```

```
Source      DF   Seq SS
x1           1   254676
x1-sq        1    21495
x2           1   279383
x1x2         1      183
x1-sqx2      1        4
```

The fitted model is $\hat{y} = 776 + .104x_1 - .000002x_1^2 + 232x_2 - .0091x_1x_2 + .00000027x_1^2x_2$.

To determine if the curvilinear relationship is different at the two locations, we test:

$$H_0 : \beta_3 = \beta_4 = \beta_5 = 0$$
$$H_a : \text{At least one } \beta_i \neq 0$$

In order to test this hypothesis, we must fit the reduced model $E(y) = \beta_0 + \beta_1 x_1 + \beta_2 x_1^2$.

Using MINITAB, the printout from fitting the reduced model is:

Regression Analysis: PeakHour versus x1, x1-sq

```
The regression equation is
PeakHour = 197 + 0.149 x1 - 0.000003 x1-sq


Predictor          Coef      SE Coef       T       P
Constant          197.5        578.9     0.34   0.734
x1              0.14921      0.05551     2.69   0.009
x1-sq       -0.00000295   0.00000132    -2.24   0.028


S = 65.4523    R-Sq = 48.3%    R-Sq(adj) = 46.8%


Analysis of Variance

Source          DF       SS       MS       F       P
Regression       2   276171   138085   32.23   0.000
Residual Error  69   295597     4284
Total           71   571767


Source   DF   Seq SS
x1        1   254676
x1-sq     1    21495
```

The fitted regression line is $\hat{y} = 197 + .149x_1 - .000003x_1^2$.

To determine if the curvilinear relationship is different at the two locations, we test:

$$H_0 : \beta_3 = \beta_4 = \beta_5 = 0$$
$$H_a : \text{At least one } \beta_i \neq 0$$

The test statistic is $F = \dfrac{(SSE_R - SSE_C)/(k-g)}{SSE_C/[n-(k+1)]} = \dfrac{(295,597 - 16,027)/(5-2)}{16,027/[72-(5+1)]} = 383.76$.

Since no α was given we will use $\alpha = .05$. The rejection region requires $\alpha = .05$ in the upper tail of the F-distribution with $v_1 = k - g = 5 - 2 = 3$ and $v_2 = n - (k+1) = 72 - (5+1) = 66$. From Table VI, Appendix D, $F_{.05} \approx 2.76$. The rejection region is $F > 2.76$.

Since the observed value of the test statistic falls in the rejection region $(F = 383.76 > 2.76)$, H_0 is rejected. There is sufficient evidence to indicate the curvilinear relationship is different at the two locations at $\alpha = .05$.

d.   Using MINITAB, the residual plots are:

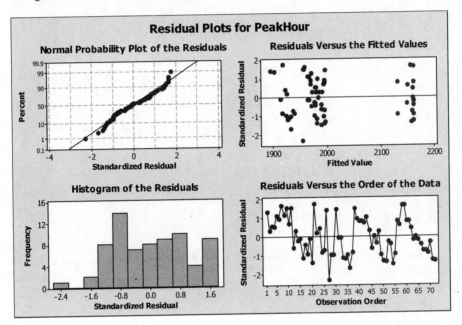

From the plot of the standardized residuals versus the fitted value, we notice that there is only one point more than 2 standard deviations from the mean and no points that are more than 3 standard deviations from the mean. Thus, there do not appear to be any outliers. There is no curve to the residuals, so we have the appropriate model. In addition, there is no cone shape to the plot, so it appears that there is no problem with constant variance.

The normal probability plot looks like a fairly straight line, so it appears that the assumption of normality is valid. Also, the histogram of the residuals is somewhat mound shaped.

12.159   a.   The model is $E(y) = \beta_0 + \beta_1 x_1 + \beta_2 x_2 + \beta_3 x_3$ where y = market share

$$x_1 = \begin{cases} 1 \text{ if M} \\ 0 \text{ otherwise} \end{cases} \qquad x_2 = \begin{cases} 1 \text{ if H} \\ 0 \text{ otherwise} \end{cases} \qquad x_3 = \begin{cases} 1 \text{ if VH} \\ 0 \text{ otherwise} \end{cases}$$

We assume that the error terms (ε_i) or y's are normally distributed at each exposure level, with a common variance. Also, we assume the ε_i's have a mean of 0 and are independent.

b.   No interaction terms were included because we have only one independent variable, exposure level. Even though we have 3 x_i's in the model, they are dummy variables and correspond to different levels of the one independent variable.

c.   Using MINITAB, the output is:

Regression Analysis: y versus x1, x2, x3

```
The regression equation is
y = 10.2 + 0.683 x1 + 2.02 x2 + 0.500 x3

Predictor        Coef      SE Coef        T        P
Constant       10.2333      0.1084    94.41    0.000
x1              0.6833      0.1533     4.46    0.000
x2              2.0167      0.1533    13.16    0.000
x3              0.5000      0.1533     3.26    0.004

S = 0.265518     R-Sq = 90.4%     R-Sq(adj) = 89.0%


Analysis of Variance

Source            DF          SS          MS         F        P
Regression         3     13.3433      4.4478     63.09    0.000
Residual Error    20      1.4100      0.0705
Total             23     14.7533


Source       DF      Seq SS
x1            1      0.1089
x2            1     12.4844
x3            1      0.7500
```

The fitted model is $\hat{y} = 10.2 + .683x_1 + 2.02x_2 + .5x_3$.

d.   To determine if the firm's expected market share differs for different levels of advertising exposure, we test:

$$H_0 : \beta_1 = \beta_2 = \beta_3 = 0$$
$$H_a : \text{At least one } \beta_i \neq 0$$

The test statistic is $F = 63.09$ and the p-value is $p = .000$. Since the p-value is less than α ($p = .000 < .05$), H_0 is rejected. There is sufficient evidence to indicate the firm's expected market share differs for different levels of advertising exposure at $\alpha = .05$.

12.161 a. $\hat{\beta}_0 = -105$ has no meaning because $x_3 = 0$ is not in the observable range. $\hat{\beta}_0$ is simply the y-intercept.

$\hat{\beta}_1 = 25$. The estimated difference in mean attendance between weekends and weekdays is 25, holding temperature and weather constant.

$\hat{\beta}_2 = 100$. The estimated difference in mean attendance between sunny and overcast days is 100, holding type of day (weekend or weekday) and temperature constant.

$\hat{\beta}_3 = 10$. The estimated change in mean attendance for each additional degree of temperature is 10, holding type of day (weekend or weekday) and weather (sunny or overcast) held constant.

b.   To determine if the model is useful for predicting daily attendance, we test:

$$H_0 : \beta_1 = \beta_2 = \beta_3 = 0$$
$$H_a : \text{At least one } \beta_i \neq 0$$

The test statistic is $F = \dfrac{R^2 / k}{(1-R^2)/[n-(k+1)]} = \dfrac{.65/3}{(1-.65)/[30-(3+1)]} = 16.10$.

The rejection region requires $\alpha = .05$ in the upper tail of the F-distribution with $v_1 = k = 3$ and $v_2 = n - (k+1) = 30 - (3+1) = 26$. From Table VI, Appendix D, $F_{.05} = 2.98$. The rejection region is $F > 2.98$.

Since the observed value of the test statistic falls in the rejection region $(F = 16.10 > 2.98)$, H_0 is rejected. There is sufficient evidence to indicate the model is useful for predicting daily attendance at $\alpha = .05$.

c.   To determine if mean attendance increases on weekends, we test:

$$H_0 : \beta_1 = 0$$
$$H_a : \beta_1 > 0$$

The test statistic is $t = \dfrac{\hat{\beta}_1}{s_{\hat{\beta}_1}} = \dfrac{25-0}{10} = 2.5$.

The rejection region requires $\alpha = .10$ in the upper tail of the t-distribution with $df = n - (k+1) = 30 - (3+1) = 26$. From Table III, Appendix D, $t_{.10} = 1.315$. The rejection region is $t > 1.315$.

Since the observed value of the test statistic falls in the rejection region $(t = 2.5 > 1.315)$, H_0 is rejected. There is sufficient evidence to indicate the mean attendance increases on weekends at $\alpha = .10$.

d.   Sunny $\Rightarrow x_2 = 1$, Weekday $\Rightarrow x_1 = 0$, Temperature $95° \Rightarrow x_3 = 95°$
$$\hat{y} = -105 + 25(0) + 100(1) + 10(95) = 945$$

e.   We are 90% confident that the actual attendance for sunny weekdays with a temperature of $95°$ is between 645 and 1245.

12.163   a. $E(y) = \beta_0 + \beta_1 x_1 + \beta_2 x_6 + \beta_3 x_7$

where $x_6 = \begin{cases} 1 \text{ if condition is good} \\ 0 \text{ otherwise} \end{cases}$ $x_7 = \begin{cases} 1 \text{ if condition is fair} \\ 0 \text{ otherwise} \end{cases}$

b.   The model specified in part **a** seems appropriate. The points for E, F, and G cluster around three parallel lines.

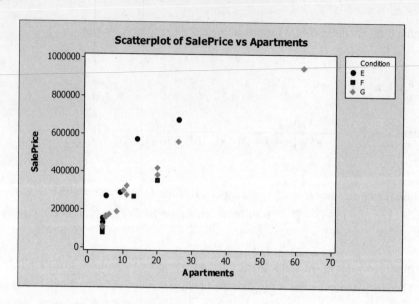

c. Using MINITAB, the output is

Regression Analysis: SalePrice versus X1, X6, X7

```
The regression equation is
SalePrice = 188875 + 15617 X1 - 103046 X6 - 152487 X7


Predictor      Coef   SE Coef      T      P
Constant      188875    28588    6.61  0.000
X1             15617     1066   14.66  0.000
X6           -103046    31784   -3.24  0.004
X7           -152487    39157   -3.89  0.001


S = 64623.6   R-Sq = 91.8%   R-Sq(adj) = 90.7%



Analysis of Variance

Source          DF          SS           MS       F      P
Regression       3  9.86170E+11  3.28723E+11   78.71  0.000
Residual Error  21  87700442851   4176211564
Total           24  1.07387E+12


Source  DF      Seq SS
X1       1  9.15776E+11
X6       1   7061463149
X7       1  63332198206
```

The fitted model is $\hat{y} = 188,875 + 15,617x_1 - 103,046x_6 - 152,487x_7$

For excellent condition, $\hat{y} = 188,875 + 15,617x_1$

For good condition, $\hat{y} = 85,829 + 15,617x_1$

For fair condition, $\hat{y} = 36,388 + 15,617x_1$

d.   Using MINITAB, the plot is:

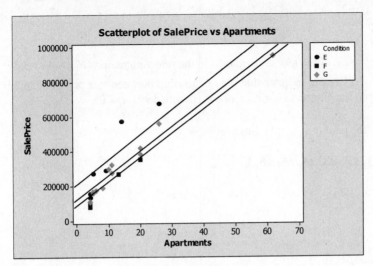

e.   We must first fit a reduced model with just x_1, number of apartments. Using MINITAB, the output is:

Regression Analysis: SalePrice versus X1

```
The regression equation is
SalePrice = 101786 + 15525 X1


Predictor     Coef   SE Coef      T       P
Constant    101786     23291    4.37   0.000
X1           15525      1345   11.54   0.000


S = 82907.5   R-Sq = 85.3%   R-Sq(adj) = 84.6%




Analysis of Variance

Source             DF           SS           MS        F      P
Regression          1   9.15776E+11  9.15776E+11   133.23  0.000
Residual Error     23   1.58094E+11   6873656705
Total              24   1.07387E+12
```

The fitted model is $\hat{y} = 101,786 + 15,525x_1$.

To determine if the relationship between sale price and number of units differs depending on the physical condition of the apartments, we test:

$$H_0 : \beta_2 = \beta_3 = 0$$
$$H_a : \text{At least one } \beta_i \neq 0$$

The test statistic is $F = \dfrac{(SSE_R - SSE_C) / (k - g)}{SSE_C / [n - (k+1)]} = \dfrac{(1.58094 \times 10^{11} - 87,700,442,851) / (3-1)}{87,700,442,851 / [25 - (3+1)]} = 8.43$

The rejection region requires $\alpha = .05$ in the upper tail of the F-distribution with $v_1 = k - g = 3 - 1 = 2$ and $v_2 = n - (k + 1) = 25 - (3 + 1) = 21$. From Table VI, Appendix D, $F_{.05} = 3.47$. The rejection region is $F > 3.47$.

Since the observed value of the test statistic falls in the rejection region $(F = 8.43 > 3.47)$, H_0 is rejected. There is evidence to indicate that the relationship between sale price and number of units differs depending on the physical condition of the apartments at $\alpha = .05$.

f.   Using MINITAB, the pairwise correlations are:

Correlations: x1, x2, x3, x4, x5, x6, x7

```
          x1        x2        x3        x4        x5        x6
x2    -0.014
       0.946

x3     0.800    -0.191
       0.000     0.361

x4     0.224    -0.363     0.167
       0.281     0.075     0.425

x5     0.878     0.027     0.673     0.089
       0.000     0.898     0.000     0.671

x6     0.175    -0.447     0.273     0.112     0.020
       0.403     0.025     0.187     0.594     0.923

x7    -0.128     0.392    -0.123     0.050    -0.238    -0.564
       0.541     0.053     0.557     0.814     0.252     0.003
```

When highly correlated independent variables are present in a regression model, the results are confusing. The researchers may only want to include one of the variables. This may be the case for the variables: x_1 and x_3, x_1 and x_5, x_3 and x_5

g.   Using MINITAB, the residual plots are:

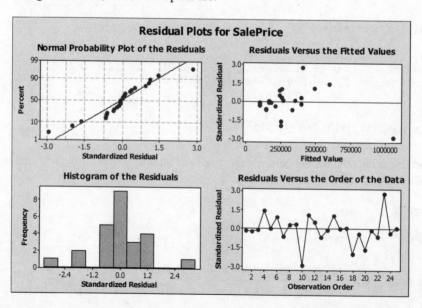

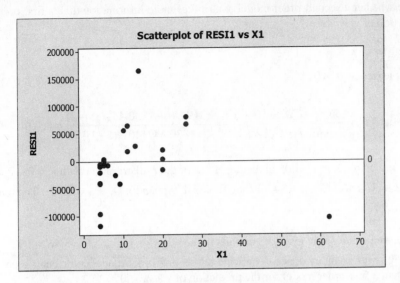

From the plots of the residuals versus the fitted values, there do not appear to be any outliers - no standardized residuals are larger than 3 in magnitude. In addition, there is no trend that would indicate non-constant variance (no funnel shape). There is a possible upside-down U shape that would indicate that the relationship between price and number of apartments might be curvilinear. In the histogram of the residuals, the plot is fairly mound-shaped, which would indicate the residuals are approximately normally distributed. Also, the normal probability plot looks to be a fairly straight line, indicating the residuals are approximately normal. In the plot of the residuals versus x_1, there is a possible upside-down U shape that would indicate that the variable number of apartments should be squared. Otherwise, all of the assumptions appear to be met.

12.165   a.   To determine whether the complete model contributes information for the prediction of y, we test:

$$H_0 : \beta_1 = \beta_2 = \beta_3 = \beta_4 = \beta_5 = 0$$
$$H_a : \text{At least one } \beta_i \neq 0$$

b. $$MSR = \frac{SS(Model)}{k} = \frac{4,911.5}{5} = 982.3 \qquad MSE = \frac{SSE}{n-(k+1)} = \frac{1,830.44}{40-(5+1)} = 53.84$$

The test statistic is $F = \dfrac{MSR}{MSE} = \dfrac{982.31}{53.84} = 18.24$.

The rejection region requires $\alpha = .05$ in the upper tail of the F-distribution with $v_1 = k = 5$ and $v_2 = n-(k+1) = 40-(5+1) = 34$. From Table VI, Appendix D, $F_{.05} \approx 2.53$. The rejection region is $F > 2.53$.

Since the observed value of the test statistic falls in the rejection region $(F = 18.24 > 2.53)$, H_0 is rejected. There is sufficient evidence to indicate that the complete model contributes information for the prediction of y at $\alpha = .05$.

c. To determine whether a second-order model contributes more information than a first-order model for the prediction of y, we test:

$$H_0 : \beta_3 = \beta_4 = \beta_5 = 0$$
$$H_a : \text{At least one } \beta_i \neq 0$$

d. The test statistic is $F = \dfrac{(SSE_R - SSE_C)/(k-g)}{SSE_C /[n-(k+1)]} = \dfrac{(3197.16 - 1830.44)/(5-2)}{1830.44/[40-(5+1)]} = 8.46$.

The rejection region requires $\alpha = .05$ in the upper tail of the F-distribution with $v_1 = k - g = 5 - 2 = 3$ and $v_2 = n - (k+1) = 40 - (5+1) = 34$. From Table VI, Appendix D, $F_{.05} \approx 2.92$. The rejection region is $F > 2.92$.

Since the observed value of the test statistic falls in the rejection region $(F = 8.46 > 2.92)$, H_0 is rejected. There is sufficient evidence to indicate the second-order model contributes more information than a first-order model for the prediction of y at $\alpha = .05$.

e. The second-order model, based on the test result in part **d**.

12.167 a. $R^2 = .78$. 78% of the total sample variation in the price of a direct burial about its mean is explained by the model that contains type of state, type of casket, and the interaction of the two.

b. To determine if the overall model is adequate, we test:

$$H_0 : \beta_1 = \beta_2 = \beta_3 = 0$$
$$H_a : \text{At least } 1 \, \beta_i \neq 0$$

The test statistic is $F = \dfrac{R^2 / k}{(1-R^2)/[n-(k+1)]} = \dfrac{.78/3}{(1-.78)/[1,437-(3+1)]} = 1693.55$.

The rejection region requires $\alpha = .05$ in the upper tail of the F-distribution with $v_1 = k = 3$ and $v_2 = n - (k+1) = 1,437 - (3+1) = 1,433$. From Table VI, Appendix D, $F_{.05} \approx 2.60$. The rejection region is $F > 2.60$.

Since the observed value of the test statistic falls in the rejection region $(F = 8.96 > 2.60)$, H_0 is rejected. There is sufficient evidence to indicate the model is adequate for the prediction of sales price at $\alpha = .05$.

c. For $x_1 = 1$ and $x_2 = 1$ (wooden casket in restrictive state),

$$\hat{y} = 1,432 + 793(1) - 252(1) + 261(1)(1) = 2,234.$$

d. For $x_1 = 1$ and $x_2 = 0$ (no casket in restrictive state), $\hat{y} = 1,432 + 793(1) - 252(0) = 261(1)(0) = 2,225$.

The difference would be $\$2,234 - \$2,225 = \$9$.

e.   For $x_1 = 0$ and $x_2 = 1$ (wooden casket in non-restrictive state),

$$\hat{y} = 1,432 + 793(0) - 252(1) = 261(0)(1) = 1,180 \ .$$

For $x_1 = 0$ and $x_2 = 0$ (no casket in non-restrictive state),

$$\hat{y} = 1,432 + 793(0) - 252(0) = 261(0)(0) = 1,432 \ .$$

The difference would be $\$1,180 - \$1,432 = -\$252$.

f.   To determine if the difference between the mean price of a direct burial with a basic wooden casket and the mean of a burial with no casket depends on whether the funeral home is in a restrictive state, we test:

$$H_0 : \beta_3 = 0$$
$$H_a : \beta_3 \neq 0$$

The test statistic is $t = \dfrac{\hat{\beta}_3 - 0}{s_{\hat{\beta}_3}} = \dfrac{261 - 0}{109} = 2.39$.

The rejection region requires $\alpha / 2 = .05 / 2 = .025$ in each tail of the t-distribution with $df = n - (k+1) = 1,437 - (3+1) = 1,433$. From Table III, Appendix D, $t_{.025} = 1.96$. The rejection region is $t < -1.96$ or $t > 1.96$.

Since the observed value of the test statistic falls in the rejection region $(t = 2.39 > 1.96)$, H_0 is rejected. There is sufficient evidence to indicate the difference between the mean price of a direct burial with a basic wooden casket and the mean of a burial with no casket depends on whether the funeral home is in a restrictive state at $\alpha = .05$.

12.169   First, we will fit the simple linear regression model $E(y) = \beta_0 + \beta_1 x_1 + \beta_2 x_2$. Using MINITAB, the results are:

Regression Analysis: y versus x1, x2

```
The regression equation is
y = - 1.57 + 0.0257 x1 + 0.0336 x2

Predictor         Coef       SE Coef             T          P
Constant        -1.5705        0.4937         -3.18      0.003
x1             0.025732       0.004024          6.40      0.000
x2             0.033615       0.004928          6.82      0.000

S = 0.4023      R-Sq = 68.1%      R-Sq(adj) = 66.4%

Analysis of Variance

Source            DF            SS            MS          F          P
Regression         2       12.7859        6.3930      39.51      0.000
Residual Error    37        5.9876        0.1618
Total             39       18.7735
```

```
Source      DF      Seq SS
x1           1      5.2549
x2           1      7.5311
```

To determine if the model is useful in the prediction of y (GPA), we test:

$$H_0 : \beta_1 = \beta_2 = 0$$
$$H_a : \text{At least one } \beta_i \neq 0$$

The test statistic is $F = 39.51$ and the p-value is $p = .000$. Since the p-value is so small, H_0 is rejected for any reasonable value of α. There is sufficient evidence to indicate at least one of the variables Verbal score or Mathematics score is useful in predicting GPA.

To determine if Verbal score is useful in predicting GPA, controlling for Mathematics score, we test:

$$H_0 : \beta_1 = 0$$
$$H_a : \beta_1 \neq 0$$

The test statistic is $t = 6.40$ and the p-value is $p = .000$. Since the p-value is so small, H_0 is rejected for any reasonable value of α. There is sufficient evidence to indicate Verbal score is useful in predicting GPA, controlling for Mathematics score.

To determine if Mathematics score is useful in predicting GPA, controlling for Verbal score, we test:

$$H_0 : \beta_2 = 0$$
$$H_a : \beta_2 \neq 0$$

The test statistic is $t = 6.82$ and the p-value is $p = .000$. Since the p-value is so small, H_0 is rejected for any reasonable value of α. There is sufficient evidence to indicate Mathematics score is useful in predicting GPA, controlling for Verbal score.

Thus, both terms in the model are significant. The R-squared value is $R^2 = .681$.
This indicates that 68.1% of the sample variance of the GPA's is explained by the model.

Now, we need to check the residuals. From MINITAB, the plots are:

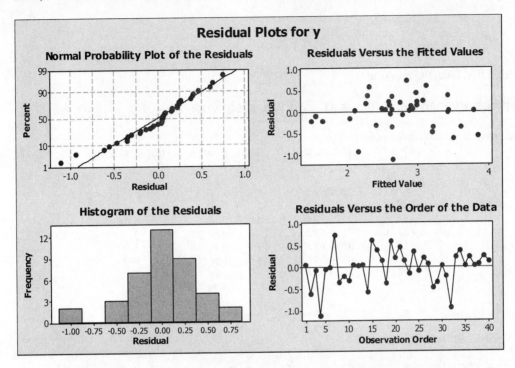

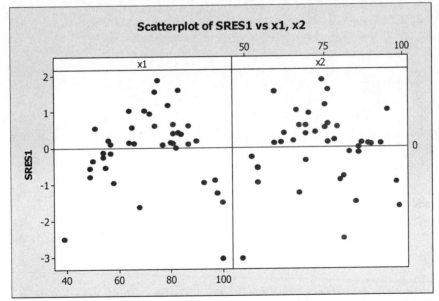

From the normal probability plot, it appears that the assumption of normality is valid. The points are very close to a straight line except for the first 2 points. The histogram of the residuals implies that the residuals are slightly skewed to the left. I would still consider the assumption to be valid. The plot of the residuals versus the fitted values indicates a random spread of the residuals between the two bands. This indicates that the assumption of equal variances is probably valid. The plot of the residuals versus x_1 indicates that the relationship between GPA and Verbal score may not be linear, but quadratic because the points form a somewhat upside down U shape. The plot of the residuals versus x_2 indicates that the relationship between GPA and Mathematics score may or may not be quadratic.

Since the plots indicate a possible 2nd order model and the R^2 value is not real large, we will fit a complete 2nd order model:

$$E(y) = \beta_0 + \beta_1 x_1 + \beta_2 x_2 + \beta_3 x_1^2 + \beta_4 x_2^2 + \beta_5 x_1 x_2$$

Using MINITAB, the results are:

Regression Analysis: y versus x1, x2, x1sq, x2sq, x1x2

```
The regression equation is
y = - 9.92 + 0.167 x1 + 0.138 x2 - 0.00111 x1sq - 0.000843 x2sq + 0.000241 x1x2


Predictor        Coef     SE Coef       T       P
Constant       -9.917       1.354    -7.32   0.000
x1            0.16681     0.02124     7.85   0.000
x2            0.13760     0.02673     5.15   0.000
x1sq       -0.0011082   0.0001173    -9.45   0.000
x2sq       -0.0008433   0.0001594    -5.29   0.000
x1x2        0.0002411   0.0001440     1.67   0.103


S = 0.187142    R-Sq = 93.7%    R-Sq(adj) = 92.7%

Analysis of Variance

Source           DF       SS       MS       F       P
Regression        5   17.5827   3.5165  100.41   0.000
Residual Error   34    1.1908   0.0350
Total            39   18.7735


Source  DF   Seq SS
x1       1   5.2549
x2       1   7.5311
x1sq     1   3.6434
x2sq     1   1.0552
x1x2     1   0.0982
```

To determine if the interaction between Verbal score and Mathematics score is useful in the prediction of y (GPA), we test:

$$H_0 : \beta_5 = 0$$
$$H_a : \beta_5 \neq 0$$

The test statistic is $t = 1.67$ and the p-value is $p = .103$. Since the p-value is not small, H_0 is not rejected for any value of $\alpha < .10$. There is insufficient evidence to indicate the interaction between Verbal score and Mathematics score is useful in predicting GPA.

Now, we will fit a model without the interaction term, but including the squared terms:

$$E(y) = \beta_0 + \beta_1 x_1 + \beta_2 x_2 + \beta_3 x_1^2 + \beta_4 x_2^2$$

Using MINITAB, the results are:

Regression Analysis: y versus x1, x2, x1sq, x2sq

```
The regression equation is
y = - 11.5 + 0.189 x1 + 0.159 x2 - 0.00114 x1sq - 0.000871 x2sq


Predictor          Coef     SE Coef        T      P
Constant        -11.458       1.019   -11.24  0.000
x1              0.18887     0.01709    11.05  0.000
x2              0.15874     0.02417     6.57  0.000
x1sq         -0.0011412   0.0001186    -9.62  0.000
x2sq         -0.0008705   0.0001626    -5.35  0.000


S = 0.191905    R-Sq = 93.1%    R-Sq(adj) = 92.3%


Analysis of Variance

Source            DF        SS       MS        F      P
Regression         4   17.4845   4.3711   118.69  0.000
Residual Error    35    1.2890   0.0368
Total             39   18.7735


Source   DF   Seq SS
x1        1   5.2549
x2        1   7.5311
x1sq      1   3.6434
x2sq      1   1.0552
```

To determine if the relationship between Verbal score and GPA is quadratic, controlling for Mathematics score, we test:

$$H_0 : \beta_3 = 0$$
$$H_a : \beta_3 \neq 0$$

The test statistic is $t = -9.62$ and the p-value is $p = .000$. Since the p-value is so small, H_0 is rejected for any reasonable value of α. There is sufficient evidence to indicate the relationship between Verbal score and GPA is quadratic, controlling for Mathematics score.

To determine if the relationship between Verbal score and GPA is quadratic, controlling for Mathematics score, we test:

$$H_0 : \beta_4 = 0$$
$$H_a : \beta_4 \neq 0$$

The test statistic is $t = -5.35$ and the p-value is $p = .000$. Since the p-value is so small, H_0 is rejected for any reasonable value of α. There is sufficient evidence to indicate the relationship between Mathematics score and GPA is quadratic, controlling for Verbal score.

Thus, both quadratic terms in the model are significant. The R-squared value is $R^2 = .913$. This indicates that 91.3% of the sample variance of the GPA's is explained by the model.

Now, we need to check the residuals. From MINITAB, the plots are:

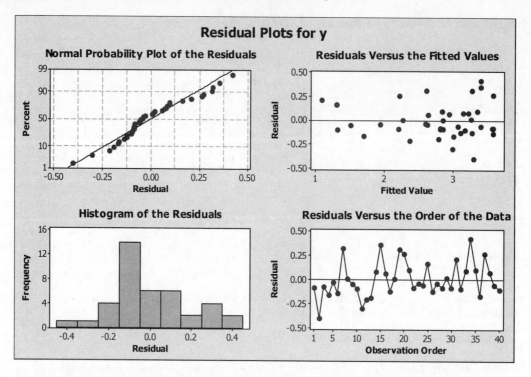

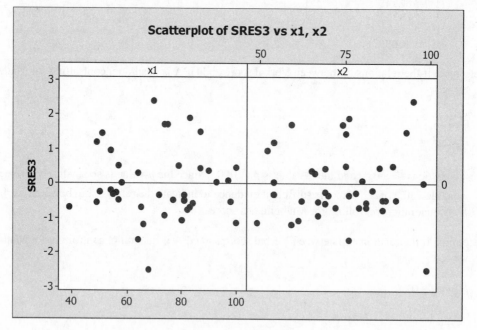

From the normal probability plot, it appears that the assumption of normality is valid. The points are very close to a straight line. The histogram of the residuals also implies that the residuals are approximately normal. The plot of the residuals versus the fitted values indicates a random spread of the residuals between the two bands. This indicates that the assumption of equal variances is probably valid. The plot of the residuals versus x_1 indicates a random spread of the residuals between the two bands. This indicates that the order of x_1 (2nd) is appropriate. The plot of the residuals versus x_2 indicates a random spread of the residuals between the two bands. This indicates that the order of x_2 (2nd) is appropriate.

The model appears to be pretty good. All terms in the model are significant, the residual analysis indicates the assumptions are met and the R-squared value is fairly close to 1. The fitted model is

$$\hat{y} = -11.5 + 0.189x_1 + 0.159x_2 - 0.0114x_1^2 - 0.000871x_2^2$$

Chapter 13
Methods for Quality Improvement: Statistical Process Control

13.1   A control chart is a time series plot of individual measurements or means of a quality variable to which a centerline and two other horizontal lines called control limits have been added. The center line represents the mean of the process when the process is in a state of statistical control. The upper control limit and the lower control limit are positioned so that when the process is in control the probability of an individual measurement or mean falling outside the limits is very small. A control chart is used to determine if a process is in control (only common causes of variation present) or not (both common and special causes of variation present). This information helps us to determine when to take action to find and remove special causes of variation and when to leave the process alone.

13.3   When a control chart is first constructed, it is not known whether the process is in control or not. If the process is found not to be in control, then the centerline and control limits should not be used to monitor the process in the future.

13.5   Even if all the points of an $\bar{x}$-chart fall within the control limits, the process may be out of control. Nonrandom patterns may exist among the plotted points that are within the control limits, but are very unlikely if the process is in control. Examples include six points in a row steadily increasing or decreasing and 14 points in a row alternating up and down.

13.7   Rule 1:   One point beyond Zone A: No points are beyond Zone A.
        Rule 2:   Nine points in a row in Zone C or beyond: No sequence of nine points are in Zone C (on one side of the centerline) or beyond.
        Rule 3:   Six points in a row steadily increasing or decreasing: No sequence of six points steadily increase or decrease.
        Rule 4:   Fourteen points in a row alternating up and down: This pattern does not exist.
        Rule 5:   Two out of three points in Zone A or beyond: There are no groups of three consecutive points that have two or more in Zone A or beyond.
        Rule 6:   Four out of five points in a row in Zone B or beyond: Points 18 through 21 are all in Zone B or beyond. This indicates the process is out of control.

        Thus, rule 6 indicates this process is out of control.

13.9   Using Table IX, Appendix D:

        a.   With $n=3$, $A_2 = 1.023$

        b.   With $n=10$, $A_2 = 0.308$

        c.   With $n=22$, $A_2 = 0.167$

13.11 a. For each sample, we compute $\bar{x}_1 = \dfrac{\sum x}{n}$ and R = range = largest measurement - smallest measurement. The results are listed in the table:

Sample No.	$\bar{x}_1$	R	Sample No.	$\bar{x}_2$	R
1	20.225	1.8	11	21.225	3.2
2	19.750	2.8	12	20.475	0.9
3	20.425	3.8	13	19.650	2.6
4	19.725	2.5	14	19.075	4.0
5	20.550	3.7	15	19.400	2.2
6	19.900	5.0	16	20.700	4.3
7	21.325	5.5	17	19.850	3.6
8	19.625	3.5	18	20.200	2.5
9	19.350	2.5	19	20.425	2.2
10	20.550	4.1	20	19.900	5.5

b. $\bar{\bar{x}} = \dfrac{\bar{x}_1 + \bar{x}_2 + \cdots \bar{x}_{20}}{k} = \dfrac{402.325}{20} = 20.11625 \qquad \bar{R} = \dfrac{R_1 + R_2 + \cdots R_{20}}{k} = \dfrac{66.2}{20} = 3.31$

c. *Centerline* $= \bar{\bar{x}} = 20.116$

From Table IX, Appendix D, with $n = 4$, $A_2 = .729$.

Upper control limit $= \bar{\bar{x}} + A_2\bar{R} = 20.116 + .729(3.31) = 22.529$

Lower control limit $= \bar{\bar{x}} - A_2\bar{R} = 20.116 - .729(3.31) = 17.703$

d. *Upper A-B boundary* $= \bar{\bar{x}} + \dfrac{2}{3}(A_2\bar{R}) = 20.116 + \dfrac{2}{3}(.729)(3.31) = 21.725$

Lower A-B boundary $= \bar{\bar{x}} - \dfrac{2}{3}(A_2\bar{R}) = 20.116 - \dfrac{2}{3}(.729)(3.31) = 18.507$

Upper B-C boundary $= \bar{\bar{x}} + \dfrac{1}{3}(A_2\bar{R}) = 20.116 + \dfrac{1}{3}(.729)(3.31) = 20.920$

Lower B-C boundary $= \bar{\bar{x}} - \dfrac{1}{3}(A_2\bar{R}) = 20.116 - \dfrac{1}{3}(.729)(3.31) = 19.312$

e.   The $\overline{x}$ -chart is:

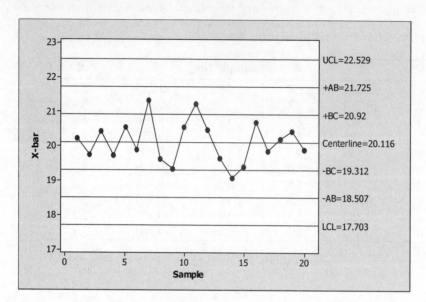

Rule 1:   One point beyond Zone A: No points are beyond Zone A.

Rule 2:   Nine points in a row in Zone C or beyond: No sequence of nine points are in Zone C (on one side of the centerline) or beyond.

Rule 3:   Six points in a row steadily increasing or decreasing: No sequence of six points steadily increase or decrease.

Rule 4:   Fourteen points in a row alternating up and down: This pattern does not exist.

Rule 5:   Two out of three points in Zone A or beyond: There are no groups of three consecutive points that have two or more in Zone A or beyond.

Rule 6:   Four out of five points in a row in Zone B or beyond: No sequence of five points has four or more in Zone B or beyond.

The process appears to be in control.

13.13   a. $\overline{\overline{x}} = \dfrac{\overline{x}_1 + \overline{x}_2 + \cdots + \overline{x}_{20}}{k} = \dfrac{1,400}{20} = 70$

b. $\overline{R} = \dfrac{R_1 + R_2 + \cdots + R_{22}}{k} = \dfrac{650}{20} = 32.5$

c.   From Table IX, Appendix D, with $n = 10$, $A_2 = .308$.

Upper control limit $= \overline{\overline{x}} + A_2\overline{R} = 70 + .308(32.5) = 80.01$

Lower control limit $= \overline{\overline{x}} - A_2\overline{R} = 70 - .308(32.5) = 59.99$

d.   *Upper A–B boundary* $= \overline{\overline{x}} + \dfrac{2}{3}\left(A_2\overline{R}\right) = 70 + \dfrac{2}{3}(.308)(32.5) = 76.67$

Lower A–B boundary $= \overline{\overline{x}} + \dfrac{2}{3}\left(A_2\overline{R}\right) = 70 - \dfrac{2}{3}(.308)(32.5) = 63.33$

Upper B–C boundary $= \overline{\overline{x}} + \dfrac{1}{3}\left(A_2\overline{R}\right) = 70 + \dfrac{1}{3}(.308)(32.5) = 73.34$

Lower B–C *boundary* $= \overline{\overline{x}} + \frac{1}{3}\left(A_2\overline{R}\right) = 70 - \frac{1}{3}(.308)(32.5) = 66.66$

The $\overline{x}$ -chart is:

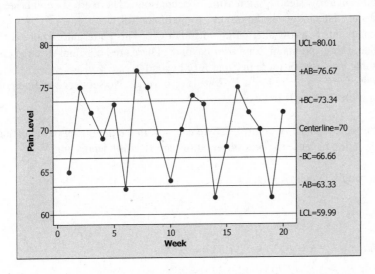

Rule 1: One point beyond Zone A: No points are beyond Zone A.

Rule 2: Nine points in a row in Zone C or beyond: No sequence of nine points are in Zone C (on one side of the centerline) or beyond.

Rule 3: Six points in a row steadily increasing or decreasing: No sequence of six points steadily increase or decrease.

Rule 4: Fourteen points in a row alternating up and down: This pattern does not exist.

Rule 5: Two out of three points in Zone A or beyond: There are no groups of three consecutive points that have two or more in Zone A or beyond.

Rule 6: Four out of five points in a row in Zone B or beyond: No sequence of five points has four or more in Zone B or beyond.

The process appears to be in control.

e.   The $\overline{x}$ -chart with the additional points is:

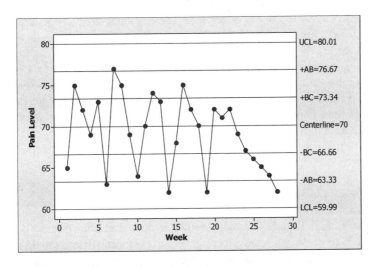

f.   Rule 1:   One point beyond Zone A: No points are beyond Zone A.
     Rule 2:   Nine points in a row in Zone C or beyond: No sequence of nine points are in Zone C (on one side of the centerline) or beyond.
     Rule 3:   Six points in a row steadily increasing or decreasing: There are six points steadily decreasing. This indicates the process is out of control.
     Rule 4:   Fourteen points in a row alternating up and down: This pattern does not exist.
     Rule 5:   Two out of three points in Zone A or beyond: There are no groups of three consecutive points that have two or more in Zone A or beyond.
     Rule 6:   Four out of five points in a row in Zone B or beyond: No sequence of five points has four or more in Zone B or beyond.

Rule 3 indicates the process is out of control. There is a shift in the pain level of the patients following the intervention because the new observations are steadily decreasing.

13.15   a.   From Table IX, Appendix D, with $n = 4$, $A_2 = .729$.

$$\bar{\bar{x}} = .6733 \text{ and } \bar{R} = .335$$

Upper control limit $= \bar{\bar{x}} + A_2\bar{R} = .6733 + .729(.335) = .9175$
Lower control limit $= \bar{\bar{x}} - A_2\bar{R} = .6733 - .729(.335) = .4291$

Upper $A - B$ *boundary* $= \bar{\bar{x}} + \dfrac{2}{3}\left(A_2\bar{R}\right) = .6733 + \dfrac{2}{3}(.729)(.335) = .8361$

Lower $A - B$ *boundary* $= \bar{\bar{x}} - \dfrac{2}{3}\left(A_2\bar{R}\right) = .6733 - \dfrac{2}{3}(.729)(.335) = .5105$

Upper $B - C$ *boundary* $= \bar{\bar{x}} + \dfrac{1}{3}\left(A_2\bar{R}\right) = .6733 + \dfrac{1}{3}(.729)(.335) = .7547$

Lower $A - B$ *boundary* $= \bar{\bar{x}} - \dfrac{1}{3}\left(A_2\bar{R}\right) = .6733 - \dfrac{1}{3}(.729)(.335) = .5919$

b.   Rule 1:   One point beyond Zone A: No points are beyond Zone A.
     Rule 2:   Nine points in a row in Zone C or beyond: There are nine points (Points 9 through 17) in a row in Zone C (on one side of the centerline) or beyond. This indicates that the process is out of control.
     Rule 3:   Six points in a row steadily increasing or decreasing: No sequence of six points steadily increase or decrease.
     Rule 4:   Fourteen points in a row alternating up and down: This pattern does not exist.
     Rule 5:   Two out of three points in Zone A or beyond: There are no groups of three consecutive points that have two or more in Zone A or beyond.
     Rule 6:   Four out of five points in a row in Zone B or beyond: No sequence of five points has four or more in Zone B or beyond.

Rule 2 indicates the process in out of control.

c.   These control limits should not be used to monitor future output because the process is out of control. One or more special causes of variation are affecting the process mean. These should be identified and eliminated in order to bring the process into control.

13.17   a. $\overline{\overline{x}} = \dfrac{\overline{x}_1 + \overline{x}_2 + \cdots + \overline{x}_{10}}{k} = \dfrac{151}{10} = 15.1$

b.   The $\overline{x}$-chart is:

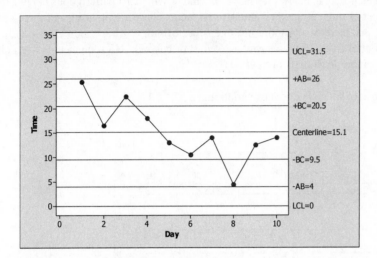

c.   Rule 1:   One point beyond Zone A: No points are beyond Zone A.

   Rule 2:   Nine points in a row in Zone C or beyond: No sequence of nine points are in Zone C (on one side of the centerline) or beyond.

   Rule 3:   Six points in a row steadily increasing or decreasing: This pattern does not exist.

   Rule 4:   Fourteen points in a row alternating up and down: This pattern does not exist.

   Rule 5:   Two out of three points in Zone A or beyond: There are no groups of three consecutive points that have two or more in Zone A or beyond.

   Rule 6:   Four out of five points in a row in Zone B or beyond: No sequence of five points has four or more in Zone B or beyond.

There is no evidence of special causes of variation.

d. $\overline{\overline{x}} = \dfrac{\overline{x}_1 + \overline{x}_2 + \cdots + \overline{x}_{14}}{k} = \dfrac{152.5}{14} = 10.9$.

The $\overline{x}$-chart is:

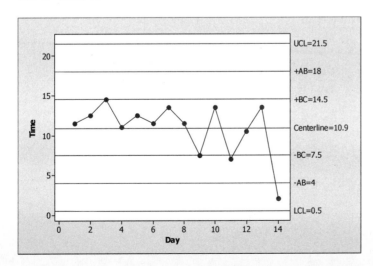

Rule 1:   One point beyond Zone A: No points are beyond Zone A.

Rule 2:   Nine points in a row in Zone C or beyond: No sequence of nine points are in Zone C (on one side of the centerline) or beyond.

Rule 3:   Six points in a row steadily increasing or decreasing: This pattern does not exist.

Rule 4:   Fourteen points in a row alternating up and down: This pattern does not exist.

Rule 5:   Two out of three points in Zone A or beyond: There are no groups of three consecutive points that have two or more in Zone A or beyond.

Rule 6:   Four out of five points in a row in Zone B or beyond: No sequence of five points has four or more in Zone B or beyond.

There is no evidence of special causes of variation.

e.   The side-by-side $\bar{x}$-charts are:

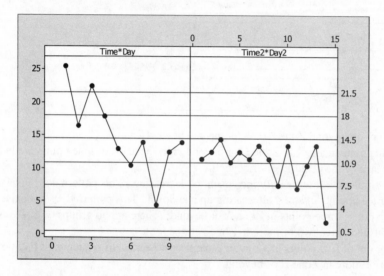

It appears that a process shift has occurred. All of the points after the implementation are below the centerline of the points before the implementation.

13.19 a.   From the problem, we are given LCL = 12.3 and UCL = 13.8. We are given the sample means for the 30 observations, but not the Ranges. Thus, we will have to compute $\bar{R}$ from the UCL and UCL. We can also compute $\bar{\bar{x}}$ from the UCL and LCL. From Table IX, Appendix D, with $n = 6$, $A_2 = .483$.

$$\bar{\bar{x}} = \frac{UCL + LCL}{2} = \frac{13.76 + 12.26}{2} = 13.01$$

$$UCL = \bar{\bar{x}} + A_2\bar{R} \Rightarrow \bar{R} = \frac{UCL - \bar{\bar{x}}}{A_2} = \frac{13.76 - 13.01}{.483} = 1.55$$

$$Upper\ A\text{-}B\ boundary = \bar{\bar{x}} + \frac{2}{3}A_2\bar{R} = 13.01 + \frac{2}{3}(.483)(1.55) = 13.51$$

$$Lower\ A\text{-}B\ boundary = \bar{\bar{x}} - \frac{2}{3}A_2\bar{R} = 13.01 - \frac{2}{3}(.483)(1.55) = 12.51$$

$$Upper\ B\text{-}C\ boundary = \bar{\bar{x}} + \frac{1}{3}A_2\bar{R} = 13.01 + \frac{1}{3}(.483)(1.55) = 13.26$$

$$Lower\ B\text{-}C\ boundary = \bar{\bar{x}} - \frac{1}{3}A_2\bar{R} = 13.01 - \frac{1}{3}(.483)(1.55) = 12.76$$

The $\bar{x}$-chart is:

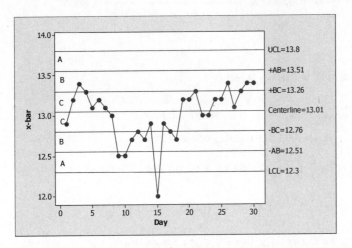

b. To determine if the process is in or out of control, we check the six rules:

Rule 1: One point beyond Zone A: There is one point beyond Zone A.

Rule 2: Nine points in a row in Zone C or beyond: Points 8 though 18 are all in the lower Zone C or below

Rule 3: Six points in a row steadily increasing or decreasing: This pattern does not exist.

Rule 4: Fourteen points in a row alternating up and down: This pattern does not exist.

Rule 5: Two out of three points in Zone A or beyond: This pattern does not exist.

Rule 6: Four out of five points in a row in Zone B or beyond: Points 11 through 156 satisfy this rule.

This process appears to be out of control. Rules 1, 2, and 6 indicate that the process is out of control.

c. Nine of these ten observations fall below the lower control limit. This would be extremely unusual if there was no under-reporting. We would conclude that there is under-reporting for the emissions data for this 10-day period.

13.21 a. The sample means and ranges are:

Sample	x-bar	Range	Sample	x-bar	Range	Sample	x-bar	Range
1	99.743	0.12	15	100.543	0.24	28	100.597	0.37
2	99.447	1.53	16	100.503	1.19	29	100.180	1.77
3	100.040	0.29	17	100.087	1.14	30	99.940	0.47
4	100.353	1.68	18	99.383	0.20	31	100.653	0.77
5	99.287	0.38	19	100.457	0.86	32	99.473	0.65
6	99.507	0.79	20	100.863	0.97	33	99.877	0.99
7	99.707	0.28	21	99.713	0.65	34	100.503	0.39
8	99.717	0.83	22	100.050	0.69	35	100.053	0.76
9	100.537	1.26	23	100.283	1.24	36	99.783	1.23
10	100.097	0.39	24	99.910	0.75	37	100.367	1.69
11	99.633	0.92	25	100.510	1.62	38	100.503	0.70
12	100.883	1.05	26	99.723	0.79	39	100.270	0.69
13	100.843	1.01	27	99.327	0.23	40	99.377	0.18
14	100.507	0.50						

$$\bar{\bar{x}} = \frac{\bar{x}_1 + \bar{x}_2 + ... + \bar{x}_{40}}{k} = \frac{4,003.229}{40} = 100.081 \quad \bar{R} = \frac{R_1 + R_2 + ... + R_{40}}{40} = \frac{32.26}{40} = .8065$$

$Centerline = \bar{\bar{x}} = 100.081$

From Table IX, Appendix D, with $n = 3$, $A_2 = 1.023$.

$Upper\ control\ limit = \bar{\bar{x}} + A_2\bar{R} = 100.081 + 1.023(.8065) = 100.906$

$Lower\ control\ limit = \bar{\bar{x}} - A_2\bar{R} = 100.081 - 1.023(.8065) = 99.256$

$Upper\ \text{A-B}\ boundary = \bar{\bar{x}} + \frac{2}{3}A_2\bar{R} = 100.081 + \frac{2}{3}(1.023)(.8065) = 100.631$

$Lower\ \text{A-B}\ boundary = \bar{\bar{x}} - \frac{2}{3}A_2\bar{R} = 100.081 - \frac{2}{3}(1.023)(.8065) = 99.531$

$Upper\ \text{B-C}\ boundary = \bar{\bar{x}} + \frac{1}{3}A_2\bar{R} = 100.081 + \frac{1}{3}(1.023)(.8065) = 100.356$

$Lower\ \text{B-C}\ boundary = \bar{\bar{x}} - \frac{1}{3}A_2\bar{R} = 100.081 - \frac{1}{3}(1.023)(.8065) = 99.806$

The $\bar{x}$ -chart is:

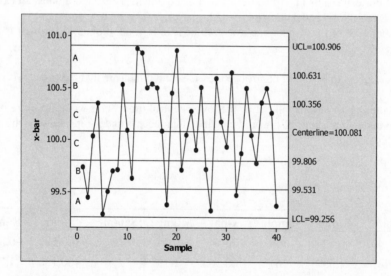

Using Rule 1, there are no points beyond Zone A. Therefore, the process appears to be in control.

b.   The sample means and ranges for the rounded data are:

Sample	x-bar	Range	Sample	x-bar	Range	Sample	x-bar	Range
1	100.000	0	15	100.667	1	28	100.333	1
2	99.333	1	16	100.667	1	29	100.000	2
3	100.000	0	17	100.333	1	30	100.000	0
4	100.333	2	18	99.000	0	31	100.667	1
5	99.000	0	19	100.667	1	32	99.667	1
6	99.667	1	20	101.333	1	33	99.667	1
7	100.000	0	21	99.667	1	34	100.333	1
8	99.667	1	22	100.000	0	35	100.000	0
9	100.667	1	23	100.333	1	36	99.667	1
10	100.000	0	24	100.000	0	37	100.333	1
11	99.667	1	25	100.667	1	38	100.333	1
12	101.333	1	26	99.667	1	39	100.333	1
13	101.333	1	27	99.000	0	40	99.000	0
14	100.333	1						

$$\bar{\bar{x}} = \frac{\bar{x}_1 + \bar{x}_2 + \dots + \bar{x}_{40}}{k} = \frac{4,003.667}{40} = 100.092 \qquad \bar{R} = \frac{R_1 + R_2 + \dots + R_{40}}{40} = \frac{30}{40} = .75$$

$Centerline = \bar{\bar{x}} = 100.092$

From Table IX, Appendix D, with $n = 3$, $A_2 = 1.023$.

$Upper\ control\ limit = \bar{\bar{x}} + A_2\bar{R} = 100.092 + 1.023(.75) = 100.859$

$Lower\ control\ limit = \bar{\bar{x}} - A_2\bar{R} = 100.092 - 1.023(.75) = 99.325$

$Upper\ \text{A-B}\ boundary = \bar{\bar{x}} + \frac{2}{3}A_2\bar{R} = 100.092 + \frac{2}{3}(1.023)(.75) = 100.604$

$Lower\ \text{A-B}\ boundary = \bar{\bar{x}} - \frac{2}{3}A_2\bar{R} = 100.092 - \frac{2}{3}(1.023)(.75) = 99.581$

$Upper\ \text{B-C}\ boundary = \bar{\bar{x}} + \frac{1}{3}A_2\bar{R} = 100.092 + \frac{1}{3}(1.023)(.75) = 100.348$

$Lower\ \text{B-C}\ boundary = \bar{\bar{x}} - \frac{1}{3}A_2\bar{R} = 100.02 - \frac{1}{3}(1.023)(.75) = 99.836$

The $\bar{x}$-chart is:

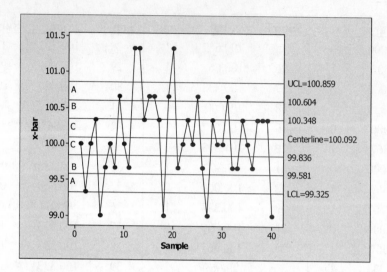

Using Rule 1, there are seven points beyond Zone A. This process appears to be out of control. When the data are rounded, the process is obviously out of control.

13.23   The control limits of the R-chart are a function of and reflect the variation in the process. If the variation is unstable (i.e., out of control), the control limits would not be constant. Under these circumstances, the fixed control limits of the $\bar{x}$-chart would have little meaning. We use the R-chart to determine whether the variation of the process is stable. If it is, the $\bar{x}$-chart is meaningful. Thus, we interpret the R-chart prior to the $\bar{x}$-chart.

13.25   a.   From Exercise 13.10, $\bar{R} = \dfrac{R_1 + R_2 + \cdots + R_{25}}{k} = \dfrac{198.7}{25} = 7.948$

Centerline $= \bar{R} = 7.948$

From Table IX, Appendix D, with $n = 5$, $D_4 = 2.114$ and $D_3 = 0$.
Upper control limit $= \bar{R}D_4 = 7.948(2.114) = 16.802$

Since $D_3 = 0$, the lower control limit is negative and is not included on the chart.

b.   From Table IX, Appendix D, with $n = 5$, $d_2 = 2.326$, and $d_3 = .864$.

Upper A–B boundary $= \bar{R} + 2d_3\dfrac{\bar{R}}{d_2} = 7.948 + 2(.864)\dfrac{7.948}{2.326} = 13.853$

Lower A–B boundary $= \bar{R} - 2d_3\dfrac{\bar{R}}{d_2} = 7.948 - 2(.864)\dfrac{7.948}{2.326} = 2.043$

Upper B–C boundary $= \bar{R} + d_3\dfrac{\bar{R}}{d_2} = 7.948 + (.864)\dfrac{7.948}{2.326} = 10.900$

Lower B–C boundary $= \bar{R} - d_3\dfrac{\bar{R}}{d_2} = 7.948 - (.864)\dfrac{7.948}{2.326} = 4.996$

c.　The *R*-chart is:

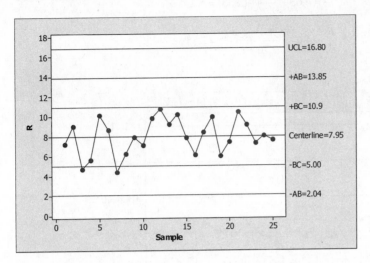

To determine if the process is in or out of control, we check the four rules:

Rule 1:　One point beyond Zone A:　No points are beyond Zone A.
Rule 2:　Nine points in a row in Zone C or beyond:　No sequence of nine points are in Zone C (on one side of the centerline) or beyond.
Rule 3:　Six points in a row steadily increasing or decreasing:　No sequence of six points steadily increase or decrease.
Rule 4:　Fourteen points in a row alternating up and down:　This pattern does not exist.

The process appears to be in control.

13.27　First, we construct an *R*-chart.

$$\bar{R} = \frac{R_1 + R_2 + \cdots + R_{20}}{k} = \frac{80.6}{20} = 4.03$$

Centerline $= \bar{R} = 4.03$

From Table IX, Appendix D, with $n = 7$, $D_3 = 0.076$ and $D_4 = 1.924$.

Upper control limit $= \bar{R}D_4 = 4.03(1.924) = 7.754$
Lower control limit $= \bar{R}D_3 = 4.03(0.076) = 0.306$

From Table IX, Appendix D, with $n = 7$, $d_2 = 2.704$ and $d_3 = .833$.

Upper A–B *boundary* $= \bar{R} + 2d_3\frac{\bar{R}}{d_2} = 4.03 + 2(.833)\frac{4.03}{2.704} = 6.513$

Lower A–B *boundary* $= \bar{R} - 2d_3\frac{\bar{R}}{d_2} = 4.03 - 2(.833)\frac{4.03}{2.704} = 1.547$

$$Upper \text{ B–C } boundary = \bar{R} + d_3\frac{\bar{R}}{d_2} = 4.03 + \frac{4.03}{2.704}(.833) = 5.271$$

$$Lower \text{ B–C } boundary = \bar{R} - d_3\frac{\bar{R}}{d_2} = 4.03 - \frac{4.03}{2.704}(.833) = 2.789$$

The *R*-chart is:

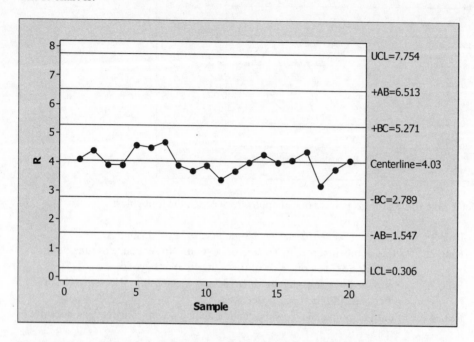

To determine if the process is in or out of control, we check the four rules:

Rule 1:   One point beyond Zone A: No points are beyond Zone A.

Rule 2:   Nine points in a row in Zone C or beyond: No sequence of nine points
are in Zone C (on one side of the centerline) or beyond.

Rule 3:   Six points in a row steadily increasing or decreasing: No sequence of six
points steadily increase or decrease.

Rule 4:   Fourteen points in a row alternating up and down: This pattern does not
exist.

The process appears to be in control. Since the process variation is in control, it is appropriate to construct the $\bar{x}$-chart.

To construct an $\bar{x}$-chart, we first calculate the following:

$$\bar{\bar{x}} = \frac{\bar{x}_1 + \bar{x}_2 + \cdots + \bar{x}_{20}}{k} = \frac{434.56}{20} = 21.728 \qquad \bar{R} = \frac{R_1 + R_2 + \cdots R_{20}}{k} = \frac{80.6}{20} = 4.03$$

$$Centerline = \bar{\bar{x}} = 21.728$$

From Table IX, Appendix D, with $n = 7$, $A_2 = .419$.

$$Upper \text{ } control \text{ } limit = \bar{\bar{x}} + A_2\bar{R} = 21.728 + .419(4.03) = 23.417$$

$$Lower \text{ } control \text{ } limit = \bar{\bar{x}} - A_2\bar{R} = 21.728 - .419(4.03) = 20.039$$

$$Upper\ A\text{-}B\ boundary = \overline{\overline{x}} + \frac{2}{3}(A_2\overline{R}) = 21.728 + \frac{2}{3}(.419)(4.03) = 22.854$$

$$Lower\ A\text{-}B\ boundary = \overline{\overline{x}} - \frac{2}{3}(A_2\overline{R}) = 21.728 - \frac{2}{3}(.419)(4.03) = 20.602$$

$$Upper\ B\text{-}C\ bondary = \overline{\overline{x}} + \frac{1}{3}(A_2\overline{R}) = 21.728 + \frac{1}{3}(.419)(4.03) = 22.291$$

$$Lower\ B\text{-}C\ boundary = \overline{\overline{x}} - \frac{1}{3}(A_2\overline{R}) = 21.728 - \frac{1}{3}(.419)(4.03) = 21.165$$

The $\overline{x}$ -chart is:

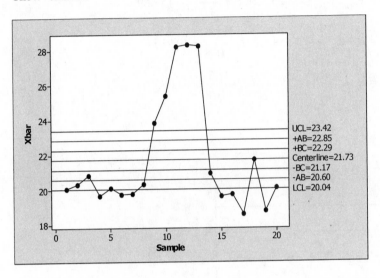

To determine if the process is in or out of control, we check the six rules:

Rule 1:   One point beyond Zone A: There are 12 points beyond Zone A. This indicates the process is out of control.

Rule 2:   Nine points in a row in Zone C or beyond: No sequence of nine points are in Zone C (on one side of the centerline) or beyond.

Rule 3:   Six points in a row steadily increasing or decreasing: Points 6 through 12 steadily increase. This indicates the process is out of control.

Rule 4:   Fourteen points in a row alternating up and down: This pattern does not exist.

Rule 5:   Two out of three points in Zone A or beyond: There are several groups of three consecutive points that have two or more in Zone A or beyond. This indicates the process is out of control.

Rule 6:   Four out of five points in a row in Zone B or beyond: Several sequences of five points have four or more in Zone B or beyond. This indicates the process is out of control.

Rules 1, 3, 5, and 6 indicate that the process is out of control.

13.29   a. $\overline{R} = \dfrac{R_1 + R_2 + \cdots R_{20}}{k} = \dfrac{650}{20} = 32.5$.

b. $Centerline = \overline{R} = 32.5$

From Table IX, Appendix D, with $n = 10$, $D_4 = 1.777$, and $D_3 = .223$.

Upper control limit $= \bar{R}D_4 = 32.5(1.777) = 57.753$

Lower control limit $= \bar{R}D_3 = 32.5(.223) = 7.248$

c. From Table IX, Appendix D, with $n = 10$, $d_2 = 3.078$, and $d_3 = .797$.

$$Upper\ A\text{–}B\ boundary = \bar{R} + 2d_3\frac{\bar{R}}{d_2} = 32.5 + 2(.797)\frac{32.5}{3.078} = 49.331$$

$$Lower\ A\text{–}B\ boundary = \bar{R} - 2d_3\frac{\bar{R}}{d_2} = 32.5 - 2(.797)\frac{32.5}{3.078} = 15.669$$

$$Upper\ B\text{–}C\ boundary = \bar{R} + d_3\frac{\bar{R}}{d_2} = 32.5 + (.797)\frac{32.5}{3.078} = 40.915$$

$$Lower\ B\text{–}C\ boundary = \bar{R} - d_3\frac{\bar{R}}{d_2} = 32.5 - (.797)\frac{32.5}{3.078} = 24.085$$

The *R*-chart is:

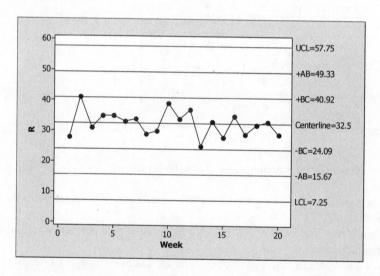

The process appears to be in control. All of the observations are very close to the centerline and none of the patterns appear in the chart.

d.   The *R*-chart with the addional points is:

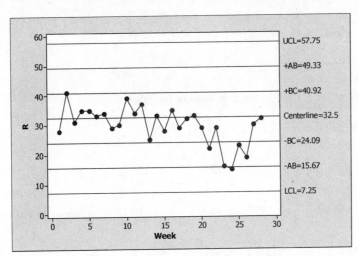

e.   To determine if the process is in or out of control, we check the four rules:

Rule 1:   One point beyond Zone A: No points are beyond Zone A.

Rule 2:   Nine points in a row in Zone C or beyond: There are nine points in Zone C (on one side of the centerline) or beyond. The last 9 points fit this pattern.

Rule 3:   Six points in a row steadily increasing or decreasing: No sequence of six points steadily increase or decrease.

Rule 4:   Fourteen points in a row alternating up and down: This pattern does not exist.

Because of Rule 2, it appears that the process variation is not in control.

13.31   a.   From Table IX, Appendix D, with $n = 4$, $D_3 = 0.000$ and $D_4 = 2.282$. $\bar{R} = .335$

Upper control limit $= \bar{R}D_4 = .335(2.282) = .764$

Since $D_3 = 0$, the lower control limit is negative and is not included on the chart.

b.   To determine if the process is in control, we check the four rules.

Rule 1:   One point beyond Zone A: No points are beyond Zone A.

Rule 2:   Nine points in a row in Zone C or beyond: There are not nine points are in a row in Zone C (on one side of the centerline) or beyond.

Rule 3:   Six points in a row steadily increasing or decreasing: No sequence of six points steadily increase or decrease.

Rule 4:   Fourteen points in a row alternating up and down: This pattern does not exist.

It appears that the process is in control.

c.   Yes. This process appears to be in control. Therefore, these control limits could be used to monitor future output.

d.   Of the 30 *R* values plotted, there are only 8 different values. Most of the *R* values take on one of three values. This indicates that the data must be discrete (take on a countable number of values), or that the path widths are multiples of each other.

13.33   a. $\bar{R} = \dfrac{R_1 + R_2 + ... + R_{16}}{16} = \dfrac{.3800}{16} = .0238$

$Centerline = \bar{R} = .0238$

From Table IX, Appendix D, with $n = 2$, $D_3 = 0.000$ and $D_4 = 3.267$.

$Upper\ control\ limit = \bar{R}D_4 = .0238(3.267) = .0778$

Since $D_3 = 0$, the lower control limit is negative and not included.

From Table IX, Appendix D, with $n = 2$, $d_2 = 1.128$ and $d_3 = .853$.

$Upper$ A-B $boundary = \bar{R} + 2d_3 \dfrac{\bar{R}}{d_2} = .0238 + 2(.853)\dfrac{.0238}{1.128} = .0598$

$Lower$ A-B $boundary = \bar{R} - 2d_3 \dfrac{\bar{R}}{d_2} = .0238 - 2(.853)\dfrac{.0238}{1.128} = -.0122$ or 0 (cannot be negative)

$Upper$ B-C $boundary = \bar{R} + d_3 \dfrac{\bar{R}}{d_2} = .0238 + (.853)\dfrac{.0238}{1.128} = .0418$

$Lower$ B-C $boundary = \bar{R} - d_3 \dfrac{\bar{R}}{d_2} = .0238 - (.853)\dfrac{.0238}{1.128} = .0058$

The R-chart is:

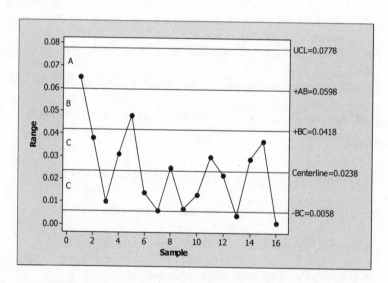

To determine if the process is in or out of control, we check the four rules:

Rule 1:   One point beyond Zone A: No points are beyond Zone A.
Rule 2:   Nine points in a row in Zone C or beyond: This pattern doe not exist.
Rule 3:   Six points in a row steadily increasing or decreasing: This pattern doe not exist.
Rule 4:   Fourteen points in a row alternating up and down: This pattern doe not exist.

The process appears to be in control.

b. $$\bar{\bar{x}} = \frac{\bar{x}_1 + \bar{x}_2 + \ldots + \bar{x}_{16}}{k} = \frac{3.5430}{16} = .2214$$

Centerline $= \bar{\bar{x}} = .2214$

From Table IX, Appendix D, with $n = 2$, $A_2 = 1.880$.

Upper control limit $= \bar{\bar{x}} + A_2\bar{R} = .2214 + 1.880(.0238) = .2661$

Lower control limit $= \bar{\bar{x}} - A_2\bar{R} = .2214 - 1.880(.0238) = .1767$

Upper A-B *boundary* $= \bar{\bar{x}} + \frac{2}{3}A_2\bar{R} = .2214 + \frac{2}{3}(1.880)(.0238) = .2512$

Lower A-B *boundar y* $= \bar{\bar{x}} - \frac{2}{3}A_2\bar{R} = .2214 + \frac{2}{3}(1.880)(.0238) = .1916$

Upper B-C *boundary* $= \bar{\bar{x}} + \frac{1}{3}A_2\bar{R} = .2214 + \frac{1}{3}(1.880)(.0238) = .2363$

Lower B-C *boundary* $= \bar{\bar{x}} - \frac{1}{3}A_2\bar{R} = .2214 - \frac{1}{3}(1.880)(.0238) = .2065$

The $\bar{x}$ -chart is:

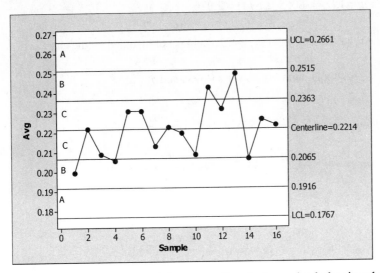

To determine if the process is in or out of control, we check the six rules:

Rule 1:   One point beyond Zone A: There are no points beyond Zone A.
Rule 2:   Nine points in a row in Zone C or beyond: This pattern does not exist.
Rule 3:   Six points in a row steadily increasing or decreasing: This pattern does not exist.
Rule 4:   Fourteen points in a row alternating up and down: This pattern does not exist.
Rule 5:   Two out of three points in Zone A or beyond: This pattern does not exist.
Rule 6:   Four out of five points in a row in Zone B or beyond: This pattern does not exist.

This process appears to be in control.

c. Based on the R-chart and the $\bar{x}$ -chart, the process appears to be in control. An estimate of the true average thickness of the expensive layer would be $\bar{\bar{x}} = .2214$.

13.35   a.   The values of R for the samples are:

Sample	R	Sample	R	Sample	R	Sample	R
1	0.12	11	0.92	21	0.65	31	0.77
2	1.53	12	1.05	22	0.69	32	0.65
3	0.29	13	1.01	23	1.24	33	0.99
4	1.68	14	0.5	24	0.75	34	0.39
5	0.38	15	0.24	25	1.62	35	0.76
6	0.79	16	1.19	26	0.79	36	1.23
7	0.28	17	1.14	27	0.23	37	1.69
8	0.83	18	0.2	28	0.37	38	0.7
9	1.26	19	0.86	29	1.77	39	0.69
10	0.39	20	0.97	30	0.47	40	0.18

$$Centerline = \bar{R} = \frac{R_1 + R_2 + \cdots R_{40}}{k} = \frac{32.26}{40} = .8065 .$$

From Table IX, Appendix D, with $n = 3$, $D_4 = 2.574$, and $D_3 = 0$.

$$Upper\ control\ limit = \bar{R}D_4 = .8065(2.574) = 2.076$$

Since $D_3 = 0$, the lower control limit is negative and is not included on the chart.

From Table IX, Appendix D, with $n = 3$, $d_2 = 1.693$, and $d_3 = .888$.

$$Upper\ \text{A–B}\ boundary = \bar{R} + 2d_3 \frac{\bar{R}}{d_2} = .8065 + 2(.888)\frac{.8065}{1.693} = 1.653$$

$$Lower\ \text{A–B}\ boundary = \bar{R} - 2d_3 \frac{\bar{R}}{d_2} = .8065 - 2(.888)\frac{.8065}{1.693} = -.040$$

$$Upper\ \text{B–C}\ boundary = \bar{R} + d_3 \frac{\bar{R}}{d_2} = .8065 + (.888)\frac{.8065}{1.693} = 1.23$$

$$Lower\ \text{B–C}\ boundary = \bar{R} - d_3 \frac{\bar{R}}{d_2} = .8065 - (.888)\frac{.8065}{1.693} = .383$$

The *R*-chart is:

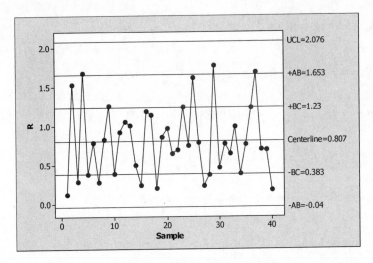

To determine if the process is in or out of control, we check the four rules:

Rule 1: One point beyond Zone A: No points are beyond Zone A.
Rule 2: Nine points in a row in Zone C or beyond: No sequence of nine points are in Zone C (on one side of the centerline) or beyond.
Rule 3: Six points in a row steadily increasing or decreasing: No sequence of six points steadily increase or decrease.
Rule 4: Fourteen points in a row alternating up and down: This pattern does not exist.

It appears that the process variation is in control.

b. The values of *R* for the rounded data are:

Sample	R	Sample	R	Sample	R	Sample	R
1	0	11	1	21	1	31	1
2	2	12	1	22	1	32	1
3	0	13	1	23	1	33	1
4	2	14	1	24	1	34	0
5	0	15	0	25	2	35	1
6	1	16	1	26	1	36	1
7	0	17	1	27	0	37	2
8	1	18	0	28	0	38	1
9	1	19	1	29	2	39	1
10	0	20	1	30	0	40	0

$$Centerline = \bar{R} = \frac{R_1 + R_2 + \cdots R_{40}}{k} = \frac{33}{40} = .825 \, .$$

From Table IX, Appendix D, with $n = 3$, $D_4 = 2.574$, and $D_3 = 0$.

$$Upper \ control \ limit = \bar{R}D_4 = .825(2.574) = 2.124$$

Since $D_3 = 0$, the lower control limit is negative and is not included on the chart.

From Table IX, Appendix D, with $n = 3$, $d_2 = 1.693$, and $d_3 = .888$.

$$Upper\ \text{A–B}\ boundary = \overline{R} + 2d_3 \frac{\overline{R}}{d_2} = .825 + 2(.888)\frac{.825}{1.693} = 1.69$$

$$Lower\ \text{A–B}\ boundary = \overline{R} - 2d_3 \frac{\overline{R}}{d_2} = .825 - 2(.888)\frac{.825}{1.693} = -.04$$

$$Upper\ \text{B–C}\ boundary = \overline{R} + d_3 \frac{\overline{R}}{d_2} = .825 + (.888)\frac{.825}{1.693} = 1.258$$

$$Lower\ \text{B–C}\ boundary = \overline{R} - d_3 \frac{\overline{R}}{d_2} = .825 - (.888)\frac{.825}{1.693} = .392$$

The R-chart for the rounded data is:

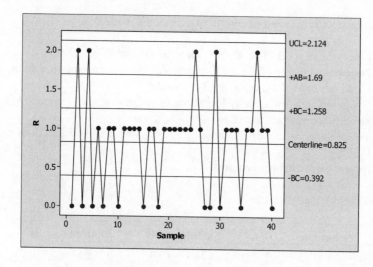

To determine if the process is in or out of control, we check the four rules:

Rule 1:   One point beyond Zone A: No points are beyond Zone A.

Rule 2:   Nine points in a row in Zone C or beyond: No sequence of nine points are in Zone C (on one side of the centerline) or beyond.

Rule 3:   Six points in a row steadily increasing or decreasing: No sequence of six points steadily increase or decrease.

Rule 4:   Fourteen points in a row alternating up and down: This pattern does not exist.

It appears that the process variation is in control. There are very few different values for R, once the data have been rounded off.

13.37   The p-chart is designed to monitor the proportion of defective units produced by a process.

13.39   The sample size is determined as follows: $n > \dfrac{9(1 - p_0)}{p_0} = \dfrac{9(1 - .08)}{.08} = 103.5 \approx 104$

13.41   a.   We must first calculate $\bar{p}$. To do this, it is necessary to find the total number of defectives in all the samples. To find the number of defectives per sample, we multiple the proportion by the sample size, 150. The number of defectives per sample are shown in the table:

Sample No.	p	No. Defectives	Sample No.	p	No. Defectives
1	.03	4.5	11	.07	10.5
2	.05	7.5	12	.04	6.0
3	.10	15.0	13	.06	9.0
4	.02	3.0	14	.05	7.5
5	.08	12.0	15	.07	10.5
6	.09	13.5	16	.06	9.0
7	.08	12.0	17	.07	10.5
8	.05	7.5	18	.02	3.0
9	.07	10.5	19	.05	7.5
10	.06	9.0	20	.03	4.5

Note: There cannot be a fraction of a defective. The proportions presented in the exercise have been rounded off. I have used the fractions to minimize the roundoff error.

To get the total number of defectives, sum the number of defectives for all 20 samples. The sum is 172.5. To get the total number of units sampled, multiply the sample size by the number of samples: $150(20) = 3000$.

$$\bar{p} = \frac{\text{Total defective in all samples}}{\text{Total units sampled}} = \frac{172.5}{3000} = .0575$$

$Centerline = \bar{p} = .0575$

$$Upper\ control\ limit = \bar{p} + 3\sqrt{\frac{\bar{p}(1-\bar{p})}{n}} = .0575 + 3\sqrt{\frac{.0575(.9425)}{150}} = .1145$$

$$Lower\ control\ limit = \bar{p} - 3\sqrt{\frac{\bar{p}(1-\bar{p})}{n}} = .0575 - 3\sqrt{\frac{.0575(.9425)}{150}} = .0005$$

b.

$$Upper\ \text{A–B}\ boundary = \bar{p} + 2\sqrt{\frac{\bar{p}(1-\bar{p})}{n}} = .0575 + 2\sqrt{\frac{.0575(.9425)}{150}} = .0955$$

$$Lower\ \text{A-B}\ boundary = \bar{p} - 2\sqrt{\frac{\bar{p}(1-\bar{p})}{n}} = .0575 - 2\sqrt{\frac{.0575(.9425)}{150}} = .0195$$

$$Upper\ \text{B-C}\ boundary = \bar{p} + \sqrt{\frac{\bar{p}(1-\bar{p})}{n}} = .0575 + \sqrt{\frac{.0575(.9425)}{150}} = .0765$$

$$Lower\ \text{B-C}\ boundary = \bar{p} - \sqrt{\frac{\bar{p}(1-\bar{p})}{n}} = .0575 - \sqrt{\frac{.0575(.9425)}{150}} = .0385$$

c.   The *p*-chart is:

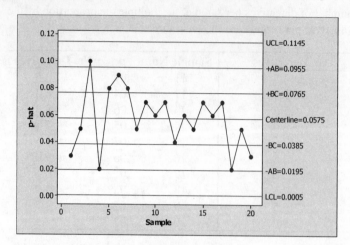

d.   To determine if the process is in or out of control, we check the four rules:

Rule 1:   One point beyond Zone A: No points are beyond Zone A.

Rule 2:   Nine points in a row in Zone C or beyond: No sequence of nine points are in Zone C (on one side of the centerline) or beyond.

Rule 3:   Six points in a row steadily increasing or decreasing: No sequence of six points steadily increase or decrease.

Rule 4:   Fourteen points in a row alternating up and down: Points 7 through 20 alternate up and down. This indicates the process is out of control.

Rule 4 indicates that the process is out of control.

e.   Since the process is out of control, the centerline and control limits should not be used to monitor future process output. The centerline and control limits are intended to represent the behavior of the process when it is under control.

13.43   a.   The attribute of interest is post-operative complications.

b.   The rational subgroups are the months.

c. $\bar{p} = \dfrac{\text{Total defective in all samples}}{\text{Total units sampled}} = \dfrac{294}{2939} = .100$

d.   The proportions are found by dividing the number of complications each month by the number of procedures each month. The proportions are:

Month	Compli-cations	Procedures	Prop.	Month	Compli-cations	Procedures	Prop.
1	14	105	.133	16	13	110	.118
2	12	97	.124	17	7	97	.072
3	10	115	.087	18	10	105	.095
4	12	100	.120	19	8	71	.113
5	9	95	.095	20	5	48	.104
6	7	111	.063	21	12	95	.126
7	9	68	.132	22	9	110	.082
8	11	47	.234	23	7	103	.068
9	9	83	.108	24	9	95	.095
10	12	108	.111	25	15	105	.143
11	10	115	.087	26	12	100	.120
12	7	94	.074	27	8	116	.069
13	12	107	.112	25	2	110	.018
14	9	99	.091	29	9	105	.086
15	15	105	.143	30	10	120	.083

e.   Since the sample sizes varied for each sample, we will use the average sample size for n:

$$n = \frac{2939}{30} \approx 98$$

$$Upper\ control\ limit = \bar{p} + 3\sqrt{\frac{\bar{p}(1-\bar{p})}{n}} = .100 + 3\sqrt{\frac{.100(.900)}{98}} = .191$$

$$Lower\ control\ limit = \bar{p} - 3\sqrt{\frac{\bar{p}(1-\bar{p})}{n}} = .100 - 3\sqrt{\frac{.100(.900)}{98}} = .009$$

$$Upper\ A\text{–}B\ boundary = \bar{p} + 2\sqrt{\frac{\bar{p}(1-\bar{p})}{n}} = .100 + 2\sqrt{\frac{.100(.900)}{98}} = .161$$

$$Lower\ A\text{–}B\ boundary = \bar{p} - 2\sqrt{\frac{\bar{p}(1-\bar{p})}{n}} = .100 - 2\sqrt{\frac{.100(.900)}{98}} = .039$$

$$Upper\ B\text{–}C\ boundary = \bar{p} + \sqrt{\frac{\bar{p}(1-\bar{p})}{n}} = .100 + \sqrt{\frac{.100(.900)}{98}} = .130$$

$$Lower\ B\text{–}C\ boundary = \bar{p} - \sqrt{\frac{\bar{p}(1-\bar{p})}{n}} = .100 - \sqrt{\frac{.100(.900)}{98}} = .070$$

f.   The *p*-chart for the data is:

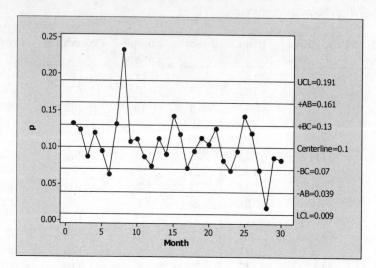

g.   To determine if the process is in or out of control, we check the four rules:

Rule 1:   One point beyond Zone A: One point is beyond Zone A.
Rule 2:   Nine points in a row in Zone C or beyond: No sequence of nine points are in Zone C (on one side of the centerline) or beyond.
Rule 3:   Six points in a row steadily increasing or decreasing: No sequence of six points steadily increase or decrease.
Rule 4:   Fourteen points in a row alternating up and down: This pattern does not exist.

Rule 1 is violated. The process appears to be out of control.

13.45   a.   To compute the proportion of defectives in each sample, divide the number of defectives by the number in the sample, 100:

$$\hat{p} = \frac{\text{No. of defectives}}{\text{No. in sample}}$$

The sample proportions are listed in the table:

Sample No.	$\hat{p}$	Sample No.	$\hat{p}$
1	.02	16	.02
2	.04	17	.03
3	.10	18	.07
4	.04	19	.03
5	.01	20	.02
6	.01	21	.03
7	.13	22	.07
8	.09	23	.04
9	.11	24	.03
10	.00	25	.02
11	.03	26	.02
12	.04	27	.00
13	.02	28	.01
14	.02	29	.03
15	.08	30	.04

To get the total number of defectives, sum the number of defectives for all 30 samples. The sum is 120. To get the total number of units sampled, multiply the sample size by the number of samples: $100(30) = 3000$.

$$\bar{p} = \frac{\text{Total defective in all samples}}{\text{Total units sampled}} = \frac{120}{3000} = .04$$

The centerline is $= \bar{p} = .04$

$$\text{Upper control limit} = \bar{p} + 3\sqrt{\frac{\bar{p}(1-\bar{p})}{n}} = .04 + 3\sqrt{\frac{.04(1-.04)}{100}} = .099$$

$$\text{Lower control limit} = \bar{p} - 3\sqrt{\frac{\bar{p}(1-\bar{p})}{n}} = .04 - 3\sqrt{\frac{.04(1-.04)}{100}} = -.019 \text{ or } 0 \text{ (cannot be negative)}$$

$$\text{Upper A–B boundary} = \bar{p} + 2\sqrt{\frac{\bar{p}(1-\bar{p})}{n}} = .04 + 2\sqrt{\frac{.04(1-.04)}{100}} = .079$$

$$\text{Lower A–B boundary} = \bar{p} - 2\sqrt{\frac{\bar{p}(1-\bar{p})}{n}} = .04 - 2\sqrt{\frac{.04(1-.04)}{100}} = .001$$

$$\text{Upper B–C boundary} = \bar{p} + \sqrt{\frac{\bar{p}(1-\bar{p})}{n}} = .04 + \sqrt{\frac{.04(1-.04)}{100}} = .060$$

$$\text{Lower B–C boundary} = \bar{p} - \sqrt{\frac{\bar{p}(1-\bar{p})}{n}} = .04 - \sqrt{\frac{.04(1-.04)}{100}} = .020$$

The *p*-chart is:

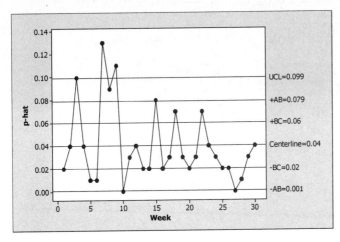

b. To determine if the process is in or out of control, we check the four rules for the *p*-chart.

Rule 1: One point beyond Zone A: There are 3 points beyond Zone A—points 2, 7, and 9.

Rule 2: Nine points in a row in Zone C or beyond: No sequence of nine points are in Zone C (on one side of the centerline) or beyond.

Rule 3: Six points in a row steadily increasing or decreasing: This pattern is not present.

Rule 4: Fourteen points in a row alternating up and down: This pattern does not exist.

The process does not appear to be in control. Rule 1 indicates that the process is out of control.

c. No. Since the process is not in control, then these control limits are meaningless.

13.47   To compute the proportion of leaky pumps in each sample, divide the number of leaky pumps by the number in the sample, 500:

$$\hat{p} = \frac{\text{No. leaky pumps}}{\text{No. in sample}}$$

The sample proportions are listed in the table:

Week	$\hat{p}$	Week	$\hat{p}$
1	0.72	8	.056
2	.056	9	.062
3	.048	10	.052
4	.052	11	.068
5	.040	12	.052
6	.112	13	.064
7	.052		

To get the total number of leaky pumps, sum the number of leaky pumps for all 13 samples. The sum is 393. To get the total number of pumps sampled, multiply the sample size by the number of samples: $500(13) = 6,500$.

$$\bar{p} = \frac{\text{Total leaky pumps in all samples}}{\text{Total pumps sampled}} = \frac{393}{6500} = .060$$

The *Centerline* is $\bar{p} = .060$

$$Upper\ control\ limit = \bar{p} + 3\sqrt{\frac{\bar{p}(1-\bar{p})}{n}} = .060 + 3\sqrt{\frac{.06(1-.06)}{500}} = .060 + .032 = .092$$

$$Lower\ control\ limit = \bar{p} - 3\sqrt{\frac{\bar{p}(1-\bar{p})}{n}} = .060 - 3\sqrt{\frac{.06(1-.06)}{500}} = .060 - .032 = .028$$

$$Upper\ \text{A-B}\ boundary = \bar{p} + 2\sqrt{\frac{\bar{p}(1-\bar{p})}{n}} = .060 + 2\sqrt{\frac{.06(1-.06)}{500}} = .060 + .021 = .081$$

$$Lower\ \text{A-B}\ boundary = \bar{p} - 2\sqrt{\frac{\bar{p}(1-\bar{p})}{n}} = .060 - 2\sqrt{\frac{.06(1-.06)}{500}} = .060 - .021 = .039$$

$$Upper\ \text{B-C}\ boundary = \bar{p} + \sqrt{\frac{\bar{p}(1-\bar{p})}{n}} = .060 + \sqrt{\frac{.06(1-.06)}{500}} = .060 + .011 = .071$$

$$Lower\ \text{B-C}\ boundary = \bar{p} - \sqrt{\frac{\bar{p}(1-\bar{p})}{n}} = .060 - \sqrt{\frac{.06(1-.06)}{500}} = .060 - .011 = .049$$

The *p*-chart is:

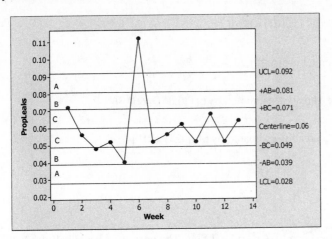

To determine if the process is in or out of control, we check the four rules:

Rule 1: One point beyond Zone A: One point lies beyond Zone A.
Rule 2: Nine points in a row in Zone C or beyond: This pattern doe not exist.
Rule 3: Six points in a row steadily increasing or decreasing: This pattern doe not exist.
Rule 4: Fourteen points in a row alternating up and down: This pattern doe not exist.

The process appears to be out of control because Rule 1 is not followed. One observation is beyond Zone A. It appears that the process is not stable.

13.49   A capability analysis is a methodology used to help determine when common cause variation is unacceptably high. If a process is not in statistical control, then both common causes and special causes of variation exist. It would not be possible to determine if the common cause variation is too high because it could not be separated from special cause variation.

13.51   One way to assess the capability of a process is to construct a frequency distribution or stem-and-leaf display for a large sample of individual measurements from the process. Then, the specification limits and the target value for the output variable are added to the graph. This is called a capability analysis diagram. A second way to assess the capability of a process is to quantify capability. The most direct way to quantify capability is to count the number of items that fall outside the specification limits in the capability analysis diagram and report the percentage of such items in the sample. Also, one can construct a capability index. This is the ratio of the difference in the specification spread and the difference in the process spread. This measure is called C_P. If C_P is less than 1, then the process is not capable.

13.53   a. $C_p = 1.00$. For this value, the specification spread is equal to the process spread. This indicates that the process is capable. Approximately 2.7 units per 1,000 will be unacceptable.

        b. $C_p = 1.33$. For this value, the specification spread is greater than the process spread. This indicates that the process is capable. Approximately 63 units per 1,000,000 will be unacceptable.

        c. $C_p = 0.50$. For this value, the specification spread is less than the process spread. This indicates that the process is not capable.

        d. $C_p = 2.00$. For this value, the specification spread is greater than the process spread. This indicates that the process is capable. Approximately 2 units per billion will be unacceptable.

13.55   The process spread is 6σ.

   a.   For $\sigma = 21$, the process spread is $6(21) = 126$.

   b.   For $\sigma = 5.2$, the process spread is $6(5.2) = 31.2$.

   c.   For $s = 110.06$, the process spread is estimated by $6(110.06) = 660.36$

   d.   For $s = .0024$, the process spread is estimated by $6(.0024) = .0144$

13.57   We know that $C_p = \dfrac{\text{USL} - \text{LSL}}{6\sigma}$

Thus, if $C_p = 2$, then $2 = \dfrac{\text{USL} - \text{LSL}}{6\sigma} \Rightarrow 12\sigma = \text{USL} - \text{LSL}$. The process mean is halfway between the USL and the LSL. Since the specification spread covers 12σ, then the USL must be $12\sigma/2 = 6\sigma$ from the process mean.

13.59   The capability index is $C_p = \dfrac{\text{USL} - \text{LSL}}{6\sigma} = \dfrac{.7 - .1}{6(.265)} = \dfrac{.6}{1.59} = .377$.

Since the capability index is less than 1, the process is not capable. The process spread is wider than the specification spread.

13.61   a.   A capability diagram is (LSL = 35 is off the chart.):

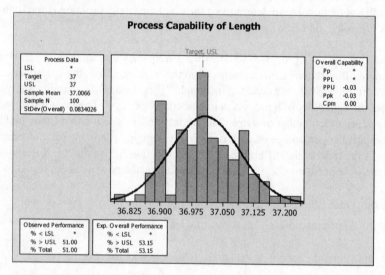

   b.   Fifty-one percent of the observations are above the upper specification limit.

   c.   From the sample, $\bar{x} = 37.007$ and $s = .0834$.

$$C_p = \frac{\text{USL} - \text{LSL}}{6s} \approx \frac{37 - 35}{6(.0834)} = \frac{2}{.5004} = 3.9968$$

d.   Since the C_P value is greater than 1, the process is capable.

From the chart, we know that 8.75% of the 80 weights fall outside the specification limits. This is also an indication that the process is not capable.

13.63   a.   The capability analysis diagram is:

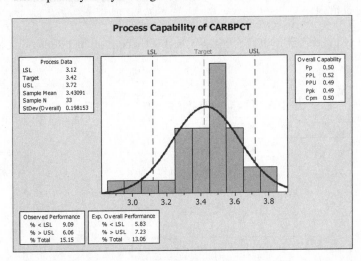

b.   Two observations are above the upper specification limit and three observations are below the lower specification limit. Thus, the proportion of measurements that fall outside the specifications is $5 / 33 = .1515$.

c.   From the sample, $\bar{x} = 3.43$ and $s = .1982$.

$$C_p = \frac{\text{USL} - \text{LSL}}{6\sigma} = \frac{3.72 - 3.12}{6(.1982)} = \frac{.6}{1.1892} = .505$$

Since the C_p value is less than 1, the process is not capable.

13.65   The quality of a good or service is indicated by the extent to which it satisfies the needs and preferences of its users. Its eight dimensions are: performance, features, reliability, conformance, durability, serviceability, aesthetics, and other perceptions that influence judgments of quality.

13.67   A system is a collection or arrangement of interacting components that has an on-going purpose or mission. A system receives inputs from its environment, transforms those inputs to outputs, and delivers those outputs to its environment.

13.69   Yes. Even though the output may all fall within the specification limits, the process may still be out of control.

13.71   Solution will vary. See Section 13.7 for Guided Solutions.

13.73   If a process is in control and remains in control, its future will be like its past. It is predictable in that its output will stay within certain limits. If a process is out of control, there is no way of knowing what the future pattern of output from the process may look like.

13.75   Control limits are a function of the natural variability of the process. The position of the limits is a function of the size of the process standard deviation. Specification limits are boundary points that define the acceptable values for an output variable of a particular product or service. They are determined by customers, management, and/or product designers. Specification limits may be either two-sided, with upper and lower limits, or one-sided with either an upper or lower limit. Specification limits are not dependent on the process in any way. The process may not be able to meet the specification limits even when it is under statistical control.

13.77   The C_P statistic is used to assess capability if the process is stable (in control) and if the process is centered on the target value.

13.79   a.   The centerline is $\bar{x} = \dfrac{\sum x}{n} = \dfrac{96}{15} = 6.4$.   The time series plot is:

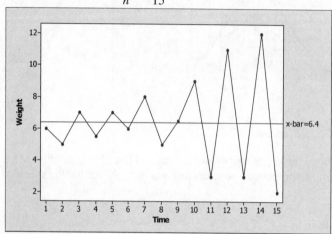

b.   The type of variation best described by the pattern in this plot is increasing variance. The spread of the measurements increases with the passing of time.

13.81   To determine if the process is in or out of control, we check the six rules:

Rule 1:   One point beyond Zone A: No points are beyond Zone A.
Rule 2:   Nine points in a row in Zone C or beyond: Points 8 through 16 are in Zone C (on one side of the centerline) or beyond. This indicates the process is out of control.
Rule 3:   Six points in a row steadily increasing or decreasing: No sequence of six points steadily increase or decrease.
Rule 4:   Fourteen points in a row alternating up and down: This pattern does not exist.
Rule 5:   Two out of three points in Zone A or beyond: No group of three consecutive points have two or more in Zone A or beyond.
Rule 6:   Four out of five points in a row in Zone B or beyond: No sequence of five points has four or more in Zone B or beyond.

Rule 2 indicates that the process is out of control. A special cause of variation appears to be present.

13.83   a.   For each sample, we compute the mean and range:

Sample	x-bar	R	Sample	x-bar	R
1	54.00	0.4	9	55.30	2.3
2	54.24	1.4	10	54.68	3.4
3	54.54	2.8	11	54.46	5.3
4	52.82	1.3	12	54.02	3.7
5	52.52	1.7	13	55.14	4.4
6	54.12	1.4	14	54.78	3.2
7	54.36	3.7	15	54.28	0.9
8	54.18	5.6	16	54.74	2.6

$$Centerline = \bar{R} = \frac{R_1 + R_2 + \cdots + R_{16}}{k} = \frac{44.1}{16} = 2.75625$$

From Table IX, Appendix D, with $n = 5$, $D_4 = 2.114$, and $D_3 = 0$.

$$Upper\ control\ limit = \bar{R}D_4 = 2.75625(2.114) = 5.827$$

Since $D_3 = 0$, the lower control limit is negative and is not included on the chart.

From Table IX, Appendix D, with $n = 5$, $d_2 = 2.326$, and $d_3 = .864$.

$$Upper\ A–B\ boundary = \bar{R} + 2d_3 \frac{\bar{R}}{d_2} = 2.75625 + 2(.864)\frac{2.75625}{2.326} = 4.804$$

$$Lower\ A–B\ boundary = \bar{R} - 2d_3 \frac{\bar{R}}{d_2} = 2.75625 - 2(.864)\frac{2.75625}{2.326} = .709$$

$$Upper\ B–C\ boundary = \bar{R} + d_3 \frac{\bar{R}}{d_2} = 2.75625 + (.864)\frac{2.75625}{2.326} = 3.780$$

$$Lower\ B–C\ boundary = \bar{R} - d_3 \frac{\bar{R}}{d_2} = 2.75625 - (.864)\frac{2.75625}{2.326} = 1.732$$

The *R*-chart is:

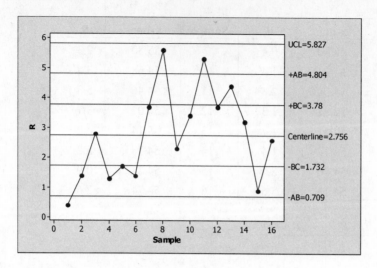

b. $Centerline = \bar{\bar{x}} = \dfrac{\bar{x}_1 + \bar{x}_2 + \cdots + \bar{x}_{16}}{k} = \dfrac{868.18}{16} = 54.26125$

From Table IX, Appendix D, with $n = 5$, $A_2 = .577$

$Upper\ control\ limit = \bar{\bar{x}} + A_2\bar{R} = 54.26125 + .577(2.75625) = 55.8516$

$Lower\ control\ limit = \bar{\bar{x}} - A_2\bar{R} = 54.26125 - .577(2.75625) = 52.6709$

$Upper\ A - B\ boundary = \bar{\bar{x}} + \dfrac{2}{3}(A_2\bar{R}) = 54.26125 + \dfrac{2}{3}(.577)(2.75625) = 55.3215$

$Lower\ A - B\ boundary = \bar{\bar{x}} - \dfrac{2}{3}(A_2\bar{R}) = 54.26125 - \dfrac{2}{3}(.577)(2.75625) = 53.2010$

$Upper\ B - C\ boundary = \bar{\bar{x}} + \dfrac{1}{3}(A_2\bar{R}) = 54.26125 + \dfrac{1}{3}(.577)(2.75625) = 54.7914$

$Lower\ B - C\ boundary = \bar{\bar{x}} - \dfrac{1}{3}(A_2\bar{R}) = 54.26125 - \dfrac{1}{3}(.577)(2.75625) = 53.7311$

The $\bar{x}$-chart is:

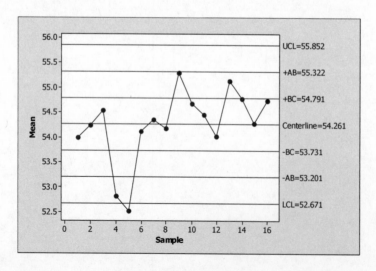

c.   For the *R*-chart: To determine if the process is in or out of control, we check the four rules:

Rule 1:   One point beyond Zone A: No points are beyond Zone A.
Rule 2:   Nine points in a row in Zone C or beyond: No sequence of nine points are in Zone C (on one side of the centerline) or beyond.
Rule 3:   Six points in a row steadily increasing or decreasing: No sequence of six points steadily increase or decrease.
Rule 4:   Fourteen points in a row alternating up and down: This pattern does not exist.

This process appears to be in control.

For the $\bar{x}$-chart: To determine if the process is in or out of control, we check the six rules:

Rule 1:   One point beyond Zone A: One point is beyond Zone A.
Rule 2:   Nine points in a row in Zone C or beyond: No sequence of nine points are in Zone C (on one side of the centerline) or beyond.
Rule 3:   Six points in a row steadily increasing or decreasing: No sequence of six points steadily increase or decrease.
Rule 4:   Fourteen points in a row alternating up and down: This pattern does not exist.
Rule 5:   Two out of three points in Zone A or beyond: There are two sets of three consecutive points (data points 3, 4, and 5 and data points 4, 5, and 6) that have two points in Zone A or beyond.
Rule 6:   Four out of five points in a row in Zone B or beyond: No sequence of five points has four or more in Zone B or beyond.

Special causes of variation appear to be present. The process appears to be out of control. Rules 1 and 5 indicate the process is out of control.

d.   Since the process is out of control, these control limits should not be used to monitor future process outputs.

13.85   a.   For each sample, we compute $\bar{x} = \dfrac{\sum x}{n}$ and R = range = largest measurement - smallest measurement.

The results are listed in the table:

Sample No.	$\bar{x}$	R	Sample No.	$\bar{x}$	R
1	4.36	7.1	11	3.32	4.8
2	5.10	7.7	12	4.02	4.8
3	4.52	5.0	13	5.24	7.8
4	3.42	5.8	14	3.58	3.9
5	2.62	6.2	15	3.48	5.5
6	3.94	3.9	16	5.00	3.0
7	2.34	5.3	17	3.68	6.2
8	3.26	3.2	18	2.68	3.9
9	4.06	8.0	19	3.66	4.4
10	4.96	7.1	20	4.10	5.5

$$\bar{\bar{x}} = \frac{\bar{x}_1 + \bar{x}_2 + \cdots + \bar{x}_{20}}{k} = \frac{77.34}{20} = 3.867 \qquad \bar{R} = \frac{R_1 + R_2 + \cdots + R_{20}}{k} = \frac{109.1}{20} = 5.455$$

First, we construct an *R*-chart.

$Centerline = \bar{R} = 5.455$

From Table IX, Appendix D, with $n = 5, D_3 = 0.000,$ and $D_4 = 2.114$.

$Upper\ control\ limit = \bar{R}D_4 = 5.455(2.114) = 11.532$

Since $D_3 = 0$, the lower control limit is negative and is not included on the chart.

$Upper\ A\text{–}B\ boundary = \bar{R} + 2d_3\dfrac{\bar{R}}{d_2} = 5.455 + 2(.864)\dfrac{(5.455)}{2.326} = 9.508$

$Lower\ A\text{–}B\ boundary = \bar{R} - 2d_3\dfrac{\bar{R}}{d_2} = 5.455 - 2(.864)\dfrac{(5.455)}{2.326} = 1.402$

$Upper\ B\text{–}C\ boundary = \bar{R} + d_3\dfrac{\bar{R}}{d_2} = 5.455 + (.864)\dfrac{(5.455)}{2.326} = 7.481$

$Lower\ B\text{–}C\ boundary = \bar{R} - d_3\dfrac{\bar{R}}{d_2} = 5.455 - (.864)\dfrac{(5.455)}{2.326} = 3.429$

The R-chart is:

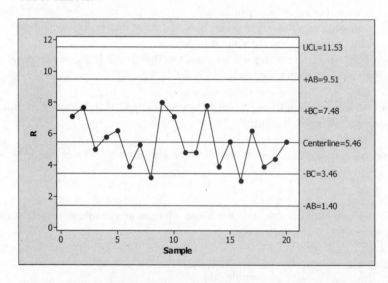

b.   To determine if the process is in or out of control, we check the four rules:

Rule 1:   One point beyond Zone A: No points are beyond Zone A.
Rule 2:   Nine points in a row in Zone C or beyond: No sequence of nine points are in Zone C (on one side of the centerline) or beyond.
Rule 3:   Six points in a row steadily increasing or decreasing: No sequence of six points steadily increase or decrease.
Rule 4:   Fourteen points in a row alternating up and down: This pattern does not exist.

The process appears to be in control. Since the process variation is in control, it is appropriate to construct the $\bar{x}$ -chart.

c.   In order for the $\bar{x}$ -chart to be valid, the process variation must be in control. The R-chart checks to see if the process variation is in control. For more details, see the answer to Exercise 13.23.

d. To construct an $\bar{x}$-chart, we first calculate the following:

$$\bar{\bar{x}} = \frac{\bar{x}_1 + \bar{x}_2 + \cdots + \bar{x}_{20}}{k} = \frac{77.24}{20} = 3.867 \qquad \bar{R} = \frac{R_1 + R_2 + \cdots + R_{20}}{k} = \frac{109.1}{20} = 5.4557$$

Centerline $= \bar{\bar{x}} = 3.867$

From Table IX, Appendix D, with $n = 5, A_2 = .577$.

Upper control limit $= \bar{\bar{x}} + A_2 \bar{R} = 3.867 + .577(5.455) = 7.015$

Lower control limit $= \bar{\bar{x}} - A_2 \bar{R} = 3.867 - .577(5.455) = .719$

Upper A–B boundary $= \bar{\bar{x}} + \frac{2}{3}(A_2\bar{R}) = 3.867 + \frac{2}{3}(.577)(5.455) = 5.965$

Lower A–B boundary $= \bar{\bar{x}} - \frac{2}{3}(A_2\bar{R}) = 3.867 - \frac{2}{3}(.577)(5.455) = 1.769$

Upper B–C boundary $= \bar{\bar{x}} + \frac{1}{3}(A_2\bar{R}) = 3.867 + \frac{2}{3}(.577)(5.455) = 4.916$

Lower B–C boundary $= \bar{\bar{x}} - \frac{1}{3}(A_2\bar{R}) = 3.867 - \frac{2}{3}(.577)(5.455) = 2.818$

The $\bar{x}$-chart is:

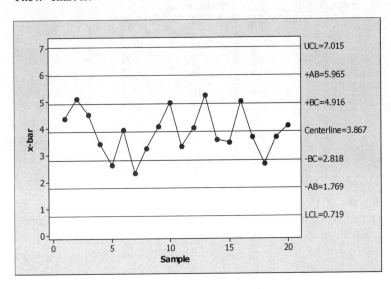

e. To determine if the process is in or out of control, we check the six rules:

Rule 1: One point beyond Zone A: No points are beyond Zone A.

Rule 2: Nine points in a row in Zone C or beyond: No sequence of nine points are in Zone C (on one side of the centerline) or beyond.

Rule 3: Six points in a row steadily increasing or decreasing: No sequence of six points steadily increases or decreases.

Rule 4: Fourteen points in a row alternating up and down: This pattern does not exist.

Rule 5: Two out of three points in Zone A or beyond: There are no groups of three consecutive points that have two or more in Zone A or beyond.

Rule 6:   Four out of five points in a row in Zone B or beyond: No sequence of five points has four or more in Zone B or beyond.

The process appears to be in control.

f.   Since both the R-chart and the $\bar{x}$-chart are in control, these control limits should be used to monitor future process output.

13.87   a.   The sample size is determined by the following: $n > \dfrac{9(1-p_0)}{p_0} = \dfrac{9(1-.06)}{.06} = 141$

The minimum sample size is 141. Since the sample size of 150 was used, it is large enough.

b.   To compute the proportion of defectives in each sample, divide the number of defectives by the number in the sample, 150:

$$\hat{p} = \frac{\text{No. of defectives}}{\text{No. in sample}}$$

The sample proportions are listed in the table:

Sample No.	$\hat{p}$	Sample No.	$\hat{p}$
1	.060	11	.047
2	.073	12	.040
3	.080	13	.080
4	.053	14	.067
5	.067	15	.073
6	.040	16	.047
7	.087	17	.040
8	.060	18	.080
9	.073	19	.093
10	.033	20	.067

To get the total number of defectives, sum the number of defectives for all 20 samples. The sum is 189. To get the total number of units sampled, multiply the sample size by the number of samples: $150(20) = 3000$.

$$\bar{p} = \frac{\text{Total defectives in all samples}}{\text{Total units sampled}} = \frac{189}{3000} = .063$$

$Centerline = \bar{p} = .063$

$Upper\ control\ limit = \bar{p} + 3\sqrt{\dfrac{\bar{p}(1-\bar{p})}{n}} = .063 + 3\sqrt{\dfrac{.063(.937)}{150}} = .123$

$Lower\ control\ limit = \bar{p} - 3\sqrt{\dfrac{\bar{p}(1-\bar{p})}{n}} = .063 - 3\sqrt{\dfrac{.063(.937)}{150}} = .003$

$Upper\ \text{A-B}\ boundary = \bar{p} + 2\sqrt{\dfrac{\bar{p}(1-\bar{p})}{n}} = .063 + 2\sqrt{\dfrac{.063(.937)}{150}} = .103$

$Lower\ \text{A-B}\ boundary = \bar{p} - 2\sqrt{\dfrac{\bar{p}(1-\bar{p})}{n}} = .063 - 2\sqrt{\dfrac{.063(.937)}{150}} = .023$

$$Upper\ \text{B-C}\ boundary = \bar{p} + \sqrt{\frac{\bar{p}(1-\bar{p})}{n}} = .063 + \sqrt{\frac{.063(.937)}{150}} = .083$$

$$Lower\ \text{B-C}\ boundary = \bar{p} - \sqrt{\frac{\bar{p}(1-\bar{p})}{n}} = .063 - \sqrt{\frac{.063(.937)}{150}} = .043$$

The *p*-chart is:

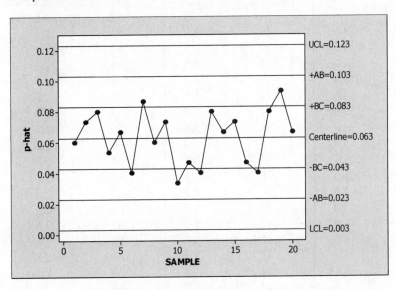

c.   To determine if the process is in or out of control, we check the four rules.

Rule 1:   One point beyond Zone A: No points are beyond Zone A.

Rule 2:   Nine points in a row in Zone C or beyond: No sequence of nine points are in Zone C (on one side of the centerline) or beyond.

Rule 3:   Six points in a row steadily increasing or decreasing: No sequence of six points steadily increase or decrease.

Rule 4:   Fourteen points in a row alternating up and down: Points 2 through 16 alternate up and down. This indicates the process is out of control.

Rule 4 indicates the process is out of control. Special causes of variation appear to be present.

e.   Since the process is out of control, the control limits should not be used to monitor future process output. It would not be appropriate to evaluate whether the process is in control using control limits determined during a period when the process was out of control.

13.89   First, we must compute the range for each sample. The range = R = largest measurement − smallest measurement. The results are listed in the table:

Sample No.	R	Sample No.	R	Sample No.	R
1	2.0	25	4.6	49	4.0
2	2.1	26	3.0	50	4.9
3	1.8	27	3.4	51	3.8
4	1.6	28	2.3	52	4.6
5	3.1	29	2.2	53	7.1
6	3.1	30	3.3	54	4.6
7	4.2	31	3.6	55	2.2
8	3.6	32	4.2	56	3.6
9	4.6	33	2.4	57	2.6
10	2.6	34	4.5	58	2.0
11	3.5	35	5.6	59	1.5
12	5.3	36	4.9	60	6.0
13	5.5	37	10.2	61	5.7
14	5.6	38	5.5	62	5.6
15	4.6	39	4.7	63	2.3
16	3.0	40	4.7	64	2.3
17	4.6	41	3.6	65	2.6
18	4.5	42	3.0	66	3.8
19	4.8	43	2.2	67	2.8
20	5.4	44	3.3	68	2.2
21	5.5	45	3.2	69	4.2
22	3.8	46	0.8	70	2.6
23	3.6	47	4.2	71	1.0
24	2.5	48	5.6	72	1.9

$$\overline{\overline{x}} = \frac{\overline{x}_1 + \overline{x}_2 + \cdots + \overline{x}_{72}}{k} = \frac{3537.3}{72} = 49.129 \qquad \overline{R} = \frac{R_1 + R_1 + \cdots + R_{72}}{k} = \frac{268.8}{72} = 3.733$$

Centerline $= \overline{\overline{x}} = 49.129$

From Table IX, Appendix D, with $n = 6, A_2 = .483$.

Upper control limit $= \overline{\overline{x}} + A_2\overline{R} = 49.129 + .483(3.733) = 50.932$

Lower control limit $= \overline{\overline{x}} - A_2\overline{R} = 49.129 - .483(3.733) = 47.326$

Upper A–B boundary $= \overline{\overline{x}} + \frac{2}{3}(A_2\overline{R}) = 49.129 + \frac{2}{3}(.483)(3.733) = 50.331$

Lower A–B boundary $= \overline{\overline{x}} - \frac{2}{3}(A_2\overline{R}) = 49.129 - \frac{2}{3}(.483)(3.733) = 47.927$

Upper B–C boundary $= \overline{\overline{x}} + \frac{1}{3}(A_2\overline{R}) = 49.129 + \frac{1}{3}(.483)(3.733) = 49.730$

Lower B–C boundary $= \overline{\overline{x}} - \frac{1}{3}(A_2\overline{R}) = 49.129 - \frac{1}{3}(.483)(3.733) = 48.528$

The $\bar{x}$-chart is:

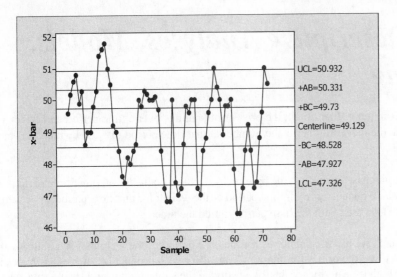

To determine if the process is in or out of control, we check the six rules:

Rule 1:   One point beyond Zone A: There are a total of 17 points beyond Zone A.

Rule 2:   Nine points in a row in Zone C or beyond: No sequence of nine points are in Zone C (on one side of the centerline) or beyond.

Rule 3:   Six points in a row steadily increasing or decreasing: There is one sequence of seven points that are steadily increasing—Points 15 through 21.

Rule 4:   Fourteen points in a row alternating up and down: This pattern does not exist.

Rule 5:   Two out of three points in Zone A or beyond: There are four groups of at least three points in Zone A or beyond—Points 12–16, Points 35–37, Points 39–41, and Points 60–63.

Rule 6:   Four out of five points in a row in Zone B or beyond: There are several groups of points that satisfy this rule.

The process appears to be out of control. Rules 1, 3, 5, and 6 indicate that the process is out of control.

No. The problem does not give the times of the shifts. However, suppose we let the first shift be from 6:00 A.M. to 2:00 P.M., the second shift be from 2:00 P.M. to 10:00 P.M., and the third shift be from 10:00 P.M. to 6:00 A.M. If this is the case, the major problems are during the second shift.

Chapter 14
Time Series: Descriptive Analyses, Models, and Forecasting

14.1   To calculate a simple index number, first obtain the prices or quantities over a time period and select a base year. For each time period, the index number is the number at that time period divided by the value at the base period multiplied by 100.

14.3   A Laspeyres index uses the purchase quantity at the base period as the weights for all other time periods. A Paasche index uses the purchase quantity at each time period as the weight for that time period. The weights at the specified time period are also used with the base period to find the index.

14.5   a.   To find Laspeyres index, we use the quantities for the base period as the weights. We multiply the quantity for quarter 1 times the prices for quarters 1 and 4 for each product (A, B, or C). We then sum the products for both time periods. Finally, we divide the sum for quarter 4 by the sum for quarter 1. The sum of the products for quarter 1 is

$100(3.25) + 20(1.75) + 50(8.00) = 325 + 35 + 400 = 760$. The sum of the products for quarter 4 is

$100(4.25) + 20(1.00) + 50(10.50) = 425 + 20 + 525 = 970$. Laspeyres index is $(970/760) \times 100 = 127.63$.

b.   To find Paasche index, we use the quantities for all time periods as weights. We multiple the quantity for each quarter and each product by the corresponding price. We then sum these products for the base period quarter 2 and the quarter for which we want to compute Paasche's index (quarter 4). The sum for quarter 2 is $300(3.50) + 100(1.25) + 20(9.35) = 1050 + 125 + 107 = 1362$. The sum of the products for quarter 4 is $300(4.25) + 100(1.00) + 20(10.50) = 1275 + 100 + 210 = 1585$. Paasche's index is $(1585/1362) \times 100 = 116.37$.

14.7   a.   To compute the simple index, divide each U.S. Beer Production value by the 1980 value, 188, and then multiply by 100.

Year	Simple Index		Year	Simple Index	
1980	(188/188) x 100 =	100.00	1996	(201/188) x 100 =	106.91
1981	(194/188) x 100 =	103.19	1997	(199/188) x 100 =	105.85
1982	(194/188) x 100 =	103.19	1998	(198/188) x 100 =	105.32
1983	(195/188) x 100 =	103.72	1999	(198/188) x 100 =	105.32
1984	(193/188) x 100 =	102.66	2000	(199/188) x 100 =	105.85
1985	(193/188) x 100 =	102.66	2001	(199/188) x 100 =	105.85
1986	(195/188) x 100 =	103.72	2002	(200/188) x 100 =	106.38
1987	(195/188) x 100 =	103.72	2003	(195/188) x 100 =	103.72
1988	(198/188) x 100 =	105.32	2004	(198/188) x 100 =	105.32
1989	(200/188) x 100 =	106.38	2005	(197/188) x 100 =	104.79
1990	(204/188) x 100 =	108.51	2006	(198/188) x 100 =	105.32
1991	(203/188) x 100 =	107.98	2007	(199/188) x 100 =	105.85
1992	(202/188) x 100 =	107.45	2008	(200/188) x 100 =	106.38
1993	(203/188) x 100 =	107.98	2009	(196/188) x 100 =	104.26
1994	(202/188) x 100 =	107.45	2010	(194/188) x 100 =	103.19
1995	(199/188) x 100 =	105.85			

The index value for 2010 is 103.19. Thus, the beer production in 2010 increased by $103.19 - 100 = 3.19\%$ over the beer production in the base year of 1980.

b. This is a quantity index because the numbers collected were the number of barrels produced rather than the price.

c. To compute the simple index, divide each U.S. Beer Production value by the 1990 value, 204, and then multiply by 100.

Year	Simple Index		Year	Simple Index	
1980	(188/204) x 100 =	92.16	1996	(201/204) x 100 =	98.53
1981	(194/204) x 100 =	95.10	1997	(199/204) x 100 =	97.55
1982	(194/204) x 100 =	95.10	1998	(198/204) x 100 =	97.06
1983	(195/204) x 100 =	95.59	1999	(198/204) x 100 =	97.06
1984	(193/204) x 100 =	94.61	2000	(199/204) x 100 =	97.55
1985	(193/204) x 100 =	94.61	2001	(199/204) x 100 =	97.55
1986	(195/204) x 100 =	95.59	2002	(200/204) x 100 =	98.04
1987	(195/204) x 100 =	95.59	2003	(195/204) x 100 =	95.59
1988	(198/204) x 100 =	97.06	2004	(198/204) x 100 =	97.06
1989	(200/204) x 100 =	98.04	2005	(197/204) x 100 =	96.57
1990	(204/204) x 100 =	100.00	2006	(198/204) x 100 =	97.06
1991	(203/204) x 100 =	99.51	2007	(199/204) x 100 =	97.55
1992	(202/204) x 100 =	99.02	2008	(200/204) x 100 =	98.04
1993	(203/204) x 100 =	99.51	2009	(196/204) x 100 =	96.08
1994	(202/204) x 100 =	99.02	2010	(194/204) x 100 =	95.10
1995	(199/204) x 100 =	97.55			

The plots of the two simple indices are:

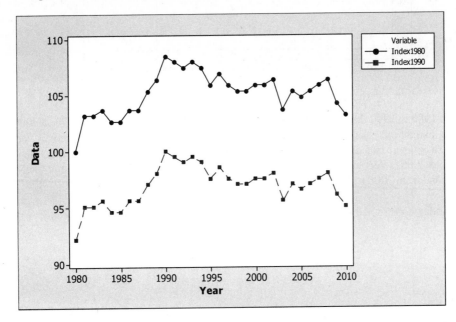

The two plots have the same shape, just at different levels. For both, there is a fairly steep increase in the indices from 1987 to 1990. After 1990, there is a fairly steady decrease in the indices.

14.9   a.   To compute the simple index, divide each natural gas price by the 1980 value, 3.68, and then multiply by 100.

Year	Simple Index		Year	Simple Index	
1980	(3.68/3.68) x 100 =	100.00	2000	(7.76/3.68) x 100 =	210.87
1990	(5.80/3.68) x 100 =	157.61	2001	(9.63/3.68) x 100 =	261.68
1991	(5.82/3.68) x 100 =	158.15	2002	(7.89/3.68) x 100 =	214.40
1992	(5.89/3.68) x 100 =	160.05	2003	(9.63/3.68) x 100 =	261.68
1993	(6.16/3.68) x 100 =	167.39	2004	(10.75/3.68) x 100 =	292.12
1994	(6.41/3.68) x 100 =	174.18	2005	(12.70/3.68) x 100 =	345.11
1995	(6.06/3.68) x 100 =	164.67	2006	(13.73/3.68) x 100 =	373.10
1996	(6.34/3.68) x 100 =	172.28	2007	(13.08/3.68) x 100 =	355.43
1997	(6.94/3.68) x 100 =	188.59	2008	(13.89/3.68) x 100 =	377.45
1998	(6.82/3.68) x 100 =	185.33	2009	(12.14/3.68) x 100 =	329.89
1999	(6.69/3.68) x 100 =	181.79	2010	(11.20/3.68) x 100 =	304.35

The plot of the index is:

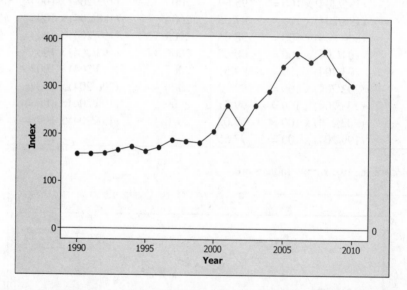

b.   From 1980 to 1990 there was an increase in the price of natural gas. From 1990 to 2000, there was again a slight increase in the price of natural gas. From 2000 to 2007, the price was very volatile, with sharp increases from 2000 to 2001, a sharp decrease from 2001 to 2002, sharp increases from 2002 to 2006, a decreases from 2006 to 2007, an increase from 2007 to 2008, and then a sharp decrease from 2008 to 2010.

c.   The index constructed is a price index since it is based on the price of natural gas.

14.11   a.   To compute the simple composite index, first sum the three values (durables, nondurables, and services) for every time period. Then, divide each sum by the sum in 1970, 649, and then multiply by 100. The simple composite index for 1970 is:

Year	Sum	Simple Composite Index-1970	Simple Composite Index-1980
1970	649	100.00	36.98
1975	1,025	157.94	58.40
1980	1,755	270.42	100.00
1985	2,667	410.94	151.97
1990	3,835	590.91	218.52
1995	4,988	768.57	284.22
2000	6,830	1,052.39	389.17
2005	8,819	1,358.86	502.51
2010	10,348	1,594.45	589.63

   b.   To update the 1970 index to the 1980 index, divide the 1970 index values by the 1970 index value for 1980, 270.42, and then multiply by 100. The 1980 simple composite index is also listed in the table in part **a**.

   c.   The graph of the two indices is:

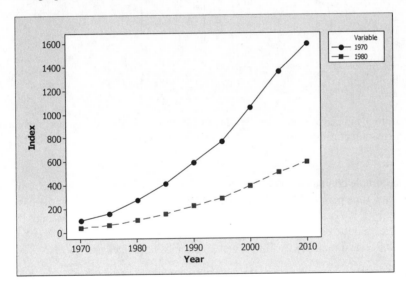

Changing the base year from 1970 to 1980 flattens out the graph. Also, the spread of the values for the 1980 index is much smaller than the spread of the values in the 1970 index.

14.13   a.   To compute the simple index for the average hourly earnings for manufacturing workers, divide the hourly earnings for each year by the hourly earnings for the base year, 10.78, and multiply by 100. To compute the simple index for the average hourly earnings for Information workers, divide the hourly earnings for each year by the hourly earnings for the base year, 13.4, and multiply by 100. To compute the simple index for the average hourly earnings for Food Service workers, divide the hourly earnings for each year by the hourly earnings for the base year, 5.7, and multiply by 100. The three indices are:

Year	Manufacturing Index	Information Index	Food Services Index
1990	100.00	100.00	100.00
2000	132.84	142.31	138.95
2005	153.62	164.63	154.39
2007	160.11	178.81	172.28
2008	164.66	184.93	179.47
2009	169.20	189.93	184.04
2010	172.63	192.99	187.37

b.   The two plots are:

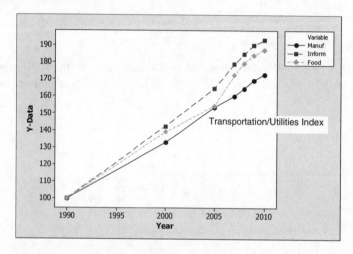

The simple earnings indices are very similar. From 1990 to 2010, the hourly earnings have increased 72.73% for the manufacturing workers, 92.99% for the information workers, and 87.37% for the food service workers.

c.   To compute the simple composite index for the hourly earnings, sum the earnings for the three industries for each time period. Then divide the sum at each year by the sum at the base year, 29.88, and multiply by 100. To compute the simple composite index for weekly hours, sum the weekly hours for the three industries for each time period. Then divide the sum at each year by the sum at the base year, 102.2, and multiply by 100. The two composite indices are:

Year	Earnings	Hours	Earnings Index	Hours Index
1990	29.88	102.2	100.00	100.00
2000	41.31	104.3	138.25	102.05
2005	47.42	102.9	158.70	100.68
2007	51.04	103.3	170.82	101.08
2008	52.76	102.9	176.57	100.68
2009	54.18	101.4	181.33	99.22
2010	55.15	102.4	184.57	100.20

d.   The plots of the two composite indices are:

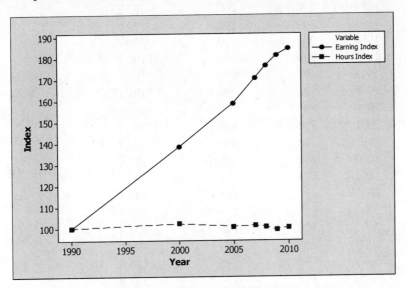

The composite earnings index increased 84.57% from 1990 to 2010. However, the composite weekly hours has increased only .2% from 1990 to 2010.

14.15   The smaller the value of w, the smoother the series. With $w = .2$, the current value receives a weight of .2 while the previous exponentially smoothed value receives a weight of .8. With $w = .8$, the current value receives a weight of .8 while the previous exponentially smoothed value receives a weight of .2. The smaller the value of w, the less chance the series can be affected by large jumps.

14.17   a.   The exponentially smoothed beer production for the first period is equal to the beer production for that period. For the rest of the time periods, the exponentially smoothed beer production is found by multiplying the beer production of that time period by $w = .2$ and adding to that $(1 - .2)$ times the exponentially smoothed value above it. The exponentially smoothed value for the second period is $.2(194) + (1 - .2)(188) = 189.2$.

The rest of the values are shown in the following table.

Year	Beer Production	Exponentially Smoothed Production $w = .2$	Exponentially Smoothed Production $w = .8$
1980	188	188.0	188.0
1981	194	189.2	192.8
1982	194	190.2	193.8
1983	195	191.1	194.8
1984	193	191.5	193.4
1985	193	191.8	193.1
1986	195	192.4	194.6
1987	195	193.0	194.9
1988	198	194.0	197.4
1989	200	195.2	199.5
1990	204	196.9	203.1
1991	203	198.1	203.0
1992	202	198.9	202.2

1993	203	199.7	202.8
1994	202	200.2	202.2
1995	199	200.0	199.6
1996	201	200.2	200.7
1997	199	199.9	199.3
1998	198	199.5	198.3
1999	198	199.2	198.1
2000	199	199.2	198.8
2001	199	199.1	199.0
2002	200	199.3	199.8
2003	195	198.5	196.0
2004	198	198.4	197.6
2005	197	198.1	197.1
2006	198	198.1	197.8
2007	199	198.3	198.8
2008	200	198.6	199.8
2009	196	198.1	196.8
2010	194	197.3	194.6

b. The exponentially smoothed beer production for the first period is equal to the beer production for that period. For the rest of the time periods, the exponentially smoothed beer production is found by multiplying .8 times the beer production of that time period and adding to that $(1-.8)$ times the value of the exponentially smoothed beer production figure of the previous time period. The exponentially smoothed beer production for the second time period is $.8(194)+(1-.8)(188)=192.8$. The rest of the values are shown in the table in part a.

c. The plot of the two series is:

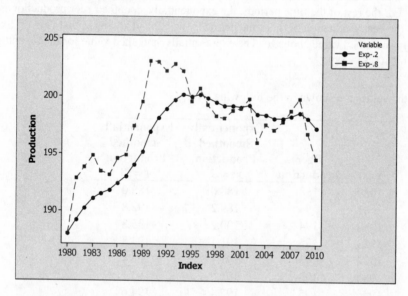

The exponentially smoothed series with $w=.2$ is smoother than the series with $w=.8$. Thus, the series with $w=.2$ best portrays the long-term trend.

14.19 a. The exponentially smoothed gold price for the first period is equal to the gold price for that period. For the rest of the time periods, the exponentially smoothed gold price is found by multiplying the price for the time period by $w = .8$ and adding to that $(1 - .8)$ times the exponentially smoothed value from the previous time period. The exponentially smoothed value for the second time period is $.8(362) + (1 - .8)(384) = 366.40$. The rest of the values are shown in the table.

Year	Price	Exponentially Smoothed $w = .8$	Year	Price	Exponentially Smoothed $w = .8$
1990	384	384.00	2001	271	272.80
1991	362	366.40	2002	310	302.56
1992	344	348.48	2003	363	350.91
1993	360	357.70	2004	410	398.18
1994	384	378.74	2005	445	435.64
1995	384	382.95	2006	603	569.53
1996	388	386.99	2007	695	669.91
1997	331	342.20	2008	872	831.58
1998	294	303.64	2009	972	943.92
1999	279	283.93	2010	1,225	1,168.78
2000	279	279.99	2011	1,572	1,491.36

   b. The plot of the two series is:

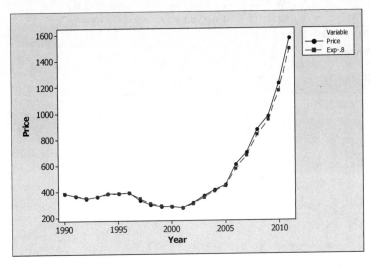

The exponentially smooth series with $w = .8$ is almost the same as the original series.

14.21 a. The exponentially smoothed imports for the first period is equal to the imports that period. For the rest of the time periods, the exponentially smoothed imports is found by multiplying $w = .1$ times the imports for that time period and adding to that $(1 - .1)$ times the value of the exponentially smoothed imports figure of the previous time period. The exponentially smoothed imports for the second time period is $.1(1,233) + (1 - .1)(1,283) = 1,278.00$. The rest of the values are shown in the table.

The same procedure is followed for $w = .9$. The exponentially smoothed imports/exports for the second time period is $.9(1,233) + (1 - .9)(1,283) = 1,238.00$. The rest of the values are shown in the table.

Year	t	Imports	Exponentially Smoothed Series $w = .1$	Exponentially Smoothed Series $w = .9$
1990	1	1,283	1,283.00	1,283.00
1991	2	1,233	1,278.00	1,238.00
1992	3	1,247	1,274.90	1,246.10
1993	4	1,339	1,281.31	1,329.71
1994	5	1,307	1,283.88	1,309.27
1995	6	1,219	1,277.39	1,228.03
1996	7	1,258	1,275.45	1,255.00
1997	8	1,378	1,285.71	1,365.70
1998	9	1,522	1,309.34	1,506.37
1999	10	1,543	1,332.70	1,539.34
2000	11	1,659	1,365.33	1,647.03
2001	12	1,770	1,405.80	1,757.70
2002	13	1,490	1,414.22	1,516.77
2003	14	1,671	1,439.90	1,655.58
2004	15	1,948	1,490.71	1,918.76
2005	16	1,738	1,515.44	1,756.08
2006	17	1,745	1,538.39	1,746.11
2007	18	1,969	1,581.45	1,946.71
2008	19	1,984	1,621.71	1,980.27
2009	20	1,594	1,618.94	1,632.63
2010	21	1,654	1,622.44	1,651.86

b.   The plot of the three series is:

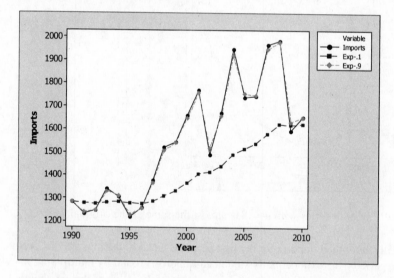

The exponentially smoothed series with $w = .9$ looks more like the original series. The closer w is to 1 the closer the exponentially smoothed curve looks like the original.

14.23 If w is small (near 0), one will obtain a smooth, slowly changing series of forecasts. If w is large (near 1), one will obtain more rapidly changing forecasts that depend mostly on the current values of the series.

14.25 a. We first compute the exponentially smoothed values $E_1, E_2, \ldots, E_t$ for years 1980 – 2007.

$$E_1 = Y_1 = 188$$

For $w = .3$, $E_2 = wY_2 + (1-w)E_1 = .3(194) + (1-.3)(188) = 189.80$
$$E_3 = wY_3 + (1-w)E_2 = .3(194) + (1-.3)(189.80) = 191.06$$
The rest of the values appear in the table.

For $w = .7$, $E_2 = wY_2 + (1-w)E_1 = .7(194) + (1-.7)(188) = 192.20$
$$E_3 = wY_3 + (1-w)E_2 = .7(194) + (1-.7)(192.20) = 193.46$$
The rest of the values appear in the table.

Year	Beer Production	Exponentially Smoothed $w = .3$	Exponentially Smoothed $w = .7$
1980	188	188.00	188.00
1981	194	189.80	192.20
1982	194	191.06	193.46
1983	195	192.24	194.54
1984	193	192.47	193.46
1985	193	192.63	193.14
1986	195	193.34	194.44
1987	195	193.84	194.83
1988	198	195.09	197.05
1989	200	196.56	199.11
1990	204	198.79	202.53
1991	203	200.05	202.86
1992	202	200.64	202.26
1993	203	201.35	202.78
1994	202	201.54	202.23
1995	199	200.78	199.97
1996	201	200.85	200.69
1997	199	200.29	199.51
1998	198	199.60	198.45
1999	198	199.12	198.14
2000	199	199.09	198.74
2001	199	199.06	198.92
2002	200	199.34	199.68
2003	195	198.04	196.40
2004	198	198.03	197.52
2005	197	197.72	197.16
2006	198	197.80	197.75
2007	199	198.16	198.62
2008	200		
2009	196		
2010	194		

To forecast using exponentially smoothed values, we use the following:

For $w=.3$:

$$F_{2008}=F_{t+1}=E_t=198.16$$
$$F_{2009}=F_{t+2}=F_{t+1}=198.16$$
$$F_{2010}=F_{t+3}=F_{t+1}=198.16$$

For $w=.7$:

$$F_{2008}=F_{t+1}=E_t=198.62$$
$$F_{2009}=F_{t+2}=F_{t+1}=198.62$$
$$F_{2010}=F_{t+3}=F_{t+1}=198.62$$

b. We first compute the Holt-Winters values for the years 1980-2007.

With $w=.7$ and $v=.3$,

$$E_2=Y_2=194$$
$$E_3=wY_3+(1-w)(E_2+T_2)=.7(194)+(1-.7)(194+6)=195.8$$

$$T_2=Y_2-Y_1=194-188=6$$
$$T_3=v(E_3-E_2)+(1-v)T_2=.3(195.8-194)+(1-.3)6=4.74$$

The rest of the E_t's and T_t's appear in the table that follows.

With $w=.3$ and $v=.7$,

$$E_2=Y_2=194$$
$$E_3=wY_3+(1-w)(E_2+T_2)=.3(194)+(1-.3)(194+6)=198.2$$

$$T_2=Y_2-Y_1=194-188=6$$
$$T_3=v(E_3-E_2)+(1-v)T_2=.7(198.2-194)+(1-.7)6=4.74$$

The rest of the E_t's and T_t's appear in the table that follows.

		Holt-Winters		Holt-Winters	
		E_t	T_t	E_t	T_t
Year	Beer	$w=.7$	$v=.3$	$w=.3$	$v=.7$
1980	188				
1981	194	194.00	6.00	194.00	6.00
1982	194	195.80	4.74	198.20	4.74
1983	195	196.66	3.58	200.56	3.07
1984	193	195.17	2.06	200.44	0.84
1985	193	194.27	1.17	198.80	-0.90
1986	195	195.13	1.08	197.03	-1.51
1987	195	195.36	0.82	195.36	-1.62
1988	198	197.46	1.20	195.02	-0.72
1989	200	199.60	1.49	196.01	0.47
1990	204	203.13	2.10	198.74	2.05
1991	203	203.67	1.63	201.45	2.52
1992	202	202.99	0.94	203.38	2.10
1993	203	203.28	0.74	204.74	1.58
1994	202	202.61	0.32	205.02	0.67

1995	199	200.18	-0.51	203.69	-0.73
1996	201	200.60	-0.23	202.37	-1.14
1997	199	199.41	-0.52	200.56	-1.61
1998	198	198.27	-0.70	198.66	-1.81
1999	198	197.87	-0.61	197.20	-1.57
2000	199	198.48	-0.25	196.64	-0.86
2001	199	198.77	-0.08	196.75	-0.18
2002	200	199.61	0.19	197.59	0.54
2003	195	196.44	-0.82	197.19	-0.12
2004	198	197.29	-0.32	197.35	0.08
2005	197	196.99	-0.31	197.30	-0.01
2006	198	197.60	-0.03	197.50	0.14
2007	199	198.57	0.27	198.04	0.42
2008	200				
2009	196				
2010	194				

To forecast using the Holt-Winters Model:

For $w = .7$ and $v = .3$,

$$F_{2008} = F_{t+1} = E_t + T_t = 198.57 + .27 = 198.84$$
$$F_{2009} = F_{t+2} = E_t + 2T_t = 198.57 + 2(.27) = 199.11$$
$$F_{2010} = F_{t+3} = E_t + 3T_t = 198.57 + 3(.27) = 199.38$$

For $w = .3$ and $v = .7$,

$$F_{2008} = F_{t+1} = E_t + T_t = 198.04 + .42 = 198.46$$
$$F_{2009} = F_{t+2} = E_t + 2T_t = 198.04 + 2(.42) = 198.88$$
$$F_{2010} = F_{t+3} = E_t + 3T_t = 198.04 + 3(.42) = 199.30$$

14.27   a.   Using MINITAB, the time series plot is:

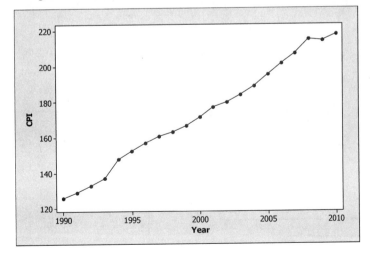

There appears to be an increasing trend in CPI over time.

b.   To compute the exponentially smoothed values, we follow these steps:

$E_1 = Y_1 = 125.8$

$E_2 = wY_2 + (1-w)E_1 = .4(129.1) + (1-.4)(125.8) = 127.12$

$E_3 = wY_3 + (1-w)E_2 = .4(132.8) + (1-.4)(127.12) = 129.39$

The rest of the values are computed in a similar manner and are listed in the table:

Year	CPI	Exponentially Smoothed $w = .4$
1990	125.8	125.80
1991	129.1	127.12
1992	132.8	129.39
1993	136.8	132.36
1994	147.8	138.53
1995	152.4	144.08
1996	156.9	149.21
1997	160.5	153.72
1998	163.0	157.43
1999	166.6	161.10
2000	171.5	165.26
2001	177.1	170.00
2002	179.9	173.96
2003	184.0	177.97
2004	188.9	182.34
2005	195.3	187.53
2006	201.6	193.16
2007	207.3	198.81
2008	215.3	205.41
2009	214.5	209.04
2010	218.1	212.67

Using MINITAB, the plot is:

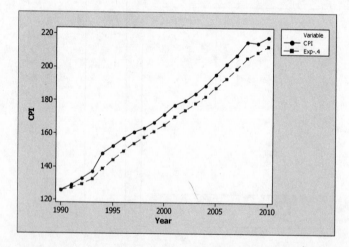

To forecast using exponentially smoothed values, we use the following: $F_{2011} = F_{t+1} = E_t = 212.67$

c.   We first compute the Holt-Winters values for the years 1990-2010. With $w = .4$ and $v = .5$,

$$E_2 = Y_2 = 129.1$$
$$E_3 = wY_3 + (1-w)(E_2 + T_2) = .4(132.8) + (1-.4)(129.1+3.3) = 132.56$$

$$T_2 = Y_2 - Y_1 = 129.1 - 125.8 = 3.3$$
$$T_3 = v(E_3 - E_2) + (1-v)T_2 = .5(132.56 - 129.1) + (1-.5)(3.3) = 3.38$$

The rest of the E_t's and T_t's appear in the table that follows.

		Holt-Winters	
		Et	*Tt*
Year	CPI	*w* = .4	*v* = .5
1990	125.8		
1991	129.1	129.10	3.30
1992	132.8	132.56	3.38
1993	136.8	136.28	3.55
1994	147.8	143.02	5.14
1995	152.4	149.86	5.99
1996	156.9	156.27	6.20
1997	160.5	161.68	5.81
1998	163.0	165.69	4.91
1999	166.6	169.00	4.11
2000	171.5	172.47	3.79
2001	177.1	176.59	3.96
2002	179.9	180.29	3.83
2003	184.0	184.07	3.80
2004	188.9	188.28	4.01
2005	195.3	193.50	4.61
2006	201.6	199.50	5.31
2007	207.3	205.81	5.81
2008	215.3	213.09	6.54
2009	214.5	217.58	5.52
2010	218.1	221.10	4.52

To forecast using the Holt-Winters Model:

For $w = .4$ and $v = .5$, $F_{2011} = F_{t+1} = E_t + T_t = 221.10 + 4.52 = 225.62$

14.29   a.   To compute the exponentially smoothed values, we follow these steps:

$$E_t = Y_1 = 1,126.2$$

For $w = .7$,

$$E_2 = wY_2 + (1-w)E_1 = .7(1,140.8) + (1-.7)(1,126.2) = 1,136.4$$
$$E_3 = wY_3 + (1-w)E_2 = .7(1,114.6) + (1-.7)(1,136.4) = 1,121.1$$

The rest of the values are computed in a similar manner and are listed in the table:

Year	Quarter	S&P 500	Exponentially Smoothed $w = .7$	Exponentially Smoothed $w = .3$
2004	1	1,126.2	1,126.2	1,126.2
	2	1,140.8	1,136.4	1,130.6
	3	1,114.6	1,121.1	1,125.8
	4	1,211.9	1,184.7	1,151.6
2005	1	1,180.6	1,181.8	1,160.3
	2	1,191.3	1,188.5	1,169.6
	3	1,228.8	1,216.7	1,187.4
	4	1,248.3	1,238.8	1,205.6
2006	1	1,294.9	1,278.1	1,232.4
	2	1,270.2	1,272.6	1,243.8
	3	1,335.8	1,316.8	1,271.4
	4	1,418.3	1,387.9	1,315.4
2007	1	1,420.9	1,411.0	1,347.1
	2	1,503.3	1,475.6	1,393.9
	3	1,526.7	1,511.4	1,433.8
	4	1,468.4	1,481.3	1,444.2
2008	1	1,322.7	1,370.3	1,407.7
	2	1,280.0	1,307.1	1,369.4
	3	1,164.7	1,207.4	1,308.0
	4	903.3	994.5	1,186.6
2009	1	797.9	856.9	1,070.0
	2	919.3	900.6	1,024.8
	3	1,057.1	1,010.1	1,034.5
	4	1,115.1	1,083.6	1,058.7
2010	1	1,169.4	1,143.7	1,091.9
	2	1,030.7	1,064.6	1,073.5
	3	1,141.2	1,118.2	1,093.8
	4	1,257.6	1,215.8	1,143.0
2011	1	1,325.8		
	2	1,320.6		
	3	1,131.4		
	4	1,257.6		

The forecasts using the exponentially smoothed values with $w = .7$ are:

$$F_{2011,1} = F_{t+1} = E_t = 1,215.8$$

$$F_{2011,2} = F_{t+2} = F_{t+1} = 1,215.8$$

$$F_{2011,3} = F_{t+3} = F_{t+1} = 1,215.8$$

$$F_{2011,4} = F_{t+4} = F_{t+1} = 1,215.8$$

b.   To compute the exponentially smoothed values, we follow these steps:

$$E_t = Y_1 = 1,126.2$$

For $w = .3$,

$E_2 = wY_2 + (1-w)E_1 = .3(1,140.8)+(1-.3)(1,126.2)=1,130.6$

$E_3 = wY_3 + (1-w)E_2 = .3(1,114.6)+(1-.3)(1,130.6)=1,125.8$

The rest of the values are computed in a similar manner and are listed in the table above.

The forecasts using the exponentially smoothed values with $w=.3$ are:

$F_{2011,1} = F_{t+1} = E_t = 1,143.0$

$F_{2011,2} = F_{t+2} = F_{t+1} = 1,143.0$

$F_{2011,3} = F_{t+3} = F_{t+1} = 1,143.0$

$F_{2011,4} = F_{t+4} = F_{t+1} = 1,143.0$

14.31 a. We first compute the exponentially smoothed values $E_1, E_2, \ldots, E_t$ for 2005 through 2011.

$E_1 = Y_1 = 424.20$

For $w=.5$,

$E_2 = wY_2 + (1-w)E_1 = .5(423.4)+(1-.5)(424.2)=423.80$

$E_3 = wY_3 + (1-w)E_2 = .5(434.2)+(1-.5)(423.8)=429.00$

The rest of the values are found in the table:

Year	Month	Gold Price	Exponentially Smoothed $w=.5$	Holt-Winters E_t $w=.5$	T_t $v=.5$
2005	Jan	424.2	424.20		
	Feb	423.4	423.80	423.40	211.70
	Mar	434.2	429.00	534.65	161.48
	Apr	428.9	428.95	562.51	94.67
	May	421.9	425.43	539.54	35.85
	Jun	430.7	428.06	503.04	-0.32
	Jul	424.5	426.28	463.61	-19.88
	Aug	437.9	432.09	440.82	-21.34
	Sep	456.0	444.05	437.74	-12.21
	Oct	469.9	456.97	447.72	-1.11
	Nov	476.7	466.84	461.65	6.41
	Dec	509.8	488.32	488.93	16.84
2006	Jan	549.9	519.11	527.84	27.88
	Feb	555.0	537.05	555.36	27.70
	Mar	557.1	547.08	570.08	21.21
	Apr	610.6	578.84	600.94	26.04
	May	676.5	627.67	651.74	38.42
	Jun	596.2	611.93	643.18	14.93
	Jul	633.8	622.87	645.95	8.85
	Aug	632.6	627.73	643.70	3.30
	Sep	598.2	612.97	622.60	-8.90
	Oct	585.8	599.38	599.75	-15.88
	Nov	627.8	613.59	605.84	-4.89
	Dec	629.8	621.70	615.37	2.32

2007	Jan	631.2	626.45	624.45	5.70
	Feb	664.7	645.57	647.42	14.34
	Mar	654.9	650.24	658.33	12.62
	Apr	679.4	664.82	675.18	14.73
	May	666.9	665.86	678.40	8.98
	Jun	655.5	660.68	671.44	1.01
	Jul	665.3	662.99	668.88	-0.78
	Aug	665.4	664.19	666.75	-1.45
	Sep	712.7	688.45	689.00	10.40
	Oct	754.6	721.52	727.00	24.20
	Nov	806.3	763.91	778.75	37.97
	Dec	803.2	783.56	809.96	34.59
2008	Jan	889.6	836.58	867.08	45.86
	Feb	922.3	879.44	917.62	48.20
	Mar	968.4	923.92	967.11	48.84
	Apr	909.7	916.81	962.83	22.28
	May	888.7	902.75	936.90	-1.82
	Jun	889.5	896.13	912.29	-13.22
	Jul	939.8	917.96	919.44	-3.03
	Aug	839.0	878.48	877.70	-22.39
	Sep	829.9	854.19	842.61	-28.74
	Oct	806.6	830.40	810.23	-30.56
	Nov	760.9	795.65	770.29	-35.25
	Dec	816.1	805.87	775.57	-14.99
2009	Jan	858.7	832.29	809.64	9.54
	Feb	943.2	887.74	881.19	40.55
	Mar	924.3	906.02	923.02	41.19
	Apr	890.2	898.11	927.20	22.69
	May	928.6	913.36	939.24	17.36
	Jun	945.7	929.53	951.15	14.64
	Jul	934.2	931.86	950.00	6.74
	Aug	949.4	940.63	953.07	4.91
	Sep	996.6	968.62	977.29	14.56
	Oct	1,043.2	1,005.91	1,017.52	27.40
	Nov	1,127.0	1,066.45	1,085.96	47.92
	Dec	1,134.7	1,100.58	1,134.29	48.12
2010	Jan	1,118.0	1,109.29	1,150.21	32.02
	Feb	1,095.4	1,102.34	1,138.81	10.31
	Mar	1,113.3	1,107.82	1,131.21	1.36
	Apr	1,148.7	1,128.26	1,140.64	5.39
	May	1,205.4	1,166.83	1,175.71	20.23
	Jun	1,232.9	1,199.87	1,214.42	29.47
	Jul	1,193.0	1,196.43	1,218.45	16.75
	Aug	1,215.8	1,206.12	1,225.50	11.90
	Sep	1,271.1	1,238.61	1,254.25	20.33
	Oct	1,342.0	1,290.30	1,308.29	37.18
	Nov	1,369.9	1,330.10	1,357.68	43.29
	Dec	1,390.6	1,360.35	1,395.79	40.70
2011	Jan	1,356.4	1,358.38	1,396.44	20.68
	Feb	1,372.7	1,365.54	1,394.91	9.57

Mar	1,424.0	1,394.77	1,414.24	14.45
Apr	1,473.8	1,434.28	1,451.25	25.73
May	1,560.4	1,497.34	1,518.69	46.58
Jun	1,528.7	1,513.02	1,546.99	37.44
Jul	1,572.8	1,542.91	1,578.61	34.53
Aug	1,755.8	1,649.36	1,684.47	70.20
Sep	1,771.9	1,710.63	1,763.29	74.50
Oct	1,665.2	1,687.91	1,751.50	31.36
Nov	1,739.0	1,713.46	1,760.93	20.39
Dec	1,652.3	1,682.88	1,716.81	-11.86

To forecast the monthly prices for 2011 using the data through December 2010:

$$F_{t+1} = E_t \qquad F_{t+1} = F_{t+i} = E_t \text{ for } i = 2, 3, \ldots$$
$$F_{t+1} = E_{\text{Dec},2010} = 1,360.35$$

Year	Month	Forecast
2011	Jan	1,360.35
	Feb	1,360.35
	Mar	1,360.35
	Apr	1,360.35
	May	1,360.35
	Jun	1,360.35
	Jul	1,360.35
	Aug	1,360.35
	Sep	1,360.35
	Oct	1,360.35
	Nov	1,360.35
	Dec	1,360.35

b. To compute the one-step-ahead forecasts for 2011, we use $F_{t+1} = E_t$, where E_t is recomputed each time period (month). The forecasts are obtained from the table in part **a**.

Year	Month	Forecast
2011	Jan	1,360.35
	Feb	1,358.38
	Mar	1,365.54
	Apr	1,394.77
	May	1,434.28
	Jun	1,497.34
	Jul	1,513.02
	Aug	1,542.91
	Sep	1,649.36
	Oct	1,710.63
	Nov	1,687.91
	Dec	1,713.46

c. First, we compute the Holt-Winters values for the years 2005-2011.

With $w = .5$ and $v = .5$,

$$E_2 = Y_2 = 423.4$$
$$E_3 = wY_3 + (1-w)(E_2 + T_2) = .5(434.2) + (1-.5)(423.4 - 0.8) = 428.40$$

$$T_2 = Y_2 - Y_1 = 423.4 - 424.2 = -0.8$$
$$T_3 = v(E_3 - E_2) + (1-v)T_2 = .5(428.40 - 423.4) + (1-.5)(-0.8) = 2.10$$

The rest of the E_t's and T_t's appear in the table in part a.

To forecast the monthly prices for 2011 using the data through December 2010:

$$F_{t+1} = E_t + T_t = 1,395.79 + 40.70 = 1,436.49$$
$$F_{t+2} = E_t + 2T_t = 1,395.79 + 2(40.70) = 1,477.19$$
$$F_{t+n} = E_t + nT_t$$

The rest of the forecasts appear in the table:

Year	Month	Forecast
2011	Jan	1,436.49
	Feb	1,477.19
	Mar	1,517.89
	Apr	1,558.59
	May	1,599.29
	Jun	1,639.99
	Jul	1,680.69
	Aug	1,721.39
	Sep	1,762.09
	Oct	1,802.79
	Nov	1,843.49
	Dec	1,884.19

To compute the one-step-ahead forecasts for 2011, we use $F_{t+1} = E_t + T_t$ where E_t and T_t are recomputed each time period. The forecasts are obtained from the table in part **a**.

$$F_{\text{Jan},2011} = E_{\text{Dec, 2010}} + T_{\text{Dec, 2010}} = 1,395.79 + 40.70 = 1436.49$$
$$F_{\text{Feb},2011} = E_{\text{Jan, 2011}} + T_{\text{Jan, 2011}} = 1,396.44 + 20.68 = 1,417.12$$

The rest of the values appear in the table:

Year	Month	Forecast
2011	Jan	1,436.49
	Feb	1,417.12
	Mar	1,404.48
	Apr	1,428.69
	May	1,476.97
	Jun	1,565.27
	Jul	1,584.43
	Aug	1,613.15
	Sep	1,754.67

Oct	1,837.79
Nov	1,782.85
Dec	1,781.32

14.33   a.   From Exercise 14.25b, the Holt-Winters forecasts for 2008-2010 using $w = .3$ and $v = .7$ are:

$$F_{2008} = 198.46$$
$$F_{2009} = 198.88$$
$$F_{2010} = 199.30$$

The errors are the differences between the actual values and the predicted values. Thus, the errors are:

$$Y_{2008} - F_{2008} = 200 - 198.46 = 1.54$$
$$Y_{2009} - F_{2009} = 196 - 198.88 = -2.88$$
$$Y_{2010} - F_{2010} = 194 - 199.30 = -5.30$$

   b.   From Exercise 14.25b, the Holt-Winters forecasts for 2008-2010 using $w = .7$ and $v = .3$ are:

$$F_{2008} = 198.84$$
$$F_{2009} = 199.11$$
$$F_{2010} = 199.38$$

The errors are:
$$Y_{2008} - F_{2008} = 200 - 198.84 = 1.16$$
$$Y_{2009} - F_{2009} = 196 - 199.11 = -3.11$$
$$Y_{2010} - F_{2010} = 194 - 199.38 = -5.38$$

   c.   For the Holt-Winters forecasts with $w = .3$ and $v = .7$,

$$\text{MAD} = \frac{\sum_{t=29}^{31} |Y_t - F_t|}{m} = \frac{|200 - 198.46| + |196 - 198.88| + |194 - 199.30|}{3} = \frac{9.72}{3} = 3.24$$

$$\text{MAPE} = \left[\frac{\sum_{t=29}^{31} \left| \frac{(Y_t - F_t)}{Y_t} \right|}{m} \right] 100$$

$$= \left[\frac{\left| \frac{200 - 198.46}{200} \right| + \left| \frac{196 - 198.88}{196} \right| + \left| \frac{194 - 199.30}{194} \right|}{3} \right] 100 = \left[\frac{.049713}{3} \right] 100 = 1.6571$$

$$\text{RMSE} = \sqrt{\frac{\sum_{t=29}^{31} (Y_t - F_t)^2}{m}} = \sqrt{\frac{(200 - 198.46)^2 + (196 - 198.88)^2 + (194 - 199.30)^2}{3}}$$

$$= \sqrt{\frac{38.756}{3}} = 3.5943$$

d. For the Holt-Winters forecasts with $w = .7$ and $v = .3$,

$$\text{MAD} = \frac{\sum_{t=29}^{31} |Y_t - F_t|}{m} = \frac{|200 - 198.84| + |196 - 199.11| + |194 - 199.38|}{3} = \frac{9.65}{3} = 3.2167$$

$$\text{MAPE} = \left[\frac{\sum_{t=29}^{31} \left| \frac{(Y_t - F_t)}{Y_t} \right|}{m} \right] 100$$

$$= \left[\frac{\left| \frac{200 - 198.84}{200} \right| + \left| \frac{196 - 199.11}{196} \right| + \left| \frac{194 - 199.38}{194} \right|}{3} \right] 100 = \left[\frac{.049399}{3} \right] 100 = 1.6466$$

$$\text{RMSE} = \sqrt{\frac{\sum_{t=29}^{31} (Y_t - F_t)^2}{m}} = \sqrt{\frac{(200 - 198.84)^2 + (196 - 199.11)^2 + (194 - 199.38)^2}{3}}$$

$$= \sqrt{\frac{39.9621}{3}} = 3.6498$$

e. Two of the three measures of forecast accuracy for the Holt-Winters forecast with $w = .7$ and $v = .3$ are smaller than the corresponding values for the Holt-Winters forecast with $w = .3$ and $v = .7$. We recommend using the Holt-Winters forecast with $w = .7$ and $v = .3$.

14.35   a. From Exercise 14.30, the forecasts for the 4 quarters of 2011 using the Holt-Winters forecasts with $w = .3$ and $v = .5$ are:

$$F_{2011,1} = 1,302.37$$
$$F_{2011,2} = 1,328.82$$
$$F_{2011,3} = 1,355.27$$
$$F_{2011,4} = 1,381.72$$

$$\text{MAD} = \frac{\sum_{t=29}^{32} |Y_t - F_t|}{m}$$

$$= \frac{|1325.8 - 1302.37| + |1320.6 - 1328.82| + |1131.4 - 1355.27| + |1257.6 - 1381.72|}{4}$$

$$= \frac{379.64}{4} = 94.91$$

$$\text{MAPE} = \left[\frac{\sum_{t=29}^{32} \left| \frac{(Y_t - F_t)}{Y_t} \right|}{m} \right] 100$$

$$= \left[\frac{\left| \frac{1325.8 - 1302.37}{1325.8} \right| + \left| \frac{1320.6 - 1328.82}{1320.6} \right| + \left| \frac{1131.4 - 1355.27}{1131.4} \right| + \left| \frac{1257.6 - 1381.72}{1257.6} \right|}{4} \right] 100$$

$$= \left[\frac{0.320463}{4} \right] 100 = 8.012$$

$$\text{RMSE} = \sqrt{ \frac{\sum_{t=29}^{32} (Y_t - F_t)^2}{m} }$$

$$= \sqrt{ \frac{(1325.8 - 1302.37)^2 + (1320.6 - 1328.82)^2 + (1131.4 - 1355.27)^2 + (1257.6 - 1381.72)^2}{4} }$$

$$= \sqrt{ \frac{66,140.0846}{4} } = 128.589$$

b. From Exercise 14.30, the forecasts for the 4 quarters of 2011 using the Holt-Winters forecasts with $w = .7$ and $v = .5$ are:

$$F_{2011,1} = 1,274.60$$
$$F_{2011,2} = 1,326.99$$
$$F_{2011,3} = 1,379.38$$
$$F_{2011,4} = 1,431.77$$

$$\text{MAD} = \frac{\sum_{t=29}^{32} |Y_t - F_t|}{m}$$

$$= \frac{|1325.8 - 1274.6| + |1320.6 - 1326.99| + |1131.4 - 1379.38| + |1257.6 - 1431.77|}{4}$$

$$= \frac{479.74}{4} = 119.935$$

$$\text{MAPE} = \left[\frac{\sum_{t=29}^{32} \left| \frac{(Y_t - F_t)}{Y_t} \right|}{m} \right] 100$$

$$= \left[\frac{\left| \frac{1325.8 - 1274.6}{1325.8} \right| + \left| \frac{1320.6 - 1326.99}{1320.6} \right| + \left| \frac{1131.4 - 1379.38}{1131.4} \right| + \left| \frac{1257.6 - 1431.77}{1257.6} \right|}{4} \right] 100$$

$$= \left[\frac{0.401131}{4} \right] 100 = 10.028$$

$$RMSE = \sqrt{\frac{\sum_{t=29}^{32}\left(Y_t - F_t\right)^2}{m}}$$

$$= \sqrt{\frac{\left(1325.8-1274.6\right)^2 + \left(1320.6-1326.99\right)^2 + \left(1131.4-1379.38\right)^2 + \left(1257.6-1431.77\right)^2}{4}}$$

$$= \sqrt{\frac{94,491.5414}{4}} = 153.697$$

c.   For all three measures of error, the Holt-Winters series with $w = .3$ and $v = .5$ is smaller than the Holt-Winters series with $w = .7$ and $v = .5$. Thus, the more accurate series would be the Holt-Winters series with $w = .3$ and $v = .5$.

14.37   a.   To compute the exponentially smoothed values, we follow these steps:

$$E_1 = Y_1 = 60,267$$
$$E_2 = wY_2 + (1-w)E_1 = .8(61,605) + (1-.8)(60,267) = 61,337.4$$
$$E_3 = wY_3 + (1-w)E_2 = .8(62,686) + (1-.8)(61,337.4) = 62,416.3$$

The rest of the values are computed in a similar manner and are listed in the table:

Year	Enroll	Exponentially Smoothed $w = .8$	Holt-Winters Et $w = .8$	Tt $v = .7$
1990	60,267	60,267.0		
1991	61,605	61,337.4	61,605.0	1338.0
1992	62,686	62,416.3	62,737.4	1194.1
1993	63,241	63,076.1	63,379.1	807.4
1994	63,986	63,804.0	64,026.1	695.1
1995	64,764	64,572.0	64,755.4	719.1
1996	65,743	65,508.8	65,689.3	869.4
1997	66,470	66,277.8	66,487.7	819.7
1998	66,983	66,842.0	67,047.9	638.0
1999	67,667	67,502.0	67,670.8	627.4
2000	68,146	68,017.2	68,176.4	542.2
2001	69,936	69,552.2	69,692.5	1223.9
2002	71,215	70,882.4	71,155.3	1391.1
2003	71,442	71,330.1	71,662.9	772.6
2004	71,688	71,616.4	71,837.5	354.0
2005	72,075	71,983.3	72,098.3	288.8
2006	73,318	73,051.1	73,131.8	810.1
2007	73,685	73,558.2	73,736.4	666.2
2008	74,079			
2009	77,288			
2010	78,519			

The forecasts for 2008-2011 using the exponential smoothing series with $w=.8$ are:

$$F_{2008} = F_{t+1} = E_t = 73,558.2$$
$$F_{2009} = F_{t+2} = F_{t+1} = 73,558.2$$
$$F_{2011} = F_{t+3} = F_{t+1} = 73,558.2$$

b. To compute the Holt-Winters values with $w=.8$ and $v=.7$:

$$E_2 = Y_2 = 61,605$$
$$E_3 = wY_3 + (1-w)(E_2 + T_2) = .8(62,686) + (1-.8)(61,605+1,338) = 62,737.4$$

$$T_2 = Y_2 - Y_1 = 61,605 - 60,267 = 1,338$$
$$T_3 = v(E_3 - E_2) + (1-v)T_2 = .7(62,737.4 - 61,605) + (1-.7)(1,338) = 1,194.1$$

The rest of the E_t's and T_t's appear in the table in part a,

The forecasts for 2008-2011 using the Holt-Winters series with $w=.8$ and $v=.7$ are:

$$F_{2008} = F_{t+1} = E_t + T_t = 73,736.4 + 666.2 = 74,402.6$$
$$F_{2009} = F_{t+2} = E_t + 2T_t = 73,736.4 + 2(666.2) = 75,068.8$$
$$F_{2011} = F_{t+3} = E_t + 3T_t = 73,736.4 + 3(666.2) = 75,735.0$$

b. For the exponential smoothing forecasts with $w=.8$:

$$MAD = \frac{\sum_{t=19}^{21} |Y_t - F_t|}{m}$$
$$= \frac{|74,079-73,558.2| + |77,288-73,558.2| + |78,519-73,558.2|}{3} = \frac{9,211.4}{3} = 3,070.467$$

$$MAPE = \left[\frac{\sum_{t=19}^{21} \left|\frac{(Y_t - F_t)}{Y_t}\right|}{m}\right]100$$

$$= \left[\frac{\left|\frac{74,079-73,558.2}{74,079}\right| + \left|\frac{77,288-73,558.2}{77,288}\right| + \left|\frac{78,519-73,558.2}{78,519}\right|}{3}\right]100$$

$$= \left[\frac{.115468}{3}\right]100 = 3.949$$

$$\text{RMSE} = \sqrt{\frac{\sum_{t=19}^{21}(Y_t - F_t)^2}{m}}$$

$$= \sqrt{\frac{(74,079 - 73,558.2)^2 + (77,288 - 73,558.2)^2 + (78,519 - 73,558.2)^2}{3}}$$

$$= \sqrt{\frac{38,792,177.32}{3}} = 3,595.932$$

For the Holt-Winters forecasts with $w = .8$ and $v = .7$:

$$\text{MAD} = \frac{\sum_{t=19}^{21}|Y_t - F_t|}{m}$$

$$= \frac{|74,079 - 74,402.6| + |77,288 - 75,068.8| + |78,519 - 75,735.0|}{3} = \frac{5,326.8}{3} = 1,775.6$$

$$\text{MAPE} = \left[\frac{\sum_{t=19}^{21}\left|\frac{(Y_t - F_t)}{Y_t}\right|}{m}\right]100$$

$$= \left[\frac{\left|\frac{74,079 - 74,402.6}{74,079}\right| + \left|\frac{77,288 - 75,068.8}{77,288}\right| + \left|\frac{78,519 - 75,735.0}{78,519}\right|}{3}\right]100$$

$$= \left[\frac{.068538}{3}\right]100 = 2.285$$

$$\text{RMSE} = \sqrt{\frac{\sum_{t=19}^{21}(Y_t - F_t)^2}{m}}$$

$$= \sqrt{\frac{(74,079 - 74,402.6)^2 + (77,288 - 75,068.8)^2 + (78,519 - 75,735.0)^2}{3}}$$

$$= \sqrt{\frac{12,780,221.6}{3}} = 2,063.995$$

For all three measures of forecast errors, the Holt-Winters forecasts have smaller errors than the exponential smoothing forecasts. Thus, the Holt-Winters forecasts are better.

14.39 a.   Let $x_1 = \begin{cases} 1 \text{ if quarter 1} \\ 0 \text{ otherwise} \end{cases}$ $x_2 = \begin{cases} 1 \text{ if quarter 2} \\ 0 \text{ otherwise} \end{cases}$ $x_3 = \begin{cases} 1 \text{ if quarter 3} \\ 0 \text{ otherwise} \end{cases}$

$t = \text{time} = 1, 2, \dots , 40$

The model is $E(Y_t) = \beta_0 + \beta_1 t + \beta_2 x_1 + \beta_3 x_2 + \beta_4 x_3$

b.   Using MINITAB, the output is:

Regression Analysis: Y versus T, X1, X2, X3

```
The regression equation is
Y = 11.5 + 0.510 T - 3.95 X1 - 2.09 X2 - 4.52 X3

Predictor          Coef      SE Coef          T          P
Constant        11.4933       0.2420      47.49      0.000
T              0.509848     0.007607      67.02      0.000
X1              -3.9505       0.2483     -15.91      0.000
X2              -2.0903       0.2477      -8.44      0.000
X3              -4.5202       0.2473     -18.28      0.000

S = 0.5528      R-Sq = 99.3%      R-Sq(adj) = 99.2%

Analysis of Variance

Source              DF           SS          MS          F          P
Regression           4      1558.79      389.70    1275.44      0.000
Residual Error      35        10.69        0.31
Total               39      1569.48

Source      DF      Seq SS
T            1     1433.96
X1           1       22.56
X2           1        0.21
X3           1      102.06
```

The fitted model is $\hat{Y}_t = 11.4933 + .5098t - 3.9505x_1 - 2.0903x_2 - 4.5202x_3$.

To determine if the model is adequate, we test:

$$H_0 : \beta_1 = \beta_2 = \beta_3 = \beta_4 = 0$$
$$H_a : \text{At least one} \beta_i \neq 0$$

The test statistic is $F = 1,275.44$.

The rejection region requires $\alpha = .05$ in the upper tail of the F-distribution with $v_1 = k = 4$ and $v_2 = n - (k+1) = 40 - (4+1) = 35$. From Table VI, Appendix D, $F_{.05} \approx 2.69$. The rejection region is $F > 2.69$.

Since the observed value of the test statistic falls in the rejection region $(F = 1,275.44 > 2.69)$, H_0 is rejected. There is sufficient evidence to indicate the model is useful at $\alpha = .05$.

c.   From MINITAB, the predicted values and prediction intervals are:

Predicted Values for New Observations

```
New Obs      Fit      SE Fit        95.0% CI            95.0% PI
1        28.4467     0.2420   ( 27.9554, 28.9379)  ( 27.2217, 29.6716)

Values of Predictors for New Observations

New Obs        T        X1        X2        X3
1           41.0      1.00  0.000000  0.000000
```

Predicted Values for New Observations

```
New Obs      Fit      SE Fit        95.0% CI              95.0% PI
2        30.8167     0.2420    (30.3254, 31.3079)  (29.5917, 32.0416)
```

Values of Predictors for New Observations

```
New Obs          T        X1        X2        X3
2             42.0   0.000000      1.00   0.000000
```

Predicted Values for New Observations

```
New Obs      Fit      SE Fit        95.0% CI              95.0% PI
3        28.8967     0.2420    (28.4054, 29.3879)  (27.6717, 30.1216)
```

Values of Predictors for New Observations

```
New Obs          T        X1        X2        X3
3             43.0   0.000000  0.000000      1.00
```

Predicted Values for New Observations

```
New Obs      Fit      SE Fit        95.0% CI              95.0% PI
4        33.9267     0.2420    ( 33.4354, 34.4179)  ( 32.7017, 35.1516)
```

Values of Predictors for New Observations

```
New Obs          T        X1        X2        X3
4             44.0   0.000000  0.000000  0.000000
```

From the above output, the predicted values and 95% prediction intervals are:

For year = 11, quarter = 1, $\hat{Y}_{41} = 28.4467$ and the 95% PI is (27.22, 29.67)

For year = 11, quarter = 2, $\hat{Y}_{42} = 30.8167$ and the 95% PI is (29.59, 32.04)

For year = 11, quarter = 3, $\hat{Y}_{43} = 28.8967$ and the 95% PI is (27.67, 30.12)

For year = 11, quarter = 4, $\hat{Y}_{44} = 33.9267$ and the 95% PI is (32.70, 35.15)

14.41   a.   Using MINITAB, the results are:

Regression Analysis: Interest versus t

```
The regression equation is
Interest = 10.5 - 0.245 t
```

```
Predictor      Coef  SE Coef      T      P
Constant    10.4993   0.3482  30.15  0.000
t          -0.24465  0.02594  -9.43  0.000
```

```
S = 0.879816   R-Sq = 80.2%   R-Sq(adj) = 79.3%
```

```
Analysis of Variance
Source            DF       SS       MS       F       P
Regression         1   68.833   68.8335   88.92   0.000
Residual Error    22   17.030    0.774
Total             23   85.863
```

Predicted Values for New Observations

```
New
Obs    Fit   SE Fit      95% CI             95% PI
  1  4.138   0.417   (3.274, 5.003)   (2.119, 6.157)
```

```
Values of Predictors for New Observations
```

```
New
Obs     t
  1   26.0
```

The fitted model is: $\hat{Y}_t = 10.4993 - .2447t$

b. For 2013, $t = 26$. The forecast for the average interest rate in 2013 is
$\hat{Y}_{26} = 10.4993 - .24465(26) = 4.138$.

From the printout, the 95% prediction interval is $(2.119, 6.157)$.

14.43 a. The regression model would be: $E(Y_t) = \beta_0 + \beta_1 t$

b. First, create dummy variables:

$$m_1 = \begin{cases} 1 \text{ if January} \\ 0 \text{ if not} \end{cases}, \quad m_2 = \begin{cases} 1 \text{ if February} \\ 0 \text{ if not} \end{cases}, \ldots, \quad m_{11} = \begin{cases} 1 \text{ if November} \\ 0 \text{ if not} \end{cases}$$

The new model is: $E(Y_t) = \beta_0 + \beta_1 x_t + \beta_2 m_1 + \beta_3 m_2 + \cdots + \beta_{12} m_{11}$

c. To determine if mean gasoline consumption varies from month to month, we test:

$$H_0 : \beta_2 = \beta_3 = \cdots = \beta_{12} = 0$$

d. Let $t = 0$ for time January, 1998. Then for January, 2013, $t = 180$. The forecast would be
$\hat{Y}_{180} = \hat{\beta}_0 + \hat{\beta}_1 x_{180} + \hat{\beta}_2$

14.45 a. Using $t = 0$ for 1980, the results using MINITAB are:

Regression Analysis: Policies versus t

```
The regression equation is
Policies = 398 - 1.67 t
```

```
Predictor      Coef   SE Coef       T       P
Constant    397.665     5.800   68.56   0.000
t           -1.6734     0.3435   -4.87   0.000
```

```
S = 16.2826    R-Sq = 45.9%    R-Sq(adj) = 43.9%
```

```
Analysis of Variance

Source            DF      SS      MS      F       P
Regression         1   6293.7  6293.7  23.74   0.000
Residual Error    28   7423.5   265.1
Total             29  13717.2
```

Predicted Values for New Observations

```
New
Obs    Fit   SE Fit       95% CI              95% PI
  1  347.46   6.10  (334.97, 359.95)  (311.85, 383.08)
```

```
Values of Predictors for New Observations
```

```
New
Obs    t
  1  30.0
```

Predicted Values for New Observations

```
New
Obs    Fit   SE Fit       95% CI              95% PI
  2  345.79   6.40  (332.68, 358.90)  (309.95, 381.63)
```

```
Values of Predictors for New Observations
```

```
New
Obs    t
  2  31.0
```

The fitted model is: $\hat{Y}_t = 397.665 - 1.6734t$

b.   From the printout, the forecasted values for 2010 and 2011 ($t = 30$ and $t = 31$) are:

$$2010: 347.46$$
$$2011: 345.79$$

c.   From the printout, the 95% prediction intervals for 2010 and 2011 are:

$$2010: (311.85, 383.08)$$
$$2011: (309.95, 381.63)$$

14.47   Autocorrelation is the correlation between time series residuals at different points in time. In the presence of autocorrelated residuals, the regression analysis tends to produce inflated t-statistics. Consequently, an analyst has a greater than α probability of committing a Type I error when testing a model parameter.

14.49   a.   For $\alpha = .05$, the rejection region is $d < d_{L,\alpha} = d_{L,.05} = 1.10$. The value of $d_{L,.05}$ is found in Table X, Appendix B, with $k = 2$, $n = 20$, and $\alpha = .05$. Also, $d_{U,.05} = 1.54$.

Since the test statistic falls between $d_{L,.05}$ and $d_{U,.05}$ $(1.10 \leq 1.10 \leq 1.54)$, no decision can be made.

b.   For $\alpha = .01$, the rejection region is $d < d_{L,\alpha} = d_{L,.01} = .86$. The value of $d_{L,.01}$ is found in Table XI, Appendix B, with $k = 2$, $n = 20$, and $\alpha = .01$. Also, $d_{U,.01} = 1.27$.

Since the test statistic falls between $d_{L,.01}$ and $d_{U,.01}$ $(.86 \leq 1.10 \leq 1.27)$, no decision can be made.

c.   For $\alpha = .05$, the rejection region is $d < d_{L,\alpha} = d_{L,.05} = 1.44$. The value of $d_{L,.05}$ is found in Table X, Appendix B, with $k = 5$, $n = 65$, and $\alpha = .05$.

Since the test statistic falls in the rejection region $(d = .95 < 1.44)$, H_0 is rejected. There is sufficient evidence to indicate positive first-order autocorrelation at $\alpha = .05$.

d.   For $\alpha = .01$, the rejection region is $d < d_{L,\alpha} = d_{L,.01} = 1.15$. The value of $d_{L,.01}$ is found in Table XI, Appendix B, with $k = 1$, $n = 31$, and $\alpha = .01$. Also, $d_{U,.01} = 1.27$.

Since the test statistic does not fall in the rejection region $(d = 1.35 \not< 1.15)$, and the test statistic is above $d_{U,.01}$ $(d = 1.35 > 1.27)$ H_0 is not rejected.

14.51   To determine if positive autocorrelation is present, we test:

H_0: No first-order autocorrelation
H_a: Positive first-order autocorrelation of residuals

The test statistics is $d = 1.77$.

For $\alpha = .05$, the rejection region is $d < d_{L,\alpha} = d_{L,.05} = .93$. The value $d_{L,.05}$ is found in Table X, Appendix D, with $k = 5$, $n = 24$, and $\alpha = .05$.

Since the observed value of the test statistic does not fall in the rejection region $(d = 1.77 \not< .93)$, H_0 is not rejected. There is insufficient evidence to indicate the time series residuals are positively autocorrelated at $\alpha = .05$.

14.53   a.   Using MINITAB, the plot of the residuals against t is:

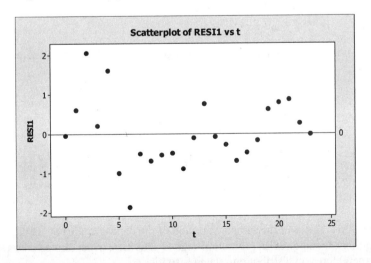

Since there appear to be groups of consecutive positive and groups of consecutive negative residuals, the data appear to be autocorrelated.

b.   Using MINITAB, the output is:

Regression Analysis: Interest versus t

```
The regression equation is
Interest = 10.5 - 0.245 t


Predictor       Coef  SE Coef       T       P
Constant     10.4993   0.3482   30.15   0.000
t           -0.24465  0.02594   -9.43   0.000


S = 0.879816   R-Sq = 80.2%   R-Sq(adj) = 79.3%


Analysis of Variance

Source           DF       SS       MS       F       P
Regression        1   68.833  68.8335   88.92   0.000
Residual Error   22   17.030    0.774
Total            23   85.863


Durbin-Watson statistic = 1.24253
```

To determine if positive autocorrelation is present, we test:

H_0: No first-order autocorrelation
H_a: Positive first-order autocorrelation of residuals

The test statistics is $d = 1.24253$.

For $\alpha = .05$, the rejection region is $d < d_{L,\alpha} = d_{L,.05} = 1.26$. The value $d_{L,.05}$ is found in Table X, Appendix D, with $k = 1$, $n = 23$, and $\alpha = .05$.

Since the observed value of the test statistic falls in the rejection region ($d = 1.24253 < 1.26$), H_0 is rejected. There is sufficient evidence to indicate the time series residuals are positively autocorrelated at $\alpha = .05$.

c.   Since the error terms are not independent, the validity of the test for the model adequacy appears to be questionable.

14.55   a.   For Bank 1, $R^2 = .914$. 91.4% of the sample variation of the deposit shares of Bank 1 is explained by the model containing expenditures on promotion-related activities, expenditures on service-related activities, and expenditures on distribution-related activities.

For Bank 2, $R^2 = .721$. 72.1% of the sample variation of the deposit shares of Bank 2 is explained by the model containing expenditures on promotion-related activities, expenditures on service-related activities, and expenditures on distribution-related activities.

For Bank 3, $R^2 = .926$. 92.6% of the sample variation of the deposit shares of Bank 3 is explained by the model containing expenditures on promotion-related activities, expenditures on service-related activities, and expenditures on distribution-related activities.

For Bank 4, $R^2 = .827$. 82.7% of the sample variation of the deposit shares of Bank 4 is explained by the model containing expenditures on promotion-related activities, expenditures on service-related activities, and expenditures on distribution-related activities.

For Bank 5, $R^2 = .270$. 27.0% of the sample variation of the deposit shares of Bank 5 is explained by the model containing expenditures on promotion-related activities, expenditures on service-related activities, and expenditures on distribution-related activities.

For Bank 6, $R^2 = .616$. 61.6% of the sample variation of the deposit shares of Bank 6 is explained by the model containing expenditures on promotion-related activities, expenditures on service-related activities, and expenditures on distribution-related activities.

For Bank 7, $R^2 = .962$. 96.2% of the sample variation of the deposit shares of Bank 7 is explained by the model containing expenditures on promotion-related activities, expenditures on service-related activities, and expenditures on distribution-related activities.

For Bank 8, $R^2 = .495$. 49.5% of the sample variation of the deposit shares of Bank 8 is explained by the model containing expenditures on promotion-related activities, expenditures on service-related activities, and expenditures on distribution-related activities.

For Bank 9, $R^2 = .500$. 50.0% of the sample variation of the deposit shares of Bank 9 is explained by the model containing expenditures on promotion-related activities, expenditures on service-related activities, and expenditures on distribution-related activities.

b. For all banks, to determine if the model is adequate, we test:

$$H_0 : \beta_1 = \beta_2 = \beta_3 = 0$$
$$H_a : \text{At least one } \beta_i \neq 0$$

For Bank 1, the p-value is $p = 0.000$. Since the p-value is less than $\alpha = .01$, H_0 is rejected. There is sufficient evidence to indicate the model is adequate at $\alpha = .01$.

For Bank 2, the p-value is $p = 0.004$. Since the p-value is less than $\alpha = .01$, H_0 is rejected. There is sufficient evidence to indicate the model is adequate at $\alpha = .01$.

For Bank 3, the p-value is $p = 0.000$. Since the p-value is less than $\alpha = .01$, H_0 is rejected. There is sufficient evidence to indicate the model is adequate at $\alpha = .01$.

For Bank 4, the p-value is $p = 0.000$. Since the p-value is less than $\alpha = .01$, H_0 is rejected. There is sufficient evidence to indicate the model is adequate at $\alpha = .01$.

For Bank 5, the p-value is $p = 0.155$. Since the p-value is not less than $\alpha = .01$, H_0 is not rejected. There is insufficient evidence to indicate the model is adequate at $\alpha = .01$.

For Bank 6, the p-value is $p = 0.012$. Since the p-value is not less than $\alpha = .01$, H_0 is not rejected. There is insufficient evidence to indicate the model is adequate at $\alpha = .01$.

For Bank 7, the p-value is $p = 0.000$. Since the p-value is less than $\alpha = .01$, H_0 is rejected. There is sufficient evidence to indicate the model is adequate at $\alpha = .01$.

For Bank 8, the p-value is $p = 0.014$. Since the p-value is not less than $\alpha = .01$, H_0 is not rejected.

There is insufficient evidence to indicate the model is adequate at $\alpha = .01$.

For Bank 9, the p-value is $p = 0.011$. Since the p-value is not less than $\alpha = .01$, H_0 is not rejected. There is insufficient evidence to indicate the model is adequate at $\alpha = .01$.

c.   To determine if positive autocorrelation is present, we test:

H_0: No positive first-order autocorrelation
H_a: Positive first-order autocorrelation of residuals

The test statistics is d.

For $\alpha = .01$, the rejection region is $d < d_{L,\alpha} = d_{L,.01} = .77$. The value $d_{L,.01}$ is found in Table XI, Appendix B, with $k = 3$, $n = 20$, and $\alpha = .01$. Also, $d_{U,.01} = 1.41$.

For Bank 1, $d = 1.3$. Since the observed value of the test statistic does not fall in the rejection region $(d = 1.3 \not< .77)$ and is not greater than $d_{U,.01}$ $(d = 1.3 \not> 1.41)$, no decision can be made at $\alpha = .01$.

For Bank 2, $d = 3.4$. Since the observed value of the test statistic does not fall in the rejection region $(d = 3.4 \not< .77)$ and is greater than $d_{U,.01}$ $(d = 3.4 > 1.41)$, H_0 is not rejected. There is insufficient evidence to indicate the time series residuals are positively autocorrelated at $\alpha = .01$.

For Bank 3, $d = 2.7$. Since the observed value of the test statistic does not fall in the rejection region $(d = 2.7 \not< .77)$ and is greater than $d_{U,.01}$ $(d = 2.7 > 1.41)$, H_0 is not rejected. There is insufficient evidence to indicate the time series residuals are positively autocorrelated at $\alpha = .01$.

For Bank 4, $d = 1.9$. Since the observed value of the test statistic does not fall in the rejection region $(d = 1.9 \not< .77)$ and is greater than $d_{U,.01}$ $(d = 1.9 > 1.41)$, H_0 is not rejected. There is insufficient evidence to indicate the time series residuals are positively autocorrelated at $\alpha = .01$.

For Bank 5, $d = .85$. Since the observed value of the test statistic does not fall in the rejection region $(d = .85 \not< .77)$ and is not greater than $d_{U,.01}$ $(d = .85 \not> 1.41)$, no decision can be made at $\alpha = .01$.

For Bank 6, $d = 1.8$. Since the observed value of the test statistic does not fall in the rejection region $(d = 1.8 \not< .77)$ and is greater than $d_{U,.01}$ $(d = 1.8 > 1.41)$, H_0 is not rejected. There is insufficient evidence to indicate the time series residuals are positively autocorrelated at $\alpha = .01$.

For Bank 7, $d = 2.5$. Since the observed value of the test statistic does not fall in the rejection region $(d = 2.5 \not< .77)$ and is greater than $d_{U,.01}$ $(d = 2.5 > 1.41)$, H_0 is not rejected. There is insufficient evidence to indicate the time series residuals are positively autocorrelated at $\alpha = .01$.

For Bank 8, $d = 2.3$. Since the observed value of the test statistic does not fall in the rejection region $(d = 2.3 \not< .77)$ and is greater than $d_{U,.01}$ $(d = 2.3 > 1.41)$, H_0 is not rejected. There is insufficient evidence to indicate the time series residuals are positively autocorrelated at $\alpha = .01$.

For Bank 9, $d = 1.1$. Since the observed value of the test statistic does not fall in the rejection region $(d = 1.1 \not< .77)$ and is not greater than $d_{U,.01}$ $(d = 1.1 \not> 1.41)$, no decision can be made at $\alpha = .01$.

14.57   a.   The simple composite index is found by summing the three worker quantities, dividing by 325.3, the sum for the base period, 2000, and multiplying by 100. The values appear in the table.

Year	Fully Permanent	Fully Not Permanent	Event Disability	Total Quantity	Index
2000	140.9	44.9	139.5	325.3	100.0
2001	142.9	45.2	141.7	329.8	101.4
2002	144.9	45.3	143.5	333.7	102.6
2003	147.0	45.0	144.9	336.9	103.6
2004	149.0	44.8	146.2	340.0	104.5
2005	151.1	44.7	147.7	343.5	105.6
2006	153.3	45.1	150.1	348.5	107.1
2007	155.4	45.6	152.3	353.3	108.6
2008	157.4	46.0	154.5	357.9	110.0
2009	159.2	44.8	150.6	354.6	109.0
2010	161.1	44.6	151.7	357.4	109.9
2011	163.1	44.3	152.6	360.0	110.7

   b.   This is a quantity index because it is based on the numbers of workers rather than prices.

   c.   The index value for 2011 is 110.7. This means that the total number of insured workers in 2011 is $110.7 - 100 = 10.7\%$ higher than in 2000.

14.59   a.   Using MINITAB, the output is:

Regression Analysis: Daily Visits versus t

```
The regression equation is
Daily Visits = 38.2 + 7.32 t

Predictor        Coef      SE Coef          T        P
Constant       38.171        4.420       8.64    0.000
t              7.3192       0.7123      10.27    0.000

S = 6.470      R-Sq = 93.0%      R-Sq(adj) = 92.1%

Analysis of Variance

Source            DF          SS          MS        F        P
Regression         1      4419.5      4419.5   105.57    0.000
Residual Error     8       334.9        41.9
Total              9      4754.4
```

Predicted Values for New Observations

```
New Obs      Fit     SE Fit        95.0% CI              95.0% PI
1         118.68       4.42   ( 108.49,  128.87)   ( 100.61,  136.75)

Values of Predictors for New Observations

New Obs         t
1            11.0
```

```
Predicted Values for New Observations
New Obs      Fit      SE Fit         95.0% CI            95.0% PI
2          126.00     5.06     ( 114.33,  137.67)  ( 107.06,  144.94)

Values of Predictors for New Observations

New Obs         t
2             12.0
```

Predicted Values for New Observations

```
New Obs      Fit      SE Fit         95.0% CI            95.0% PI
3          133.32     5.72     ( 120.13,  146.51)  ( 113.40,  153.24)

Values of Predictors for New Observations

New Obs         t
3             13.0
```

The fitted regression line is: $\hat{Y}_t = 38.171 + 7.319t$

The forecasts for the next 3 years are:

$$\hat{Y}_{11} = 38.171 + 7.319(11) = 118.68$$

$$\hat{Y}_{12} = 38.171 + 7.319(12) = 126.00$$

$$\hat{Y}_{13} = 38.171 + 7.319(13) = 133.32$$

b. From the printout, the 95% prediction intervals for the 3 years are:

    Year 11:   (100.61, 136.75)
    Year 12:   (107.06, 144.94)
    Year 13:   (113.40, 153.24)

c. There are basically two problems with using simple linear regression for predicting time series data. First, we must predict values of the time series for values of time outside the observed range. We observe data for time periods 1, 2, …, t and use the regression model to predict values of the time series for $t + 1$, $t + 2$, … . The second problem is that simple linear regression does not allow for any cyclical effects such as seasonal trends.

d. We could use an exponentially smoothed series to forecast patient visits or we could use a Holt-Winters series to forecast patient visits.

14.61 a. To compute the Holt-Winters series, we use:

$E_2 = Y_2 = 10.86$
$E_3 = wY_3 + (1-w)(E_2 + T_2)$
$\quad = .3(12.07) + (1-.3)(10.86 + .40)$
$\quad = 11.50$

$T_2 = Y_2 - Y_1 = 10.86 - 10.46 = .40$
$T_3 = v(E_3 - E_2) + (1-v)T_2$
$\quad = .7(11.50 - 10.86) + (1-.7)(.40)$
$\quad = .57$

The rest of the values appear in the table:

| | | Holt-Winters | |
| | | E_t | T_t |
Year	Interest	$w = .3$	$v = .7$
1987	10.46		
1988	10.86	10.86	0.40
1989	12.07	11.50	0.57
1990	9.97	11.44	0.13
1991	11.14	11.44	0.04
1992	8.27	10.52	-0.64
1993	7.17	9.07	-1.21
1994	8.28	7.99	-1.12
1995	7.86	7.17	-0.91
1996	7.76	6.71	-0.59
1997	7.57	6.55	-0.29
1998	6.92	6.46	-0.15
1999	7.46	6.65	0.09
2000	8.08	7.15	0.37
2001	7.01	7.37	0.26
2002	6.56	7.31	0.04
2003	5.89	6.91	-0.27
2004	5.86	6.41	-0.43
2005	5.93	5.96	-0.44
2006	6.47	5.81	-0.24
2007	6.40	5.82	-0.07
2008	6.23	5.89	0.03
2009	5.38	5.76	-0.08
2010	4.86	5.44	-0.25

The forecasts for 2011-2013 using the Holt-Winters series with $w = .3$ and $v = .7$ are:

$$F_{2011} = F_{t+1} = E_t + T_t = 5.44 + (-.25) = 5.19$$
$$F_{2012} = F_{t+2} = E_t + 2T_t = 5.44 + 2(-.25) = 4.94$$
$$F_{2013} = F_{t+3} = E_t + 3T_t = 5.44 + 3(-.25) = 4.69$$

From Exercise 14.41, the forecasts for 2011-2013 are:

2011: $\hat{Y}_{24} = 10.4993 - .2447(24) = 4.63$

2012: $\hat{Y}_{25} = 10.4993 - .2447(25) = 4.38$

2013: $\hat{Y}_{25} = 10.4993 - .2447(26) = 4.14$

The forecasts from the Holt-Winters series are larger than those of the regression forecasts.

14.63   a.   Using MINITAB, the printout from fitting the model $E(Y_t) = \beta_0 + \beta_1 t$ starting with $t = 0$ is:

Regression Analysis: Price versus t

```
The regression equation is
Price = 42.6 + 0.449 t


Predictor      Coef   SE Coef       T       P
Constant     42.561    4.183   10.18   0.000
t            0.4489    0.3410    1.32   0.203


S = 10.1460    R-Sq = 8.0%   R-Sq(adj) = 3.4%


Analysis of Variance

Source            DF       SS      MS      F       P
Regression         1    178.4   178.4   1.73   0.203
Residual Error    20   2058.8   102.9
Total             21   2237.3

Durbin-Watson statistic = 1.75313
```

Predicted Values for New Observations

```
New
Obs    Fit   SE Fit      95% CI              95% PI
  1  52.44     4.48  (43.10, 61.78)   (29.30, 75.57)
```

Values of Predictors for New Observations

```
New
Obs     t
  1  22.0
```

Predicted Values for New Observations

```
New
Obs    Fit  SE Fit      95% CI              95% PI
  2  52.89    4.78  (42.92, 62.86)   (29.49, 76.28)
```

Values of Predictors for New Observations

```
New
Obs     t
  2  23.0
```

The fitted model is $\hat{Y}_t = 42.561 + .4489t$.

b.   The plot of the data is:

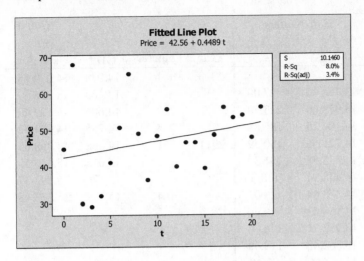

c.   From the printout in part a, $F_{2012} = 52.44$ and $F_{2013} = 52.89$.

d.   Also from the printout in part a, the 95% prediction intervals are:

2012: (29.30, 75.57)   We are 95% confident that the actual closing price for 2012 will be between 29.30 and 75.57.

2013: (29.49, 76.28)   We are 95% confident that the actual closing price for 2013 will be between 29.49 and 76.28.

e.   To determine if autocorrelation is present, we test:

H_0: Autocorrelation is not present
H_a: Autocorrelation is present

The test statistic is $d = 1.75313$.

Since α is not given, we will use $\alpha = .10$. The rejection region is $d < d_{L,\alpha/2} = d_{L,.05} = 1.24$ or $4 - d < d_{L,.05} = 1.24$, where $d_{L,.05}$ is from Table X, Appendix D, for $k = 1$, $n = 22$, and $\alpha = .10$.

Since the observed value of the test statistic does not fall in the rejection region $(d = 1.75313 \not< 1.24)$, H_0 is not rejected. There is insufficient evidence to indicate that autocorrelation is present at $\alpha = .10$.

14.65   To compute the Holt-Winters values for the years 2007-2011:

With $w = .5$ and $v = .5$,

$$E_2 = Y_2 = 13{,}738$$
$$E_3 = wY_3 + (1-w)(E_2 + T_2) = .5(13{,}951) + (1-.5)(13{,}738 + 227) = 13{,}958.00$$

$$T_2 = Y_2 - Y_1 = 13{,}738 - 13{,}511 = 227$$
$$T_3 = v(E_3 - E_2) + (1-v)T_2 = .5(13{,}958.00 - 13{,}738) + (1-.5)(227) = 223.50$$

The rest of the values appear in the table:

Year	Quarter	GDP	Holt-Winters Et w = .5	Tt v = .5	Year	Quarter	GDP	Holt-Winters Et w = .5	Tt v = .5
2007	1	13,511			2010	1	14,278	14,079.75	65.63
	2	13,738	13,738.00	227.00		2	14,468	14,306.69	146.29
	3	13,951	13,958.00	223.50		3	14,606	14,529.49	184.54
	4	14,031	14,106.25	185.88		4	14,755	14,734.52	194.78
2008	1	14,151	14,221.56	150.59	2011	1	14,868	14,898.65	179.46
	2	14,295	14,333.58	131.30		2	15,013	15,045.55	163.18
	3	14,413	14,438.94	118.33		3	15,176	15,192.37	155.00
	4	14,200	14,378.64	29.02		4	15,319	15,333.18	147.91
2009	1	13,894	14,150.83	-99.40
	2	13,854	13,952.71	-148.76
	3	13,921	13,862.48	-119.49
	4	14,087	13,914.99	-33.49

The forecasts for the four quarters of 2012 are:

$$F_{2012,1} = F_{t+1} = E_t + T_t = 15,333.18 + 147.91 = 15,481.09$$

$$F_{2012,2} = F_{t+2} = E_t + 2T_t = 15,333.18 + 2(147.91) = 15,629.00$$

$$F_{2012,3} = F_{t+3} = E_t + 3T_t = 15,333.18 + 3(147.91) = 15,776.91$$

$$F_{2012,4} = F_{t+4} = E_t + 4T_t = 15,333.18 + 4(147.91) = 15,924.82$$

14.67 Once you find the 2012 GDP values, you would use the following formulas to compute the criteria to evaluate the forecasts.

Holt forecasts:

$$MAD = \frac{\sum_{t=n+1}^{n+m}|Y_t - F_t|}{m} = \frac{|Y_1 - 15,481.09| + |Y_2 - 15,629.00| + |Y_3 - 15,776.91| + |Y_4 - 15,924.82|}{4}$$

$$MAPE = \left[\frac{\sum_{t=20}^{23}\left|\frac{(Y_t - F_t)}{Y_t}\right|}{m}\right]100 = \left[\frac{\left|\frac{Y_{20}-15,481.09}{Y_{20}}\right| + \left|\frac{Y_{21}-15,629.00}{Y_{21}}\right| + \left|\frac{Y_{22}-15,776.91}{Y_{22}}\right| + \left|\frac{Y_{23}-15,924.82}{Y_{23}}\right|}{4}\right]100$$

$$RMSE = \sqrt{\frac{\sum_{i=20}^{23}(Y_t - F_t)^2}{m}} = \sqrt{\frac{(Y_{20}-15,481.09)^2 + (Y_{21}-15,629.00)^2 + (Y_{22}-15,776.91)^2 + (Y_{23}-15,924.82)^2}{4}}$$

Simple linear regression forecasts:

$$MAD = \frac{\sum_{t=n+1}^{n+m}|Y_t - F_t|}{m} = \frac{|Y_1 - 15,088.1| + |Y_2 - 15,160.6| + |Y_3 - 15,233.2| + |Y_4 - 15,305.7|}{4}$$

$$\text{MAPE} = \left[\frac{\sum\limits_{t=20}^{23}\frac{|(Y_t - F_t)|}{Y_t}}{m}\right]100 = \left[\frac{\left|\frac{Y_{20}-15,088.1}{Y_{20}}\right| + \left|\frac{Y_{21}-15,160.6}{Y_{21}}\right| + \left|\frac{Y_{22}-15,233.2}{Y_{22}}\right| + \left|\frac{Y_{23}-15,305.7}{Y_{23}}\right|}{4}\right]100$$

$$\text{RMSE} = \sqrt{\frac{\sum\limits_{i=20}^{23}(Y_t - F_t)^2}{m}} = \sqrt{\frac{(Y_{20}-15,088.1)^2 + (Y_{21}-15,160.6)^2 + (Y_{22}-15,233.2)^2 + (Y_{23}-15,305.7)^2}{4}}$$

Seasonal linear regression forecasts:

$$\text{MAD} = \frac{\sum\limits_{t=n+1}^{n+m}|Y_t - F_t|}{m} = \frac{|Y_1 - 14,990.8| + |Y_2 - 15,124.0| + |Y_3 - 15,263.8| + |Y_4 - 15,328.8|}{4}$$

$$\text{MAPE} = \left[\frac{\sum\limits_{t=20}^{23}\frac{|(Y_t - F_t)|}{Y_t}}{m}\right]100 = \left[\frac{\left|\frac{Y_{20}-14,990.8}{Y_{20}}\right| + \left|\frac{Y_{21}-15,124.0}{Y_{21}}\right| + \left|\frac{Y_{22}-15,263.8}{Y_{22}}\right| + \left|\frac{Y_{23}-15,328.8}{Y_{23}}\right|}{4}\right]100$$

$$\text{RMSE} = \sqrt{\frac{\sum\limits_{i=20}^{23}(Y_t - F_t)^2}{m}} = \sqrt{\frac{(Y_{20}-14,990.8)^2 + (Y_{21}-15,124.0)^2 + (Y_{22}-15,263.8)^2 + (Y_{23}-15,328.8)^2}{4}}$$

To determine which forecasting model performs best, one would select the model with the smallest value for the particular criterion.

14.69   a.   Real income $1990 = \dfrac{\$50,000}{125.8} \times 100 = \$39,745.63$

Real income $2010 = \dfrac{\$95,000}{218.1} \times 100 = \$43,558.00$

The real income for 2010 was greater than that for 1990. Since the real income in 2010 is greater than that in 1990, you would be able to buy more in 2010 than in 1990.

   b.   Let x = monetary income in 2010. Then $\dfrac{x}{218.1} = \dfrac{\$20,000}{125.8}$. Solving for x, we get $x = \$34,674.09$.

14.71   a.   To determine if the overall model contributes information for the prediction of future spot exchange rates for the British pound, we test:

$$H_0: \beta_1 = 0$$
$$H_a: \beta_1 \neq 0$$

The test statistic is $F = \dfrac{R^2 / k}{(1 - R^2) / [n - (k+1)]} = \dfrac{.957 / 1}{(1 - .957) / [81 - (1+1)]} = 1758.21$

The rejection region requires $\alpha = .05$ in the upper tail of the F-distribution with $v_1 = k = 1$ and $v_2 = n - (k + 1) = 81 - (1 + 1) = 79$. From Table VI, Appendix B, $F_{.05} \approx 3.96$. The rejection region is $F > 3.96$.

Since the observed value of the test statistic falls in the rejection region $(F = 1758.21 > 3.96)$, H_0 is rejected. There is sufficient evidence to indicate the overall model contributes information for the prediction of future spot exchange rates for the British pound at $\alpha = .05$.

b.   The value of s is .025. Almost all of the observations will fall within $\pm 2s$ or $\pm 2(.025)$ or $\pm.05$ of their least squares predicted values.

  $R^2 = .957$. 95.7% of the sample variation in the future spot exchange rates for the British pound values are explained by the model containing the forward exchange rate.

c.   To determine if positive autocorrelation is present, we test:

  H_0: No first-order autocorrelation
  H_a: Positive first-order autocorrelation of residuals

  The test statistics is $d = 0.962$.

  For $\alpha = .05$, the rejection region is $d < d_{L,\alpha} = d_{L,.05} = 1.61$. The value $d_{L,.05}$ is found in Table X, Appendix B, with $k = 1$, $n = 81$, and $\alpha = .05$.

  Since the observed value of the test statistic falls in the rejection region $(d = 0.962 < 1.61)$, H_0 is rejected. There is sufficient evidence to indicate the time series residuals are positively autocorrelated at $\alpha = .05$.

d.   No. Since the error terms do not appear to be independent, the validity of the test for model adequacy is in question.

Chapter 15
Nonparametric Statistics

15.1   The sign test is preferred to the *t*-test when the population from which the sample is selected is not normal.

15.3   a. $P(x \geq 7) = 1 - P(x \leq 6) = 1 - .965 = .035$

b. $P(x \geq 5) = 1 - P(x \leq 4) = 1 - .637 = .363$

c. $P(x \geq 8) = 1 - P(x \leq 7) = 1 - .996 = .004$

d. $P(x \geq 10) = 1 - P(x \leq 9) = 1 - .849 = .151$

$\mu = np = 15(.5) = 7.5$ and $\sigma = \sqrt{npq} = \sqrt{15(.5)(.5)} = 1.9365$

$P(x \geq 10) \approx P\left(z \geq \dfrac{(10 - .5) - 7.5}{1.9365}\right) = P(z \geq 1.03) = .5 - .3485 = .1515$ (Using Table II, Appendix D)

e. $P(x \geq 15) = 1 - P(x \leq 14) = 1 - .788 = .212$

$\mu = np = 25(.5) = 12.5$ and $\sigma = \sqrt{npq} = \sqrt{25(.5)(.5)} = 2.5$

$P(x \geq 15) \approx P\left(z \geq \dfrac{(15 - .5) - 12.5}{2.5}\right) = P(z \geq .80) = .5 - .2881 = .2119$ (Using Table II, Appendix D)

15.5   To determine if the median is greater than 75, we test:

$H_0 : \eta = 75$
$H_a : \eta > 75$

The test statistic is S = number of measurements greater than 75 = 17.

The *p*-value $= P(x \geq 17)$ where x is a binomial random variable with $n = 25$ and $p = .5$. From Table I,

$p\text{-value} = P(x \geq 17) = 1 - P(x \leq 16) = 1 - .946 = .054$

Since the *p*-value is less than α $(p = .054 < .10)$, H_0 is rejected. There is sufficient evidence to indicate the median is greater than 75 at $\alpha = .10$.

We must assume the sample was randomly selected from a continuous probability distribution.

Note: Since $n \geq 10$, we could use the large-sample approximation.

15.7   a.   To determine if the median income of graduates of the MBA program is more than $125,000, we test:

$$H_0 : \eta = 125,000$$
$$H_a : \eta > 125,000$$

b.   The test statistic is $S = \{$Number of observations greater than $125,000\} = 9$.

The p-value $= P(x \geq 9)$ where x is a binomial random variable with $n = 15$ and $p = .5$. From Table I,

$$p - \text{value} = P(x \geq 9) = 1 - P(x \leq 8) = 1 - .696 = .304$$

Since the p-value is not less than α $(p = .304 \not< .05)$, H_0 is not rejected. There is insufficient evidence to indicate the median income of graduates of the MBA program is more than $125,000 at $\alpha = .05$.

c.   We must assume only that the sample is selected randomly from a continuous probability distribution.

15.9   To determine if half of all stocks with suspended short-sales have a positive return rate, we test:

$$H_0 : \eta = 0$$
$$H_a : \eta \neq 0$$

$S_1 = \{$Number of measurements $< 0\} = 11$.
$S_2 = \{$Number of measurements $> 0\} = 6$.

The test statistic is $S = $ Larger of S_1 and $S_2 = 11$.

The p-value $= 2P(x \geq 11)$ where x is a binomial random variable with $n = 17$ and $p = .5$. Using MINITAB,

$$p - \text{value} = 2P(x \geq 11) = 2(1 - P(x \leq 10)) = 2(1 - .834) = .332$$

Since the p-value is not less than α $(p = .332 \not< .05)$, H_0 is not rejected. There is insufficient evidence to indicate half of all stocks with suspended short-sales have a positive return rate at $\alpha = .05$.

15.11   To determine if the median radon exposure is less than 6,000, we test:

$$H_0 : \eta = 6,000$$
$$H_a : \eta < 6,000$$

The test statistic is $S = $ number of measurements less than $6,000 = 9$.

The p-value $= P(x \geq 9)$ where x is a binomial random variable with $n = 12$ and $p = .5$. Using MINITAB,

$$p - \text{value} = P(x \geq 9) = 1 - P(x \leq 8) = 1 - .927 = .073$$

Since the p-value is less than α $(p = .073 < .10)$, H_0 is rejected. There is sufficient evidence to indicate the median radon exposure is less than 6,000 at $\alpha = .10$.

No, the tombs should not be closed.

15.13   To determine if the median productivity z-score of all such Ph.D. programs differs from 0, we test:

$$H_0 : \eta = 0$$
$$H_a : \eta \neq 0$$

$S_1 = \{\text{Number of observations} < 0\} = 8$
$S_2 = \{\text{Number of observations} > 0\} = 2$

The test statistic is $S = \text{larger of } S_1 \text{ and } S_2 = 8$.

The *p*-value $= P(x \geq 8)$ where x is a binomial random variable with $n = 10$ and $p = .5$. Using Table I, Appendix D, $p - \text{value} = 2P(x \geq 8) = 2(1 - P(x \leq 7)) = 2(1 - .945) = .110$

Since the *p*-value is not less than α $(p = .110 \not< .05)$, H_0 is not rejected. There is insufficient evidence to indicate the median productivity z-score of all such Ph.D. programs differs from 0 at $\alpha = .05$.

15.15   To determine if the distribution of A is shifted to the left of distribution B, we test:

H_0: The two sampled populations have identical distributions
H_a: The probability distribution for population A is shifted to the left of population B.

The test statistic is $z = \dfrac{T_1 - \dfrac{n_1(n_1 + n_2 + 1)}{2}}{\sqrt{\dfrac{n_1 n_2 (n_1 + n_2 + 1)}{12}}} = \dfrac{173 - \dfrac{15(15 + 15 + 1)}{2}}{\sqrt{\dfrac{15(15)(15 + 15 + 1)}{12}}} = -2.47$

The rejection region requires $\alpha = .05$ in the lower tail of the *z*-distribution. From Table II, Appendix D, $z_{.05} = 1.645$. The rejection region is $z < -1.645$.

Since the observed value of the test statistic falls in the rejection region $(z = -2.47 < -1.645)$, H_0 is rejected. There is sufficient evidence to indicate the distribution of A is shifted to the left of distribution B at $\alpha = .05$.

15.17

Sample from Population 1	Rank	Sample from Population 2	Rank
15	13	5	2.5
10	8.5	12	10.5
12	10.5	9	6.5
16	14	9	6.5
13	12	8	4.5
8	4.5	4	1
		5	2.5
		10	8.5
$T_1 = 62.5$		$T_2 = 42.5$	

a.   To determine if there is a shift in the locations of the probability distributions, we test:

H_0: The two sampled populations have identical probability distributions
H_a: The probability distribution for population 1 is shifted to the left or to the right of that for population 2

The test statistic is $T_1 = 62.5$ since sample A has the smallest number of measurements.

The null hypothesis will be rejected if $T_1 \leq T_L$ or $T_1 \geq T_U$ where T_L and T_U correspond to $\alpha = .05$ (two-tailed), $n_1 = 6$ and $n_2 = 8$. From Table XII, Appendix D, $T_L = 29$ and $T_U = 61$.

Reject H_0 if $T_1 \leq 29$ or $T_1 \geq 61$.

Since $T_1 = 62.5 \geq 61$, H_0 is rejected. There is sufficient evidence to indicate population 1 is shifted to the left or right of population 2 at $\alpha = .05$.

b.   To determine if the distribution of population 1 is shifted to the right of that for population 2, we test:

H_0: The two sampled populations have identical probability distributions
H_a: The probability distribution for population 1 is shifted to the right of population 2

The test statistic remains $T_1 = 62.5$.

The null hypothesis will be rejected if $T_1 \geq T_U$ where T_U corresponds to $\alpha = .05$ (one-tailed), $n_1 = 6$ and $n_2 = 8$. From Table XII, Appendix D, $T_U = 58$.

Reject H_0 if $T_1 \geq 58$.

Since $T_1 = 62.5 \geq 58$, H_0 is rejected. There is sufficient evidence to indicate population 1 is shifted to the right of population 2 at $\alpha = .05$.

15.19   a.   The ranks of the data are:

Old Design	Rank	New Design	Rank
210	9	216	16.5
212	13.5	217	18.5
211	11	162	4
211	11	137	1
190	7	219	20
213	15	216	16.5
212	13.5	179	6
211	11	153	3
164	5	152	2
209	8	217	18.5
	$T_1 = 104$		$T_2 = 106$

b.   The sum of the ranks is $T_1 = 104$.

c.   The sum of the ranks is $T_2 = 106$.

d.   Since $n_1 = n_2 = 10$, either T_1 or T_2 can be used. We will pick $T_1 = 104$.

e. To determine if the distributions of bursting strengths differ for the two designs, we test:

H_0: The two sampled populations have identical probability distributions
H_a: The probability distribution of the new design is located to the right or left of that for the old design.

The test statistic is $T_1 = 104$.

The null hypothesis will be rejected if $T_1 \leq T_L$ or $T_1 \geq T_U$ where T_L and T_U correspond to $\alpha = .05$ (two-tailed) and $n_1 = n_2 = 10$. From Table XII, Appendix D, $T_L = 79$ and $T_U = 131$.

Reject H_0 if $T_1 \leq 79$ or $T_1 \geq 131$.

Since $T_1 = 104 \not\leq 79$ and $T_1 = 104 \not\geq 131$, H_0 is not rejected. There is insufficient evidence to indicate the distributions of bursting strengths differ for the two designs at $\alpha = .05$.

15.21   a. The Wilcoxon Rank Sum Test would be appropriate for analyzing these data.

b. To determine if the low-handicapped golfers have a higher X-factor than high-handicapped golfers, we test:

H_0: The probability distributions of the X-factors for low-handicapped and high handicapped golfers are identical
H_a: The probability distribution of the X-factors for low-handicapped golfers is shifted to the right of that for high-handicapped golfers

c. The rejection region is $T_2 \leq 41$, from Table XII, Appendix D, with $n_1 = 8$, $n_2 = 7$, and $\alpha = .05$.

d. Since the p-value is not less than α ($p = .487 \not< .05$), H_0 is not rejected. There is insufficient evidence to indicate that low-handicapped golfers have a higher X-factor than high-handicapped golfers at $\alpha = .05$.

15.23   a. To determine if the distribution of the recalls for those receiving audiovisual presentation differs from that of the recalls of those receiving only the visual presentation, we test:

H_0: The two sampled distributions are identical
H_a: The distribution of recalls for those receiving audiovisual presentation is shifted to the right or left of that for those receiving only visual presentation

b. First, we rank all of the data:

Audiovisual Group				Video Only Group			
Recall	Rank	Recall	Rank	Recall	Rank	Recall	Rank
0	1.5	1	5	6	34.5	6	34.5
4	24	2	12	3	19	2	12
6	34.5	6	34.5	6	34.5	3	19
6	34.5	1	5	2	12	1	5
1	5	3	19	2	12	3	19
2	12	0	1.5	4	24	2	12
2	12	2	12	7	40	5	28
6	34.5	5	28	6	34.5	2	12
6	34.5	4	24	1	5	4	24
4	24	5	28	3	19	6	34.5
		$T_1 = 385.5$				$T_2 = 434.5$	

The test statistic is $z = \dfrac{T_1 - \dfrac{n_1(n_1 + n_2 + 1)}{2}}{\sqrt{\dfrac{n_1 n_2 (n_1 + n_2 + 1)}{12}}} = \dfrac{385.5 - \dfrac{20(20 + 20 + 1)}{2}}{\sqrt{\dfrac{20(20)(20 + 20 + 1)}{12}}} = -.66$

c.   The rejection region requires $\alpha / 2 = .10 / 2 = .05$ in each tail of the z-distribution. From Table II, Appendix D, $z_{.05} = 1.645$. The rejection region is $z < -1.645$ or $z > 1.645$.

d.   Since the observed value of the test statistic does not fall in the rejection region ($z = -.66 \not< -1.645$), H_0 is not rejected. There is insufficient evidence to indicate the distribution of the recalls for those receiving audiovisual presentation differs from that of the recalls of those receiving only the visual presentation at $\alpha = .10$. This supports the researchers' theory.

15.25   a.   Using MINITAB, the histograms of the data are:

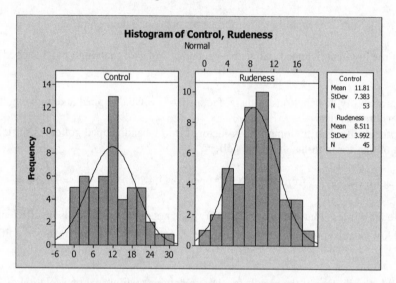

As you can see from the above graphs, the distribution for the control group is skewed to the right while the distribution for the Rudeness group is fairly normal.

b.   We first rank the data:

Control Group				Rudeness Condition			
Score	**Rank**	**Score**	**Rank**	**Score**	**Rank**	**Score**	**Rank**
1	5.5	9	42	4	17	7	30.5
24	96	12	66.5	11	58.5	11	58.5
5	22	18	85.5	18	85.5	4	17
16	81.5	5	22	11	58.5	13	73
21	93.5	21	93.5	9	42	5	22
7	30.5	30	98	6	25.5	4	17
20	91	15	78	5	22	7	30.5
1	5.5	4	17	11	58.5	8	36
9	42	2	9	9	42	3	12.5
20	91	12	66.5	12	66.5	8	36
19	88	11	58.5	7	30.5	15	78
10	50	10	50	5	22	9	42
23	95	13	73	7	30.5	16	81.5
16	81.5	11	58.5	3	12.5	10	50
0	2	3	12.5	11	58.5	0	2
4	17	6	25.5	1	5.5	7	30.5
9	42	10	50	9	42	15	78
13	73	13	73	11	58.5	13	73
17	84	16	81.5	10	50	9	42
13	73	12	66.5	7	30.5	2	9
0	2	28	97	8	36	13	73
2	9	19	88	9	42	10	50
12	66.5	12	66.5	10	50		
11	58.5	20	91				
7	30.5	3	12.5				
1	5.5	11	58.5				
19	88						
		$T_1 = 2,964.5$				$T_2 = 1,886.5$	

To determine if the distribution of the rudeness condition is shifted to the left of that for the control group, we test:

H_0: The distributions of the two sampled populations are identical
H_a: The distribution of the rudeness group scores is shifted to the left of that for the control group

The test statistic is $z = \dfrac{T_1 - \dfrac{n_1(n_1+n_2+1)}{2}}{\sqrt{\dfrac{n_1 n_2(n_1+n_2+1)}{12}}} = \dfrac{2,964.5 - \dfrac{53(53+45+1)}{2}}{\sqrt{\dfrac{53(45)(53+45+1)}{12}}} = 2.43$

The rejection region requires $\alpha = .01$ in the upper tail of the z-distribution. From Table II, Appendix D, $z_{.01} = 2.33$. The rejection region is $z > 2.33$.

Since the observed value of the test statistic falls in the rejection region ($z = 2.43 > 2.33$), H_0 is rejected. There is sufficient evidence to indicate the distribution of the rudeness condition scores is shifted to the left of that for the control group at $\alpha = .01$.

c.   Since the sample sizes for both groups were over 30, the Central Limit Theorem applies. Thus, the parametric 2-sample test in Exercise 8.21 is appropriate.

15.27   a.   Using MINITAB, histograms of the two data sets are:

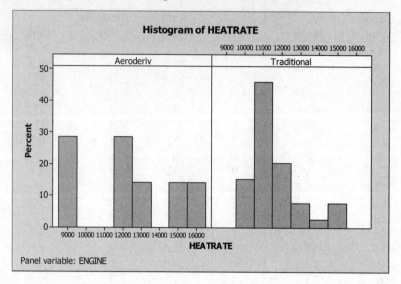

From the histograms, the data for each group do not look like they are mound-shaped. The variance of the aeroderivative engines is greater than that of the traditional engines. Thus, the assumptions of normal distributions and equal variances necessary for the t-test are probably not met.

   b.   The p-value = .3431. Since this p-value is not small, H_0 is not rejected. There is no evidence to indicate that the heat rate distribution of the traditional turbine engines is shifted to the right or left of that for the aeroderivative turbine engines for any reasonable value of α.

15.29   a.   The test statistic is the smaller of T_- or T_+.

The rejection region is $T \leq 152$, from Table XIII, Appendix D, with $n = 30$, $\alpha = .10$, and two-tailed.

   b.   The test statistic is T_-.

The rejection region is $T_- \leq 60$, from Table XIII, Appendix D, with $n = 20$, $\alpha = .05$, and one-tailed.

   c.   The test statistic is T_+.

The rejection region is $T_+ \leq 0$, from Table XIII, Appendix D, with $n = 8$, $\alpha = .005$, and one-tailed.

15.31   a.   The hypotheses are:

H_0:   The two sampled populations have identical probability distributions
H_a: The probability distributions for population A is shifted to the right of that for population B

b.   Some preliminary calculations are:

Treatment		Difference	Rank of Absolute
A	B	A - B	Difference
54	45	9	5
60	45	15	10
98	87	11	7
43	31	12	9
82	71	11	7
77	75	2	2.5
74	63	11	7
29	30	−1	1
63	59	4	4
80	82	−2	2.5
			$T_- = 3.5$

The test statistic is $T_- = 3.5$.

The rejection region is $T_- \leq 8$, from Table XIII, Appendix D, with $n = 10$ and $\alpha = .025$.

Since the observed value of the test statistic falls in the rejection region $(T_- = 3.5 \leq 8)$, H_0 is rejected. There is sufficient evidence to indicate the responses for A tend to be larger than those for B at $\alpha = .025$.

15.33 a.   In order for the confidence interval to be valid, the distribution of the differences must be normal. This may not be the case.

b.   For this paired comparison, the appropriate nonparametric test is the Wilcoxon Signed Rank Test. To determine if there is a difference in the true THM means between the original holes and their twin holes, we test:

H_0: The distributions of the THM values for the original holes and their twins are identical
H_a: The distribution of the THM values for the original holes is shifted to the right or left of that for the twin holes.

c & d. The differences and the ranks are in the following table:

Location	1st Hole	2nd Hole	Diff $1^{st} - 2^{nd}$	Rank of Absolute Difference
1	5.5	5.7	-0.2	3.5
2	11.0	11.2	-0.2	3.5
3	5.9	6.0	-0.1	1.5
4	8.2	5.6	2.6	15
5	10.0	9.3	0.7	6
6	7.9	7.0	0.9	7
7	10.1	8.4	1.7	13.5
8	7.4	9.0	-1.6	12
9	7.0	6.0	1.0	8
10	9.2	8.1	1.1	9
11	8.3	10.0	-1.7	13.5
12	8.6	8.1	0.5	5
13	10.5	10.4	0.1	1.5
14	5.5	7.0	-1.5	11
15	10.0	11.2	-1.2	10
				$T_- = 55$

e. $T_- = 3.5 + 3.5 + 1.5 + 12 + 13.5 + 11 + 10 = 55$ and $T_+ = 15 + 6 + 7 + 13.5 + 8 + 9 + 5 + 1.5 = 65$

f.   The test statistic is the smaller of T_- and T_+ which is $T_- = 55$.

The rejection region is $T_- \leq 25$, from Table XIII, Appendix D, with $n = 15$ and $\alpha = .05$.

Since the observed value of the test statistic does not fall in the rejection region ($T_- = 55 \nleq 25$), H_0 is not rejected. There is insufficient evidence to indicate that there is a difference in the true THM means between the original holes and their twin holes at $\alpha = .05$.

15.35   a.   The test statistic is $z = \dfrac{T_- - \dfrac{n(n+1)}{4}}{\sqrt{\dfrac{n(n+1)(2n+1)}{24}}} = \dfrac{11.50 - \dfrac{31(31+1)}{4}}{\sqrt{\dfrac{31(31+1)(2(31)+1)}{24}}} = -4.63$.

b.   To determine if handling a museum object has a positive impact on a sick patient's well-being, we test:

H_0: The distributions of patients' heath statuses before and after handling museum pieces are identical

H_a: The distribution of patients' heath statuses after handling museum pieces is shifted to the right of the distribution before handling museum pieces

The test statistic is $z = -4.63$. From the printout, the two-tailed p-value is $p = .000$. The one-tailed p-value is $p = .000 / 2 = .000$.

Since the p-value is less than α ($p = .000 < .01$), H_0 is rejected. There is sufficient evidence to indicate handling a museum object has a positive impact on a sick patient's well-being at $\alpha = .01$.

15.37   To determine if the photo-red enforcement program is effective in reducing red-light-running crash incidents at intersections, we test:

H_0: The two sampled populations have identical probability distributions
H_a: The probability distribution after the camera installation is shifted to the left of that before the camera installation

From the printout, the test statistic is $T = 79$ and the p-value is $p = .011$. Since the p-value is so small, H_0 is rejected. There is sufficient evidence to indicate the photo-red enforcement program is effective in reducing red-light-running crash incidents at intersections for any value of α greater than .011.

15.39

Operator	Before Policy	After Policy	Difference	Rank of Absolute Difference
1	10	5	5	5.5
2	3	0	3	4
3	16	7	9	8
4	11	4	7	7
5	8	6	2	2.5
6	2	4	−2	2.5
7	1	2	−1	1
8	14	3	11	9
9	5	5	0	(eliminated)
10	6	1	5	5.5
				$T_- = 3.5$
				$T_+ = 41.5$

To determine if the distributions of the number of complaints differs for the two time periods, we test:

H_0: The distributions of the number of complaints for the two years are the same
H_a: The distribution of the number of complaints after the policy change is shifted to the right or left of the distribution before the policy change.

The test statistic is $T_- = 3.5$.

Since no α is given we will use $\alpha = .05$. The null hypothesis will be rejected if $T_- \leq T_o$ where T_o corresponds to $\alpha = .05$ (two-tailed) and $n = 9$. From Table XIII, Appendix D, $T_o = 6$.

Reject H_0 if $T_- \leq 6$.

Since the observed value of the test statistic falls in the rejection region $(T_- = 3.5 \leq 6)$, H_0 is rejected. There is sufficient evidence to indicate the distributions of the complaints are different for the two years at $\alpha = .05$.

15.41   a.   Some preliminary calculations are:

Circuit	Standard Method	Huffman-coding Method	Difference S-H	Rank of Absolute Differences
1	0.80	0.78	0.02	2
2	0.80	0.80	0.00	(eliminated)
3	0.83	0.86	-0.03	3
4	0.53	0.53	0.00	(eliminated)
5	0.50	0.51	-0.01	1
6	0.96	0.68	0.28	8
7	0.99	0.82	0.17	5
8	0.98	0.72	0.26	7
9	0.81	0.45	0.36	9
10	0.95	0.79	0.16	4
11	0.99	0.77	0.22	6
				$T_- = 4$

To determine if the Huffman-coding method yields a smaller mean compression ratio, we test:

H_0: The two sampled populations have identical probability distributions.
H_a: The probability distribution of the Standard Method is shifted to the right of that for the Huffman-coding Method.

The test statistic is $T_- = 4$.

The rejection region is $T_- \leq 8$, from Table XIII, Appendix D, with $n = 9$ and $\alpha = .05$ (one-tailed).

Since the observed value of the test statistic falls in the rejection region $(T_- = 4 \leq 8)$, H_0 is rejected. There is sufficient evidence to indicate the Huffman-coding method yields a smaller mean compression ratio at $\alpha = .05$

b.   In Exercise 8.39, we concluded that the Huffman-coding method yields a smaller mean compression ratio than the standard method which is the same as the conclusion above.

15.43   The χ^2 distribution provides an appropriate characterization of the sampling distribution of H if the p sample sizes exceed 5.

15.45   a.   A completely randomized design was used.

b.   The hypotheses are:

H_0: The three probability distributions are identical
H_a: At least two of the three probability distributions differ in location

c.   The rejection region requires $\alpha = .01$ in the upper tail of the χ^2 distribution with df $= k - 1 = 3 - 1 = 2$. From Table IV, Appendix D, $\chi^2_{.01} = 9.21034$. The rejection region is $H > 9.21034$.

d. Some preliminary calculations are:

I		II		III	
Observation	**Rank**	**Observation**	**Rank**	**Observation**	**Rank**
66	13	19	2	75	14.5
23	3	31	6	96	19
55	10	16	1	102	21
88	18	29	4	75	14.5
58	11	30	5	98	20
62	12	33	7	78	16
79	17	40	8		
49	9				
	$R_A = 93$		$R_B = 33$		$R_C = 105$

$$\bar{R}_A = \frac{R_A}{8} = \frac{93}{8} = 11.625 \qquad \bar{R}_B = \frac{R_B}{7} = \frac{33}{7} = 4.714$$

$$\bar{R}_C = \frac{R_C}{6} = \frac{105}{6} = 17.5 \qquad \bar{R} = \frac{n+1}{2} = \frac{21+1}{2} = 11$$

The test statistic is:

$$H = \frac{12}{n(n+1)} \sum n_j (\bar{R}_j - \bar{R})^2$$

$$= \frac{12}{21(22)} \left[8(11.625 - 11)^2 + 7(4.714 - 11)^2 + 6(17.5 - 11)^2 \right] = 13.85$$

Since the observed value of the test statistic falls in the rejection region $(H = 13.85 > 9.21034)$, H_0 is rejected. There is sufficient evidence to indicate at least two of the three probability distributions differ in location at $\alpha = .01$.

15.47 a. To determine if the distributions of recalls differ among the three groups, we test:

H_0: The three probability distributions are identical
H_a: At least two of the three probability distributions differ in location

b. The test statistic is $H = 36.04$ and the p-value is $p = 0.000$.

c. Since the p-value is less than α $(p = 0.000 < .01)$, H_0 is rejected. There is sufficient evidence to indicate that at least two of the distributions of recalls differ in location at $\alpha = .01$.

15.49 a. To determine if the distributions of office rental growth rates differ among the four market cycle phases, we test:

H_0: The four probability distributions are identical
H_a: At least two of the growth rate distributions differ

b.   The ranks of the measurements are:

Phase I	Rank	Phase II	Rank	Phase III	Rank	Phase IV	Rank
2.7	9	10.5	20	6.1	14	−1.0	4.5
−1.0	4.5	11.5	23	1.2	7	6.2	15.5
1.1	6	9.4	19	11.4	22	−10.8	1
3.4	10	12.2	24	4.4	13	2.0	8
4.2	12	8.6	18	6.2	15.5	−1.1	3
3.5	11	10.9	21	7.6	17	−2.3	2
	$R_1 = 52.5$		$R_2 = 125$		$R_3 = 88.5$		$R_4 = 34$

c.   The rank sums appear in the table above.

$$\bar{R}_1 = \frac{R_1}{n_1} = \frac{52.5}{6} = 8.75 \qquad \bar{R}_2 = \frac{R_2}{n_2} = \frac{125}{6} = 20.833 \qquad \bar{R}_3 = \frac{R_3}{n_3} = \frac{88.5}{6} = 14.75$$

$$\bar{R}_4 = \frac{R_4}{n_4} = \frac{34}{6} = 5.667 \qquad \bar{R} = \frac{n+1}{2} = \frac{24+1}{2} = 12.5$$

The test statistic is

$$H = \frac{12}{n(n+1)} \sum n_j (\bar{R}_j - \bar{R})^2$$

$$= \frac{12}{24(24+1)} \left[6(8.75-12.5)^2 + 6(20.833-12.5)^2 + 6(14.75-12.5)^2 + 6(5.667-12.5)^2 \right] = 16.23$$

d.   The rejection region requires $\alpha = .05$ in the upper tail of the χ^2 distribution with $df = k - 1 = 4 - 1 = 3$. From Table IV, Appendix D, $\chi^2_{.05} = 7.81473$. The rejection region is $H > 7.81473$.

e.   Since the observed value of the test statistic falls in the rejection region $(H = 16.23 > 7.81473)$, H_0 is rejected. There is sufficient evidence to indicate the distributions of office rental growth rates differ among the four market cycle phases at $\alpha = .05$.

15.51   a.   The *F*-test would be appropriate if:

1.   All *k* populations sampled from are normal.
2.   The variances of the *k* populations are equal.
3.   The *k* samples are independent.

b.   The variances for the three populations are probably not the same and the populations are probably not normal.

c.   To determine whether the salary distributions differ among the three cities, we test:

H_0: The three probability distributions are identical
H_a: At least two of the three probability distributions differ in location

Some preliminary calculations are:

Atlanta	Rank	Los Angeles	Rank	Washington, D.C.	Rank
39,600	1	47,400	4	43,000	2
89,900	19	140,000	21	81,900	16
66,700	11	68,000	12	53,000	6
43,900	3	48,700	5	77,600	14
82,200	17	74,400	13	78,200	15
88,600	18	102,000	20	56,800	8
64,800	10	54,500	7	60,000	9
	$R_1 = 79$		$R_2 = 82$		$R_3 = 70$

$$\bar{R}_1 = \frac{R_1}{n_1} = \frac{79}{7} = 11.286 \qquad\qquad \bar{R}_2 = \frac{R_2}{n_2} = \frac{82}{7} = 11.714$$

$$\bar{R}_3 = \frac{R_3}{n_3} = \frac{70}{7} = 10 \qquad\qquad \bar{R} = \frac{n+1}{2} = \frac{21+1}{2} = 11$$

The test statistic is

$$H = \frac{12}{n(n+1)} \sum n_j (\bar{R}_j - \bar{R})^2 = \frac{12}{21(21+1)} \left[7(11.286 - 11)^2 + 7(11.714 - 11)^2 + 7(10 - 11)^2 \right] = 0.29$$

The rejection region requires $\alpha = .05$ in the upper tail of the χ^2 distribution with df $= k - 1 = 3 - 1 = 2$. From Table IV, Appendix D, $\chi^2_{.05} = 5.99147$. The rejection region is $H > 5.99147$.

Since the observed value of the test statistic does not fall in the rejection region $(H = .29 \not> 5.99147)$, H_0 is not rejected. There is insufficient evidence to indicate the salary distributions differ among the three cities at $\alpha = .05$.

We must assume we have independent random samples, sample sizes greater than or equal to 5 from each population, and that all populations are continuous.

15.53   Some preliminary calculations:

Honey Dosage				DM Dosage				No Dosage			
Change	Rank	Change	Rank	Change	Rank	Change	Rank	Change	Rank	Change	Rank
12	88	12	88	4	12	6	24.5	5	18.5	5	18.5
11	78.5	8	47	6	24.5	8	47	8	47	11	78.5
15	102	12	88	9	59	12	88	6	24.5	9	59
11	78.5	9	59	4	12	12	88	1	3	5	18.5
10	70.5	11	78.5	7	35	4	12	0	1	6	24.5
13	96.5	15	102	7	35	12	88	8	47	8	47
10	70.5	10	70.5	7	35	13	96.5	12	88	8	47
4	12	15	102	9	59	7	35	8	47	6	24.5
15	102	9	59	12	88	10	70.5	7	35	7	35
16	105	13	96.5	10	70.5	13	96.5	7	35	10	70.5
9	59	8	47	11	78.5	9	59	1	3	9	59
14	99	12	88	6	24.5	4	12	6	24.5	4	12
10	70.5	10	70.5	3	6	4	12	7	35	8	47
6	24.5	8	47	4	12	10	70.5	7	35	7	35
10	70.5	9	59	9	59	15	102	12	88	3	6
8	47	5	18.5	12	88	9	59	7	35	1	3
11	78.5	12	88	7	35			9	59	4	12
12	88							7	35	3	6
								9	59		
		$R_1 = 2,549$				$R_2 = 1,693.5$				$R_3 = 1,322.5$	

$$\bar{R}_1 = \frac{R_1}{n_1} = \frac{2549}{35} = 72.829 \qquad \bar{R}_2 = \frac{R_2}{n_2} = \frac{1693.5}{33} = 51.318$$

$$\bar{R}_3 = \frac{R_3}{n_3} = \frac{1322.5}{37} = 35.743 \qquad \bar{R} = \frac{n+1}{2} = \frac{105+1}{2} = 53$$

To determine if the distributions of improvement scores for the three groups differ in location, we test:

H_0: The three probability distributions are identical

H_a: At least two of the three improvement distributions differ in location

The test statistic is

$$H = \frac{12}{n(n+1)}\sum n_j(\bar{R}_j - \bar{R})^2$$

$$= \frac{12}{105(105+1)}\left[35(72.829-53)^2 + 33(51.318-53)^2 + 37(35.743-53)^2\right] = 26.82$$

The rejection region requires $\alpha = .01$ in the upper tail of the χ^2 distribution with df $= k-1 = 3-1 = 2$. From Table IV, Appendix D, $\chi^2_{.01} = 9.21034$. The rejection region is $H > 9.21034$.

Since the observed value of the test statistic falls in the rejection region ($H = 26.82 > 9.21034$), H_0 is rejected. There is sufficient evidence to indicate the distributions of improvement scores for the three groups differ in location at $\alpha = .01$.

15.55 a. The hypotheses are:

H_0: The probability distributions for three treatments are identical
H_a: At least two of the probability distributions differ in location

b. The rejection region requires $\alpha = .10$ in the upper tail of the χ^2 distribution with df $= k - 1 = 3 - 1 = 2$. From Table IV, Appendix D, $\chi^2_{.10} = 4.60517$. The rejection region is $F_r > 4.60517$.

c. Some preliminary calculations are:

Block	A	Rank	B	Rank	C	Rank
1	9	1	11	2	18	3
2	13	2	13	2	13	2
3	11	1	12	2.5	12	2.5
4	10	1	15	2	16	3
5	9	2	8	1	10	3
6	14	2	12	1	16	3
7	10	1	12	2	15	3
		$R_A = 10$		$R_B = 12.5$		$R_C = 19.5$

$$\bar{R}_A = \frac{R_A}{b} = \frac{10}{7} = 1.429 \qquad \bar{R}_B = \frac{R_B}{b} = \frac{12.5}{7} = 1.786 \qquad \bar{R}_C = \frac{R_C}{b} = \frac{19.5}{7} = 2.786$$

$$\bar{R} = \frac{1}{2}(k+1) = \frac{1}{2}(3+1) = 2$$

The test statistic is

$$F_r = \frac{12b}{k(k+1)} \sum (\bar{R}_j - \bar{R})^2 = \frac{12(7)}{3(3+1)}[(1.429-2)^2 + (1.786-2)^2 + (2.786-2)^2] = 6.93$$

Since the observed value of the test statistic falls in the rejection region $(F_r = 6.93 > 4.60517)$, H_0 is rejected. There is sufficient evidence to indicate the effectiveness of the three different treatments differ at $\alpha = .10$.

15.57 a. The data are not independent. Each subject had measurements for each of the 4 time segments. Thus, the data are blocked. It would realistic to assume that the data might not be normally distributed, so the use of a nonparametric test would be appropriate. Thus, the Friedman test would be appropriate.

b. The test statistic is $F_r = 14.37$ and the p-value is $p = .002$.

c. Since the p-value is less than α $(p = .002 < .01)$, H_0 is rejected. There is sufficient evidence to indicate the distribution of walking times differ for the four time segments at $\alpha = .01$.

15.59   a.   From the printout, the rank sums are 23 (before), 32 (after 2 months), and 35 (after 2 days).

b. $\bar{R}_1 = \dfrac{R_1}{b} = \dfrac{23}{15} = 1.533$ $\bar{R}_2 = \dfrac{R_2}{b} = \dfrac{32}{15} = 2.133$ $\bar{R}_3 = \dfrac{R_3}{b} = \dfrac{35}{15} = 2.333$

$$\bar{R} = \frac{1}{2}(k+1) = \frac{1}{2}(3+1) = 2$$

$$F_r = \frac{12b}{k(k+1)}\sum(\bar{R}_j - \bar{R})^2 = \frac{12(15)}{3(3+1)}[(1.533-2)^2 + (2.133-2)^2 + (2.333-2)^2] = 5.2$$

c.   From the printout, the test statistic is $F_r = 5.20$ and the p-value is $p = .074$.

d.   To determine if the distributions of the competence levels differ in location among the 3 time periods, we test:

H_0: The probability distributions of the three sampled populations are the same
H_a: At least two of the distributions of the competence levels differ in location

The test statistic is $F_r = 5.20$ and the p-value is $p = .074$. Since the p-value is not small, we would not reject H_0 for any values of $\alpha < .074$. There is insufficient evidence to indicate the distributions of the competence levels differ in location among the 3 time periods for $\alpha < .074$.

If we use $\alpha = .10$, then we would reject H_0.

15.61   Using MINITAB, the results of analyzing the data using Friedman's test are:

Friedman Test: Score versus Item blocked by Review
```
S = 29.11   DF = 10   P = 0.001
S = 31.39   DF = 10   P = 0.001 (adjusted for ties)

                     Sum
              Est     of
Item  N    Median   Ranks
 1    5     3.500    40.0
 2    5     2.500    28.5
 3    5     3.864    46.5
 4    5     3.591    40.0
 5    5     2.455    23.0
 6    5     3.591    41.0
 7    5     3.500    37.0
 8    5     3.227    32.0
 9    5     2.636    23.5
10    5     1.091     9.5
11    5     1.045     9.0

Grand median = 2.818
```

To determine if the distributions of the 11 item scores are different, we test:

H_0: The distributions of the 11 item scores are identical
H_a: At least two of the distributions of the item scores differ in location

From the printout, the test statistic is $F_r = 29.11$ and the p-value is $p = .001$. Since the p-value is so small, H_0 is rejected for any reasonable value of α. There is sufficient evidence to indicate that the distributions of the 11 item scores differ in location at any reasonable value of α.

15.63   Some preliminary calculations are:

Student	Rank Live Plant	Rank Plant Photo	Rank No Plant
1	1	2	3
2	2	3	1
3	3	2	1
4	1	2	3
5	2	3	1
6	3	2	1
7	2	1	3
8	1	3	2
9	2	1	3
10	2	1	3
	$R_1 = 19$	$R_2 = 20$	$R_3 = 21$

$$\bar{R}_1 = \frac{R_1}{n_1} = \frac{19}{10} = 1.9 \qquad \bar{R}_2 = \frac{R_2}{n_2} = \frac{20}{10} = 2 \qquad \bar{R}_3 = \frac{R_3}{n_3} = \frac{21}{10} = 2.1 \qquad \bar{R} = \frac{k+1}{2} = \frac{3+1}{2} = 2$$

To determine if the students' finger temperatures depend on the experimental conditions, we test:

H_0: The probability distributions of finger temperatures are the same for the three conditions
H_a: At least two probability distributions of finger temperatures differ in location

The test statistic is $F_r = \dfrac{12b}{k(k+1)} \sum (\bar{R}_j - \bar{R})^2 = \dfrac{12(10)}{3(3+1)} \left((1.9-2)^2 + (2-2)^2 + (2.1-2)^2 \right) = 0.2$

Since no α was given, we will use $\alpha = .05$. The rejection region requires $\alpha = .05$ in the upper tail of the χ^2 distribution with df $= k-1 = 3-1 = 2$. From Table IV, Appendix D, $\chi^2_{.05} = 5.99147$. The rejection region is $F_r > 5.99147$.

Since the observed value of the test statistic does not fall in the rejection region $(F_r = 0.2 \not> 5.99147)$, H_0 is not rejected. There is insufficient evidence to indicate that the students' finger temperatures depend on the experimental conditions at $\alpha = .05$.

Because the value of the test statistic is so small, H_0 would not be rejected for any reasonable value of α.

15.65   Some preliminary calculations are:

Metal	I	Rank	II	Rank	III	Rank
1	4.6	2	4.2	1	4.9	3
2	7.2	3	6.4	1	7.0	2
3	3.4	1.5	3.5	3	3.4	1.5
4	6.2	3	5.3	1	5.9	2
5	8.4	3	6.8	1	7.8	2
6	5.6	2	4.8	1	5.7	3
7	3.7	1.5	3.7	1.5	4.1	3
8	6.1	1	6.2	2	6.4	3
9	4.9	3	4.1	1	4.2	2
10	5.2	3	5.0	1	5.1	2
		$R_1 = 23$		$R_2 = 13.5$		$R_3 = 23.5$

$$\bar{R}_1 = \frac{R_1}{n_1} = \frac{23}{10} = 2.3 \qquad \bar{R}_2 = \frac{R_2}{n_2} = \frac{13.5}{10} = 1.35 \qquad \bar{R}_3 = \frac{R_3}{n_3} = \frac{23.5}{10} = 2.35 \qquad \bar{R} = \frac{k+1}{2} = \frac{3+1}{2} = 2$$

To determine if there is a difference in the probability distributions of the amounts of corrosion among the three types of sealers, we test:

H_0:   The probability distributions of corrosion amounts are identical for the three types of sealers
H_a: At least two of the probability distributions differ in location

The test statistic is $F_r = \dfrac{12b}{k(k+1)} \sum (\bar{R}_j - \bar{R})^2 = \dfrac{12(10)}{3(3+1)} \left((2.3-2)^2 + (1.35-2)^2 + (2.35-2)^2 \right) = 6.35$

The rejection region requires $\alpha = .05$ in the upper tail of the χ^2 distribution with df $= k-1 = 3-1 = 2$. From Table IV, Appendix D, $\chi^2_{.05} = 5.99147$. The rejection region is $F_r > 5.99147$.

Since the observed value of the test statistic falls in the rejection region $(F_r = 6.35 > 5.99147)$, H_0 is rejected. There is sufficient evidence to indicate a difference in the probability distributions among the three types of sealers at $\alpha = .05$.

15.67   a.   From Table XIV with $n = 10$, $r_{s,\alpha/2} = r_{s,.025} = .648$. The rejection region is $r_s < -.648$ or $r_s > .648$.

b.   From Table XIV with $n = 20$, $r_{s,\alpha} = r_{s,.025} = .450$. The rejection region is $r_s > .450$.

c.   From Table XIV with $n = 30$, $r_{s,\alpha} = r_{s,.01} = .432$. The rejection region is $r_s < -.432$.

15.69   Since there are no ties, we will use the shortcut formula.

a.   Some preliminary calculations are:

x Rank (u_i)	y Rank (v_i)	$d_i = u_i - v_i$	d_i^2
3	2	1	1
5	4	1	1
2	5	−3	9
1	1	0	0
4	3	1	1
			Total = 12

$$r_s = 1 - \frac{6\sum d_i^2}{n(n^2-1)} = 1 - \frac{6(12)}{5(5^2-1)} = 1 - .6 = .4$$

b.

x Rank (u_i)	y Rank (v_i)	$d_i = u_i - v_i$	d_i^2
2	3	−1	1
3	4	−1	1
4	2	2	4
5	1	4	16
1	5	−4	16
			Total = 38

$$r_s = 1 - \frac{6\sum d_i^2}{n(n^2-1)} = 1 - \frac{6(38)}{5(5^2-1)} = 1 - 1.9 = -.9$$

c.

x Rank (u_i)	y Rank (v_i)	$d_i = u_i - v_i$	d_i^2
1	2	−1	1
4	1	3	9
2	3	−1	1
3	4	−1	1
			Total = 12

$$r_s = 1 - \frac{6\sum d_i^2}{n(n^2-1)} = 1 - \frac{6(12)}{4(4^2-1)} = 1 - 1.2 = -.2$$

d.

x Rank (u_i)	y Rank (v_i)	$d_i = u_i - v_i$	d_i^2
2	1	1	1
5	3	2	4
4	5	−1	1
3	2	1	1
1	4	−3	9
			Total = 16

$$r_s = 1 - \frac{6 \sum d_i^2}{n(n^2-1)} = 1 - \frac{6(16)}{5(5^2-1)} = 1 - .8 = .2$$

15.71 a.   Some preliminary calculations:

x	Rank, u	y	Rank, v	u^2	v^2	uv
28.582	2	3	2	4	4	4
24.374	1	1	1	1	1	1
31.666	3	10	5	9	25	15
40.530	6	14	6	36	36	36
38.808	5	7	4	25	16	20
33.309	4	4	3	16	9	12
	$\sum u = 21$		$\sum v = 21$	$\sum u^2 = 91$	$\sum v^2 = 91$	$\sum uv = 88$

$$SS_{uv} = \sum uv - \frac{\left(\sum u\right)\left(\sum v\right)}{n} = 88 - \frac{21(21)}{6} = 14.5 \qquad SS_{uu} = \sum u^2 - \frac{\left(\sum u\right)^2}{n} = 91 - \frac{(21)^2}{6} = 17.5$$

$$SS_{vv} = \sum v^2 - \frac{\left(\sum v\right)^2}{n} = 91 - \frac{(21)^2}{6} = 17.5 \qquad r_s = \frac{SS_{uv}}{\sqrt{SS_{uu}\,SS_{vv}}} = \frac{14.5}{\sqrt{17.5(17.5)}} = .8286 \, .$$

b.   To determine if there is positive rank correlation between total US births and the number of software millionaire birthdays, we test:

$$H_0 : \rho_s = 0$$
$$H_a : \rho_s > 0$$

The test statistic is $r_s = .8286$.

Reject H_0 if $r_s > r_{s,\alpha}$ where $\alpha = .05$ and $n = 6$:

Reject H_0 if $r_s > .829$ (from Table XIV, Appendix D).

Since the observed value of the test statistic does not fall in the rejection region ($r_s = .8286 \not> .829$), H_0 is not rejected. There is insufficient evidence to indicate total US births and the number of software millionaire birthdays are positively rank correlated at $\alpha = .05$.

c. Some preliminary calculations:

x	Rank, u	y	Rank, v	u^2	v^2	uv
2	2.5	3	2	6.25	4	5
2	2.5	1	1	6.25	1	2.5
23	5	10	5	25	25	25
38	6	14	6	36	36	36
9	4	7	4	16	16	16
0	1	4	3	1	9	3
	$\sum u = 21$		$\sum v = 21$	$\sum u^2 = 90.5$	$\sum v^2 = 91$	$\sum uv = 87.5$

$$SS_{uv} = \sum uv - \frac{\left(\sum u\right)\left(\sum v\right)}{n} = 87.5 - \frac{21(21)}{6} = 14 \qquad SS_{uu} = \sum u^2 - \frac{\left(\sum u\right)^2}{n} = 90.5 - \frac{(21)^2}{6} = 17$$

$$SS_{vv} = \sum v^2 - \frac{\left(\sum v\right)^2}{n} = 91 - \frac{(21)^2}{6} = 17.5 \qquad r_s = \frac{SS_{uv}}{\sqrt{SS_{uu} SS_{vv}}} = \frac{14}{\sqrt{17(17.5)}} = .8117 .$$

d. To determine if there is positive rank correlation between the number of software millionaire birthdays and the number of CEO birthdays, we test:

$$H_0 : \rho_s = 0$$
$$H_a : \rho_s > 0$$

The test statistic is $r_s = .8117$.

Reject H_0 if $r_s > r_{s,\alpha}$ where $\alpha = .05$ and $n = 6$.

Reject H_0 if $r_s > .829$ (from Table XIV, Appendix D).

Since the observed value of the test statistic does not fall in the rejection region $(r_s = .8117 \not> .829)$, H_0 is not rejected. There is insufficient evidence to indicate the number of software millionaire birthdays and the number of CEO birthdays are positively rank correlated at $\alpha = .05$.

15.73   a. **Navigability**: $r_s = .179$. Since this value is close to 0, there is a very weak positive rank correlation between the ranks of organizational internet use and the ranks of navigability.

Transactions: $r_s = .334$. Since this value is relatively close to 0, there is a weak positive rank correlation between the ranks of organizational internet use and the ranks of transactions.

Locatability: $r_s = .590$. Since this value is about half way between 0 and 1, there is a moderate positive rank correlation between the ranks of organizational internet use and the ranks of locatability.

Information Richness: $r_s = -.115$. Since this value is close to 0, there is a very weak negative rank correlation between the ranks of organizational internet use and the ranks of information richness.

Number of files: $r_s = .114$. Since this value is close to 0, there is a very weak positive rank correlation between the ranks of organizational internet use and the ranks of number of files.

b. For each indicator, we will test:

$$H_0: \rho_s = 0$$
$$H_a: \rho_s > 0$$

Navigability: $p\text{-value} = p = .148$. Since the p-value is greater than $\alpha = .10$, H_0 is not rejected. There is insufficient evidence to indicate a positive rank correlation between organizational internet use and navigability.

Transactions: $p\text{-value} = p = .023$. Since the p-value is less than $\alpha = .10$, H_0 is rejected. There is sufficient evidence to indicate a positive rank correlation between organizational internet use and transactions.

Locatability: $p\text{-value} = p = .000$. Since the p-value is less than $\alpha = .10$, H_0 is rejected. There is sufficient evidence to indicate a positive rank correlation between organizational internet use and locatability.

Information Richness: $p\text{-value} = p = .252$. Since the p-value is greater than $\alpha = .10$, H_0 is not rejected. There is insufficient evidence to indicate a positive rank correlation between organizational internet use and information richness.

Number of files: $p\text{-value} = p = .255$. Since the p-value is greater than $\alpha = .10$, H_0 is not rejected. There is insufficient evidence to indicate a positive rank correlation between organizational internet use and number of files.

15.75   Some preliminary calculations are:

Punish	Rank, u	Payoff	Rank, v	u^2	v^2	uv
0	1	0.50	13	1	169	13
1	2	0.20	9	4	81	18
2	3	0.30	11.5	9	132.25	34.5
3	4	0.25	10	16	100	40
4	5	0.00	6	25	36	30
5	6	0.30	11.5	36	132.25	69
6	7	0.10	7	49	49	49
8	8	-0.20	3.5	64	12.25	28
10	9	0.15	8	81	64	72
12	10	-0.30	1	100	1	10
14	11	-0.10	5	121	25	55
16	12	-0.20	3.5	144	12.25	42
17	13	-0.25	2	169	4	26
	$\sum u = 91$		$\sum v = 91$	$\sum u^2 = 819$	$\sum v^2 = 818$	$\sum uv = 486.5$

$$SS_{uv} = \sum uv - \frac{\left(\sum u\right)\left(\sum v\right)}{n} = 486.5 - \frac{91(91)}{13} = -150.5$$

$$SS_{uu} = \sum u^2 - \frac{\left(\sum u\right)^2}{n} = 819 - \frac{91^2}{13} = 182 \qquad SS_{vv} = \sum v^2 - \frac{\left(\sum v\right)^2}{n} = 818 - \frac{91^2}{13} = 181$$

$$r_s = \frac{SS_{uv}}{\sqrt{SS_{uu}SS_{vv}}} = \frac{-150.5}{\sqrt{182(181)}} = -.829$$

To determine if "punishers tend to have lower payoffs", we test:

$$H_0 : \rho_s = 0$$
$$H_a : \rho_s < 0$$

The test statistic is $r_s = -.829$

Since no α was given, we will use $\alpha = .05$.

Reject H_0 if $r_s < -r_{s,\alpha}$ where $\alpha = .05$ and $n = 13$.

Reject H_0 if $r_s < -.475$ (from Table XIV, Appendix D)

Since the observed value of the test statistic falls in the rejection region $(r_s = -.829 < -.475)$, H_0 is rejected. There is sufficient evidence to indicate "punishers tend to have lower payoffs" at $\alpha = .05$.

15.77 **Method I and Method II**: $r_s = .189$. Since this value is close to 0, there is a very weak positive rank correlation between the ranks of Method I and the ranks of Method II.

Method I and Method III: $r_s = .592$. Since this value is about half way between 0 and 1, there is a moderate positive rank correlation between the ranks of Method I and the ranks of Method III.

Method I and Method IV: $r_s = .340$. Since this value is fairly close to 0, there is a weak positive rank correlation between the ranks of Method I and the ranks of Method IV.

Method II and Method III: $r_s = .205$. Since this value is close to 0, there is a very weak positive rank correlation between the ranks of Method II and the ranks of Method III.

Method II and Method IV: $r_s = .324$. Since this value is fairly close to 0, there is a weak positive rank correlation between the ranks of Method II and the ranks of Method IV.

Method III and Method IV: $r_s = .314$. Since this value is fairly close to 0, there is a weak positive rank correlation between the ranks of Method III and the ranks of Method IV.

15.79 Some preliminary calculations:

2011	Rank, u	2012	Rank, v	Difference, d_i	d_i^2
82.7	20	76.94	6	14	196
81.4	19	84.84	19	0	0
81.32	18	85.82	20	-2	4
81	17	77.15	7	10	100
80.87	16	82.78	18	-2	4
80.46	15	78.93	14	1	1
79.63	14	77.59	9	5	25
79.53	13	80.04	16	-3	9
79.25	12	79.31	15	-3	9
79.02	11	82.11	17	-6	36

78.46	10	75.79	4	6	36
77.95	9	78.07	12	-3	9
77.91	8	71.43	1	7	49
77.51	7	76.81	5	2	4
77.44	6	78.46	13	-7	49
77.29	5	77.46	8	-3	9
77.24	4	73.92	2	2	4
76.85	3	77.73	11	-8	64
76.5	2	77.7	10	-8	64
76.45	1	74.26	3	-2	4

$$\sum d_i^2 = 676$$

$$r_s = 1 - \frac{6\sum d_i^2}{n(n^2-1)} = 1 - \frac{6(676)}{20(20^2-1)} = .492$$

To determine if the true rank correlation between global pulse scores of firms in 2011 and 2012 is positive, we test:

$$H_0 : \rho_s = 0$$
$$H_a : \rho_s > 0$$

The test statistic is $r_s = .492$.

Reject H_0 if $r_s > r_{s,\alpha}$ where $\alpha = .01$ and $n = 20$.

Reject H_0 if $r_s > .534$ (from Table XIV, Appendix D).

Since the observed value of the test statistic does not fall in the rejection region ($r_s = .492 \not> .534$), H_0 is not rejected. There is insufficient evidence to indicate the true rank correlation between global pulse scores of firms in 2011 and 2012 is positive at $\alpha = .01$.

15.81   a.   Some preliminary calculations are:

Pair	x	Rank, u	y	Rank, v	u^2	v^2	uv
1	19	5	12	5	25	25	25
2	27	7	19	8	49	64	56
3	15	2	7	1	4	1	2
4	35	9	25	9	81	81	81
5	13	1	11	4	1	16	4
6	29	8	10	2.5	64	6.25	20
7	16	3.5	16	6	12.25	36	21
8	22	6	10	2.5	36	6.25	15
9	16	3.5	18	7	12.25	49	24.5
		$\sum u_i = 45$		$\sum v_i = 45$	$\sum u_i^2 = 284.5$	$\sum v_i^2 = 284.5$	$\sum u_i v_i = 248.5$

$$SS_{uv} = \sum u_i v_i - \frac{\sum u_i v_i}{n} = 248.5 - \frac{45(45)}{9} = 23.5$$

$$SS_{uu} = \sum u_i^2 - \frac{\left(\sum u_i\right)^2}{n} = 284.5 - \frac{45^2}{9} = 59.5 \qquad SS_{vv} = \sum v_i^2 - \frac{\left(\sum v_i\right)^2}{n} = 284.5 - \frac{45^2}{9} = 59.5$$

To determine if the Spearman rank correlation differs from 0, we test:

$$H_0: \rho_s = 0$$
$$H_a: \rho_s \neq 0$$

The test statistic is $r_s = \dfrac{SS_{uv}}{\sqrt{SS_{uv}SS_{vv}}} = \dfrac{23.5}{\sqrt{59.5(59.5)}} = .39$

Reject H_0 if $r_s < -r_{s,\alpha/2}$ or $r_s > r_{s,\alpha/2}$ where $\alpha/2 = .025$ and $n = 9$:

Reject H_0 if $r_s < -.683$ or $r_s > .683$ (from Table XIV, Appendix D)

Since the observed value of the test statistic does not fall in the rejection region $(r_s = .39 \not> .683)$, H_0 is not rejected. There is insufficient evidence to indicate that Spearman's rank correlation between x and y is significantly different from 0 at $\alpha = .05$.

b. Use the Wilcoxon signed rank test. Some preliminary calculations are:

Pair	x	y	Difference	Rank of Absolute Difference
1	19	12	7	3
2	27	19	8	4.5
3	15	7	8	4.5
4	35	25	10	6
5	13	11	2	1.5
6	29	10	19	8
7	16	16	0	(eliminated)
8	22	10	12	7
9	16	18	-2	1.5
				$T_- = 1.5$

To determine if the probability distribution of x is shifted to the right of that for y, we test:

H_0: The probability distributions are identical for the two variables
H_a: The probability distribution of x is shifted to the right of the probability distribution of y

The test statistic is $T = T_- = 1.5$.

Reject H_0 if $T \leq T_0$ where T_0 is based on $\alpha = .05$ and $n = 8$ (one-tailed):

Reject H_0 if $T \leq 6$ (from Table XIII, Appendix D).

Since the observed value of the test statistic falls in the rejection region $(T = 1.5 \leq 6)$, H_0 is rejected. There is sufficient evidence to conclude that the probability distribution of x is shifted to the right of that for y at $\alpha = .05$.

15.83 Some preliminary calculations are:

Block	1	Rank	2	Rank	3	Rank	4	Rank	5	Rank
1	75	4	65	1	74	3	80	5	69	2
2	77	3	69	1	78	4	80	5	72	2
3	70	4	63	1.5	69	3	75	5	63	1.5
4	80	3.5	69	1	80	3.5	86	5	77	2
	$R_1 = 14.5$		$R_2 = 4.5$		$R_3 = 13.5$		$R_4 = 20$		$R_5 = 7.5$	

$$\bar{R}_1 = \frac{R_1}{b} = \frac{14.5}{4} = 3.625 \qquad \bar{R}_2 = \frac{R_2}{b} = \frac{4.5}{4} = 1.125 \qquad \bar{R}_3 = \frac{R_3}{b} = \frac{13.5}{4} = 3.375 \qquad \bar{R}_4 = \frac{R_4}{b} = \frac{20}{4} = 5$$

$$\bar{R}_5 = \frac{R_5}{b} = \frac{7.5}{4} = 1.875 \qquad \bar{R} = \frac{k+1}{2} = \frac{5+1}{2} = 3$$

To determine whether at least two of the treatment probability distributions differ in location, use Friedman F_r test.

H_0:   The five treatments have identical probability distributions
H_a: At least two of the populations have probability distributions differ in location

The test statistic is

$$F_r = \frac{12b}{k(k+1)} \sum (\bar{R}_j - \bar{R})^2 = \frac{12(4)}{5(5+1)} \left((3.625-3)^2 + (1.125-3)^2 + (3.375-3)^2 + (5-3)^2 + (1.875-3)^2 \right) = 14.9$$

The rejection region requires $\alpha = .05$ in the upper tail of the χ^2 distribution with df $= k - 1 = 5 - 1 = 4$. From Table IV, Appendix D, $\chi^2_{.05} = 9.48773$. The rejection region is $F_r > 9.48773$.

Since the observed value of the test statistic falls in the rejection region $(F_r = 14.9 > 9.48773)$, H_0 is rejected. There is sufficient evidence to indicate that at least two of the treatment means differ in location at $\alpha = .05$.

15.85   a.   Since the data are not normal, we will use the Wilcoxon Rank Sum test. There is some concern with this test as there are many ties in the data. One of the assumptions for the Wilcoxon Rank Sum test is that the data are continuous, with relatively few ties.

b.   To determine if the scores of those in the CMC group tend to be lower than the scores of those in the FTF group, we test:

H_0: The two sampled populations have identical probability distributions
H_a: The probability distribution of the FTF is located to the right of that for the CMC group.

c.   Since $n_1 = n_2 = 24$, the large sample test statistic must be used. The rejection region requires $\alpha = .10$ in the lower tail of the z-distribution. From Table II, Appendix D, $z_{.10} = 1.28$. The rejection region is $z < -1.28$.

d. Some preliminary calculations are:

CMC	Rank	CMC	Rank	FTF	Rank	FTF	Rank
4	34.5	3	13.5	5	47	4	34.5
3	13.5	3	13.5	4	34.5	4	34.5
3	13.5	2	2	4	34.5	4	34.5
4	34.5	4	34.5	4	34.5	4	34.5
3	13.5	2	2	3	13.5	4	34.5
3	13.5	4	34.5	3	13.5	3	13.5
3	13.5	5	47	3	13.5	3	13.5
3	13.5	4	34.5	4	34.5	3	13.5
4	34.5	4	34.5	3	13.5	4	34.5
4	34.5	4	34.5	3	13.5	4	34.5
3	13.5	5	47	3	13.5	2	2
4	34.5	3	13.5	3	13.5	4	34.5
		$T_1 = 578$				$T_2 = 598$	

The test statistic is $z = \dfrac{T_1 - \dfrac{n_1(n_1 + n_2 + 1)}{2}}{\sqrt{\dfrac{n_1 n_2 (n_1 + n_2 + 1)}{12}}} = \dfrac{578 - \dfrac{24(24 + 24 + 1)}{2}}{\sqrt{\dfrac{24(24)(24 + 24 + 1)}{12}}} = \dfrac{-10}{48.4974} = -.206$

Since the observed value of the test statistic does not fall in the rejection region $(z = -.206 \not< -1.28)$, H_0 is not rejected. There is insufficient evidence to indicate the scores of those in the CMC group tend to be lower than the scores of those in the FTF group at $\alpha = .10$.

15.87   a. To calculate the median, we first arrange the data in order from the smallest to the largest:

22, 28, 32, 33, 39, 41, 43, 43, 45, 47, 50, 54, 54, 59, 62

Since n is odd, the median is the middle number, which is 43.

b. To determine if the median age of the terminated workers exceeds the entire company's median age, we test:

$H_0 : \eta = 37$

$H_a : \eta > 37$

c. The test statistic is S = number of measurements greater than 37 = 11.

The p-value = $P(x \geq 11)$ where x is a binomial random variable with $n = 15$ and $p = .5$. From Table I, Appendix D, $p - \text{value} = P(x \geq 11) = 1 - P(x \leq 10) = 1 - .941 = .059$.

Since no α value was given, we will use $\alpha = .05$. Since the p-value is greater than α ($p = .059 > .05$), H_0 is not rejected. There is insufficient evidence to indicate that the median age of the terminated workers exceeds the entire company's median age at $\alpha = .05$.

(Note: If $\alpha = .10$ was used, the conclusion would be to reject H_0.)

d.   Since the conclusion using $\alpha = .10$ is to reject H_0 and conclude that there is sufficient evidence to indicate that the median age of the terminated workers exceeds the entire company's median age, we would advise the company to reevaluate its planned RIF. With the proposed sample, there is evidence that the company is discriminating with respect to age.

15.89   a.   Some preliminary calculations are:

Brand	Expert 1	Expert 2	Difference d_i	d_i^2
A	6	5	1	1
B	5	6	−1	1
C	1	2	−1	1
D	3	1	2	4
E	2	4	−2	4
F	4	3	1	1
				$\sum d_i^2 = 12$

$$r_s = 1 - \frac{6\sum d_i^2}{n(n^2-1)} = 1 - \frac{6(12)}{6(6^2-1)} = 1-.343 = .657$$

b.   To determine if there is a positive correlation in the rankings of the two experts, we test:

$$H_0 : \rho_s = 0$$
$$H_a : \rho_s > 0$$

The test statistic is $r_s = .657$.

Reject H_0 if $r_s > r_{s,\alpha}$ where $\alpha = .05$ and $n = 6$. From Table XIV, Appendix D, $r_{s,.01} = .829$. Reject H_0 if $r_s > .829$.

Since the observed value of the test statistic does not fall in the rejection region $(r_s = .657 \not> .829)$, H_0 is not rejected. There is insufficient evidence to indicate a positive correlation in the rankings of the two experts at $\alpha = .05$.

15.91   a.   Since only 70 of the 80 customers responded to the question, only the 70 will be included.

To determine if the median amount spent on hamburgers at lunch at McDonald's is less than $2.25, we test:

$$H_0 : \eta = 2.25$$
$$H_a : \eta < 2.25$$

S = number of measurements less than 2.25 = 20.

The test statistic is $z = \frac{(S-.5)-.5n}{.5\sqrt{n}} = \frac{(20-.5)-.5(70)}{.5\sqrt{70}} = -3.71$

Since no α was given in the exercise, we will use $\alpha = .05$. The rejection region requires $\alpha = .05$ in the upper tail of the z-distribution. From Table II, Appendix D, $z_{.05} = 1.645$. The rejection region is $z > 1.645$.

Since the observed value of the test statistic does not fall in the rejection region ($z = -3.71 \not> 1.645$), H_0 is not rejected. There is insufficient evidence to indicate that the median amount spent on hamburgers at lunch at McDonald's is less than \$2.25 at $\alpha = .05$.

    b.   No. The survey was done in Boston only. The eating habits of those living in Boston are probably not representative of all Americans.

    c.   We must assume that the sample is randomly selected from a continuous probability distribution.

15.93   From MINITAB, the results of running a Friedman's test are:

Friedman Test: Rank versus Group blocked by Theme

```
S = 0.93   DF = 3   P = 0.819
S = 1.08   DF = 3   P = 0.782 (adjusted for ties)

                       Sum
                        of
Group   N  Est Median  Ranks
1      12     5.1250    27.0
2      12     6.1250    32.5
3      12     5.6250    29.0
4      12     6.1250    31.5

Grand median = 5.7500
```

To determine if the atlas theme ranking distributions of the four groups differ, we test:

    H_0: The probability distributions of the atlas theme rankings are the same for the four groups
    H_a: The probability distributions of at least two atlas theme rankings differ in location

The test statistic is $F_r = .93$ and the p-value is $p = .819$. Since the p-value is so large, there is no evidence to reject H_0 for any reasonable value of α. There is insufficient evidence to indicate that the atlas theme ranking distributions of the four groups differ.

15.95   a.   We first rank all the data:

Firms with Successful MIS (1)				Firms with Unsuccessful MIS (2)			
Score	**Rank**	**Score**	**Rank**	**Score**	**Rank**	**Score**	**Rank**
52	5	90	25.5	60	10.5	65	12.5
70	15	75	17	50	4	55	7
40	1.5	80	19	55	7	70	15
80	19	95	29.5	70	15	90	25.5
82	21	90	25.5	41	3	85	22
65	12.5	86	23	40	1.5	80	19
59	9	95	29.5	55	7	90	25.5
60	10.5	93	28				
$T_1 = 290.5$				$T_2 = 174.5$			

To determine whether the distribution of quality scores for the successfully implemented systems differs from that for the unsuccessfully implemented systems, we test:

H_0: The two sampled distributions are identical

H_a: The probability distribution for the successful MIS is shifted to the right or left of that for the unsuccessful MIS

The test statistic is $z = \dfrac{T_1 - \dfrac{n_1(n_1+n_2+1)}{2}}{\sqrt{\dfrac{n_1 n_2 (n_1+n_2+1)}{12}}} = \dfrac{290.5 - \dfrac{16(16+14+1)}{2}}{\sqrt{\dfrac{16(14)(16+14+1)}{12}}} = 1.77$

The rejection region requires $\alpha/2 = .05/2 = .025$ in each tail of the z-distribution. From Table II, Appendix D, $z_{.025} = 1.96$. The rejection region is $z < -1.96$ or $z > 1.96$.

Since the observed value of the test statistic does not fall in the rejection region ($z = 1.77 \not> 1.96$), H_0 is not rejected. There is insufficient evidence to indicate the distribution of quality scores for the successfully implemented systems differs from that for the unsuccessfully implemented systems at $\alpha = .05$.

b. We could use the two-sample t-test if:

1. Both populations are normal.
2. The variances of the two populations are the same.

15.97 a. To determine if the median level differs from the target, we test:

$H_0 : \eta = .75$

$H_a : \eta \neq .75$

b. S_1 = number of observations less than .75 and S_2 = number of observations greater than .75.

The test statistic is S = larger of S_1 and S_2.

The p-value $= 2P(x \geq S)$ where x is a binomial random variable with $n = 25$ and $p = .5$. If the p-value is less than $\alpha = .10$, reject H_0.

c. A Type I error would be concluding the median level is not .75 when it is. If a Type I error were committed, the supervisor would correct the fluoridation process when it was not necessary. A Type II error would be concluding the median level is .75 when it is not. If a Type II error were committed, the supervisor would not correct the fluoridation process when it was necessary.

d. S_1 = number of observations less than .75 = 7 and S_2 = number of observations greater than .75 = 18.

The test statistic is S = larger of S_1 and S_2 = 18.

The p-value $= 2P(x \geq 18)$ where x is a binomial random variable with $n = 25$ and $p = .5$. From Table I, p-value $= 2P(x \geq 18) = 2(1 - P(x \leq 17)) = 2(1 - .978) = 2(.022) = .044$

Since the p-value $= .044 < \alpha = .10$, H_0 is rejected. There is sufficient evidence to indicate the median level of fluoridation differs from the target of .75 at $\alpha = .10$.

e.   A distribution heavily skewed to the right might look something like the following:

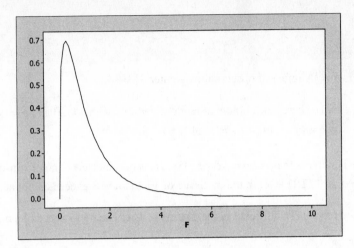

One assumption necessary for the *t*-test is that the distribution from which the sample is drawn is normal. A distribution which is heavily skewed in one direction is not normal. Thus, the sign test would be preferred.

15.99   Since the data are already ranked, it is clear that:

$$R_1 = 19 \qquad R_2 = 21.5 \qquad R_3 = 27.5 \qquad R_4 = 32$$

$$\bar{R}_1 = \frac{R_1}{n_1} = \frac{19}{10} = 1.9 \qquad \bar{R}_2 = \frac{R_2}{n_2} = \frac{21.5}{10} = 2.15 \qquad \bar{R}_3 = \frac{R_3}{n_3} = \frac{27.5}{10} = 2.75 \qquad \bar{R}_4 = \frac{R_4}{n_4} = \frac{32}{10} = 3.2$$

$$\bar{R} = \frac{k+1}{2} = \frac{4+1}{2} = 2.5$$

To determine if the probability distributions of ratings differ for at least two of the items, we test:

H_0: The probability distributions of responses are identical for the four aspects
H_a: At least two of the probability distributions differ in location

The test statistic is

$$F_r = \frac{12b}{k(k+1)} \sum (\bar{R}_j - \bar{R})^2 = \frac{12(10)}{4(4+1)} \left((1.9-2.5)^2 + (2.15-2.5)^2 + (2.75-2.5)^2 + (3.2-2.5)^2 \right) = 6.21$$

The rejection region requires $\alpha = .05$ in the upper tail of the χ^2 distribution with df $= k-1 = 4-1 = 3$. From Table IV, Appendix D, $\chi^2_{.05} = 7.81473$. The rejection region is $F_r > 7.81473$.

Since the observed value of the test statistic does not fall in the rejection region $(F_r = 6.21 \not> 7.81473)$, H_0 is not rejected. There is insufficient evidence to conclude that at least two of the probability distributions of ratings differ at $\alpha = .05$.

15.101   a.   To determine if the median TCDD level in the fat tissue of Vietnam vets exceeds 3 ppt, we test:

$$H_0 : \eta = 3$$
$$H_a : \eta > 3$$

The test statistic is $S = \{$Number of observations greater $3\} = 14$.

The p-value $= P(x \geq 14)$ where x is a binomial random variable with $n = 20$ and $p = .5$. From Table I, Appendix D, $p - \text{value} = P(x \geq 14) = 1 - P(x \leq 13) = 1 - .942 = .058$.

Since the p-value is not less than α ($p = .058 \not< .05$), H_0 is not rejected. There is insufficient evidence to indicate the median TCDD level in the fat tissue of Vietnam vets exceeds 3 ppt at $\alpha = .05$.

b.   To determine if the median TCDD level in the plasma of Vietnam vets exceeds 3 ppt, we test:

$$H_0 : \eta = 3$$
$$H_a : \eta > 3$$

The test statistic is $S = \{$Number of observations greater $3\} = 12$.

The p-value $= P(x \geq 12)$ where x is a binomial random variable with $n = 20$ and $p = .5$. From Table I, Appendix D, $p - \text{value} = P(x \geq 12) = 1 - P(x \leq 11) = 1 - .748 = .252$.

Since the p-value is not less than α ($p = .252 \not< .05$), H_0 is not rejected. There is insufficient evidence to indicate the median TCDD level in the plasma of Vietnam vets exceeds 3 ppt at $\alpha = .05$.

c.   Some preliminary calculations are:

Vet	Fat	Plasma	Difference	Rank
1	4.9	2.5	2.4	11.5
2	6.9	3.5	3.4	16
3	10.0	6.8	3.2	15
4	4.4	4.7	-0.3	4
5	4.6	4.6	0.0	(eliminated)
6	1.1	1.8	-0.7	8
7	2.3	2.5	-0.2	2.5
8	5.9	3.1	2.8	14
9	7.0	3.1	3.9	17
10	5.5	3.0	2.5	13
11	7.0	6.9	0.1	1
12	1.4	1.6	-0.2	2.5
13	11.0	20.0	-9.0	19
14	2.5	4.1	-1.6	9
15	4.4	2.1	2.3	10
16	4.2	1.8	2.4	11.5
17	41.0	36.0	5.0	18
18	2.9	3.3	-0.4	5
19	7.7	7.2	0.5	6.5
20	2.5	2.0	0.5	6.5
			$T_- = 50$	
			$T_+ = 140$	

To determine if the distribution of TCDD levels in fat is shifted above or below that of the distribution of TCDD levels in plasma, we test:

H_0: The probability distributions for the two populations are identical

H_a: The probability distribution of TCDD levels in fat is shifted above or below that of the distribution of TCDD levels in plasma

The test statistic is T = smaller of T_- or $T_+ = 50$.

Reject H_0 if $T \leq T_0$ where T_0 is based on $\alpha = .05$ and $n = 19$ (two-tailed).

Reject H_0 if $T \leq 46$ (from Table XIII, Appendix D)

Since the observed value of the test statistic does not fall in the rejection region $(T = 50 \not\leq 46)$, H_0 is not rejected. There is insufficient evidence to indicate the distribution of TCDD levels in fat is shifted above or below that of the distribution of TCDD levels in plasma at $\alpha = .05$.

d.   Some preliminary calculations are:

Vet	Fat	u	Plasma	v	u^2	v^2	uv
1	4.9	11	2.5	6.5	121	42.25	71.5
2	6.9	14	3.5	12	196	144	168
3	10.0	18	6.8	16	324	256	288
4	4.4	8.5	4.7	15	72.25	225	127.5
5	4.6	10	4.6	14	100	196	140
6	1.1	1	1.8	2.5	1	6.25	2.5
7	2.3	3	2.5	6.5	9	42.25	19.5
8	5.9	13	3.1	9.5	169	90.25	123.5
9	7.0	15.5	3.1	9.5	240.25	90.25	147.25
10	5.5	12	3.0	8	144	64	96
11	7.0	15.5	6.9	17	240.25	289	263.5
12	1.4	2	1.6	1	4	1	2
13	11.0	19	20.0	19	361	361	361
14	2.5	4.5	4.1	13	20.25	169	58.5
15	4.4	8.5	2.1	5	72.25	25	42.5
16	4.2	7	1.8	2.5	49	6.25	17.5
17	41.0	20	36.0	20	400	400	400
18	2.9	6	3.3	11	36	121	66
19	7.7	17	7.2	18	289	324	306
20	2.5	4.5	2.0	4	20.25	16	18
		$\sum u = 210$		$\sum v = 210$	$\sum u^2 = 2868.5$	$\sum v^2 = 2868.5$	$\sum uv = 2718.75$

$$SS_{uv} = \sum uv - \frac{\left(\sum u\right)\left(\sum v\right)}{n} = 2718.75 - \frac{210(210)}{20} = 513.75$$

$$SS_{uu} = \sum u^2 - \frac{\left(\sum u\right)^2}{n} = 2868.5 - \frac{210^2}{20} = 663.5$$

$$SS_{vv} = \sum v^2 - \frac{\left(\sum v\right)^2}{n} = 2868.5 - \frac{210^2}{20} = 663.5$$

$$r_s = \frac{SS_{uv}}{\sqrt{SS_{uu}SS_{vv}}} = \frac{513.75}{\sqrt{663.5(663.5)}} = .774$$

To determine if there is a positive association between the two TCDD measures, we test:

$$H_0 : \rho_s = 0$$
$$H_a : \rho_s > 0$$

The test statistic is $r_s = .774$.

Reject H_0 if $r_s > r_{s,\alpha}$ where $\alpha = .05$ and $n = 20$.

Reject H_0 if $r_s > .377$ (from Table XIV, Appendix D)

Since the observed value of the test statistic falls in the rejection region $(r = .774 > .377)$, H_0 is rejected. There is sufficient evidence to indicate there is a positive association between the two TCDD measures at $\alpha = .05$.

15.103   Using MINITAB, the results of the Wilcoxon Rank Sum Test (Mann-Whitney Test) for each of the variables are:

Mann-Whitney Test and CI: CREATIVE-S, CREATIVE-NS

```
             N   Median
CREATIVE-S   47  5.0000
CREATIVE-NS  67  4.0000


Point estimate for ETA1-ETA2 is 1.0000
95.0 Percent CI for ETA1-ETA2 is (0.9999,1.0000)
W = 3734.5
Test of ETA1 = ETA2 vs ETA1 not = ETA2 is significant at 0.0000
The test is significant at 0.0000 (adjusted for ties)
```

Mann-Whitney Test and CI: INFO-S, INFO-NS

```
          N   Median
INFO-S    47  5.000
INFO-NS   67  5.000


Point estimate for ETA1-ETA2 is 0.000
95.0 Percent CI for ETA1-ETA2 is (-0.000,1.000)
W = 2888.5
Test of ETA1 = ETA2 vs ETA1 not = ETA2 is significant at 0.2856
The test is significant at 0.2743 (adjusted for ties)
```

Mann-Whitney Test and CI: DECPERS-S, DECPERS-NS

```
             N   Median
DECPERS-S    47  3.000
DECPERS-NS   67  2.000
```

```
Point estimate for ETA1-ETA2 is -0.000
95.0 Percent CI for ETA1-ETA2 is (-0.000,1.000)
W = 2963.5
Test of ETA1 = ETA2 vs ETA1 not = ETA2 is significant at 0.1337
The test is significant at 0.1228 (adjusted for ties)
```

Mann-Whitney Test and CI: SKILLS-S, SKILLS-NS

```
            N   Median
SKILLS-S   47   6.0000
SKILLS-NS  67   5.0000


Point estimate for ETA1-ETA2 is 1.0000
95.0 Percent CI for ETA1-ETA2 is (0.9999,1.9999)
W = 3498.5
Test of ETA1 = ETA2 vs ETA1 not = ETA2 is significant at 0.0000
The test is significant at 0.0000 (adjusted for ties)
```

Mann-Whitney Test and CI: TASKID-S, TASKID-NS

```
            N   Median
TASKID-S   47   5.000
TASKID-NS  67   4.000


Point estimate for ETA1-ETA2 is 1.000
95.0 Percent CI for ETA1-ETA2 is (-0.000,1.000)
W = 3028.0
Test of ETA1 = ETA2 vs ETA1 not = ETA2 is significant at 0.0614
The test is significant at 0.0566 (adjusted for ties)
```

Mann-Whitney Test and CI: AGE-S, AGE-NS

```
          N  Median
AGE-S    47  47.000
AGE-NS   67  45.000


Point estimate for ETA1-ETA2 is 1.000
95.0 Percent CI for ETA1-ETA2 is (-1.000,4.001)
W = 2891.5
Test of ETA1 = ETA2 vs ETA1 not = ETA2 is significant at 0.2779
The test is significant at 0.2771 (adjusted for ties)
```

Mann-Whitney Test and CI: EDYRS-S, EDYRS-NS

```
           N   Median
EDYRS-S   47   13.000
EDYRS-NS  67   13.000


Point estimate for ETA1-ETA2 is -0.000
95.0 Percent CI for ETA1-ETA2 is (0.000,-0.000)
W = 2664.0
Test of ETA1 = ETA2 vs ETA1 not = ETA2 is significant at 0.8268
The test is significant at 0.8191 (adjusted for ties)
```

A summary of the tests above and the *t*-tests from Chapter 8 are listed in the table:

Variable	Wilcoxon Test Statistic, T_2	*p*-value	*t*	*p*-value
CREATIVE	3734.5	0.000	8.847	0.000
INFO	2888.5	0.274	1.503	0.136
DECPERS	2963.5	0.123	1.506	0.135
SKILLS	3498.5	0.000	4.766	0.000
TASKID	3028.0	0.057	1.738	0.087
AGE	2891.5	0.277	0.742	0.460
EDYRS	2664.0	0.819	-0.623	0.534

The *p*-values for the Wilcoxon Rank Sum Tests and the *t*-tests are similar and the decisions are the same.

Since the sample sizes are large ($n = 47$ and $n = 67$), the Central Limit Theorem applies. Thus, the *t*-tests (or *z*-tests) are valid. One assumption for the Wilcoxon Rank Sum test is that the distributions are continuous. Obviously, this is not true. There are many ties in the data, so the Wilcoxon Rank Sum tests may not be valid.